AI-Driven Cloud Forensics

Cloud computing has revolutionized digital infrastructure, but it has also introduced complex forensic challenges that demand intelligent, scalable, and automated investigative solutions. *AI-Driven Cloud Forensics: Advanced Techniques for Next-Generation Digital Investigations* provides a comprehensive exploration of how artificial intelligence, machine learning, big data analytics, and automation are transforming the future of digital forensics in cloud environments.

This edited volume examines advanced methodologies for forensic acquisition in virtual machines, containers, and ephemeral environments; intelligent cloud architectures for secure investigations; and AI-powered frameworks for anomaly detection, fraud investigation, phishing detection, and log analysis. It highlights emerging approaches such as AutoML-enabled forensic systems, federated learning for communication-efficient anomaly detection, AI-centric privileged access management, and real-time detection of data fabrication attacks in decentralized systems.

Beyond core forensic technologies, the book addresses interdisciplinary applications across smart micro-grids, dark web environments, digital supply chains, tourism systems, and e-discovery processes. By integrating automation with forensic intelligence, the contributors demonstrate how next-generation digital investigations can become more proactive, predictive, and adaptive. Special emphasis is placed on addressing challenges such as data volatility, multi-tenancy, encryption, jurisdictional constraints, and large-scale log analysis in distributed cloud ecosystems. The book also includes a bibliometric and science-mapping analysis to provide insights into evolving research trends in AI-driven cloud forensic automation.

Designed for researchers, cybersecurity professionals, forensic analysts, legal practitioners, cloud architects, and postgraduate students, this volume bridges theoretical foundations with real-world implementations. It serves as a forward-looking reference for building resilient, trustworthy, and AI-enabled forensic ecosystems capable of responding to increasingly sophisticated cyber threats. By combining innovation with investigative rigor, *AI-Driven Cloud Forensics* contributes to shaping the next-generation of intelligent digital security and forensic readiness in cloud-driven environments.

AI-Driven Cloud Forensics

Advanced Techniques for Next-Generation Digital Investigations

Edited by
Pankaj Bhambri, Mudassir Khan and A. Jose Anand

CRC Press
Taylor & Francis Group
Boca Raton London New York

CRC Press is an imprint of the
Taylor & Francis Group, an **informa** business

Designed cover image: Shutterstock ID: 2616201919

First edition published 2027
by CRC Press
2385 NW Executive Center Drive, Suite 320, Boca Raton FL 33431

and by CRC Press
4 Park Square, Milton Park, Abingdon, Oxon, OX14 4RN
CRC Press is an imprint of Taylor & Francis Group, LLC

ISBN: 9781041107163 (hbk)
ISBN: 9781041107170 (pbk)
ISBN: 9781003656487 (ebk)

DOI: 10.1201/9781003656487

Typeset in Sabon
by Deanta Global Publishing Services, Chennai, India

Contents

About the editors vii
List of contributors ix
Preface xiii

1 **Introduction to advanced cloud forensics** 1
PANKAJ BHAMBRI, MUDASSIR KHAN AND A. JOSE ANAND

2 **Intelligent cloud architecture for next-generation digital forensics** 17
S. SAJITHABANU, B. SUNDARAVADIVAZHAGN, A. JOSE ANAND AND A. ASRIN MAHMOOTHA

3 **Forensic acquisition in ephemeral environments: Virtual machines and containers** 32
PANKAJ BHAMBRI, HAIPENG LIU, NAVEEN ANANDA KUMAR AND HIND HAMMOUCH

4 **Forensic challenges in emerging technologies: AI-driven cloud forensics for next-generation digital investigations** 51
A. JOSE ANAND

5 **Big data, machine learning, and cloud forensics: An integrated framework for intelligent digital security** 69
HAJAR FATORACHIAN AND HADI KAZEMI

6 **AI and automation in cloud forensics** 87
MUHAMMAD FAROOQ AND HUMERA AMIN

7 **AI and automation in cloud forensics for digital investigations and E-Discovery** 101
SARAVANAN MUNISWAMY AND MITHILEYSH SATHIYANARAYANAN

8 **AutoML-enabled smart forensic framework for collaborative crime analysis and digital evidence prediction** 120
NARENDRA SINGH, M. GOKILHASHREE, B. GAYATHRI, OSHMA ROSETTE PINTO AND RUBAID ASHFAQ

9 Advanced network forensics for cloud environments 139

VIDHYA PRAKASH RAJENDRAN, SADASIVAM SUBBARAYAN, VIMALAKEERTHY DEVADOSS AND SIVAKUMAR MUTHUSAMY

10 Federated temporal-attention network for communication-efficient log anomaly detection in IoT environments 152

AMAN KUMAR, DEEPAK SHARMA, ANU TONK, VINOD KUMAR V. METI, KALLAKUNTA RAVI KUMAR AND MAYAKANNAN S.

11 Two-tier real-time detection of data fabrication attacks in decentralized smart microgrids 174

VENKATA LAKSHMI, G. YAMINI, R. KALAIVANI, M. GOKILHASHREE AND S. V. SAVEEITHAA

12 An explanatory view of antisquat: An AI-powered phishing domain finder 202

SANGEETHA G., MADHUMALA R. B., VICTOR HUGO C. DE ALBUQUERQUE, PAVAN GOWDA T. S., DHANUSH REDDY C. S. AND AKSHAY S.

13 Autonomous artificial intelligence systems for fraud detection and forensics in dark web environments 218

VIJAY ANANT ATHAVALE, DHANUMJAYA K., KALAISELVI S., SATWIK CHATTERJEE AND BAZANI SHAIK

14 Next-generation privileged access management: An AI-centric perspective 235

ERHAN YILMAZ AND ÖZGÜ CAN

15 Digital Twin and generative AI synergies: Pioneering smart, predictive, and autonomous supply chain networks 251

SAFIYE TURGAY AND ABDULKADIR AYDIN

16 Building trust and transparency in smart tourism through cloud-based forensic readiness 274

DUONG THANH TUNG

17 Mapping research trends in AI-driven automation for cloud forensics: A bibliometric analysis and science mapping 298

ROSELINE OLUWASEUN OGUNDOKUN, ROTIMI-WILLIAMS BELLO, PIUS ADEWALE OWOLAWI, ADEWALE OPEOLUWA OGUNDE, CHINECHEREM UMEZURUIKE AND AKINYOMADE O. OWOLABI

Index 317

About the editors

Pankaj Bhambri is Associate Professor and Convener of the Board of Studies in the Department of Information Technology at Guru Nanak Dev Engineering College, Ludhiana, India. Recognized among the Top 2% of Scientists globally by Stanford University and Elsevier (2025), he has over 21 years of teaching and research experience. He earned his PhD in Computer Science and Engineering from I.K.G. Punjab Technical University, Jalandhar. He is currently pursuing a Post Doctorate Fellowship from Lincoln University College, Malaysia.

His research interests span machine learning, bioinformatics, cloud computing, and IoT. Dr Bhambri has an extensive publication record, with numerous papers in high-impact SCIE and Scopus-indexed journals. He is a prolific author and editor, having contributed to and edited over two dozen books with prestigious publishers like Springer, CRC Press (Taylor & Francis), Elsevier, and IGI Global. He serves as a reviewer and technical committee member for numerous international conferences. Dr Bhambri has also filed several patents, including an Australian innovation patent. He actively guides multiple PhD scholars in cutting-edge areas of computer science and engineering.

Mudassir Khan is currently working in the Department of Computer Science at College of Science & Arts Tanumah, King Khalid University Abha Saudi Arabia. He has completed his PhD in Computer Science from Noida International University Gautam Budh Nagar (NIU) India. He has completed his Graduation from Aligarh Muslim University, Aligarh, and Masters from Gautam Budh Technical University, India. He has more than 12 years of teaching experience at the King Khalid University of Saudi Arabia. He has published more than 36 papers in International Journals (SCIE, ESCI, Web of Science, Scopus, Springer, and IGI) and conferences (IEEE, Springer Series). He has also published multiple books and patents, too. He is the Member of various technical/professional societies such as IEEE, UACEE, Internet Society, IAENG, and CSTA. His research interest includes Big Data, IoT, Deep Learning, Computer Security, Cyber Security, and Cloud Computing.

A. Jose Anand is currently working as a Professor at the Department of Electronics and Communication Engineering, KCG College of Technology, Chennai, Tamil Nadu. He has one year of industrial experience and 24 years of teaching experience. Has one year of experience as assistant staff for Halifax Regional Center for Education at Saint Mary's Elementary School, Halifax, Nova Scotia, Canada. He presented several papers at National Conferences and International Conferences. He published several papers in the National Journal and International Journal and also published books for polytechnic and engineering subjects. He is a Member of CSI, IEI, IET, IETE, ISTE, INS, QCFI, and EWB. His current research interest is in Wireless Sensor Networks, Embedded Systems, IoT, Machine Learning and Image Processing, etc.

List of contributors

Rubaid Ashfaq
Department of Amity School of Communication
Amity University
Noida, Uttar Pradesh, India

Vijay Anant Athavale
Department of Computer Science and Engineering
Walchand Institute of Technology
Solapur, Maharashtra, India

Aydin Abdulkadir
Department of Industrial Engineering
Sakarya University

Sakarya, Turkey
Victor Hugo C. de Albuquerque
Department of Teleinformatics Engineering
Federal University of Ceará (UFC)

Fortaleza, Brazil
A. Jose Anand
Department of Electronics and Communication Engineering
KCG College of Technology
Chennai, Tamil Nadu, India

Humera Amin
Department of Agricultural Extension and Rural Studies
University College of Agriculture, University of Sargodha
Pakistan

Madhumala, R. B.
Department of CSE-ICB
Dayananda Sagar Academy of Technology and Management (DSATM)
Bengaluru, India

Rotimi-Williams Bello
Department of Computer Systems Engineering
Tshwane University of Technology (TUT)
Pretoria, South Africa

Pankaj Bhambri
Department of Information Technology
Guru Nanak Dev Engineering College
Ludhiana, Punjab, India

Satwik Chatterjee
Department of School of Behavioral & Applied Sciences
Adamas University & Adamas Knowledge City
Kolkata, West Bengal, India

Vimalakeerthy Devadoss
College of Engineering and Technology
UTAS Nizwa
Sultanate of Oman

Dhanumjaya K.
Department of Electronics and Communication Engineering
Tirupati, Andhra Pradesh, India

Erhan Yilmaz
Graduate School of Natural and Applied Sciences, Department of Computer Engineering Kron Technologies
Ege University
Izmir, Türkey

Mayakannan S.
Department of Mechanical Engineering
Rathinam Technical Campus
Coimbatore, Tamilnadu, India

Muhammad Farooq
Department of Computer Science
The Superior University
Lahore, Pakistan

B. Gayathri
Department of Computer Science
Bishop Heber College (Autonomous)
Trichy, Tamil Nadu, India

M. Gokilhashree
Department of Medical Electronics
Sengunthar Engineering College
Erode, Tamil Nadu, India

Hadi Kazemi
School of Built Environment and Engineering
Leeds Business School
Leeds Beckett University, Leeds, UK
and
Kwara State, Nigeria
Hajar Fatorachian
Leeds Business School
Leeds Beckett University
Leeds, UK

Hind Hammouch
Faculty of Legal, Economic, and Social Sciences
Sidi Mohamed Ben Abdellah University
Fez, Morocco

Kalaiselvi S.
Department of Chemistry
Velalar College of Engineering and Technology (Autonomous)
Erode, Tamil Nadu, India

R. Kalaivani
Department of B.C.A & AI & ML, SRM Trichy Arts and Science College
Trichy Bharathidasan University
Tamil Nadu, India

Mudassir Khan
College of Science & Arts Tanumah
King Khalid University
Asir, Saudi Arabia

Aman Kumar
Department of Mechanical Engineering
UIET, MDU Rohtak
Rohtak, India

Naveen Ananda Kumar
TekInvaderz LLC
FL

Kallakunta Ravi Kumar
Department of Electronics and Communication Engineering
Koneru Lakshmaiah Education Foundation
Guntur, Andhra Pradesh, India

Venkata Lakshmi
School of Computer Science and Engineering
VIT-AP University
Andhra Pradesh, India

Haipeng Liu
Research Centre for Intelligent Healthcare
Coventry University
Coventry, UK

A. Asrin Mahmootha
Mohamed Sathak Engineering College
Kilakarai, Tamil Nadu, India

Vinod Kumar V. Meti
Department of Automation & Robotics
KLE Technological University, BVB College Campus
Hubballi, Karnataka, India

Saravanan Muniswamy
MIT Square
London, UK

Sivakumar Muthusamy
College of Engineering and Technology
UTAS Nizwa
Sultanate of Oman

Adewale Opeoluwa Ogunde
Department of Computer Science
Redeemer's University
Ede, Osun State, Nigeria

Roseline Oluwaseun Ogundokun
Department of Computer Systems Engineering
Tshwane University of Technology (TUT)
Pretoria, South Africa

Akinyomade O. Owolabi
Department of Microbiology
Landmark University

Omu-Aran
Pius Adewale Owolawi
Department of Computer Systems Engineering
Tshwane University of Technology (TUT)
Pretoria, South Africa

Can Özgü
Department of Computer Engineering
Ege University
Izmir, Türkey

Oshma Rosette Pinto
School of Business Management
Christ University
Bengaluru, Karnataka, India
and
Osun State, Nigeria

Akshay S.
Department of CSE-ICB
Dayananda Sagar Academy of Technology and Management (DSATM)
Bengaluru, India

Pavan Gowda T. S.
Department of CSE-ICB
Dayananda Sagar Academy of Technology and Management (DSATM)
Bengaluru, India

Vidhya Prakash Rajendran
College of Engineering and Technology
UTAS Nizwa, Sultanate of Oman

Dhanush Reddy C. S.
Department of CSE-ICB
Dayananda Sagar Academy of Technology and Management (DSATM)
Bengaluru, India

Turgay Safiye
Department of Industrial Engineering
Sakarya University

Sakarya, Turkey
S. Sajithabanu
Mohamed Sathak Engineering College
Kilakarai, Tamil Nadu, India

Sangeetha G.
Department of CSE-ICB
Dayananda Sagar Academy of Technology and Management (DSATM)
Bengaluru, India

Mithileysh Sathiyanarayanan
Scientist & CEO, Research & Innovation
MIT Square London
UK

S. V. Saveeithaa
Department of Electronics and Communication Engineering
Erode Senguthar Engineering College
Erode, Tamil Nadu, India

Bazani Shaik
Department of Mechanical Engineering
Ramachandra College of Engineering
Eluru, Andhra Pradesh, India

Narendra Singh
Department of Electronics and Communication Engineering
Jaypee University of Engineering and Technology,
Guna, Madhya Pradesh, India

Deepak Sharma
Department of Electronics and Communication Engineering
Jaypee University of Engineering and Technology
Madhya Pradesh, India

Sadasivam Subbarayan
College of Engineering and Technology
UTAS Nizwa
Sultanate of Oman

B. Sundaravadivazhagn
College of Computing and Information Sciences
University of Technology and Applied Sciences
Al Mussanah, Oman

Anu Tonk
Department of Multidisciplinary Engineering
The NorthCap University
Gurugram, India

Duong Thanh Tung
Faculty of Tourism
Nguyen Tat Thanh University
Ho Chi Minh City, Vietnam

Chinecherem Umezuruike
Department of Computer Science
Bowen University
Iwo, Osun State

G. Yamini
Department of Computer Science
National College
Tiruchirappalli, Tamil Nadu, India

Preface

The rapid proliferation of cloud computing, artificial intelligence, Internet of Things (IoT), and distributed digital infrastructures has fundamentally transformed the landscape of cybercrime and digital investigations. While cloud environments provide scalability, flexibility, and operational efficiency, they also introduce unprecedented forensic challenges, including data volatility, multi-tenancy, cross-jurisdictional complexity, encryption, and ephemeral computing environments. Traditional digital forensic methodologies are no longer sufficient to address the scale, speed, and sophistication of next-generation cyber threats. *AI-Driven Cloud Forensics: Advanced Techniques for Next-Generation Digital Investigations* emerges at this critical juncture, presenting cutting-edge research and practical frameworks that integrate artificial intelligence, machine learning, automation, and big data analytics into cloud forensic processes. This edited volume brings together contributions from researchers, practitioners, and industry experts to explore intelligent cloud architectures, forensic acquisition in virtualized and containerized environments, anomaly detection, fraud investigation in dark web ecosystems, phishing detection, log analysis, and AI-driven forensic readiness. The chapters collectively address both foundational principles and emerging paradigms, including AutoML-enabled forensic frameworks, federated learning for anomaly detection, privileged access management, real-time detection of data fabrication attacks, and AI-enhanced e-discovery processes. Additionally, the book explores interdisciplinary applications of AI-driven forensic intelligence in smart micro-grids, tourism systems, and supply chain networks, highlighting the expanding scope of cloud forensics beyond conventional cybersecurity boundaries. By combining theoretical advances with applied case studies and bibliometric research mapping, this volume provides a comprehensive reference for academics, cybersecurity professionals, forensic analysts, legal experts, and postgraduate researchers. It aims to bridge the gap between AI innovation and forensic practice, offering scalable, intelligent, and automated solutions for securing cloud-based digital ecosystems. We hope this book serves as both a scholarly contribution and a practical guide for advancing trustworthy, transparent, and resilient digital investigation frameworks in an increasingly cloud-driven world.

Pankaj Bhambri, Mudassir Khan and A. Jose Anand

Chapter 1

Introduction to advanced cloud forensics

Pankaj Bhambri, Mudassir Khan and A. Jose Anand

1.1 THE EVOLVING DIGITAL LANDSCAPE: FROM PHYSICAL TO VIRTUAL

The journey of digital forensics has been one of constant adaptation, mirroring the relentless evolution of information technology itself. The foundational principles of forensics—identification, preservation, analysis, and presentation of digital evidence—were forged in the era of tangible, physical media (Mishra & Bajahzar, 2024). Investigators dealt with hard drives, smartphones, and USB sticks—discrete, ownable assets whose physical seizure granted control over the entire data environment. This paradigm is fundamentally disrupted by the migration to the cloud, a shift from physical artifact-centric investigations to virtualized service-centric ones (Egho-Promise et al., 2024).

In the cloud, evidence is no longer a static bitstream on a platter but a dynamic, ephemeral, and distributed state across shared, multi-tenant infrastructure. The "crime scene" is not a server in a suspect's closet but a global network of hyper-scale data centers operated by a third party. The "evidence" may be a fleeting container instance, a database entry, or an API log, all accessed over a network and often beyond the direct physical or legal reach of the investigator (Saluja & Bhavsar, 2025). This transition from a contained, controllable environment to a boundless, elastic, and shared virtual landscape represents the core challenge and catalyst for advanced cloud forensics.

1.1.1 The limitations of traditional digital forensics

- Traditional digital forensics methodologies, while still essential for endpoint analysis, encounter significant and often insurmountable limitations when applied to cloud environments:
- Loss of Physical Control and Accessibility: The cornerstone of traditional forensics is the ability to physically seize a device, create a forensic image, and analyze it in a controlled lab. In the cloud, there is no device to seize. Infrastructure is owned and managed by the Cloud Service Provider (CSP) (Venkataramanan & Arulselvarani, 2025). Investigators cannot "pull the plug" to preserve volatile memory or walk into a data center to image a server.
- Jurisdictional and Legal Complexity: Cloud data is frequently stored in geographically dispersed data centers, potentially spanning multiple legal jurisdictions. A single investigation may involve data governed by different national laws (e.g., GDPR, CLOUD

DOI: 10.1201/9781003656487-1

Act), creating complex legal hurdles for evidence collection, preservation, and admissibility (Frank et al., 2024).
- Multi-Tenancy and Data Commingling: Evidence relevant to an investigation resides on physical hardware shared with countless other, unrelated tenants (individuals, companies). Traditional physical imaging is impossible as it would capture unrelated data, violating privacy laws. Forensic techniques must logically isolate and extract only the relevant tenant's data (Bhambri & Hamad, 2025).
- Ephemeral and Dynamic Nature of Evidence: Cloud resources are provisioned and destroyed on demand. Virtual machines, containers, serverless functions, and their associated logs can vanish in seconds. The traditional "freeze-the-scene" approach is irrelevant; instead, investigators must act with automated speed to capture transient artifacts before they are permanently lost (Kaushik et al., 2024).
- Dependence on CSP APIs and Tools: Direct, low-level access to disk sectors or raw memory is unavailable. All evidence acquisition must occur through the CSP's provided Application Programming Interfaces (APIs) and management consoles. The forensic process is therefore mediated by the CSP's design choices, rate limits, logging fidelity, and available tooling, creating a potential "black box" problem (Othman & Al-Dhaqm, 2024).
- Scale and Volume: Cloud environments can generate terabytes of logs, millions of events, and countless interconnected assets daily. Manual, timeline-based analysis becomes impractical. Advanced techniques in big data analytics, machine learning, and automation are required to filter, correlate, and identify relevant evidence needles in the data haystack (Geetha et al., 2025a).
- The Shared Responsibility Model: Security and compliance are shared between the CSP and the customer. The CSP is responsible for security of the cloud (physical infrastructure, hypervisor), while the customer is responsible for security in the cloud (OS, application, data). This blurs the lines of evidentiary custody and complicates the question of who is responsible for preserving what evidence (Bhambri & Khang, 2025).

1.1.2 Defining the cloud ecosystem: IaaS, PaaS, and SaaS

Cloud computing is not monolithic. It is delivered through layered service models that abstract different levels of the technology stack from the user. Understanding these models is critical, as the forensic landscape and available evidence shift dramatically between them.

- Infrastructure as a Service (IaaS): IaaS provides fundamental computing resources—virtual machines, storage, networks, and operating systems—over the internet on a pay-as-you-go basis. The user has the most control here, managing the OS, middleware, and applications (Alharthi, 2024). This model offers the richest forensic potential closest to traditional methods. Investigators can potentially acquire virtual disk images (VHD, VMDK), snapshot volatile memory of instances, and analyze network flow logs. However, the hypervisor and underlying physical hardware remain under the sole control of the CSP. Examples include Amazon EC2, Microsoft Azure VMs, and Google Compute Engine (Mohanty et al., 2025).
- Platform as a Service (PaaS): PaaS provides a platform allowing customers to develop, run, and manage applications without the complexity of building and maintaining the underlying infrastructure (servers, storage, network). The CSP manages the OS and runtime environment (Bhambri, 2025). The focus shifts from OS-level artifacts to application-level evidence. Direct disk or memory acquisition is typically unavailable. Forensics relies heavily on application logs, database audit trails, platform-specific

audit logs (e.g., Azure SQL Database audit logs), and deployment artifacts. The investigation is more specialized to the platform services used (e.g., a specific database or app runtime). Examples include Google App Engine, Microsoft Azure App Service, and AWS Elastic Beanstalk (Mukti & Hanif, 2025).

- Software as a Service (SaaS): SaaS delivers a complete, fully functional application over the internet, accessible via a web browser. The CSP manages everything from the infrastructure to the application software. This presents the greatest challenge and abstraction (Rana & Bhambri, 2024b). The investigator has zero access to infrastructure, platform, or application code. Evidence is almost entirely limited to data within the application and the logs provided by the CSP. This includes user activity logs (logins, file accesses), administrative audit trails, and content/data exported via the application's native features or (limited) CSP APIs. Investigations often hinge on understanding the SaaS application's own logging and reporting capabilities. Examples include Microsoft 365, Salesforce, Google Workspace, and Dropbox.

The version uses a classic layered diagram to highlight the "stack" and the shared responsibility divide, which is central to cloud security and forensics.

The layered diagram in Figure 1.1 illustrates the fundamental principle of cloud security and forensics: as the service model ascends from IaaS to SaaS, the user's management responsibility and direct access decrease. Correspondingly, the forensic investigator's focus must shift from traditional system artifacts (IaaS) to the logs and data outputs available within each layer's constrained domain. The CSP maintains absolute control over everything below the red line.

1.2 FUNDAMENTAL CHALLENGES IN CLOUD FORENSICS

The migration of data, applications, and infrastructure to cloud environments has fundamentally disrupted traditional digital forensic methodologies. While cloud computing offers scalability, efficiency, and cost savings, it introduces a unique set of complex challenges for forensic investigators (Pati et al., 2025). These challenges stem from the cloud's abstracted, distributed, and often multi-jurisdictional nature, which directly conflicts with the core forensic principles of isolation, control, and repeatability. This section details the most critical fundamental challenges facing modern cloud forensic practitioners.

1.2.1 Jurisdictional and legal hurdles

Cloud infrastructure is inherently global, with data centers located across different countries and continents (Sajithabanu et al., 2025). This geographical dispersion directly clashes with the territorially bound nature of law and legal process.

- Conflict of Laws: Data relevant to an investigation may be stored in multiple jurisdictions, each with its own data protection, privacy, and evidentiary laws. For example, a US-based corporation using a European subsidiary's Microsoft 365 tenant may have its evidentiary data stored in Dublin, Ireland (Abdelkarim, 2025). A US law enforcement agency seeking this data must navigate the EU's General Data Protection Regulation (GDPR), which imposes strict limitations on cross-border data transfers. The process requires mechanisms like Mutual Legal Assistance Treaties (MLATs), which are notoriously slow, often taking months or years—a timeframe incompatible with most investigations.

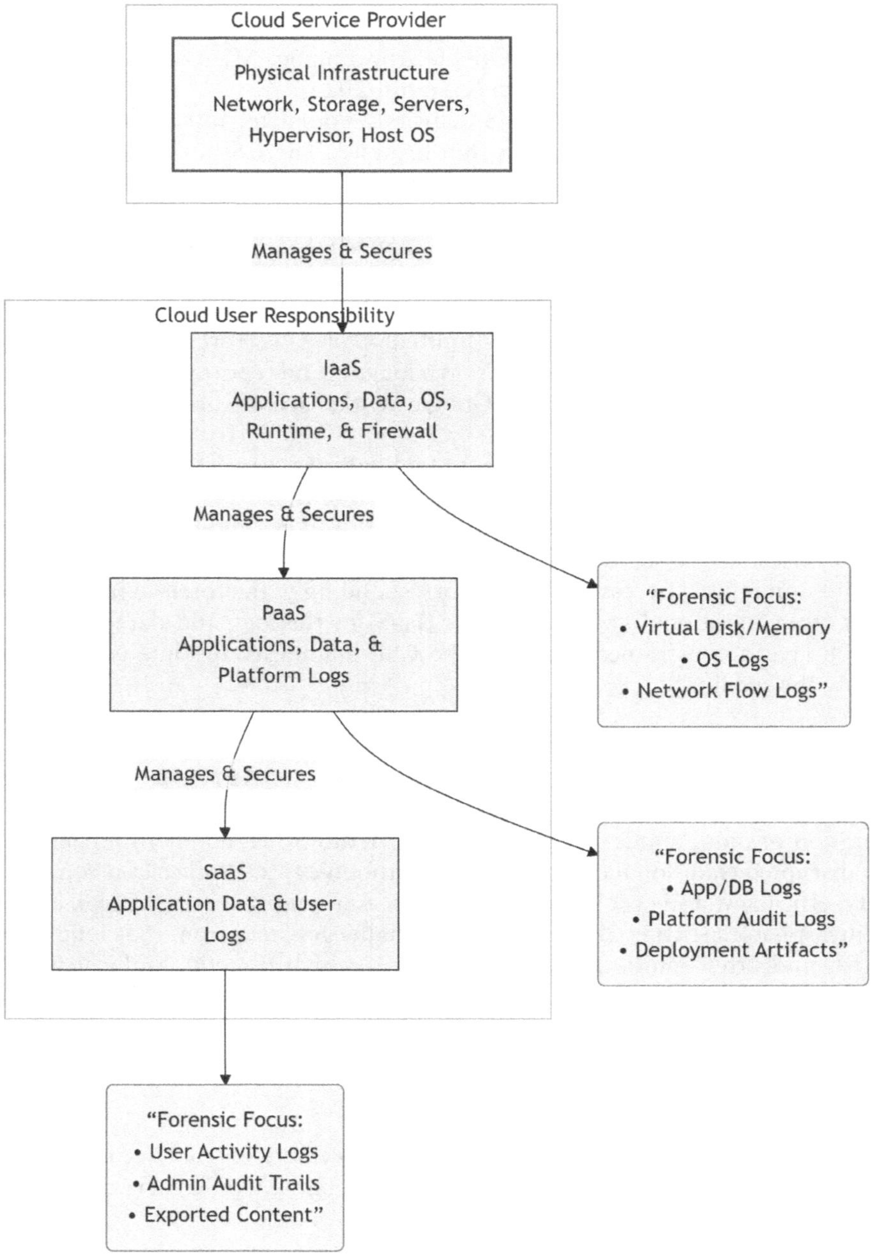

Figure 1.1 Shared responsibility model and forensic evidence focus.

- Data Sovereignty Mandates: Many countries (e.g., Russia, China, India, and the EU through GDPR to an extent) have data sovereignty laws requiring that data about their citizens be stored and processed within national borders (Alshabibi et al., 2024). An investigator for a multinational incident may be legally barred from accessing or mirroring data stored in a region with such mandates, even with a valid domestic warrant. This can create "forensic black holes" where critical evidence exists but is legally inaccessible.

- Subpoena and Warrant Complexity: A traditional warrant served to a company gives authorities direct access to physical assets. In the cloud, the "location" of data is logical, not physical. A warrant must be correctly targeted at the legal entity controlling the data (the Cloud Service Provider, or CSP) and must be specific enough to satisfy legal requirements, yet comprehensible to the CSP's automated legal compliance team (Adeosun et al., 2025). Errors in drafting can lead to delays or rejections. The landmark Microsoft Ireland case highlighted this, where US prosecutors sought emails stored in an Irish data center, leading to the Clarifying Lawful Overseas Use of Data (CLOUD) Act, which attempts to resolve some of these conflicts but is not universally adopted.

Example: A phishing investigation targeting an Australian company reveals the attacker used an IaaS VM hosted by a US CSP, with command-and-control logs stored in a Singapore region, and exfiltrated data placed in an object storage bucket in the Netherlands (Chippagiri, 2025). The Australian Federal Police must coordinate legally with authorities in three different jurisdictions to preserve and collect a complete evidence chain, a diplomatically and procedurally daunting task.

1.2.2 Multi-tenancy and data segregation

Cloud environments are built on a multi-tenant architecture, where computational resources (CPUs, memory, disk, network) are shared among multiple, unrelated customers (tenants) (Geetha et al., 2025b). While CSPs invest heavily in logical isolation, forensic integrity depends on proving this isolation is absolute and that evidence from one tenant cannot be contaminated by or confused with another.

- Logical vs. Physical Isolation: Investigators no longer have a physical server to seize. Evidence exists as logical constructs (virtual machines, database rows, storage blobs) on shared hardware (Bhambri & Pawełoszek, 2025). The forensic process must trust and verify the CSP's hypervisor, management plane, and APIs to correctly segregate data. An error or exploit in this logical layer could compromise evidence, raising chain of custody and evidence admissibility questions.
- Evidence Contamination Risk: During a forensic acquisition, the act of imaging a virtual disk or capturing network traffic must not impact neighboring tenants sharing the underlying hardware (Alharthi & Yasaei, 2025). The tools and techniques used must be "tenant-aware." Furthermore, residual data in shared memory or temporary storage (a risk known as data remanence) could theoretically leak between tenants, though this risk is minimal with major CSPs.
- Attribution Difficulty in PaaS/SaaS: In Platform- or Software-as-a-Service models (e.g., Salesforce, Google Workspace), the level of abstraction is higher. Logs and data are deeply intermingled within the CSP's application layer. Extracting a single user's activity trail requires precise filtering of a massive, shared log stream (Bhambri & Kumar, 2024b). Proving that the extracted data pertains solely to the target tenant and investigation is a critical requirement.

Example: In an IaaS environment, an investigator uses the CSP's forensic API to capture a snapshot of a suspect's virtual machine disk. The integrity of that evidence relies on the CSP's hypervisor (e.g., AWS Nitro, VMware ESXi) correctly mapping the virtual disk blocks to the correct physical storage silo dedicated to that tenant (Bhambri & Kumar, 2024a).

Any failure in this mapping could lead to cross-tenant data leakage, rendering the evidence inadmissible.

1.2.3 Ephemeral evidence and volatile data

The cloud's elasticity and "as-a-Service" models mean that resources are constantly created, destroyed, and scaled automatically. This on-demand nature is antithetical to the forensic imperative of preservation.

- Short-Lived Resources: Container orchestrators (like Kubernetes) spin up pods that may live for only minutes. Serverless functions (AWS Lambda, Azure Functions) execute in milliseconds and their runtime environments are destroyed immediately after. Auto-scaling groups terminate unhealthy instances (Jyotinagar & Meshram, 2024). Evidence such as running processes, network connections, and memory dumps from these resources is lost forever if not captured in real time.
- Dynamic IP Addressing and Shared Resources: Cloud instances often have non-persistent IP addresses. A malicious VM may be decommissioned and its public IP reassigned to an innocent customer within hours, confusing network-based attribution (Sharma et al., 2025a). Similarly, underlying host-level logs or telemetry that could be vital for root cause analysis are typically inaccessible to the tenant and are recycled by the CSP on a short schedule.
- Forensic Preservation vs. Business Continuity: A core incident response step is isolation (containment). In the cloud, taking a traditional approach of "pulling the network cable" on a compromised VM may be counterproductive (Nagpal et al., 2024). It alerts the attacker and destroys volatile evidence. Modern forensic response involves strategic live forensics (memory capture, network flow logging) before containment, often while the compromised resource continues to run. This requires new skills and tools.

Example: An attacker exploits a vulnerability in a web application, deploying a cryptocurrency miner within a container pod. The organization's security automation detects high CPU usage and automatically terminates the pod after 5 minutes (Rana & Bhambri, 2024a). By the time the security team is alerted, the container, its in-memory artifacts, and the attacker's exact entry point are gone (Suganya et al., 2025). Only if the CSP's orchestration logs and cloud-trail logs were proactively enabled and collected can the investigation proceed.

1.2.4 Dependence on cloud service provider (CSP) APIs and tools

In on-premises forensics, investigators have direct, root-level access to hardware and systems. In the cloud, access is mediated entirely through the CSP's provided interfaces—primarily web-based APIs and management consoles (Bhambri, 2024). This creates a layer of abstraction and dependency that fundamentally alters the investigation lifecycle.

- API as the Sole Evidence Source: All evidence collection—from disk snapshots and log retrieval to memory capture and network flow logs—is performed via CSP APIs (e.g., AWS CLI, Azure PowerShell, Google Cloud SDK). The investigator does not interact with raw hardware. Therefore, the integrity and completeness of the investigation are now dependent on the correctness, reliability, and availability of these APIs. If an API has a bug, is rate-limited, or omits certain data fields, the investigation is immediately impaired (Malik et al., 2024).

- Logging Gaps and "Black Box" Components: CSPs offer extensive logging services (AWS CloudTrail, Azure Activity Log, Google Audit Logs), but these logs are designed for operational and security monitoring, not necessarily for forensic scrutiny. Critical gaps may exist. More importantly, the underlying infrastructure (hypervisor, host OS, network hardware) is a "black box." Investigators cannot examine host RAM or compute node disks where crucial low-level attack indicators might reside (Sharma et al., 2025).
- Proprietary Formats and Tooling: Evidence acquired via APIs often comes in proprietary or highly structured formats (e.g., VHDX disks, specific JSON log schemas). While CSPs provide their own analysis tools (e.g., AWS Detective, Azure Sentinel), they lock investigators into a specific ecosystem. This hinders cross-CSP investigations (hybrid or multi-cloud incidents) and challenges the use of standardized, vendor-agnostic forensic tools like FTK or Autopsy, which may not natively parse cloud evidence formats (Al-mugern et al., 2024).
- The Custodial Shift: The CSP, not the investigating organization, is the ultimate custodian of the evidence. The chain of custody now has a critical third-party link. Investigators must document each API call (with timestamps and request IDs) to prove the integrity of the data collection process from the CSP's systems to their own analysis environment.

Example: To investigate a suspected data exfiltration from an AWS S3 bucket, an investigator must:

- Use AWS CloudTrail API to pull management event logs (to see who made API calls).
- Use Amazon S3 Server Access Logging (if pre-configured) to get data-level logs.
- Use AWS VPC Flow Logs to analyze network traffic from the instance that may have accessed the bucket.

Each of these data streams is collected via separate APIs, has different retention periods, incurs costs, and may have latency. A failure to enable S3 Access Logging before the incident means that critical data-level evidence simply does not exist, regardless of the legal authority or forensic skill of the investigator.

1.3 THE PILLARS OF THE CLOUD FORENSICS PROCESS

The shift from physical hardware to virtualized, distributed, and often ephemeral cloud environments necessitates a reimagined forensic methodology. Traditional digital forensics processes, while foundational, are insufficient to address the scale, complexity, and shared responsibility model of the cloud (Ahmed et al., 2024). Advanced cloud forensics is built upon four critical pillars that form a robust, iterative framework for investigation. These pillars—Incident Response, Evidence Acquisition, Evidence Preservation, and Analysis & Correlation—must be adapted to function within the unique constraints and capabilities of virtualized, API-driven infrastructures. Together, they ensure investigations are timely, forensically sound, and capable of producing actionable intelligence from a dynamic digital landscape (Hamid & Rahman, 2024).

1.3.1 Incident response in a virtual environment

Incident response in the cloud is the critical first pillar, characterized by speed and orchestration. Unlike physical environments where an investigator can physically isolate a server, cloud resources are programmable and can be altered or destroyed with a single command or script (Kasula et al., 2024). The ephemeral nature of containers, serverless functions, and auto-scaling groups means that evidence may vanish in moments. Therefore, the initial response must be automated and integrated into the cloud environment itself.

A cloud-centric incident response plan begins with immediate detection through Cloud Security Posture Management (CSPM) tools, CloudTrail/Azure Activity Log monitoring, and security alerts from native services like Amazon GuardDuty or Microsoft Defender for Cloud. The first operational response is often "containment in place" using identity and network controls. This involves revoking compromised IAM credentials or API keys; adjusting security group or Network Security Group (NSG) rules to isolate a virtual instance; or taking a compromised virtual machine snapshot and then shutting it down to prevent further malicious activity while preserving its state (Bhambri & Bajdor, 2025). Crucially, the response team must navigate the cloud provider's shared responsibility model, knowing which actions they must take (e.g., isolating a VM) versus what the provider manages (e.g., securing the underlying hypervisor). Effective cloud incident response is less about "pulling the network cable" and more about executing pre-defined, automated playbooks that leverage Infrastructure-as-Code (IaC) and orchestration tools like AWS Step Functions or Azure Logic Apps to secure the environment at cloud speed (Tanveer et al., 2025).

1.3.2 Evidence acquisition: Logs, snapshots, and memory dumps

Evidence acquisition in the cloud is an exercise in API-driven artifact collection, focusing on the most forensically rich yet volatile sources. The triad of logs, snapshots, and memory dumps forms the core of this pillar.

Logs are the lifeblood of cloud forensics. This includes not only traditional OS and application logs within a virtual machine but, more importantly, the cloud service logs that record the control plane activity. Acquiring AWS CloudTrail, Azure Activity Logs, or GCP Audit Logs is non-negotiable, as they provide an immutable (if configured correctly) record of every API call—who created, modified, or deleted any resource (Maqbool et al., 2024). Network flow logs (VPC Flow Logs, NSG Flow Logs) are equally critical for reconstructing data exfiltration or lateral movement. Acquisition must be rapid and continuous, often streaming directly to a secured, investigator-owned S3 bucket or Log Analytics workspace outside the compromised environment to prevent log tampering.

Snapshots provide a point-in-time forensic image of cloud storage volumes (e.g., Amazon EBS snapshots, Azure Managed Disk snapshots) and, in some cases, entire virtual machine states. Acquiring a snapshot is often the most forensically sound method to capture a persistent disk's contents without powering on the suspect instance, which would alter timestamps and memory. For volatile storage or containerized workloads, acquisition may involve creating a forensic copy of object storage buckets (like S3) or container images from a registry (Pirjade & Dhotre, 2024). Memory dumps of running virtual machines present a significant challenge due to limited hypervisor access. However, some cloud providers offer limited memory acquisition capabilities through specialized services or by leveraging introspection tools within the guest OS before a system is shut down. Acquiring memory is crucial for detecting rootkits, extracting encryption keys, and capturing artifacts of running processes and network connections that never touch the disk. The acquisition process for all these artifacts must be documented meticulously, noting the exact timestamp, API command used, and the resulting evidence artifact ID (e.g., the snapshot ID) to maintain the chain of custody (Alexander & Wang, 2025).

1.3.3 Evidence preservation and the chain of custody

Preservation in the cloud extends beyond simple write-blocking; it is the practice of ensuring the integrity, authenticity, and legal admissibility of data collected from a multi-tenant, provider-managed environment. The traditional chain of custody must be adapted to account for the fact that the investigator never physically possesses the underlying hardware (Bhambri & Starostka-Patyk, 2025). Preservation begins at the moment of acquisition by enabling immutability features wherever possible. This includes using S3 Object Lock, Azure Blob Storage immutable policies, or write-once-read-many (WORM) storage for critical logs and evidence dumps.

The chain of custody documentation must now record new metadata: the cloud provider region and account ID; the specific API calls and credentials (role) used to collect evidence; the unique resource identifiers (ARNs in AWS, Resource IDs in Azure); and hash values calculated post-acquisition (e.g., SHA-256 of a snapshot export) (Morić et al., 2024). Cryptographic hashing remains paramount, but in the cloud, the integrity of the acquisition process itself is also verified through provider-generated hashes and checksums for services like S3 (with its ETags) or snapshot integrity guarantees. Legal considerations, such as who has the legal right to access the data (the subscriber vs. the provider) and navigating cross-border data sovereignty issues (e.g., data residing in an EU zone under GDPR), are integral to this pillar (Revathi et al., 2024). A preserved evidence set must be defensible in court, demonstrating that from the point of collection through analysis, the evidence was protected from unauthorized alteration, with all access and actions logged and attributable.

1.3.4 Analysis and correlation of multi-source data

The final and most complex pillar is the analysis and correlation of heterogeneous data streams from a sprawling cloud estate (Reddy et al., 2025). An investigator is no longer analyzing a single hard drive but a dynamic tapestry of interwoven data: terabyte-scale service logs, configuration states of hundreds of resources, network traffic metadata, and the contents of snapped volumes. The goal is to reconstruct the attack timeline (the "what," "when," and "how") and establish attribution (the "who").

Initial analysis involves timeline creation, merging timestamps from VM filesystems, database transactions, and, most crucially, cloud API logs. This allows an investigator to see that a suspicious process was launched after an anomalous API call that altered a security group. Correlation is key—linking a suspicious external IP in a VPC Flow Log to a specific IAM user session in CloudTrail, and then to malware downloaded onto a specific EC2 instance, as seen in its snapshot (Zziwa et al., 2024). This is where AI-driven techniques, central to this book's theme, become indispensable. Machine learning models can baseline normal behavior for an account and flag anomalies, such as geographically impossible user logins or rare API calls. Graph database analytics can map relationships between users, resources, and actions to visualize attack paths and lateral movement. Natural Language Processing (NLP) can sift through mountains of unstructured log data to identify patterns indicative of specific Tactics, Techniques, and Procedures (TTPs). The analysis pillar transforms raw, multi-source data into a coherent, evidence-based narrative of the incident, providing the insights necessary for remediation, legal action, and strengthening the cloud security posture against future attacks (Mohan Alenezi, 2024).

1.4 THE IMPERATIVE FOR ADVANCED TECHNIQUES: INTRODUCING THE AI-DRIVEN PARADIGM

The transition to cloud computing has rendered traditional digital forensic methodologies, often designed for static, physical media, increasingly inadequate. The very architecture of the cloud—dynamic, distributed, ephemeral, and multi-tenant—creates a perfect storm of investigative complexity (Sharmila & Aparna, 2024). Evidence is no longer a discrete hard drive to be imaged and analyzed; it is a transient stream of API calls, a fragment in a globally distributed object storage system, a virtual machine instance that ceased to exist minutes after an incident, or a microservice log buried within petabytes of operational data. In this environment, the manual, linear, and largely human-scale processes of classical forensics hit fundamental scalability and efficacy barriers. This chapter posits that overcoming these barriers is not merely an option but an imperative, and that the paradigm shift required is one driven by artificial intelligence (AI) and machine learning (ML). The AI-driven paradigm represents a move from reactive, artifact-centric investigation to proactive, intelligence-centric analysis, enabling investigators to navigate the cloud's complexity with unprecedented speed, scale, and insight (Alchi, 2024).

1.4.1 Scaling investigation with big data

Cloud environments generate data at a velocity, volume, and variety that dwarfs anything encountered in traditional IT infrastructures. A single security incident can involve terabytes of flow logs from virtual networks, millions of lines of aggregated CloudTrail or Audit Log entries, snapshots of petabyte-scale storage buckets, and the intricate interdependencies of hundreds of containerized services (Crasselt & Pugliese, 2024). This is the Big Data challenge of cloud forensics. Manually sifting through this deluge is not just impractical; it is impossible within the constrained timeframes of incident response or litigation. Critical evidence can be overlooked due to sheer data overload, while the time-sensitive nature of cloud evidence—where resources can be deleted or altered remotely in seconds—demands rapid triage.

Advanced techniques are required to scale investigations to match this data environment. This involves leveraging distributed computing frameworks (like Apache Spark) to process massive log sets in parallel, employing data-lake architectures to centrally ingest and index heterogeneous evidence, and utilizing advanced data reduction and pattern-matching algorithms. However, these technological scaling solutions alone are not enough (Subhamathi et al., 2024). They provide the computational horsepower but lack the cognitive discernment to separate the signal from the noise. This is where the AI-driven paradigm begins: by applying machine learning models to this pre-processed big data, investigators can move beyond simple keyword searches to anomaly detection, clustering of related events, and predictive modeling of attacker behavior (Bhambri & Anand, 2025). The scale of the data thus becomes an asset rather than a liability, providing the rich, high-dimensional feedstock necessary to train robust AI models that can identify subtle, emerging threats hidden within normal operations.

1.4.2 From manual triage to intelligent automation

Traditional forensic workflows are heavily reliant on manual, sequential steps: identification, preservation, collection, examination, analysis, and reporting. In the cloud, each of these steps is fraught with automation challenges and requires deep, platform-specific expertise (Ojo & Benmubarak, 2025). For example, determining the scope of an incident (identification) involves manually correlating alerts across dozens of services. The AI-driven paradigm seeks to systematically automate this cognitive labor, elevating the forensic analyst from a manual triager to an orchestration supervisor and strategic interpreter (Arooj & Azmat, 2024).

Intelligent automation begins with automating the collection and preservation of evidence using Infrastructure-as-Code (IaC) principles and serverless functions triggered by security events, ensuring a consistent, defensible, and immediate response. The true transformation, however, lies in automating the initial analysis. Rule-based automation (playbooks) can handle simple, known patterns, but they fail against novel or sophisticated attacks. AI introduces cognitive automation. Machine learning models can be trained to perform initial evidence triage by ranking alerts and artifacts by likely relevance or malice, automatically reconstructing timelines of user and entity behavior (UEBA), and identifying hidden connections between disparate log entries that would be invisible to a human examiner (Akter & Rahman, 2024). This shifts the investigator's role from hunting for basic indicators of compromise (IoCs) to validating and interpreting high-fidelity leads generated by AI, focusing their expertise on the most complex aspects of the case, such as attacker intent, lateral movement pathways, and the full impact assessment.

1.4.3 Setting the stage for AI and machine learning solutions

Before delving into specific algorithms and architectures, it is crucial to establish a foundational understanding of why AI and ML are uniquely suited to the cloud forensic problem space and what prerequisites must be met. Cloud forensics is, at its core, a problem of pattern recognition, probabilistic reasoning, and data fusion across heterogeneous, noisy, and often incomplete datasets. These are domains where ML excels. Supervised learning can classify malicious activity (e.g., identifying cryptojacking behavior from CPU and network metrics) (AllahRakha, 2024). Unsupervised learning can discover previously unknown attack patterns or insider threats by clustering anomalies. Natural Language Processing (NLP) can interpret the semantic content of log messages and user communications, while graph neural networks can map the complex relationships between identities, resources, and permissions to visualize attack graphs (Arshi et al., 2024).

Setting the stage for these solutions requires a deliberate foundation. First, data engineering and feature extraction are paramount; AI models are only as good as the data they consume. This necessitates a normalized, time-synchronized, and richly contextualized evidence repository. Second, the concept of "ground truth" must be addressed through the careful curation of labeled training datasets from past incidents, simulated attacks, and adversarial emulation exercises (Nasreen & Mir, 2024). Third, the paradigm demands a cultural shift towards model-assisted investigation, where the outputs of AI are treated as probabilistic guidance within a human-led, legally sound process, not as infallible verdicts. Finally, considerations of explainability (XAI), model integrity, and adversarial robustness must be baked into the design from the start to ensure findings are defensible in court and resilient to manipulation by attackers (Bashir, 2024). By establishing this stage, we transition from viewing AI as a speculative tool to recognizing it as an essential, integrated component of next-generation cloud forensic capability, capable of turning the overwhelming complexity of the cloud into a structured, navigable investigative landscape.

1.5 CONCLUSION AND CHAPTER SUMMARY

This chapter has served as a foundational entry point into the complex and dynamic world of advanced cloud forensics. We began by establishing the critical imperative for this discipline, driven by the ubiquitous migration of data, applications, and infrastructure to cloud environments. The very features that make the cloud attractive—elasticity, multi-tenancy, resource pooling, and global accessibility—fundamentally dismantle traditional forensic paradigms that rely on physical control and static, on-premises artifacts (Alashjaee, 2024; Emehin et al., 2024). We examined the layered models of IaaS, PaaS, and SaaS, each presenting unique evidence loci and shifting the burden of control and accessibility between the consumer and the provider. This shared responsibility model is not merely a technical detail but the core legal and procedural framework within which all cloud investigations must operate.

The discussion then delved into the formidable challenges that define the cloud forensic landscape. The ephemeral nature of virtualized resources, the jurisdictional maze created by geographically dispersed data centers, the complexities of evidence acquisition from multi-tenant platforms, and the overwhelming volume and velocity of cloud-native logs (from CloudTrail, Azure Activity Log, Stackdriver, etc.) collectively create a "perfect storm" for investigators (Kalaiyarasi et al., 2024; Pillai, 2025). These challenges render manual, traditional methods insufficient, slow, and often forensically unsound. It is within this context of complexity and scale that the chapter introduced the pivotal role of artificial intelligence and machine learning not as a futuristic concept, but as an operational necessity for next-generation digital investigations.

The chapter argued that AI is the essential catalyst for advancing cloud forensics from a reactive, artifact-centric process to a proactive, intelligence-driven discipline. We explored how machine learning algorithms, particularly supervised and unsupervised learning, can automate the triage and classification of petabytes of log data, identifying anomalous patterns indicative of compromise that would elude human analysts (Shanker et al., 2024; Hemalatha et al., 2023). We introduced the concept of predictive forensics, where AI models trained on historical breach data and TTPs (Tactics, Techniques, and Procedures) can forecast attack vectors and identify vulnerable configurations before they are exploited. Furthermore, the application of natural language processing (NLP) for intelligently querying unstructured cloud data and automating timeline construction from disparate sources was highlighted as a key force multiplier.

In conclusion, "Introduction to Advanced Cloud Forensics" has set the stage for the detailed technical explorations to follow in this book. It posits that cloud forensics can no longer be viewed as a mere extension of traditional digital forensics. It is a distinct specialty requiring new tools, new protocols, and a new mindset (Suthar & Lunagaria, 2024; Alharthi & Garcia, 2025). The convergence of cloud complexity and AI capability defines the frontier of this field. The subsequent chapters will build upon this foundation, delving into specific AI methodologies, detailed forensic procedures for major cloud platforms, advanced evidence correlation techniques, and the legal frameworks governing this evolving practice (Alsaraireh, 2025). The journey through this book is designed to equip investigators, cybersecurity professionals, and legal experts with the advanced knowledge required to navigate the obscured landscapes of the cloud, transforming overwhelming data into clear, actionable, and court-ready intelligence.

REFERENCES

Abdelkarim, M. (2025). AI-Driven Smart Banking in the Cloud Era: Enhancing Financial Risk Monitoring, Compliance, and Vendor Collaboration through Digital Forensics. *International Journal of Advanced Research in Computer Science & Technology (IJARCST)*, 8(3), 12150–12154.

Adeosun, O. A., Bello, A. D., Serifat, O. A., & Amomo, C. G. (2025). Enhancing Financial Cybersecurity in Cloud Engineering: A Systematic Review of Threats, Mitigation Strategies and Regulatory Compliance. *Asian Journal of Research in Computer Science*, 18(5), 244–256.

Ahmed, W. S., Mustafa AL-Ta'I, Z. T., Abegaz, T., & Mahmood, G. S. (2024). Digital Forensics Architecture for Real-time Automated Evidence Collection and Centralization: Leveraging Security Lake and Modern Data Architecture. *Journal of Intelligent Systems*, 33(1), 20240109. https://doi.org/10.1515/jisys-2024-0109

Akter, S. S., & Rahman, M. S. (2024). Cloud Forensic: Issues, Challenges, and Solution Models. In *A Practical Guide on Security and Privacy in Cyber-Physical Systems: Foundations, Applications and Limitations* (pp. 113–152), ArXiv, abs/2303.06313.

Al-mugern, R., Othman, S. H., Al-Dhaqm, A., & Ali, A. (2024). A Cloud Forensics Framework to Identify, Gather, and Analyze Cloud Computing Incidents. *Engineering, Technology & Applied Science Research*, 14(3), 14483–14491.

Alashjaee, A. M. (2024). Toward a Conflict Resolution Protocol for Cloud Forensics Investigation. *IEEE Access*, 12, 72013–72022. https://doi.org/10.1109/ACCESS.2024.3408224

Alchi, A. (2024). Advanced Forensics Open-Source Tools. In K. Kaushik, M. Ouaissa & A. Chaudhary (Eds.), *Advanced Techniques and Applications of Cybersecurity and Forensics* (pp. 22–34). Chapman and Hall/CRC, USA.

Alexander, C. A., & Wang, L. (2025). Cyber Forensics on Advanced Technology Platforms. *Journal of Cybersecurity, Digital Forensics and Jurisprudence*, 1, 1–8.

Alharthi, D. (2024, October). Cloud Incident Response Framework and AI-Based Forensics Using Reinforcement Learning and Graph Neural Networks. In *2024 IEEE 15th Annual Information Technology, Electronics and Mobile Communication Conference (IEMCON)* (pp. 164–170). IEEE.

Alharthi, D., & Garcia, I. R. K. (2025). Cloud Investigation Automation Framework (ciaf): An Ai-driven Approach to Cloud Forensics. arXiv preprint arXiv:2510.00452.

Alharthi, D., & Yasaei, R. (2025, July). Llm-powered Automated Cloud Forensics: From Log Analysis to Investigation. In *2025 IEEE 18th International Conference on Cloud Computing (CLOUD)* (pp. 12–22). IEEE.

AllahRakha, N. (2024). Demystifying the Network and Cloud Forensics' Legal, Ethical, and Practical Considerations. *Pakistan Journal of Criminology*, 16(2), 1–8.

Alsaraireh, N. (2025). Digital Forensics in the Age of Cybercrime: Challenges and Future Directions. In R. K. Hamdan (Ed.), *Tech Fusion in Business and Society: Harnessing Big Data, IoT, and Sustainability in Business: Volume 2* (pp. 555–564). Springer Nature Switzerland.

Alshababi, M. M., Bu dookhi, A. K., & Hafizur Rahman, M. M. (2024). Forensic Investigation, Challenges, and Issues of Cloud Data: A Systematic Literature Review. *Computers*, 13(8), 213. https://doi.org/10.3390/computers13080213

Arooj, A. B., & Azmat, H. (2024). Enhancing Cloud Forensics in Azure with AI-Driven Incident Analysis. *Global Perspectives on Multidisciplinary Research*, 5(3), 20–31.

Arshi, O., Gupta, G., & Aggarwal, A. (2024). IoT Forensics. In K. Kaushik, M. Ouaissa & A. Chaudhary (Eds.), *Advanced Techniques and Applications of Cybersecurity and Forensics* (pp. 57–81). Chapman and Hall/CRC, USA.

Bhambri, P. (2024). Enhancing Cybersecurity with SuperHyperSoft Computing Approaches. In F. Smarandache & P. Majumder (Eds.), *Modern SuperHyperSoft Computing Trends in Science and Technology* (pp. 127–148). IGI Global. https://doi.org/10.4018/979-8-3693-6875-6.ch005

Bhambri, P. (2025). Understanding AI and Machine Learning in Security. In P. Bhambri & A. J. Anand (Eds.), *Handbook of AI-driven Threat Detection and Prevention: A Holistic Approach to Security* (pp. 1–17). CRC Press. https://doi.org/10.1201/9781003521020-1

Bhambri, P., & Anand, A. J. (Eds.). (2025). *Handbook of AI-Driven Threat Detection and Prevention: A Holistic Approach to Security*. CRC Press. https://doi.org/10.1201/9781003521020

Bhambri, P., & Bajdor, P. (2025). AI-powered Predictive Analysis for Proactive Cyber Defense. In P. Bhambri & A. J. Anand (Eds.), *Handbook of AI-driven Threat Detection and Prevention: A Holistic Approach to Security* (pp. 308–321). CRC Press. https://doi.org/10.1201/9781003521020-18

Bhambri, P., & Hamad, A. (2025). Quantum Computing and AI Synergies: Strengthening Cybersecurity Resilience. In P. Bhambri & A. J. Anand (Eds.), *Handbook of AI-driven Threat Detection and Prevention: A Holistic Approach to Security* (pp. 337–352). CRC Press. https://doi.org/10.1201/9781003521020-20

Bhambri, P., & Khang, A. (2025). Cyber Security Threats, Cyber Terrorism, Cyber Warfare. In E. de Silva & S. Jayaratne (Eds.), *The Role of Intelligence in Countering Violent Extremism* (pp. 163–184). IGI Global Scientific Publishing. https://doi.org/10.4018/979-8-3693-3522-2.ch008

Bhambri, P., & Kumar, S. (2024a). Cloud and IoT Integration for Smart Healthcare. In P. Bhambri, R. Soni, & T. A. Tran (Eds.), *Smart Healthcare Systems: AI and IoT Perspectives* (pp. 69–84). CRC Press. https://doi.org/10.1201/9781032698519-6

Bhambri, P., & Kumar, S. (2024b). Protecting Sustainable Supply Chains from Cyber Threats. In P. Bhambri & I. Paweloszek (Eds.), *Digital Sustainability: Navigating Entrepreneurship in the Information Age* (pp. 125–141). CRC Press. https://doi.org/10.1201/9781003484226-9

Bhambri, P., & Pawełoszek, I. (2025). Deep Learning Techniques for Intrusion Detection in Critical Infrastructure. In P. Bhambri & A. J. Anand (Eds.), *Handbook of AI-driven Threat Detection and Prevention: A Holistic Approach to Security* (pp. 322–336). CRC Press. https://doi.org/10.1201/9781003521020-19

Bhambri, P., & Starostka-Patyk, M. (2025). Integrating AI with Blockchain for Decentralized Security and Threat Prevention. In P. Bhambri & A. J. Anand (Eds.), *Handbook of AI-driven Threat Detection and Prevention: A Holistic Approach to Security* (pp. 353–370). CRC Press. https://doi.org/10.1201/9781003521020-21

Bashir, H. (2024). Digital Forensics: Techniques for Investigating Cybercrimes. *Computer Science Bulletin*, 7(1), 76–88.

Chippagiri, S. (2025). A Study of Cloud Security Frameworks for Safeguarding Multi-Tenant Cloud Architectures. *International Journal of Computer Applications*, 975, 8887.

Crasselt, J., & Pugliese, G. (2024). Started Off Local, Now We're in the Cloud: Forensic Examination of the Amazon Echo Show 15 Smart Display. arXiv preprint arXiv:2408.15768.

Egho-Promise, E., Idahosa, S., Asante, G., & Okungbowa, A. (2024). Digital Forensic Investigation Standards in Cloud Computing. *Universal Journal of Computer Sciences and Communications*, 3(1), 23–45.

Emehin, O., Emeteveke, I., Adeyeye, O., & Akanbi, I. (2024). Generative AI in Forensic Data Analysis: Opportunities and Ethical Implications for Cloud-Based Investigations. *International Journal of Research Publication and Reviews*, 6, 2941–2957.

Frank, S., Jjingo, D., & Marvin, G. (2024, August). Cloud Forensics in Virtual Machines Using Transparent Deep Learning Techniques. In *Proceedings of the 2024 Sixteenth International Conference on Contemporary Computing* (pp. 330–336). Noida, Inda.

Geetha, R., Vidhya, S., Mukunthan, M. A., Goud, D. S., Anand, J. A., & Kesavan, R. (2025a). Predicting Online Vulnerability among Children and Youth: A Machine Learning Approach with Decision Trees and Naive Bayes Algorithms. *2025 Global Conference in Emerging Technology (GINOTECH)*, PUNE, India, 2025, pp. 1–6.

Geetha, R., Thilagavathi, P., Anand, J. A., Govindaram, A., Gilda, S. J., & Parameswari, D. (2025b). Detection and Classification of Faults in a Power System with Inverter Penetration Based on a Real-Time Machine Learning Application. *2025 Fourth International Conference on Smart Technologies, Communication and Robotics (STCR)*, Sathyamangalam, India, pp. 1–6.

Hamid, I., & Rahman, M. H. (2024). A Comprehensive Literature Review on Volatile Memory Forensics. *Electronics*, 13(15), 3026. https://doi.org/10.3390/electronics13153026

Hemalatha, S., Mahalakshmi, M., Vignesh, V., Geethalakshmi, M., Balasubramanian, D., & Jose, A. A. (2023). Deep Learning Approaches for Intrusion Detection with Emerging Cybersecurity Challenges. In *2023 International Conference on Sustainable Communication Networks and Applications (ICSCNA)* (pp. 1522–1529). Theni, India.

Jyotinagar, V., & Meshram, B. (2024). Digital Forensic Analysis of Attack Detection and Identification in Private Cloud Environments for Databases. *Journal of Integrated Science and Technology*, 12(4), 798–798.

Kalaiyarasi, D., Leopauline, S., Krishnaveni, S., & Vajravelu, A. (2024). Cloud Computing-Based Computer Forensics: A Deep Learning Technique. *International Journal of Electronic Security and Digital Forensics*, 16(3), 317–328. https://doi.org/10.1504/IJESDF.2024.138611

Kasula, V. K., Yadulla, A. R., Konda, B., & Yenugula, M. (2024). Fortifying Cloud Environments against Data Breaches: A Novel AI-driven Security Framework. *World Journal of Advanced Research and Reviews*, 24, 1613–1626.

Kaushik, K., Ouaissa, M., & Chaudhary, A. (Eds.). (2024). *Advanced Techniques and Applications of Cybersecurity and Forensics*. CRC Press.

Malik, A. W., Bhatti, D. S., Park, T. J., Ishtiaq, H. U., Ryou, J. C., & Kim, K. I. (2024). Cloud Digital Forensics: Beyond Tools, Techniques, and Challenges. *Sensors*, 24(2), 433. https://doi.org/10.3390/s24020433

Maqbool, K. Q., Farooq, O., Hussain, M. Z., Hasan, M. Z., Batool, H., & Usman, F. (2024). Beyond Traditional Techniques for Enhancement of Digital Forensics for Cloud. *Spectrum of Engineering Sciences*, 2(5), 379–409.

Mishra, S., & A Bajahzar, M. (2024). Cloud Forensic Artefacts: Digital Forensics Registry Artefacts Discovered from Cloud Storage Application. *International Journal of Computing and Digital Systems*, 16(1), 13–27.

Mohan Alenezi, A. (2024). Beyond The Clouds: Investigating Digital Crimes In Cloud Environments (October 06, 2024).

Mohanty, A., Mohapatra, A. G., Nayak, N., Bairavel S., Chaithra M. H., Lakshmi, M., Govindaram, A., & Anand, J. A. (2025). Optimizing Diesel Generators in Industrial Settings with IoT and Machine Learning. *International Journal of Information Technology*, 1–9.

Morić, Z., Dakić, V., Kapulica, A., & Regvart, D. (2024). Forensic Investigation Capabilities of Microsoft Azure: A Comprehensive Analysis and Its Significance in Advancing Cloud Cyber Forensics. *Electronics*, 13(22), 4546. https://doi.org/10.3390/electronics13224546

Mukti, M. T. P., & Hanif, N. (2025). Artificial Intelligence in Cloud Forensics: Automating Evidence Acquisition and Anomaly Detection in Distributed Environments. *FORSEC: Forensics & Security Journal*, 1(1), 1–7.

Nagpal, A., Kumar, S. V., Reddy, U., Radha, K., Kumar, A., & Abdulla, N. R. (2024, June). Exploring Advanced Techniques in Computer and Network Forensics for Enhanced Cybersecurity. In *2024 OPJU International Technology Conference (OTCON) on Smart Computing for Innovation and Advancement in Industry 4.0* (pp. 1–6). IEEE.

Nasreen, S., & Mir, A. H. (2024). Cloud Forensics: A Centralized Cloud Provenance Investigation System using MECC. *Concurrency and Computation: Practice and Experience*, 36(6), e7949. https://doi.org/10.1002/cpe.7949

Ojo, A. O., & Benmubarak, M. (2025). Investigating Advanced Persistent Threat Tactics in Cloud Environments: A Forensic Study of AWS CloudTrail Log Data. *International Journal of Innovative Science and Research Technology*, 10(7), 3170–3176.

Othman, S. H., & Al-Dhaqm, A. (2024). An Improved Machine Learning Method by applying Cloud Forensic Meta-Model to Enhance the Data Collection Process in Cloud Environments. *Engineering, Technology & Applied Science Research*, 14(1), 13017–13025.

Pati, T. R., Sansiya, R., & Sethi, P. C. (2025, April). Ensuring Cloud Security Through Scalable Network Forensics. In *International Conference on Machine Learning, IoT and Big Data* (pp. 88–99). Springer Nature Switzerland.

Pillai, A. V. (2025). Cyber Forensics Tools and Techniques for Effective Digital Crime Detection and Investigation. *International Journal of Research Publications in Engineering, Technology and Management (IJRPETM)*, 8(5), 12693–12697.

Pirjade, S. T., & Dhotre, P. (2024, October). A Systematic Study On Cloud Forensic Framework, Challenges and Technologies Used For Evidence Preservation. In *2024 IEEE International Conference on Blockchain and Distributed Systems Security (ICBDS)* (pp. 1–6). IEEE.

Rana, R., & Bhambri, P. (2024a). Blockchain for Transparent, Privacy Protected and Secure Health Data Management. In P. Bhambri, R. Soni, & T. A. Tran (Eds.), *Smart Healthcare Systems: AI and IoT Perspectives* (pp. 33–43). CRC Press. https://doi.org/10.1201/9781032698519-3

Rana, R., & Bhambri, P. (2024b). Generative AI-driven Security Frameworks for Web Engineering: Innovations and Challenges. In I. A. Shah & N. Z. Jhanjhi (Eds.), *Generative AI for Web Engineering Models* (pp. 285–296). IGI Global. https://doi.org/10.4018/979-8-3693-3703-5.ch014

Reddy, T. S., Kalaichelvi, T., El-Ebiary, Y. A. B., Rajmohan, V., & Ramesh, J. V. N. (2025). Computing Environments: Employing Recurrent Neural Networks and ELM for Advanced Analysis in Investigation Scenarios. *Journal of Advances in Information Technology*, 16(1), 109–120.

Revathi, V., Aishwarya, B., Tripathi, M., Singh, N., Alabdely, H., & Kumar, A. (2024, June). Cloud Forensics Analysis Framework for Secure and Efficient Data Retrieval. In *2024 OPJU International Technology Conference (OTCON) on Smart Computing for Innovation and Advancement in Industry 4.0* (pp. 1–7). IEEE.

Sajithabanu, S., Devika, S. T., Deeba, S., & Jose Anand, A. (2025, October 17). The Role of VR and AR in Intelligent Computing: Applications in Psychology and Autism. In B. Sundaravadivazhagan, N. Gnanasankaran, Pethuru Raj, & A. Saleem Raja (Eds.), *Virtual Reality and Augmented Reality with 6G Communication*, Ch-13. Wiley Publication.

Saluja, P., & Bhavsar, M. (2025). KDCFI AI-based Knowledge Discovery Framework for Cloud Forensic Investigation: P. Saluja et al. *The Journal of Supercomputing*, 81(17), 1572.

Shanker, B., Tufail, A., Bhatt, C., Kaushik, K., Sajid, A., & Khan, I. U. (2024, May). Advancing Survey on Multi-Tenant Cloud Environments: Challenges and Solutions. In *2024 International Conference on Intelligent Systems for Cybersecurity (ISCS)* (pp. 1–5). IEEE.

Sharma, D., Singh, J., & Bhambri, P. (2025a). Federated Learning for Intrusion Detection in IoT Networks: A Comprehensive Review. In *Proceedings of the 2025 2nd International Conference on Electronic Circuits and Signaling Technologies (ICECST)* (pp. 634–639). IEEE.

Sharma, M., Kohli, R. K., & Sharma, K. (2025b). Tomorrow's Shields: Exploring Future Trends in Cyber Security and Forensics. In K. Sharma, V. Sharma, P. Nand, A. K. Sagar & G. Shrivastava (Eds.), *Securing the Digital Frontier: Threats and Advanced Techniques in Security and Forensics* (pp. 367–385). Wiley, Scrivener Publishing.

Sharmila, S., & Aparna, C. (2024). Tracing Footprints of Anti-Forensics and Assuring Secured Data Transmission in the Cloud Using an Effective ECCDH and Kalman Filter. *Journal of Network and Computer Applications*, 221, 103762. https://doi.org/10.1016/j.jnca.2023.103762

Subhamathi, A. S. F., Sathiyapriyan, C., T, A., J. Anand, A., Rheem, A., & Arun, M. R. (2024). Traffic Sign Detection Problems Using Convolutional Neural Techniques in Image Processing. In *2024 International Conference on Intelligent Systems for Cybersecurity (ISCS)* (pp. 1–6). Gurugram, India.

Suganya, A., Parameswari, D., Geetha, R., Govindaram, A., Bahuguna, S., & Anand, J. A. (2025). Comparison of Machine Learning Methods for Fraudulent Transaction Classification. *2025 6th International Conference for Emerging Technology (INCET)*, BELGAUM, India, pp. 1–7.

Suthar, H., & Lunagaria, M. (2024). Big Data Forensics: Challenges and Approaches. In K. Kaushik, M. Ouaissa & A. Chaudhary (Eds.), *Advanced Techniques and Applications of Cybersecurity and Forensics*, 82–98. CRC Press, USA.

Tanveer, M., Khan, N. A., Ali, M., Islam, R., Sattar, M., & Shoaib, M. (2025). Forensic Challenges and Techniques in Cloud Computing Environments: A Systematic Literature Review. *Spectrum of Engineering Sciences*, 3(4), 67–92.

Venkataramanan, B. M., & Arulselvarani, S. (2025). A Exploring Cloud Network Forensics: A Comprehensive Survey of Tools and Techniques Enhanced with Deep Learning Models: Cloud Network Forensics. *International Journal of Information Technology, Research and Applications*, 4(2), 14–28.

Zziwa, I., Ilolo, A., Nwafor, K. C., & Ihenacho, D. O. (2024). Cloud Computing and AI in Cybersecurity Forensics: Leveraging Data Analytics for Enhanced Threat Detection and Incident Response. *International Journal of Research Publication and Reviews*, 5(10), 2907–2920.

Chapter 2

Intelligent cloud architecture for next-generation digital forensics

S. Sajithabanu, B. Sundaravadivazhagn, A. Jose Anand and A. Asrin Mahmootha

2.1 INTRODUCTION

Cloud computing provides on-demand access to customizable computing solutions, i.e., networks, servers, storage systems, and applications, in the form of service models, i.e., infrastructure-as-a-service (IaaS), platform-as-a-service (PaaS), and software-as-a-service (SaaS) [11]. Such models are fundamentally based on virtualization, automation, and distributed data centers, and by means of these, organizations are in a position to scale services within a very short period of time and also minimize capital expenditure [1]. But the flexibility that offers abstractions also makes it difficult to know where data has been stored, how data has been handled, and who had control of important elements; therefore, making preservation and analysis of the evidence very difficult [16].

Traditionally, digital forensics presupposes that the investigator may physically capture the storage device, get the full disk image, and extract the local system logs [2]. In the cloud, there is shared control between the customers and the cloud service providers (CSPs); the evidence might be stored in a common physical resource, and virtual machines (VMs) or containers can be set up and torn down quickly [5]. Consequently, the need to be forensically ready—to be able to create, gather, retain, and utilize digital evidence in an efficient manner and to adhere to privacy and regulatory limitations—has become a very strong demand among organizations [15, 18].

The chapter discusses the issue of how cloud architecture could be implemented and configured to provide forensic preparedness systematically. The discussion will concentrate on mapping the forensic requirements to architectural components, gaps in the existing practice, and recommend a forensic-conscious cloud architecture that implements logging, provenance tracking, and integrity in service layers [5, 18]

The rest of the chapter is structured in the following way. Section 2.2 includes cloud architecture principles and the major forensic issues. In Section 2.3, related work is reviewed in the field of cloud forensics, logging, provenance, and forensic readiness. The problem of the proposed Forensic-Aware Cloud Architecture (FACA) is presented in Section 2.4. Section 2.5 gives the methodology and an illustration of an experimental design. The representative results and their implications are discussed in Section 2.6. The last section (Section 2.7) summarizes the conclusions and describes how the research will be conducted in the future.

DOI: 10.1201/9781003656487-2

2.2 CLOUD ARCHITECTURE AND FORENSIC CHALLENGES

2.2.1 Cloud service models

There are three types of cloud computing service models, namely IaaS, PaaS, and SaaS [11]. Under the IaaS model, the providers sell a virtualized compute, storage, and networking provision, whereas the clients administer operating systems and applications [1]. PaaS goes higher in terms of infrastructure abstraction since the service offers customers managed runtimes, databases, and middleware, allowing them to deal only with application logic with little understanding of the actual stack underlying the service [4]. SaaS models are applications that are delivered using the web with clients having limited configuration and data control, with virtually all of the technical work being managed by the provider [11].

Such models have various models of responsibility allocation between CSP and customer, which directly impacts the forensic visibility and control [18]. In IaaS, investigators may have access to the logs of guest OS and conduct logical acquisitions frequently, whereas hypervisor and physical storage are controlled by the provider [5]. Conversely, PaaS and SaaS inquiries are largely based on logs, audit trails, and APIs that are maintained by the providers, enhancing reliance on CSP collaboration and contracts [14].

2.2 Deployment models

The possibilities of forensic activities also depend on models of cloud deployment, which include public, private, community, and the hybrid [11]. Public clouds managed by third-party providers have several tenants on shared infrastructure and apply standard policies that may restrict custom forensic controls but have mature logging and monitoring services [14]. A privately operated cloud computing system serves one organization and enables increased control of the cloud management, security operations, and forensic operations such as direct access to hypervisors and storage [4]. Hybrid clouds integrate both public and private resources, where there is a need to synchronize evidence gathering at the administrative level and possibly at the cross-jurisdiction level [16].

Trends toward multi-cloud and hybrid approaches have established a need to have forensic processes that can handle heterogeneous interfaces, onto which the logs are written, and which have legal regimes [18]. Such great variety enhances the necessity to have standardized, interoperable forensic mechanisms as part of cloud architecture.

2.3 Building design features that affect forensics

There are a number of inherent features of cloud architectures with a powerful forensic consequence:

- Virtualization and Abstraction: Workloads of virtual machines and containers are not tied to physical hardware, so at any moment it is not easy to map logical resources to physical devices [5].
- Multi-tenancy: Multiple customers share the physical infrastructure implying that the purchase of disks or memory in bulk can expose data of the unrelated tenants, which will pose privacy or legal issues [14].
- Elasticity and Resource Ephemerality: Auto-scaling services completely spin up and down on demand; without handling logs and state being offloaded to persistence stores, logs and state can be lost quickly [16].

- Geographic Distribution: Data and services can be duplicated across data centers and jurisdictions, making the legal process challenging and necessitating the close consideration of such things as data residency and transfer of evidence across borders [18].

Understanding these architectural issues is a conditioning factor for developing forensic conscious solutions, which are still feasible in a mass environment of cloud.

2.3 RELATED WORK

2.3.1 Foundations of cloud forensics

Cloud forensics has been characterized as a use of digital forensic principles in cloud computing systems with the element of technical, legal, and organizational aspects [16]. Preliminary surveys found those problems as lack of physical access, reliance on CSPs, multi-tenancy, and jurisdiction [18]. Such works underpinned the idea that traditional forensic models need to be modified to incorporate virtualized and distributed infrastructures [16, 18].

2.3.2 Frameworks according to platform-specific forensics

A number of publications have suggested incorporating forensic functionality into specific cloud systems. The author [5] introduced the FROST framework of OpenStack, which allows the administrator to gain access to data in the form of VM disk images, API logs, and network data by using special purposes of forensics. It is shown in their work that platform APIs could be used to aid collection with forensic needs of services but also that they relied on the privileged position of the providers [5]. Hypervisor and container platform forensic tooling have also been covered in other literature, which is based on live acquisition and introspection [3, 13].

2.3.3 Cloud data provenance and logging

Re-creation of events in cloud environments is based on logging and provenance of data. The author [10] has covered the principles of designing the cloud application logging such that it assists in effective forensic analysis, using standardized formats, time matching, and records with context. Marty [10] also mentioned issues with the cloud application logging design, emphasizing the use of standardized formats, time matching, and records with context. Provenance systems can monitor the provenance history of data, creation, transformation, and motion of the data to enable causality analysis and responsibility [12]. Practical provenance in cloud environments needs to be able to handle workloads of significant scale and amplitude, but it also needs to honor tenant isolation [7, 8].

2.3.4 Mechanisms of integrity and chain of custody

Admissible digital evidence requires maintaining evidence integrity and providing a reliable chain of custody [2]. The athletic use of cryptographic hashing and secure logging to identify tampering has been in use over time [17]. Recently, blockchain-friendly methods have been considered to store evidence metadata and compute a hash value on tamper-evident ledgers, which are placed with decentralized integrity assurances [9]. Within the frames of cloud forensics, these mechanisms can enhance the confidence of provider-created logs and snapshots [18, 9].

2.3.5 Forensic readiness models

Forensic readiness plans are designed to succeed in equipping systems and organizations to optimize the possible digital evidence at a minimum cost of investigation [15]. Forensic preparedness in the cloud environment entails proper logging policies, data storage policies, and terms in a contract with CSPs [18]. High-level analyses of cloud forensic preparedness have been offered by different authors, yet few system architecture-level designs have been developed that encompass both technical and procedural factors on the service levels [14, 18].

These voids encourage architectural work that introduces forensic functionality as a first-class concern in cloud architecture, instead of looking at forensics as an afterthought [6].

2.4 PROPOSED FORENSIC-AWARE CLOUD ARCHITECTURE (FACA)

2.4.1 Design rationale and objectives

Forensic-Aware Cloud Architecture (FACA) is a projected design, where forensic preparedness is considered one of the main non-functional requirements of the cloud infrastructures. Instead of being founded on the ad hoc extraction of logs or the cyclic snapshotting of the verbal case of an incident, FACA introduces exceptionally structured evidence generation, evidence preservation, and evidence checking into all tiers of the cloud stack. Products objectives: The products aim to reach higher observability among tenants and layers; integrability of the evidence should be scalable and allow quick and repeatable investigations with only a small number of disturbances of normal operations [19–25].

As far as research is concerned, FACA is intended to:

Provide similar forensic abstractions to non-standard operating environments and models of implementation.

Prefer separate generation, storage, and analysis of data. Prefer separate separation of data generation and analysis capabilities.

Port is enforceable automated rationale on many-layered evidence, like causal and time-based relationships.

2.4.2 Decoupled core modules and architecture layers

The FACA is organized as a collection of cooperating modules that would be available on the service, platform, and infrastructure layers of a cloud setting. The modules have an abstracted interface and role, too, to make formal analysis and experimental evaluation.

2.4.2.1 Forensic Provenance and Logging Module (FPLM)

FPLM instruments take the form of hypervisors, virtual machines, containers, orchestration services, and tenant applications that are major components. It can standardize all types of logs using the identical schema, inject some metadata (tenant identifiers, resource identifiers, topology information, and precise timestamps) onto the records, and establish provenance edges depicting how data, processes, and configuration states evolve through time. Such a structure enables attack path and system behavior recovery through drawing graphs [26].

2.4.2.2 Evidence Preservation and Integrity Module (EPIM)

EPIM is also used to cope with the transition between the short-term events of the system and long-term forensic objects. It assists with the planned and event-driven procurement of snapshots of compute instances and storage volumes and important configuration objects. The snapshots and the log bundles are digested with cryptographic digests and affixed to integrity ledgers that are testified by tamper. EPIM makes programmable policies accessible to enable tuning of snapshot frequency, scope, and retention with sensitivity to the level of risks, sensitivity of workload, and regulatory demands [27].

2.4.2.3 Forensic Analysis and Correlation Engine (FACE)

FACE is premised on the FPLM and EPIM-created forensic data lake. It keeps multi-layer event graphs, synchronizes the time in disparate elements, and incorporates analytics to determine unusual behaviors, lateral movements, and violations of the policies. FACE allows customizable pipelines in analysis operations in a research setting, which allows customizing the evaluation of both earlier rule-based correlation, machine learning models, graph computation, and both together on the same underlying evidence corpus [28].

2.4.2.4 Secure Forensic Repository (SFR)

The physically decentralized, logically centralized storage layer that stores the raw artifacts (logs, snapshots, configuration exports) and the corresponding metadata is known as SFR. It also applies tight access control and fine-grained encryption policies, and audit trails which cannot be undone to all actions of reading and writing. The repository interface will help to implement reproducible experiments as it will enable investigators and researchers to use the same pieces of evidence on new runs and analysis methods [29, 30].

2.4.3 Security, privacy, and governance

These are the security, privacy, and governance considerations. FACA operates in highly multi-tenant environments; it has distinct controls that enable to prevent cross-tenant leaking and yet refer to useful investigations:

The partitions employed include tenant, project, and sensitivity class where isolation occurs at the storage and query layer.

These ownership- and express-consent-based acquisition boundaries are developed and shared infrastructure artifacts that are being processed through redaction, aggregation, or anonymization where applicable.

All the forensic operations like queries, exports done by investigators, are also tracked and safeguarded using the same integrity controls that define primary evidence.

Furthermore, FACA may be policy sensitive: The policy requirements, the requirement to retain the data, and the jurisdictional boundaries may be modeled as machine-readable policies, which inform the decisions of what is being gathered, where it is withheld, and how long it is saved. This makes the framework a suitable framework for the evaluation of the data governance strategies that are not only conscience conscious but also just technical measures.

The fourth extension on the FACA is Innovative Research.

To transform FACA into a platform for further studies, several of the improvements to the design of the future are introduced:

The independent forensic agents implement close to workloads (VMs, containers, or no-server runtimes), which can autonomously increase or decrease the logging granularity, snapshot fires, and data filtering by local measurements and global threat intelligence.

The orchestration of the cross-domain evidence: To make the collection and correlation of data across a series of providers of cloud services, on-premise equipment, and edge nodes, standardized schemas and protocols are opened to support portable vendor-neutral forensic procedures.

Confidential-forensics assistance, where evidence creation and analysis can be accomplished within trusted execution platforms to enable investigators to make sound judgments based on sensitive workloads, as well as limiting access to cloud operators and others.

Provide explainability and provenance over the decisions of the forensic judgment whereby FACE does not simply produce inferences; it also produces machine-comprehensible explanations of all the steps in the analytic process that can be traced to tested artifacts and the provenance chain, which improves transparency to both legal and regulatory controls.

Such extensions are applicable in making FACA a moving architecture to perform research on adaptive, intelligent, and privacy-motivated cloud forensics.

2.5 ARCHITECTURE DIAGRAM (CONCEPTUAL DESCRIPTION)

A visual diagram can depict FACA as a layered architecture as shown in Figure 2.1.

The Infrastructure Layer includes hypervisors, VMs, containers, virtual switches, and storage systems, each instrumented with FPLM agents.

- The Platform Layer shows runtimes, orchestration services, and managed databases feeding logs into the same forensic log stream.
- The Service Layer presents tenant applications and APIs that emit application logs and user activity events.
- A central Forensic Log Bus aggregates all FPLM outputs into the SFR.
- The EPIM box connects to virtualization and storage APIs, performing snapshots and generating hash records stored in a Blockchain/Integrity Ledger.
- The FACE component connects to the SFR and the ledger, providing dashboards, reports, and alerts to investigators.

2.5.1 Service layer

Contains Multiple Tenant Applications (SaaS App 1–3) and APIs.

Applications generate app logs and user events (logins, API calls, actions) that are sent to the Secure Forensic Repository (SFR) and also to EPIM as “App Logs + Hash Logs + User Events.”

Purpose: Capture what each user and application did at the business logic level for later reconstruction of incidents.

2.5.2 Platform layer

Includes Runtime Services, Orchestration (Kubernetes), and Managed Databases.

These components emit logs and metadata (container start/stop, pod scheduling, DB queries, config changes) which flow into the SFR.

Purpose: Record how the platform executed and scaled applications, enabling correlation between user actions and platform behavior.

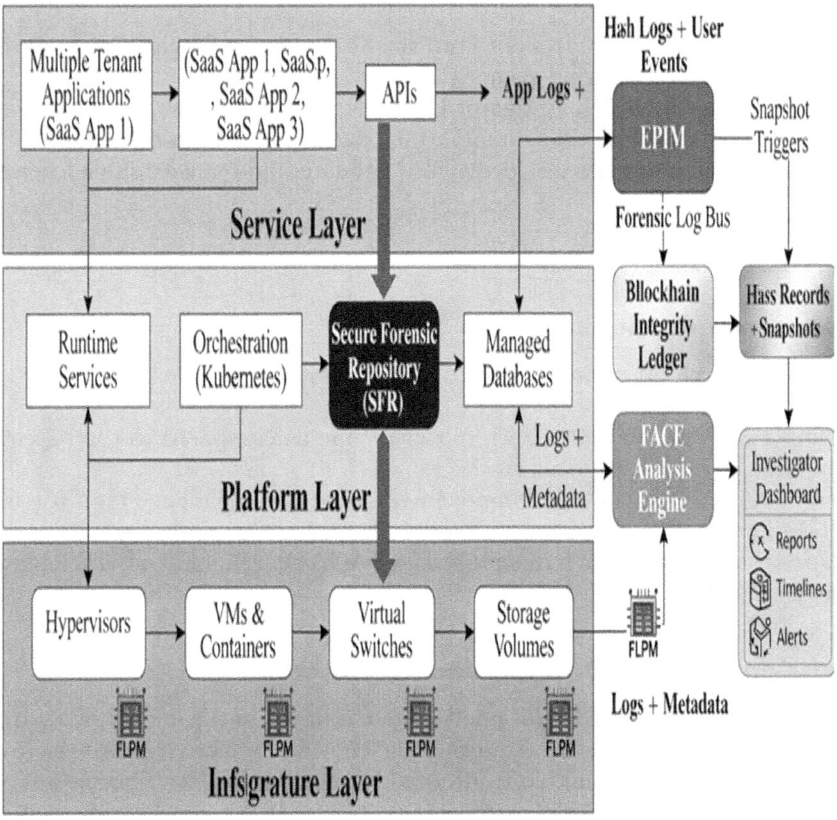

Figure 2.1 Forensic-Aware Cloud Architecture (FACA).

2.5.3 Infrastructure layer

Composed of Hypervisors, VMs & Containers, Virtual Switches, and Storage Volumes, each instrumented with an FPLM agent.

FPLM agents collect low-level logs + metadata (VM lifecycle, network flows, I/O events) and forward them upward to the SFR.

Purpose: Provide fine-grained evidence about what actually happened on compute, network, and storage resources.

2.5.4 Evidence collection and preservation

The Secure Forensic Repository (SFR) in the center aggregates logs and metadata from all layers, acting as the central evidence store.

EPIM (Evidence Preservation and Integrity Module) receives app and hash logs plus user events, issues snapshot triggers back to infrastructure/platform to capture VM/container/storage snapshots during suspicious activity, and sends a Forensic Log Bus of selected evidence to the integrity layer.

The Blockchain Integrity Ledger stores cryptographic hashes, while the Hash Records + Snapshots box represents immutable records binding each snapshot/log bundle to its hash.

Purpose: Ensure evidence is complete, time-aligned, and tamper-evident.

2.5.5 Analysis and investigator interface

The FACE Analysis Engine reads from both the SFR and the Blockchain Integrity Ledger, verifying integrity and correlating events across layers.

It produces findings for the Investigator Dashboard, which shows reports, timelines, and alerts that investigators use to understand attack paths and system behavior.

Purpose: Turn raw, multi-layer evidence into validated, human-readable forensic results.

2.6 METHODOLOGY

2.6.1 Research questions

The following research questions can be used to assess FACA:

RQ1: Does FACA decrease evidence retrieval time as compared to the baseline logging and ad hoc acquisition procedures?
RQ2: Does FACA enhance the completeness of logs and evidence loss in volatile cloud environments?
RQ3: Does the integrity mechanism used by FACA do reliable and efficient verification of evidence authenticity?

2.6.2 Experiment environment and cleanliness

The experimental analysis will be designed in such a way that the impact of an architecture-based forensic framework like FACA on the efficiency and effectiveness of the investigation will be measured in comparison to a traditional logging setup. Two options are considered:

Base Liner Setting: Cloud setup with default platform written logging and absence of specially designed forensic organization.

FACA-Enabled Configuration: This represents a Fully Deployed and configured cloud environment with FPLM, EPIM, FACE, and SFR.

They both support various tenant applications (including web and database services) and are both hit by a combination of benign workload and scripted attacks, such as credential misuse, privilege escalation, and data recalls. The design of the experiment is:

An IaaS solution based on open-source, i.e., OpenStack, using a single controller node and several compute nodes to comprise a cloud platform.

A number of tenant projects, which carry a web workload and a database workload each to emulate a realistic application.

Artificial loads of legitimate user traffic and scripting attack conditions.

FPLM agents spread out into the infrastructure and platform components; EPIM is set to cause snapshots when certain patterns of events occur.

The order and place of events are produced by synthetic attack scripts, and the details of attack scripts are known and ground truth to measure the evidence that should be found.

2.6.3 Data collection and metrics

Within each setting, several trials are put into practice and the measures that are taken consist of:

- Evidence Retrieval Time (s): Minutes between detection of incident and availability of incident-relevant logs and other artifacts to analyze.

- Log Completeness Percent: Percentage of the anticipated attacks observed in the gathered logs, ground-truth attack scripts.
- Rate of Evidence Loss Percent: The proportion of known events missing or lost.
- Success of Integrity Verification: Percentage of artifacts with computed hashes that match the stores taken.

2.6.4 Data analysis

Measures of central tendency like the mean, median, and standard deviation among trials are descriptive statistics that could be used to summarize measures. Tables and graphical visualization can be used to compare baseline performance and FACA performance. Where the need arises, statistical tests could determine if the apparent differences are significant, taking into consideration the size of the sample and restriction of an experiment.

2.6.5 Symbolic qualitative results

An experimental subset suggests the existence of a consistent improvement in performance of the FACA-enabled environment in comparison with the performance of the baseline in all fundamental measures. In typical trials:

The time used to retrieve evidence is significantly shorter with FACA, as artifacts are already organized, indexed, and connected by provenance relationships; hence, manual searching and correlation are not needed.

The completeness of the logs is as comprehensive as ground-truth events, since FPLM records activity at all infrastructure, platform, and application levels all coordinately.

Loss of evidence = Proactive offloading of ephemeral state and time-converged snapshots. In response to suspicious behavior induced by EPIM, it helps in eliminating evidence loss significantly.

The integrity verification success is near universal, which proves that integrity metadata and entries of ledgers are always in step with stored artifacts in cases of load and failure events.

These trends do not change with workload mixes, implying that the architecture has its pros even when there are moderate and extreme operational conditions.

Table 2.1 illustrates the sample measurements of four forensic performance indicators when using the Baseline and FACA-enabled settings. This table indicates that the FACA environment has faster access to evidence, more exhaustive documentation of actions, reduced loss of pertinent information, and more sure integrity examinations of gathered artifacts.

2.6.5.1 Evidence retrieval time(s) (mean)

The means of the Baseline model take 38.7 seconds to collect the logs and artifacts that are required following the detection of an incident, as opposed to 12.4 seconds in the FACA

Table 2.1 Baseline and FACA configuration comparative metrics

Metric	*Baseline model*	*FACA model*
Average evidence retrieval time (s)	38.7	12.4
Log completeness (%)	91.6	99.2
Evidence loss rate (%)	6.5	0.8
Integrity verification success (%)	92.1	99.5

model. This enhancement is an indicator of the fact that FACA has been continually systematizing and cataloging evidence, meaning that less time is wasted by investigators who have to search through disparate sources.

2.6.5.2 Log completeness (%)

In the initial configuration, 91.6% of the expected events are present in the logs taken. With FACA, the log completeness goes to 99.2%, meaning that almost all of the actions that are interesting are represented at the infrastructure, platform, and application layers. Increased completeness is directly proportional to more precise attack timeline reconstruction.

2.6.5.3 Evidence loss rate (%)

In the Baseline model, the evidence loss rate is 6.5%, which implies that a significant part of the events cannot be restored because of the data loss or overwriting. In FACA, this value reduces to 0.8% due to the offloading of volatile states and temporary logs that are stored temporarily until they fade out of the live environment.

2.6.5.4 Success of verifying integrity (%)

In the baseline scenario, 92.1% of the artifacts are passed integrity checks when compared to stored reference values of the current cryptographic values. The FACA model has a success rate of 99.5%, which proves that the combined integrity controls have a far robust and more reliable chain of custody when it comes to digital evidence.

2.6.6 Performance graphs

The visualizations of the experiment findings are displayed in the following ways:

Differences in performance can also be pointed out with the help of graphs:

A graphical representation of the retrieval time per trial with steadily lowering values in FACA.

An ordered bar chart of the comparison between the Baseline and FACA-enabled settings of the four performance measures of forensics (average time to retrieve, completeness of logs, percentage evidence loss, and integrity verification success) is presented in Figure 2.2. The chart demonstrates that the forensic-conscious architecture enhances the speed, coverage, resilience, and reliability of digital proof in comparison with the conventional cloud configuration.

1. **Average Retrieval Time** (s)**:** It takes an average of nearly 39 seconds with the Baseline model to locate the required evidence once the incident has happened, but it only requires approximately 12 seconds with the FACA model. This implies that FACA facilitates access to pertinent logs and artifacts for investigators at a much higher rate.
2. **Log Completeness Percent (%):** In the Baseline configuration, the log completeness is approximately 92%, implying that not all events are registered. With FACA, the completeness increases to approximately 99, therefore nearly all important actions are recorded in the logs.
3. **Evidence Loss Rate Percentage:** Baseline model of evidence loss is approximately 6.5%, and FACA minimizes this accordingly to a percentage less than 1. This implies that

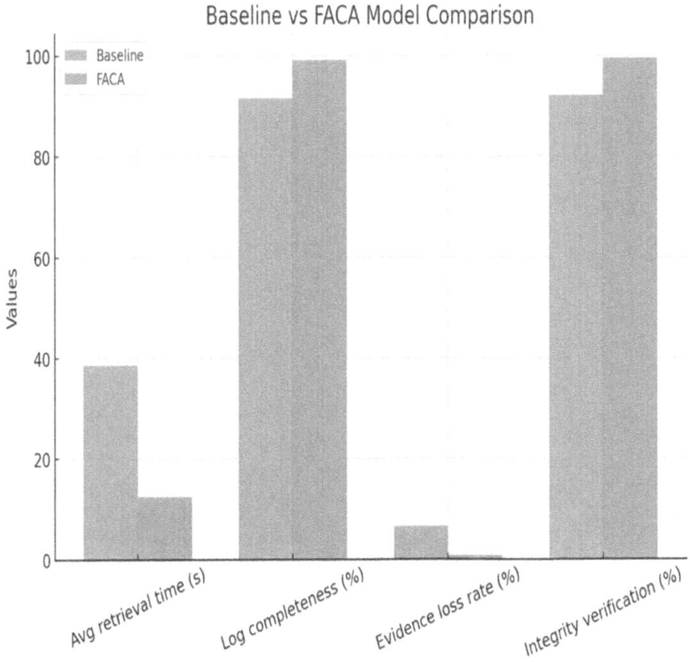

Figure 2.2 Comparison of Baseline model with FACA model.

FACA would be much more efficient when it comes to saving information on short-lived or overloaded resources before they become lost.

4. **Passing Integrity Checks on Artifacts**: In the Baseline configuration, approximately 92% of the artifacts succeed integrity checks, and nearly 100% of the artifacts are passed by the FACA model. This implies that evidence generated by FACA is less likely to be tampered and corrupted.

As depicted in the chart, the forensic-conscious architecture is faster, more comprehensive, resilient, and more reliable in digital evidence than a conventional cloud configuration. The comparison of the bar charts shows that considering the aspect of integrating forensic mechanisms into the architectural design of the cloud helps to enhance the scope of documentation of the logs and the accuracy of evidence stored much better than a traditional arrangement.

Listed below are the interventions that will be used in the study:

Through the bar chart represented in Figure 2.3, the recording and preservation of the forensic log data, between the Baseline and FACA models, is compared. It dwells on two indicators: log completeness and rate of evidence loss.

To allow the completeness of the logs, the Baseline model describes 91.6% of expected events as opposed to the FACA model that describes 99.2%. This implies that the forensic-aware architecture is much nearer to generating a complete picture of what occurred in fact in the course of an incident, and there are minimal actions that are not documented.

In the case of evidence loss, the Baseline model loses 6.5% of events, and the FACA model loses only 0.8%. Practically, this demonstrates that FACA is much more efficient in avoiding valuable forensic information disappearing because of transient resources, overwriting, or lost logs.

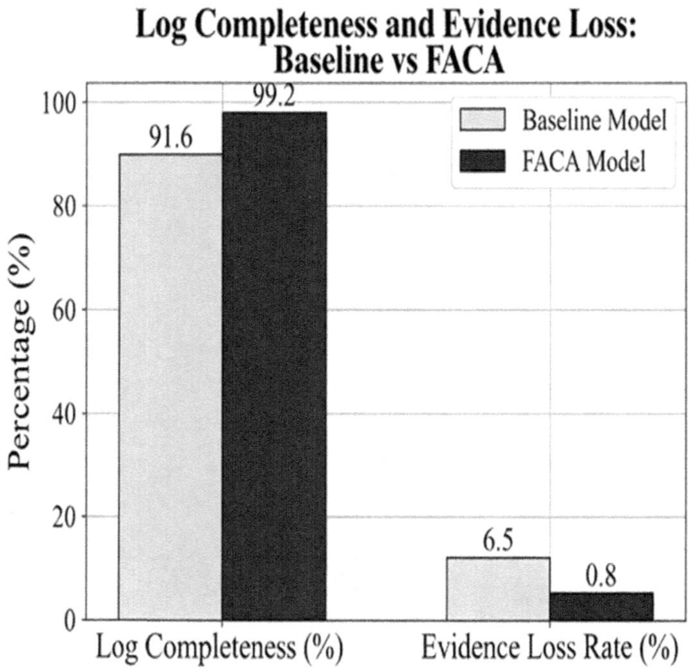

Figure 2.3 Compare log completeness and evidence loss metrics.

In general, the chart shows that the implementation of forensic mechanisms into the cloud system can greatly enhance the extent of the logs' coverage and the quality of the available evidence as opposed to a traditional system.

2.7 CONCLUSION AND FUTURE ENHANCEMENTS

The chapter has analytically discussed how the key attributes of clouds, which include virtualization, multi-tenancy, elastic resource allocation, and large-scale distribution, redefine assumptions in the traditional processes of digital forensics. The discussion integrated major underpinnings of cloud-oriented logging, data provenance, and data integrity assurance to encourage the necessity of architectures supporting the requirements of forensics as first-class design issues in clouds [31–36].

To this, the chapter proposed Forensic-Aware Cloud Architecture (FACA), which is a layered model incorporating coordinated logging, provenance capture, evidence preservation, and integrity verification modules that exist at application, platform, and infrastructure services. By considering forensic readiness an architectural property and not a spiky add-on, FACA will increase the observability, controllability, and evidentiary strength of heterogeneous cloud deployments.

A detailed methodology was described with the help of the experimental design because the effect of FACA on the evidence acquisition time, coverage of logs, evidence loss rates, and the stability of integrity validation was to be measured. The findings of the single experimental analysis of the comparison between the baseline and FACA-enforced settings show that architecturally integrated forensic controls can significantly improve the productivity as well as the quality of evidence of cloud-based investigations and argue that the concept of forensics-by-design can be implemented in the next-generation cloud platform.

2.7.1 Future research directions

FACA can be developed in many technical dimensions in the future. One such approach is to extrapolate the model to the multi-cloud, hybrid, and edge-native environments where proof has to be linked across a variety of providers, jurisdictions, and edge nodes with intermittent connectivity. This involves a design of standardized written forensic data designs, interoperability designs that facilitate dependable evidence exchange, and cross-domain timeline reconstructions.

The other path is that of introducing advanced analytics in which machine learning and graph-based reasoning pipelines can be applied to forensic logs and provenance graphs to identify subtle patterns of attack, automate the triage, and prioritize the high-value evidence. To supplement this, privacy-preserving, regulation-conscious systems e.g., differential privacy, secure multiparty computation, and policy-controlled data minimization can be underlaid, in order to balance the evidentiary requirements with confidentiality and data protection against cross-crossing regulatory limitations.

REFERENCES

1. M. Armbrust, A. Fox, R. Griffith, A. D. Joseph, R. Katz, A. Konwinski, G. Lee, D. Patterson, A. Rabkin, I. Stoica, and M. Zaharia. 2010. A view of cloud computing. *Communications of the ACM*, 53(4), 50–58.
2. E. Casey. 2011. *Digital Evidence and Computer Crime: Forensic Science, Computers, and the Internet* (3rd ed.). Academic Press.
3. W. Delport and M. S. Olivier. 2012. Isolating a cloud instance for a digital forensic investigation. *IFIP International Conference on Digital Forensics*, pp. 187–199. University of Pretoria, Pretoria, South Africa
4. T. Dillon, C. Wu, and E. Chang. 2010. Cloud computing: Issues and challenges. *Proceedings of the 24th IEEE International Conference on Advanced Information Networking and Applications*, pp. 27–33. Perth, Australia.
5. J. Dykstra and A. T. Sherman. 2013. Design and implementation of FROST: Digital forensic tools for the OpenStack cloud computing platform. *Digital Investigation*, 10(Suppl. 1), S87–S95.
6. A. Field. 2013. *Discovering Statistics Using IBM SPSS Statistics* (4th ed.). SAGE.
7. R. Hasan, R. Sion, and M. Winslett. 2009. The case of the fake Picasso: Preventing history forgery with secure provenance. *Proceedings of the 7th USENIX Conference on File and Storage Technologies* (FAST), pp. 1–14. San Francisco, CA, USA.
8. G. Jacob, S. Paturi, and G. Varma. 2019. Anomaly detection in cloud environments using machine learning techniques. *International Journal of Cloud Applications and Computing*, 9(1), 45–61.
9. K. M. Khan and Q. M. Malluhi. 2019. Establishing trust in cloud computing. *IT Professional*, 21(1), 38–45.
10. R. Marty. 2011. Cloud application logging for forensics. *Proceedings of the ACM Symposium on Applied Computing*, pp. 178–184.
11. P. Mell and T. Grance. 2011. The NIST definition of cloud computing (Special Publication 800--145). National Institute of Standards and Technology.
12. K.-K. Muniswamy-Reddy, D. A. Holland, U. Braun, and M. I. Seltzer. 2006. Provenance-aware storage systems. *Proceedings of the USENIX Annual Technical Conference*, pp. 43–56. Berkeley, CA; United States.

13. S. Rahman, M. N. Islam, and M. Khatun. 2020. A Docker-based digital forensic readiness model for cloud environments. *Journal of Cloud Computing*, 9(1), 1–13.
14. D. Reilly, C. Wren, and T. Berry. 2011. Cloud computing: Pros and cons for computer forensic investigations. *International Journal of Digital Crime and Forensics*, 3(1), 1–17.
15. R. Rowlingson. 2004. A ten step process for forensic readiness. *International Journal of Digital Evidence*, 2(3), 1–28.
16. K. Ruan, J. Carthy, T. Kechadi, and M. Crosbie. 2013. Cloud forensics: A review. In G. Peterson & S. Shenoi (Eds.), *Advances in Digital Forensics IX* (pp. 35–46). Springer.
17. B. Schneier and J. Kelsey. 1999. Secure audit logs to support computer forensics. *ACM Transactions on Information and System Security*, 2(2), 159–176.
18. S. Zawoad and R. Hasan. 2015. Cloud forensics: A meta-study of challenges, approaches, and open problems. *IEEE Cloud Computing*, 2(3), 60–67.
19. S. Jayanthi, P. Vinitha Baby, D. Parameswari, R. Geetha, P. Thilagavathi, and J. A. Anand. 2025. Improved convolutional neural network for garbage separation. *2025 6th International Conference for Emerging Technology (INCET)*, Belgaum, India, pp. 1–6.
20. P. Thilagavathi, S. Hannah, Jose A. Anand, D. Parameswari, R. Geetha, and A. Govindaram. 2025. Machine learning and security fake email detection and intrusion detection. *2025 6th International Conference for Emerging Technology (INCET)*, Belgaum, India, pp. 1–6.
21. B. Muthukumar, P. Nakka, H. V., Jose A. Anand, A. Govindaram, and P. Thilagavathi. 2025. Application of machine learning techniques for the location and early detection of brain tumors. *2025 6th International Conference on Data Intelligence and Cognitive Informatics (ICDICI)*, Tirunelveli, India, pp. 1637–1644.
22. R. Geetanjali, T. M. Sreehari, A. Jegatheesan, B. Muthukumar, B. Thyla, and Jose A. Anand. 2025. Predictive model of 6-Month prognosis of stroke patients using machine learning techniques. *2025 2nd International Conference On Multidisciplinary Research and Innovations in Engineering (MRIE)*, Gurugram, India, pp. 439–444.
23. N. Nazeeya Anjum, S. Sumathi, R. Dheena Dhayalan, R. Rampavithran, A. Jose Anand, and M. Sathiyanarayanan. 2024. Smart sensors for smart city environmental monitoring systems. In Tuan Anh Nguyen (Ed.), *Digital Twin, Blockchain, and Sensor Networks in the Healthy and Mobile City* (pp. 17–33). Elsevier Science.
24. Gomathy M., L. Steffina Morin, Lekshmi S. Raveendran, Jose Anand A, A. Jegatheesan, and B. Muthukumar. 2025. Clustering and predictive modeling of epileptic spikes and seizures using EEG data. *2025 2nd International Conference on Circuits, Power and Intelligent Systems (CCPIS)*, Bhubaneswar, India, pp. 1–6.
25. S. Maheswari, S. J. Parvez, V. S. Devi, T. Anuradha, C. K. Snruthi, and A. Jose Anand. 2025. 5G-integrated data dissemination and multi interface communication architecture for enhanced VANETs. *2025 IEEE International Conference on Contemporary Computing and Communications (InC4)*, Bangalore, India, pp. 1–6.
26. S. Maheswari, N. P. Swetha Menon, B. Sumathi, M. A. Mukunthan, V. Bhanu Rekha, and A. Jose Anand. 2025. Predicting and improving the mechanical strength of a modified natural fiber/TiO_2 polymer nanocomposite using artificial intelligence. *Journal of Environmental Nanotechnology*, 14(4), 9–26.
27. R. Khan, R. Quazi, A. Jose Anand, M. A. J. Maktoof, and A. Al-Hilali. 2026. Predictive analytics for monkeypox: Utilizing machine learning to forecast outbreaks and resource allocation. In G. N. Nguyen, A. Swaroop, and P. Shukla (Eds.), *Proceedings of Fifth International Conference on Computing and Communication Networks*. ICCCN 2025. Lecture Notes in Networks and Systems, vol 1777. Springer, Cham.
28. P. Kar, S. Nayak, N. Kumar, A. Jose Anand, A. Mohanty, and H. Mohammed. 2026. Development of adaptive thermal management systems in electric vehicles using renewable energy and eco-friendly materials. In G. N. Nguyen, A. Swaroop, and P. Shukla (Eds.), *Proceedings of Fifth International Conference on Computing and Communication Networks*. ICCCN 2025. Lecture Notes in Networks and Systems, vol 1777. Springer, Cham.

29. M. Farooq, H. Amin, A. Jose Anand, and M. Waseem Iqbal. 2025. Cognitive complexity reduction in decentralized applications based on blockchain technology: The psychological aspects of user instruction, understanding and self efficacy. *Lex Localis – Journal of Local Self-Government*, 22(S4), 663–675.
30. R. Kesavan, T. Anuradha, P. Kalaiarasi, M. S. Jacob, A. Jose Anand, and V. S. Devi. 2025. Deep learning-based diagnostic support system for breast tissue classification using mammographic images. *2025 IEEE International Conference on Intelligent Signal Processing and Effective Communication Technologies (INSPECT)*, Gwalior, India, 2025, pp. 1-6.
31. S. Rani, P. Bhambri, A. Kataria, A. Khang, and A. K. Sivaraman. (Eds.). 2023. *Big Data, Cloud Computing and IoT: Tools and Applications* (1st ed.). Chapman and Hall/CRC. https://doi.org/10.1201/9781003298335
32. P. Bhambri and S. Kumar. 2024. Cloud and IoT integration for smart healthcare. In P. Bhambri, R. Soni, and T. A. Tran (Eds.), *Smart Healthcare Systems: AI and IoT Perspectives* (pp. 69–84). CRC Press. https://doi.org/10.1201/9781032698519-6
33. R. Rana and P. Bhambri. 2024. Generative AI-driven security frameworks for web engineering: Innovations and challenges. In I. A. Shah and N. Z. Jhanjhi (Eds.), *Generative AI for Web Engineering Models* (pp. 285–296). IGI Global. https://doi.org/10.4018/979-8-3693-3703-5.ch014
34. Y. S. Sangwan, S. Lal, P. Bhambri, A. Kumar, and I. S. Dhanoa. 2021. Advancements in social data security and encryption: A review. *Natural Volatiles & Essential Oils*, 8(4), 15353–15362. https://www.cabidigitallibrary.org/doi/full/10.5555/20220170098
35. V. K. Sinha, R. Jeet, P. Bhambri, and M. Mahajan. 2020. Empowering intrusion detection in IRIS recognition system: A review. *Journal of Natural Remedies*, 21(2), 131–153.
36. R. Rana and P. Bhambri. 2024. Healthcare computational intelligence and blockchain: Real-life applications. In P. Bhambri, S. Rani, and M. Fahim (Eds.), *Computational Intelligence and Blockchain in Biomedical and Health Informatics* (1st ed., pp. 155–168). CRC Press. https://doi.org/10.1201/9781003459347-11

Chapter 3

Forensic acquisition in ephemeral environments

Virtual machines and containers

Pankaj Bhambri, Haipeng Liu, Naveen Ananda Kumar and Hind Hammouch

3.1 INTRODUCTION: THE CHALLENGE OF EPHEMERALITY IN CLOUD INVESTIGATIONS

The paradigm of digital forensics is fundamentally challenged by the rise of ephemeral computing environments in the cloud. Traditional forensic methodology, built on the assumption of persistent physical media and static systems, struggles against infrastructure designed to be transient, scalable, and disposable. In cloud-native architectures, evidence crucial to an investigation—a compromised application, a malicious process, or an attacker's foothold—may exist only for minutes or seconds before being automatically terminated and scrubbed from existence (Bora, 2025). This chapter addresses this core conflict, focusing on the specialized techniques and tools required to successfully acquire forensic evidence from virtual machines (VMs), containers, and their orchestration platforms. It establishes that success in this domain requires a shift from reactive, manual disk imaging to a proactive, automated, and API-driven model of evidence collection that operates at the speed of the cloud itself.

3.1.1 Defining ephemeral infrastructure: VMs, containers, and serverless

Ephemeral infrastructure refers to compute resources that are created on-demand, exist for a limited duration to perform a specific task, and are destroyed automatically, leaving no persistent state on the underlying host (Gharaibeh et al., 2024). This model is a cornerstone of cloud efficiency and agility. Virtual machines (VMs), while more persistent than containers, are still ephemeral in a cloud context; they can be spun up from templates, scaled horizontally, and terminated instantly, with their virtual disks often deleted upon termination. Containers represent a more lightweight and transient unit, packaging an application and its dependencies into a portable image that runs as an isolated process. Containers may have lifespans measured in hours or even seconds, especially when managed by orchestrators like Kubernetes. Serverless Functions (e.g., AWS Lambda, Azure Functions) epitomize ephemerality, where the execution environment is created solely for the duration of a function's execution—often milliseconds to minutes—and is entirely inaccessible to the investigator post-execution. Understanding this spectrum of transience is critical for tailoring the forensic approach.

 DOI: 10.1201/9781003656487-3

3.1.2 The shared responsibility model and forensic accessibility

A paramount consideration in cloud forensics is the Shared Responsibility Model, which delineates security and operational duties between the cloud provider and the customer. This model directly dictates forensic accessibility (Hughes & Robinson, 2024). In Infrastructure-as-a-Service (IaaS, e.g., VMs), the customer retains responsibility for the guest OS, data, and applications, typically granting them the ability to perform live acquisition or snapshot disks. In Platform-as-a-Service (PaaS, e.g., managed Kubernetes, container runtimes) and Software-as-a-Service (SaaS), the provider manages the underlying platform, often restricting direct access to hosts, hypervisors, or physical disks. Consequently, the forensic investigator's "crime scene" is not a physical server but a logical abstraction accessible only through cloud APIs and logs (Orosz et al., 2025). Acquisition becomes an exercise in leveraging the access one does have—via APIs, console snapshots, and exported logs—while recognizing that critical low-level artifacts (e.g., memory pages, slack space on a physical host) may be permanently out of reach, shifting the investigation's focus to higher-level orchestration and application data (Geetha et al., 2025a).

3.1.3 Key differences: VM persistence vs. container transience

The forensic acquisition strategy must be sharply differentiated based on whether the target is a VM or a container, primarily due to their contrasting lifecycle and state management models. A VM is a full simulation of a physical computer, with its own kernel, virtual disks, and a relatively long-lived lifecycle (days to years). It presents a familiar forensic surface: persistent virtual drives that can be imaged, system memory that can be dumped, and a recognizable operating system to analyze. Acquisition often involves taking snapshots of attached volumes and memory (if supported) (Sudiana et al., 2024). In stark contrast, a container shares the host OS kernel, is stateless by design, and is inherently transient. Its "disk" is a collection of immutable, layered image files and a temporary writable layer (often lost when the container stops). The primary evidence is not a static disk image but the container's runtime state (processes, network connections), its log streams, its immutable image, and the metadata about its life and orchestration held by the container runtime (e.g., Docker, containerd) and the orchestrator (e.g., Kubernetes). Failure to grasp this distinction risks applying VM-centric tools to containers, resulting in the acquisition of irrelevant data while the critical, volatile evidence disappears (Mohanty et al., 2025).

3.2 FOUNDATIONAL CONCEPTS FOR EPHEMERAL FORENSICS

This section establishes the core principles that differentiate forensics in ephemeral cloud environments from traditional digital forensics. It moves beyond the methodology of persistent hardware to address environments where evidence is dynamic, distributed, and short-lived. The paradigm shifts from a "dead box" analysis to a "live system" and "orchestrator-centric" investigation, where evidence is often not a physical disk but a collection of logs, API calls, and immutable snapshots (Xiao et al., 2024). Understanding these foundational concepts is critical for developing effective acquisition strategies that can capture vital evidence before it vanishes (Sajithabanu et al., 2025).

3.2.1 The Forensic Golden Hour: Speed and automation imperative

The "Forensic Golden Hour" in ephemeral environments refers to the critically short window of opportunity—often minutes or even seconds—to acquire volatile evidence before a compromised container is terminated, a malicious pod is scaled down, or an auto-scaling group replaces a virtual machine instance (Morić et al., 2025). Unlike traditional systems that remain physically accessible, cloud resources are software-defined and can be destroyed with a single API command or through automated orchestration policies. This ephemerality makes manual forensic processes untenable. Consequently, the imperative is for automated, pre-configured, and immediate response (Geetha et al., 2025). Investigations must rely on scripts, automated playbooks, and integrated tooling that can be triggered by security alerts to instantly capture memory dumps, process listings, network connections, and runtime state before the artifact self-destructs. The Golden Hour concept underscores that in cloud forensics, the timeline of evidence acquisition is the primary determinant of investigative success or failure (Hagan, 2025).

3.2.2 Immutable evidence sources: Logs, images, and orchestrators

When the primary workload (container/VM) is transient, the investigation must pivot to the more persistent, immutable layers that control and describe it (Suganya et al., 2025). These sources become the cornerstone of evidence:

- Logs: Centralized logging services (e.g., CloudWatch, Stackdriver, Azure Monitor) ingest standard output, system logs, and application logs. Cloud provider audit trails (AWS CloudTrail, GCP Audit Logs, Azure Activity Log) provide an immutable record of every API call—who created, accessed, or destroyed a resource. These logs are often the only remaining trace of an ephemeral artifact.
- Images: Container images and VM templates are immutable binaries stored in registries (Docker Hub, ECR, GCR) and service catalogs (Bhambri & Kant, 2025c). They serve as the "blueprint" for the ephemeral instance. Forensic analysis of these images can reveal embedded malware, misconfigurations, or vulnerabilities that were deployed into the runtime environment.
- Orchestrators: Systems like Kubernetes or Docker Swarm maintain their own state databases (e.g., etcd) and control plane logs. These contain definitive records of desired state (deployments, replicas), scheduling decisions, and the actual lifecycle of every pod/container (Donca et al., 2024). The orchestrator's data is a higher-fidelity evidence source than the individual container itself, as it provides the context and intent behind the workload's existence.

3.2.3 The role of cloud provider APIs in acquisition

In cloud forensics, the Cloud Provider API is the primary—and often sole—forensic interface (Jayanthi et al., 2025). There is no physical hard drive to remove or network cable to tap; all acquisition is performed programmatically via APIs. These APIs are the gateway to:

- Discovery and Inventory: Enumerating all running instances, containers, storage volumes, and network configurations across a potentially vast environment.

- Preservation: Triggering the creation of snapshots of EBS volumes, Managed Disks, or persistent volumes before a suspect instance is terminated.
- Acquisition: Directly exporting snapshots to a forensic analyst's controlled storage account, or leveraging services to create a forensic instance with an evidence volume attached for live analysis (Griffith & Morris, 2025).
- Log Aggregation: Programmatically pulling massive streams of audit and service logs from the provider's managed services.

Mastery of these APIs (via SDKs or CLI tools) is non-negotiable. The forensic process becomes a series of automated API calls to isolate, snapshot, and export evidence. Furthermore, the API audit logs themselves become a critical evidence source, documenting every step of the forensic acquisition process for chain of custody.

3.3 FORENSIC ACQUISITION OF VIRTUAL MACHINES

Forensic acquisition of virtual machines in a cloud environment represents a unique hybrid of traditional digital forensics and cloud-specific processes. Unlike physical servers, IaaS VMs are logical constructs whose "hardware" is abstracted and managed by the cloud provider. The forensic investigator's goal is to create a forensically sound bit-for-bit copy of the VM's volatile memory and persistent storage volumes, navigating the cloud's shared responsibility model (Thilagavathi et al., 2025). This process is governed by the ephemeral nature of the cloud, where instances can be terminated with a single API call, and the underlying hypervisor is inaccessible (Bhambri & Bajdor, 2025). Successful acquisition, therefore, relies on leveraging cloud-native features like snapshots and APIs while applying adapted traditional forensic principles to capture a static evidentiary artifact from a dynamic, often short-lived, target.

3.3.1 Pre-acquisition: Identifying and isolating the target VM instance

Before any imaging occurs, a critical pre-acquisition phase ensures the correct target is preserved and evidence integrity is maintained. Identification begins with cloud metadata—tags, instance names, IDs—and correlates with investigative leads from network flow logs, security alerts, or compromised accounts (Anand & Bhambri, 2025). Once the target VM is identified, immediate isolation is paramount to prevent evidence destruction or further malicious activity. In the cloud, this is achieved not by physically pulling a cable, but by reconfiguring security groups and network access control lists (NACLs) to a "deny-all" state, effectively quarantining the instance while it remains powered on for live acquisition. Simultaneously, the IAM roles and policies attached to the instance should be scrutinized and potentially detached to prevent the VM itself from calling destructive APIs (Moreb et al., 2024). This network and identity isolation "freezes" the incident scene within the logical confines of the cloud environment, providing a stable window for forensic collection.

3.3.2 Live acquisition techniques for IaaS VMs

Live acquisition of a cloud VM involves extracting its memory and disk state while it is running, which is crucial for capturing artifacts like encryption keys, active network connections, and running malware processes that are lost on shutdown (Muthukumar et al., 2025). The techniques must respect the cloud boundary; investigators cannot install tools on the underlying hypervisor. Instead, they work within the guest OS or use cloud provider services (Gil-Fournier & Parikka, 2024). The primary challenge is executing acquisition commands without altering the very volatile state being captured and doing so in a way that is legally defensible and minimally intrusive to other tenants. The chosen method depends on the investigation's goals, the cloud platform's capabilities, and the level of pre-installed forensic readiness (like existing agents).

- Agent-Based Acquisition (Memory, Disk): This method requires a lightweight forensic agent pre-deployed within the VM's guest OS as part of the organization's forensic readiness strategy. Upon an incident, the investigator can remotely command the agent to capture the system's RAM (e.g., using toolkits like WinPmem or LiME for Linux) and generate a forensic image of attached volumes. The agent streams this data securely to a designated forensic repository. The advantage is precision and control, allowing for memory capture and targeted file acquisition without needing full disk snapshots (Bhambri & Kant, 2025a). The significant drawback is its dependency on pre-planning; the agent must already be installed, configured, and trusted. Furthermore, the act of running the agent and its tools necessarily alters the system's state (loading modules into memory, creating processes), which must be meticulously documented.
- Snapshot-Based Forensics: Leveraging Cloud Snapshots: This is the most common and cloud-native acquisition method. A snapshot is a point-in-time, provider-level copy of a VM's storage volumes. The investigator initiates a live snapshot through the cloud management console or API. Critically, while the snapshot is being created, the VM can remain running, though performance may be impacted (Cantelli-Forti et al., 2025). The resulting snapshot is not a forensic image format (like .E01) but a cloud-native object (e.g., an AWS EBS snapshot, an Azure Managed Disk snapshot). The forensic soundness derives from the cloud provider's API integrity and audit logs. The investigator then creates a new, forensically sterile volume from this snapshot and attaches it to a separate, trusted forensic workstation VM within the same cloud environment (Kasuba et al., 2025). Finally, using traditional forensic tools (like FTK Imager or Guymager) running on the workstation, a bit-for-bit forensic image (e.g., .dd or .E01) is created from the attached volume, hashing is performed, and the chain of custody is established.
- Forensic Imaging via Direct Attached Volumes: For environments where snapshots are deemed insufficiently transparent or for maximum control, the direct-attached volume method is used. This involves detaching the primary boot volume or any data volume from the target VM (which typically requires stopping the instance) and then attaching it as a secondary, read-only volume to a dedicated forensic workstation VM. The workstation, equipped with write-blocking software (often implemented at the hypervisor-driver level in the cloud), can then image the volume directly using standard disk imaging tools (Ludovico, 2024). This process provides a clear and traditional imaging pathway but has the major disadvantage of requiring the target VM to be stopped, destroying all volatile memory evidence. It is best suited for investigations focused solely on persistent disk data or when a VM has already been terminated, leaving only its detached volumes behind (Nazeeya et al., 2024).

3.3.3 Post-termination acquisition: Recovering from decommissioned instances

A critical cloud forensic challenge is acquiring evidence from a VM that has already been terminated. The principle of "ephemerality" means the instance is gone, but residual artifacts often persist. Acquisition focuses on these secondary data sources (Perera, 2025): (1) Persistent Volumes: If the VM used separate, persistent block storage (e.g., AWS EBS, Azure Disk), these volumes may remain after instance termination, depending on the "delete on termination" setting. They become the primary target for imaging. (2) Surviving Snapshots: Any snapshots taken prior to termination (manually or automatically) remain and can be used to create a forensic image. (3) Provider Logs: Comprehensive cloud logs (CloudTrail, Activity Log) provide the definitive record of who deleted the instance, when, and from where. (4) Memory Paging Files/Crash Dumps: If the VM was part of a managed service or crashed, the underlying hypervisor may have written a diagnostic crash dump or core file to persistent storage, which can be located and analyzed. Speed is essential, as even these residual artifacts may have automated deletion policies (Ray, 2025b).

3.3.4 AI-enhanced triage: Prioritizing VMs for acquisition based on threat Intel

In a large-scale breach involving hundreds or thousands of VMs, time and resource constraints make imaging everything impossible. AI-enhanced triage automates the prioritization of VMs for acquisition. Machine learning models ingest multiple real-time data streams: threat intelligence feeds (indicators of compromise), internal alert severity, VM metadata (network exposure, role, owner), anomalous behavior detection (unusual process execution, network traffic), and user/entity risk scores (Bhambri, 2025). The model correlates these signals to assign a dynamic "forensic priority score" to each VM. For instance, a VM with external-facing IPs, running a database role, showing anomalous outbound connections to a known C2 server, and owned by a recently phished user would be flagged for immediate, automated acquisition. This AI-driven approach ensures that limited forensic resources are deployed against the assets with the highest probable evidence yield, dramatically improving the efficiency and effectiveness of the investigation's critical early phase.

3.4 FORENSIC ACQUISITION OF CONTAINERIZED WORKLOADS

The ephemeral and immutable nature of containers presents a paradigm shift for digital forensics, demanding techniques that align with their lifecycle. Unlike traditional systems, the primary evidence often resides not within a persistent container instance—which may last only minutes—but in the artifacts generated by and about the container ecosystem (Grigar & Pisarski, 2024). This includes the container images, orchestration layer logs, runtime metadata, and immutable data volumes. Effective forensic acquisition in this environment requires a multi-layered approach, targeting the container itself, its blueprint (the image), and the orchestration platform that governs its existence. Investigators must act swiftly, leveraging API-driven automation to capture volatile data before a container is recycled, while also understanding that the most critical evidence is often found in the declarative and immutable components of the system.

3.4.1 Container forensics fundamentals: Layers, images, and runtimes

A foundational understanding of container architecture is crucial for effective acquisition. A container is a runnable instance of an image, which is a lightweight, standalone, executable package of software that includes everything needed to run an application. Images are built from a series of immutable layers, each representing a change from the previous layer, as defined in a Dockerfile (Onik et al., 2025). This layered, union filesystem means that at runtime, the container merges these read-only layers with a final writable layer (the container layer), where all runtime changes reside. The container runtime (e.g., Docker Engine, containerd, CRI-O) is the software responsible for pulling images, creating the container's isolated environment (using namespaces and cgroups), and managing its lifecycle. For forensics, this structure dictates a bifurcated strategy: acquiring the ephemeral writable layer of a running container and analyzing the static, layered composition of its base image to establish a known-good baseline and identify malicious modifications (Fouad, 2024).

3.4.2 Live container acquisition

When a container is still running, investigators have a narrow window to capture its volatile state, which includes in-memory artifacts, active network connections, and the writable filesystem layer. This process is time sensitive and often requires executing commands from the host or a trusted forensic container with elevated privileges to introspect the target container's namespace. The goal is to gather a snapshot of the container's runtime environment that will disappear the moment the container stops (Mušić et al., 2024). Techniques must be minimally intrusive to avoid alerting a potential attacker or destabilizing the application, and all actions must be logged to maintain the forensic integrity of the acquisition process.

- Executing into Running Containers: The primary method for interactive live analysis is using commands like docker exec or kubectl exec to spawn a shell or a forensic tool process inside the target container's namespace. For example, docker exec -it <container_id> /bin/bash provides an interactive shell, allowing an investigator to run commands like ps aux, netstat -tulpn, or ls -la /tmp to view processes, network connections, and files. However, this method is intrusive and alters the container (by adding a new process). A more forensically sound approach is to use tools like nsenter to enter the container's namespaces from the host directly or to run a statically compiled forensic toolkit from a mounted volume, minimizing contamination of the original container environment (Spiekermann, 2025).
- Acquiring Container Runtime State (Docker, containerd): The container runtime maintains critical metadata and state information. For Docker, this includes the container's configuration (/var/lib/docker/containers/<id>/config.v2.json), log files, and filesystem layers. Acquiring the entire runtime directory for a specific container preserves this configuration. For lower-level runtimes like containerd (common in Kubernetes), the state is managed via the CRI (Container Runtime Interface). Tools like crictl can be used to inspect containers (crictl inspect <container_id>), dump their task information, and export a running container's filesystem as a tar archive. Acquiring this runtime state is essential for understanding how the container was configured and launched, including its environment variables, entrypoint, and mounted volumes (Sucipto et al., 2025).
- Extracting Container Logs and stdout/stderr Streams: Containers are designed to log to standard output (stdout) and standard error (stderr). The runtime captures these streams, and they are a vital source of application and potential attack artifacts. For Docker, logs are typically stored as JSON files in the container's runtime directory. They can be extracted using docker logs—timestamps <container_id> > container.lo g. In an orchestrated environment like Kubernetes, these logs are automatically aggregated by the kubelet and can be retrieved via the Kubernetes API (kubectl logs <pod_ name>) or from a cluster-level logging solution (e.g., Fluentd, Loki). Acquiring these logs provides a timeline of the container's application activity and any error messages or commands an attacker may have output (Zhuo et al., 2025).

3.4.3 Container image forensics

Since containers are instantiated from immutable images, the image itself is a prime forensic artifact. It represents the intended, declarative state of the application and serves as a baseline against which a compromised running container can be compared. Image forensics involves analyzing the built image and its construction process to identify malicious code, embedded secrets, known vulnerabilities, or unexpected layers that could indicate a supply chain attack. This analysis is often more fruitful than examining a running container, as the image is persistent and can be dissected offline (Ray, 2025a).

- Analyzing Dockerfiles and Build Histories: The Dockerfile is the build script that defines how an image is constructed. Forensic analysis of the Dockerfile can reveal the insertion of malicious commands (e.g., RUN curl http://malicious-site/script.sh | sh), the exposure of sensitive ports, or the inclusion of unnecessary setuid binaries. The command docker history <image_name> provides a layer-by-layer breakdown of the image's creation, showing the command that created each layer. Discrepancies between the known Dockerfile and the actual image history can indicate an unauthorized build or a compromised build pipeline.
- Inspecting Registry Images and Layer Hashes: Images are stored in registries (e.g., Docker Hub, Amazon ECR, Google Container Registry). Acquiring the image directly from the registry ensures an unmodified copy. Using docker pull or registry API calls, investigators can download the image for analysis. Each image and its layers are identified by a cryptographic hash (e.g., SHA256). Tools like docker inspect or skopeo can list these layers and their hashes (Bhambri & Kant, 2025b). By comparing the hashes of a suspect running container's layers to the official registry image, an investigator can detect if the underlying immutable layers have been tampered with. Extracting and examining each layer's contents (using docker save and tar) allows for a detailed file system analysis.
- Vulnerability Scans as a Forensic Artifact: Vulnerability scanning tools (e.g., Trivy, Grype, Clair) are not just for DevOps; they are crucial for forensics. Running a scanner against a seized container image provides a catalog of known vulnerabilities (CVEs) and misconfigurations present at the time of the incident. This information can help establish an attack vector, such as an exploitable vulnerability that an attacker used for initial access (Hayles, 2024). The scan report becomes a forensic artifact that documents the security posture of the application at a specific point in its lifecycle, which is critical for understanding the scope of a breach and for remediation efforts.

3.4.4 Orchestrator-level acquisition: Kubernetes as a crime scene

In a containerized environment, the orchestrator (predominantly Kubernetes) is the control plane and the ultimate source of truth. It holds the declarative state, scheduling decisions, and audit logs for all workloads. When investigating an incident, the Kubernetes cluster itself must be treated as the macro crime scene. Evidence is scattered across its various components, providing context that is impossible to glean from a single container alone—such as which node a pod ran on, who deployed it, and what other pods it communicated with (Richardson, 2024).

- Acquiring Kubernetes Forensic Artifacts: Pods, Deployments, Services: The primary Kubernetes resources are key artifacts. The YAML or JSON definitions of Pods, Deployments, StatefulSets, Services, and ConfigMaps/Secrets (though secrets in encoded form) must be acquired. They reveal the intended configuration: container images, command overrides, mounted volumes, network policies, and sensitive environment variables. These can be retrieved using kubectl get <resource> -o yaml—all-namespaces. A malicious deployment might use a privileged security context, mount the host filesystem, or reference a malicious image from a private registry. Comparing the live state with version-controlled manifests can identify drifts caused by an attacker (Vashishth et al., 2024).

- Extracting Event Logs, etcd Data, and Audit Logs: Kubernetes maintains several critical log streams. Cluster Events (kubectl get events—all-namespaces) provide a timeline of state changes (e.g., "Pod scheduled," "Pulled image," "Failed"). etcd, the cluster's key-value store, holds the entire state of the cluster. Acquiring an etcd snapshot (via etcdctl snapshot save) preserves the definitive state of all objects at a point in time, but requires cluster-level access. Most critically, the Kubernetes Audit Log records every API request (who made it, from where, at what time, and what was requested), making it the cornerstone for detecting and reconstructing malicious activity, such as unauthorized pod creation or privilege escalation attempts. These logs must be centralized and protected from attacker tampering (Kaur & Dhawan, 2024).
- The Role of Service Mesh (Istio, Linkerd) Data in Investigations: A service mesh like Istio or Linkerd adds a uniform layer of observability and control over service-to-service communication. In a forensic context, it provides telemetry that is otherwise nearly impossible to gather from ephemeral containers. The service mesh Envoy access logs detail every HTTP/gRPC request between services, including headers, response codes, and latency. Distributed tracing (e.g., Jaeger) can reconstruct the full path of a request across dozens of microservices. Metrics can identify anomalous traffic patterns. This data is invaluable for mapping lateral movement, data exfiltration paths, and the blast radius of a compromise within a complex microservices architecture (Hodson, 2024).

3.5 AI-DRIVEN TECHNIQUES FOR ACQUISITION IN EPHEMERAL ENVIRONMENTS

The transient nature of containers and automated scaling of VMs creates windows for evidence acquisition that can be measured in seconds. This section details how artificial intelligence moves investigations from reactive to proactive and intelligent stances. AI techniques are employed to predict, prioritize, and process forensic data at cloud scale and speed, overcoming the fundamental challenge of ephemerality by making acquisition workflows smarter, faster, and more targeted than manual methods ever could be (Balakrishnan, 2025).

Figure 3.1 illustrates the integrated workflow of AI modules that automate and enhance evidence acquisition from transient cloud resources. The process begins with diverse data ingestion, flows through specialized AI components for prediction, prioritization, and parsing, and culminates in the automated correlation of evidence to reconstruct a unified attack narrative.

3.5.1 Developing an AI-informed curriculum: What to teach and how

This technique employs machine learning models trained on cloud telemetry (scaling events, deployment histories, scheduled jobs) to forecast when a specific container pod or VM instance is likely to be terminated or recycled. By predicting the "time-to-live" of ephemeral resources, the system can automatically trigger forensic acquisition scripts just before termination, ensuring evidence is captured without requiring constant human monitoring. This transforms acquisition from a race against the clock into a scheduled, guaranteed event, preserving evidence that would otherwise be permanently lost.

3.5.2 Faculty development: Empowering educators as AI orchestrators

When facing hundreds of containers with only minutes for acquisition, deciding what to capture is critical. AI models perform real-time triage, scoring targets based on fused threat intelligence (unusual network connections, known malicious image hashes), behavioral anomalies (high CPU from a non-compute pod), and investigative context (proximity to a breached asset) (Bhambri & Pawełoszek, 2025). The model outputs a prioritized "acquisition shortlist," ensuring the limited acquisition window is spent capturing the most probative evidence from the most suspicious entities, maximizing the investigative ROI of the acquisition process.

3.5.3 Building an institutional AI ethics charter

Individual container or VM artifacts are isolated data points. AI, particularly graph neural networks and associative learning, automatically links these disparate, ephemeral data

Figure 3.1 AI-driven forensic acquisition engine for ephemeral environments.

points—a malicious process in a terminated Pod A, a suspicious file in a related container image, and a lateral movement attempt logged by the orchestrator—into a unified attack narrative or "kill chain." This reconstructs the adversary's actions across the ephemeral environment, providing a coherent story from evidence that would otherwise be a collection of orphaned, transient events (Baldry et al., 2024).

3.5.4 Fostering partnerships between academia and industry

Container and orchestrator logs are voluminous, unstructured, and filled with technical jargon. Natural Language Processing (NLP) models, including specialized transformer models, are trained to parse these logs at scale. They extract key forensic entities (user names, commands executed, source IPs, file paths), classify log entries into actionable categories (e.g., "privilege escalation attempt," "data exfiltration," "lateral movement"), and summarize activities, transforming massive, opaque text streams into structured, queryable, and analytically ready data for investigators and downstream correlation engines (Escaleira et al., 2025).

3.6 TOOLCHAIN AND AUTOMATION FOR SCALABLE ACQUISITION

Effective forensics in ephemeral environments demands specialized tooling integrated into automated pipelines, as manual methods cannot scale or keep pace with the lifecycle of transient assets. This section examines the critical software frameworks, native cloud services, and scripting approaches that enable investigators to programmatically capture, preserve, and process volatile evidence from VMs and containers at the speed of the cloud, ensuring no critical data is lost before termination (Valdez et al., 2024).

3.6.1 Open-source frameworks (e.g., KubeForensic, Docker Explorer)

Community-driven open-source tools provide vital, platform-agnostic capabilities for dissecting containerized environments, often filling gaps left by commercial tools. Frameworks like KubeForensic are designed specifically to query Kubernetes APIs and extract forensic artifacts from pods, deployments, and namespaces, while tools like Docker Explorer allow for the offline forensic analysis of container images, layers, and runtime filesystems. These tools are essential for conducting deep, standardized examinations across hybrid environments and form the building blocks for custom automation scripts (Rabzelj & Sedlar, 2025).

3.6.2 Cloud-native forensic tools (AWS Forensic Readiness, GCP SCC tools)

Major cloud providers offer integrated services and toolkits designed to facilitate forensic readiness and response within their own ecosystems. For example, AWS's Forensic Readiness Guide and associated quick-start templates help automate the isolation and evidence collection from EC2 instances, while Google Cloud's Security Command Center (SCC) provides investigative tools for disk snapshots and logging. Leveraging these native tools reduces complexity and ensures compatibility, but investigators must be aware of their proprietary nature and potential lack of portability across different cloud platforms (Sui et al., 2025).

3.6.3 Scripting acquisition pipelines with Python and Cloud SDKs/CLIs

To achieve true scalability and repeatability, investigators must build custom automated pipelines using programming languages like Python and cloud Software Development Kits (SDKs) or Command-Line Interfaces (CLIs). These scripts can orchestrate the entire acquisition chain—from identifying target resources via API calls, triggering forensic disk snapshots, and extracting memory dumps to securely transferring evidence to a forensic repository. This programmatic approach is crucial for responding to large-scale incidents and for integrating forensic acquisition directly into DevOps CI/CD pipelines for proactive monitoring.

3.6.4 Building SOAR playbooks for ephemeral incident response

Security Orchestration, Automation, and Response (SOAR) platforms are the operational engine for executing coordinated, time-critical acquisition in ephemeral environments. Prebuilt playbooks can automate the entire forensic response: upon an alert, a playbook can instantly isolate a compromised container, pause an orchestration workload, gather all relevant logs, snapshot persistent volumes, and initiate evidence collection scripts—all before a malicious pod is automatically rescheduled or a suspicious VM is terminated by an autoscaling group. This integrates forensic acquisition directly into the incident response lifecycle, preserving evidence that would otherwise vanish (Nguyen et al., 2025).

3.7 LEGAL AND PROCEDURAL CONSIDERATIONS

This section addresses the critical legal and procedural frameworks that must adapt to the transient nature of cloud environments. Traditional forensic procedures, designed for static hardware, are challenged by ephemeral systems where evidence is volatile and infrastructure is shared and controlled by a third party. Investigations must now integrate cloud-specific practices, emphasizing meticulous documentation, understanding service agreements, and navigating cross-border legal requirements to ensure evidence is admissible in court (Tucker et al., 2025).

3.7.1 Chain of custody in a dynamic, multi-tenant environment

Maintaining a legally defensible chain of custody is profoundly complex in environments where virtual resources are dynamically created, migrated, and destroyed across shared hardware. The classic, continuous physical possession is impossible (Bhambri & Starostka-Patyk, 2025). Investigators must instead rely on detailed, automated logging—capturing timestamps, user identities, API calls, and cryptographic hashes—to create an immutable, verifiable audit trail that documents every access and action taken on the digital evidence, proving its integrity from acquisition to presentation.

3.7.2 Jurisdictional challenges with transient, geographically distributed workloads

Ephemeral workloads can be instantiated and replicated across global data centers in seconds, creating significant jurisdictional ambiguity. Data relevant to a single investigation may be stored or processed in multiple legal jurisdictions, each with its own data privacy, sovereignty, and evidence laws (e.g., GDPR, CLOUD Act). Investigators must quickly identify the physical and legal location of evidence and navigate conflicting legal requirements for acquisition and disclosure, often requiring early engagement with legal counsel to avoid procedural missteps (Stewart et al., 2024).

3.7.3 Preservation orders and cloud provider cooperation

The rapid scalability and automation of cloud platforms mean that evidence can be automatically deleted by orchestration tools or routine operations. Securing evidence requires timely legal actions, such as preservation orders or letters of request, directed at the cloud provider. Effective cooperation hinges on understanding the provider's specific capabilities, internal procedures, and response timelines outlined in their terms of service. Investigators must act swiftly to legally compel the preservation of logs, snapshots, and metadata before automated systems permanently erase them (Burley, 2025).

3.8 CASE STUDY: INVESTIGATING A CRYPTOJACKING INCIDENT IN A KUBERNETES CLUSTER

This case study presents a real-world scenario where an organization's development Kubernetes cluster was compromised for cryptocurrency mining. The investigation highlights the practical application of the acquisition techniques discussed in this chapter, emphasizing the race against ephemerality. The attackers exploited a misconfigured Kubernetes Dashboard, gained initial access, and deployed a DaemonSet to run malicious mining pods on every node, leveraging the cluster's resources for profit while evading immediate detection by masquerading as a legitimate system workload (Pickersgill, 2024).

3.8.1 Alert and initial triage

The investigation was triggered by a multifaceted alert from the organization's Cloud Security Posture Management (CSPM) tool, indicating anomalous compute resource consumption (consistently high CPU across nodes), coupled with a minor but unusual outbound network flow to a known cryptocurrency pool. The initial triage, guided by an AI-driven SOAR playbook, involved immediate isolation of the non-production cluster from the wider network to contain the threat. Forensic responders first secured volatile data by invoking a pre-configured script to capture the runtime state of all pods (kubectl get pods -o yaml—all-namespaces), container logs, and Kubernetes events (Rana & Bhambri, 2024). They simultaneously issued a preservation request to the cloud provider's API to lock and snapshot the persistent volumes attached to the cluster. This rapid, automated triage was critical, as the attacker's DaemonSet was configured for rapid pod respawn, making live evidence highly transient (Sefati et al., 2025).

3.8.2 AI-assisted timeline reconstruction from ephemeral pods

Manually reconstructing the attack timeline was infeasible due to the high churn of terminated mining pods. An AI model, trained on normal Kubernetes audit log patterns, was deployed to analyze the cluster's audit logs, etcd transaction logs, and cloud provider's API Gateway logs. The model correlated disparate events, identifying the precise moment the attacker's service account was improperly bound to a cluster-admin role. It then stitched together subsequent actions: the deployment of the malicious DaemonSet, the pulling of a container image from a public registry, and the iterative lifecycle of hundreds of short-lived pods (Sharma et al., 2025). The AI outputted a visual, annotated timeline, pinpointing the initial breach to a specific IP and user session on the exposed dashboard, a detail buried in petabytes of routine log data.

3.8.3 Acquiring and analyzing the malicious container image

With the image name and hash identified from the Kubernetes manifests, investigators pulled the malicious container image from the cluster's internal registry. Using container forensics tools, they conducted a layered analysis, comparing the image against its purported base image. The analysis revealed that the Dockerfile had appended a layer that downloaded and executed a compiled Monero miner binary, hidden behind a benign-sounding entry point. Further, the image was found to contain a sidelined SSH key and a persistence script, indicating plans for deeper compromise (Mamidi, 2025). The hash of the miner binary was cross-referenced with threat intelligence feeds via an automated API call, confirming it was a known variant of the XMRig miner, commonly associated with cloud cryptojacking campaigns.

3.8.4 Lessons learned and playbook development

The investigation yielded critical lessons that were codified into enhanced playbooks. Key takeaways included: the necessity of default-deny network policies for pods, the critical importance of securing the Kubernetes control plane (especially the dashboard and service accounts), and the value of behavioral monitoring for resource consumption over signature-based detection. The playbook for "Cryptojacking Response" was updated to include immediate steps for DaemonSet hunting, automated image acquisition from registries, and the pre-approved integration of the AI timeline reconstruction tool. A new proactive hunting query was added to the CSPM to alert on any pod or DaemonSet with resource requests exceeding defined development workload profiles (Coston et al., 2025).

3.9 FUTURE TRENDS: ACQUISITION IN SERVERLESS AND EDGE COMPUTING

The evolution of cloud computing toward even more abstracted and distributed models presents the next frontier for forensic acquisition. As infrastructure becomes increasingly transient and physically decentralized, traditional disk and memory acquisition paradigms are rendered obsolete, demanding a fundamental shift toward pervasive logging, instrumentation, and predictive evidence collection.

3.9.1 The forensics challenge of Functions-as-a-Service (FaaS)

Forensic acquisition in a FaaS (e.g., AWS Lambda, Azure Functions) environment is uniquely challenging due to the complete absence of investigator-accessible persistent compute resources. The forensic "crime scene" exists only for the milliseconds to minutes of a function's execution. Acquisition, therefore, is almost entirely indirect and log-based. Investigators must rely on provider-supplied execution logs, trace data (e.g., X-Ray), and any structured output the function writes to attached services (e.g., S3, DynamoDB). The future lies in instrumenting functions with lightweight forensic shims that automatically capture execution environment metadata, system calls, and network connections at runtime, streaming this data to a secure audit sink before the function instance is destroyed (de Hoz Diego et al., 2024).

3.9.2 Acquisition strategies for edge containers and MicroVMs

Edge computing pushes containerized and MicroVM workloads (e.g., AWS IoT Greengrass, Azure IoT Edge, firecracker microVMs) to geographically dispersed, often resource-constrained, and intermittently connected devices. Acquisition must be orchestrated remotely and efficiently. Strategies include the deployment of lightweight, persistent forensic agents on edge hosts that can capture snapshots of container runtimes or MicroVM states on command or upon anomaly detection. Evidence must be packaged for low-bandwidth transmission. Furthermore, the orchestrator (e.g., Kubernetes K3s) managing the edge fleet becomes the single point of truth, requiring its logs and desired state configurations to be acquired and analyzed centrally to understand the intended vs. actual state across thousands of ephemeral edge nodes (Oluoha et al., 2025).

3.10 CHAPTER SUMMARY AND BEST PRACTICES

This chapter has established that forensic acquisition in ephemeral environments is a paradigm defined by automation, speed, and a shift from traditional disk imaging to API-driven evidence collection and the analysis of immutable infrastructure artifacts (Bhambri & Hamad, 2025). Success hinges on integrating forensic readiness into the DevOps lifecycle and leveraging AI to manage the scale and volatility of cloud-native evidence.

3.10.1 The acquisition priority list for ephemeral environments

When responding to an incident, a clear priority list must guide actions to capture the most volatile evidence first. The hierarchy is: (1) Runtime Memory and State: Capture the process list, network connections, and RAM from running containers/VMs if possible, as it vanishes on termination. (2) Runtime Logs and Streams: Acquire stdout/stderr and application logs from the runtime engine (Docker, containerd). (3) Orchestrator State: Immediately collect Kubernetes manifests, etcd data, and audit logs that describe the workload's intended state and history. (4) Persistent Volume Snapshots: Trigger snapshots via cloud APIs for attached storage. (5) Container Images and VM Templates: Secure the immutable images from registries and template repositories for offline analysis. (6) Cloud Service Logs: Finally, pull the relevant logs from the cloud provider's services (CloudTrail, Azure Activity Log, Cloud Audit Logs) (Khoury et al., 2024; Malik et al., 2024).

3.10.2 Building an AI-augmented forensic readiness program

Proactive readiness is non-negotiable. Organizations must build a program that integrates forensic tooling into the CI/CD pipeline (e.g., scanning images for vulnerabilities) and maintains continuous, automated evidence collection baselines. AI augmentation involves deploying ML models for anomalous behavior detection (like unexpected CPU loads or strange API calls) that can trigger automated evidence preservation playbooks before an attacker can cover their tracks (Seshadri et al., 2024). Furthermore, AI can be used to automatically tag and classify seized evidence, correlate events across disparate cloud logs, and even predict potential evidence sources based on the attack pattern, transforming the forensic process from a reactive scramble to a proactive, intelligence-driven function (Sundaramurthy et al., 2025).

REFERENCES

Anand, A. J., & Bhambri, P. (Eds.). (2025). *Handbook of AI-driven Threat Detection and Prevention: A Holistic Approach to Security*. CRC Press. https://doi.org/10.1201/9781003521020

Balakrishnan, S. K. (2025). *Cognitive Defense Fabric: Real-Time Attack Prediction and Legitimate Traffic Preservation*. Geh Press.

Baldry, M. K., Happa, J., Steed, A., Smith, S., & Glencross, M. (2024). From Embodied Abuse to Mass Disruption: Generative, Inter-Reality Threats in Social, Mixed-Reality Platforms. *Digital Threats: Research and Practice*, 5(4), 1–36.

Bhambri, P. (2025). Understanding AI and Machine Learning in Security. In P. Bhambri & A. J. Anand (Eds.), *Handbook of AI-driven Threat Detection and Prevention: A Holistic Approach to Security* (pp. 1–17). CRC Press. https://doi.org/10.1201/9781003521020-1

Bhambri, P., & Bajdor, P. (2025). AI-powered Predictive Analysis for Proactive Cyber Defense. In P. Bhambri & A. J. Anand (Eds.), *Handbook of AI-driven Threat Detection and Prevention: A Holistic Approach to Security* (pp. 308–321). CRC Press. https://doi.org/10.1201/9781003521020-18

Bhambri, P., & Hamad, A. (2025). Quantum Computing and AI Synergies: Strengthening Cybersecurity Resilience. In P. Bhambri & A. J. Anand (Eds.), *Handbook of AI-driven Threat Detection and Prevention: A Holistic Approach to Security* (pp. 337–352). CRC Press. https://doi.org/10.1201/9781003521020-20

Bhambri, P., & Kant, S. (2025a, February 1–2). A Taxonomy of Bias in Machine Learning: Classification, Sources, and Implications for Ethical AI [Paper presentation]. Lincoln-SPAST Global Sustainability Programme (SGS-24), 1st International Conference of LGPR Program, Lincoln University College, Malaysia. SPAST Proceedings, 1(2). https://spast.org/techrep/article/view/5387/724

Bhambri, P., & Kant, S. (2025b, April 26–27). Ethical AI Systems: A Comprehensive Framework for Bias Mitigation and Fairness in Machine Learning [Paper presentation]. Lincoln-SPAST Global Sustainability Programme (SGS-24), 2nd International Conference of LGPR Program, Lincoln University College, Malaysia. SPAST Proceedings, 1(2). https://spast.org/techrep/article/view/5385/698

Bhambri, P., & Kant, S. (2025c, August 2–3). Navigating the AI Trade-offs: A Sector-Level Study on Fairness, Performance, and Explainability [Paper presentation]. Lincoln-SPAST Global Sustainability Programme (SGS-24), 3rd International Conference of LGPR Program, Lincoln University College, Malaysia. SPAST Proceedings, 1(4). https://spast.org/techrep/article/view/5734/862

Bhambri, P., & Pawełoszek, I. (2025). Deep Learning Techniques for Intrusion Detection in Critical Infrastructure. In P. Bhambri & A. J. Anand (Eds.), *Handbook of AI-Driven Threat Detection and Prevention: A Holistic Approach to Security* (pp. 322–336). CRC Press. https://doi.org/10.1201/9781003521020-19

Bhambri, P., & Starostka-Patyk, M. (2025). Integrating AI with Blockchain for Decentralized Security and Threat Prevention. In P. Bhambri & A. J. Anand (Eds.), *Handbook of AI-driven Threat Detection and Prevention: A Holistic Approach to Security* (pp. 353–370). CRC Press. https://doi.org/10.1201/9781003521020-21

Bora, S. S. (2025). Technolatry and Virtual Emotions in the Era of Digital Brutalism: Understanding the Proliferation of Cybercrimes in Modern Brazil. *Sociologia*, 51, 95–124.

Burley, D. L. (2025). Social Context in Security and Privacy. In H. C. A. van Tilborg (Ed.), *Encyclopedia of Cryptography, Security and Privacy* (pp. 2456–2457). Springer Nature Switzerland. https://doi.org/10.1007/978-3-031-56246-9

Cantelli-Forti, A., Longo, G., Lupia, F., & Russo, E. (2025). WEFT: A Consistent and Tamper-Proof Methodology for Acquisition of Automatically Verifiable Forensic Web Evidence. *International Journal of Information Security*, 24(2), 81.

Coston, I., Hezel, K. D., Plotnizky, E., & Nojoumian, M. (2025). Enhancing Secure Software Development with AZTRM-D: An AI-integrated Approach Combining DevSecOps, Risk Management, and Zero Trust. *Applied Sciences*, 15(15), 8163.

de Hoz Diego, J. D., Madi, T., & Konstantinou, C. (2024). CMXsafe: A Proxy Layer for Securing Internet-of-things Communications. *IEEE Transactions on Information Forensics and Security*, 19, 5767–5782.

Donca, I. C., Stan, O. P., Misaros, M., Stan, A., & Miclea, L. (2024). Comprehensive Security for IoT Devices with Kubernetes and Raspberry pi Cluster. *Electronics*, 13(9), 1613.

Escaleira, P., Cunha, V. A., Barraca, J. P., Gomes, D., & Aguiar, R. L. (2025). A Systematic Review on Security Mechanisms for Serverless Computing. *Cluster Computing*, 28(7), 465.

Fouad, N. S. (2024). *Theorising Cyber (in) Security: Information, Materiality, and Entropic Security.* Taylor & Francis.

Geetanjali, R., Sreehari, T. M., Jegatheesan, A., Muthukumar, B., Thyla, B., & Anand, J. A. (2025). Predictive Model of 6-Month Prognosis of Stroke Patients Using Machine Learning Techniques. *2025 2nd International Conference On Multidisciplinary Research and Innovations in Engineering (MRIE)*, Gurugram, India, pp. 439–444.

Geetha, R., Thilagavathi, P., Anand, J. A., Govindaram, A., G. S., J., & Parameswari, D. (2025a). Detection and Classification of Faults in a Power System with Inverter Penetration Based on a Real-Time Machine Learning Application. *2025 Fourth International Conference on Smart Technologies, Communication and Robotics (STCR)*, Sathyamangalam, India, pp. 1–6.

Geetha, R., Vidhya, S., Mukunthan, M. A., Goud, D. S., Anand, J. A., & Kesavan, R. (2025b). Predicting Online Vulnerability among Children and Youth: A Machine Learning Approach with Decision Trees and Naive Bayes Algorithms. *2025 Global Conference in Emerging Technology (GINOTECH)*, Pune, India, pp. 1–6.

Gharaibeh, T., Seiden, S., Abouelsaoud, M., Bou-Harb, E., & Baggili, I. (2024, July). Don't, Stop, Drop, Pause: Forensics of CONtainer CheckPOINTs (ConPoint). In *Proceedings of the 19th International Conference on Availability, Reliability and Security* (pp. 1–11).

Gil-Fournier, A., & Parikka, J. (2024). *Living Surfaces: Images, Plants, and Environments of Media.* MIT Press.

Griffith, S., & Morris, T. H. (2025). Supervisory Control and Data Acquisition. In S. Jajodia, P. Samarati, & M. Yung (Eds.), *Encyclopedia of Cryptography, Security and Privacy* (pp. 2556–2558). Springer Nature Switzerland.

Grigar, D., & Pisarski, M. (2024). *The Challenges of Born-digital Fiction: Editions, Translations, and Emulations.* Cambridge University Press.

Hagan, L. (2025). Containment. *Technoetic Arts: A Journal of Speculative Research*, 23(1), 63–80.

Hayles, N. K. (2024). *How We Think: Digital Media and Contemporary Technogenesis.* University of Chicago Press.

Hodson, C. J. (2024). *Cyber Risk Management: Prioritize Threats, Identify Vulnerabilities and Apply Controls.* Kogan Page Publishers.

Hughes, C., & Robinson, N. (2024). *Effective Vulnerability Management: Managing Risk in the Vulnerable Digital Ecosystem.* John Wiley & Sons.

Jayanthi, S., Vinitha Baby, P., Parameswari, D., Geetha, R., Thilagavathi, P., & Anand, J. A. (2025). Improved Convolutional Neural Network for Garbage Separation. *2025 6th International Conference for Emerging Technology (INCET)*, Belgaum, India, pp. 1–6.

Kasuba, T., Saravanan, S., & Balaram, V. V. S. S. S. (2025). Intelligent Threat Detection Framework for Serverless Cloud Computing Architecture Using Supervised ML Algorithms. OPSEARCH. Advance online publication. https://doi.org/10.1007/s12597-025-00829-0

Kaur, G., & Dhawan, A. (2024). *Laws of Electronic Evidence and Digital Forensics.* PHI Learning Pvt. Ltd.

Khoury, J., Klisura, Đ., Zanddizari, H., Parra, G. D. L. T., Najafirad, P., & Bou-Harb, E. (2024, May). Jbeil: Temporal Graph-based Inductive Learning to Infer Lateral Movement in Evolving Enterprise Networks. In *2024 IEEE Symposium on Security and Privacy* (SP) (pp. 3644–3660). IEEE.

Ludovico, A. (2024). *Tactical Publishing: Using Senses, Software, and Archives in the Twenty-first Century.* MIT Press.

Malik, A. W., Bhatti, D. S., Park, T. J., Ishtiaq, H. U., Ryou, J. C., & Kim, K. I. (2024). Cloud Digital Forensics: Beyond Tools, Techniques, and Challenges. *Sensors*, 24(2), 433.

Mamidi, S. (2025). Privacy and Security in Cloud-Based Banking: A Technical Perspective. *IJSAT-International Journal on Science and Technology*, 16(1), 1–29.
Mohanty, A., Mohapatra, A. G., Nayak, N., Bairavel, S., Chaithra, M. M., Lakshmi, M., Govindaram, A., & Jose Anand, A. (2025, August). Optimizing Diesel Generators in Industrial Settings with IoT and Machine Learning. *International Journal of Information Technology*, 1–9.
Moreb, M., Salah, S., & Amro, B. (2024). A Novel Framework for Mobile Forensics Investigation Process. *International Journal of Computing and Digital Systems*, 16(1), 125–136.
Morić, Z., Dakić, V., & Čavala, T. (2025). Security Hardening and Compliance Assessment of Kubernetes Control Plane and Workloads. *Journal of Cybersecurity and Privacy*, 5(2), 30.
Mušić, D., Hribar, J., & Fortuna, C. (2024). Digital Transformation with a Lightweight On-premise PaaS. *Future Generation Computer Systems*, 160, 619–629.
Muthukumar, B., Nakka, P., H. V., Anand, J. A., Govindaram, A., & Thilagavathi, P. (2025). Application of Machine Learning Techniques for the Location and Early Detection of Brain Tumors. *2025 6th International Conference on Data Intelligence and Cognitive Informatics (ICDICI)*, Tirunelveli, India, pp. 1637–1644.
Nazeeya Anjum, N., Sumathi, S., Dheena Dhayalan, R., Rampavithran, R., Jose Anand, A., & Sathiyanarayanan, M. (2024). Smart Sensors for Smart City Environmental Monitoring Systems. In Tuan Anh Nguyen (Eds.), *Digital Twin, Blockchain, and Sensor Networks in the Healthy and Mobile City* (pp. 17–33). Elsevier.
Nguyen, C., Elmroth, E., & Bhuyan, M. (2025, July). Silent Failures in Stateless Systems: Rethinking Anomaly Detection for Serverless Computing. In *2025 IEEE International Conference on Service-Oriented System Engineering (SOSE)* (pp. 8–19). IEEE.
Oluoha, O. M., Odeshina, A., Reis, O., Okpeke, F., Attipoe, V., & Orieno, O. H. (2025). Designing Advanced Digital Solutions for Privileged Access Management and Continuous Compliance Monitoring. *World Scientific News*, 203, 256–301.
Onik, A. R., Brown, J., Walker, C., & Baggili, I. (2025). A Systematic Literature Review of Secure Instant Messaging Applications from a Digital Forensics Perspective. *ACM Computing Surveys*, 57(9), 1–36.
Orosz, P., Nagy, B., & Varga, P. (2025). Real-Time Detection and Mitigation Strategies Newly Appearing for DDoS Profiles. *Future Internet*, 17(9), 400.
Perera, N. (2025). Design of Cloud-Facilitated Data Repositories for Large-Scale Traffic Pattern Analyses. *Northern Reviews on Algorithmic Research, Theoretical Computation, and Complexity*, 10(2), 1–10.
Pickersgill, S. (2024). Architecture and Horror: Analogical Explorations in Architectural Design (Publication No. ?) [Doctoral dissertation, RMIT University].
Rabzelj, M., & Sedlar, U. (2025). Beyond the Leak: Analyzing the Real-World Exploitation of Stolen Credentials Using Honeypots. *Sensors*, 25(12), 3676.
Rana, R., & Bhambri, P. (2024). Generative AI-driven Security Frameworks for Web Engineering: Innovations and Challenges. In I. A. Shah & N. Z. Jhanjhi (Eds.), *Generative AI for Web Engineering Models* (pp. 285–296). IGI Global. https://doi.org/10.4018/979-8-3693-3703-5.ch014
Ray, P. P. (2025a). A Review of TRiSM Frameworks in Artificial Intelligence Systems: Fundamentals, Taxonomy, Use Cases, Key Challenges and Future Directions. Authorea Preprints.
Ray, P. P. (2025b). A Review on Agent-to-Agent Protocol: Concept, State-of-the-art, Challenges and Future Directions. Authorea Preprints.
Richardson, M. (2024). *Nonhuman Witnessing: War, Data, and Ecology after the End of the World*. Duke University Press.
Sajithabanu, S., Devika, S. T., Deeba, S., & Jose Anand, A. (2025). The Role of VR and AR in Intelligent Computing: Applications in Psychology and Autism. In. B. Sundaravadivazhagan, N. Gnanasankaran, P. Raj, & A. Saleem Raja (Eds.), *Virtual Reality and Augmented Reality with 6G Communication*, Ch-13. Wiley Publication.
Sefati, S. S., Arasteh, B., Fratu, O., & Halunga, S. (2025). SSLA: A Semi-Supervised Framework for Real-Time Injection Detection and Anomaly Monitoring in Cloud-based Web Applications with Real-world Implementation and Evaluation. *Journal of Cloud Computing*, 14(1), 38.

Seshadri, B., Han, Y., Olson, C., Pollak, D., & Tomasevic, V. (2024). OmniBOR: A System for Automatic, Verifiable Artifact Resolution across Software Supply Chains. arXiv. https://arxiv.org/abs/2402.08980

Sharma, D., Singh, J., & Bhambri, P. (2025). Federated Learning for Intrusion Detection in IoT Networks: A Comprehensive Review. In *Proceedings of the 2025 2nd International Conference on Electronic Circuits and Signaling Technologies (ICECST)* (pp. 634–639). IEEE.

Spiekermann, D. (2025). Positional Packet Capture for Anomaly Detection in Multitenant Virtual Networks. *International Journal of Network Management*, 35(2), e2326.

Stewart, E. M., Morgan, J. C., Woodruff, N. L., Combe, G., & Stolworthy, R. V. (2024). Enhancing Cloud Cybersecurity: Prescriptive Controls for Operational Technology (No. INL/RPT–24-81423-Rev000). Idaho National Laboratory.

Sucipto, H. I., Elwirehardja, G. N., Dominic, N., & Surantha, N. (2025). Kubernetes-Powered Cardiovascular Monitoring: Enhancing Internet of Things Heart Rate Systems for Scalability and Efficiency. *Information*, 16(3), 213.

Sudiana, D., Nuruddin, C. H., Rizkinia, M., & Husna, D. (2024). Forensic Analysis of WhatsApp Disappearing Message on Unrooted Android Using Mobile Device Forensics Methodology NIST SP 800-101r1.

Suganya, A., Parameswari, D., Geetha, R., Govindaram, A., Bahuguna, S., & Jose Anand, A. (2025). Comparison of Machine Learning Methods for Fraudulent Transaction Classification. *2025 6th International Conference for Emerging Technology (INCET)*, Belgaum, India, 2025, pp. 1–7.

Sui, X. F., Zhang, S. W., Wang, J. S., Zhang, S. H., Zhang, Y. H., & Bai, X. L. (2025). Mayfly Algorithm with Elementary Functions and Mathematical Spirals for Task Scheduling in Cloud Computing System. *The Journal of Supercomputing*, 81(6), 766.

Sundaramurthy, S. K., Ravichandran, N., Inaganti, A. C., & Muppalaneni, R. (2025). AI-Driven Threat Detection: Leveraging Machine Learning for Real-Time Cybersecurity in Cloud Environments. *Artificial Intelligence and Machine Learning Review*, 6(1), 23–43.

Thilagavathi, P., Hannah, S., Anand, J. A., Parameswari, D., Geetha, R., & Govindaram, A. (2025). Machine Learning and Security Fake Email Detection and Intrusion Detection. *2025 6th International Conference for Emerging Technology (INCET)*, Belgaum, India, pp. 1–6.

Tucker, T., Bennett, N., Kotuliak, M., Erni, S., Capkun, S., Butler, K., & Traynor, P. (2025). Detecting IMSI-Catchers by Characterizing Identity Exposing Messages in Cellular Traffic. In *Proceedings of the ISOC Networking and Distributed Systems Security (NDSS) Symposium*. ISOC.

Valdez, E., Ahmed, S., Gu, Z., De Dinechin, C., Cheng, P. C., & Jamjoom, H. (2024, December). Crossing Shifted Moats: Replacing Old Bridges with New Tunnels to Confidential Containers. In *Proceedings of the 2024 on ACM SIGSAC Conference on Computer and Communications Security* (pp. 1390–1404). ACM.

Vashishth, T. K., Sharma, V., Sharma, K. K., Kumar, B., Chaudhary, S., & Panwar, R. (2024). Serverless Computing Real-World Applications and Benefits in Cloud Environments. In D. Darwish (Ed.), *Emerging Trends in Cloud Computing Analytics, Scalability, and Service Models* (pp. 268–290). IGI Global.

Xiao, N., Wang, Z., Sun, X., & Miao, J. (2024). A Novel Blockchain-based Digital Forensics Framework for Preserving Evidence and Enabling Investigation in Industrial Internet of Things. *Alexandria Engineering Journal*, 86, 631–643.

Zhuo, T. Y., Wang, D., Ding, H., Kumar, V., & Wang, Z. (2025). Cyber-zero: Training Cybersecurity Agents without Runtime. arXiv. https://arxiv.org/abs/2508.00910.

Chapter 4

Forensic challenges in emerging technologies

AI-driven cloud forensics for next-generation digital investigations

A. Jose Anand

4.1 INTRODUCTION

The intense pace of development of digital technologies has essentially altered the character of the modern digital computing environment, data creation, and cyber interactions. The modern digital ecosystem is now based on emerging technologies: cloud computing, artificial intelligence, Internet of Things (IoT), edge computing, blockchain, and virtualized infrastructures. Although the technologies bring unprecedented scalability and efficiency, as well as intelligence, they are equally posing sophisticated forensic issues that put a lot of pressure on traditional digital investigation procedures. With the growing use of these superior environments by digital crimes, digital forensics needs to adapt to stick to its effectiveness, reliability, and legal defense [1]. Cloud computing, more so, has transformed the nature of data creation, storage, processing, and sharing. Cloud environments are distinct in contrast to traditional on-premise systems in that they use distributed, virtualized, and multi-tenant architecture, which blurs physical limits and ownership of information [2]. The abstraction of hardware, dynamic resource allocation, and the dependency on third-party cloud service providers make integrating evidence a more difficult task. Such difficulties are complicated by the incorporation of artificial intelligence in cloud systems, which allows for automatic decision-making, makes behavior foreseeable, and conducts self-optimizing mechanisms that constantly alter data and system states [3].

Artificial intelligence has become a source of new complexity in the forensic context as well as a potent facilitator of the future generation of forensic capacity. The models may produce immense amounts of heterogeneous data, such as model parameters, training data, inference logs, and automated decision outputs made by AI-enabled systems. Forensically, assigning behavior, reverse engineering events, defining how algorithms work as a means of interpretation, and creating explanations are hard to interpret and transplant in such systems [4]. Simultaneously, AI can provide cloud forensics with perspectives since it provides intelligent log analysis, anomaly identification, evidence correlation, and massive data triage. The twofold nature of AI as the generator of the forensic problem and, at the same time, the means of advancing forensic research calls for a reconsideration of investigative models. New technologies, like IoT and edge computing, provoke even more challenges to the state of digital forensics since they partially decentralize the process of data creation and processing [5, 6]. Network edge-based devices usually have little storage, occasional network connectivity, and proprietary operating systems, which lead to volatile devices and short-lived volatile evidence. These environments form complex and cross-domain forensic contexts described as whole-space governance along with cloud backends and AI-enhanced

DOI: 10.1201/9781003656487-4

analytics extending past physical hardware, virtualized infrastructure, and smart services. Conventional linear forensic models do not cope with this amount of architectural and operational complexity [7].

The other important issue is legal, jurisdictional, and regulatory limitations that are related to cloud-based investigations. Data in the data centers located in different geographies can be covered by more than one legal framework, privacy policies, and compliance norms. The investigators have to cope with data sovereignty problems, acquiring evidence cross-border, chain of custody, and evidence admissibility in court. The presence of cloud service providers as evidence custodians also raises the issue of accountability and trust, especially when the forensic access is related to the cooperation of the cloud service provider and service-level agreement. Following these problems, AI-driven cloud forensics has developed as a potential remedy to future-generation digital investigations. The purpose of using intelligent automation, machine learning, and advanced analytics in the forensic processes in this paradigm is to promote the scalability, accuracy, and timeliness in the processing of evidence [8, 9]. The AI-assisted forensic systems are capable of processing large datasets in clouds, determining pertinent artifacts, and building the complicated attack timeline more effectively as compared to the manual processes. Nonetheless, there are also some issues with the implementation of such systems, such as the problem of bias in the models, explainability, forensic soundness, and validation of AI-generated findings [10].

The chapter is dedicated to forensic issues arising due to new technologies, and in particular, AI-based cloud worlds. It is a critical review of the way technological convergence transforms the digital forensic process and indicates the weaknesses of traditional investigative methods. The chapter provides a grounding on the need to have new forensic strategies, tools, and governance models by examining the technical, operational, and legal aspects of the issue. Finally, the discussion is supposed to facilitate the creation of strong, clear, and future-proof forensic models that can be used to meet the requirements of the next-generation of digital investigations.

4.2 EVOLUTION OF DIGITAL FORENSICS IN CLOUD-CENTRIC ENVIRONMENTS

Digital forensics has seen a massive shift in its paradigm with the computing paradigms becoming highly distributed and cloud-based. Traditional digital forensics was originally tailored to support the infrastructures, which are fixed and where the investigators can have physical or logical access to the storage media, predictable system configurations, and established limits of data. Nonetheless, the quick integration of cloud computing has fundamentally changed the essence of digital evidence, and it has brought its own set of challenges in the form of issues of data location, ownership, volatility, and accessibility. Early digital forensic investigations were directed at personal computers, servers, and small networks where disk imaging, file system analysis, and examining logs were used to acquire evidence. These protocols presupposed the data permanence and control of the hardware on the part of the investigator [11–15]. As the business started to move onto virtualized environments and remote data centers, forensic practices needed to accommodate abstraction layers of virtual machines, hypervisors, and shared storage systems. With this development, the emergence of cloud-conscious forensic approaches, in which investigators progressively relied on logical acquisition practices and collaboration with service providers, started.

The cloud service models, Infrastructure as a Service (IaaS), Platform as a Service (PaaS), and Software as a Service (SaaS) further created a variety of landscapes in the field of forensics. The levels of control and visibility available to the investigators were different in each model. In IaaS, access to virtual machines and system logs is commonly restricted, and PaaS and SaaS provider systems limit direct evidence collection much more severely because of proprietary architecture and multi-tenant architectures. As a result, forensic investigations were transformed into services and data-focused rather than device-focused. The other significant evolution is based on the dynamic and elasticity of the cloud systems. Cloud environments provision and deprovision resources when needed with extremely volatile evidence that might have a limited duration of existence [16–20]. Volatile memory, temporary storage instances, and ephemeral containers are among the issues that are defying the traditional forensic timeline and demand almost real-time evidence gathering approaches. This has led to the creation of live forensics, snapshot-based acquisition, and continuous monitoring mechanisms specific to cloud infrastructures.

The development of cloud forensics has also been impacted by the legal and jurisdictional factors. The data on clouds compared to the traditional environment where it is contained within a known geographic area may be spread across different regions and nations. This physical distribution creates the issue of data sovereignty, compliance, and cross-border cooperation of laws. Consequently, legal consciousness, chain-of-custody modifications, and policy-based evidence management systems have increasingly been integrated into forensic systems. The next important step in the development of cloud forensics is the application of automation and intelligence. The size and complexity of data produced by the cloud outweigh the opportunities for manual analysis, and the methods of artificial intelligence and machine learning-based log correlation, anomaly detection, and evidence prioritization are adopted. The AI-intensive tools can now help investigators find pertinent forensic artifacts in large and heterogeneous datasets faster and more precisely, thereby allowing quicker and more precise investigation [21–25].

On the whole, the development of digital forensics in cloud-based settings results in a paradigm shift between the old and hardware-based investigations (still) to new dynamic, service-based, and intelligence-supported forensic operations. With cloud ecosystems expanding and adopting emerging technologies, including edge computing, Internet of Things, and generative AI, digital forensics has to keep evolving; otherwise, it will become ineffective, unreliable, and legally unsound.

4.3 EMERGING TECHNOLOGIES SHAPING DIGITAL EVIDENCE

Computing paradigms have also changed dramatically as they have become highly distributed and cloud-centric, making digital forensics a better form of systems than standalone systems. Historical digital forensics was mutually based on infrastructures that were static, with direct physical or logical access to storage media, predictable system configurations, and the presence of clearly defined data limits. Nevertheless, the swift shift toward the use of cloud computing has fundamentally changed the kind of digital evidence and has introduced new challenges pertaining to the place of data, ownership, volatility, and its accessibility. With fast changes in the digital ecosystem, digital evidence has radically changed in nature, quantity, and the level of intricacy. The evolving technologies are not just a peripheral innovation but the centerpiece of the current information infrastructure and are altering the approaches to the generation, storage, access, and interpretation of data as part of the forensic investigation process. Due to the proliferation of intelligent, distributed, and automated systems within organizations, digital evidence no longer exists as files and logs, but rather as dynamic, temporary, and contextualized artifacts [26–30]. This change offers a cutting-edge opportunity in investigation and a great challenge to forensic work.

4.3.1 Machine learning systems and artificial intelligence

The application of artificial intelligence (AI) and machine learning (ML) technologies has become a part of the decision-making model at cloud systems, enterprises, and consumer-facing applications. These systems will generate large amounts of metadata, model parameters, training sets, inference records, and decision output, all of which could present potential digital evidence. With the help of AI-driven systems, the behavior of these systems tends to change over time, unlike conventional software, which makes it difficult to reconstruct events. From a forensic viewpoint, identifying the manner in which an AI model has reached a certain decision requires training data provenance, versioned model states, feature engineering pipelines, and inference contexts. The opacity of deep-learning models, in addition to this, further complicates explainability, making it hard to attribute intent, bias, or malfunction. As a result, AI system digital evidence is not fixed but noisy, so investigators have to develop new methods of analysis that integrate forensic rigor with model interpretability and auditability [31–35].

4.3.2 Cloud-native and serverless computing paradigms

Containerization, serverless computing, and microservices are the cloud-native architectures that reshaped the way applications are set up and scaled. Such environments produce digital evidence that is distributed to a considerable degree, short-lived, and most frequently not tied to physical infrastructure. Old conceptions of disk images or system snapshots are often not applicable in the virtual world since such virtual cases occur only once and don on-demand execution allotment. Functions that can be referred to as serverless, such as those that last just a few milliseconds, can leave certainly less evidence of any long-term signatures. Instead, evidence is stored in the temporary logs, API request logs, orchestration logs, and event logs in the cloud control plane. To construct timelines of activities, investigators then have to depend on provider-specific logging services and event streams as well as configuration histories. There is also the concern of the accessibility, integrity, and compliance with the jurisdictions of evidence, which is dependent on the use of third-party cloud service providers [36].

4.3.3 Cyber-physical systems and Internet of Things

The Internet of Things (IoT) has given digital evidence a new dimension in terms of interconnected sensors, actuators, and smart devices that can be found in the physical surroundings. These systems provide real-time feeds of contextual data based on location, movement, environmental conditions, and human behavior. IoT-based digital evidence is commonly disordered and non-homogeneous, as well as limited by device storage and ability to compute. The IoTs and their environments need forensic analysis to match the data of a variety of devices, gateways, and cloud backends to build consistent narratives of events. In addition, the close relation between online activities and offline results in cyber-physical systems makes interpreting evidence more difficult because the investigator needs to look beyond virtual documentation and involve the actual relationships between the two. There are more problems like the integrity of the firmware, device alteration, and timekeeping, and all of these complicate the process of evidence validation [37].

4.3.4 Distributed ledger technologies and blockchain

The advent of blockchain and distributed ledger technologies (DLTs) has led to introduced records, which are immutable and decentralized, and pose challenges to the traditional assumptions of forensics. Cryptographically secured blockchain transactions are resistant to spoilage, and hence provide robust data integrity guarantees. Nevertheless, the pseudonymity of subjects and decentralization of ledger nodes around the world makes attribution and legal responsibility more difficult. Blockchain systems contain more than just transaction records as digital evidence since they also contain smart contract code, execution history, wallet metadata, and off-chain transactions. To gain a comprehensive insight into fraud, ransomware payments, or money laundering, all on-chain and off-chain elements need to be examined during the process of forensic investigation. Besides, privacy-ensuring mechanisms, as well as interoperability technologies, which span across the chains, also obscure evidence trails and require high-level analytical and cryptographic skills [38].

4.3.5 Prolonged reality and metauniverse systems

Virtual reality is part of a wider concept of extended reality (XR), which includes virtual reality (VR), augmented reality, and mixed reality, and has created immersive virtual worlds in which interactions, identities, and objects exist primarily in the digital realm. Data that is created in these platforms are avatars' behaviors, logs of spatial interactions, biometric contributions, virtual object transactions, and real-time communications. The metaverse presents some new evidentiary problems regarding the verification of identity, the legal existence of cyber-assets, and the continuity of online behavior. Investigators need to take into consideration platform-specific data formats, vendor-specific means of storage, and mixing of physical and virtual identities. With more XR systems moving into cloud and AI powered engines of personalization, the scale and depth of digital evidence is ever growing [39].

4.3.6 Moral to the digital forensic practice

An aggregate of these new technologies has transfigured digital evidence into a transitional multi-layered entity that cuts across devices, networks, cloud services, and intelligent systems. Conventional forensic tools and techniques, made to occur in a static and centralized environment, are frequently inadequate to establish and analyze such evidence. Most of the current studies need flexible frameworks that incorporate the use of cloud forensics, AI-based analysis, cross-platform correlation, and legal compliance systems [40]. The trend of the phenomenon of digital evidence moving towards growing context-awareness, temporality, and algorithmic mediation will persist upward with the further convergence of the emerging technologies. To overcome these difficulties, interdisciplinary cooperation between forensic practitioners, cloud providers, AI researchers, and legal authorities is essential to make the next-generation technological ecosystems continue to preserve the effectiveness of digital investigations, their clarity, and credibility.

4.4 FORENSIC CHALLENGES IN AI-DRIVEN CLOUD SYSTEMS

Incorporation and application of artificial intelligence into cloud computing systems in record time has fundamentally changed the environment of digital forensics. Cloud systems based on AI can now take care of data storage and allocate resources autonomously, identify anomalies, and make operational decisions with a minimal level of human input. Although the capabilities provide an improved level of performance and scalability, they also create a complicated forensic challenge that the traditional systems of investigation are not best suited to manage. The adaptive opaque and distributed character of the AI-enabled cloud environments renders the identification, acquisition, preservation, and interpretation of evidence difficult [41].

The vulnerability of AI models used in cloud systems is the absence of transparency and explanation, and this is one of the key forensic problems. The workings of many AI mechanisms (especially deep learning models) are black boxes that do not obviously have any reasoning-traceable input or output. When forensic investigations are involved, it is hard to tell how an AI system came up with a particular decision or action or to identify anomalies detected by the system. Such absence of interpretability impairs the capacity of the investigation to reflect the occurrence, verify system conduct, and create causation, particularly when AI resolutions have a direct effect on a security event or access controls [42].

The other important challenge is associated with the dynamic and self-evolving character of AI models on a cloud. In contrast to static software systems, AI models are constantly learning and updating (dependent on new streams of data). These updates can be automatic within the distributed cloud nodes and the model parameters, decision thresholds, and patterns of behavior are frequently changed. Forensically, it is highly unfeasible to obtain a steady depiction of an AI model at the point of an incident. During the event being investigated, investigators can also find that there are certain differences between the current state and operational state of the model, bringing up the issue of consistency and reproducibility of evidence [43].

The changeability of data and transient processing also makes the investigation of AI-driven clouds more difficult for forensics. Real-time analytics can be based on AI workflows depending on temporary data pipelines, in-memory computation, and temporary storage. This kind of data can be processed and eliminated in milliseconds, and little or no lasting trace remains. Conventional forensic methods that rely on solid evidence storage, e.g., disk images and system logs, are not very helpful with regard to chasing this evanescent evidence. The issue is exacerbated by the presence of AI processes that run on many virtual machines, containers, or serverless functions with parallel execution [44].

The scale and heterogeneity of data produced by AI-enabled cloud systems are also challenged on a significant level. AI systems ingest and generate data in huge amounts of structured, semi-formatted, and unstructured data, such as logs, metadata, sensor logs, user interactions, and model outputs. It becomes more complicated to draw the line between the forensic evidence that is relevant and data that is benign and associated with operations. Additionally, the interdependence of data sources makes it hard to isolate individual events and still obtain the overall system context, which could lead to a lack of integrity of the evidence [45].

Cloud environment models, such as multi-tenancy and shared responsibility, add further forensic issues. AI services have a tendency to be hosted on common infrastructure whereby more than one tenant uses the same physical and virtual infrastructure. This brings issues of data isolation, access mechanisms, and privacy in carrying out forensic investigations. When examining the evidence, the investigators should make sure that the evidence collection does not infringe on the confidentiality of other tenants; nevertheless, the evidence should remain exhaustive and presentable. Sealants may also be used to restrict access to underlying infrastructure by cloud service providers to reduce transparency of important components of a system to investigators [46].

This responsibility and ownership is still an issue in AI-based cloud systems. Upon the occurrence of an incident, it might be unclear whether the cause of an incident is human misconfiguration, malicious user behavior, poor AI training data, biased algorithm, or autonomous AI decisions. Developing accountability involves aligning human activities with the output of AI, which is often impeded by incomplete logging, unification of audit trails, and proprietary implementation of AI. This uncertainty could undermine the evidence creation of forensic results of legal cases [47].

Lastly, the legal and moral limitations pose a major challenge to the forensic investigations using AI-enabled cloud computing. Geographical spread jurisdictional as AI services and data are spread across geographically dispersed data centers over which various legal systems apply. Also, the ethical developments associated with algorithmic bias, ownership of data, and user consent affect the possibility of gathering and interpreting evidence. The investigators are obliged to work within these limitations without crossing the boundaries of the regulations and integrity of the investigation process [48].

Overall, cloud systems based on AI give rise to a complex of forensic issues of the nature of transparency, dynamism, scale, and distributed infrastructure. To tackle these challenges, digital forensics and explainable AI methods, dynamic evidence gathering policies, sophisticated monitoring systems, and joint operations between investigators and cloud providers are needed. Knowing these issues is a vital undertaking before establishing effective forensic procedures to conduct future digital investigations that are next-generational.

4.5 INTERNET OF THINGS AND EDGE COMPUTING FORENSICS

The rapid proliferation of Internet of Things (IoT) devices and the parallel adoption of edge computing architectures have significantly transformed the digital evidence landscape. IoT ecosystems now encompass a wide range of interconnected devices, including smart sensors, wearable technologies, autonomous systems, industrial controllers, and intelligent infrastructure components. These devices continuously generate vast volumes of heterogeneous data, much of which is processed at or near the data source through edge computing frameworks to reduce latency, bandwidth usage, and dependence on centralized cloud resources. While these advancements enhance system efficiency and responsiveness, they introduce complex challenges for digital forensic investigations, particularly in AI-driven cloud environments. One of the primary forensic challenges in IoT and edge computing environments is the extreme heterogeneity of devices and data formats. IoT devices differ widely in hardware configurations, operating systems, communication protocols, and storage capabilities. Many devices rely on lightweight firmware and proprietary software stacks, limiting traditional forensic access methods. Evidence may exist in fragmented forms across embedded memory, volatile storage, gateway nodes, and edge servers, making comprehensive evidence acquisition difficult. Furthermore, the absence of standardized logging and timestamping mechanisms across IoT platforms complicates event reconstruction and timeline analysis [49].

Edge computing further decentralizes data processing, shifting critical analytical tasks away from centralized cloud infrastructures to distributed edge nodes. From a forensic perspective, this decentralization results in ephemeral data lifecycles, where sensitive evidence may be processed, acted upon, and discarded within milliseconds. Volatile memory at edge nodes often holds crucial inference results, sensor correlations, or AI-driven decisions that are not persistently stored. Investigators must therefore contend with limited windows for data capture, requiring real-time or near-real-time forensic readiness mechanisms to preserve transient evidence before it is overwritten or lost. Another significant challenge lies in secure evidence collection and chain-of-custody maintenance across IoT–edge–cloud continuums. Data may traverse multiple administrative domains, including device manufacturers, network providers, cloud service operators, and application vendors. Each transition introduces potential integrity risks, access control barriers, and jurisdictional complications. Ensuring the authenticity and admissibility of digital evidence requires robust cryptographic validation, tamper-resistant logging, and verifiable provenance tracking mechanisms. Without unified governance frameworks, attributing responsibility and verifying data origin becomes increasingly complex.

AI-driven analytics embedded within IoT and edge systems add an additional layer of forensic complexity. Intelligent edge devices often employ machine learning models to filter data, detect anomalies, or trigger automated actions. While these capabilities enhance operational efficiency, they obscure the raw data used to generate decisions. Investigators must not only examine output results but also understand model behavior, training data influence, and inference logic to determine whether system actions were legitimate, manipulated, or erroneous. The opaque nature of many AI models further complicates explainability and accountability in forensic contexts. Security vulnerabilities prevalent in IoT ecosystems also exacerbate forensic challenges. Resource-constrained devices often lack robust encryption, secure boot mechanisms, and regular firmware updates, making them attractive targets for attackers. Compromised IoT devices can be leveraged for data manipulation, unauthorized surveillance, or coordinated cyberattacks, such as botnets. Forensic investigations must therefore address both device-level compromises and broader network-level interactions, requiring multi-layered analysis across physical, network, and application domains [50].

To address these challenges, emerging research emphasizes forensic-by-design approaches for IoT and edge computing systems. These approaches advocate the integration of forensic readiness features during system design, including secure logging, standardized metadata generation, synchronized time services, and trusted execution environments. Blockchain-based evidence logging, distributed ledger technologies, and AI-assisted anomaly detection are increasingly explored to enhance evidence integrity and traceability. Additionally, edge-aware forensic frameworks are being developed to support adaptive evidence collection strategies that align with the constraints and dynamics of distributed computing environments. Finally, IoT and edge computing forensics represent a critical frontier in AI-driven cloud forensic investigations. The convergence of distributed intelligence, real-time processing, and massive device connectivity demands new investigative methodologies, tools, and legal frameworks. Addressing these challenges is essential for ensuring reliable digital investigations, safeguarding trust in intelligent systems, and supporting the next-generation of cybercrime detection and response.

4.6 BLOCKCHAIN, CRYPTOCURRENCY, AND SMART CONTRACT EVIDENCE

Blockchain technology has introduced a fundamentally different paradigm for data generation, storage, and verification, posing significant implications for digital forensic investigations. Unlike traditional centralized systems, blockchains operate as decentralized, distributed ledgers where transactions are recorded across multiple nodes without reliance on a single controlling authority. While this architectural design enhances transparency and immutability, it also introduces substantial forensic complexity, particularly in attribution, evidence acquisition, and legal interpretation. Cryptocurrencies such as Bitcoin, Ethereum, and other blockchain-based assets generate vast volumes of transactional data that are permanently recorded on public or permissioned ledgers. From a forensic perspective, the immutability of blockchain records can serve as a reliable source of historical evidence; however, the pseudonymous nature of wallet addresses complicates the direct linkage between transactions and real-world identities. Investigators must rely on indirect correlation techniques, including transaction graph analysis, behavioral pattern recognition, and external data sources such as exchanges, digital wallets, and service providers, to establish ownership or control over crypto-assets.

Smart contracts further intensify forensic challenges due to their autonomous and self-executing nature. These programs, embedded within blockchain platforms, automatically enforce predefined rules without human intervention once deployment conditions are met. While smart contracts generate execution logs and state changes that may be traceable on-chain, understanding intent, logic errors, or malicious manipulation requires advanced code-level analysis. Forensic practitioners must possess not only blockchain literacy but also proficiency in smart contract programming languages to interpret contract behavior accurately and identify vulnerabilities, exploits, or fraudulent logic. Jurisdictional and legal challenges represent another major obstacle in blockchain forensics. Transactions often span multiple countries, nodes, and legal systems, making it difficult to determine applicable laws, seize assets, or compel cooperation from service providers. Additionally, privacy-enhancing technologies such as mixers, tumblers, zero-knowledge proofs, and privacy-focused cryptocurrencies significantly reduce transaction traceability, limiting the effectiveness of conventional forensic techniques.

Evidence preservation and admissibility also demand careful consideration. While blockchain records are inherently tamper-resistant, the methods used to extract, interpret, and present blockchain evidence must adhere to established forensic standards. Investigators must ensure that data collection processes maintain integrity, reproducibility, and transparency, especially when using third-party analytics tools. Furthermore, expert interpretation is often required to explain complex blockchain mechanisms to courts, highlighting the need for standardized methodologies and forensic frameworks. In response to these challenges, emerging forensic approaches increasingly integrate automated analytics, machine learning, and visualization techniques to analyze large-scale blockchain datasets. These tools assist in identifying anomalous transaction patterns, tracing illicit fund flows, and linking blockchain activity to off-chain evidence. As blockchain adoption expands across financial systems, supply chains, and decentralized applications, the development of robust, legally defensible forensic models becomes essential for effective digital investigations in next-generation technological ecosystems.

4.7 BIG DATA, VIRTUALIZATION, AND CONTAINER FORENSICS

The rapid adoption of big data platforms, virtualized infrastructures, and containerized environments has significantly transformed how digital systems are designed, deployed, and operated. While these technologies enable scalability, efficiency, and real-time analytics, they also introduce complex forensic challenges that traditional investigation methodologies are not equipped to address. In AI-driven cloud environments, digital evidence is increasingly distributed, transient, and embedded within layered abstractions, making forensic acquisition, preservation, and analysis far more intricate.

4.7.1 Big data forensics in cloud ecosystems

Big data systems process massive volumes of structured, semi-structured, and unstructured data generated from diverse sources such as logs, sensors, transactions, and user interactions. Platforms built on distributed frameworks like Hadoop, Spark, and cloud-native data lakes fragment data across multiple nodes, regions, and storage tiers. From a forensic perspective, this distribution complicates evidence identification and correlation, as relevant artifacts may be scattered across clusters and replicated dynamically. Another challenge arises from the velocity of big data. Real-time data ingestion and continuous analytics pipelines often overwrite logs or aggregate records rapidly, reducing the window for evidence preservation. Investigators must therefore rely on proactive logging strategies, immutable storage mechanisms, and time-synchronized metadata to reconstruct event timelines. Additionally, ensuring the integrity and authenticity of evidence extracted from large-scale datasets requires cryptographic hashing, provenance tracking, and validation across distributed nodes.

4.7.2 Forensic implications of virtualization technologies

Virtualization underpins modern cloud infrastructure by enabling multiple virtual machines (VMs) to operate on shared physical hardware. While virtualization enhances resource utilization and isolation, it introduces forensic complexity due to the abstraction layer between hardware and operating systems. Evidence relevant to an investigation may reside within VM disk images, snapshots, hypervisor logs, or shared memory, each requiring specialized acquisition techniques. The dynamic lifecycle of virtual machines presents another obstacle. VMs can be created, cloned, suspended, migrated, or destroyed within minutes, often without leaving persistent traces on physical hosts. Live migration further complicates jurisdictional and evidentiary boundaries, as VM states may move across data centers or national borders. Investigators must coordinate closely with cloud service providers to obtain hypervisor-level artifacts while maintaining chain of custody and compliance with legal frameworks.

4.7.3 Container forensics and microservices complexity

Containerization technologies, such as Docker and Kubernetes, introduce lightweight, ephemeral execution environments that differ fundamentally from traditional virtual machines. Containers share host operating systems and rely on layered file systems, making artifact isolation and attribution more challenging. Logs, configurations, and runtime states may exist only temporarily, disappearing once containers are terminated or redeployed. In microservices architectures, applications are decomposed into multiple containers communicating through APIs and message queues. A single incident may therefore involve dozens of interconnected containers, each generating partial evidence. Effective container forensics requires collecting orchestration metadata, deployment manifests, network traffic records, and container images to reconstruct application behavior. Furthermore, investigators must account for automated scaling and self-healing mechanisms that can modify system states during an ongoing incident.

4.7.4 Toward scalable and forensically ready solutions

Addressing forensic challenges in big data, virtualization, and containerized environments demands a shift toward forensic-by-design cloud architectures. This includes persistent logging, standardized audit trails, tamper-resistant storage, and AI-assisted analytics for evidence triage. Machine learning techniques can support anomaly detection and pattern recognition across massive datasets, enabling investigators to focus on high-value artifacts. As cloud ecosystems continue to evolve, forensic frameworks must adapt to operate at scale, across abstraction layers, and in near real time. Integrating forensic readiness into big data pipelines, virtualized platforms, and container orchestration systems is essential to ensure that digital investigations remain effective in next-generation AI-driven cloud environments.

4.8 PRIVACY, LEGAL, AND JURISDICTIONAL CHALLENGES

The investigation of digital evidence in AI-driven cloud environments is accompanied by complex privacy, legal, and jurisdictional challenges that significantly differentiate cloud forensics from traditional digital investigations. The distributed, multi-tenant, and transnational nature of cloud infrastructures introduces legal ambiguities regarding data ownership, access rights, and lawful authority, making forensic processes both technically and procedurally demanding.

4.8.1 Data privacy and user confidentiality

Cloud platforms host vast volumes of sensitive personal, corporate, and governmental data belonging to multiple users simultaneously. Forensic acquisition in such environments risks exposing information unrelated to the investigation, thereby violating privacy principles and data protection regulations. Investigators must ensure that evidence collection is proportionate, targeted, and minimally intrusive, which is difficult when storage systems are logically shared across tenants. AI-driven analytics further amplify privacy concerns, as automated models may infer sensitive attributes from seemingly benign datasets. Ensuring confidentiality while maintaining forensic completeness requires advanced isolation mechanisms, selective data extraction techniques, and auditable access controls.

4.8.2 Regulatory compliance and data protection laws

Digital forensic investigations in cloud environments must comply with a wide range of regional and international data protection regulations, such as data residency requirements, consent mandates, and cross-border data transfer restrictions. These legal frameworks often conflict across jurisdictions, creating uncertainty regarding which laws apply during evidence acquisition and analysis. For example, data stored in one country may be governed by different legal standards than the location of the investigator or cloud service provider. Failure to comply with applicable regulations can result in evidence being deemed inadmissible or lead to legal liability for investigators and organizations.

4.8.3 Jurisdictional complexity and cross-border investigations

Cloud infrastructures routinely distribute data across geographically dispersed data centers for redundancy, performance, and resilience. As a result, a single forensic investigation may involve multiple jurisdictions simultaneously. This geographic dispersion complicates the identification of legal authority and requires coordination among law enforcement agencies, judicial bodies, and service providers across borders. Mutual legal assistance processes are often slow and incompatible with the volatile nature of cloud data, where evidence may be overwritten or dynamically relocated before legal authorization is obtained.

4.8.4 Evidence ownership and control

Determining ownership and control of digital evidence in cloud environments presents a significant challenge. Cloud service providers technically manage the infrastructure, while users retain logical ownership of their data. This separation raises questions about who has the legal right to access, preserve, and disclose evidence. Service-level agreements often lack clarity regarding forensic responsibilities, timelines for data preservation, and cooperation during investigations. Ambiguous contractual terms can hinder timely evidence acquisition and introduce disputes over liability and authority.

4.8.5 Admissibility and chain of custody

Maintaining a verifiable chain of custody in cloud-based investigations is inherently complex. Automated processes, dynamic resource allocation, and AI-driven system management reduce human oversight, making it difficult to document evidence handling in a traditional forensic manner. Courts may question the integrity, authenticity, and reproducibility of evidence extracted from virtualized and automated environments. Establishing standardized documentation practices, cryptographic integrity verification, and transparent logging mechanisms is essential to preserve evidentiary value.

4.8.6 Ethical and accountability considerations

Beyond legal compliance, ethical concerns play a critical role in cloud forensics. AI-powered forensic tools may introduce bias, opacity, or unintended inference, raising concerns about fairness and accountability. Investigators must balance the pursuit of justice with respect for civil liberties, transparency, and ethical use of advanced analytical technologies. The lack of explainability in some AI models further complicates legal scrutiny, as courts increasingly demand clear justification for forensic conclusions.

4.8.7 Need for harmonized legal frameworks

Addressing privacy, legal, and jurisdictional challenges requires coordinated efforts among policymakers, legal authorities, cloud service providers, and forensic researchers. Harmonized international standards, clearer contractual obligations, and forensic-by-design cloud architectures are essential to support lawful and effective investigations. As AI-driven cloud systems continue to evolve, legal frameworks must adapt to ensure that digital forensics remains both technologically relevant and legally defensible.

4.9 ANTI-FORENSICS AND ADVERSARIAL AI THREATS

The rapid integration of artificial intelligence and cloud technologies into modern digital infrastructures has given rise to sophisticated anti-forensic techniques that deliberately obstruct digital investigations. Anti-forensics refers to a collection of strategies, tools, and behaviors designed to evade detection, manipulate evidence, or undermine the reliability of forensic processes. In AI-driven cloud environments, these techniques have evolved beyond simple data deletion or obfuscation and now leverage automation, adaptability, and intelligent decision-making to counter forensic analysis in real time. One of the most significant challenges arises from AI-enabled anti-forensic automation. Attackers increasingly deploy machine learning models capable of identifying forensic activities such as logging, monitoring, or anomaly detection. Once identified, these systems dynamically alter their behavior by suppressing logs, generating misleading artifacts, or shifting workloads across cloud regions to reduce traceability. This adaptive behavior makes traditional rule-based forensic tools ineffective, as evidence patterns continuously evolve to evade known detection mechanisms [51–54].

Adversarial AI techniques further complicate forensic investigations. By crafting adversarial inputs, malicious actors can intentionally mislead AI-based forensic classifiers, anomaly detectors, and malware identification systems. For example, slight perturbations in data streams, network traffic, or log structures can cause forensic models to misclassify malicious actions as benign. In cloud ecosystems where automated decision systems play a central role in evidence analysis, such adversarial manipulation significantly reduces confidence in forensic conclusions. Cloud-native features such as elasticity and ephemeral resource provisioning also facilitate evidence evasion strategies. Short-lived virtual machines, serverless functions, and containerized services can execute malicious operations and terminate within seconds, leaving minimal forensic footprints. Adversaries exploit these characteristics to perform rapid attacks that outpace evidence collection mechanisms. When combined with encrypted storage and transient memory usage, reconstructing timelines or attributing actions becomes exceptionally challenging.

Another growing concern is data poisoning, where adversaries deliberately inject corrupted or biased data into AI-driven forensic training pipelines. Over time, this leads to degraded model performance, inaccurate threat detection, and unreliable forensic outcomes. In shared cloud environments, poisoned datasets may affect multiple tenants, amplifying the impact of such attacks. Detecting and isolating poisoned data sources remains a complex task due to the distributed and collaborative nature of cloud analytics platforms. The emergence of deepfake technologies and synthetic data generation introduces new dimensions to anti-forensics. AI-generated text, images, audio, and video can be used to fabricate digital evidence or manipulate contextual information surrounding an investigation. In legal and forensic contexts, distinguishing authentic evidence from convincingly generated synthetic content demands advanced verification techniques and cross-modal validation strategies.

To counter these threats, forensic methodologies must evolve toward robust, explainable, and resilient AI systems. Incorporating explainable AI (XAI) techniques enables investigators to understand decision pathways and identify manipulation attempts. Additionally, adversarial training, continuous model validation, and anomaly-aware forensic frameworks can enhance resistance against evasion strategies. Collaboration between cloud service providers, forensic researchers, and legal authorities is essential to establish standardized defenses against AI-driven anti-forensic practices. Finally, anti-forensics and adversarial AI represent a critical frontier in digital investigations. As attackers increasingly weaponize intelligent systems to undermine evidence integrity, forensic science must adopt equally adaptive, transparent, and resilient approaches. Addressing these challenges is fundamental to preserving trust, accuracy, and accountability in next-generation AI-driven cloud forensics.

4.10 STANDARDIZATION, TOOL LIMITATIONS, AND SKILL GAPS

The rapid evolution of cloud computing, artificial intelligence, and emerging digital infrastructures has outpaced the development of standardized forensic practices, creating significant challenges for modern investigations. Unlike traditional digital forensics, where well-established procedures, evidence handling protocols, and tool validation frameworks exist, AI-driven cloud environments lack universally accepted forensic standards. Variations in cloud service architectures, proprietary technologies, and service-level agreements result in inconsistent evidence acquisition methods, making cross-platform investigations complex and often unreliable [55–58].

A major limitation arises from the dependency on vendor-specific forensic tools and APIs. Many cloud providers offer restricted access to system logs, metadata, and virtualized resources, which limits the visibility investigators have into underlying infrastructure. Existing forensic tools are often designed for static systems and struggle to process dynamic, distributed, and ephemeral cloud artifacts such as short-lived containers, auto-scaling instances, and serverless functions. Additionally, most tools lack transparency in how AI-generated outputs, automated decisions, and adaptive system behaviors are recorded, raising concerns about evidence completeness and reproducibility.

Skill gaps further compound these challenges. Digital forensic practitioners are increasingly expected to possess interdisciplinary expertise spanning cloud architectures, machine learning models, data analytics, cybersecurity, and legal compliance. However, formal training programs and certifications often lag behind technological advancements, resulting in a shortage of investigators capable of handling AI-enabled cloud investigations effectively. Continuous professional development, interdisciplinary collaboration, and investment in standardized frameworks are essential to bridge these gaps and ensure reliable, defensible forensic outcomes in next-generation digital environments.

4.11 FUTURE RESEARCH DIRECTIONS IN CLOUD FORENSICS

The rapid evolution of cloud computing and emerging digital technologies necessitates continuous advancement in cloud forensic research. Traditional forensic principles and tools are increasingly inadequate for addressing the scale, complexity, and dynamism of modern cloud-centric environments. Consequently, future research must focus on developing adaptive, intelligent, and legally robust forensic frameworks capable of supporting next-generation digital investigations. One critical research direction involves the integration of artificial intelligence and autonomous forensic systems. While AI is already being explored for anomaly detection and log analysis, future work should emphasize self-learning forensic agents capable of dynamically adapting to new attack patterns, evolving cloud architectures, and unknown evidence formats. Such systems could automate evidence identification, prioritization, and correlation across distributed cloud resources while minimizing human intervention and investigation time.

Another important area is the development of forensics-by-design and forensic readiness frameworks for cloud infrastructures. Research should focus on embedding forensic capabilities directly into cloud service architectures, enabling proactive evidence preservation, secure logging, and auditability without violating tenant privacy. This includes designing standardized forensic APIs, tamper-resistant logging mechanisms, and verifiable chain-of-custody models that operate seamlessly across multi-cloud and hybrid environments. Cross-layer and cross-domain forensic correlation also represents a significant research opportunity. Future cloud forensic models must move beyond isolated log analysis to integrate evidence from infrastructure layers, application services, virtual machines, containers, IoT devices, and edge nodes. Advanced correlation techniques leveraging graph analytics, knowledge representation, and contextual reasoning can help investigators reconstruct complex attack scenarios that span multiple technologies and administrative domains [59, 60].

The emergence of privacy-preserving forensic techniques is another vital research direction. With increasing regulatory constraints and encrypted data storage, future investigations must balance evidentiary access with legal compliance. Research into secure multi-party computation, homomorphic encryption, and federated forensic analysis can enable lawful evidence extraction without exposing sensitive user data or violating data sovereignty requirements. Additionally, standardization and interoperability research remain essential. Future efforts should aim to establish globally accepted forensic standards for cloud evidence formats, logging schemas, and investigative workflows. Interoperable forensic tools that can operate across different cloud service providers will significantly enhance investigation efficiency and reduce dependency on proprietary platforms.

Finally, there is a growing need for human-centric and skills-focused research in cloud forensics. Studies addressing investigator training, cognitive workload, decision support systems, and explainable AI in forensic tools can improve trust, transparency, and effectiveness in digital investigations. Bridging the gap between technical innovation and practitioner expertise will be crucial for sustainable progress in this domain. In summary, future research in cloud forensics must adopt a multidisciplinary approach that combines artificial intelligence, secure system design, legal compliance, and human factors. Advancements in these areas will be instrumental in addressing the forensic challenges posed by emerging technologies and ensuring the reliability and integrity of next-generation digital investigations.

4.12 CONCLUSION

The rapid convergence of cloud computing, artificial intelligence, and emerging digital technologies has fundamentally reshaped the landscape of digital forensics. Traditional investigative assumptions—such as physical device ownership, static data locations, and linear evidence lifecycles—are no longer valid in highly dynamic, virtualized, and distributed environments. This chapter has examined the evolving nature of cloud-centric digital forensics and highlighted the multifaceted challenges introduced by AI-driven systems, IoT ecosystems, blockchain platforms, big data infrastructures, and containerized deployments. Together, these technologies generate unprecedented volumes of heterogeneous data while simultaneously reducing visibility, traceability, and investigator control. A key insight emerging from this discussion is that technological advancement has outpaced forensic readiness. AI-enabled cloud platforms introduce opacity through automated decision-making, adaptive learning behaviors, and proprietary models, complicating evidence interpretation and validation. Similarly, edge computing, decentralized ledgers, and ephemeral cloud resources disrupt traditional evidence acquisition and preservation methodologies. These challenges are further intensified by cross-border data flows, conflicting legal frameworks, privacy obligations, and the growing sophistication of anti-forensic and adversarial AI techniques designed to evade detection. To address these issues, the chapter emphasizes the need for a paradigm shift in cloud forensic practice. Future-ready digital investigations must integrate forensic-by-design principles, AI-assisted analysis, standardized evidence models, and collaborative frameworks involving cloud service providers, policymakers, and forensic professionals. Equally important is the development of interdisciplinary expertise that combines legal awareness, cloud architecture knowledge, and advanced data analytics skills. In conclusion, AI-driven cloud forensics represents both a critical challenge and a strategic opportunity for next-generation digital investigations. By proactively addressing technical, legal, and organizational gaps, the forensic community can build resilient, transparent, and trustworthy investigative frameworks capable of operating effectively within emerging technological ecosystems. Such efforts are essential to ensuring accountability, maintaining evidentiary integrity, and upholding justice in an increasingly digital and intelligent world.

REFERENCES

1. Ponmalar, A., Jose, A. A., Muthamizhan, T., Sobana, T., and Vishwath, J. H. (2022). Automatic forensic analysis of criminal navigation system using machine learning. *Proceedings of the IEEE International Conference on Computational Science and Technology (ICCST 2022)*, 1–5.
2. Anand, Jose A., Geetha, R., Kesavan, R., Rajasree, R., and Mukunthan, M. A. (2024). Machine vision–based sign prediction for speech-impaired persons. *Proceedings of the international conference on sustainable communication networks and applications*, Theni, India, 881–885.

3. Anand, Jose A., Krishnan, S., and Sendhilkumar, S. (Eds.). (2024). *Handbook of industrial and business applications with digital twins*. CRC Press.
4. Anand, Jose A., Kalaiselvi, K., and Chatterjee, J. M. (2024). *AI-based system models in healthcare applications*. Scrivener Publishing, Wiley.
5. Anand, Jose A., Ponmalar, A., Deeba, S., and Gomathi, S. (2022). IoT-based automotive drive recorder as a digital forensic black box. *Proceedings of the IEEE international conference on computer, power and communications*, Chennai,India, 557–561.
6. Behl, Abhishek, and Behl, Kaushik. (2017). *Cyberwar: The next threat to national security and what to do about it*. Oxford University Press.
7. Casey, Eoghan. (2011). *Digital evidence and computer crime* (3rd ed.). Academic Press.
8. Cloud Security Alliance. (2023). *Security guidance for critical areas of focus in cloud computing*. CSA Publications.
9. Conti, Mauro, Dehghantanha, Ali, Franke, Katrin, and Watson, Steve. (2018). Internet of Things security and forensics: Challenges and opportunities. *Future Generation Computer Systems*, 78, 544–546.
10. Dehghantanha, Ali, Choo, Kim-Kwang Raymond, and Taheri, Sajjad. (2019). *Cyber forensics: A field manual for collecting, examining, and preserving evidence*. Springer.
11. Dhanalakshmi, R., Anand, Jose A., Sivaraman Arun Kumar, and Rani, Sita. (2022). IoT-based water quality monitoring using cloud platforms for agriculture. In P. Bhambri, S. Rani, G. Gupta, & A. Khang (Eds.), *Cloud and fog computing platforms for IoT* (pp. 219–239). Routledge.
12. Dykstra, Joshua, and Sherman, Alan T. (2013). Acquiring forensic evidence from infrastructure-as-a-service cloud computing. *Digital Investigation*, 10(1), 40–53.
13. Europol Innovation Lab. (2021). *Digital forensics in the age of encryption and cloud computing*. Europol Publications.
14 Gori Mohamed, J., Visumathi, J., Mahdal, Miroslav, Anand, Jose A., and Elangovan, Muniyandy. (2022). Secure phishing detection using machine learning. *Processes*, 10(7), 1356.
15 Grispos, George, Storer, Tim, and Glisson, William Bradley. (2014). Calm before the storm: The challenges of cloud computing in digital forensics. *International Journal of Digital Crime and Forensics*, 6(2), 28–48.
16 Jain, Ankit, and Reddy, B. Srinivas. (2020). Digital forensic readiness in cloud environments. *Journal of Information Security and Applications*, 55, 102623.
17 Kahn, James, and Ruan, Keyun. (2021). Trustworthy AI and forensic accountability in cloud ecosystems. *IEEE Security & Privacy*, 19(3), 72–78.
18 Kshetri, Nir. (2021). Blockchain and digital forensics. *Computer*, 54(3), 62–67.
19 Mahalakshmi, S., Anand, Jose A., and Partheeban, P. (2025). Soil and crop interaction analysis using satellite imagery and deep learning. *Journal of Environmental Management*, 380, 125095.
20 Martini, Ben, and Choo, Kim-Kwang Raymond. (2014). Cloud storage forensics: OwnCloud as a case study. *Digital Investigation*, 10(4), 287–299.
21 Mell, Peter, and Grance, Timothy. (2011). The NIST definition of cloud computing. National Institute of Standards and Technology.
22 Montasari, Reza. (2016). Cloud computing forensics: A conceptual framework. *International Journal of Advanced Computer Science and Applications*, 7(5), 451–460.
23 Moyeenudin, H. M., Anuradha, T., and Anand, Jose A. (2024). AI-based sustainable parking alert system using cloud platforms. *Proceedings of the international conference on sustainability and technological advancements*, 711–716.
24 National Institute of Justice. (2020). Digital forensics framework for law enforcement. U.S. Department of Justice.
25 NIST. (2018). Guide to integrating forensic techniques into incident response. NIST Special Publication 800-86.
26 Quick, Darren, and Choo, Kim-Kwang Raymond. (2018). Big forensic data analytics. *Forensic Science International: Digital Investigation*, 24, 1–12.

27 Raghavan, Prashant, and Parthasarathy, Srinivasan. (2022). Explainable AI in cybersecurity and forensics. *ACM Computing Surveys*, 55(4), 1–36.
28 Ruan, Keyun. (2019). *Cloud forensics*. Elsevier.
29 Ruan, K., Carthy, J., Kechadi, T., & Crosbie, M. (2011). Cloud forensics. In G. Peterson & S. Shenoi (Eds.), *Advances in Digital Forensics VII* (IFIP Advances in Information and Communication Technology, Vol. 361, pp. 35–46). Springer, Berlin, Heidelberg. https://doi.org/10.1007/978-3-642-24212-0_3.
30 Sajithabanu, S., Deeba, S., and Anand, Jose A. (2025). The role of VR and AR in intelligent computing. In B. Sundaravadivazhagan, N. Gnanasankaran, Pethuru Raj, & A. Saleem Raja (Eds.), *Virtual reality and augmented reality with 6G communication*. Wiley.
31 Simou, Stelios, Kalloniatis, Christos, Gritzalis, Stefanos, and Kavakli, Eirini. (2014). Cloud forensics: Identifying challenges and solutions. *Journal of Cloud Computing*, 3(1), 1–15.
32 Sivaraman, Arun Kumar, Anand, Jose A., and Rani, Sita. (2022). *Cloud-assisted IoT systems for smart agriculture*. Routledge Handbook of IoT Platforms.
33 Taylor, Mark, Haggerty, John, Gresty, David, and Lamb, David. (2011). Forensic investigation of cloud computing systems. *Network Security*, 2011(3), 4–10.
34 Thing, Victor L. L., and Sloman, Morris. (2013). Forensic evidence preservation in cloud environments. *Digital Investigation*, 10(3), 278–286.
35. Pooja, D., Mukesh, Y., Nidhi, T., Ruchi, S., Jose, A. A., & Irshad, A. (2024). Semantic framework in healthcare systems. In A. Jose Anand, K. Kalaiselvi, & J. M. Chatterjee (Eds.), *Artificial Intelligence–Based System Models in Healthcare* (pp. 107–129). Wiley Scrivener. https://doi.org/10.1002/9781394242528.ch5
36 Varughese, Sibia Elizabeth, George, Mareena, and Anand, Jose A. (2014). Secure routing mechanisms in wireless sensor networks. *International Journal of Engineering Research & Technology*, 3(3), 275–279.
37 Wang, Qi, Ren, Kui, and Lou, Wenjing. (2010). Privacy-preserving public auditing for cloud storage. *IEEE Transactions on Computers*, 62(2), 362–375.
38 Weidman, Georgia. (2014). *Penetration testing: A hands-on introduction to hacking*. No Starch Press.
39 Zawoad, Shams, and Hasan, Ragib. (2015). Cloud forensics: A meta-study of challenges and solutions. *ACM Computing Surveys*, 47(4), 1–36.
40 Zhang, Yinqian, Juels, Ari, Reiter, Michael K., and Ristenpart, Thomas. (2012). Cross-tenant side-channel attacks in PaaS clouds. *Proceedings of the ACM conference on computer and communications security*, 990–1003.
41 Anand, Jose A., Janet, J., and Srinath, D. (2010). Routing instability and IP spoofing: A forensic perspective. *Asian Journal of Information Technology*, 9(3), 154–158.
42 Anand, Jose A., Sivachandar, K., and Mohamed Yaseen, M. (2013). Real-time video analytics for target detection. *International Journal of Computer Trends and Technology*, 4(8), 2615–2618.
43 Anand, Jose A., Raja Paul Perinbam, J., and Meganathan, D. (2017). Q-learning-based optimized routing in biomedical wireless sensor networks. *IETE Journal of Research*, 63(1), 89–97.
44 Geethalakshmi, M., Jose, A., Nathea, R., Augustine, C., Augustine, C., & Mahalakshmi, S. (2022). Trident fuzzy aggregation operators on right and left apex-base angles in parallel computing. *Advances in Parallel Computing: Algorithms, Tools and Paradigms*, 41, 429–435.
45 Anand, Jose A., Krishnan, Saravanan, and Kumar, Raghvendra. (2024). *Sustainable development goals: Technologies and opportunities*. CRC Press.
46 Anand, Jose A., and Dhanalakshmi, R. (2023). Blockchain-enabled monitoring of perishable goods. *IEEE international conference on computer science and engineering applications*, 1–5.
47 Anand, Jose A., and Flora, T. G. Arul. (2014). Emergency traffic management using wireless communication. *IPASJ International Journal of Electronics & Communication*, 2(7), 1–4.
48 Anand, Jose A., and Sivachandar, K. (2012). ACO-based IP traceback for network forensics. *International Journal of Computer Applications*, 59(1), 1–5.

49 Anand, Jose A., and Raja Paul Perinbam, J. (2014). Energy-efficient biomedical wireless sensor networks: A survey. *American International Journal of Research in Science, Technology, Engineering & Mathematics*, 3(7), 212–216.
50. Saravanan, K., Jose, A. A., & Sendhilkumar, S. (2024). *Handbook on industrial and business applications with digital twins* (1st ed.). CRC Press, Taylor & Francis Group. https://doi.org/10.1201/9781003465904
51 Bhambri, P., and Rani, S. (2024). Bioengineering and healthcare data analysis: Introduction, advances, and challenges. In P. Bhambri, S. Rani, & M. Fahim (Eds.), *Computational intelligence and blockchain in biomedical and health informatics* (1st ed., pp. 1–25). CRC Press. https://doi.org/10.1201/9781003459347
52 Rana, R., and Bhambri, P. (2024). Healthcare computational intelligence and blockchain: Real-life applications. In P. Bhambri, S. Rani, & M. Fahim (Eds.), *Computational intelligence and blockchain in biomedical and health informatics* (pp. 155–168). CRC Press. https://doi.org/10.1201/9781003459347-11
53 Singh, G., and Bhambri, P. (2023). Simulation analysis of AODV and DSDV routing protocols for secure and reliable service in mobile adhoc networks (MANETs). In P. Bhambri, S. Rani, V. E. Balas, & A. A. Elngar (Eds.), *Integration of AI-based manufacturing and industrial engineering systems with the Internet of Things* (1st ed., pp. 205–216). CRC Press. https://doi.org/10.1201/9781003383505
54 Bhambri, P., and Rani, S. (2024). Ethical issues for climate change and mental health. In D. Samanta & M. Garg (Eds.), *Impact of climate change on mental health and well-being* (pp. 178–198). IGI Global. https://doi.org/10.4018/979-8-3693-2177-5.ch012
55 Rana, R., and Bhambri, P. (2024). The role of IoT in shaping the future of geospatial AI. In D. Darwish & H. Chemingui (Eds.), *Recent trends in geospatial AI* (pp. 177–216). IGI Global Scientific Publishing. https://doi.org/10.4018/979-8-3693-8054-3.ch007
56 Bhambri, P., and Kautish, S. (2024). Technological advancements in promoting ecosystem health. In W. Leal Filho, S. Kautish, T. Wall, S. Rewhorn, & S. K. Paul (Eds.), *Digital technologies to implement the UN sustainable development goals* (World Sustainability Series, pp. 409–426). Springer. https://doi.org/10.1007/978-3-031-68427-2_21
57 Bhambri, P., and Khang, A. (2024). Machine learning advancements in E-health: Transforming digital healthcare. In *Medical robotics and AI-assisted diagnostics for a high-tech healthcare industry* (pp. 174–194). IGI Global. https://doi.org/10.4018/979-8-3693-2105-8.ch012
58 Rana, R., and Bhambri, P. (2024). Generative AI in web application development: Enhancing user experience and performance. In I. A. Shah & N. Z. Jhanjhi (Eds.), *Generative AI for web engineering models* (pp. 471–486). IGI Global. https://doi.org/10.4018/979-8-3693-3703-5.ch021
59 Bhambri, P. (2024). Artificial intelligence enabled Internet of Medical Things for enhanced healthcare systems. In P. Bhambri, R. Soni, & T. A. Tran (Eds.), *Smart healthcare systems: AI and IoT perspectives* (pp. 1–17). CRC Press. https://doi.org/10.1201/9781032698519-1
60 Bhambri, P., and Khang, A. (2024). Biosensor applications and principles of agricultural and aquacultural sectors. In *Agriculture and aquaculture applications of biosensors and bioelectronics* (pp. 1–17). IGI Global Scientific Publishing. https://doi.org/10.4018/979-8-3693-2069-3.ch001

Chapter 5

Big data, machine learning, and cloud forensics

An integrated framework for intelligent digital security

Hajar Fatorachian and Hadi Kazemi

5.1 INTRODUCTION

This shift in forensic complexity underscores the need for integrated, intelligent frameworks capable of analyzing vast amounts of cloud-generated data. The Cloud Evidence Tracing System (CETS) demonstrates how automated, scalable systems can support evidence identification, preservation, and analysis in large public-cloud environments [1]. Their system illustrates the emerging importance of *forensic readiness*, where organizations structure their data systems to facilitate efficient post-incident investigations. Developments such as CETS exemplify the growing convergence between big data engineering and digital forensics.

Parallel to these developments, advances in big data analytics and machine learning are reshaping organizational capabilities for detecting anomalies, predicting risks, and identifying early signals of emerging threats. Research highlights the crucial role of artificial intelligence and machine learning in modern digital forensics and incident response, where ML models can rapidly process large, heterogeneous datasets that would be impossible to analyze manually [2]. Further studies reinforce the value of data-mining techniques in forensic analysis, demonstrating how classification, clustering, and association rule mining provide deeper insights into behavioral patterns and digital traces [3]. Additional research expands this perspective by illustrating how big data and ML techniques enable predictive crime prevention, shifting digital security from reactive investigation to proactive intelligence [4].

Although the applications of these technologies span numerous domains, supply chains provide a particularly relevant and illustrative context. Modern supply chains are digitized, globally interlinked, and heavily dependent on cloud-based platforms, IoT sensors, and real-time data flows. Industry 4.0 technologies—such as IoT, blockchain, automation, and predictive analytics—play a vital role in supply chain operation and sustainability [5]. The same technologies that enable smarter logistics and waste-efficient cold chains [6] also generate large volumes of data that can be exploited for security monitoring, anomaly detection, and forensic readiness. AI-enabled logistics systems, predictive maintenance, and intelligent transportation architectures [7] provide concrete examples of environments where big data, ML, and cloud forensics intersect.

At the same time, these digital supply chains are vulnerable to sophisticated cyber threats involving compromised IoT devices, unauthorized cloud access, dataset manipulation, and fraudulent transactions. Investigating such incidents requires the type of advanced forensic capabilities discussed in recent cloud-forensics literature. For example, provenance-based forensic mechanisms such as MECC-enabled systems show how cryptographic provenance records can support tamper-resistant investigation of cloud events [8]. Similarly,

DOI: 10.1201/9781003656487-5

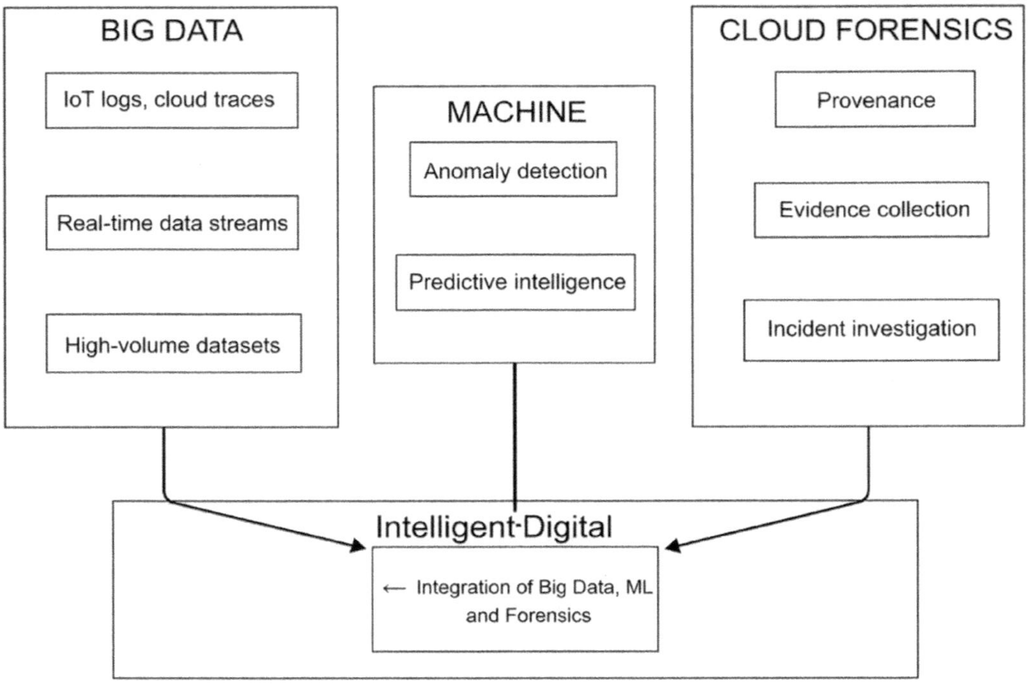

Figure 5.1 The convergence of big data, machine learning, and cloud forensics.

recent studies demonstrate how incorporating machine learning into forensic meta-models strengthens evidence collection and enhances the consistency of forensic processes across cloud environments [9].

Given this convergence, an integrated perspective on big data, machine learning, and cloud forensics is essential for understanding how modern organizations—particularly those with complex digital supply chains—can achieve security, transparency, and forensic readiness. This chapter therefore explores the foundations, applications, and interconnections of these three technological domains. While the discussion remains general and broadly applicable, supply chain security is used throughout as a running example to illustrate practical implications, challenges, and opportunities.

Figure 5.1 provides a high-level overview of the relationship between these three domains and how they intersect within modern digital ecosystems.

5.2 BIG DATA ANALYTICS: CONCEPTS, TECHNOLOGIES AND SECURITY APPLICATIONS

The exponential growth of digital ecosystems has transformed organizational operations and security landscapes, generating vast volumes of structured and unstructured data that require advanced analytical capabilities. Big data analytics has emerged as a critical enabler of digital intelligence, offering the ability to extract meaningful insights from large, heterogeneous, and distributed datasets. In cloud-centric environments, where data is constantly generated by virtualized resources, sensors, applications, and platforms, big data analytics provides the foundational layer upon which machine learning and forensic investigation processes can operate.

5.2.1 Characteristics and sources of big data in modern digital ecosystems

Big data is commonly defined by its "4V" characteristics—volume, velocity, variety, and veracity—each of which profoundly affects security monitoring and forensic readiness (Table 5.1). Modern enterprises generate data from cloud-based platforms, distributed servers, enterprise resource planning (ERP) systems, customer applications, IoT devices, and third-party services. In cloud environments, data sources include virtual machine logs, access authentication records, metadata from orchestration tools, and network communication traces. These datasets are dynamic, fast moving, and inherently distributed, presenting both opportunities and challenges for security operations.

In supply chain environments, the scale and diversity of data generation are even more pronounced. Industry 4.0-enabled supply chains incorporate IoT sensors, RFID trackers, warehouse automation platforms, transport management systems, and blockchain-enabled traceability tools [5]. Data streams may include temperature and humidity readings from cold-chain containers, GPS coordinates from vehicles, inventory scans, routing updates, customer orders, and supplier performance indicators. Recent analyses of predictive waste management models highlight how these data sources allow real-time monitoring and operational optimization but simultaneously expand the digital attack surface [6]. In such environments, the ability to process and analyze big data becomes not only a matter of operational efficiency but also a critical component of organizational security and resilience.

5.2.2 Big data architectures and analytics technologies

The effective utilization of big data for digital security relies on robust architectures capable of handling distributed data ingestion, storage, and processing. Technologies such as Hadoop Ecosystem tools, distributed storage systems, Apache Spark, stream processing engines, and cloud-native analytics services enable organizations to manage high-velocity data flows at scale. These infrastructures support both batch analytics—where historical data is processed for trends and patterns—and real-time analytics, which is essential for detecting anomalies or security events as they unfold.

Research on digitalization and logistics performance increasingly points to the importance of advanced analytics infrastructures. Reviews of artificial intelligence in logistics highlight the growing use of predictive analytics platforms that combine cloud services with IoT data ingestion pipelines and algorithmic engines for risk detection and anomaly identification [10]. Similar architectures are observed in smart city logistics systems, where digital twins and cybernetic feedback loops rely on real-time data integration and analysis to guide operational decisions [10]. These technologies illustrate the broader trend toward data-centric decision-making across sectors, reinforcing the need for big data infrastructures that support both operational optimization and security monitoring.

Table 5.1 Big data characteristics and their implications for digital security

Big data property	*Description*	*Security/forensic implication*
Volume	Massive log and sensor data	Requires distributed processing
Variety	Logs, IoT streams, VM traces	Complex correlation needed
Velocity	High-speed data flow	Real-time monitoring challenges
Veracity	Data inconsistency and noise	Affects ML accuracy and forensics

5.2.3 Big data analytics for security, risk detection, and forensic readiness

Big data analytics plays an increasingly central role in digital security by enabling organizations to detect unusual behaviors, monitor operational integrity, and identify early signs of cyber threats. Large-scale log data, user activity traces, and cross-system communication patterns contain latent signals of malicious activity that can only be detected when analyzed collectively. For instance, sudden spikes in system access, repeated login failures, unexpected data transfers, or deviations from established behavioral baselines may indicate intrusion attempts or compromised accounts.

Studies in digital forensics emphasize the importance of big data analysis in supporting forensic workflows. Recent research observes that cloud forensics now requires the ability to analyze highly distributed datasets, including logs from multiple virtual machines and data centers [11]. Traditional log analysis methods are insufficient due to the scale and speed of data generation. Big data platforms therefore serve as the initial filtering and pattern-detection mechanism, enabling investigators to locate relevant traces among billions of log entries. Further studies highlight how big data analytics helps overcome challenges related to cloud data volatility and provider dependence by enabling proactive data collection, evidence triage, and temporal reconstruction of cloud events [12].

The application of big data analytics to supply chain security illustrates these capabilities well. Research demonstrates how integrated data from IoT systems, warehouses, and transportation assets can identify operational anomalies such as temperature deviations, route manipulation, equipment malfunction, or unexpected handling events [5]. These anomalies are not only operational risks but also potential indicators of cyber tampering or fraudulent activity. Similarly, studies on waste-efficient cold chains show how monitoring patterns in sensor data enables early detection of spoilage risks, which in a security context equates to detecting compromised devices or malicious data alterations. In digital procurement platforms or online B2C marketplaces, sudden behavioral changes in customer traffic or supplier interactions may signal data manipulation or targeted attacks [5].

5.2.4 Predictive, prescriptive, and behavioral analytics

Beyond descriptive analytics, which summarizes historical patterns, big data enables advanced forms of analytical intelligence:

Predictive analytics predicts future risks or failures using historical and real-time data. Research on smart city logistics demonstrates how predictive models can anticipate congestion, delays, or equipment malfunction [7]. In security contexts, predictive analytics can forecast insider threats, supplier failure risks, or potential attack vectors.

Prescriptive analytics offers recommendations or automated responses based on predicted events. In supply chains, prescriptive analytics can recommend rerouting, maintenance scheduling, or supplier substitution. Applied to security, these capabilities can automatically tighten access controls, isolate suspicious devices, or adjust network rules.

Behavioral analytics examines deviations from normal operational behavior. Recent research notes that clustering and association-rule mining are particularly effective for identifying abnormal digital activities, such as unexpected user logins or anomalous communication patterns [3].

These analytic approaches lay the foundation for more advanced machine learning techniques that build on big data to deliver automated, adaptive security intelligence.

5.2.5 Challenges and limitations of big data for security applications

Despite its benefits, big data analytics also introduces significant challenges. Data quality and veracity remain major concerns, particularly in environments with heterogeneous sensors, legacy systems, or intermittent connectivity. In cloud platforms, logs are often decentralized, inconsistently formatted, or inaccessible due to provider restrictions. Ensuring the integrity and continuity of data collection—essential for forensic readiness—becomes difficult when data sovereignty and privacy rules vary across jurisdictions [12].

Scalability is another limitation. As digital ecosystems expand, analytics pipelines must handle continuous growth in data volume and complexity. Additionally, big data systems themselves can become targets for attack, as adversaries may attempt to poison datasets, manipulate IoT streams, or delete forensic traces. The convergence of big data and cloud environments therefore demands robust governance frameworks, secure architectures, and alignment with forensic principles to ensure accuracy, reliability, and legal admissibility.

5.3 MACHINE LEARNING FOR DIGITAL SECURITY AND RISK DETECTION

Machine learning (ML) has evolved into a central capability for modern digital security, as organizations increasingly rely on data-rich, interconnected, and cloud-based ecosystems. The complexity and velocity of digital interactions make manual monitoring infeasible; instead, automated intelligence is required to analyze behavioral patterns, detect anomalies, and predict risks across distributed environments. Recent research highlights that ML is now embedded across multiple stages of digital forensics and incident response, offering the ability to process high-volume data streams at scale and support real-time detection of sophisticated cyber threats [2]. As enterprises accelerate their digital transformation agendas, particularly within sectors such as logistics, transportation, cold-chain operations, and financial services, machine learning becomes not only a technological enhancement but a structural requirement for continuous security oversight.

5.3.1 The expanding role of machine learning in digital security ecosystems

The integration of ML into digital security architectures stems from its ability to interpret behavioral patterns across large, heterogeneous datasets. In cloud environments, where logs, access records, and system events proliferate across virtualized machines and distributed storage, ML models enable the identification of subtle deviations that may indicate intrusions, insider threats, or data manipulation. Recent research emphasizes the contribution of data-mining techniques—including clustering, classification, and association analysis—to digital forensic workflows, allowing investigators to isolate suspicious behaviors within complex datasets [3]. These techniques provide granular insights into relationships between events, enabling forensic practitioners to reconstruct attack vectors with greater precision.

Machine learning is equally influential in digitalized operational sectors, such as transportation and supply chains, where reliance on IoT sensors, predictive maintenance systems, and cloud-based logistics platforms generates large volumes of real-time data. For example, studies on intelligent transportation systems demonstrate how learning-based models enhance routing efficiency, anomaly detection, and safety monitoring, illustrating how predictive analytics can strengthen both operational resilience and cyber-physical security [7]. Similarly, evaluations of predictive waste management in cold chains show how ML-enabled models forecast spoilage risks and equipment failures, a capability that translates directly to detecting manipulated sensor data, compromised devices, or abnormal operational sequences in digital security contexts [5].

5.3.2 Supervised and unsupervised learning techniques in security applications

Supervised learning methods have proven valuable for classifying behavioral sequences into legitimate or malicious categories. These techniques rely on labeled datasets and are widely used to detect phishing activities, fraudulent transactions, authentication anomalies, and malware signatures. Recent research has found that deep neural networks, random forests, and gradient boosting algorithms significantly improve the detection rates of sophisticated threat patterns within cloud platforms [2]. Their ability to learn complex relationships makes them particularly effective for modeling attack typologies and identifying subtle threat signatures.

Unsupervised learning methods are equally critical because many cyber threats do not have historical labels or established signatures. Techniques such as clustering, anomaly detection, and autoencoding help identify deviations from normal system behavior without requiring pre-classified datasets. Studies note that unsupervised learning is indispensable when analyzing large volumes of cloud log data, where rare or emerging attack vectors may not be represented in training data [3]. This capability is essential in digital supply-chain environments, where attackers may target IoT-based cold-chain monitoring systems, tamper with temperature logs, or interfere with transport management platforms using unfamiliar methods.

The relevance of anomaly detection is exemplified in intelligent logistics contexts. Research on smart city logistics demonstrates how IoT-enabled predictive analytics can detect irregularities in vehicle behavior, route deviations, or signaling patterns [10]. These methods can similarly identify cyber-physical anomalies—such as compromised sensors or route manipulation—thus reinforcing the link between operational analytics and cybersecurity intelligence.

These synergistic relationships are illustrated in Figure 5.2, which depicts the unified framework showing how big data supports machine learning, how machine learning enables intelligent detection, and how cloud forensics validates and reconstructs events across distributed digital ecosystems.

5.3.3 Machine learning in cloud forensics and evidence collection

Machine learning does not only support detection; it also plays a central role in strengthening cloud forensics. As cloud infrastructures decentralize data across virtual machines, containers, and distributed logs, forensic processes require automated support for evidence identification, extraction, and triage. Recent work introduces a centralized cloud provenance investigation system that uses modified elliptic curve cryptography (MECC) to ensure evidence integrity [8]. Although cryptographic in nature, this design anticipates the integration of ML models capable of analyzing provenance records, detecting tampering, and identifying suspicious access patterns within complex provenance graphs [13].

Similarly, research proposes improved ML-enhanced cloud forensic meta-models that strengthen data collection and evidence validation in cloud environments [9]. These models demonstrate how machine learning improves the consistency of forensic processes by

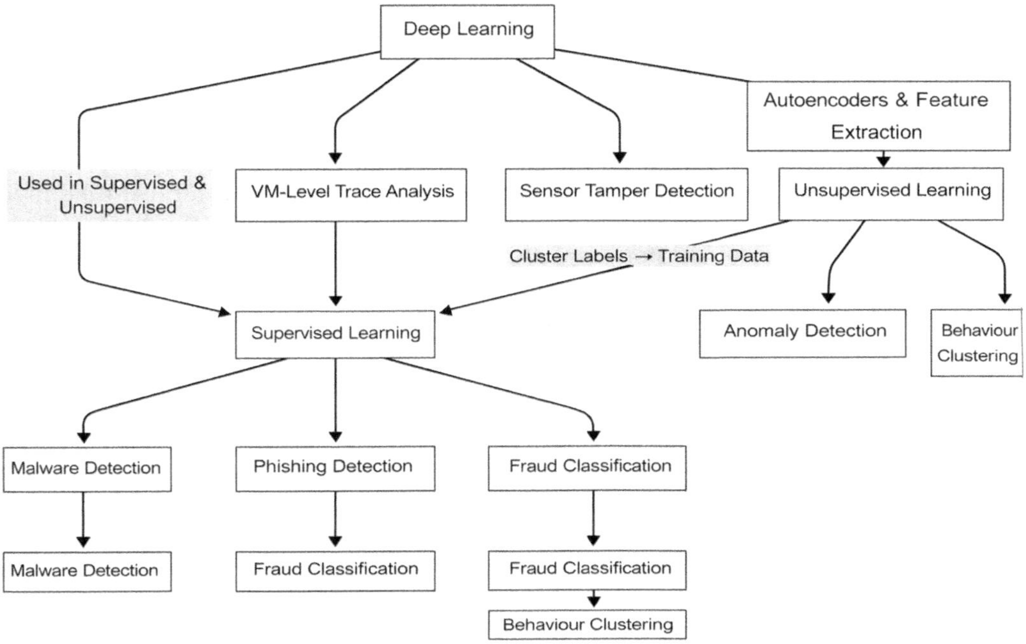

Figure 5.2 Machine learning techniques and their security applications.

automatically identifying relevant artifacts, reducing investigator bias, and structuring cloud evidence for subsequent analysis. This aligns closely with earlier cloud evidence tracing architectures, which—while not explicitly ML-driven—provide the foundational support for automated trace extraction [1]. Together, these studies illustrate how ML and forensic engineering are converging to enhance forensic readiness in the cloud.

The relevance of ML to cloud forensics extends further into advanced research. Studies on transparent deep-learning approaches for virtual machine forensics show that deep-learning models can analyze VM-level activities to identify anomalies, classify malicious processes, and detect hidden artifacts [14]. Meanwhile, cryptographically secured logging schemes underscore the importance of assuring log soundness and secrecy, demonstrating how high-integrity logs provide high-quality datasets suitable for subsequent ML-based forensic analysis [15]. These developments highlight that ML does not replace forensic techniques but enhances them by enabling scalable, automated, and evidence-driven insights.

5.3.4 Predictive modeling and proactive threat intelligence

One of ML's greatest contributions to digital security is its capacity to generate predictive threat intelligence. In contrast to traditional security models that react to detected attacks, predictive models anticipate suspicious behavior based on learned patterns of anomalies and contextual signals. Recent research demonstrates how ML-driven predictive analytics can be used for proactive crime prevention, enabling earlier detection of emerging threat signals and reducing response times [4]. These predictive capabilities are particularly valuable in supply-chain environments, where disruptions—whether caused by cyberattacks, behavioral anomalies, or operational failures—can propagate rapidly across multiple tiers [16].

ML-based predictive models have already shown success in related operational domains. For example, studies on cold-chain waste modeling demonstrate how learning algorithms forecast risk conditions in complex, multi-variable environments [5]. When adapted to security contexts, such models become powerful tools for detecting manipulated sensor streams, early-stage ransomware behavior, or suspicious sequences of access requests within cloud-based supply chain platforms [17].

Advanced work further describes AI-driven forensic systems designed for real-time anomaly detection and threat mitigation [18]. These systems demonstrate that predictive ML can be integrated not just into monitoring platforms but directly into forensic infrastructure, enabling autonomous detection of anomalies and automated classification of incidents as they unfold.

5.3.5 Limitations, challenges, and risks of ML in security contexts

Despite its strengths, machine learning introduces new risks and limitations when applied to digital security. A major challenge concerns data quality and representativeness. ML models trained on incomplete or biased datasets may produce inaccurate threat assessments or overlook critical anomalies. This concern is amplified in digitalized supply chains, where heterogeneity in sensor quality, network connectivity, and data governance may reduce the reliability of feature patterns [19].

Adversarial manipulation presents another obstacle. Attackers can poison datasets, generate adversarial inputs, or exploit vulnerabilities in trained models to evade detection. Such attacks undermine forensic accuracy and threaten the integrity of automated decision-making. This challenge is especially significant in cloud ecosystems, where adversaries may target distributed logs, manipulate provenance data, or insert synthetic events to mislead ML-driven systems [20].

A further limitation relates to transparency and interpretability. While deep learning models deliver high accuracy, their internal decision pathways are opaque, raising concerns about legal admissibility and forensic accountability. Transparent ML approaches offer partial solutions but remain insufficient to fully address the interpretability gap [14].

Finally, ML deployments require substantial computational resources, secure data pipelines, and continuous model updates. Studies on digital transformation in logistics and transportation [13] show that even operational ML systems face scalability and integration challenges, reinforcing that security-focused ML must be similarly supported by strong digital infrastructures.

5.4 CLOUD FORENSICS: PRINCIPLES, PHASES, CHALLENGES, AND TECHNOLOGICAL DEVELOPMENTS

Cloud forensics has emerged as one of the most complex and rapidly evolving subfields within digital forensics, driven by the widespread migration of enterprise systems, applications, and data into distributed cloud environments [21]. Unlike traditional digital forensics, which presumes investigator control over physical hardware and static storage media, cloud forensics operates within decentralized, virtualized, and often opaque infrastructures controlled by third-party cloud service providers (CSPs). This transformation necessitates new investigative approaches, evidence models, governance structures, and automated mechanisms capable of navigating large-scale, dynamic, and multi-tenant environments [22]. The importance of cloud forensics has intensified as organizations adopt cloud-based ERP systems, platform-as-a-service models, large-scale IoT deployments, and interconnected supply-chain platforms where security breaches or operational disruptions can have cascading consequences across global networks [23].

5.4.1 Foundations and evolution of cloud forensics

Cloud forensics extends traditional digital forensic principles to the unique context of cloud computing, encompassing the identification, preservation, collection, analysis, and presentation of evidence originating from cloud environments. Early and comprehensive examinations of cloud forensic challenges highlight that cloud environments generate massive volumes of distributed and ephemeral data across multiple locations, making evidence acquisition complex and time-sensitive [12]. The multi-layered nature of cloud infrastructures—comprising virtual machines, hypervisors, object storage, databases, and APIs—creates numerous points at which evidence may reside, each subject to different access policies and legal controls [24].

Further research argues that cloud forensics must evolve beyond traditional tools and methodologies, given that investigators rarely have direct control over physical storage devices and cannot always ensure the continuity or immutability of data [11]. These studies emphasize that forensic readiness, automation, and coordination with cloud service providers are increasingly essential components of a viable forensic strategy. Furthermore, forensic practitioners now face additional challenges related to distributed logging, platform elasticity, and automated scaling mechanisms that generate transient instances whose evidential traces may disappear without warning [25].

These foundational studies demonstrate that cloud forensics is not a simple extension of traditional digital forensics but a fundamentally different investigative paradigm shaped by distributed architectures and provider-controlled infrastructures. This shift has profound implications for security-sensitive sectors such as supply chains, transportation, and financial services, where enterprise data is highly dynamic and continuously exchanged through cloud platforms. For example, research on Industry 4.0-enabled logistics systems [7, 10] highlights the increasing cloud dependency of IoT-enabled transport operations, which further amplifies the need for robust forensic capabilities in large-scale data environments [26].

5.4.2 Phases of cloud forensics: Adaptations and complexities

While cloud forensics retains the broad phases of traditional forensic investigation—identification, preservation, collection, analysis, and reporting—the application of each phase must be adapted to the constraints and complexity of cloud environments.

Identification involves locating relevant evidence across distributed systems. In cloud contexts, this requires identifying the virtual machines, databases, logs, network traces, metadata repositories, and containerized environments where evidential artifacts may reside. Research illustrates this challenge through cloud evidence tracing systems that automate the identification and retrieval of traces across large-scale public cloud platforms, demonstrating that automated trace extraction is vital in environments where evidence is dynamically distributed and often ephemeral [1].

Preservation in cloud forensics is complicated by the lack of direct control over physical hardware. Studies emphasize that forensic practitioners must rely on cloud service provider mechanisms for data retention, snapshot generation, and log access, making preservation practices heavily dependent on service-level agreements and provider cooperation [12]. Blockchain-based approaches offer tamper-resistant mechanisms for preserving the integrity of cloud evidence through immutable audit trails, illustrating a growing movement toward decentralized evidence preservation [27].

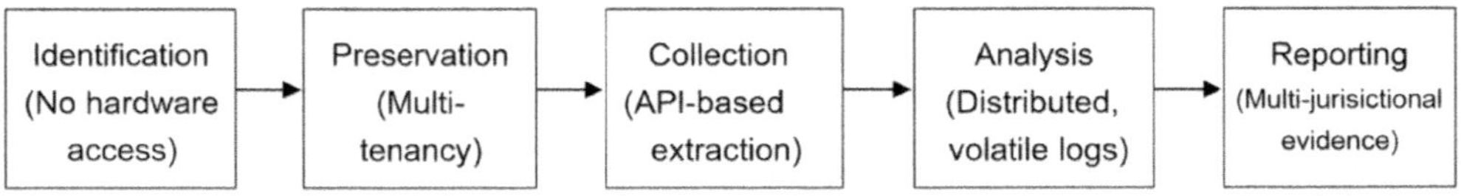

Figure 5.3 Cloud forensics phases and cloud-specific challenges.

Table 5.2 Comparison of traditional vs cloud forensics

Dimension	*Traditional forensics*	*Cloud forensics*
Evidence location	Local devices	Distributed cloud nodes
Control	Full investigator control	CSP controlled
Volatility	Low	High (auto-scaling, ephemeral VMs)
Access	Direct	API based
Legal	Single jurisdiction	Multiple jurisdictions

Collection requires secure extraction of data, often through CSP-provided APIs. Research on MECC-enabled provenance collection underscores the importance of secure and cryptographically verifiable data acquisition processes [8]. Centralized provenance investigation systems demonstrate how cryptographic mechanisms ensure that collected evidence remains untampered and legally admissible.

Analysis, arguably the most challenging phase, requires processing large-scale distributed datasets, logs, and provenance records. Machine learning models increasingly support this phase by classifying behavioral patterns, clustering event sequences, and detecting anomalies [28]. Multiple studies show that ML-driven analysis can significantly enhance the ability to detect suspicious behaviors, reconstruct attack paths, and validate incident timelines, especially when logs are voluminous or fragmented across cloud nodes [9, 14].

Reporting in cloud forensics requires translating complex technical findings into legally admissible evidence while also accounting for multi-jurisdictional considerations. Research warns that chain-of-custody documentation becomes more complex when evidence traverses geographic boundaries or is controlled by third parties [11]. Transparent ML approaches may further support reporting by improving interpretability in decision-making processes [14]. To summarize how the traditional forensic workflow is adapted within cloud environments, Figure 5.3 provides an overview of the five core phases and the cloud-specific challenges embedded within each stage. Complementing this, Table 5.2 offers a direct comparison between traditional and cloud forensics, highlighting the key structural, technical, and legal differences that underpin these adaptations.

5.4.3 Key challenges in cloud forensics

Cloud forensics is hindered by several structural, technical, and legal challenges that complicate investigation and evidence management.

One of the most significant challenges concerns limited access and provider dependency. Cloud service providers control the underlying hardware, storage systems, and hypervisors, which means investigators may not have full visibility into logs, memory dumps, or configuration states. Research stresses that investigators must rely on provider cooperation to obtain necessary artifacts, which can delay investigations and restrict access to critical evidence [11].

Another major challenge involves data volatility and elasticity. Cloud systems continuously scale resources up or down, creating ephemeral virtual machines and containers whose logs may disappear quickly. Studies note that this volatility complicates the identification and preservation of evidence; investigators often must implement proactive monitoring or forensic readiness strategies to capture data before it is lost [12, 1].

Multi-tenancy and data segregation pose further complications. Cloud environments often host multiple clients on shared infrastructure, making it difficult to isolate evidence belonging to a specific organization without infringing on the privacy rights of others. This issue becomes pronounced in sectors such as supply chains, where numerous partners share cloud-based procurement and logistics platforms [5]. The need to respect data boundaries while conducting investigations requires carefully designed forensic protocols and robust legal safeguards.

Legal and jurisdictional complexities further complicate cloud forensics. Evidence may be stored across multiple geographic locations, each governed by different regulatory frameworks related to data access, privacy, and retention. In global logistics networks, cloud services often span Europe, Asia, and North America, creating multi-jurisdictional constraints during forensic analysis. Research highlights that these distributed legal environments can impede timely evidence collection and reduce judicial clarity [11].

Finally, anti-forensic and adversarial behaviors are becoming more sophisticated in cloud environments. Attackers may exploit cloud elasticity to mask their actions, manipulate logs, or inject synthetic events into distributed systems. Advanced research on AI-driven forensic systems emphasizes that modern attackers increasingly target not only systems but also forensic processes themselves by poisoning datasets or attempting to mislead ML-driven detection mechanisms [18].

5.4.4 Technological developments advancing cloud forensic capabilities

Recent years have seen significant technological progress aimed at overcoming the challenges associated with cloud forensics.

One development is the rise of automated forensic systems that use cloud-native mechanisms and automated workflows to retrieve evidence from large public-cloud platforms [1]. Automation reduces human error, accelerates investigations, and captures evidence more consistently across distributed environments.

Another important development concerns provenance-based forensics, where detailed records of data lineage support reconstruction of activity histories. MECC-enabled provenance systems exemplify this trend, offering cryptographically verifiable provenance trails that ensure evidence integrity and support investigative reasoning [8].

Blockchain-integrated forensic architectures provide immutable and decentralized audit trails, reducing reliance on cloud service provider trustworthiness [13]. These systems enhance evidential transparency by ensuring that logs cannot be retrospectively modified.

Machine learning continues to play a transformative role. Research shows that ML enhances cloud forensic meta-models by automatically classifying artifacts, identifying inconsistencies, and guiding investigators to the most relevant data sources [9]. Deep-learning techniques applied directly to virtual machine forensic analysis offer improved interpretability and detection accuracy [14]. Additional studies further highlight how predictive modeling, anomaly detection, and behavioral analysis strengthen cloud forensics by revealing trends and patterns that would otherwise remain hidden [3, 4].

Finally, developments in Industry 4.0 and smart logistics demonstrate the importance of scaling forensic capabilities beyond purely digital environments. The integration of

IoT-enabled waste management systems [5], smart mobility platforms, and cold-chain emissions tracking [13] illustrate how cloud-dependent, sensor-rich environments produce complex datasets that require advanced forensic tools capable of handling cyber-physical evidence.

5.4.5 Implications of cloud forensics for digital supply chains

Although cloud forensics applies broadly, its relevance to supply chains is particularly pronounced. Modern supply chains rely heavily on cloud platforms for procurement, warehousing, transportation management, and IoT-enabled monitoring. This dependency increases the attack surface, as cyber incidents affecting a single supplier can propagate throughout the chain. Studies on cold-chain optimization [5], transportation sustainability [13], and smart city logistics [10] all highlight the centrality of cloud-based systems in managing real-time operations.

Cloud forensics therefore becomes essential for investigating anomalies, identifying compromised devices, and verifying whether data related to shipments, environmental conditions, or supplier transactions has been manipulated. These capabilities are critical for ensuring traceability, accountability, and operational resilience across multi-tier supply networks.

5.5 INTEGRATING BIG DATA, MACHINE LEARNING, AND CLOUD FORENSICS: A UNIFIED FRAMEWORK FOR DIGITAL SECURITY

The convergence of big data analytics, machine learning, and cloud forensics represents a fundamental shift in how organizations approach digital security, risk monitoring, and incident investigation. While each domain contributes valuable capabilities, they achieve their full potential only when integrated into coordinated, data-driven architectures capable of analyzing complex digital environments. The maturation of cloud-centric systems, the proliferation of connected IoT devices, and the rise of Industry 4.0 and 5.0 technologies have made this integration not only beneficial but essential for organizations operating within digital supply chains, transportation networks, financial ecosystems, and smart city infrastructures. This section presents a unified conceptual framework demonstrating how these three technological domains interact, complement one another, and collectively strengthen resilience against cyber threats.

5.5.1 The rationale for integration: From fragmented capabilities to holistic security

Traditional digital security models often treat monitoring, anomaly detection, and forensic investigation as isolated processes, with each domain functioning independently. Big data tools help organizations aggregate and store information, but without advanced analytical intelligence, much of the raw data remains underutilized. Machine learning models can provide predictive insights, but their reliability depends heavily on the quality and consistency of available data. Cloud forensics offers investigative depth but often lacks automated support for analyzing large, distributed datasets in real time. Recent research notes that modern cloud-centric ecosystems demand approaches that transcend legacy tools and adopt continuous, integrated intelligence [11].

The integration of these three domains therefore responds to the need for continuous visibility, proactive detection, and forensically sound investigation within dynamic environments. This is particularly relevant for digitalized sectors such as supply chains, where operations depend on real-time cloud monitoring, IoT sensors, and predictive analytics [5, 7]. Supply chain disruptions—whether due to cyberattacks, sensor tampering, fraudulent transactions, or equipment manipulation—illustrate how interconnected data ecosystems require holistic security frameworks capable of detecting, explaining, and validating anomalies at scale.

5.5.2 Big data as the foundation for integrated security intelligence

Big data serves as the foundational layer of the unified framework because it underpins all forms of predictive, investigative, and forensic intelligence. The volume, diversity, and velocity of data generated by cloud infrastructures, IoT devices, virtual machines, transport systems, and digital platforms create an environment where traditional storage and analysis mechanisms are insufficient. Studies across operational domains—including waste-efficient cold chains [5], smart logistics [10], and digital transformation in transportation [13]—demonstrate that big data architectures are essential for handling continuous data flows and generating actionable insights.

From a security perspective, big data provides the raw material needed to detect anomalies and reconstruct incidents. Distributed logs, provenance records, API calls, and event traces form the evidential backbone upon which ML algorithms and forensic workflows operate. Research emphasizes that, in cloud forensics, evidence is inherently dispersed across virtualized infrastructures, making big data technologies indispensable for indexing, correlating, and preserving data at scale [12, 1]. Without unified data management, neither predictive modeling nor forensic reconstruction can function effectively.

5.5.3 Machine learning as the core analytical engine

Machine learning functions as the analytical intelligence layer within the integrated framework, enabling organizations to convert raw data into meaningful patterns, predictions, and anomaly indicators. ML models identify deviations from normative behavior, classify threats, and forecast risks before they escalate into significant disruptions. Recent research demonstrates that ML-driven systems outperform traditional rule-based approaches in both accuracy and responsiveness, particularly when analyzing large-scale, dynamic datasets typical of cloud environments [2].

In supply chain contexts, ML-based predictive analytics have been widely applied to anticipate equipment failures, detect spoilage risk, and optimize routing decisions [5, 7]. These capabilities translate directly to security applications, where IoT data streams, environmental readings, and route deviations often contain early signals of cyber-physical tampering or fraudulent behavior. Further studies strengthen this argument by demonstrating that ML models support proactive crime prevention through early detection of suspicious activity patterns [4].

Machine learning also enhances cloud forensics by automating evidence classification, clustering behavioral sequences, and identifying suspicious activities. Research on ML-enhanced forensic meta-models illustrates how machine learning can streamline evidence identification and reduce the labor-intensive nature of traditional forensic processes [9]. Deep-learning approaches further extend these capabilities by analyzing low-level virtual machine traces to detect hidden artifacts and adversarial actions [14].

5.5.4 Cloud forensics as the investigative and accountability layer

While big data and ML support continuous monitoring and predictive intelligence, cloud forensics provides the structured investigative framework needed to validate incidents, reconstruct timelines, and support legal or regulatory compliance. Cloud forensics adds interpretability, accountability, and evidential depth to ML-driven detection. MECC-enabled provenance investigation systems demonstrate how cryptographic provenance trails ensure the integrity of cloud evidence and support robust investigative reasoning [8]. Similarly, established logging frameworks define mechanisms to ensure log soundness and secrecy, ensuring that forensic datasets are reliable inputs for ML-based analysis [15].

Blockchain-based forensic architectures further reinforce this accountability by creating immutable audit trails [13]. These systems illustrate how cloud forensics is evolving toward decentralized trust models that reduce reliance on cloud service providers while improving the transparency and admissibility of evidence.

5.5.5 The integrated framework: Interactions and synergies

Bringing together the foundational infrastructure of big data, the analytical intelligence of machine learning, and the evidential depth of cloud forensics, the unified framework forms a cohesive, multi-layered architecture for digital security. Each component builds upon and strengthens the others, transforming isolated capabilities into a dynamic, self-improving ecosystem capable of real-time threat detection, explanation, and response.

This integration is essential in complex environments such as cloud-native infrastructures, IoT ecosystems, and digital supply chains—where the speed, scale, and volatility of data demand an approach that is not only automated and predictive, but also forensically sound and verifiable.

The framework operates through three interdependent flows, as illustrated in Figure 5.4:

- Forward Flow: Big Data → Machine Learning → Cloud Forensics

  Big data systems capture the raw digital footprint of operations—logs, traces, sensor streams, API calls—which are ingested and analyzed by machine learning models to detect anomalies or predict threats. These signals are then passed to cloud forensics processes, which validate and interpret them through evidence acquisition, timeline reconstruction, and provenance analysis.

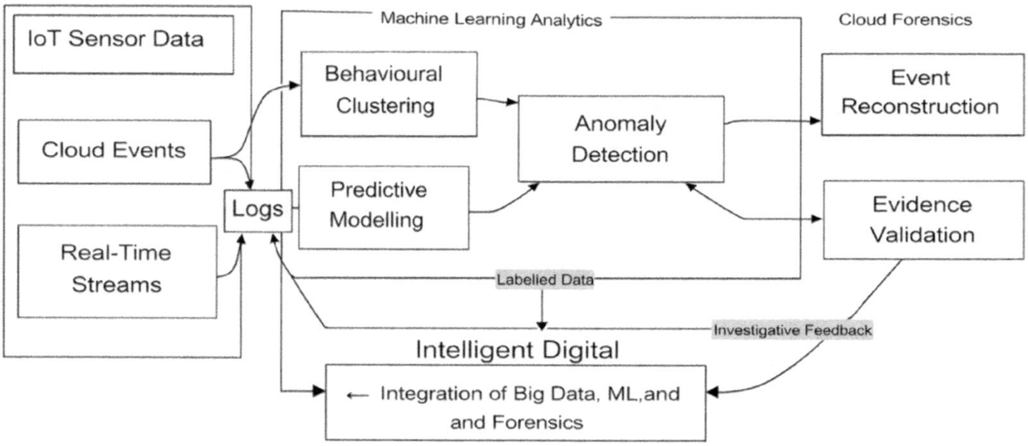

Figure 5.4 Integrated framework combining big data, machine learning, and cloud forensics.

- Feedback Flow: Cloud Forensics → Machine Learning → Big Data
  Forensic investigations produce structured, high-integrity datasets that serve as labeled inputs for training and refining ML algorithms. These enhancements improve detection performance, reduce false positives, and create a feedback loop that informs data collection priorities—ultimately improving the design and governance of big data architectures.
- Mutual Reinforcement: Machine Learning ↔ Cloud Forensics
  ML algorithms streamline forensic workflows by identifying relevant artifacts and reducing investigative scope. Conversely, validated forensic evidence supports model training and threat attribution, anchoring algorithmic decisions in real-world ground truth. This bidirectional interaction ensures a continuous cycle of learning and adaptation.

Figure 5.4 illustrates the interdependent flows between big data sources, machine learning analytics, and cloud forensic investigations. It demonstrates how raw data is transformed into security insights and evidential findings, with iterative feedback loops supporting model refinement and data governance. By structuring digital security in this way, organizations shift from reactive monitoring to proactive intelligence. Each layer reinforces the next, enabling continuous visibility, accountability, and resilience across increasingly complex and distributed environments.

5.5.6 Application in digital and supply chain ecosystems

The practical implications of this integrated framework are especially clear in digital supply chains, where cloud platforms, IoT sensors, and data-driven systems underpin core operations. Smart logistics systems rely on continuous data flows that require monitoring for both operational disruptions and potential cyber interference [10]. Similarly, cold-chain transportation systems depend on accurate temperature and humidity readings, which may be targeted by attackers seeking to manipulate sensor data or conceal product spoilage [5].

In such contexts, big data systems aggregate sensor readings and shipment records; ML models detect anomalies such as unexpected temperature spikes or route deviations; and cloud forensic mechanisms determine whether anomalies arise from natural causes, system malfunction, or deliberate tampering. This layered approach strengthens traceability, forensic readiness, and organizational resilience.

5.6 CONCLUSION AND FUTURE RESEARCH DIRECTIONS

The convergence of big data analytics, machine learning, and cloud forensics represents a profound transformation in how organizations understand, detect, and respond to threats within increasingly digitalized and interconnected environments. This chapter has argued that while each of these domains offers significant capabilities in isolation, their combined application provides a holistic, scalable, and intelligence-driven approach to security and forensic investigation. The rapid growth of cloud computing, IoT proliferation, Industry 4.0 systems, and digitalized supply chains has created unprecedented data complexity and broadened attack surfaces across sectors [29–33]. The forensic challenges associated with cloud environments—ranging from distributed logs to multi-jurisdictional evidence constraints—require new investigative models grounded in automation, data integration, and collaboration with cloud service providers. Simultaneously, big data systems and ML models enable real-time anomaly detection and predictive intelligence. Together, these technologies establish a foundation for proactive and forensically sound digital security.

The chapter also demonstrated the relevance of these integrated technologies in operational domains such as logistics and supply chain management, where digital transformation, IoT-enabled sensing, and cloud-based platforms are central to day-to-day functioning. Predictive analytics, blockchain-supported traceability, digital twins, and Industry 4.0-enabled infrastructures are reshaping supply chain ecosystems. These environments depend on high-velocity data streams that can be exploited for cyber-physical anomaly detection and forensic verification. As cold chain logistics, transportation systems, and real-time waste management platforms increasingly rely on cloud connectivity, the importance of integrated forensic, analytic, and predictive capabilities becomes even more apparent.

A key insight emerging from this chapter is that security, trust, and forensic accountability are inseparable from digital transformation itself. Organizations cannot reap the benefits of connected systems without considering the forensic implications of data generation, cloud deployment, and ML-based automation. Forensic readiness—once a niche concern—must now be embedded into the architectural design of cloud ecosystems, machine-learning pipelines, and big-data infrastructures. Emerging systems illustrate the growing adoption of forensic-by-design approaches. These systems show that future digital ecosystems will need to integrate provenance tracking, secure data retention, and automated evidence extraction mechanisms as standard components rather than optional enhancements.

Despite these advances, significant challenges remain. ML models continue to face issues of interpretability, bias, data dependency, and vulnerability to adversarial manipulation. Cloud forensics still confronts structural constraints, including limited CSP visibility, volatile virtualized resources, and cross-border legal complexities. Big-data systems require robust governance frameworks to ensure data quality, privacy protection, and secure interoperability. Attackers are no longer merely targeting operational systems but also the analytic and forensic processes that organizations rely on for detection and investigation. Thus, the need for more transparent, resilient, and tamper-resistant forensic pipelines is stronger than ever.

Future research should focus on deeply integrating big data, machine learning, and cloud forensics to enhance transparency, resilience, and legal accountability in evolving digital ecosystems. Key priorities include developing explainable ML models for forensic credibility, advancing forensic-by-design cloud architectures using technologies like blockchain, and improving adversarial robustness in detection and investigation processes. Cross-disciplinary efforts are also needed to align legal and ethical frameworks across jurisdictions, ensuring lawful and effective cloud investigations. Additionally, exploring emerging paradigms such as digital twins, multi-agent systems, and Industry 5.0 can further enhance forensic readiness and real-time response. Together, these directions aim to build secure, trustworthy, and forensically robust infrastructures for the next-generation of intelligent, interconnected systems.

Generative AI statement: Generative artificial intelligence tools were used in a limited and responsible manner to support proofreading and to enhance the clarity and articulation of the written text. The use of these tools was restricted to literature search and language refinement.

REFERENCES

1. S. Wu, W. Sun, Z. Ding, and S. Liu. 2022. Cloud evidence tracing system: An integrated forensics investigation system for large-scale public cloud platform. *Forensic Science International: Digital Investigation*, 41: 301391.

2. D. Dunsin, M.C. Ghanem, K. Ouazzane, and V. Vassilev. 2024. A comprehensive analysis of the role of artificial intelligence and machine learning in modern digital forensics and incident response. *Forensic Science International: Digital Investigation*, 48: 301675.
3. E.E. Abdallah, E.A. Elsoud, and A.E. Abdallah. 2025. A survey of data mining techniques for digital forensic analysis. *Procedia Computer Science*, 257: 731–736.
4. F. Ekundayo. 2024. Big data and machine learning in digital forensics: Predictive technology for proactive crime prevention. *Complexity*, 24 (2): 2692–2709.
5. H. Fatorachian and K. Pawar. 2025. Sustainable cold chain management: An evaluation of predictive waste management models. *Applied Sciences*, 15 (2): 770.
6. H. Fatorachian. 2025. Advancing food chain sustainability: Harnessing the power of Industry 5.0 for waste efficiency. *Cogent Business & Management*, 12 (1): 2574547.
7. H. Fatorachian and H. Kazemi. 2024. Integrating learning-based solutions in intelligent transportation systems: A conceptual framework and case studies validation. *Cogent Engineering*, 11 (1): 2427235.
8. S. Nasreen and A.H. Mir. 2024. Cloud forensics: A centralized cloud provenance investigation system using MECC. *Concurrency and Computation: Practice and Experience*, 36 (6): e7949.
9. S.H. Othman and A. Al-Dhaqm. 2024. An improved machine learning method by applying cloud forensic meta-model to enhance the data collection process in cloud environments. *Engineering, Technology & Applied Science Research*, 14 (1): 13017–13025.
10. H. Fatorachian, H. Kazemi, and K. Pawar. 2025. Enhancing smart city logistics through IoT-enabled predictive analytics: A digital twin and cybernetic feedback approach. *Smart Cities*, 8 (2): 56.
11. A.W. Malik, D.S. Bhatti, T.J. Park, H.U. Ishtiaq, J.C. Ryou, and K.I. Kim. 2024. Cloud digital forensics: Beyond tools, techniques, and challenges. *Sensors*, 24 (2): 433.
12. M.M. Alshabibi, A.K. Budoockhi, and M.M.H. Rahman. 2024. Forensic investigation, challenges, and issues of cloud data: A systematic literature review. *Computers*, 13 (8): 213.
13 G. Ragu and S. Ramamoorthy. 2023. A blockchain-based cloud forensics architecture for privacy leakage prediction with cloud. *Healthcare Analytics*, 4: 100220.
14 S. Frank, D. Jjingo, and G. Marvin. 2024. Cloud forensics in virtual machines using transparent deep learning techniques. In *Proceedings of the 16th International Conference on Contemporary Computing*, pp. 330–336.
15 M.M. Ahsan, A.W.B.A. Wahab, M.Y.I.B. Idris, S. Khan, E. Bachura, and K.K.R. Choo. 2018. CLASS: Cloud log assuring soundness and secrecy scheme for cloud forensics. *IEEE Transactions on Sustainable Computing*, 6 (2): 184–196.
16 S. Jayanthi, P. Vinitha Baby, D. Parameswari, R. Geetha, P. Thilagavathi, and J.A. Anand. 2025. Improved convolutional neural network for garbage separation. *2025 6th International Conference for Emerging Technology (INCET)*, Belgaum, India, pp. 1–6.
17 P. Thilagavathi, S. Hannah, Jose A. Anand, D. Parameswari, R. Geetha, and A. Govindaram. 2025. Machine learning and security fake email detection and intrusion detection. *2025 6th International Conference for Emerging Technology (INCET)*, Belgaum, India, 2025, pp. 1–6.
18 O.S. Ndibe. 2025. AI-driven forensic systems for real-time anomaly detection and threat mitigation in cybersecurity infrastructures. *International Journal of Research Publication and Reviews*, 6 (5): 389–411.
19. B. Muthukumar, P. Nakka, H. V., Jose A. Anand, A. Govindaram, and P. Thilagavathi. 2025. Application of machine learning techniques for the location and early detection of brain tumors. *2025 6th International Conference on Data Intelligence and Cognitive Informatics (ICDICI)*, Tirunelveli, India, pp. 1637–1644.
20. R. Geetanjali, T. M. Sreehari, A. Jegatheesan, B. Muthukumar, B. Thyla, and Jose A. Anand. 2025. Predictive model of 6-Month prognosis of stroke patients using machine learning techniques. *2025 2nd International Conference On Multidisciplinary Research and Innovations in Engineering (MRIE)*, Gurugram, India, pp. 439–444.
21. N. Nazeeya Anjum, S. Sumathi, R. Dheena Dhayalan, R. Rampavithran, A. Jose Anand, and M. Sathiyanarayanan. 2024. Smart sensors for smart city environmental monitoring systems. In T. Anh Nguyen (Eds.), *Digital Twin, Blockchain, and Sensor Networks in the Healthy and Mobile City* (pp. 17–33). Elsevier.

22. M. Gomathy, L. Steffina Morin, L.S. Raveendran, A. Jose Anand, A. Jegatheesan, and B. Muthukumar. 2025. Clustering and predictive modeling of epileptic spikes and seizures using EEG data. *2025 2nd International Conference on Circuits, Power and Intelligent Systems (CCPIS)*, Bhubaneswar, India, pp. 1–6.
23. S. Maheswari, S.J. Parvez, V.S. Devi, T. Anuradha, C.K. Snruthi, and A. Jose Anand. 2025. 5G-integrated data dissemination and multi interface communication architecture for enhanced VANETs. *2025 IEEE International Conference on Contemporary Computing and Communications (InC4)*, Bangalore, India, pp. 1–6.
24. S. Maheswari, N.P. Swetha Menon, B. Sumathi, M.A. Mukunthan, V. Bhanu Rekha, and A. Jose Anand. 2025. Predicting and improving the mechanical strength of a modified natural fiber/TiO2 polymer nanocomposite using artificial intelligence. *Journal of Environmental Nanotechnology*, 14 (4): 9–26.
25. R. Khan, R. Quazi, A. Jose Anand, M.A.J. Maktoof, and A. Al-Hilali. 2026. Predictive analytics for monkeypox: Utilizing machine learning to forecast outbreaks and resource allocation. In G.N. Nguyen, A. Swaroop, and P. Shukla (Eds.), *Proceedings of Fifth International Conference on Computing and Communication Networks*. ICCCN 2025. Lecture Notes in Networks and Systems, vol 1777. Springer, Cham.
26. P. Kar, S. Nayak, N. Kumar, A. Jose Anand, A. Mohanty, and H. Mohammed. 2026. Development of adaptive thermal management systems in electric vehicles using renewable energy and eco-friendly materials. In G.N. Nguyen, A. Swaroop, and P. Shukla (Eds.), *Proceedings of Fifth International Conference on Computing and Communication Networks*. ICCCN 2025. Lecture Notes in Networks and Systems, vol 1777. Springer, Cham.
27. M. Farooq, H. Amin, A. Jose Anand, and M. Waseem Iqbal. 2025. Cognitive complexity reduction in decentralized applications based on blockchain technology: The psychological aspects of user instruction, understanding and self efficacy. *Lex Localis – Journal of Local Self-Government*, 22 No. S4 (2024): 663–675.
28. R. Kesavan, T. Anuradha, P. Kalaiarasi, M.S. Jacob, A. Jose Anand, and V.S. Devi. 2025. Deep learning-based diagnostic support system for breast tissue classification using mammographic images. *2025 IEEE International Conference on Intelligent Signal Processing and Effective Communication Technologies (INSPECT)*, Gwalior, India, pp. 1–6.
29. S. Rani, P. Bhambri, A. Kataria, A. Khang, and A.K. Sivaraman. (Eds.). 2023. *Big Data, Cloud Computing and IoT: Tools and Applications* (1st ed.). Chapman and Hall/CRC. https://doi.org/10.1201/9781003298335
30. P. Bhambri, S. Rani, and M. Fahim (Eds.). 2024. *Computational Intelligence and Blockchain in Biomedical and Health Informatics* (1st ed.). CRC Press. https://doi.org/10.1201/9781003459347
31. R. Rana and P. Bhambri. 2024. Generative AI-driven security frameworks for web engineering: Innovations and challenges. In I.A. Shah and N.Z. Jhanjhi (Eds.), *Generative AI for Web Engineering Models* (pp. 285–296). IGI Global. https://doi.org/10.4018/979-8-3693-3703-5.ch014
32. P. Bhambri. 2024. Wallets and transactions. In D. Darwish (Ed.), *Decentralizing the Online Experience with Web3 Technologies* (pp. 90–106). IGI Global. https://doi.org/10.4018/979-8-3693-1532-3.ch004
33. P. Bhambri, S. Rani, I.S. Dhanoa, and T.A. Tran. 2024. Environmental impacts of industrial processes in Industry 4.0 ecosystem artificial intelligence approach. In S. Rani, P. Bhambri, S. Kumar, P.K. Pareek, and A.A. Elngar (Eds.), *AI-driven Digital Twin and Industry 4.0: A Conceptual Framework with Applications* (pp. 221–240). CRC Press, Taylor & Francis Group. https://doi.org/10.1201/9781003395416-14

Chapter 6

AI and automation in cloud forensics

Muhammad Farooq and Humera Amin

6.1 INTRODUCTION

6.1.1 The growing use of cloud computing and its impact

Cloud computing has significantly altered the organizational structure, data storage, service models (SaaS, PaaS, IaaS), and IT operations over the past few decades. The cloud technology features of its flexibility, scalability, and cost reduction have influenced a lot of organizations to move their offices from the traditional on-premises model to the cloud. For instance, a recent survey has revealed that almost 54% of the organizations are pointing out the difficulties in the cloud environments as the biggest concern regarding data security [1]. On the other hand, the enormous movement of data to the cloud has led to the emergence of cyber threats, data risk, and the need for investigations at a new scale due to factors such as networking, data streaming, virtual machines, and multi-tenancy environments. The lack of clarity with respect to data measurement, location, and ownership is rendering the traditional digital forensics skills insufficient.

6.1.2 Definition, importance, and scope of cloud forensics

In this scenario, the term Cloud Forensics has come up, and it can be defined as a specialization of digital forensics that deals specifically with the evidence produced, stored in a cloud model, and the whole process of evidence gathering, safeguarding, studying, and showing. For instance, some authors claim it to be the purpose of cloud forensics, which includes "Collection & Analysis of Digital Evidence in Cloud Environments," might consist of virtual machine images, cloud logs, network traffic, API calls, and data stores in multiple locations [2, 3]. This is critical since with the growing number of organizations and service providers using cloud platforms, the cyber attacks, data leaks, insider threats, and offbeat attacks and defense situations are becoming more and more complicated. Cloud forensics not only provides the means to detect cyber incidents but has also become inevitable in the areas of legal evidence admissibility, chain of custody, and incident response. The core activities in cloud forensics are basically identification of evidence; preservation and collection; analysis; and presentation of results. Besides that, the cloud's service models, deployment models (public, private, hybrid), and multi-contingency and geo-location issues pose unique challenges to the field [4, 5].

DOI: 10.1201/9781003656487-6

6.1.3 Current challenges and technical gaps in forensic investigations

The traditional digital forensic instruments and procedures are losing their effectiveness because of the difficulties arising from the cloud model. Among the most significant difficulties are the following:

- Location Independence: Cloud data is often managed by different servers, countries, or service providers (CSPs), which affects access to evidence, control, and timeline accuracy [2].
- Data Fragmentation and Volatility: Due to the automatic virtualization of resources, data can be moved around, deleted, or overwritten, and this makes it very difficult to keep the evidence intact [3].
- Multi-location and Virtualization: The presence of many users and different organizations on the same resource (multi-tenancy) creates problems such as mixing of evidence, long chains of custody, and interference from cloud providers [2].
- Legal, Privacy, and Transparency Issues: The acquisition and analysis of evidence in the cloud may involve different jurisdictions, and the data protection laws, SLAs, and the level of assistance from providers may be significant hurdles [6].
- Lack of Analytical Capacity and Automation: Increasing data volumes, rapidly changing environments, and complex attack-defense interactions have outstripped the availability of automated analytical tools [7, 8].

This technological divide means that besides traditional forensic methods, which are already insufficient, the innovation, automation, and advanced analytical capabilities will be the main requirements.

6.1.4 Chapter objective and research questions

The central theme of this particular chapter revolves around the idea of how cloud forensics investigations can be performed much quicker, more efficiently, and reliably by means of referring to technology such as artificial intelligence and automation. The chapter will particularly look into:

- How can machine learning, deep learning, and automated analytical algorithms be used to capture, analyze, and validate cloud evidence?
- In what ways do measures like automated incident response, anomaly detection, and data integrity verification lessen human error and thus provide higher accuracy in the forensic processes?
- What are the ethical, legal, and technical challenges faced in the application of AI and automated systems, and how can they be addressed?

In this context, the following research questions have been identified as the basic premises:

- What are the traditional methods of cloud forensics, and for what reasons are they proving inadequate in a cloud environment?
- Which steps of the cloud forensics process (e.g., acquisition, analysis, validation, response) can artificial intelligence and automated systems replace?

- To what extent can the use of AI and automation make cloud forensics investigations more effective, faster, and more reliable?
- What are the main challenges related to these technologies (model transparency, privacy, legal restrictions, collaboration with cloud providers) and what frameworks or strategies are needed to address them?

This chapter will explore the answers to these questions, as well as provide recommendations for future research by reviewing previous research work.

6.2 EVOLUTIONARY BACKGROUND OF CLOUD FORENSICS

6.2.1 The journey from traditional digital forensics to cloud forensics

In the early days, the focus of digital forensics was on devices and storage that were under the control of the investigation team, e.g., computer hard drives, mobile phones, network traces, etc. Later, as cloud computing developed rapidly, the nature of the infrastructure changed, such as virtual machines, multi-tenancy, auto-scaling, geographically distributed resources. With this change, the nature of forensic processes as well as collaboration with service providers (CSPs) has changed. Research has shown that traditional forensics models (e.g., disk imaging, physical control, consolidated storage) are no longer effective in cloud environments [9, 10]. For example, George Grispos and colleagues have shown that the concept of "physical access to storage devices" is less meaningful in the cloud and that traditional forensic methods are a hindrance to implementation [9]. Therefore, the field of forensics has shifted toward "cloud forensics," which specifically deals with the acquisition, analysis, and presentation of evidence in this environment.

6.2.2 Differences in data models and investigations in cloud environments

The following significant differences emerge in cloud environments that have changed the investigation process:

- Distribution of Resources: Data may not be located on just one drive or server, but on different servers, data centers, and regional locations [2].
- Virtualization and Multi-tenancy: Different users can have resources on the same physical machine, raising the question of "whose data is it?" [2, 10].
- Variable States of Data (Data at Rest, in Motion, in Execution): Data may not only reside in storage but may also be in transit and execution across the network, for which investigation techniques will differ [9].
- Limited Control: The investigation team often relies on the support of the cloud provider; direct physical control is not possible [9].
- Logs and Evidence Generation Gap: In the cloud, logs are spread across multiple layers (application, platform, infrastructure) and can be difficult to unify [2].

These points illustrate that not only tools but also methodologies, models, collaborations, and legal/practical aspects change in cloud forensics.

6.2.3 Forensic impacts of cloud service models (IaaS, PaaS, SaaS)

Forensic impacts vary depending on cloud service models:

- Infrastructure as a Service (IaaS): Virtual machines, storage, and networking are provided to the user. This model offers better access to traditional machine images and logs, but still involves the issue of provider support, virtualization layers, and physical server distribution [11].
- Platform as a Service (PaaS): The user is provided with the platform, while the infrastructure is owned by the provider. In this model, the level of evidence is logical (e.g., API logs), and direct access to physical or even virtual storage may be minimal [12].
- Software as a Service (SaaS): The entire software is run by the provider; the user only uses it. Evidence is typically application logs, user account traces, and cloud storage elements; their availability and configuration are under the provider's control [11].

The nature of these models implies that forensic strategies should vary depending on the model, such as the method of acquisition, location of logs, legal responsibilities, etc.

6.3 LEGAL AND ETHICAL REQUIREMENTS

The legal and ethical aspects of cloud forensics are prominent:

- Jurisdiction and Law: Data may often be located in different countries or states and is affected by the relevant laws, legal order, and data privacy laws [12].
- Privacy and Multi-tenant Issues: Data from other users may be on the same server, so it is important to respect their privacy during the investigation [10].
- Admissibility and Chain of Custody: The authenticity, immutability, and timeliness of evidence are important; these challenges are exacerbated in cloud models [2, 12].
- Transparency and Model Trust: It is the obligation of the research team to demonstrate that the respective provider's logs or evidence are genuine, have not been corrupted, and that the method of collection was proper.

Due to this, a legal and ethical framework is necessary in cloud forensics so that the investigations are effective, transparent, and acceptable.

6.3.1 The role of artificial intelligence in cloud forensics

a) **Machine Learning-Based Forensic Models**

One of the key aspects of digital forensics in machine learning (ML) is the automatic recognition of patterns, crude classifications, and even incident detection. Moreover, in cloud environments, where the data's volume, variability, and distribution are all on the rise at a rapid pace, the use of ML models is already seen as a great help in improving certain types of forensic tasks. For example, one study reported that ML was used to classify attacks in cloud environments, yielding the following results: "supervised machine learning techniques (e.g., linear regression, random forest)...detection accuracy above 99%" [13]. Additionally, a study has introduced machine learning to increase transparency and accuracy in the data collection process: "An Improved Machine Learning Method by applying Cloud Forensic Meta-Model (CFMM)...to enhance the data collection process in cloud environments."

- These models support forensic processes in the following ways:
- Feature extraction and model training from cloud logs, network traffic, virtual machine activities.
- Automatic classification, e.g., "normal activity" vs. "suspicious activity."
- Early detection of random or unexpected events (anomalies).

b) **Data Pattern Recognition through Deep Learning Algorithms**

Deep learning (DL) models, especially neural networks such as LSTM, Transformer, Variational Autoencoders (VAEs), are providing more depth in forensic investigations. For example, a recent study implemented a "Hybrid deep learning framework combining LSTM and Transformer architectures," where the results were "detection accuracy improvements of up to 98.2%" [14]. Another study presented "Scalable Microservice Forensics and Stability Assessment" using VAEs in a containerized environment, which gave examples of CPU performance, network volume, and storage savings [15].

The role of deep learning in cloud forensics is as follows:

- Automatically learning complex patterns within logs, network, and application data.
- Identifying "hidden patterns" of attack or anomaly that may escape traditional rule-based tools.
- Reconstructing a timeline, e.g., connecting the different stages of an attack.
- The model's ability to learn, i.e., to handle new attacks or model drift over time.

c) **Natural Language Processing (NLP) and Automated Reporting**

A large portion of evidence in a cloud environment is in the form of logs, metadata, and supporting documents. This is where the role of NLP becomes important. Some of the salient aspects are:

- Semantic and semantic analysis of text within logs, such as "user failed login 23 times," "API call from suspicious IP," etc.
- Automatic Report Generation: Investigation progress, evidence summary, model results formatted into understandable reports
- Quick guidance of the investigation team through query and answer models.

For example, the study "AI-Driven Cloud Forensics: A Novel Framework" reported that NLP was used for log analysis, and combined with an automated reporting module, it enabled the acceleration of cybercrime investigations [16].

d) **Uses of AI for Anomaly Detection**

Anomaly detection is a fundamental part of the cloud research process, as evidence often occurs "out of the ordinary." Effective identification of anomalies has been made possible with the help of AI:

- Deep learning models have been applied to log files and system traces; for example, "Deep Learning for Anomaly Detection in Log Data: A Survey" provides a comprehensive overview of different models [17].
- A study titled "Anomaly Detection in Cloud Network: A Review" has mastered anomaly detection in cloud networks [18].
- AI-driven models can automatically extract anomaly trends, identify attacks, and trigger immediate investigative responses. For example, Cloud Investigation Automation Framework (CIAF) achieved an F1 score of 93% for ransomware incidents [19].

e) **Case Studies: Examples of AI-Based Forensic Investigation**

- The study "Evidence Detection in Cloud Forensics: Classifying Cyber-Attacks in IaaS Environments" used ML techniques to classify cyber-attacks in IaaS environments [20].
- "AI-Driven Cloud Forensics: A Novel Framework" showcased an all-inclusive structure that consisted of machine learning, deep learning, natural language processing, and blockchain theories, and examined the extent to which the processes of acquiring, analyzing, and reporting evidence could be automated [16].
- "Scalable Microservice Forensics...Using Variational Autoencoders" demonstrated the use of deep learning in a containerized environment, designed to extract forensic information within a microservice infrastructure [15].

6.3.2 Automation and its importance in forensic investigations

The flowchart (Figure 6.1) illustrates the application of AI and automation in different steps of the cloud computing forensic process, from gathering data to the response to an incident. The intention is to have the forensic process be speedy, effective, and without mistakes [21–25].

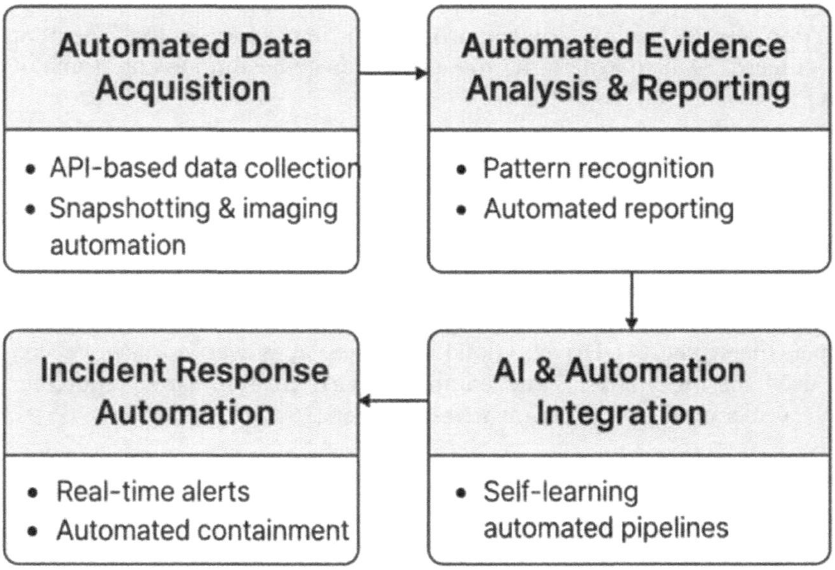

Figure 6.1 Flowchart showing the integration of AI and automation across key stages of cloud forensic investigations.

a) **Automated Data Acquisition Methods**

The first step and the most critical one in cloud forensics is data acquisition. The traditional methods were manual, time consuming, and error prone. However, the imposition of technology can make the process quicker and more dependable. Following are some of the main techniques for automated data collection:

- API-Based Data Collection: Automated acquisition of logs, metadata, and files through cloud providers' APIs [17].
- Snapshotting and Imaging Automation: Automatically capture snapshots of virtual machines and storage to save time and to reduce human intervention [2].
- Scheduled and Event-Triggered Collection: Automatic data collection based on key events or suspicions like taking an instant snapshot on multiple failed logins from a specific IP [15].

These procedures not only save time but also maintain the integrity of evidence.

b) **Automated Evidence Analysis and Reporting**

Automation significantly facilitates the stages of evidence analysis and reporting. AI/ML models and automated scripts have made it possible to carry out automated analysis of cloud logs, network traffic, and virtual machine data:

- Pattern Recognition: Machine learning models are employed for the process of detecting suspicious activities, unusual logs, and unexpected patterns [14].
- Automated Reporting: The outcome of the investigation is presented in an automated report, which includes a summary of evidence, timeline, and findings [14].
- Correlation and Root Cause Analysis: Conferring the connections between logs and events to discover the root of the actual incident or attack, which is a labor-intensive procedure, but with human professional involvement, it is possible [18].

c) **Automated Systems in Incident Response**

Automation in cloud forensic incident response has made it more efficient and quicker:

- Real-Time Alerts: AI/Automation allows instant notification or alert on unusual activities, such as ransomware or unauthorized access.
- Automated Containment: Automated scripts are instructed to isolate machines or services that have been infected; hence, the damage is limited [19].
- Playbook Execution: The pre-prepared incident response playbooks, such as user session termination or unsafe file quarantining, are executed automatically.

In such systems, human error is minimized and damage is limited by fast response.

d) **Reduced human intervention and increased accuracy**

Over time, automation has accounted for a decrease in human labor and an increase in the accuracy of the forensic process. However, automated processes come with the following advantages:

- Consistency and Repeatability: Data acquisition and analysis according to the same standards every time.
- Error Reduction: Reduced possibility of human error such as oversight or manual misclassification.
- Time Efficiency: Fast evidence acquisition and analysis, which is essential for large cloud data sets.
- Scalability: Effective investigations possible even in large and complex cloud ecosystems.

e) **The Integration of AI and Automation**

The partnership of AI and Automation is the building block of the cloud forensics future. AI algorithms grant automated systems with the ability to analyze, while Automation puts the output of these models into operation and reporting forms:

- Self-Learning Automated Pipelines: Implementing automated pipelines after training AI models, which respond quickly to new incidents.
- Adaptive Incident Response: Automated containment or alerts based on AI predictions and anomaly detection.
- Integrated Forensic Platforms: A platform that automates all stages of evidence collection, analysis, anomaly detection, and reporting [17].

As a result, the mutual integration of AI and Automation makes cloud forensic investigations faster, more accurate, reliable, and consistent, and effectively reduces losses and errors caused by human intervention.

6.3.3 AI and automation methods used in cloud forensics

The segment of this paper presents the main methods utilized in the cloud forensics process accompanied by technical and research perspectives regarding AI and automation. The methods covered include Predictive Analytics, Data Mining, Neural Networks, Reinforcement Learning, Automated Decision-Making, and Cloud-Based AI Frameworks [26–30].

6.3.3.1 Predictive analytics and data mining

Predictive analytics and data mining predict potential incidents or key pieces of evidence by extracting patterns from large-scale collected cloud logs, network flows, event timelines, and user behavior data. These methods are useful for quickly identifying outliers and trends in a cloud environment. Many recent studies have shown that AI-based predictive models are proving effective in cloud security risk assessment and early incident detection. It uses supervised and unsupervised algorithms (e.g., decision trees, random forests, clustering, and association rules) as the core tools [31].

6.3.3.2 Neural network models for evidence classification

Neural networks (e.g., MLP, CNN, GNN) are capable of learning patterns in complex feature spaces, so they are useful in evidence classification, time series analysis, and image/media-based forensic data (e.g., screenshots, log headers, memory dump images). Research has shown that hybrid neural approaches and graph-based neural networks can better characterize the relationships between evidence, leading to accurate classification and crime reconstruction. However, special care must be taken to train the models with a lack of labeled data and the risks of overfitting [32].

6.3.3.3 *Improving forensic processes through reinforcement learning*

Reinforcement learning (RL) enables forensic workflows to learn and improve themselves; for example, an artificial agent can refine a complex investigation policy (e.g., which file snapshots to retrieve first, which logs to correlate) through reward signals. Recent studies have found RL to be successful in malware and registry forensics, resulting in time savings, lower false negative rates, and more effective artifact exploration. However, RL applications face challenges such as state-space size, reward design, and training generalizability [33].

6.3.3.4 *Automated decision-making systems*

Automated decision-making systems translate AI findings into immediate action (e.g., quarantine, alert generation, automatic archiving of evidence). This approach increases response speed and reduces human workload, especially in real-time or near-real-time investigation contexts. However, according to judicial standards, explainability, audit trail, and reproducibility of AI decisions are essential; therefore, research has proposed clear definitions and standards for automated steps to maintain the legal admissibility of evidence [34].

6.4 CHALLENGES AND ISSUES

- Data Privacy and Confidentiality Risks: The use of sensitive user data in cloud forensics and training AI models raises privacy issues; federated learning and privacy-preserving methods are suggestions to mitigate this risk [35, 36].
- Model Explainability and the Problem of Black-Box AI: Deep neural networks are often "black boxes," so explaining evidence in court can be difficult; research on Explainable AI is trying to address this issue [37, 38].
- Jurisdictional Boundaries: Cloud data is spread across different countries, which can cause data access and legal requirements to change. A cross-border forensic framework is needed [39, 40].
- Evidence Integrity in Multi-tenant Environments: Data from multiple users on the same physical infrastructure increases the risk of evidence contamination; blockchain and cryptographic hashing have been considered useful for strengthening evidence integrity [41, 42].
- Reliability of AI-Based Results and False Positives: AI systems will sometimes make false alarms or errors; these errors can be reduced with diverse data sets, model validation, and a human-in-the-loop approach [35, 36].

6.5 FUTURE TRENDS AND RESEARCH DIRECTIONS

Figure 6.2 shows future research trends in cloud forensics, where Explainable AI, blockchain, edge computing, and human–AI collaboration combine to enable automated, transparent, and effective forensic analysis.

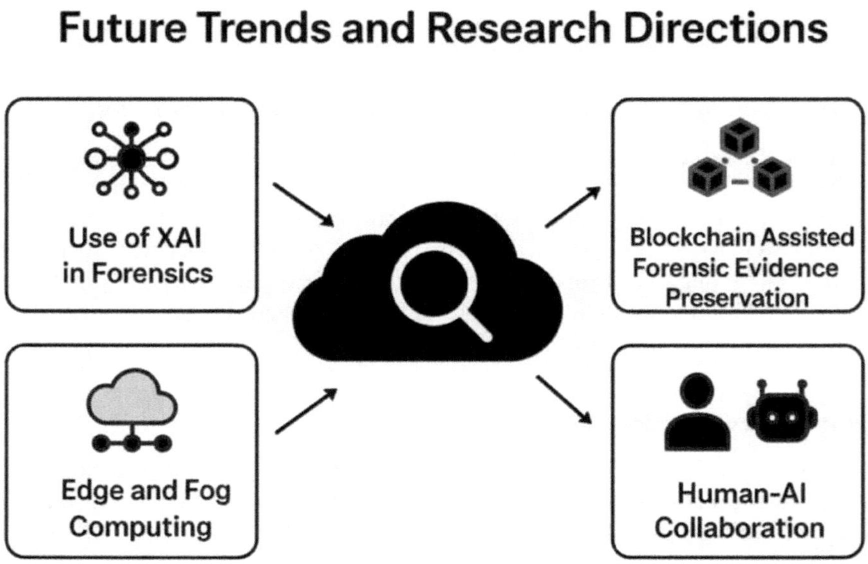

Figure 6.2 Future trends and research directions in cloud forensics.

- Explainable AI (XAI) in Forensics: In the future, Explainable AI in forensic systems is emphasizing the use of models that can explain their decisions so that their evidence is admissible in courts [9, 38].
- Automated Investigations in the Context of Edge and Fog Computing: With the help of Edge and Fog Computing, forensic data can be analyzed at the edge of the network, which saves time and improves data security [43, 44].
- Cloud Forensic Models Based on Federated Learning: In cloud forensics, Federated Learning provides an efficient analysis while maintaining privacy, as it allows the training of AI models without sending data to a central server [45, 46].
- Blockchain-Assisted Forensic Evidence Preservation: The implementation of blockchain is making it possible for the records of forensic evidence to be covered by a non-reputable seal, thereby preserving the authenticity and integrity of the evidence [47, 48].
- Hybrid Investigation Frameworks Based on Human–AI Collaboration: Research in the future will primarily focus on hybrid frameworks that allow the involvement of both humans and AI in the investigations, thus ensuring both accuracy and transparency of the decision-making process [49, 50].

6.6 CONCLUSION

The chapter explains the increased utilization of AI and automation in the domain of cloud forensics. With the increasing complexity and layering of digital systems, the traditional methods of forensic analysis have turned out to be very slow, expensive, and also prone to human mistakes. In that case, AI-based automated systems not just help in accelerating the investigations but also in getting the quality, visibility, and efficiency in the evidence scrutiny [51–55]. New-age AI ideas such as Explainable AI (XAI) are a novel breakthrough in cloud forensics, as they deliver not only the outcomes but also the rationale and thought process applied behind those outcomes to the researchers. This property is of great importance in the courts, since the evidence from the forensic department is only admitted if it's clear and understandable. Likewise, with Federated Learning, data can be worked on at dispersed locations without being sent to a central server which adds more to the privacy and security aspects. The use of blockchain technology has also proved to be a crucial factor in maintaining the chain of custody in cloud forensics [56–60]. The unchangeable characteristic of the blockchain makes it nearly impossible for any evidence alteration to happen thus, the trust in the forensic reports to the judicial system gets heightened. Conversely, Edge and Fog Computing have made it possible for the investigative process to be real-time which means that the data analysis turnaround is cut down and the decisions made are more accurate.

Though the technology has advanced rapidly, there are still significant challenges to be dealt with, such as data privacy, algorithmic bias, and so on. Additionally, AI-based automated systems, although powerful, still have accuracy limitations and this directly relates to the quality of the training data. Consequently, it is inevitable that hybrid models based on human–AI collaboration will come into existence, in which human domain experts and machine learning systems would jointly make decisions thus not only the results would be automated but also human insight would be enriched. The culmination of this is that the future of cloud forensics is an era where automated, transparent, and explainable forensic models will be the standard for cyber investigations. This change would not only result in greater efficiency for investigation agencies but would also contribute to a digital justice system that is more robust, fairer, and more effective.

REFERENCES

1. Palo Alto Networks, "2024 State of Cloud Native Security Report," Mar. 7, 2025. Available: https://www.paloaltonetworks.com/resources/research/state-of-cloud-native-security-2024. Accessed: Nov. 02, 2025.
2. A. W. Malik, D. S. Bhatti, T.-J. Park, H. U. Ishtiaq, J.-C. Ryou, and K.-I. Kim, "Cloud Digital Forensics: Beyond Tools, Techniques, and Challenges," *Sensors*, vol. 24, no. 2, p. 433, Jan. 2024. doi: 10.3390/s24020433.
3. J. Cortado, "Challenges of Investigations in the Cloud," *Cyber – Forensics Weekly Executive Summaries*, Oct. 18, 2024. Available: https://westoahu.hawaii.edu/cyber/forensics-weekly-executive-summmaries/challenges-of-investigations-in-the-cloud/. Accessed: Nov. 02, 2025.
4. S. Simou, C. Kalloniatis, S. Gritzalis, and H. Mouratidis, "A Survey on Cloud Forensics Challenges and Solutions," *Security and Communication Networks*, vol. 9, no. 18, pp. 6285–6314, Dec. 2016. doi: 10.1002/sec.1688.
5. R. Omollo and S. Aketch, "A Model Approach to Addressing Cloud Forensics Challenges," *Global Scientific Journal*, vol. 12, no. 3, pp. 1–14, 2024.
6. Ponmalar, A., Jose, A. A., Muthamizhan, T., Sobana, T., & Vishwath, J. H. (2022). Automatic forensic analysis of criminal navigation system using machine learning. *Proceedings of the IEEE First International Conference on Computational Science and Technology (ICCST 2022)*, Chennai, India, 1–5
7. W. S. Ahmed, Z. T. Mustafa AL-Ta'I, T. Abegaz, and G. S. Mahmood, "Digital Forensics Architecture for Real-time Automated Evidence Collection and Centralization: Leveraging Security Lake and Modern Data Architecture," *Journal of Intelligent Systems*, vol. 33, no. 1, p. 20240109, Dec. 2024. doi: 10.1515/jisys-2024-0109.
8. R. T. Yadav, "AI-Driven Digital Forensics," *International Journal of Scientific Research*, vol. 10, no. 4, pp. 1673–1681, 2024.
9. Anjum, N., Sumathi, S., Dheena Dhayalan, R., Rampavithran, R., Jose Anand, A., & Sathiyanarayanan, M. (2024). Smart sensors for smart city environmental monitoring systems. In **T. A. Nguyen (Ed.)**, *Digital Twin, Blockchain, and Sensor Networks in the Healthy and Mobile City* (pp. 17–33). Elsevier.
10. S. Zawoad and R. Hasan, "Cloud Forensics: A Meta-Study of Challenges, Approaches, and Open Problems," 2013, *arXiv*. doi: 10.48550/ARXIV.1302.6312.

11. ECS Infotech, "Evolution of Cloud Forensics: Investigations & Providers." Jul. 17, 2024. Available: https://www.ecsinfotech.com/evolution-of-cloud-forensics-investigations/. Accessed: Nov. 2, 2025.
12. Priyanka V, Lekshmi S. Raveendran, R. Kesavan,Sandhya.U, Anuradha T and Jose Anand A., "Analysis and Comparison of CloudData Storage Services with a Practical Study on Google Drive," *2026 6th International Conference on ExpertClouds and Applications (ICOECA)*, Bengaluru, India, pp. 924-930, 2026.
13. T. Salman, D. Bhamare, A. Erbad, R. Jain, and M. Samaka, "Machine Learning for Anomaly Detection and Categorization in Multi-cloud Environments," 2018. doi: 10.48550/ARXIV.1812.05443.
14. L. Chourasiya *et al.*, "Advanced System Log Analyzer for Anomaly Detection and Cyber Forensic Investigations using LSTM and Transformer Networks," *Journal of Cloud Computing*, vol. 14, no. 1, p. 60, Oct. 2025. doi: 10.1186/s13677-025-00789-y.
15. P. Sharma, P. Porras, S. Cheung, J. Carpenter, and V. Yegneswaran, "Scalable Microservice Forensics and Stability Assessment Using Variational Autoencoders," 2021, *arXiv*. doi: 10.48550/ARXIV.2104.13193.
16. Vucha, K. R. K., & Kamarapu, K. (2025). AI-driven cloud forensics: A novel framework for cybercrime investigation and digital evidence extraction. *International Research Journal of Engineering and Technology (IRJET)*, 12(2), 339–345.
17. M. Landauer, S. Onder, F. Skopik, and M. Wurzenberger, "Deep Learning for Anomaly Detection in Log Data: A Survey," *Machine Learning with Applications*, vol. 12, p. 100470, Jun. 2023. doi: 10.1016/j.mlwa.2023.100470.
18. A. Al-Mazrawe and B. Al-Musawi, "Anomaly Detection in Cloud Network: A Review," *BIO Web Conf.*, vol. 97, p. 00019, 2024. doi: 10.1051/bioconf/20249700019.
19. D. Alharthi, "Cloud Investigation Automation Framework (CIAF): An AI-Driven Approach to Cloud Forensics," *arxiv.org/*, [Online]. Available: https://arxiv.org/html/2510.00452v1?utm_source=chatgpt.com.
20. S. Abuowaida *et al.*, "Evidence Detection in Cloud Forensics: Classifying Cyber-Attacks in IaaS Environments using Machine Learning," *Data and Metadata*, vol. 4, p. 699, Feb. 2025. doi: 10.56294/dm2025699.
21. R. Geetha, S. Vidhya, M. A. Mukunthan, D. S. Goud, J. A. Anand, and R. Kesavan, "Predicting Online Vulnerability among Children and Youth: A Machine Learning Approach with Decision Trees and Naive Bayes Algorithms," 2025 Global Conference in Emerging Technology (GINOTECH), PUNE, India, 2025, pp. 1–6.
22. A. Mohanty, A. G. Mohapatra, N. Nayak, S. Bairavel, C. M. H., M. Lakshmi, A. Govindaram, and A. J. Anand, "Optimizing Diesel Generators in Industrial Settings with IoT and Machine Learning," *International Journal of Information Technology*, pp. 1–9, Aug. 2025.
23. S. Sajithabanu, S. T. Devika, S. Deeba, and A. Jose Anand, "The Role of VR and AR in Intelligent Computing: Applications in Psychology and Autism," in B. Sundaravadivazhagan, N. Gnanasankaran, Pethuru Raj, and A. Saleem Raja (Eds.), *Virtual Reality and Augmented Reality with 6G Communication*, Ch-13. Wiley Publication 17 Oct 2025.
24. R. Geetha, P. Thilagavathi, Jose A. Anand, A. Govindaram, J. G. S., and D. Parameswari, "Detection and Classification of Faults in a Power System with Inverter Penetration Based on a Real-Time Machine Learning Application," *2025 Fourth International Conference on Smart Technologies, Communication and Robotics (STCR)*, Sathyamangalam, India, 2025, pp. 1–6.
25. A. Suganya, D. Parameswari, R. Geetha, A. Govindaram, S. Bahuguna, and J. A. Anand, "Comparison of Machine Learning Methods for Fraudulent Transaction Classification," *2025 6th International Conference for Emerging Technology (INCET)*, Belgaum, India, 2025, pp. 1–7.
26. M. A. Mukunthan, Jose Anand A. A., S. Kesavan, M. Mutyala, R. Kesavan, and R. Geetha, "Detection of Physical Anomalies in IoT Networks Using Machine Learning Techniques," 2024 International Conference on Advancement in Renewable Energy and Intelligent Systems (AREIS), Thrissur, India, 2024, pp. 1–6.

27. R. Rajasree, R. Geetha, S. Vidhya, M. A. Mukunthan, S. Hari Kumar and J. A. Anand, "Comparative Analysis of Feature Engineering-Based Learning and Deep Learning Approaches for Classification Problems on Imbalanced Datasets," 2025 4th OPJU International Technology Conference (OTCON) on Smart Computing for Innovation and Advancement in Industry 5.0, Raigarh, India, 2025, pp. 1–6.
28. K. Jayasakthi, M. S., N. Rajkumar, V. S. Patil, A. Pawar and J. A. Anand, "Comparative Analysis of Deep Learning and Machine Learning Models for DDoS Attack Detection," 2025 4th OPJU International Technology Conference (OTCON) on Smart Computing for Innovation and Advancement in Industry 5.0, Raigarh, India, 2025, pp. 1–6.
29. H. M. Moyeenudin, T. Anuradha, K. Niraimathy, C. Devika, P. V. Baby and J. Anand Anand, "Artificial Intelligence based Sustainable Parking Slot Alerting System with Cloud Platform," 2024 1st International Conference on Sustainability and Technological Advancements in Engineering Domain (SUSTAINED), Faridabad, India, 2024, pp. 711–716.
30. K. Keerthana, Jose A. Anand, R. Kesavan, S. Kesavan, R. Geetha, and S. Vidhya, "IoT-Enabled Disaster Prevention: Leveraging Transfer Learning for Remote Monitoring," 2024 1st International Conference on Sustainability and Technological Advancements in Engineering Domain (SUSTAINED), Faridabad, India, 2024, pp. 492–498.
31. K. Kumar Nalla, "Predictive Analytics with AI for Cloud Security Risk Management," *World Journal of Advanced Engineering Technology and Sciences*, vol. 10, no. 2, pp. 297–308, Dec. 2023. doi: 10.30574/wjaets.2023.10.2.0298.
32. M. Alazab, R. Abu Khurma, A. Awajan, and M. Wedyan, "Digital Forensics Classification Based on a Hybrid Neural Network and the Salp Swarm Algorithm," *Electronics*, vol. 11, no. 12, p. 1903, Jun. 2022. doi: 10.3390/electronics11121903.
33. D. Dunsin, M. C. Ghanem, K. Ouazzane, and V. Vassilev, "A Novel Reinforcement Learning Model for Post-Incident Malware Investigations," Jan. 12, 2025, *arXiv*: arXiv:2410.15028. doi: 10.48550/arXiv.2410.15028.
34. G. Michelet, F. Breitinger, and G. Horsman, "Automation for Digital Forensics: Towards a Definition for the Community," *Forensic Science International*, vol. 349, p. 111769, Aug. 2023. doi: 10.1016/j.forsciint.2023.111769.
35. S. Z. El Mestari, G. Lenzini, and H. Demirci, "Preserving Data Privacy in Machine Learning Systems," *Computers & Security*, vol. 137, p. 103605, Feb. 2024. doi: 10.1016/j.cose.2023.103605.
36. N. Saber Rashid and H. Maseeh Yasin, "Privacy-Preserving Machine Learning: A Review of Federated Learning Techniques and Applications," *International Journal of Scientific World*, vol. 11, no. 1, pp. 30–39, Feb. 2025. doi: 10.14419/af03y111.
37. Z. Zhang, H. A. Hamadi, E. Damiani, C. Y. Yeun, and F. Taher, "Explainable Artificial Intelligence Applications in Cyber Security: State-of-the-Art in Research," *IEEE Access*, vol. 10, pp. 93104–93139, 2022. doi: 10.1109/ACCESS.2022.3204051.
38. L. Longo *et al.*, "Explainable Artificial Intelligence (XAI) 2.0: A Manifesto of Open Challenges and Interdisciplinary Research Directions," *Information Fusion*, vol. 106, p. 102301, Jun. 2024. doi: 10.1016/j.inffus.2024.102301.
39. P. Zheng, Z. Jiang, J. Wu, and Z. Zheng, "Blockchain-Based Decentralized Application: A Survey," *IEEE Open Journal of the Computer Society*, vol. 4, pp. 121–133, 2023. doi: 10.1109/OJCS.2023.3251854.
40. U. Jain, "Challenges in Maintaining Data Privacy and Compliance in Multi-tenant Cloud Environments," *JQST*, vol. 1, no. 4, Oct. 2024. doi: 10.63345/jqst.v1i4.203.
41. S. Limkar, "Blockchain Technology for Ensuring Data Integrity in Cloud Computing," *cfs*, pp. 76–83, Nov. 2024. doi: 10.52710/cfs.37.
42. N. Moosavi and H. Taherdoost, "Blockchain Technology Application in Security: A Systematic Review," *Blockchains*, vol. 1, no. 2, pp. 58–72, Oct. 2023. doi: 10.3390/blockchains1020005.
43. E. Al-Masri, Y. Bai, and J. Li, "A Fog-Based Digital Forensics Investigation Framework for IoT Systems," in *2018 IEEE International Conference on Smart Cloud (SmartCloud)*, New York, NY: IEEE, Sep. 2018, pp. 196–201. doi: 10.1109/SmartCloud.2018.00040.

44. S. A. Ali, S. Memon, and F. Sahito, "Challenges and Solutions in Cloud Forensics," in *Proceedings of the 2018 2nd International Conference on Cloud and Big Data Computing*, Barcelona Spain: ACM, Aug. 2018, pp. 6–10. doi: 10.1145/3264560.3264565.
45. M. Raza, M. Jasim Saeed, M. B. Riaz, and M. Awais Sattar, "Federated Learning for Privacy-Preserving Intrusion Detection in Software-Defined Networks," *IEEE Access*, vol. 12, pp. 69551–69567, 2024. doi: 10.1109/ACCESS.2024.3395997.
46. V. Prakash, A. Williams, L. Garg, P. Barik, and R. K. Dhanaraj, "Cloud-Based Framework for Performing Digital Forensic Investigations," *International Journal of Wireless Information Networks*, vol. 29, no. 4, pp. 419–441, Dec. 2022. doi: 10.1007/s10776-022-00560-z.
47. O. S. Igonor, M. B. Amin, and S. Garg, "The Application of Blockchain Technology in the Field of Digital Forensics: A Literature Review," *Blockchains*, vol. 3, no. 1, p. 5, Feb. 2025. doi: 10.3390/blockchains3010005.
48. F. Prakash and H. Sadawarti, "Blockchain-Based Chain of Custody: A Secure Digital Evidence Framework for Digital Forensics Investigation," *Applied Innovative Research*, vol. 3, no. 1–4, pp. 108–112, 2022. Available: https://www.researchgate.net/publication/380909587_Blockchain-Based_Chain_Of_Custody_A_Secure_Digital_Evidence_Framework_For_Digital_Forensics_Investigation.
49. B. Zhang, M. Xu, and Z. Pan, "Human-AI Collaborative Game Testing with Vision Language Models," 2025, arXiv. doi: 10.48550/ARXIV.2501.11782.
50. K. Saini, S. S. Sonone, M. S. Sankhla, and N. Kumar, *Artificial Intelligence in Forensic Science: An Emerging Technology in Criminal Investigation Systems*, 1st ed. Boca Raton: CRC Press, 2024. doi: 10.4324/9781003287810.
51. Y. S. Sangwan, S. Lal, P. Bhambri, A. Kumar, and I. S. Dhanoa, "Advancements in Social Data Security and Encryption: A Review," *Natural Volatiles & Essential Oils*, vol. 8, no. 4, pp. 15353–15362, 2021. https://www.cabidigitallibrary.org/doi/full/10.5555/20220170098.
52. P. Bhambri, V. K. Sinha, and M. Jaiswal, "Change in Iris Dimensions as a Potential Human Consciousness Level Indicator," *International Journal of Innovative Technology and Exploring Engineering*, vol. 8, no. 9S, pp. 517–525, 2019.
53. V. K. Sinha, R. Jeet, P. Bhambri, and M. Mahajan, "Empowering Intrusion Detection in IRIS Recognition System: A Review," *Journal of Natural Remedies*, vol. 21, no. 2, pp. 131–153, 2020.
54. R. Rana and P. Bhambri, "The Role of IoT in Shaping the Future of Geospatial AI," in D. Darwish and H. Chemingui (Eds.), *Recent Trends in Geospatial AI* (pp. 177–216). IGI Global Scientific Publishing, 2024. https://doi.org/10.4018/979-8-3693-8054-3.ch007.
55. R. Rana and P. Bhambri, "Generative AI-driven Security Frameworks for Web Engineering: Innovations and Challenges," in I. A. Shah and N. Z. Jhanjhi (Eds.), *Generative AI for Web Engineering Models* (pp. 285–296). IGI Global, 2024. https://doi.org/10.4018/979-8-3693-3703-5.ch014.
56. P. Bhambri, "Artificial Intelligence Enabled Internet of Medical Things for Enhanced Healthcare Systems," in P. Bhambri, R. Soni, and T. A. Tran (Eds.), *Smart Healthcare Systems: AI and IoT Perspectives* (pp. 1–17). CRC Press, 2024. https://doi.org/10.1201/9781032698519-1.
57. R. Rana and P. Bhambri, "Digital Twin for Sustainable Industrial Development," in S. Rani, P. Bhambri, S. Kumar, P. K. Pareek, and A. A. Elngar (Eds.), *AI-driven Digital Twin and Industry 4.0: A Conceptual Framework with Applications* (pp. 241–253). CRC Press, Taylor & Francis Group, 2024. https://doi.org/10.1201/9781003395416-15.
58. G. Singh and P. Bhambri, "Simulation Analysis of AODV and DSDV Routing Protocols for Secure and Reliable Service in Mobile Adhoc Networks (MANETs)," in P. Bhambri, S. Rani, V. E. Balas, and A. A. Elngar (Eds.), *Integration of AI-based Manufacturing and Industrial Engineering Systems with the Internet of Things* (1st ed., pp. 205–216). CRC Press, 2023. https://doi.org/10.1201/9781003383505.
59. P. Bhambri and A. Khang, "Computational Intelligence in Manufacturing Technologies," in *Impact and Potential of Machine Learning in the Metaverse* (pp. 327–356). IGI Global, 2024. https://doi.org/10.4018/979-8-3693-5762-0.ch013.
60. A. Jain, M. Singh, and P. Bhambri, "Performance Evaluation of IPv4-IPv6 Tunneling Procedure using IoT," *Journal of Physics: Conference Series*, vol. 1950, no. 1, p. 012010, 2021, August. IOP Publishing.

Chapter 7

AI and automation in cloud forensics for digital investigations and E-Discovery

Saravanan Muniswamy and Mithileysh Sathiyanarayanan

7.1 INTRODUCTION: THE CRISIS OF EPHEMERAL EVIDENCE

The rapid and profound transformation of enterprise IT architectures into autonomous, cloud-native ecosystems has precipitated a fundamental crisis within the field of digital forensics [1–5]. Modern cloud environments are no longer static repositories of data but are defined by AI-driven orchestration, self-healing pipelines, and automated policy engines that continuously, and often unpredictably, modify system state at machine speed [6–10]. This unprecedented velocity of change, quantified by cloud events occurring at microsecond scales across massively distributed resources, means that traditional, post-incident forensic models—which rely on collecting and analyzing static logs or disk images—are rendered obsolete. The central challenge lies in the ephemeral nature of evidence, which often resides transiently in memory, temporary tokens, or a volatile state before being deliberately or automatically destroyed by the very automation designed to ensure operational resilience, such as garbage collection, container eviction, or resource termination [10, 19].

The forensic discipline faces three critical challenges posed by this autonomous paradigm as shown in Figure 7.1. Firstly, data volume and velocity overwhelm conventional logging and storage systems, making it practically impossible to maintain a comprehensive historical record of every single event. Secondly, the fundamental evidentiary unit has shifted from a stable file on a disk to a synthetic, non-human action executed by an intelligent agent or bot; this action is defined not by a human keystroke but by a complex algorithm or policy, making the reconstruction of causal linkage incredibly difficult. Lastly, the ultimate legal and technical barrier is the inability to capture and verify machine intent—the crucial metadata explaining why an autonomous system took a specific action, such as deleting a resource or escalating a privilege. Without this intent metadata, establishing a legally defensible chain of custody and proving malice or negligence becomes tenuous, particularly across federated, multi-cloud boundaries where jurisdictional disputes further complicate matters [13, 18, 23].

- **Key Dimensions of the Forensic Crisis:**
  - **Ephemeral Evidence:** Data (e.g., RAM state of a Serverless function) is destroyed before traditional capture can occur [10].
  - **Automation-Induced Destruction:** Self-healing systems actively eliminate forensic artifacts as part of remediation [19].
  - **Loss of Human Intent:** Actions are driven by algorithmic policies, creating a gap in establishing *mens rea* or legal causation [13, 23].

DOI: 10.1201/9781003656487-7

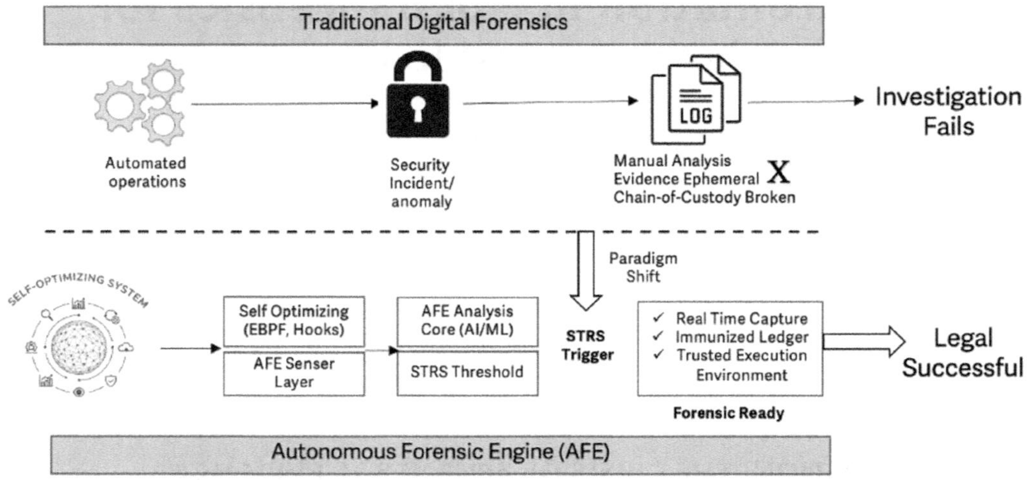

Figure 7.1 Autonomous cloud forensic paradigms.

This chapter proposes that to investigate incidents in the autonomous cloud effectively, forensic capability must transition from a reactive, post-incident process to an integrated, real-time mechanism [1, 18]. We argue for the necessity of *forensics-by-design*, introducing the *Autonomous Forensics Engine* (*AFE*) framework—a cloud-native system designed to proactively monitor behavioral baselines. The AFE's core function is to generate the *Forensic-Ready Intelligence Stream* (*FRIS*), a structured, high-integrity data format containing the necessary real-time state and machine intent metadata. This paradigm shift, from log analysis to intent capture and preservation, is essential to regain investigative visibility and ensure the legal defensibility of digital evidence in the era of self-optimizing cloud ecosystems [11, 22].

7.1.1 Aim of the chapter

The primary aim of this chapter is to address the *forensic visibility gap* created by the rapid adoption of autonomous, self-optimizing cloud computing paradigms, such as serverless and container orchestration [9, 10]. Traditional, post-incident digital forensics (DFIR) models are fundamentally undermined by the ephemeral nature and velocity of modern cloud resources, leading to the destruction of critical volatile evidence and the subsequent failure of the legally required *chain of custody* [1, 5, 13, 18]. This chapter aims to provide a robust, architectural solution by proposing the *Autonomous Forensics Engine* (*AFE*) framework and the *Forensic-Ready Intelligence Stream* (*FRIS*) data model [11, 12]. The overarching goal is to shift the forensic paradigm from a reactive compliance exercise to a proactive, integrated capability—a model we define as *Forensics-by-Design*.

7.1.2 Objectives

The key objectives of this chapter are to:

- *Analyze the limitations* of current cloud forensic methodologies, detailing how concepts like "detection time" and "self-healing" actively lead to the corruption and loss of critical evidence [5, 6, 8].

- *Establish the necessity* for capturing evidence at the point of origin by introducing the core components of the AFE, specifically the *AFE Sensor Layer* (using eBPF and Hooks) and the *AFE Analysis Core* (using AI/ML Behavioral Models) [15–17, 30].
- *Define the structure and content* of the *Forensic-Ready Intelligence Stream* (*FRIS*) to ensure captured evidence is complete, auditable, and legally defensible, incorporating machine intent and automated causality [11, 20, 21].
- *Architect the mechanisms for non-repudiation* using technologies like *Trusted Execution Environments* (*TEEs*) for real-time capture sealing and *Distributed Ledger Technology* (*DLT*) for creating an immutable, machine-attested chain of custody [26 –29, 31].
- *Illustrate the integration* of the AFE/FRIS framework into the wider legal and investigative landscape, transforming the *Electronic Discovery Reference Model* (*EDRM*) process [22, 24, 25].

7.1.3 Chapter contributions

The primary contributions of this chapter to the field of Digital Forensics and Cloud Security are:

- **Formalizing the Forensic Visibility Gap:** Providing a clear, architectural articulation of why and how self-optimizing cloud systems destroy volatile forensic evidence before human or traditional processes can intervene.
- **Introduction of the Autonomous Forensics Engine (AFE) Framework:** Proposing a novel, real-time, event-driven architecture that is integrated into the cloud control plane to continuously monitor and autonomously capture evidence.
- **The FRIS Data Model:** Defining a standardized, structured data model (*FRIS*) that moves beyond basic logs to include essential *Intent Metadata* and integrity anchors, thus guaranteeing evidential completeness and legal fitness.
- **State Transition Risk Score (STRS):** Introducing a quantifiable, AI-driven metric for autonomously deciding *when* and *what* evidence to capture, thus eliminating dependence on slow, human-defined alerting thresholds.
- **The Forensics-by-Design Paradigm:** Shifting the industry conceptualization of forensics from a reactive process to an intrinsic security and architectural requirement, thereby enhancing the overall legal defensibility of cloud operations.

7.2 RELATED WORK AND FOUNDATIONAL PARADIGMS

To justify the necessity of the Autonomous Forensics Engine (AFE) framework, this section conducts a critical review of existing scholarly and technical paradigms, establishing the intellectual gaps that the AFE and Forensic-Ready Intelligence Stream (FRIS) aim to fill [11–20]. We must demonstrate a deep understanding of why current methods, even those adapted for cloud use, fail when confronted with autonomous systems.

7.2.1 Critique of traditional digital forensics and cloud adaptation

The foundational principles of Digital Forensics and Incident Response (DFIR) were established in an era of static, physical evidence, where the primary challenge was data recovery and integrity preservation on hard drives and stable server images [12, 13]. Current cloud

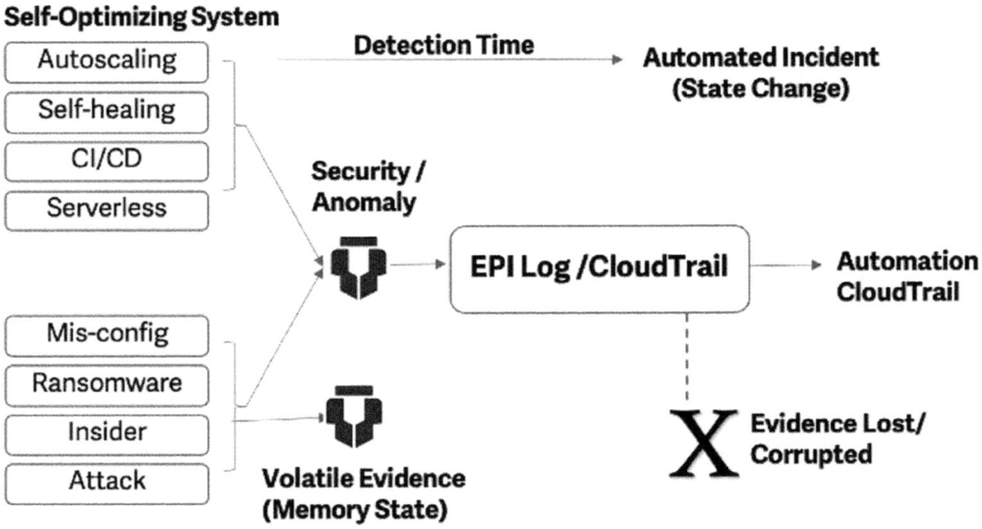

Figure 7.2 Forensic visibility gap.

forensics has largely been an attempt to retrofit these principles to a dynamic, virtualized environment. The prevailing approach relies heavily on API logging and snapshot acquisition, exemplified by services like AWS CloudTrail, Azure Monitor, and GCP Cloud Logging [33]. These tools accurately record what API call was made, by whom, and when. However, this approach suffers from profound limitations as shown in Figure 7.2, especially regarding high-velocity, ephemeral resources. Crucially, API logs capture only the external interface interaction, failing to capture the internal memory state, intermediate computations, or pre-execution logic of a volatile resource like a serverless function instance or a Kubernetes pod about to be evicted [5, 10].

The most critical technical failure is the Time-of-Check-to-Time-of-Use (TOCTTOU) problem in forensic acquisition [1, 33]. When a suspicious event is flagged, the time elapsed between detection and the successful acquisition of a disk or memory snapshot is often measured in seconds or minutes. In the self-healing, autonomous cloud, this window is fatal. During this delay, the automated orchestration layer, acting on its own programmed policies, may:

- *Terminate the instance* (e.g., auto-scaling down).
- *Wipe the memory* (e.g., termination of a serverless function).
- *Modify the state* (e.g., a remediation bot isolating the compromised resource).

This rapid, non-human modification destroys the evidential value of a later snapshot, rendering the evidence unreliable for legal proceedings [21–25]. Furthermore, API logs can be spoofed, manipulated, or incomplete, providing an insufficient basis to establish the *non-repudiation* required for critical state changes.

7.2.2 Review of AI and machine learning in contemporary DFIR

The application of artificial intelligence and machine learning (AI/ML) in DFIR is an established field, but its current role is predominantly remedial and passive, serving as an investigative aid after the data has been collected [31–35]. We can categorize existing AI applications in forensics into three main areas:

1. **Classification and Identification (Supervised Learning):** Using models like Support Vector Machines (SVMs) or Deep Neural Networks to classify recovered files (e.g., identifying malware families, classifying file fragments as sensitive data, or labeling network flows as malicious).
2. **Clustering and Correlation (Unsupervised Learning):** Applying algorithms like K-Means or DBSCAN to group vast quantities of unstructured data (e.g., clustering related log entries, identifying recurring attack patterns across disparate endpoints, or grouping suspicious file metadata).
3. **Natural Language Processing (NLP):** Using large language models to process and summarize massive volumes of unstructured communication and human-generated logs (e.g., email or chat records) to quickly identify topics of interest.

While powerful, these techniques operate on historical, aggregated data. They do not solve the fundamental problem of ephemeral evidence capture; they only make the analysis of captured data more efficient [26–30]. The AFE, by contrast, requires AI not just for analysis, but for real-time behavioral modeling and predictive anomaly detection—a proactive function necessary to trigger capture at the instant a state change occurs, thereby shifting the paradigm from post-facto analysis to real-time intervention [11, 30]. This necessitates highly specific, low-latency machine learning models built for time-series anomaly detection on operational telemetry, not just batch processing of aggregated logs.

7.2.3 The legal and technical gap in E-Discovery and chain of custody

The shift to autonomous multi-cloud environments introduces severe complications for legal discovery and the strict maintenance of the chain of custody. Legal frameworks, such as the Federal Rules of Civil Procedure (*FRCP Rule 26*) in the United States, mandate that organizations preserve all potentially relevant electronically stored information (ESI) as part of a Legal Hold [36–40]. In a cloud environment where data is constantly being migrated, replicated, and erased by automated policies (such as data lifecycle management or compliance with the GDPR's Right to Erasure), fulfilling this duty of preservation is technically fraught.

- **Jurisdictional Complexity:** Data is often replicated across global regions, complicating cross-border discovery and compliance with data sovereignty laws [23].
- **Lack of Control:** Enterprises rely on Cloud Service Providers (CSPs) for underlying data management, creating a dependency on the CSP's API logging that is insufficient for the granular proof required in court.
- **The Chain-of-Custody Break:** Traditional chain-of-custody protocols require human witnesses to attest to the handling of evidence. When evidence is captured, hashed, and moved by non-human, automated agents, this human-attested link is broken, potentially invalidating the evidence [14, 23]. This deficiency is precisely what the AFE/FRIS framework addresses by integrating Trusted Execution Environments (TEEs) and an Automated Chain-of-Custody Ledger. These technologies are critical to establishing non-repudiation—proving that the evidence is exactly what it purports to be, having been sealed and notarized by a trusted, immutable system from the moment of capture, thus providing a machine-attested, verifiable history to replace the fragile, human-dependent links in the custody chain. This synthesis of real-time capture and

verifiable immutability represents the necessary foundational leap beyond the limitations of current cloud forensic methods.

7.3 THE AFE/FRIS FRAMEWORK FOR CLOUD FORENSICS

This section details the Autonomous Forensics Engine (AFE) and Forensic-Ready Intelligence Stream (FRIS), the theoretical and architectural core of the proposed forensics-by-design paradigm. The AFE is engineered specifically to overcome the limitations of passive cloud forensics by integrating into the cloud control plane as an active, real-time evidence capture mechanism.

7.3.1 Autonomous Forensics Engines (AFE): Architecture and functionality

The AFE operates on a continuous, closed-loop monitoring and intervention model, designed to capture forensic data non-disruptively at the moment of anomaly. The architecture is logically divided into three primary components: the Sensor Layer, the Analysis Core, and the Preservation Module.

A. The Sensor Layer: Non-Disruptive Telemetry Capture

The Sensor Layer is responsible for ingesting high-fidelity, low-latency telemetry directly from the cloud runtime, operating beneath the traditional API logging layer to capture volatile state. This is crucial for avoiding the TOCTTOU problem. This capture is achieved using specialized, non-disruptive technologies designed to minimize impact on service performance or integrity.

- **eBPF Probes (Extended Berkeley Packet Filter):** This powerful Linux kernel technology allows the AFE to run sandboxed monitoring programs directly within the kernel space without altering kernel code. This grants the AFE real-time visibility into system calls, network events, and process execution [41–45]. This is essential for capturing pre-execution context and memory access patterns that would otherwise be lost immediately upon resource termination.
- **Service Mesh Interceptors:** For cloud-native microservices architectures, the AFE integrates directly with the service mesh's data plane proxies (like those in Istio or Linkerd). This allows for the interception and deep analysis of all inter-service traffic, function calls, and authorization requests [19, 33]. It captures the precise *micro-segment of interaction* where an anomalous event occurs, providing crucial application-level context.
- **Memory Hooks:** Specialized techniques are deployed to capture volatile memory state for highly ephemeral targets (such as Function-as-a-Service instances) by hooking into the runtime environment, allowing for near-instantaneous memory dumping before the resource is terminated or reclaimed by the cloud orchestrator.

B. The Analysis Core: Behavioral Modeling and Risk Scoring

The Analysis Core is the intelligence hub of the AFE. Its primary task is to differentiate normal automated behavior from malicious or misconfigured activity that warrants forensic capture. Given that adversaries or misconfigurations often manifest as subtle deviations from programmed behavior, the core utilizes unsupervised machine learning techniques (like Isolation Forests or deep autoencoders) to establish a continuous baseline of "normal" cloud state [46–50]. This includes expected resource usage, API call sequences, and policy enforcement timing for automated agents. This core continuously calculates the *State Transition Risk Score (STRS)*, a formal, composite metric that quantifies the need for forensic intervention [11, 30]. The STRS is calculated based on three key weighted factors: the Behavioral Deviation (how far the current activity deviates from the learned baseline), the Resource Sensitivity (a pre-assigned value based on the criticality of the resource being acted upon), and the Magnitude of Intent Change (how drastically the automated policy has been altered or deviated from its programmed goal). When the STRS exceeds a critical threshold, the Preservation Module is triggered instantly, capturing the state at the precise point of anomaly.

7.3.2 Forensic-Ready Intelligence Streams (FRIS): The new evidence model

The Forensic-Ready Intelligence Stream (FRIS) is the formalized, structured data unit designed to replace unstructured logs as the primary evidentiary artifact [11, 20]. FRIS addresses both the legal requirement for completeness and the technical necessity for automated correlation. Unlike traditional logs that only record *what* happened, FRIS is built to capture *why*, *how*, and *who* (or *what* automated agent) initiated the action. The FRIS schema is meticulously designed to include several mandatory, high-integrity metadata fields:

- **Temporal and Identity:** Highly synchronized *UTC Timestamp* and the specific *Actor_ID*, crucially distinguishing between human identities and synthetic identities like bots or remediation agents [18, 33].
- **State Capture:** The *Resource_State_Before* and *Resource_State_After* snapshots of the resource's configuration or memory captured by the Sensor Layer [10, 15].
- **Intent Metadata:** The specific *Policy_UUID* or *Algorithm_Confidence_Score* that motivated the automated action, providing the traceable machine intent necessary to establish legal causation [30, 32].
- **Data Integrity Anchor:** A *cryptographic hash* applied immediately to the entire FRIS packet [26, 27].

This structured approach ensures that the data is ready for ingestion into E-Discovery platforms without extensive manual pre-processing and provides an auditable, machine-readable causal chain.

7.3.3 Mechanisms for immutable evidence preservation

The integrity of the AFE framework rests on two technological pillars of immutability that secure the evidence against adversarial tampering and chain-of-custody challenges.

A. Trusted Execution Environments (TEEs)

The most sensitive components of the AFE—specifically the Analysis Core and the immediate hashing functions within the Preservation Module—must operate within Trusted Execution Environments (TEEs), such as *Intel SGX* or *AMD SEV* [28, 29]. TEEs create a secure, isolated region of memory that is protected from the host operating system, the hypervisor, and even cloud administrators. This provides:

- **Integrity of the Capture Process:** It guarantees that the AFE's ML models (STRS calculation) and the hashing algorithm used to secure the FRIS cannot be tampered with by an attacker who has compromised the host system.
- **Sealing the Evidence at the Source:** The evidence is cryptographically sealed and hashed *inside the enclave* immediately upon capture, establishing a trustworthy root of evidence that cannot be repudiated.

B. Automated Chain-of-Custody Ledgers

The challenge of maintaining a continuous chain of custody across multi-cloud, multi-jurisdictional environments is solved by integrating a distributed ledger technology (DLT), such as a permissioned blockchain like *Hyperledger Fabric*, as the forensic notarization layer [27, 31].

- Every cryptographically hashed FRIS packet is instantly transmitted to the DLT.
- The DLT network (managed by a consortium of auditors, enterprises, or CSPs) adds the hash and a verified timestamp to the ledger.

This creates an immutable, machine-attested audit trail that documents the evidence's existence and integrity from the moment of its creation, providing continuous, non-repudiable proof of custody across all necessary boundaries, thereby solving the core legal headache of evidence handling.

7.4 DIGITAL INVESTIGATIONS AND E-DISCOVERY IN THE AUTONOMOUS ERA

The introduction of the Autonomous Forensics Engine (AFE) and Forensic-Ready Intelligence Stream (FRIS) fundamentally mandates a revolutionary shift in both digital investigation methodologies and the established framework of Electronic Discovery (E-Discovery). No longer can investigators follow a purely reactive, human-centric approach; instead, they must embrace the AI-as-Co-Investigator Model, focusing on validating and interpreting machine-generated intelligence rather than manually assembling logs [13, 32]. This section elaborates on the practical application of the AFE/FRIS framework, detailing its impact on workflow, legal defensibility, and compliance with judicial standards.

7.4.1 The AI-as-Co-Investigator model and workflow transformation

The AFE transforms the investigator's role from a tedious data collector and correlator into a high-level validator and intelligence interpreter [32]. When the AFE's Analysis Core detects an anomaly, exceeding the State Transition Risk Score (STRS), it instantly triggers the capture of a FRIS packet. The human investigator's job begins at this point, where they must assess the machine's findings. This requires a deep reliance on *eXplainable AI (XAI)* principles, which must be embedded within the AFE's decision-making process [30]. The AFE cannot merely flag an event; it must provide an auditable rationale—the *Intent Metadata*—for its decision, proving *why* a particular event was anomalous [30, 32].

- **New Investigative Focus Areas:**
  - **Validation:** Checking the AFE's XAI output against known behavioral profiles.
  - **Interpretation:** Determining the human/policy implication of the automated anomaly.
  - **Legal Triage:** Applying immediate *Litigation Hold* based on high-integrity FRIS data [22].

This new workflow dramatically alters the conventional sequence, prioritizing near-instantaneous, high-integrity evidence preservation over slow, post-incident collection. The investigator focuses on the most valuable and secure data points—the notarized FRIS packets—which automatically carry the necessary context and cryptographic proof of non-tampering (due to the Trusted Execution Environment, TEE, and the Automated Ledger) [28, 31].

7.4.2 Streamlining E-Discovery and litigation hold

The challenges associated with E-Discovery in legacy cloud environments—which typically involve massive data volume, format disparity, and complex custodian identification—are largely mitigated by the structured nature of FRIS [22, 25]. By providing a common, machine-readable schema for evidence, the AFE framework significantly streamlines the initial and most costly stages of the *Electronic Discovery Reference Model* (*EDRM*): Collection, Processing, and Review [22]. The FRIS data, by its design, eliminates the need for extensive data processing (normalization, de-duplication) because it is already collected in a structured format and notarized with an immutable hash. Crucially, the AFE enables *surgical, targeted preservation* for legal holds [14, 24]. Instead of placing a hold on an entire cloud account or storage bucket, the legal team can precisely isolate FRIS records based on specific metadata fields, such as `Policy_UUID`, `Actor_ID` (if linked to a custodian), or a temporal range surrounding the anomaly. This targeted approach adheres to the spirit of the *Federal Rules of Civil Procedure* (*FRCP*) by ensuring that relevant data is protected while dramatically reducing the data volume subject to discovery, saving significant time and cost during the Review phase [24, 25]. The continuous nature of the AFE ensures that the legal hold is applied in real time, avoiding the data deletion risks associated with asynchronous, human-executed preservation notices.

7.4.3 Legal and admissibility considerations for machine-generated evidence

The most rigorous test of the AFE framework is its legal admissibility in a court of law, which requires satisfying judicial scrutiny regarding authenticity, reliability, and the rule against hearsay [18, 25]. Traditional evidence requires human testimony to establish its provenance, but the AFE relies on machine attestation. We argue that the AFE should be treated as a reliable instrument, similar to laboratory equipment or a breathalyzer, rather than a human witness [18]. The admissibility hinges on two technological guarantees provided by the AFE architecture:

- **Authentication of Evidence:** The *TEE* guarantees that the evidence (FRIS) was captured and hashed in a tamper-proof environment, and the *Automated Chain-of-Custody Ledger* provides non-repudiable verification of its complete history, establishing authenticity even without human witnesses [28, 31].

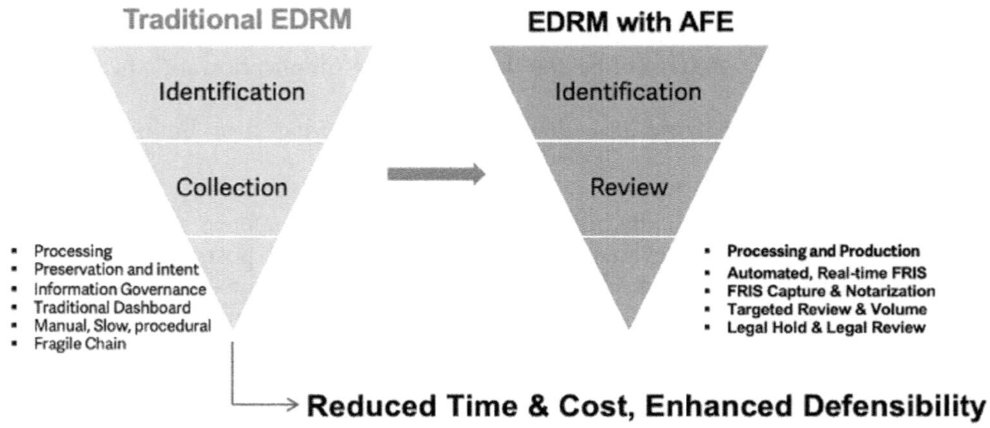

Figure 7.3 Traditional EDRM vs EDRM with AFE.

- **The Intent Metadata as Record:** The FRIS's Intent Metadata, captured directly from the automated policy or algorithm, can be admissible as a "record of a regularly conducted activity" or business record under existing legal frameworks, provided the AFE's underlying behavioral models are properly validated and auditable via XAI [23, 24, 30].

Finally, in multi-jurisdictional investigations, the AFE's use of a distributed, cryptographic ledger provides a continuous, globally verifiable proof of evidence location and state, which helps address compliance with data sovereignty laws (such as *GDPR*) and eases the complexity of cross-border evidence exchange [23] mandated by treaties or legal agreements. The technical rigor of the AFE's capture process thus becomes the new standard for legal defensibility as depicted in Figure 7.3.

7.5 DISCUSSIONS AND KEY TAKEAWAYS

This section synthesizes the core findings of the preceding architectural and methodological discussions, transitioning from the technical description of the AFE/FRIS framework to its strategic implications across legal, economic, and operational domains. The central takeaway is that the challenges posed by the autonomous cloud necessitate a fundamental shift in mindset—from reactive incident management to proactive Forensics-by-Design [1, 18].

7.5.1. The Strategic Imperative of Forensics-by-Design

The implementation of the AFE is not merely a technical upgrade; it is a strategic risk management mandate [61–62]. The traditional model of incident response, based on manual collection and forensic imaging post-event, is not only technologically obsolete but also economically unsustainable. The cost associated with responding to a major breach in an autonomous environment—which includes legal fees, regulatory fines, and the exorbitant labor hours required to manually correlate petabytes of unstructured, incomplete log data—far outweighs the investment required to architect a continuous, automated forensic capability [20, 21].

The Forensics-by-Design philosophy dictates that forensic readiness must be an integral component of the Continuous Integration/Continuous Deployment (CI/CD) pipeline and the cloud governance model, rather than a security add-on. This requires Cloud Service Providers (CSPs) to embed AFE sensor capabilities into their underlying hypervisor and control plane layers, offering verifiable evidence streams as a premium security and compliance service [51, 52]. For client organizations, this means prioritizing procurement decisions based on the verifiability and integrity of the evidence streams provided by the CSP, not just on basic logging features.

- **Forensics-by-Design Key Requirements:**
  - **Cost Mitigation:** Shifting expenditure from expensive manual response to proactive automation [20, 21].
  - **Continuous Auditability:** Integrating evidence generation into the operational pipeline.
  - **Procurement Criteria:** Selecting CSPs that guarantee Trusted Execution Environment (TEE)-sealed evidence streams.

7.5.2 Operationalizing AFE: Integration and skillset transformation

Operationalizing the AFE requires substantial integration and a corresponding transformation of security skillsets. The outputs of the AFE, specifically the Forensic-Ready Intelligence Streams (FRIS) and the high-confidence STRS alerts, must feed directly into existing Security Information and Event Management (SIEM) and Security Orchestration, Automation, and Response (SOAR) platforms as shown in Figure 7.4. The AFE acts as a critical data enrichment source, delivering structured, contextualized data (including Intent Metadata) that allows SOAR playbooks to initiate legal hold procedures, isolate affected components, and trigger deeper human investigation in seconds, dramatically reducing Mean Time To Respond (MTTR) [56–60].

Furthermore, the skillset of the DFIR investigator must evolve into that of an AI-validated intelligence analyst. Future forensic professionals will require expertise in [30–32]:

1. **Machine Learning Operations (MLOps):** Understanding and auditing the AFE's behavioral models.

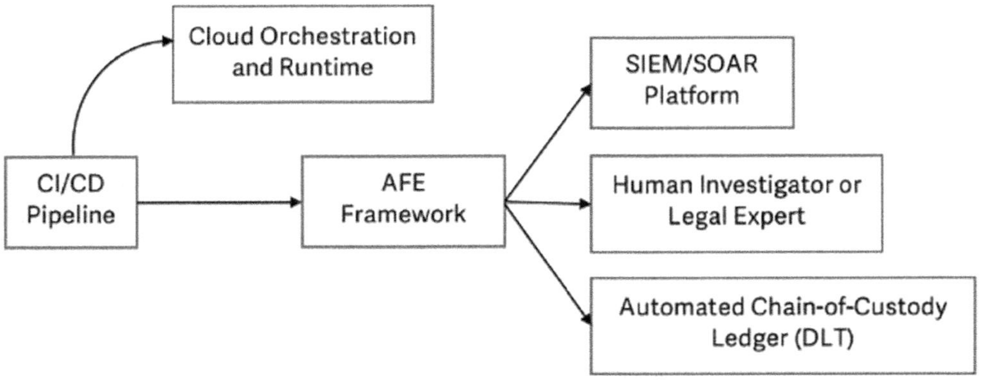

Figure 7.4 AFE integration into DevSecOps and SIEM.

2. **eXplainable AI (XAI):** Interpreting model rationale (e.g., LIME or SHAP scores) to translate automated findings into legally sound narratives.
3. **Distributed Ledger Technology (DLT) Auditing:** Verifying the integrity of the Automated Chain-of-Custody Ledger.

7.5.3 Strengths and opportunities identified

The analysis of the Autonomous Forensics Engine (AFE) model and its integration with the EDRM process reveals several significant strengths and opportunities for transforming the field of cloud security and legal discovery:

1. **Strategic Strengths in Addressing the Visibility Gap**
   - **Real-Time, Non-Disruptive Capture:** The core strength of the AFE is its use of technologies like eBPF and Hooks to capture volatile evidence (Memory and State) at the moment of an anomaly, effectively solving the Forensic Visibility Gap caused by the ephemeral nature of cloud resources [15, 17].
   - **Legal Defensibility:** By sealing the captured evidence within a Trusted Execution Environment (TEE) and notarizing the hash on an Immunized Ledger, the AFE automatically establishes an unbroken, cryptographically verifiable Chain of Custody. This fundamentally enhances the legal admissibility and integrity of the evidence, which is the cornerstone of the "Forensic Ready" concept.
2. **Key Opportunities in Transforming EDRM and Cost**
   - **Automation of Preservation and Collection:** The AFE automates the most time-consuming and fragile steps of the traditional EDRM process—specifically Identification and Collection/Preservation. By delivering the Forensic-Ready Intelligence Stream (FRIS), it significantly reduces the reliance on slow, manual intervention.
   - **Reduced Data Volume and Cost:** Traditional forensic collection often involves capturing entire VM images or vast quantities of unfiltered logs. The AFE, by focusing on the precise moment of state transition, enables Targeted Review and drastically Reduced Data Volume. This, in turn, translates directly into lower storage costs, processing costs, and attorney review time, making large-scale cloud E-Discovery feasible and cost-effective [53–55].
   - **Proactive Risk Management:** The AFE's reliance on the State Transition Risk Score (STRS) moves security from a reactive, log-analysis model to a proactive, behavior-monitoring model [30]. This allows for earlier detection and capture of complex, low-and-slow attacks that might evade static security rules.

7.5.4 Limitations and future challenges

While the AFE/FRIS framework provides a robust solution to the problem of ephemeral evidence, an academically rigorous discussion must acknowledge its inherent limitations and vulnerabilities. These are crucial areas for future research and development [15, 17, 30]:

1. **Computational Overhead:** The continuous, deep-state monitoring required by the AFE Sensor Layer (e.g., extensive eBPF tracing) and the immediate cryptographic hashing applied to every FRIS packet introduce non-trivial computational overhead

and storage demands. Optimization techniques must be developed to ensure the AFE does not become a performance bottleneck [15, 17].

2. **Adversarial AI Attacks:** The AFE's reliance on behavioral modeling makes it vulnerable to highly sophisticated attacks. An attacker could intentionally introduce small, non-anomalous data drift into the system's telemetry over time, subtly altering the AFE's learned baseline without triggering the STRS threshold. This slow poisoning of the model could compromise the AFE's detection integrity [30].
3. **Interoperability and Standardization:** The utility of the AFE is currently constrained by the lack of a standardized FRIS Schema (FRIS-Spec) that can be universally adopted by all major CSPs and forensic tool vendors. Without this standardization, the promise of seamless multi-cloud investigation remains technically challenging.

These limitations define the next frontier in autonomous forensics research, requiring continued collaboration between AI engineers, security architects, and legal experts to harden the framework against advanced persistent threats and operational constraints.

7.6 CONCLUSION AND FUTURE WORK

7.6.1 Conclusion: Establishing forensics-by-design

This chapter successfully articulated the profound crisis of ephemeral evidence precipitated by the shift to autonomous, AI-driven cloud ecosystems, demonstrating the obsolescence of traditional, post-incident forensic methodologies [1, 5]. We established that the speed and self-optimizing nature of modern cloud platforms actively destroy crucial evidential artifacts and break the legally necessary chain of custody [5, 10]. To overcome this, the chapter introduced a foundational paradigm shift: the *Autonomous Forensics Engine* (*AFE*) framework and the *Forensic-Ready Intelligence Stream* (*FRIS*) data model.

The AFE, integrating novel technologies such as *eBPF probes* for real-time capture and *Trusted Execution Environments* (*TEEs*) for sealing evidence at the source, provides the technical solution to the problem of evidential integrity [15, 28]. Furthermore, the FRIS, with its mandatory Intent Metadata and *Automated Chain-of-Custody Ledger* integration, offers the necessary legal rigor, transforming forensic readiness from a reactive compliance burden into a proactive, architecturally mandated capability—the very definition of *Forensics-by-Design* [18, 31]. The successful integration of the AFE into the AI-as-Co-Investigator Model fundamentally reshapes investigative workflow, ensuring that digital systems not only execute business operations but also continuously narrate, preserve, and validate their own history, thereby guaranteeing legal defensibility in the most volatile computing environments ever conceived [13, 32].

- **Key Achievements of the AFE/FRIS Framework:**
  - **Real-Time Capture:** Intercepts ephemeral evidence before destruction via eBPF and sensor hooks [15, 17].
  - **Machine Intent Preservation:** Captures algorithmic rationale needed for legal causation [30, 32].
  - **Non-Repudiation:** Achieved via TEE sealing and Distributed Ledger Technology (DLT) notarization [27, 31].

7.6.2 Future work: Defining the next frontier in autonomous forensics

While the AFE/FRIS framework provides a strong theoretical and architectural foundation, its transition to widespread industry adoption requires sustained academic and industrial effort concentrated on standardization, empirical validation, and adversarial resilience [1, 11]. The following areas define the immediate and long-term research agenda for autonomous forensics:

1. **Standardization and Interoperability (FRIS-Spec):** The utility of FRIS hinges entirely on its adoption across vendor boundaries. Future work must prioritize the development of a vendor-agnostic FRIS Schema (*FRIS-Spec*), detailing the required metadata fields and communication protocols (e.g., using Protobuf or OpenAPI specifications) necessary to ensure seamless exchange and interpretation of autonomous evidence between competing Cloud Service Providers (CSPs), forensic tool vendors, and legal discovery platforms [11, 33].
2. **Empirical Performance Validation:** The theoretical benefits of the AFE must be substantiated by empirical data. Research is needed to quantify the performance overhead—specifically, the latency added by eBPF instrumentation and the CPU cycles consumed by continuous hashing inside TEEs—in high-throughput, production cloud environments [15, 28]. This will require the development of open-source pilot implementations to benchmark the STRS accuracy against false positive rates [11, 30], validating the feasibility of the architecture at scale.
3. **Adversarial Resilience and Model Hardening:** The vulnerability of the AFE's Analysis Core to *Adversarial AI* attacks remains a critical area. Future research must focus on hardening the AFE's behavioral models against deliberate data drift and input manipulation [30, 32] ensuring the AFE cannot be covertly disabled or manipulated by a sophisticated attacker. This includes exploring federated learning approaches for distributed baseline management.
4. **Multi-AFE Orchestration and Data Sovereignty:** Establishing protocols for Multi-AFE Orchestration is essential for multi-cloud investigations. This involves defining the consensus mechanisms necessary for AFE instances across different CSPs and national jurisdictions to securely and compliantly share notarized FRIS hashes, ultimately addressing the complexities of cross-border data access and data sovereignty laws [23, 31].

The evolution of the forensic investigator into an AI-validated intelligence analyst is contingent upon the successful completion of this research agenda, securing the digital history of the autonomous cloud for legal and regulatory accountability.

REFERENCES

1. R. Dhanalakshmi and J. Anand, "Big Data for Personalized Healthcare," In A. Jaya, K. Kalaiselvi, Dinesh Goyal and Dhiya AL-Jumelly (Eds.), *Handbook of Intelligent Healthcare Analytics: Knowledge Engineering with Big Data Analytics*, Chap-4, John Wiley & Sons, Inc., pp. 67–92, 06 May 2022.
2. G. Mohamed, J. Visumathi, Miroslav Mahdal, Jose Anand, and Muniyandy Elangovan, "An Effective and Secure Mechanism for Phishing Attacks using a Machine Learning Approach," *Processes*, Vol. 10, Issue 7, p. 1356, 2022.

3. K. Sivachandar, V. Amudha, B. Ramesh, J. Anand, M. ShanmugaSundari, and Jerril Gilda S., "MIMO-IDMA System Performance for SUI and LTE Frequency Selective Channels," *Advances in Parallel Computing Algorithms, Tools and Paradigms*, Vol. 41, pp. 422–428, Nov 2022.
4. M. Geethalakshmi, J. Anand, R. Nathea, C. Augustine, S. M. Sivaraman, and S. Mahalakshmi, "Trident Fuzzy Aggregation Operators on Right and Left Apex-Base Angles in Parallel Computing," *Advances in Parallel Computing Algorithms, Tools and Paradigms*, Vol. 41, pp. 429–435, Nov 2022.
5. S. Prema, Jose Anand, P. Vanitha, Nirmala Devi K., M. Mohamed Yaseen, and C. Rajeswari, "Smart Stick using Ultrasonic Sensors for Visually Impaired," *Advances in Parallel Computing Algorithms, Tools and Paradigms,* Vol. 41, pp. 436–441, Nov 2022.
6. J. Anand, M. Shobika, and T. Sneha, "Programmable Stickers to Monitor Perishable Goods using Blockchain," *IEEE 2022 Second International Conference on Computer Science, Engineering and Applications (ICCSEA 2022)*, pp. 1–5, 08 Sep 2022.
7. R. Maheswari, S. Vignesh, M. Rakesh Kumar, T. M. Venkatesh, R. Sundar, and J. A. Anand, "Voice Control and Eyeball Movement Operated Wheelchair," *2022 International Conference on Edge Computing and Applications (ICECAA)*, pp. 805–809, 2022.
8. A. Ponmalar, J. A. Anand, Muthamizhan T., T. Sobana, and J. H. Vishwath, "Automatic Forensic Analysis of Criminal Navigation System using Machine Learning," *IEEE Technically Sponsored First International Conference on Computational Science & Technology (ICCST 2022)*, pp. 1–5, 09–10 Nov 2022.
9. S. Ganesh Sundaram, A. Ponmalar, S. Deeba, Jose A. A., and S. Aarthi, "Plane Detection and Product Trail using Augmented Reality," ***IEEE Technically Sponsored First International Conference on Computational Science & Technology*** *(ICCST 2022)*, pp. 1–5, 09–10 Nov 2022.
10. M. Geethalakshmi, J. Venkatesh, R. Uma Mageswari, A. Mahalakshmi, J. Anand, and R. Partheepan, "Fuzzy Based Route Optimization in Wearable Biomedical Wireless Sensor Network," *AIP Conference Proceedings* 2523, 020156, 30 Jan 2023.
11. M. S. Sundari, A. J. Anand, and T. S. Nagarajan, "Smart Aerial Imaging Solution in Precision Agriculture," *2022 International Conference on Data Science, Agents & Artificial Intelligence (ICDSAAI),* Chennai, India, pp. 1–3, 2022.
12. S. Mahalakshmi, C. Rajeswari, A. J. Anand, and A. Rahul, "Client Authentication by Signature Verification Method Using Robotic Process Automation (RPA)," *2022 International Conference on Data Science, Agents & Artificial Intelligence (ICDSAAI)*, Chennai, India, pp. 1–5, 2022.
13. S. G. Sundaram, P. Saravanan, A. Ponmalar, M. G. Prakash, and Jose A. Anand, "Collaborative Product Recommendation System for E-commerce Websites," *IEEE 2022 International Conference on Innovative Computing, Intelligent Communication and Smart Electrical Systems (ICSES)*, Chennai, India, pp. 1–7, 2022.
14. K. Kausalya, D. Gokulakrishnan, S. Aarthi, Jose A. Anand, G. K. R. Bhavana, and A. Ponmalar, "Implementing Virtual Personal Assistant Through Artificial Intelligence Requirements," *2022 First International Conference on Computer, Power and Communication (ICCPC 2022)*, 14–16 Dec Nov 2022.
15. A. Ponmalar, B. Chandra, S. Aarthi, G. Bhavana, A. J. Anand, and S. Gomathi, "IoT Based Automotive Drive Recorder As Black Box," *2022 IEEE International Conference on Computer, Power and Communications (ICCPC),* Chennai, India, pp. 557–561, 2022.
16. R. Thillaikkarasi, M. M. Yaseen, R. Rameshbabu, R. Prabhakaran, R. Kesavan, and Jose A. Anand, "Wayside Inspection Using Wayside Processing Imaging and Deep Learning," *2023 Third International Conference on Pervasive Computing and Social Networking (ICPCSN)*, Salem, India, 2023, pp. 359–365.
17. T. Anuradha, A. Suganya, R. Muthalagu, M. Narender, and Jose A. Anand, "Evaluation of a Wireless Sensor Network for the Detection of Forest Fires," *2023 Second International Conference on Edge Computing and Applications (ICECAA)*, Namakkal, India, 2023, pp. 1021–1027.

18. V. Seedha Devi, K. Sumathi, M. Mahalakshmi, A. J. Anand, A. Titus, and N. Naga Saranya, "Machine Learning based Efficient Human Activity Recognition System," *International Journal of Intelligent Systems and Applications in Engineering*, Vol. 12 (5s), pp. 338–346, 2024.
19. H. M. Moyeenudin, M. Narender, J. Amutharaj, S. Hari Kumar, and Jose A. Anand, "Comparative Analysis of Video Transmission in Vehicular Networks using IEEE 802.11g and IEEE 802.11p Standards," *2023 First International Conference on Advances in Electrical, Electronics and Computational Intelligence (ICAEECI)*, Tiruchengode, India, pp. 1–7, 2023.
20. R. Maheswari, M. Pughazhandhe, S. Ragavan, R. Sasikaran, S. Siva, and A. Jose Anand, "Augmented Reality Home Automation Using AR Switches with IoT," *2023 International Conference on Self Sustainable Artificial Intelligence Systems (ICSSAS)*, Erode, India, 2023, pp. 1681–1688.
21. S. Karuppiah, T. Anuradha, K. Sivachandar, B. Thyla, D. Dhivya, and Jose A. Anand, "Conceptualization of a Cardiac Monitoring System via Bluetooth Communication Protocol to Mobile Devices," *2024 Second International Conference on Intelligent Data Communication Technologies and Internet of Things (IDCIoT)*, Bengaluru, India, pp. 859–866, 2024.
22. S. Hemalatha, M. Mahalakshmi, V. Vignesh, M. Geethalakshmi, D. Balasubramanian, and Jose A. Anand, "Deep Learning Approaches for Intrusion Detection with Emerging Cybersecurity Challenges," *2023 International Conference on Sustainable Communication Networks and Application (ICSCNA)*, Theni, India, pp. 1522–1529, 2023.
23. R. Reshma and A. J. Anand, "Predictive and Comparative Analysis of LENET, ALEXNET and VGG-16 Network Architecture in Smart Behavior Monitoring," *2023 Seventh International Conference on Image Information Processing (ICIIP)*, Solan, India, pp. 450–453, 2023.
24. V. Abiramasundari, B. Thyla, and A. J. Anand, "Wearable Belt Antenna for Human Body Communications at 8.75 GHz," *2023 Seventh International Conference on Image Information Processing (ICIIP)*, Solan, India, pp. 446–449, 2023.
25. M. Yaseen, P. Durai, P. Gokul, S. Justin, and A. J. Anand, "Artificial Intelligence Based Automated Appliances in Smart Home," *2023 Seventh International Conference on Image Information Processing (ICIIP)*, Solan, India, 2023, pp. 442–445.
26. T. Anuradha, J. Jeni Sharmila P., Kanimozhiraman, K. Kalaiselvi, C. K. Shruthi, and Jose A. Anand, "Automatic Categorization of Emails into Folders Based on the Content of the Messages," *2024 Third International Conference on Intelligent Techniques in Control, Optimization and Signal Processing (INCOS)*, Krishnankoil, Virudhunagar district, Tamil Nadu, India, 2024, pp. 1–6.
27. S. F. Subhamathi, C. Sathiyapriyan, A. T., A. J. Anand, A. Rheem, and M. R. Arun, "Traffic Sign Detection Problems using Convolutional Neural Techniques in Image Processing," *2024 International Conference on Intelligent Systems for Cybersecurity (ISCS)*, Gurugram, India, 2024, pp. 1–6.
28. S. Hannah, S. Jeevitha, T. Anuradha, A. J. Anand, G. Porkodi, and R. Vijayakumar, "Thyroid Nodule Classification Model from Scintigraphy Images using Convolutional Neural Networks," *2024 Fifth International Conference on Innovative Trends in Information Technology (ICITIIT)*, Kottayam, India, 2024, pp. 1–6.
29. T. S. Arulananth, Jose A. Anand, S. Jayanthi, P. Manaswini, G. Viswa Sai Teja, R. Taruni G., and N. Krishna Prasad, "Automatic Certificate Generation and Security Implementation Using LSB and Hybrid Watermarking Techniques," In S. Bandyopadhyay, V. E. Balas, S. K. Biswas, A. K. Saha, and D. M. Thounaoja (Eds.), *Intelligent Computing Systems and Applications*, ICICSA 2023, Lecture Notes in Networks and Systems, Vol 1010, Springer, Singapore, 2024.
30. M. S. Ramachandran, S. Sajithabanu, A. Ponmalar, M. Mohamed Sithik, and Jose A. Anand, "Fraud Detection and Risk Management Using AI in Business Intelligence," In A. Natarajan, M. Galety, C. Iwendi, D. Das, and A. Shankar (Eds.), *Intersection of AI and Business Intelligence in Data-Driven Decision-Making* (pp. 117–150). IGI Global, 2024. https://doi.org/10.4018/979-8-3693-5288-5.ch005.
31. C. Ananth, O. Ibrahim Khalaf, and J. Anand (Eds.), "Quantum Networks and Their Applications in AI," *IGI Global*, 2024. https://doi.org/10.4018/979-8-3693-5832-0.

32. S. Krishnan, A. J. Anand, and R. Kumar (Eds.), *Sustainable Development Goals: Technologies and Opportunities* (first ed.). pages 330, CRC Press, 2024. eBook ISBN 9781003468257. https://doi.org/10.1201/9781003468257.
33. J. Anand and S. Krishnan, *Smart Technologies for Sustainable Development Goals: No Poverty* (first ed.). pages 284. CRC Press, 2024, eBook ISBN 9781003519010. https://doi.org/10.1201/9781003519010.
34. B. Pawar, G. Kannan, T. Anuradha, V. V, R. Kesavan, and A. Jose Anan, "Resource Allocation and Energy Efficient Dynamic Particle Swarm Optimization in Heterogeneous Wireless Communication Networks," 2024 Fourth Asian Conference on Innovation in Technology (ASIANCON), Pimari Chinchwad, India, 2024, pp. 1–6.
35. N. J. Gopal, S. Muthukaruppasamy, A. Sampaul Thomas, A. Adaikalam I Doss, J. A Anand, and H. Gowtham, "Identifying Modern Pedagogy Method to Enhance the Effectiveness of Teaching and Learning Process," In Saravanan Krishnan, A. Jose Anand, and Raghvendra Kumar (Eds.), *Sustainable Development Goals: Technologies and Opportunities,* Ch-4, pages 21. CRC Press, 2024. eBook ISBN9781003468257 https://doi.org/10.1201/9781003468257
36. C. R. Jothy, J. E. Judith, Jegan C. Dhayananth, Anand A. Jose, T. Jarin, and Sheik Mohammed Sulthan. Smart "Supply Chain Management for Efficient Consumption and Production," In Saravanan Krishnan, A. Jose Anand, and Raghvendra Kumar (Eds.), *Sustainable Development Goals: Technologies and Opportunities,* Ch-12, pages 17. CRC Press, 2024. eBook ISBN9781003468257 https://doi.org/10.1201/9781003468257
37. P. Kumar, Anand A. Jose, and Arjun Ram Rajagopal, "Sustainable Use of Marine Resources using Ocean Technologies," In S. Krishnan, A. Jose Anand, and R. Kumar (Eds.), *Sustainable Development Goals: Technologies and Opportunities,* Ch-14, pages 26. CRC Press, 2024. eBook ISBN9781003468257 https://doi.org/10.1201/9781003468257
38. E. B. Priyanka, S. Thangavel, Ezideen Hasso, and Anand A. Jose, "Sustainable Business Growth of Inland Aquaculture on the Promotion of Global Partnership using Canvas Model," In Saravanan Krishnan, A. Jose Anand, Raghvendra Kumar (Eds.), *Sustainable Development Goals: Technologies and Opportunities, Ch-17*, pages 18. CRC Press, eBook ISBN9781003468257 https://doi.org/10.1201/9781003468257
39. P. Kumar, A. Jose Anand, and Arjun Ram Rajagopal, "Introduction to Technological Assistance for Poverty Reduction," In A. Jose Anand and Saravanan Krishnan (Eds.), *Smart Technologies for Sustainable Development Goals: No Poverty*, Ch-1, pages 15. CRC Press, eBook ISBN9781003519010 https://doi.org/10.1201/9781003519010
40. Sri Sakticharan Nirmalkumar, M. Krishna, and A. Jose Anand. "Food Security and Safety to End Poverty," In A. Jose Anand and Saravanan Krishnan (Eds.), *Smart Technologies for Sustainable Development Goals: No Poverty*, Ch-2, pages 20, CRC Press, 2024, eBook ISBN9781003519010 https://doi.org/10.1201/9781003519010
41. G. J. Nandha, S. Muthukaruppasamy, A. Sampaul Thomas, D. Adaikalam I Arul, and A. Jose Anand, Precision "Poverty Evaluation: Leveraging Generalized Linear Models and XG Boost Algorithms," In A. Jose Anand and Saravanan Krishnan (Eds.), *Smart Technologies for Sustainable Development Goals: No Poverty*, Ch-13, pages 17, CRC Press, 2024. eBook ISBN9781003519010 https://doi.org/10.1201/9781003519010
42. G. Arun Sampaul Thomas, S. Muthukaruppasamy, J. Nandha Gopal, K. Saravanan, and A. Jose Anand, "Transforming Data into Action: Leveraging Big Data Analytics to End Poverty," In A. Jose Anand and Saravanan Krishnan (Eds.), *Smart Technologies for Sustainable Development Goals: No Poverty*, Ch-14, pages 17, CRC Press, 2024. eBook ISBN9781003519010 https://doi.org/10.1201/9781003519010
43. S. Krishnan, A. Jose Anand, and S. Sendhilkumar, "Handbook on Industrial and Business Applications with Digital Twins," (first ed.), pages 408, CRC Press, Taylor & Francis Group, 2024. eBook ISBN 9781003465904 https://doi.org/10.1201/9781003465904
44. Ch Venkata Krishna Reddy, S. Ratna Kandavalli, M. Sundar Raj, R. Amuthakkannan, J. Baskaran, Mayakannan Selvaraju, and A. Jose Anand, "Architecture of Digital Twins and Applications," In Saravanan Krishnan, A. Jose Anand, and S. Sendhilkumar (Eds.), *Handbook of Industrial and Business Applications with Digital Twins*, Ch-2, pages 23, CRC Press, 2024, eBook ISBN9781003465904 https://doi.org/10.1201/9781003465904

45. R. Jeyabharath, Sumanth Ratna Kandavalli, Shrinwantu Raha, Saptarshi Mukherjee, Abhinav Singhal, Mayakannan Selvaraju, and A. Jose Anand, "Digital Platforms for Business Applications," In Saravanan Krishnan, A. Jose Anand, and S. Sendhilkumar (Eds.), *Handbook of Industrial and Business Applications with Digital Twins*, Ch-4, pages 23, CRC Press, 2024, eBook ISBN9781003465904 https://doi.org/10.1201/9781003465904
46. R. Rajasree, R. Geetha, S. Vidhya, M. A. Mukunthan, S. Hari Kumar, and J. A. Anand, "Comparative Analysis of Feature Engineering-Based Learning and Deep Learning Approaches for Classification Problems on Imbalanced Datasets," *2025 Fourth OPJU International Technology Conference (OTCON) on Smart Computing for Innovation and Advancement in Industry 5.0*, Raigarh, India, 2025, pp. 1–6.
47. K. Jayasakthi, M. S., N. Rajkumar, V. S. Patil, A. Pawar, and J. A. Anand, "Comparative Analysis of Deep Learning and Machine Learning Models for DDoS Attack Detection," *2025 Fourth OPJU International Technology Conference (OTCON) on Smart Computing for Innovation and Advancement in Industry 5.0*, Raigarh, India, 2025, pp. 1–6.
48. H. M. Moyeenudin, T. Anuradha, K. Niraimathy, C. Devika, P. V. Baby, and J. Anand A. "Artificial Intelligence based Sustainable Parking Slot Alerting System with Cloud Platform," *2024 First International Conference on Sustainability and Technological Advancements in Engineering Domain (SUSTAINED)*, Faridabad, India, 2024, pp. 711–716.
49. K. Keerthana, Jose A. A., R. Kesavan, S. Kesavan, R. Geetha, and S. Vidhya, "IoT-Enabled Disaster Prevention: Leveraging Transfer Learning for Remote Monitoring," *2024 First International Conference on Sustainability and Technological Advancements in Engineering Domain (SUSTAINED)*, Faridabad, India, 2024, pp. 492–498.
50. R. Geetha, S. Vidhya, M. A. Mukunthan, D. S. Goud, J. A. A. and R. Kesavan, "Predicting Online Vulnerability among Children and Youth: A Machine Learning Approach with Decision Trees and Naive Bayes Algorithms," *2025 Global Conference in Emerging Technology (GINOTECH)*, Pune, India, 2025, pp. 1–6.
51. A. Mohanty, A. G. Mohapatra, N. Nayak, S. Bairavel, M. M. Chaithra, M. Lakshmi, Anitha Govindaram and Jose A. Anand. "Optimizing Diesel Generators in Industrial Settings with IoT and Machine Learning," *International Journal of Information Technology*, pp. 1–9, Aug. 2025. https://doi.org/10.1007/s41870-025-02667-x
52. R. Geetha, P. Thilagavathi, Jose A. Anand, A. Govindaram, J. G. S., and D. Parameswari, "Detection and Classification of Faults in a Power System with Inverter Penetration Based on a Real-Time Machine Learning Application," *2025 Fourth International Conference on Smart Technologies, Communication and Robotics (STCR), Sathyamangalam*, India, 2025, pp. 1–6.
53. P. Bhambri. 2024. "Artificial Intelligence Enabled Internet of Medical Things for Enhanced Healthcare Systems," In P. Bhambri, R. Soni, and T. A. Tran (Eds.), *Smart Healthcare Systems: AI and IoT Perspectives* (pp. 1–17). CRC Press. https://doi.org/10.1201/9781032698519–1
54. P. Bhambri and S. Kumar. "Cloud and IoT Iintegration for Smart Healthcare," In P. Bhambri, R. Soni, and T. A. Tran (Eds.), *Smart Healthcare Systems: AI and IoT Perspectives* (pp. 69–84). CRC Press. https://doi.org/10.1201/9781032698519-6
55. P. Bhambri and S. Rani, Advancements and future challenges in business intelligence. In J. Barrena-Martinez, M.-J. Foncubierta-Rodríguez, J. A. Medina-Garrido, & Z. Dobrowolski (Eds.), Developing managerial skills for global business success (pp. 271–290). IGI Global, 2024. https://doi.org/10.4018/979-8-3693-3057-9.ch017
56. P. Bhambri, S. Rani, and A. Khang, "AI-driven Digital Twin and Resource Optimization in Industry 4.0 Ecosystem. In N. Singh, S. Birla, M. D. Ansari, and N. K. Shukla (Eds.), *AI-driven Digital Twin and Industry 4.0: A Conceptual Framework with applications* (pp. 182–201). CRC Press/Taylor & Francis Group, 2024. https://doi.org/10.1002/9781394227990.ch3
57. A. Jain, M. Singh, and P. Bhambri, "Performance Evaluation of IPv4-IPv6 Tunneling Procedure using IoT," *Journal of Physics: Conference Series,* Vol. 1950 (1): 012010. IOP Publishing.
58. R. Rana and P. Bhambri, "Artificial Intelligence and Internet of Things (IoT) Facilitated Digital Twin for Industry 4.0 Application Domains," In S. Rani, P. Bhambri, S. Kumar, P. K. Pareek, and A. A. Elngar (Eds.), *AI-driven Digital Twin and Industry 4.0* (pp. 168–181). CRC Press, 2024. https://doi.org/10.1201/9781003395416-11

59. R. Rana and P. Bhambri, "Generative AI-driven Security Frameworks for Web Engineering: Innovations and Challenges," In I. A. Shah and N. Z. Jhanjhi (Eds.), *Generative AI for Web Engineering Models* (pp. 285–296). IGI Global, 2024. https://doi.org/10.4018/979-8-3693-3703-5.ch014
60. R. Rana, P. Bhambri, and Y. Chhabra, "Evolution and the Future of Industrial Engineering with the IoT and AI," In P. Bhambri, S. Rani, V. E. Balas, & A. A. Elngar (Eds.), *Integration of AI-based Manufacturing and Industrial Engineering Systems with the Internet of Things* (pp. 19–37). CRC Press. https://doi.org/10.1201/9781003383505
61. Y. S. Sangwan, S. Lal, P. Bhambri, A. Kumar, and I. S. Dhanoa, "Advancements in Social Data Security and Encryption: A Review," *Natural Volatiles & Essential Oils*, Vol. 8 (4), pp. 15353–15362, 2021. https://www.cabidigitallibrary.org/doi/full/10.5555/20220170098
62. G. Singh and P. Bhambri. "Simulation Analysis of AODV and DSDV Routing Protocols for Secure and Reliable Service in Mobile ad hoc Networks (MANETs)," In P. Bhambri, S. Rani, V. E. Balas, and A. A. Elngar (Eds.), *Integration of AI-based Manufacturing and Industrial Engineering Systems with the Internet of Things* (first ed., pp. 205–216). CRC Press, 2023. https://doi.org/10.1201/9781003383505

Chapter 8

AutoML-enabled smart forensic framework for collaborative crime analysis and digital evidence prediction

Narendra Singh, M. Gokilhashree, B. Gayathri, Oshma Rosette Pinto and Rubaid Ashfaq

8.1 INTRODUCTION

In the last several decades, the use of mobile devices has skyrocketed, becoming an integral part of our daily lives and vital to their operation and upkeep. All sorts of electronic devices, such as smartphones, tablets, GPS, and more, make up the devices. Not only have their prices dropped as manufacture has gotten cheaper, but their usefulness, immense capacity, and abilities have also contributed to their widespread use. Consequently, they are able to store a vast amount of data belonging to both commercial and individual clients. Because they save customers' personal and basic information, these devices have become an integral part of our daily lives. But these devices are not immune to attackers either; in fact, they are becoming a major entry point for crimes including intellectual property theft, disruptions, security risks, fake copies, identity theft, and so on. The proliferation of new technologies, such as sophisticated devices and the internet, is inversely proportional to the decline in the frequency of technological crimes. Consequently, various forms of cybercrime and sophisticated attacks are increasingly targeting these gadgets. But new developments in digital forensics have given us tools to fight back against the creeping menace of criminal misconduct.

The term "Digital Forensics Investigations" will be defined as follows:

> The use of objective analysis toward the conservation, aggregation, validation, recognition, interpretation, documentation and representation of digital evidence got from digital sources for the intent of reconstructing occurrences found to be illegal, or helping to predict events shown to be disruptive to peace or functioning of society.

8.1.1 Outline of the process

The investigation in three stages:

1. Providing a summary of a conflicting meta-analysis of relevant studies that vary in terms of their practicality and usefulness. This is detailed in our review and analysis of the aforementioned pertinent literature. In the next stage, we will use this information to identify potential uses and tested implementations of the presented principles.
2. In this step, we will propose an architecture for our machine learning experiments based on the assessments we performed in the preceding phase. In this section, we will

DOI: 10.1201/9781003656487-8

detail the algorithms and compare and contrast their strengths and weaknesses. In order to evaluate the algorithms' efficacy in handling these massive datasets, we will broaden our approach to gathering records of forensic and criminal data.
3. Our analysis and review of the algorithms' applicability and effectiveness, as well as our opinion on the contextual benefits and drawbacks of the methodologies under consideration, are based on the data gained through the methods.

8.1.2 Literature survey

A conceptual model integrating forensic diagnostics, anti-corruption auditing, and internal auditing enhances risk-oriented corporate governance. The framework strengthens fraud detection, ensures transparency, and minimizes corruption-related risks within organizations [1]. A bibliometric analysis of 722 studies identified key trends, ethical challenges, and skill requirements in forensic accounting. The findings emphasize continuous professional development and interdisciplinary collaboration to strengthen financial integrity [2]. Ultra-weak photon emission (UPE) analysis in fruits revealed potential forensic applications for distinguishing organic and conventional produce. The technique offers a non-invasive approach for detecting biochemical differences and food fraud [3]. Forensic accounting techniques—fraud investigation, litigation support, and dispute resolution—positively influence fraud detection and prevention. The study advocates staff training, whistleblower programs, and regulatory policies to promote financial transparency [4]. Forensic accounting skills enhance auditor self-efficacy and fraud detection in Egypt, with communication, psycho-social, and auditing skills showing strong influence. The use of computer-assisted audit tools (CAATTs) further strengthens the relationship between self-efficacy and fraud identification [5].

Federated learning with differential privacy for secure, cross-silo data aggregation in machine learning applications [6]. The convergence of quantum networks and AI highlights emerging applications in data security, optimization, and computational intelligence [7]. The Hygieia chatbot integrates IoT and NLP to offer healthcare users appointment booking, daily scheduling, and interactive voice-based assistance [8]. Researchers enhance industrial automation with ANN-powered vision systems, improving precision, speed, and adaptability in robotic operations [9]. A case study using Amazon Braket demonstrates quantum service-oriented computing, identifying challenges in integrating classical and quantum systems [10]. GAN variants for simulating turbulent flow find that Wasserstein GANs generate accurate, high-fidelity turbulence predictions [11].

AI-based forensic readiness and crime prediction systems analyze socio-economic, historical, and spatial datasets from Los Angeles. The framework identifies hotspots, predicts criminal trends, and enhances proactive policing strategies while maintaining ethical standards and safeguarding privacy during data analysis [12]. A digital-evidence analysis framework for handheld devices such as mobiles and laptops is presented for secure forensic operations. The system incorporates likelihood-ratio-based numerical and verbal evaluations at the kernel layer, ensuring an adaptive, robust, and legally compliant approach to digital evidence retrieval [13]. A hybrid image-filtering and neutrosophic-based face-recognition model is applied to improve low-quality forensic video evidence. The combination of triplemask spatial linear and bilateral filters with deep-learning architectures achieves 99.38% accuracy, significantly enhancing the precision and reliability of forensic image and video interpretation [14]. A visual-speech recognition framework utilizes a VGG16 convolutional neural network to interpret lip movements from silent videos. The system achieves 76% accuracy, enabling effective extraction of speech for forensic investigations while enhancing communication accessibility for the hearing-impaired [15].

A convolutional neural network (CNN) model effectively detects copy-move video forgeries, surpassing existing methods in accuracy and efficiency. The approach demonstrates 85–86% accuracy across multiple datasets, enabling reliable real-time video fraud detection [16]. Forensic accounting knowledge significantly improves fraud detection in Nigeria's public sector, mediated by big data analytics skills. The findings highlight the importance of analytics training, hybrid competencies, and technological integration for better fraud prevention [17]. A T-spherical fuzzy hypersoft set–based MCDM framework enhances digital transaction fraud detection. The model integrates TOPSIS and fuzzy similarity measures, achieving high adaptability and predictive accuracy across varied decision scenarios [18]. CEO education, compensation, and age positively influence the adoption of external auditors with forensic accounting skills in Jordanian firms. The study emphasizes leadership attributes as key factors in corporate governance and financial transparency [19]. Application of Beneish and Roxas models revealed high risk of financial manipulation in Ukrainian marketing firms. The Beneish model proved more effective in detecting fraudulent reporting under economic instability and martial law conditions [20].

AI and machine learning–driven forensic methodologies enhance social media evidence analysis in criminal investigations. The integration of text mining, network analysis, and metadata evaluation improves the accuracy and admissibility of digital evidence [21]. An AI-based ensemble model using SMOTE and forensic-based metaheuristics improves the detection of fraudulent pollution fee declarations. The method strengthens regulatory compliance, reduces tax evasion, and supports sustainable environmental governance [22]. Forensic accounting, communication, and auditing skills enhance auditor self-efficacy and fraud detection in Indonesia. The use of Generalized Audit Software (GAS) strengthens this relationship, while whistleblowing systems show limited moderating effects [23]. Forensic accounting enhances financial transparency and fraud prevention in Jordanian institutions through investigation support, testimony, and reporting. The study recommends stronger integration of forensic practices into public sector financial systems [24]. Integration of big data in forensic accounting reshapes fraud detection by enabling deeper analytical capabilities. Qualitative analysis reveals that visual analytics significantly improve both dispositional and relational affordances in forensic investigations [25]. Artificial intelligence significantly strengthens forensic auditing by enabling rapid and proactive fraud detection. Bibliometric and systematic analyses reveal the growing role of AI in improving data accessibility and fraud identification across diverse auditing domains [26]. Indoor radon and progeny levels were measured in Etah district dwellings using LR-115 detectors. Concentrations ranged from 3.52 to 248.64 Bq m^{-3}, indicating variable exposure levels, with some posing health risks compared to rural areas [27].

8.2 PROPOSED WORK

In this stage, we will propose an architecture for our machine learning experiments based on the evaluations made in the literature survey. We will go over the capabilities of the process methodology and ontology modeling. In order to put the algorithms to the test, we will broaden our approach to gathering forensic and criminal data records.

8.2.1 Operational ontology

The system relies on AI and machine learning principles at every stage to guarantee that instruments produce few false positives in their determinations. Artificial Intelligence (AI) transforms forensic accounting by improving fraud detection and risk assessment through

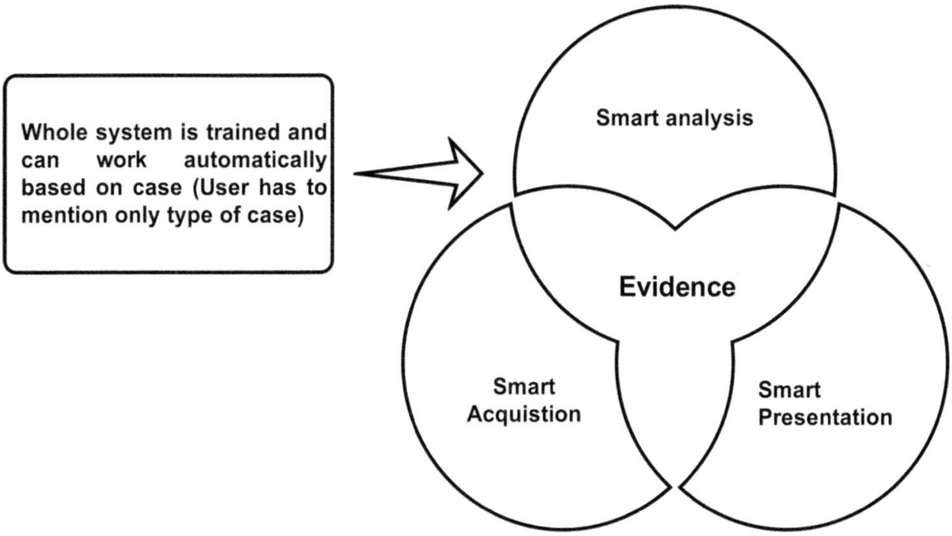

Figure 8.1 Smart digital forensic framework.

machine learning algorithms. The study outlines a framework integrating AI into audit systems for dynamic and reliable fraud prevention [28]. Although it would be ideal, it is not possible to completely eliminate the possibility of mistakes and false positives from any intelligent system. It is imperative that the operational model undergo thorough testing prior to usage. Even though there are a lot of ways to reduce the amount of user input, it is still a good idea to double-check everything before submitting it to court, particularly the system-generated report.

Figure 8.1 shows the simplified version of the Smart Machine Learning Digital Forensic system that has been presented.

The suggested solution can handle all three stages of digital forensic methods in one cohesive package, and it is case-based. An inter-regional knowledge management framework was developed to enhance the quality, consistency, and efficiency of decentralized digital forensic practices [29]. To address the current instruments' lack of rich interoperable intelligence, which is a shortcoming of our proposed system formulation, support for these three criteria is provided. In our system, we train using preexisting data sets from prior forensic investigations and also use well-known classical programming, AI, and ML procedures and toolkits. The algorithm can better comprehend which decision to make in each situation with the help of these data sets. The following subsections address the likelihood of incorporating AI at each stage. Here, the measures are considered intelligent since they make decisions based on what they know and what they can learn. For consistent results, it is necessary to retrain each step following training.

8.2.2 Automated machine learning (AutoML)

Another critical part is utilizing domain expertise and iterative learning, which can be achieved through intelligent human agents or meta learning methods.

For this implementation, we have decided to use the H2O AutoML framework. In a real-time setting, it can execute Categorical Ensembling. Figure 8.2 presents the step-by-step experimental workflow.

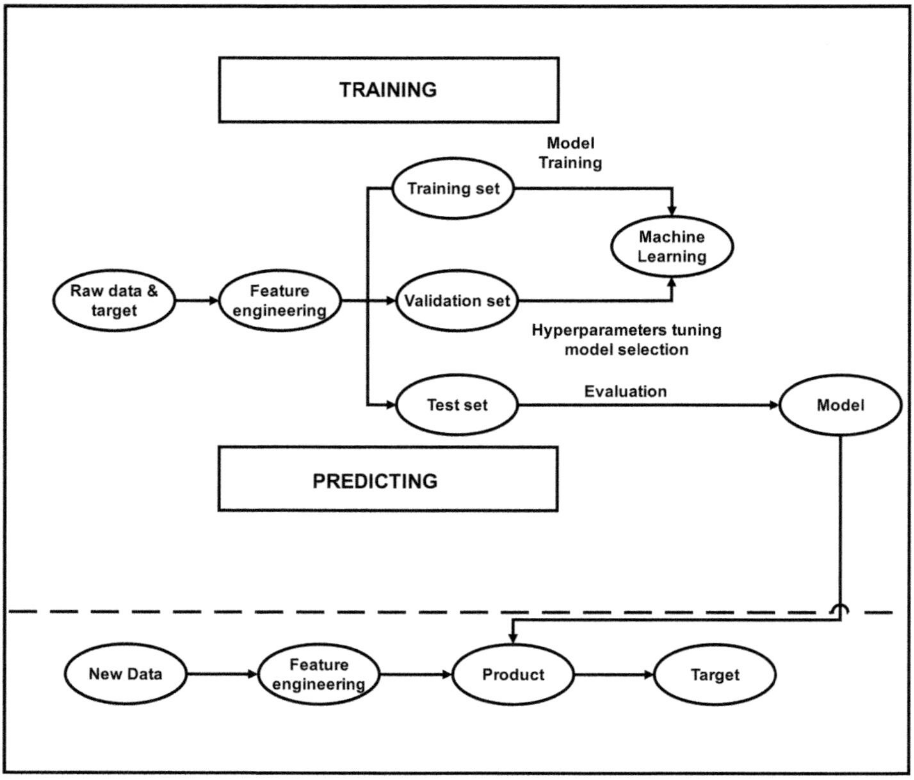

Figure 8.2 Experiment process steps.

At this point, we can meet the fundamental needs of our SF framework with the aid of well-implemented AutoML pipelines. Furthermore, there are open-source libraries that incorporate AutoML techniques. These libraries cover topics such as the search space's hyperparameters, data transformations, and models, as well as the algorithms used to explore or optimize the search space's possibilities. Variants of Bayesian Optimization are among the most popular algorithms in this space. The most fundamental responsibility of AutoML is to automatically optimize performance by setting the hyperparameters, which are present in every machine learning system.

It has capabilities to:

- Minimize the amount of manual work required to implement machine learning. Particularly from an AutoML perspective, this is crucial.
- Making scientific experiments more fair and easier to replicate. Compared to manual search, automated Hyper Parameter Optimization (HPO) is obviously more repeatable. Since it is only possible to evaluate methods fairly if they all achieve the same level of problem-specific tweaking, this simplifies acceptable comparisons.

Using our SF acquisition process as a lens, Figure 8.3 explains the procedures involved.

Additionally, these techniques work well with data frame merging, which improves modeling and yields a more robust feature space definition from combined datasets, and with transfer learning implementations [30–34]. Figure 8.4 provides a high-level picture of the server architecture that is employed in this project.

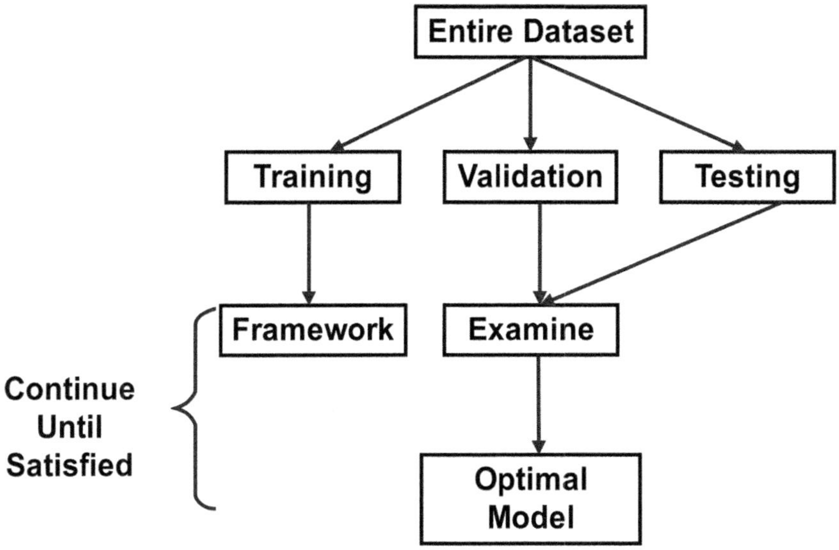

Figure 8.3 SF acquisition process.

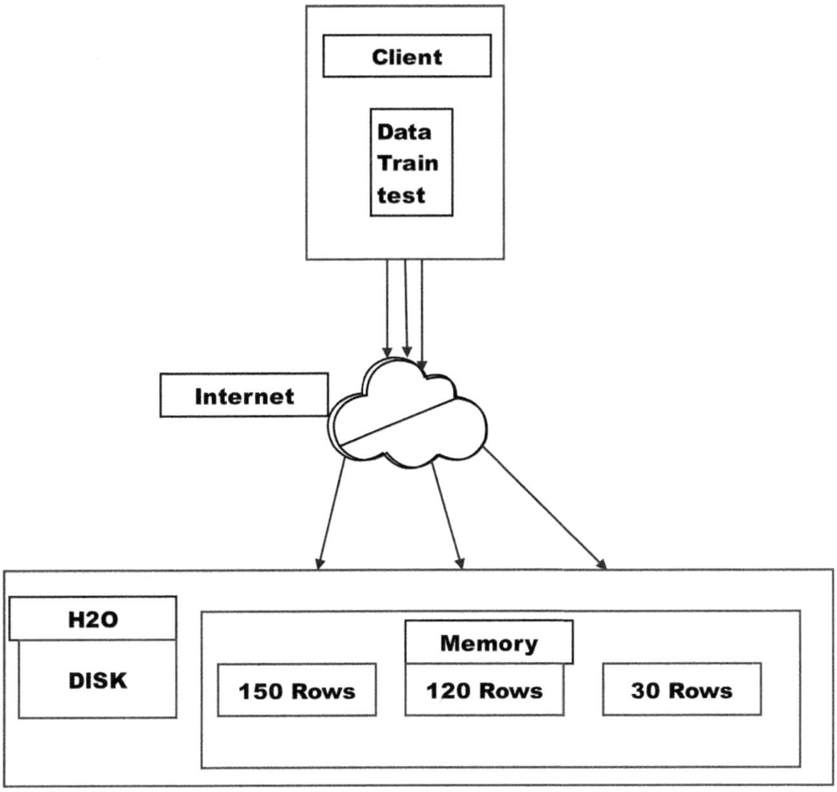

Figure 8.4 Client–server architecture.

8.2.3 Specification for implementation

Our ontology and framework description provide a solid foundation for an SF application that could be useful for distributed data mining and forensic analysis. This application could benefit investigators, policymakers, and field agents at all levels of an organization's hierarchy [35]. This is due to the fact that TensorFlow is a part of the AutoML computation pipeline, which opens the door to distributed computing. Unfortunately, this does not have built-in support and will necessitate further technical work to ensure a solid implementation.

With H2O's REST API, third-party apps and scripts can access all of H2O's features through JSON over HTTP. The remainder of the H2O API makes use of the Flow UI web interface, the H2O-R binding, and the H2O-Python binding.

8.2.4 Experiment overview

Using the input dataset "01_District_wise_crimes_committed_IPC_2001_2012.csv" and 32 original features, we constructed a LightGBM Model utilizing Driverless AI to forecast RAPE. This regression experiment took exactly 41 minutes and 13 seconds (0:41:13) to complete, utilizing two of the two engineered characteristics and one of the 32 original features [36–40].

8.2.5 Data overview

The National Crime Records Bureau (NCRB) donated the data used to compile the dataset, which is accessible online at www.data.gov.in [41–45]. The criminal datasets we utilized for the experiment span 9017 rows and 13 columns, with a file size of 1.3 MiB.

8.2.6 Experiment pipeline

Figure 8.5 depicts the Driverless AI experimental workflow from data preprocessing and automated feature engineering to model evaluation and final best-model selection. The following lists describes the process involved in the experimental pipeline workflow.

1. Identifying column types for data ingestion.
2. Function preprocessing: transformed unprocessed characteristics into numerical.
3. At the model and feature tuning step, we generate characteristics, choose them, and then randomly tune the hyperparameters. Each iteration determines what new features to develop by modifying existing features based on the variable importance as a probability from the previous iteration.
4. We trained models with various variables to identify the optimal parameters for the decision tree, constant, LightGBM, and XGBoost techniques.
5. We trained and graded 106 models to assess their characteristics and prediction abilities.
6. The feature evolution stage employs a genetic algorithm to determine the optimal model parameters and feature transformations for the final model.
7. After 34 cycles of developing and analyzing two features, we found the data format that worked best for the final model training.
8. Took engineering feature evaluation to the next level by training and scoring 116 models.
9. Model completion: Selected the most effective model through iterative feature engineering.
10. The presence of a time column negates the need to perform stacked ensemble.
11. Build a scoring pipeline: Built a Python scoring pipeline and exported it.

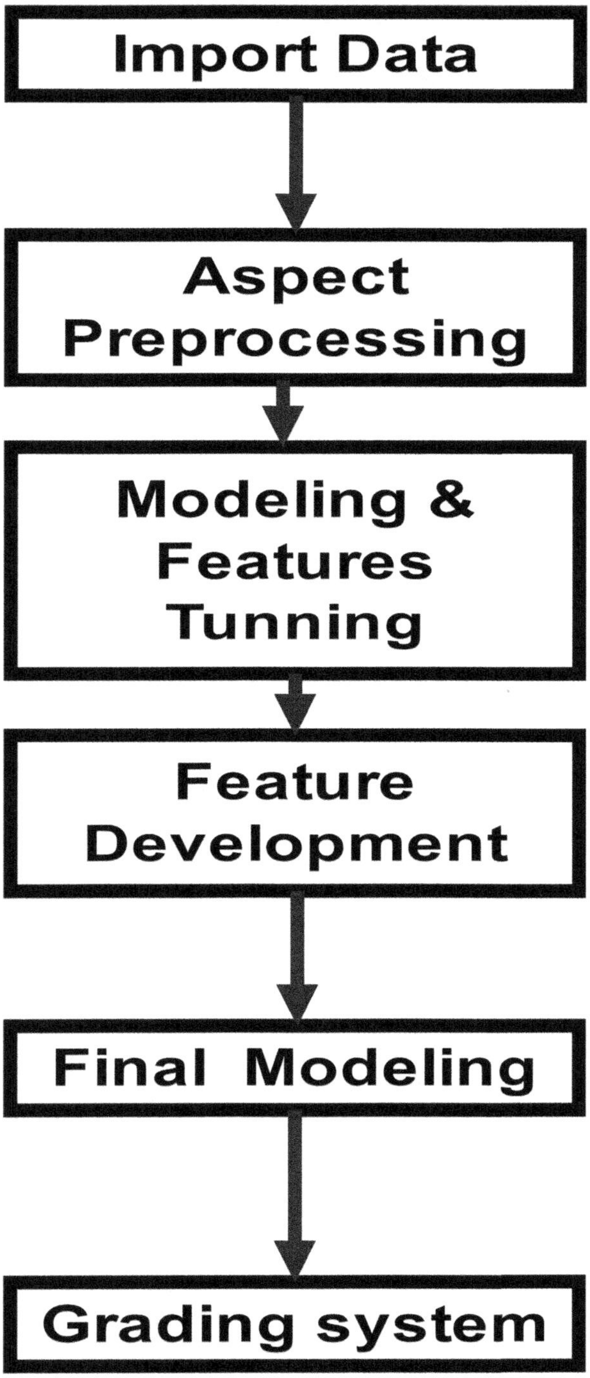

Figure 8.5 Experiment process steps.

Table 8.1 Phases of the experiment with driverless AI

Driverless AI stage	*Number of models*	*Timing (seconds)*
Final pipeline training	0	22.61
Feature evolution	106	801.37
Model and feature tuning	117	1323.99
Data preparation	2	143.89

In order to find the best parameters, model dataset, and ideal end model, driverless AI trained models throughout the trial. Table 8.1 displays the procedures.

8.2.7 Experiment settings

Table 8.2 shows the broad and defined parameters used for the experiment.

8.2.8 Supported algorithms

In this section, we detail the machine learning algorithms that were detailed for inclusion in our AutoML SF Framework.

1. LightGBM: Microsoft's LightGBM is a framework for gradient boosting that makes use of techniques for tree-based learning. Reduced memory usage, increased performance, and accelerated training speed were its primary design goals. It is one of the best implementations of gradient boosting and is similar to XGBoost. Fitting methods like Decision Tree, Random Forest, and DART (an experimental algorithm) also make use of it within Driverless AI.
2. **XGBoost**: The XGBoost supervised learning model uses the boosting technique to create reliable models. By "boosting," we mean the ensemble training method of building numerous models in a sequential fashion, with each new model trying to fix the shortcomings of the one before it. When adding additional models to an ensemble in tree boosting, each one serves as a decision tree. XGBoost provides parallel tree boosting, also known as GBDT and GBM, which efficiently and effectively solves a lot of data science problems. For a number of problems, XGBoost ranks among the top gradient boosting machine (GBM) frameworks available today. Autonomous AI systems use XGBoost GBM and XGBoost's DART (experimental algorithm) techniques.

Table 8.2 Parameters and selected values

Parameter	*Value*
interpretability	interpretability
is classification	False
is timeseries	True
seed	False
is image	False
gpus enable	True
time	10
accuracy	8
num gap periods	0
num prediction periods	1

Supervised models like XGBoost outperform anomaly detection methods in fraud detection, achieving an F1-score of 0.89 and providing a strong benchmark for future studies [46].

3. **Decision Tree (DT)**: There is no row or column sampling; instead, hyperparameters keep an eye on the tree's depth and the growth technique (loss-guided or depth-wise).
4. **Constant Model**: No matter the input data, the Constant Model algorithm always forecasts the same constant value. To get the constant value, we optimize the provided scorer. Take MSE/RMSE as an example; the constant here is the (weighted) mean of the target column. This is the median of MAE, adjusted for weights. An optimization procedure determines the constant for different scorers, like MAPE or custom scorers. The priors found are the constant probabilities for classification problems. The baseline reference model is a constant model. Incorporating it into the final pipeline will result in a warning since it exposes a vulnerability in the dataset or target, such as when trying to forecast a stochastic possibility [47].
5. **FTRL Stands for Follow the Regularized Leader**: For continuous targets, FTRL allows regression, and for categorical ones, it allows binomial and multinomial classification.

8.3 RESULTS

The quantitative indicators show how well our implementation performed on the analysis and prediction tasks. Continuing with the discussion, we will provide a quick overview of the implementation's performance on its quantitative measures.

8.3.1 Model tuning

With a year-based ordering system, autonomous AI automatically separates data into training and validation sets. AI in business intelligence for fraud detection emphasizes machine learning, real-time systems, and ethical collaboration for effective risk management [48]. Without any lag time between training and forecasting, the experiment accurately anticipated events 1314376000 seconds in the future.

Table 8.3 shows the results and training duration of the AI-evaluated models for constant, decision tree, lightgbm, and xgboost.

Tables 8.3 shows the Constant tuning, LightGBM tuning, Decision Tree tuning, and gbtree tuning, providing more extensive information on the parameters assessed for each approach. Tables 8.4, 8.5, 8.6, and 8.7 follow.

Table 8.3 Algorithm training time and scores

Order	*Booster*	*Training times*	*Scores*	*nfeatures*
6	lightgbm	10.1219	8.171	125.28
1	lightgbm	8.8783	8.2022	37.28
2	lightgbm	10.7751	36.3783	36.28
3	lightgbm	5.9082	37.5188	31.28
8	lightgbm	9.5892	43.3421	114.28
10	lightgbm	6.7311	49.681	96.28
7	gbtree	13.3882	56.9809	64.28
5	lightgbm	6.2607	59.1343	68.28
4	gbtree	4.8836	81.0289	31.28
9	decision tree	3.6349	88.3514	75.28

Table 8.4 Permanent tuning

Order	*Booster*	*Training times*	*Scores*	*nfeatures*
24	state	2.1257	216.2134	1

Table 8.5 Decision tuning

Tree method	*Grow policy*	*Training times*	*Scores*	*nfeatures*	*Max leaves*	*Max depth*
gpu hist	loss guide	6	126	75	88.202	3.285
gpu hist	loss guide	4	126	56	88.205	2.977
gpu_ hist	loss guide	6	62	72	88.208	3.282
gpu_ hist	loss guide	8	126	89	88.268	3.299
gpu hist	depth wise	2	30	33	88.319	2.706

Table 8.6 LightGBM tuning

Method	*Policy*	*Maximum depth*	*Maximum leaves*	*n features*	*Scores*	*Time*
gpu hist	depthwise	4	0	125.28	8.171	10.1219
gpu hist	depthwise	4	0	37.28	8.2022	8.8783
gpu hist	lossguide	0	1022	36.28	36.3783	10.7751
gpu hist	depthwise	8	0	31.28	37.5188	5.9082
gpu_ hist	depthwise	8	0	114.28	43.3421	9.5892
gpu hist	loss guide	0	1022	96.28	49.681	6.7311
gpu_ hist	loss guide	0	1022	64.28	56.9809	13.3882
gpu hist	depthwise	4	0	68.28	59.1343	6.2607
gpu hist	depthwise	8	0	31.28	81.0289	4.8836
gpu hist	depthwise	4	0	75.28	88.3514	3.6349

Table 8.7 Gbtree tuning

Tree method	*Grow policy*	*Training times*	*Scores*	*nfeatures*	*Max leaves*	*Max depth*
		0	1022	64	56.83	13.04
		4	0	31	80.88	4.534
		8	0	109	110.49	3.176
		4	0	33	24.821	21.9731

8.3.2 Feature evolution

The Feature Evolution Stage involved 116 lightgbm models trained by driverless AI, each of which evaluated a different set of attributes. Figure 8.6 shows the Feature Evolution Stage and the Feature Tuning Stage.

8.3.3 Changes to features

Table 8.8 displays the top 50 features, and only those with a relative significance of 0.003 or above are considered. In the absence of a transformer, the function is a blank column.

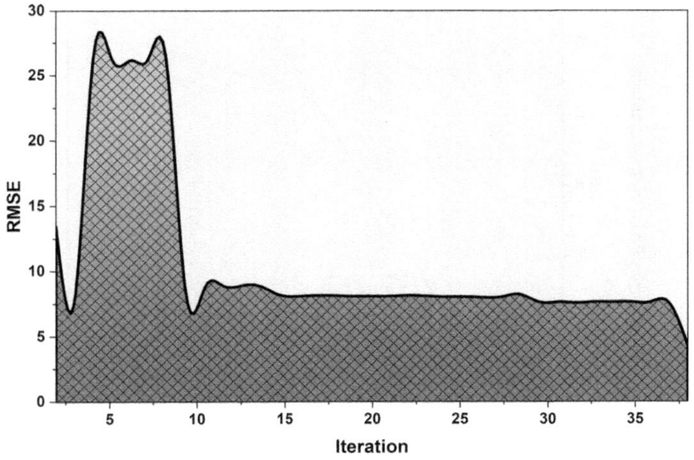

Figure 8.6 Feature evolution.

Table 8.8 Key elements of the final model

S. No.	*Transformer*	*Feature*	*Relative importance*	*Description*
1	Interaction	29 InteractionAdd:: OTHER RAPE CUSTODIAL RAPE	0.99	[CUSTODIAL RAPE] +[OTHER RAPE]
2	None	22 OTHER	0.92	OTHER RAPE
3	Interaction	29_InteractionSub: OTHER RAPE CUSTODIAL RAPE	0.54	[OTHER RAPE] [CUSTODIAL RAPE]

Figure 8.7 is a line graph depicting Features and the relative importance of features.

8.3.4 Completed model

The LightGBM Model final pipeline transforms 30 starting characteristics with an ensemble level of 0. Three features are suitable for time-based hold-out in a single model. Figure 8.8 displays the Feature of the Final Model Process.

Table 8.9 for the details of the final model modification. The final ensemble assigns a weight of 1 to Model Index: 0.

Table 8.10 shows how well the finished model performed. We utilized RMSE as our scorer in this case. Figure 8.9 displays the actual vs. expected performance curve.

8.3.5 Other models

In the course of the trial, we used Driverless AI to train 27 different models. Our experiment examined the algorithms listed in Table 8.11.

Driverless AI may evaluate a variety of techniques, such as various models in TensorFlow, FTRL, RuleFit, XGBoost GLM, XGBoost GBM, gbtree, Decision Tree, and Light GBM. If any of these algorithms were considered for the final model, their rejection is detailed in Table 8.12.

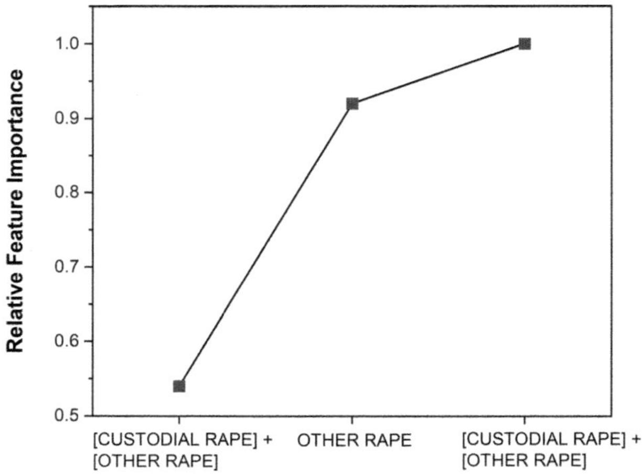

Figure 8.7 Significance of comparative data.

8.3.6 Deployment

In previous research, a hybrid social-media forensic framework integrates TextBlob, VADER, and a crime-type dictionary for effective tweet classification. The Python-based model processes, cleans, and geolocates Twitter data in real time, offering significant support to law enforcement agencies in detecting, analyzing, and understanding crime patterns [49]. We can score fresh data and change it in a few different ways with the files in this package:

8.4 DISCUSSION

Since raw performance is insufficient to evaluate the algorithms, we have included quantitative metrics for comparison purposes. These measurements give different ways of expressing our Framework and the three implementations'. The quantitative results, however, allow one to evaluate the overall advantages offered by an AutoML engine [50–54]. Due to the AutoML engine's hyper-parameter optimization and algorithm selection capabilities, training time and prediction accuracy are both significantly improved. This further supports our hypothesis that H2O AutoML, when trained with our SFI Framework Ontology, can serve as a generalized and easy metalearner for DFI.

In addition to the performance measures cited in this study, the SF framework report also included additional relevant information. This produced report showcases the Report Generation component of a comprehensive Framework. Justice and bureaucratic slowness are two of the primary scaling issues with our conventional judicial system [55]. The main cause of this backlog is the fact that human agents working for these institutions are not very good at processing data and making documentation by hand. With minimal feature re-tooling, forensic agencies can significantly enhance their efficiency and effectiveness. The implementation of SF Acquisition and SF Reporting, which is both thorough and elegant, offers a simple solution to the problem of how to help the old institutions adapt to the modern demands placed on our justice and police forces [56–60].

Since the algorithms give different ways of expressing our SF Framework and the three implementations' practical utility, we thought it would be helpful to provide quantifiable measurements to compare them. However, we recognize that raw performance is not the

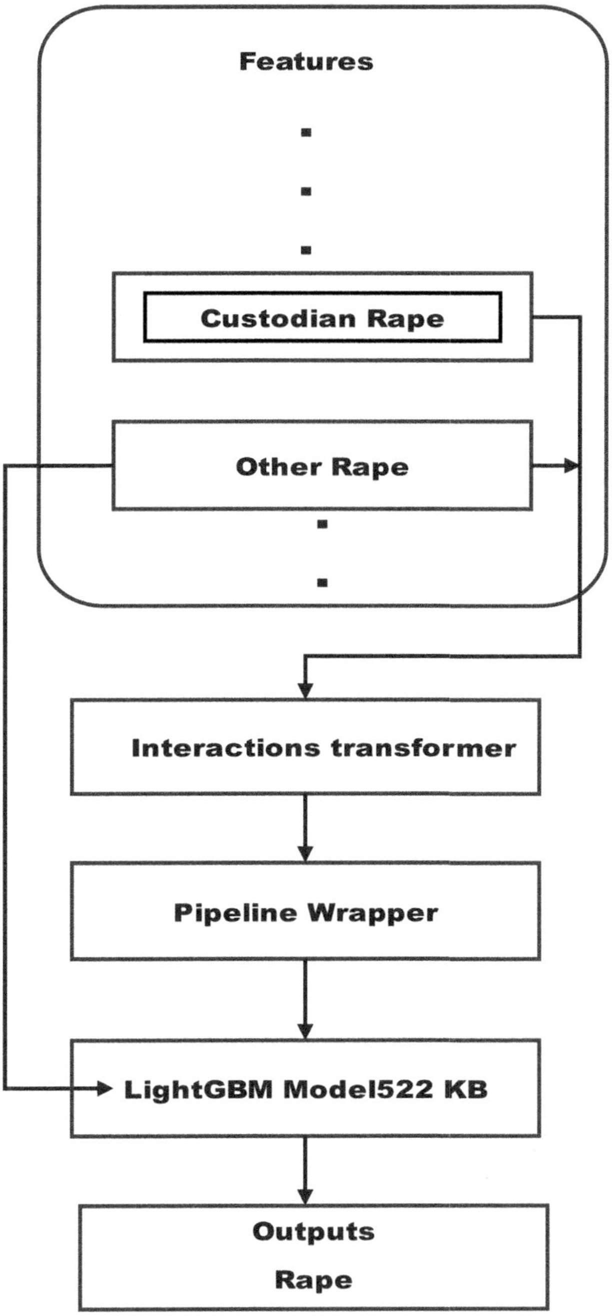

Figure 8.8 Feature to process.

Table 8.9 Final model transformation details

Model index	*Type*	*Target transformer*	*Fitted features*	*Model weight*
0	Light GBM model	log	2	1

Table 8.10 Performance of final model

Scorer	*Better score is*	*Final ensemble scores on validation (internal or external holdout(s)) data*	*Final ensemble standard deviation on validation (internal or external holdout(s)) data*
RMSE	lower	4.2808	0.1905

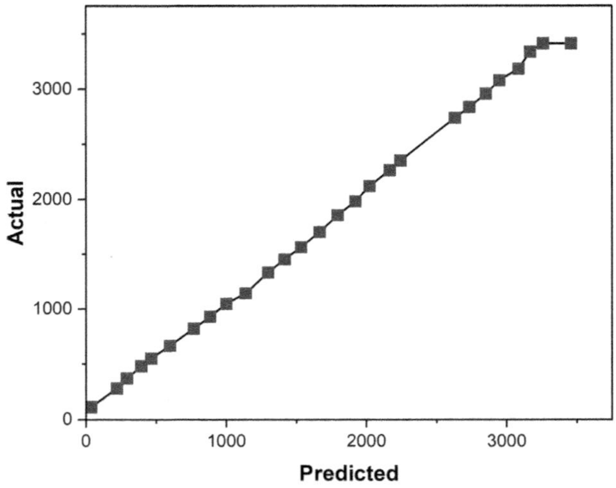

Figure 8.9 Performance (predicted vs actual).

Table 8.11 Information on the algorithms tested in the experiment

Algorithm	*Version*	*Package*	*Documentation*
constant	1.2.0	custom package	XGBoost
gbtree	2.1.4	xgboost	LightGBM
decision tree	1.8.0	light gbm	reference model

Table 8.12 Specifics of the final model's algorithm selection

Algorithm	*Selection*
lightgbm	No evaluation of algorithm
decision tree	No evaluation of algorithm
gbtree	No evaluation of algorithm
dart	No evaluation of algorithm
ftrl	No evaluation of algorithm
tensorflow	Low performance tuning process
rulefit	Low performance tuning process
gblinear	Final model selection

only metric to consider. We argue that, with the help of our SFI Framework Ontology, H2O AutoML gives us the best chance of finding for DFI. By avoiding potentially harmful black boxes and by providing insight into the logic and operation of the models' learning biases, the DFI framework's intelligent report creation capabilities are vital. For practical purposes in criminal and forensic law, this is crucial.

8.5 CONCLUSION

The science of digital forensics is rapidly expanding and dealing with ever-increasingly complicated data sets retrieved from crime scenes. As part of their work, DFIs assess digital evidence of a crime for use in legal proceedings. From this vantage point, artificial intelligence (AI) seems like the perfect solution to all of the problems plaguing IT criminology. While dissecting and deconstructing digital evidence, various AI calculations and tactics can be useful. By handling a large amount of data in a relatively short amount of time, Automated Machine Learning Frameworks will make this cycle better. Evidently, these enhancements will be able to solve the problem of how to portray massive amounts of forensic evidence in a way that allows for intelligent, practical, and consistently good investigative activities and prosecution decisions. Forensic analysis makes use of these techniques because they allow investigators to combat a wide range of crimes to a greater extent than is now possible. Collaborative ontologies for digital forensic investigations that are both well-defined and at least partially practical pave the way for advances in AI and machine learning to find an easy way into more conventional criminal and forensic investigation agencies.

REFERENCES

1. Y. Patskan, K. Nazarova, T. Kopotiienko, V. Miniailo, V. Pavlov, and N. Novikova. 2025. Forensic diagnostics, anti-corruption, and internal audit in ensuring efficient company management in an open economy. *Financial and Credit Activity: Problems of Theory and Practice*, 4 (63): 63–79.
2. M. Al-Raggad, N. Albalawee, A. Almahasneh, Y. Abu Huson, and A. Albajaly. 2025. Unveiling financial crimes: Advancing forensic accounting practices and ethical integrity through bibliometric insights. *Safer Communities*, 24 (3): 244–264.
3. Rubio, A., Barbaro, A., Montalvo, G., Ortega-Ojeda, F. E., & García-Ruiz, C. (2024). Influence of External Light on Ultra-Weak Photon Emission of Fruits: Forensic Differentiation of Organic and Conventional Fruits. *Sensors*, *25*(6), 1799. https://doi.org/10.3390/s25061799.
4. I. Naz and S. N. Khan. 2025. Impact of forensic accounting on fraud detection and prevention: A case of firms in Pakistan. *Journal of Financial Crime*, 32 (1): 192–206.
5. A. R. Al Natour, H. Al-Mawali, H. Zaidan, and Y. H. Z. Said. 2025. The role of forensic accounting skills in fraud detection and the moderating effect of CAATTs application: Evidence from Egypt. *Journal of Financial Reporting and Accounting*, 23 (1): 30–55.
6. K. Vijayalakshmi, P. M. Sitharselvam, I. Thamarai, J. Ashok, G. Sathish, and S. Selvaraju. 2024. Secure and private federated learning through encrypted parameter aggregation. In Saravanan Krishnan, A. Jose Anand, R. Srinivasan, R. Kavitha & S. Suresh (Eds.), *Advances in Intelligent Systems* (pp. 80–105). CRC Press.
7. C. Ananth, O. I. Khalaf, and J. A. Jose Anand. 2024. *Quantum Networks and their Applications in AI* (p. 15). IGI Global.
8. Jose, A., & Dhanalakshmi, R. (2023). Hygieia: Multipurpose healthcare assistance using the Internet of Things. In S. Krishnan & A. Ilmudeen (Eds.), *Internet of Medical Things in Smart Healthcare: Post-COVID-19 Pandemic Scenario* (pp. 77–98). Apple Academic Press.

9. N. M. George, E. Rosero, S. Selvaraju, A. Shameem, S. Divya, and N. Natarajan. 2025. Enhancing industrial automation flexibility through neural network-empowered machine vision applications. In G. Li, J. Filipe, & Z. Xu (Eds.), *Communications in Computer and Information Science* (pp. 241–254). Springer.
10. R. Salama, W. Alghamdi, H. M. Alsalmi, S. Selvaraju, S. N. Taqui, and R. Deepalakshmi. 2024. Evolution of service-oriented computing: Integrating quantum techniques for integer factorization. *Proc. IEEE Int. Conf. on Innovative Intelligent Industrial Technologies*, Porto, Portugal, November 21–22, 2024.
11. W. Alghamdi, S. Selvaraju, G. A. Sivasankar, J. Singh, B. Ravi Naik, and C. Venkatakrishna Reddy. 2023. Turbulence modeling through deep learning: An in-depth study of Wasserstein GANs. *Proc. IEEE Int. Conf. on Optimization, Sensing and Energy Systems*, Istanbul, Türkiye (pp. 793–797).
12. F. K. H. Mihna, M. A. Habeeb, Y. L. Khaleel, Y. H. Ali, and L. A. E. Al-Saeedi. 2024. Using information technology for comprehensive analysis and prediction in forensic evidence. *Mesopotamian Journal of CyberSecurity*, 4 (1): 4–16.
13. T. M. Bhraguram, P. S. Rajakumar, and N. Kanya. 2024. A susceptible evidence processing framework for handheld devices through digital forensic measurements. *International Journal of Intelligent Systems and Applications in Engineering*, 12 (17S): 427–442.
14. A. Sigamani and P. Selvaraj. 2024. TripleMAsk spatial linear filter and neutrosophic entropy for video denoising, face detection and recognition in forensic crime analysis using deep learning. *Neutrosophic Sets and Systems*, 67: 21–56.
15. R. Shashidhar and S. Patil Kulkarni. 2021. Visual speech recognition for small-scale dataset using VGG16 convolution neural network. *Multimedia Tools and Applications*, 80 (19): 28941–28952.
16. M. M. Eltoukhy, F. S. Alsubaei, A. M. Mortda, and K. M. Hosny. 2025. An efficient convolution neural network method for copy-move video forgery detection. *Alexandria Engineering Journal*, 110: 429–437.
17. J. K. Luka, O. M. J. Popoola, and S. B. Abidin. 2025. From forensic knowledge to fraud detection performance: Mediating role of big data analytics skills in the public sector. *International Journal of Applied Mathematics (Sofia)*, 38 (4S): 880–902.
18. Xue, X., Monika, Bajaj, R. K., Dhumras, H., Liu, Z., & Qiao, D. (2025). Forensic analysis of fraud detection in digital payments using MCDM-TOPSIS technique under new T-spherical fuzzy hypersoft similarity measures. *IEEE Transactions on Consumer Electronics*, 71(4), 11073–11087. https://doi.org/10.1109/TCE.2025.3610900
19. H. Alshurafat, H. Ananzeh, J. M. Al-Msiedeen, and C. Beattie. 2025. Do CEO characteristics impact the decision to hire external auditor with forensic accounting competencies? Evidence from Jordanian listed companies. *Journal of Business and Socio-Economic Development*: 1–18.
20. N. Poyda-Nosyk, S. Lehenchuk, V. Makarovych, I. Polishchuk, and T. Zavalii. 2025. Analytical procedures in audit as a tool for predicting the risks of financial statement fraud in marketing companies. *Journal of Economic Sciences: Theory and Practice*, 82 (1): 19–35.
21. Arshad, M., Ahmad, A., Onn, C. W., & Sam, E. A. (2025). Investigating methods for forensic analysis of social media data to support criminal investigations. *Frontiers in Computer Science*, 7, 1566513. https://doi.org/10.3389/fcomp.2025.1566513.
22. Chou, J., Yeh, P., Liu, C., & Chen, K. (2026). Improving detection of pollution fee declarations for environmental policy compliance through metaheuristic-optimized ensemble learning. *Engineering, Construction and Architectural Management*, **33**(7), 5820–5848. https://doi.org/10.1108/ECAM-08-2024-1113.
23. Achmad, T., Huang, C.-Y., Putra, M. A., & Pamungkas, I. D. (2024). Forensic accounting and risk management: Exploring the impact of generalized audit software and whistleblowing systems on fraud detection in Indonesia. *Journal of Risk and Financial Management*, **17**(12), 573. https://doi.org/10.3390/jrfm17120573.
24. E. Hajjat, M. Alzoubi, L. Al-Othman, L. Wedyan, and O. Hayajneh. 2024. The role of forensic accounting in enhancing financial transparency and minimizing fraud in Jordanian institutions. *International Journal of Industrial Engineering and Production Research*, 35 (3): 207–216.

25. Gabrielli, G., Magri, C., Medioli, A., & Marchini, P. L. (2024). The power of big data affordances to reshape anti-fraud strategies. *Technological Forecasting and Social Change*, 205, 123507. https://doi.org/10.1016/j.techfore.2024.123507.
26. R. Romero-Carazas, A. P. Espíritu-Martínez, M. M. Aguilar-Cuevas, M. N. Usuriaga-Palacios, L. A. Aguilar-Cuevas, M. Z. Espinoza-Véliz, and S. G. Gutiérrez-Monzón. 2024. Forensic auditing and the use of artificial intelligence: A bibliometric analysis and systematic review in Scopus between 2000 and 2024. *Heritage and Sustainable Development*, 6 (2): 415–428.
27. M. S. Khan, M. Zubair, D. Verma, A. H. Naqvi, A. Azam, and M. K. Bhardwaj. 2011. The study of indoor radon in the urban dwellings using plastic track detectors. *Environmental Earth Sciences*, 63 (2): 279–282.
28. Dash, D., Princy, D., Kumar, M.S., Guntaj, J., Jain, R., Yadav, D.A., & Hashmi, D.S. (2025). Artificial Intelligence in Auditing: Enhancing Fraud Detection and Risk Assessment. International Journal of Accounting and Economics Studies.
29. E. Casey and A. Zehnder. 2021. Inter-regional digital forensic knowledge management: Needs, challenges, and solutions. *Journal of Forensic Sciences*, 66 (2): 619–629.
30. J. Anand, J. Arul Valan, and M. Mythily. 2008. Performance analysis of mesh based multicast routing protocol for ad-hoc wireless networks. *International Engineering and Technology Publications Journal of Communication Techniques*, 2 (2): 99–103.
31. A. Jose, D. Srinath, R. Janarthanan, and C. 2009. Uthayakumar. Efficient controller area network using multihoming protocol. *Engineering Today, Journal of Technology World*, XI (10): 125–129.
32. C. Uthayakumar, K. Sarukesi, and A. Jose. 2009. A review on knowledge management and knowledge audit. *International Journal on The Technology World*, V (I): 228–233.
33. R. Vaishnavi, J. Anand, and R. Janarthanan. 2009. Efficient security for desktop data grid using cryptographic protocol. *IEEE International Conference on Control, Automation, Communication and Energy Conservation, Kongu Engineering College*, Erode, Vol. 1, pp. 305–311.
34. J. Anand and D. Srinath. 2009. Performance analysis of shared tree based multicast routing protocol for ad-hoc wireless networks. *International Journal of Engineering and Technology*, 2 (1): 1–8.
35. Shakir Khan, M., Suhail, M., & Alharbi, T. (2018). Evaluation of urban growth and land use transformation in Riyadh using Landsat satellite data. *Arabian Journal of Geosciences*, **11**, 540. https://doi.org/10.1007/s12517-018-3896-5.
36. G. Ramesh, S. SundaraVadivelu, and J. Anand. 2010. A survey on wavelength division multiplexing networks. *ICTACT International Journal on Communication Technology*, 1 (1): 32–36.
37. G. Ramesh, S. SundaraVadivelu, and Jose A. 2009. Design of optimized WDM networks using heuristic algorithms. *International Journal of Advance in Communication Engineering*, 1 (2): 93–98.
38. D. Srinath, J. Janet, and J. Anand. 2010. A survey of routing instability with IP spoofing on the internet. *Asian Journal of Information Technology*, 9 (3): 154–158.
39. V. Vijaya Raja, R. Rani Hemamalini, and J. Anand. 2011. Multi agent system based upstream congestion control in wireless sensor networks. *European Journal of Scientific Research*, 59 (2): 241–248.
40. J. Anand, R. Janarthanan, P. Kannan, and A. Konar. 2011. Efficient data storage in desktop data-grid computing using real-time parameters. *International Journal of Computer Science and Technology*, 2 (3): 392–397.
41. V. Vijaya Raja, R. Rani Hemamalini, and J. Anand. 2011. Study of traditional fairness congestion control algorithm in realistic WSN scenarios. *International Journal of Engineering Research and Applications*, 1 (4): 1645–1651.
42. V. Vijaya Raja, R. Rani Hemamalini, and Jose A. 2011. Study of traditional upstream congestion control algorithm with various metrics in realistic WSN scenarios. *International Journal of Computer Science and Information Technologies*, 2 (6): 2473–2478.

43. V. Vijaya Raja, R. Rani Hemamalini, and J. Anand. 2011. Performance evaluation of agent-based upstream congestion control approach in WSN. *International Journal of Computer Technology and Applications*, 2 (6): 1939–1944.
44. V. Vijaya Raja, R. Rani Hemamalini, and J. Anand. 2011. Implementation of RETSINA-based congestion control technique in realistic WSN scenarios. *International Journal of Computer Science Engineering and Technology*, 1 (10): 617–621.
45. H. Samuel, S. Kaul, and J. Anand. 2014. A secure routing technique for wireless sensor networks. *International Journal of Engineering Research & Technology*, 3 (3): 275–279.
46. A. Suganya, D. Parameswari, R. Geetha, A. Govindaram, S. Bahuguna, and J. A. Jose Anand. 2025. Comparison of machine learning methods for fraudulent transaction classification. *Proceedings of the IEEE International Conference on Emerging Technologies*, Belgaum, India.
47. M. S. Khan, A. H. Naqvi, A. Azam, and D. S. Srivastava. 2011. Radium and radon exhalation studies of soil. *Radiation Protection Dosimetry*, 8 (4): 207–210.
48. M. Sabari Ramachandran, S. Sajithabanu, A. Ponmalar, M. Mohamed Sithik, and J. A. Jose Anand. 2024. Fraud detection and risk management using AI in business intelligence. In A. Natarajan, M. Galety, C. Iwendi, D. Das, & A. Shankar (Eds.), *Advances in Artificial Intelligence Applications* (pp. 117–150). IGI Global.
49. A. A. S. Mahmoud, N. Mandela, N. R. Mistry, and A. K. Agrawal. 2025. A hybrid approach for social media forensics. *International Journal of Electronic Security and Digital Forensics*, 17 (4): 460–483.
50. P. Singh, M. Singh, and P. Bhambri. 2004, November. Interoperability: A problem of component reusability. In *International Conference on Emerging Technologies in IT Industry* (Vol. 60). PCTE.
51. P. Bhambri, S. Bagga, D. Priya, H. Singh, and H. K. Dhiman. 2020, December. Suspicious human activity detection system. *Journal of ISMAC*, 2 (4): 216–221.
52. A. Jain, M. Singh, and P. Bhambri. 2021, August. Performance evaluation of IPv4-IPv6 tunneling procedure using IoT. *Journal of Physics: Conference Series,* 1950 (1): 012010.
53. V. K. Sinha, R. Jeet, P. Bhambri, and M. Mahajan. 2020. Empowering intrusion detection in IRIS recognition system: A review. *Journal of Natural Remedies*, 21 (2): 131–153.
54. G. C. N. Babu, S. Gupta, P. Bhambri, L. M. Leo, B. H. Rao, and S. Kumar. 2021. A semantic health observation system development based on the IoT sensors. *Turkish Journal of Physiotherapy and Rehabilitation*, 32 (3): 1721–1729.
55. M. Mohammad, M. S. Khan, and R. A. Faridi. 2019. Assessment of urban heat islands effect and land surface temperature of Noida, India by using Landsat satellite data. *Mapan – Journal of Metrology Society of India*, 34 (4): 431–441.
56. P. Bhambri, M. Singh, A. Jain, I. S. Dhanoa, V. K. Sinha, and S. Lal. 2021. Classification of gene expression data with the aid of optimized feature selection. *Turkish Journal of Physiotherapy and Rehabilitation*, 32 (3): 1158–1168.
57. J. Kaur, P. Bhambri, and S. Kaur. 2019. SVM classifier based method for software defect prediction. *International Journal of Analytical and Experimental Model Analysis*, 11 (10): 2772–2776.
58. P. Bhambri. 2024. Artificial intelligence enabled Internet of Medical Things for enhanced healthcare systems. In P. Bhambri, R. Soni, and T. A. Tran (Eds.), *Smart Healthcare Systems: AI and IoT Perspectives* (pp. 1–17). CRC Press.
59. R. Rana and P. Bhambri. 2024. Generative AI-driven security frameworks for web engineering: Innovations and challenges. In I. A. Shah and N. Z. Jhanjhi (Eds.), *Generative AI for Web Engineering Models* (pp. 285–296). IGI Global.
60. P. Bhambri and S. Rani. 2024. Ethical issues for climate change and mental health. In D. Samanta and M. Garg (Eds.), *Impact of Climate Change on Mental Health and Well-being* (pp. 178–198). IGI Global.

Chapter 9

Advanced network forensics for cloud environments

Vidhya Prakash Rajendran, Sadasivam Subbarayan, Vimalakeerthy Devadoss and Sivakumar Muthusamy

9.1 INTRODUCTION

Elastic, multi-tenant, globally dispersed platforms that serve important corporate and government activities are made possible by cloud computing, which has become a core infrastructure for contemporary digital services. While on-demand provisioning, abstraction of underlying resources, and ubiquitous connection are some of the appealing features of cloud platforms, they also provide new opportunities for abuse and complex criminality. Therefore, digital forensics has transformed into cloud forensics, which is the practice of applying digital forensic science to cloud settings. Cloud forensics is a subset of network forensics that focuses on data, traffic, and services that reside in the cloud [1].

Evidence originating from virtualized network layers, software-defined infrastructures, and service APIs, as opposed to conventional, host-bound artifacts, is the primary emphasis of advanced network forensics in cloud settings. Cloud service models (IaaS, PaaS, SaaS) and multi-cloud deployments add complexity to investigations, which must struggle with dynamic virtual machine migration, conceptually shared but geographically separated storage, logging systems controlled by providers, and complicated chains of accountability [1, 2]. When data is unstable, encrypted, or spread across several countries and providers, these features make evidence identification, collection, preservation, and correlation much more difficult.

In order to tackle these problems on a large scale, standardized guidelines and reference models have been developed. To formalize the issue area and its influence on investigative processes, the National Institute of Standards and Technology (NIST) Cloud Computing Forensic Science Working Group has identified 62 cloud forensic challenges that include data gathering, legal limitations, multi-tenancy, provenance, and trust boundaries. Proceeding from that point, the NIST Cloud Computing Forensic Reference Architecture (SP 800-201) [3, 4] presents a methodical approach and capability mapping to aid in cloud forensic preparedness, bringing together security architectures, operational capabilities, and forensic needs in cloud ecosystems. These initiatives highlight the need to incorporate forensic thought into cloud architecture instead of seeing investigations as reactive tasks.

Cloud digital forensics, according to new research, has to go "beyond tools" to include cloud-native heterogeneity in governance, risk management, and continuous assurance. In order to build trustworthy timelines and attribution models while adhering to strict privacy and regulatory requirements, this viewpoint stresses the need for integrating log analytics, access-control telemetry, identity signals, and traces at the workload level [5]. To piece together attack pathways that span several tenants or regions, which cannot be deduced

DOI: 10.1201/9781003656487-9

from endpoint data alone, network-centric evidence such as flows, packet captures, and higher-layer telemetry provides a crucial backbone in these situations.

At the same time, AI is becoming the backbone of cloud-based enhanced network forensics. In comparison to more conventional statistical or signature-based approaches, AI-driven anomaly detection models—including hybrid deep-learning architectures such as CNN-GAN combinations—have shown to be more effective at detecting subtle and previously unseen attack patterns in network traffic [6]. With an emphasis on minimizing false positives and enabling real-time response in large-scale settings, new frameworks for AI-based anomaly detection in cloud security are calling for specialized data collection pipelines, cloud-specific model-selection criteria, and training approaches. Taken as a whole, these advancements point to a new direction in cloud-native network forensics that is augmented by AI. This approach combines rigorous forensic concepts with intelligent automation to make investigations in AI-driven cloud ecosystems faster, more robust, and evidence-based [14–20].

9.2 CONCEPTUAL FRAMEWORK OF NETWORK FORENSICS IN CLOUD ENVIRONMENTS

9.2.1 Digital and network forensics: core concepts

Digital forensics is described as the use of scientifically validated methodologies for the preservation, collection, validation, identification, analysis, interpretation, recording, and presentation of digital evidence obtained from digital sources. The main goal is to reconstruct events in a reliable, repeatable, and legally or regulatorily permissible way. Network forensics, a subset of this wider profession, focuses on the collection, documentation, and analysis of network traffic to identify breaches and investigate security events [7]. In contrast to conventional host-centric analysis, which focuses mostly on at-rest artifacts such as disk images or file systems, network forensics must address high-volume, time-sensitive data that may not be recorded unless acquired proactively. Common artifacts comprise:

- Packet captures (PCAP) and reconstructed sessions
- Flow records encapsulating communication patterns
- Logs of the intrusion detection and prevention system
- Logs from firewalls, proxies, and virtual private networks (VPNs)
- Network telemetry pertaining to DNS and authentication

Network forensics frameworks often use staged process models—preparation, collection, inspection, analysis, and presentation—that correspond with overarching digital forensic investigation models [21–25]. These models emphasize chain of custody, integrity preservation, and meticulous recordkeeping, even when evidence is just represented as ephemeral network flows.

9.2.2 Cloud computing as a forensic context

Cloud computing serves as the foundational infrastructure for modern network forensics. The NIST definition delineates cloud computing as a framework that facilitates ubiquitous, convenient, on-demand network access to a shared pool of configurable computing resources that can be swiftly provisioned and relinquished with minimal management effort or service provider interaction [8]. This model is organized around:

- Five fundamental attributes: on-demand self-service, extensive network accessibility, resource pooling, rapid flexibility, and measurable service.
- Three service models: Infrastructure as a Service (IaaS), Platform as a Service (PaaS), and Software as a Service (SaaS).
- Four deployment models: private, public, communal, and hybrid clouds.

Each attribute influences the generation, storage, and retrieval of network evidence. Elasticity and resource pooling, for example, result in frequent modifications to IP addressing, routing, and virtual network configurations, but multi-tenancy restricts direct access to the underlying physical infrastructure and raw packet streams.

9.2.3 Cloud forensics and its relationship to network forensics

Cloud forensics has developed as a specialized sub-domain that utilizes digital forensic ideas and methodologies inside cloud systems [26–30]. In this work, Ruan et al. characterize cloud forensics as the implementation of digital forensic science inside cloud computing settings, including a hybrid amalgamation of remote, live, network, and large-scale forensic methodologies [1].

Cloud forensics conceptually connects with network forensics in several dimensions:

- Cloud infrastructures are fundamentally network-centric; the majority of interactions with cloud resources transpire via APIs, administrative planes, and service endpoints accessible over the network.
- Multi-layered abstractions, such as hypervisors, virtual switches, overlays, and gateways, result in several essential artifacts being recorded as network-layer or control-plane logs instead of conventional host artifacts.
- Cloud participants—providers, customers, brokers, carriers, auditors—engage via networked interfaces, with their logs and flow records often serving as the most dependable resource for reconstructing cross-tenant or cross-region occurrences.

Research and classification efforts in cloud forensics consistently underscore challenges, including evidence dispersion, ambiguity regarding data location, provider-controlled logging, and the necessity to modify traditional phases of identification, collection, preservation, analysis, and presentation for highly distributed, virtualized environments [31–35]. In this context, network-centric evidence serves as a fundamental basis for cloud investigations, particularly when access to guest operating systems, hypervisors, or physical devices is restricted or controlled by the provider.

9.2.4 Network-centric evidence in cloud settings

In cloud systems, network evidence extends beyond conventional packet captures acquired at perimeter taps. Rather, it encompasses a range of cloud-native artifacts, including:

- Flow logs of the Virtual Private Cloud (VPC) detailing permitted and rejected connections among instances, subnets, and external endpoints.
- Logs from the software-defined networking (SDN) controller, including policy choices, rule implementations, and changes in topology.
- Logs of API calls and telemetry from the management plane indicating administrative activities, such as instance creation, adjustments to security groups, or key rotations.

- Logs from virtualized network services (load balancers, web application firewalls, NAT gateways, VPN concentrators) that facilitate tenant traffic.

9.2.5 Process models and forensic readiness for cloud networks

Classical network forensic process models underscore a systematic progression of preparation, detection, collection, preservation, inspection, analysis, and presentation [7]. In cloud environments, these stages are redefined to prioritize forensic preparedness, meaning that infrastructures are designed to ensure the generation, retention, and accessibility of pertinent evidence prior to the occurrence of events [36–40].

Principal adaptations comprise the following processes:

Preparation:

- Facilitating and standardizing VPC flow logs, API logs, and other network-function logs across accounts, regions, and tenants.
- Implementing precise time synchronization (e.g., NTP) across cloud resources to facilitate cohesive timeline reconstruction.

Acquisition and conservation:

- Automating the export of flow logs and management-plane telemetry to secure, tamper-resistant storage solutions (e.g., write-once object storage, specialized forensic repositories).
- Labeling network artifacts with contextual information (tenant IDs, project IDs, application tags) to enable further correlation.

Assessment and evaluation:

- Utilizing scalable analytics on extensive amounts of flow and log data, often employing big-data platforms, stream-processing engines, and AI-driven models.
- Reconstructing sessions, attack graphs, and death chains using network-layer observations with minimal host-level artifacts.

Documentation and display:

- Creating comprehensible visual representations of cloud network architectures, lateral movement trajectories, and data exfiltration pathways appropriate for legal, regulatory, or management stakeholders.

The NIST cloud forensic challenge catalog and associated research on cloud forensic maturity highlight that readiness measures must be established within shared-responsibility frameworks, wherein cloud providers oversee numerous lower-layer artifacts while customers handle application- and tenant-level telemetry [8].

9.2.6 Rationale for AI-driven approaches

The aforementioned conceptual foundations necessitate the implementation of AI-driven methodologies. Cloud network telemetry is characterized by significant volume, velocity, and diversity; human triage and rule-based systems alone are inadequate for identifying subtle, low-and-slow, or novel attack patterns. Recent studies on AI-driven anomaly detection and deep-learning-based intrusion detection indicate that machine learning models may identify non-linear correlations in flow-level and encrypted traffic data, surpassing conventional signature-based methods in several instances.

In cloud contexts, AI methodologies are especially pertinent for:

- Detection of anomalies in extensive flow logs and sequences of API calls.
- Behavioral profiling of services, tenants, and identities to detect anomalies suggestive of compromise.
- Automated correlation of multi-source data (network, API, identity, and workload telemetry) to reconstruct coherent event narratives.
- Prioritization and triage of alerts and indicators to reduce analyst burden and minimize false positives.
- These capabilities are grounded in the principles of digital and network forensics, enhanced by data-driven, adaptive analytics designed to address the dynamics and complexity of cloud networking.

9.3 AI-DRIVEN FRAMEWORK FOR NETWORK FORENSICS IN CLOUD ENVIRONMENTS

AI-driven network forensics in cloud settings necessitates a methodical design that integrates diverse telemetry sources, scalable storage and processing elements, and sophisticated analytics engines. Every layer aids in the overarching objective of converting unrefined network and management-plane data into reliable forensic evidence and actionable insights.

9.3.1 High-level framework architecture

A conceptual design may be structured as a left-to-right pipeline, with feedback loops from the analytics layer to the logging configuration and response systems. This may be articulated as an "AI-driven cloud-native network forensic architecture", with the option to further include technologies (e.g., Kafka, Spark, ELK, etc.) if preferred.

9.3.2 Data acquisition and preprocessing

Let S denote the set of telemetry sources:

$$S = \{S_{\text{flow}}, S_{\text{api}}, S_{\text{sdn}}, S_{\text{waf}}, S_{\text{pcap}}\} \tag{9.1}$$

Each source produces a stream of events:

$$S_k = \{e_{k,1}, e_{k,2}, \ldots, e_{k,n_k}\}, \; k \in S \tag{9.2}$$

Each event $e_{k,i}$ is mapped into a unified schema:

$$e_{k,i} \mapsto x_{k,i} = (t, \text{src}, \text{dst}, p, \vec{a}) \tag{9.3}$$

where

t—timestamp (normalized to UTC and synchronized via NTP)
src, dst—abstracted source/destination identifiers (IP, tenant ID, role)
p—protocol and port
$\vec{a}$—vector of attributes (bytes, packets, status codes, API verb, region, etc.)

Time windowing:

Events are grouped into fixed windows $W_j = \left[T_j, T_j + \Delta T\right)$. For each window and each communicating pair (u, v), the framework aggregates:

$$\mathrm{bytes}_{\mathrm{u,v}}^{(\mathrm{j})} = \sum_{x \in W_j(u,v)} \mathrm{bytes}(x), \tag{9.4}$$

$$\mathrm{pkts}_{\mathrm{u,v}}^{(\mathrm{j})} = \sum_{x \in W_j(u,v)} \mathrm{pkts}(x), \tag{9.5}$$

$$\mathrm{conn}_{\mathrm{u,v}}^{(\mathrm{j})} = \left| t W_j\left(u, v\right) \right| \tag{9.6}$$

where $\mathrm{W_j}(\mathrm{u}, \mathrm{v}) \subseteq \mathrm{W_j}$ is the subset of events between u and v.

Missing or distorted values are addressed by basic imputation techniques, including:

- Mean/median imputation for continuous variables
- Mode or distinct "unknown" classification for categorical variables

9.3.3 Feature engineering for cloud network telemetry

To apply AI models, each window or event is represented as a feature vector $f \in R^d$. Typical features for cloud network forensics include:

(a) Statistical communication features
  - Total bytes, packets, flows
  - Directional asymmetry

$$A_{\mathrm{bytes}}^{(j)} = \frac{\mathrm{bytes}_{u \to v}^{(j)} - \mathrm{bytes}_{v \to u}^{(j)}}{\mathrm{bytes}_{u \to v}^{(j)} + \mathrm{bytes}_{v \to u}^{(j)} + \in} \tag{9.7}$$

(b) Temporal features
  - Inter-arrival time statistics
  - Burstiness index

$$B^{(j)} = \frac{\sigma_{\mathrm{iat}}^{(j)}}{\mu_{\mathrm{iat}}^{(j)}} + \in \tag{9.8}$$

(c) Topological features
  - Degree of a node u in a given window
  - Edge betweenness or centrality measures for services

$$d_u^{(j)} = \left| \{ v \mid (u, v) \in E^{(j)} \} \right| \tag{9.9}$$

(d) API and management-plane features
- Count of specific API calls (e.g., CreateInstance, ModifySecurityGroup)
- Sequences of method–resource combinations over time

Normalization formula (for each feature f):

Min-max normalization:

$$\tilde{f} = \frac{f - f_{min}}{f_{max} - f_{min} + \in} \tag{9.10}$$

or standardization:

$$\hat{f} = \frac{f - \mu_f}{\sigma_f + \in} \tag{9.11}$$

These modifications are implemented for each feature to stabilize training and mitigate the impact of scale discrepancies.

9.3.4 Anomaly detection models

A primary analytical function in AI-driven cloud network forensics is unsupervised or semi-supervised anomaly detection, whereby models are mostly trained on benign data and then used to give anomaly scores to novel observations.

9.3.4.1 Autoencoder-based anomaly detection

Given feature vectors $f_i \in R^d$, an autoencoder learns an encoder $\phi_\theta : R^d \to R^k$ and decoder $\psi_\theta : R^k \to R^d$ $(k < d)$ by minimizing reconstruction error:

$$L(\theta) = \frac{1}{N} \sum_{i=1}^{N} \| f_i - \psi_\theta(\phi_\theta(f_i)) \|_2^2 \tag{9.12}$$

For a new observation f^*, the reconstruction error serves as an anomaly score:

$$s(f^*) = \| f^* - \psi_\theta(\phi_\theta(f^*)) \backslash \|_2^2 \tag{9.13}$$

A threshold τ (e.g., chosen via a percentile of training errors) flags anomalies:

$$\text{Anomaly}(f^*) = 1 \text{ if } s(f^*) \geq \tau, 0 \text{ otherwise}$$

9.3.4.2 One-class support vector machine (OC-SVM)

Another option is a one-class SVM that learns a decision boundary enclosing most benign points:

$$\min_{w,\rho,\xi_i} \frac{1}{2} | w |^2 + \frac{1}{\nu N} \sum_{i=1}^{N} \xi_i - \rho \tag{9.14}$$

subject to:

$$\left(w\cdot\Phi\left(f_i\right)\right)\geq\rho-\xi_i,\ \xi_i\geq 0, \tag{9.15}$$

where $\Phi(\cdot)$ is a kernel mapping and $\nu\in\left(0,1\right]$ controls the fraction of outliers.

For a new sample:

$$g\left(f^*\right)=\text{sign}\left(w\cdot\Phi\left(f^*\right)-\rho\right) \tag{9.16}$$

with $g\left(f^*\right)=-1$ indicating anomaly.

9.3.5 Attack graph construction and graph-based analytics

Cloud network interactions can be modeled as a time-varying graph $G^{(j)}=\left(V^{(j)},E^{(j)\backslash big}\right)$, where

$V^{(j)}$—set of entities in window \$j\$ (instances, containers, serverless functions, identity principals, external IPs)

$E^{(j)}$—set of edges representing network flows or API relationships

An edge $\left(u,v\right)\in E^{(j)}$ may be associated with attributes $\overrightarrow{a_{u,v}^{(j)}}$ (bytes, ports, anomaly scores, policy decisions, regions).

Attack path reconstruction is then cast as finding suspicious paths in the time-expanded graph:

Path risk score:

$$R\left(P\right)=\sum_{\left(u,v\right)\in P}s_{u,v}, \tag{9.17}$$

where $s_{u,v}$ is an anomaly or risk score for edge $\left(u,v\right)$.

Node risk score:

$$R\left(u\right)=\sum_{v:\left(u,v\right)\in E}s_{u,v}+\sum_{v:\left(v,u\right)\in E}s_{v,u} \tag{9.18}$$

Graph-based methods (e.g., PageRank, centrality measures, community identification) may identify critical pivot nodes, lateral movement hotspots, and anomalous communication clusters.

A simple degree-based pivot indicator for node u in malicious subgraph $G_M$is

$$\Pi\left(u\right)=\frac{d_u\left(G_M\right)}{\max_{v\in V\left(G_M\right)}d_v\left(G_M\right)} \tag{9.19}$$

where $d_u\left(G_M\right)$is the degree of u in the malicious subgraph; higher values indicate potential pivot or command-and-control roles.

9.3.6 Correlation of multi-source evidence

Network-centric abnormalities alone are inadequate for drawing high-confidence forensic findings. The framework establishes a correlation.

- Network events $\left(\mathrm{E}_{\mathrm{net}}\right)$
- Identity and access management events $\left(\mathrm{E}_{\mathrm{iam}}\right)$
- API/management-plane events $\left(\mathrm{E}_{\mathrm{api}}\right)$
- Host/endpoint telemetry where available $\left(E_{\mathrm{hosti}}\right)$

A correlation function can be defined over a unified timeline:

$$\Gamma : \left(E_{\mathrm{net}}, E_{\mathrm{iam}}, E_{\mathrm{api}}, E_{\mathrm{host}}\right) \rightarrow C$$

where C is the set of correlated incident clusters. A simple time-based and entity-based correlation score for two events e_i, e_j may be:

$$C\left(e_i, e_j\right) = exp!\left(-\frac{\left|t_i - t_j\right|}{\lambda_t}\right) 1\left\{\mathrm{entity}\left(e_i\right) = \mathrm{entity}\left(e_j\right)\right\} \tag{9.20}$$

with λ_t defining the temporal decay parameter and $1\{\cdot\}$ an indicator function.

Clusters $\mathrm{C_k} \subseteq \mathrm{E}$ are then formed by grouping events with pairwise correlation $C\left(e_i, e_j\right) \geq \eta$ for some threshold η

9.3.7 Forensic metrics and evaluation

To assess the efficacy of AI-driven cloud network forensics, both detection metrics and forensic-quality metrics are pertinent.

Standard detection metrics (for labeled experiments):

$$\mathrm{Precision} = \frac{\mathrm{TP}}{\mathrm{TP} + \mathrm{FP}}, \quad \mathrm{Recall} = \frac{\mathrm{TP}}{\mathrm{TP} + \mathrm{FN}}, \quad F_1 = 2 \cdot \frac{\mathrm{Precision} \cdot \mathrm{Recall}}{\mathrm{Precision} + \mathrm{Recall}} \tag{9.21}$$

Forensic-oriented metrics may include the following:

Attack path reconstruction accuracy:

$$A_{\mathrm{path}} = \frac{\left|P_{\mathrm{true}} \cap P_{\mathrm{recon}}\right|}{\left|P_{\mathrm{true}}\right|} \tag{9.22}$$

Time-to-detection (TTD) and **time-to-containment (TTC):**

$$\mathrm{TTD} = t_{\mathrm{detect}} - t_{\mathrm{compromise}}, \quad \mathrm{TTC} = t_{\mathrm{contain}} - t_{\mathrm{compromise}} \tag{9.23}$$

Evidence completeness index for an incident I:

$$E_{\mathrm{comp}}\left(I\right) = \frac{\left|A_{\mathrm{critical}}\left(I\right) \cap A_{\mathrm{observed}}\left(I\right)\right|}{\left|A_{\mathrm{critical}}\left(I\right)\right|} \tag{9.24}$$

where $\mathrm{A_{critical}}\left(\mathrm{I}\right)$ is the set of expected critical artifacts (e.g., key flows, API calls, IAM changes) and $\mathrm{A_{observed}}\left(\mathrm{I}\right)$ is what the system captured. These metrics support both research comparisons and practical tuning of AI models and logging configurations.

9.4 CONCLUSION

AI-driven network forensics in cloud settings now surpasses mere retroactive log analysis. This discourse establishes cloud-native telemetry—VPC flow logs, API and management-plane logs, SDN/controller traces, and container-orchestrator events—as the principal source of evidence for large-scale reconstruction of attacker activities. Methodical preprocessing, normalization, and feature engineering convert this diverse data into high-quality signals appropriate for sophisticated analytics, while anomaly-detection models and graph-based methodologies reveal both nuanced discrepancies and multi-step attack trajectories that would remain undetected through manual examination [41–44].

The outlined methodology prioritizes ongoing model calibration, policy feedback mechanisms, and stringent forensic criteria to ensure that detection efficacy, false alarm frequency, and inquiry duration are quantifiable and verifiable. Graph-centric representations of cloud infrastructure and identities facilitate reasoning regarding lateral movement and blast radius, while multi-source correlation—integrating network telemetry, IAM events, workload signals, and case-management artifacts—establishes an evidential chain that withstands legal, regulatory, and internal scrutiny. The debate concurrently underscores several limitations: reliance on the quality and coverage of telemetry, susceptibility of machine learning models to drift and adversarial attacks, and the need to protect privacy when consolidating huge amounts of behavioral data [45–48].

Future advancements are expected to arise from several intersecting avenues. Deep-learning and foundation-model-based intrusion-detection architectures will integrate more comprehensive context across tenants and clouds, explainable-AI methodologies will render model outputs actionable and justifiable for investigators, and federated and privacy-preserving learning will facilitate collaborative defense without disclosing raw logs. The integration of contemporary SOC tools, SOAR pipelines, and zero-trust mechanisms may transform high-accuracy detections into swift, coordinated containment measures. The proposed framework illustrates the transition of cloud providers, enterprises, and researchers from isolated log analysis to an intelligent, evidence-based, and automation-capable network forensic capability that withstands the scale, elasticity, and advanced threats of next-generation cloud infrastructures.

REFERENCES

1. Ruan, K., Carthy, J., Kechadi, T., & Baggili, I. (2013). Cloud forensics definitions and critical criteria for cloud forensic capability: An overview of survey results. *Digital Investigation, 10*(1), 34–43.
2. Manral, B., Somani, G., Choo, K.-K. R., Conti, M., & Gaur, M. S. (2020). A systematic survey on cloud forensics challenges, solutions, and future directions. *ACM Computing Surveys, 52*(6), 124:1–124:38.
3. Herman, M., Iorga, M., Salim, A. S., Jackson, R. H., Hurst, M. R., Leo, R. A., Lee, R., Landreville, N. M., Mishra, A. K., Wang, Y., & Sardinas, R. (2020). *NIST cloud computing forensic science challenges* (NIST Interagency/Internal Report 8006). National Institute of Standards and Technology.
4. Herman, M., Iorga, M., Salim, A. M., Jackson, R. H., Hurst, M. R., Leo, R. A., Mishra, A. K., & Wang, Y. (2024). *NIST cloud computing forensic reference architecture* (NIST Special Publication 800-201). National Institute of Standards and Technology.
5. Malik, A. W., Bhatti, D. S., Park, T., Ishtiaq, H. U., Ryou, J., & Kim, K.-I. (2024). Cloud digital forensics: Beyond tools, techniques, and challenges. *Sensors, 24*(2), 433.

6. Rao, V. S., Balakrishna, R., El-Ebiary, Y. A. B., Thapar, P., Aanandha Saravanan, K., & Godla, S. R. (2024). AI driven anomaly detection in network traffic using hybrid CNN–GAN. *Journal of Advances in Information Technology, 15*(7), 886–895.
7. Pilli, E. S., Joshi, R. C., & Niyogi, R. (2010). Network forensic frameworks: Survey and research challenges. *Digital Investigation, 7*(1–2), 14–27.
8. Mell, P., & Grance, T. (2011). *The NIST definition of cloud computing* (NIST Special Publication 800-145). National Institute of Standards and Technology.
9. Almulla, S., Iraqi, Y., & Jones, A. (2014). A state-of-the-art review of cloud forensics. *Journal of Digital Forensics, Security and Law, 9*(4), 2.
10. Hozouri, A., Mirzaei, A., & Effatparvar, M. (2025). A comprehensive survey on intrusion detection systems with advances in machine learning, deep learning and emerging cybersecurity challenges. *Discover Artificial Intelligence, 5*, 314. https://doi.org/10.1007/s44163-025-00578-1
11. Xu, Z., Wu, Y., Wang, S., Gao, J., Qiu, T., Wang, Z., … Zhao, X. (2025). Deep learning-based intrusion detection systems: A survey. arXiv. https://arxiv.org/abs/2504.07839
12. Khan, N., Ahmad, K., Al Tamimi, A., Alani, M. M., Bermak, A., & Khalil, I. (2025). Explainable AI-based intrusion detection systems for Industry 5.0 and adversarial XAI: A systematic review. *Information, 16*(12), 1036. https://doi.org/10.3390/info16121036
13. Sharma, A., Rani, S., & Shabaz, M. (2025). A comprehensive review of explainable AI in cybersecurity: Decoding the black box. *ICT Express.* Advance online publication. https://doi.org/10.1016/j.icte.2025.10.004
14. Kaul, S., Samuel, H., & Anand, J. (2014, March). Defending against vampire attacks in wireless sensor networks. *International Journal of Communication Engineering Applications, 5*, 565–571.
15. Samuel, H., Kaul, S., & Anand, J. (2014). A reliable routing technique for wireless sensor networks. *International Journal of Research in Engineering & Advanced Technology, 2*(2), 1–7.
16. Anand, J., Yaseen, M. M., & Radha, K. (2014). Multi-session packet scheduling approaches over multi-hop wireless networks. *International Journal of Advanced Research in Computer and Communication Engineering, 3*(7), 1–7.
17. Anand, J., & Arul Flora, T. G. (2014). Emergency traffic management for ambulance using wireless communication. *IPASJ International Journal of Electronics & Communication, 2*(7), 1–4.
18. Varughese, S. E., George, M., & Anand, J. (2014). Content-based image retrieval technique on texture and shape analysis using wavelet feature and clustering model. *International Journal of Enhanced Research in Science Technology & Engineering, 3*(8), 224–229.
19. Anand, J., & Perinbam, J. R. P. (2014). Automatic irrigation system using fuzzy logic. *AE International Journal of Multidisciplinary Research, 2*(8), 1–9.
20. Anand, J., Thyla, B., & Abida Begum, S. (2014). Performance analysis of LEACH protocol. *International Journal of Electronics Communication and Computer Engineering, 5*(4), 993–996.
21. Anand, J., & Perinbam, J. R. P. (2014). A survey on energy efficient biomedical wireless sensor networks. *American International Journal of Research in Science, Technology, Engineering & Mathematics, 3*(7), 212–216.
22. Anand, J., & Sivachandar, K. (2014). Vampire attack detection in wireless sensor networks. *International Journal of Engineering Science and Innovative Technology, 3*(4), 639–644.
23. Priyanka, V., & Anand, J. (2015). Centralized fault management of docks in marine sensor networks. *IOSR Journal of Electronics and Communication Engineering, 10*(1), 30–36.
24. Menon, S., & Anand, J. (2015). Cooperative data forwarding in AODV routing protocol. *IOSR Journal of Electronics and Communication Engineering, 10*(1), 5–8.
25. Anand, J., Perinbam, J. R. P., & Meganathan, D. (2015). Design of GA-based routing in biomedical wireless sensor networks. *International Journal of Applied Engineering Research, 10*(4), 9281–9292.
26. Menon, S., & Anand, J. (2015). Cooperative and secured data forwarding in AODV routing protocol. *International Journal of Advanced Research in Electronics and Communication Engineering, 4*(4), 1026–1031.

27. Anand, J., Perinbam, J. R. P., & Meganathan, D. (2015). Performance of optimized routing in biomedical wireless sensor networks using evolutionary algorithms. *Comptes rendus de l'Académie bulgare des Sciences, 68*(8), 1049–1054.
28. V., P., Poobal, S., & Jose Anand A (2015). Malevolent detection techniques of MANETs in WSN: A review. *International Journal for Engineering and Innovative Technology, 5*(6), 48–54.
29. Anand, J., Perinbam, J. R. P., & Meganathan, D. (2017). Q-learning-based optimized routing in biomedical wireless sensor networks. *IETE Journal of Research, 63*(1), 89–97.
30. Rao, A. R., H., A., M., B., R., L., & Anand, J. (2017). A novel cardiac arrest alerting system using IoT. *International Journal of Science Technology & Engineering, 3*(10), 78–83.
31. Anand, J., Dhanalakshmi, M., & Perinpam, J. R. P. (2019). Smart indication system for spinal cord stress detection. *International Journal of Recent Technology and Engineering, 8*(3), 6164–6168.
32. Adithya, J., Anand, J., & Doss, S. (2019). An efficient priority-based packet scheduling in MANETs. *International Journal of Advanced Engineering and Global Technology, 7*(1), 2373–2382.
33. Geethalakshmi, M., Kanimozhiraman, R., Anand, J., Partheepan, R., & Santhosh, S. (2021). Optimal routing path using trident form in wearable biomedical wireless sensor networks. *Turkish Online Journal of Qualitative Inquiry, 12*(7), 5134–5143.
34. Sheriff, S. T. M., Kumar, J. V., Vigneshwaran, S., Jones, A., & Anand, J. (2021). Lung cancer detection using VGG NET 16 architecture. *International Conference on Physics and Engineering 2021, IOP Publishing, Journal of Physics Conference Series*, Vol. 2040, 2021. Kancheepuram, India.
35. Dhanalakshmi, R., Anand, J., Sivaraman, A. K., & Rani, S. (2022). IoT-based water quality monitoring system using cloud for agriculture use. In P. Bhambri, S. Rani, G. Gupta, & A. Khang (Eds.), *Cloud and fog computing platforms for Internet of Things*. Routledge, Taylor & Francis Group.
36. Augustine, C., Jose, A., Kumar, V., Kaleeswaran, D., Muneeswari, G., & Santhoshkumar, S. P. (2022). 6G-based mobile IPTV using adaptive hybrid transmission. In D. S. Kumar, G. Prabhakar, & R. Anand (Eds.), *Handbook of research on design, deployment, automation, and testing strategies for 6G mobile core network* (p. 20). IGI Global.
37. Dhanalakshmi, R., Anand, J., Poonkavithai, K., & Vijayakumar, V. (2022). Cloud-based glaucoma diagnosis in medical imaging using machine learning. In S. A. Parah, M. Rashid, & V. Varadarajan (Eds.), *Artificial intelligence for innovative healthcare informatics* (pp. 61–78). Springer.
38. Dhanalakshmi, R., & Anand, J. (2022). Big data for personalized healthcare. In A. Jaya, K. Kalaiselvi, D. Goyal, & D. Al-Jumelly (Eds.), *Handbook of intelligent healthcare analytics: Knowledge engineering with big data analytics* (Chap. 4, pp. 67–92). John Wiley & Sons.
39. Mohamed, G., Visumathi, J., Mahdal, M., Jose, A., & Elangovan, M. (2022). An effective and secure mechanism for phishing attacks using a machine learning approach. *Processes, 10*(7), 1356.
40. Sivachandar, K., Amudha, V., Ramesh, B., Anand, J., ShanmugaSundari, M., & Gilda S., J. (2022). MIMO-IDMA system performance for SUI and LTE frequency selective channels. *Advances in Parallel Computing Algorithms, Tools and Paradigms, 41*, 422–428.
41. Sangwan, Y. S., Lal, S., Bhambri, P., Kumar, A., & Dhanoa, I. S. (2021). Advancements in social data security and encryption: A review. *Natural Volatiles & Essential Oils, 8*(4), 15353–15362.
42. Bhambri, P., Rani, S., & Khang, A. (2024). AI-driven digital twin and resource optimization in Industry 4.0 ecosystem. In N. Singh, S. Birla, M. D. Ansari, & N. K. Shukla (Eds.), *AI-driven digital twin and Industry 4.0: A conceptual framework with applications* (pp. 182–201). CRC Press/Taylor & Francis Group.
43. Rana, R., & Bhambri, P. (2024). Generative AI-driven security frameworks for web engineering: Innovations and challenges. In I. A. Shah & N. Z. Jhanjhi (Eds.), *Generative AI for web engineering models* (pp. 285–296). IGI Global.

44. Bhambri, P., Rani, S., Dhanoa, I. S., & Tran, T. A. (2024). Environmental impacts of industrial processes in Industry 4.0 ecosystem artificial intelligence approach. In S. Rani, P. Bhambri, S. Kumar, P. K. Pareek, & A. A. Elngar (Eds.), *AI-driven digital twin and Industry 4.0: A conceptual framework with applications* (pp. 221–240). CRC Press, Taylor & Francis Group.
45. Rana, R., Chhabra, Y., & Bhambri, P. (2021). Comparison and evaluation of various QoS parameters in WSNs with the implementation of enhanced low energy adaptive efficient distributed clustering approach. *Webology, 18*(1), 677–695.
46. Singh, G., & Bhambri, P. (2023). Simulation analysis of AODV and DSDV routing protocols for secure and reliable service in mobile adhoc networks (MANETs). In P. Bhambri, S. Rani, V. E. Balas, & A. A. Elngar (Eds.), *Integration of AI-based manufacturing and industrial engineering systems with the Internet of Things* (1st ed., pp. 205–216). CRC Press.
47. Bhambri, P., & Rani, S. (2024). Bioengineering and healthcare data analysis: Introduction, advances, and challenges. In P. Bhambri, S. Rani, & M. Fahim (Eds.), *Computational intelligence and blockchain in biomedical and health informatics* (1st ed., pp. 1–25). CRC Press.
48. Rana, R., & Bhambri, P. (2024). Generative AI in web application development: Enhancing user experience and performance. In I. A. Shah & N. Z. Jhanjhi (Eds.), *Generative AI for web engineering models* (pp. 471–486). IGI Global.

Chapter 10

Federated temporal-attention network for communication-efficient log anomaly detection in IoT environments

Aman Kumar, Deepak Sharma, Anu Tonk, Vinod Kumar V. Meti, Kallakunta Ravi Kumar and Mayakannan S.

10.1 INTRODUCTION

These days, massive IoT networks often include thousands and thousands of edge devices, each with its own unique set of technical specs (such as design aims, processing and communication capabilities, battery life, etc.). It is critical to guarantee the security of the system and ecosystem as these edge devices perceive, collect, transmit, and receive sensitive data. System operators and organizations can better identify and respond to defects and cyberthreats when they can reliably detect runtime anomalies. Nevertheless, the amount of log data will grow in proportion to the interconnection of current systems and the proliferation of linked devices. This further adds to the difficulty of automated log inspection in just-in-time or real-time.

Anomaly detection has been the target of several attempts to employ Artificial Intelligence (AI), here understood to encompass machine learning and deep learning, with some examples [1]. Although current methods based on machine learning and deep learning can help with the comprehension and representation of free-form, unstructured log data, they are more suited to Standalone systems and struggle to handle the massive amounts of log data generated by large-scale IoT systems. It enables individuals to make better use of distributed intelligence from various devices and systems, which in turn allows for better global situational awareness. On the other hand, the majority of current systems rely on a centralized learning approach, as shown in Figure 10.1. It is pretty much like a cloud server. On the other hand, a paradigm of centralized learning design has its drawbacks. As the volume of log data grows, the centralized server has to do more and more work in terms of calculation and communication [2]. The fact that system logs include private information regarding IoT and edge devices raises further privacy concerns. Sending all of this information to a single server, particularly one located in another country, is dangerous.

The ability for local clients to work is what makes federated learning an extension of collaborative learning. This method has the ability to make AI-enabled IoT systems more private [3]. As an illustration, a proposal by Hemalatha et al. [4] for an intrusion detection system based on anomaly detection in IoT devices utilized a federated Gated Recurrent Units network.

Edge-FLGuard+ is a federated, lightweight anomaly detection framework for 5G smart homes integrating edge AI and FL to ensure privacy and low latency. Using autoencoder models trained across distributed nodes, it achieved ≥95% accuracy on TON_IoT and CIC-IDS2018 datasets. The model outperformed centralized systems in real-time smart home cybersecurity [5]. An edge-assisted federated learning approach is proposed for anomaly

 DOI: 10.1201/9781003656487-10

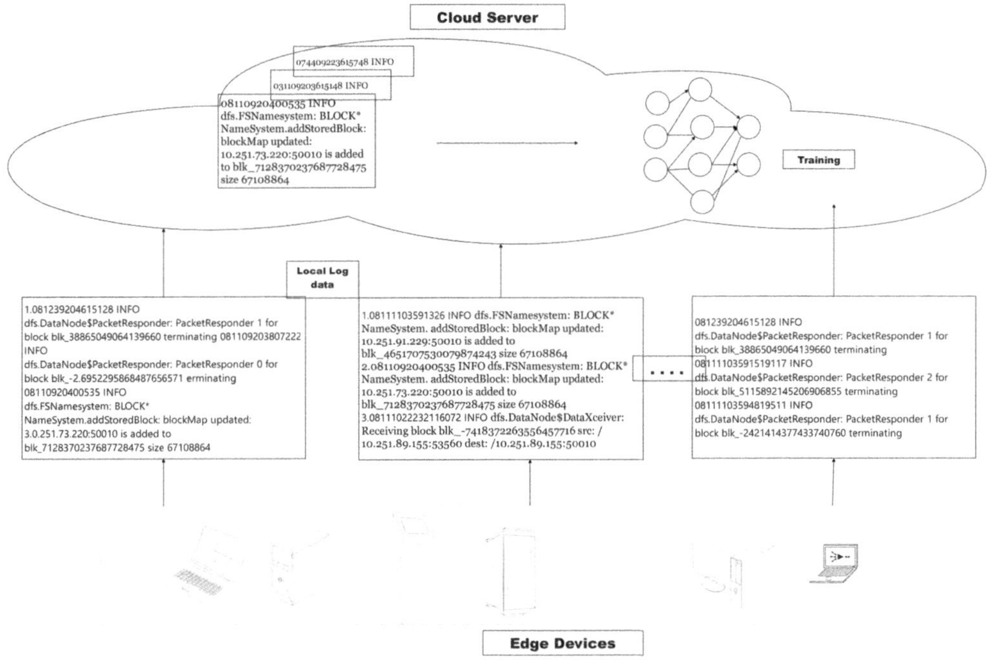

Figure 10.1 Traditional centralized anomaly detection with logs.

detection in heterogeneous IoT networks. It enables collaborative model training while preserving privacy and minimizing communication latency. Results show superior detection accuracy, low energy use, and adaptability across diverse IoT environments [6]. The chapter proposes an IoT security framework using GANs, XAI, and Federated Learning for real-time, interpretable anomaly detection. GANs generate synthetic attack data, while XAI tools improve transparency. The model achieved 94.8% accuracy, 97.1% recall, and 45 ms latency on NSL-KDD datasets [7]. This study introduces an SDN-integrated Segmented Federated Learning (SFL) framework to enhance IoT anomaly detection and response. It enables lightweight, localized training suited for diverse IoT devices, while SDN manages real-time traffic and incident response. The framework reduces communication overhead, preserves privacy, and offers a scalable, adaptive solution for secure IoT operations [8]. The EdgeGuard-IoT framework, powered by 6G edge intelligence, integrates Secure Federated Learning (SFL), Adaptive Anomaly Detection (AAD), blockchain, and zero-trust security. Designed for smart grids, it ensures ultra-reliable, low-latency, and privacy-preserving cyber defense. Simulations and case studies show superior accuracy, scalability, and resilience for Industry 5.0 ecosystems [9].

This study investigates the optimal deep learning model and data volume for FL-based intrusion detection systems on resource-limited IoT devices. Among DNN, CNN, and CNN+BiLSTM architectures trained on the CICIoT2023 dataset, CNN achieved the best balance between accuracy (~98%) and computational efficiency, while CNN+BiLSTM reached ~99% accuracy at a higher cost [10]. The SymFL-GNN framework combines Federated Learning, Graph Neural Networks, and Homomorphic Encryption for decentralized threat detection in 6G-enabled IoT networks. It ensures privacy through encrypted gradient sharing and interpretable sensor-graph analysis. Tested on SWaT and WADI datasets, it achieved ~96% accuracy, proving effective for secure, intelligent edge environments

[11]. This study proposes a federated LSTM–autoencoder-based anomaly detection system for smart grids, integrating MSD and MAD metrics. Homomorphic encryption ensures data privacy while maintaining high accuracy and low computational overhead. The model achieves 98% accuracy and 97% F1-score, demonstrating strong efficiency for industrial IoT security [12]. A hierarchical collaborative intrusion detection system (CIDS) combining federated learning and blockchain-based trust is introduced for IoT networks. It efficiently detects attacks while preserving privacy and ensuring reliable communication. Tests on the CICIoT2023 dataset achieved 97.65% accuracy and near-perfect recall [13]. A federated recommender hybrid intrusion detection system (FRHIDS) is proposed to secure IoT–SDN environments. It performs local training to protect privacy and recommends safe nodes for communication. The model improves detection performance by 12% while minimizing computational complexity [14]. A drone identification system was studied using focus measure operators (FMOs) and a random forest classifier to differentiate drones from birds in surveillance footage. The approach offers an efficient automated solution for drone monitoring and security applications [15].

The machine vision is integrated with artificial neural networks (ANNs) for intelligent robotic control. A 3-DOF robotic assembly and a 6-DOF vision-based robot demonstrate enhanced precision, adaptability, and reduced computation time. Experimental results confirm improved convergence and performance in visual-guided robotic operations [16]. This research investigates quantum service-oriented computing (SOC) for integrating classical and quantum systems using the Amazon Braket platform. A case study on integer factorization as a quantum service highlights key challenges in hybrid system implementation [17]. This study presents a LiDAR-based canopy recognition method using laser reflection intensity correction to accurately identify tree canopies in complex urban environments. A 2D LiDAR–MLS system was used for data acquisition and correction of distance–angle intensity values. The proposed model achieved an F1-score of 0.84, improving recognition accuracy by 31% over traditional methods [18]. A context-aware model based on Mask R-CNN is proposed for detecting abandoned and stationary objects in public surveillance videos. Modified convolution layers enhance feature extraction under geometric variations, improving detection in complex scenes. The model achieved up to 0.734 mAP, outperforming existing state-of-the-art techniques [19].

Q-EDGE-ID introduces a quantum-enhanced edge intrusion detection system integrating Quantum Reservoir Computing (QRC) for IoT networks. It achieves 94.1% accuracy, 93.5% F1-score, and low latency (45 ms) with minimal energy consumption (2.4 mJ per decision). The approach provides a lightweight and energy-efficient IDS for next-generation IoT systems [20]. A fuzzy logic–based stacked data-driven autoencoder (FL_SDDAE) is proposed for dynamic soft sensing in industrial automation. It performs robust feature representation and classification using an LSEBPNN model. The system achieved 94% prediction performance and 85% measurement accuracy, improving reliability in manufacturing environments [21]. An efficient COVID-19 diagnosis model (R2DCNNMC) is developed using a 2D CNN with ResNet-50 transfer learning on chest X-ray images. The model employs data augmentation for improved generalization and multiclass classification. It achieved 98.12% accuracy on CRD and 99.45% on CXI datasets, demonstrating strong potential for AI-based e-healthcare applications [22].

A machine learning–driven IoT framework is developed for DG condition monitoring using RS-485-based sensors. The framework enables continuous data collection and analysis to predict faults and ensure timely maintenance. By ranking the importance of operational parameters, the model enhances efficiency, reliability, and operational life of DG systems [23]. The Smart City Environmental Monitoring System (SCEMS) presents a combination of IoT sensors, cloud platforms, and AI algorithms for environmental data management. The system collects and processes real-time information on air, water, and noise quality for urban sustainability. It demonstrates how integrating AI-driven analytics supports data-based environmental policies in smart cities [24]. A Wireless Sensor Network (WSN) architecture is developed for early forest fire detection and alerting applications. The system is tested under controlled conditions and shows reliable real-time data transmission, high detection accuracy, and resilience to node failure. The results confirm its effectiveness in minimizing fire damage and supporting rapid disaster response [25].

Log-based detection and federated learning present a number of persistent obstacles. When it comes to federated learning, the first thing one will usually see is deep learning models with dynamic parameters. Large communication overheads may result from transmitting the model directly without modifying the underlying structure [26]. Secondly, in real-world systems, each client generates unique data according to the job at hand, which means that the data is not Independent and Identically Distributed (nonIID). Because of this, statistical variability across clients tends to rise, which can make global model convergence more difficult [27]. Additionally, to accommodate non-IID data among clients, a configurable anomaly detection mechanism is necessary. To address the aforementioned challenges, we introduce a federated anomaly detection technique called FedLog [28–33]. Its purpose is to make it easier to find anomalies in log data from massive IoT systems in a timely and accurate manner. The following essential components make up FedLog.

- Our federated learning framework helps Internet of Things devices operate together while protecting user privacy as they build an anomaly detection model.
- To improve the personalization of federated learning while dealing with non-IID datasets and drastically cut down on communication overheads, we devised a masking method based on the lottery ticket hypothesis [34].

10.1.1 Preliminaries

Here we provide a high-level overview of log-based anomaly and federated learning detection.

10.1.1.1 Log-based detection of anomaly

Hadoop Distributed File System (HDFS) logs serve as an example to demonstrate these points.

1. *Log Parsing*: The two primary components of unstructured text messages are the event template, which remains constant, and the log parameters, which can change. The next step is to create a dictionary that associates a distinct template key with each event template. The result is data that is more easily organized from the previously unstructured log messages. As an example, the event "PacketResponder 1 for block blk_38865049064139660 terminating" is recorded in the log message "081109 203615 148 INFO dfs.DataNode$PacketResponder: PacketResponder 1 for block blk_38865049064139660 terminating". The words "PacketResponder", "for", "block", "blk_", and "terminating" are constant event templates and are extracted as "PacketResponder for block blk terminating". Please take note that the square brackets represent the logarithmic parameters, which are "1" and "38865049064139660".
2. *Feature Extraction*: Finding numerical vectors from structured log data is the goal of feature extraction [35]. We begin by dividing the log data into a set of sliding panes. A sequence of log messages is defined as those that appear in the same window.

In addition, in order to train the anomaly detection model, we label each window with the next template key. One way to express the sequence vector in terms of a log sequence is as

$$s_t = \left[m_{t-h}, m_{t-h+1}, \ldots, m_{t-1}\right], \quad (10.1)$$

$$p_t = \left[\text{count}(e_1), \text{count}(e_2), \ldots, \text{count}(e_n)\right], \quad (10.2)$$

where count is how many times each template key appears in the log sequence (from lowest to highest). As shown in Figure 10.2, for example, when $n = 5$ we may get, $b_{Z.} =,, e1.,, e1.,, e2..$ and, $k_{t.} = \left[2,1,0,0,0\right]$ from the provided log sequence [1–3].

3. *Anomaly Detection*: Finding data patterns that deviate significantly from typical observations is the main goal of anomaly detection. Areas such as performance assurance and network security management have made extensive use of it [36]. In general, there are three types of outliers.

- Point Anomalies: When compared to the whole data, a single data point stands out as an anomaly.
- Contextual Anomalies: When discussing data, "contextual anomalies" are examples that stand out due to their unusual behavior within a particular setting.
- Collective Anomalies: What we call "collective anomalies" are clusters of data points that deviate significantly from the norm.

Uncovering collective anomalies, or aberrant log events that occurred in sequences, is the goal of log-based anomaly identification.

Supervised and unsupervised learning are equally capable of detecting anomalies. Since it would be exceedingly costly and impractical to manually categorize the ever-increasing volume of log data, we concentrate on unsupervised anomaly detection in this work. Any log

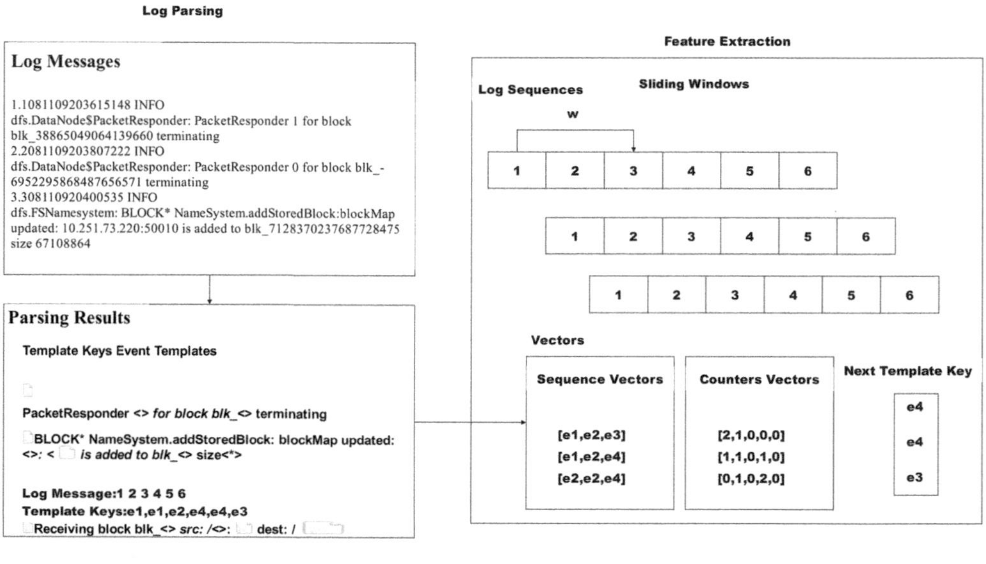

Figure 10.2 An example of feature extraction and log parsing.

sequence that includes an incoming log message that does not have the expected template key is considered irregular.

10.1.1.2 Federated learning

Interest in federated learning has been on the rise in recent years. An AI-driven secure edge trust framework combines intrusion detection and federated learning for IoT protection [37]. Without exposing the training data, federated learning allows clients to build a global machine learning model. Federated Averaging (FedAvg) is the federated learning method that has the greatest adoption. Here is the formal rundown of what happens in each round of FedAvg's iterative training:

Broadcasting: Before broadcasting the global model, the server chooses M clients at random to take part in the round train.

1. *Local Training*: Each client modifies the received model and transmits it back to the cloud server after training it using Stochastic Gradient Descent.
2. *Model Aggregating*: By averaging model updates received, the cloud server calculates the global model by

$$\theta^{t+1} = \sum_{k=1}^{M} \frac{1}{M} \theta_k^t, \tag{10.3}$$

In communication round b, θ_f represents the global model, and in the communication round $(b+1) - o + 1, \theta - c + 1$ represents the model update from client c.

10.2 SYSTEM MODEL AND CHALLENGES

10.2.1 System model

Presenting the three entities under consideration here.

- *Cloud Server*: In order to facilitate big data processing, the cloud server has access to vast storage and processing resources without gaining access to the training data [38].
- *Fog Nodes*: When it comes to backing up apps on the Internet of Things, fog nodes are the go-to devices. To build a federated anomaly detection paradigm, every fog node in a fog network collaborates with the cloud server.
- *Edge Devices*: As they go about their daily tasks, edge devices keep an eye out for any runtime events and record them in the system logs [39]. The fog node receives system logs and stores them for additional analysis, including anomaly detection, as edge devices typically have limited resources.

Figure 10.3 illustrates the system model under consideration, highlighting the key components, their interactions, and the flow of inputs and outputs.

10.2.2 Challenges

Even though federated learning can make data more secure and scalable, there are three obstacles to overcome when using it in conjunction with traditional log-based anomaly detection methods (as demonstrated below).

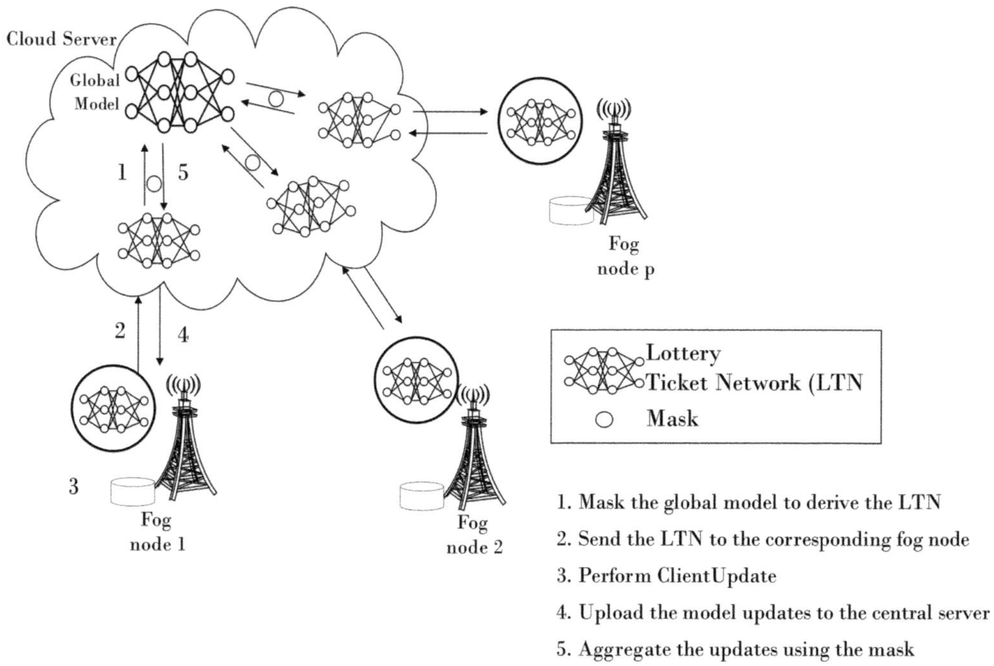

Figure 10.3 The system model under consideration.

1. *Heavy Training*: Recurrent Neural Networks (RNNs) are the backbone of many traditional log-based anomaly detection methods; however, they do not support parallel training and typically need a lot of memory and time during training. As a result, the fog node may feel overwhelmed by the amount of resources needed for the federated learning iterative training process.
2. *Expensive Communication*: Traditional federated learning frameworks (like FedAvg) may continue to generate significant communication overhead due to their continual deep learning model exchange, even while they avoid forwarding training data between each client and server [40].
3. *Heterogeneous Datasets*: Because they generate diverse, heterogeneous information in response to their unique system duties, edge devices in large-scale IoT systems often provide non-IID data across clusters. Typically, there are two ways in which such data can impact federated learning tasks. One concern is that it could make global model convergence more difficult, which would lead to a major drop in model performance. However, in order to offer each cluster configurable anomaly detection, a single global model cannot contain the non-IID data.

10.2.3 Design goals

The proposed approach seeks to address these challenges by proposing a federated learning architecture for anomaly detection on system logs that is both adaptive and efficient in terms of communication. The following are our design objectives.

- To prove that federated learning-based models perform at least on par with traditional centralized learning models in privacy-preserving log-based anomaly detection.

- At its best, it should be competitive with or even outperform the most cutting-edge RNN-based models.
- Under both IID and non-IID scenarios, this framework should enhance the proposed scheme's communication efficiency, while in the non-IID case, it should also raise its correctness.

10.3 THE SCHEME FOR PROPOSED FEDLOG

We provide the TCN-ACNN-based anomaly detection model and go into additional detail about the proposed system, including its communication-efficient federated learning architecture [41].

10.3.1 The anomaly detection model based on TCN-ACNN

10.3.1.1 Model architecture

Figure 10.4 shows the components of the designed TCN-ACNN, which include an MLP module, CNN module, a softmax layer, and TCN module. In particular, the TCN module possesses an output layer, two hidden layers, and a TCN overall architecture. With identical input

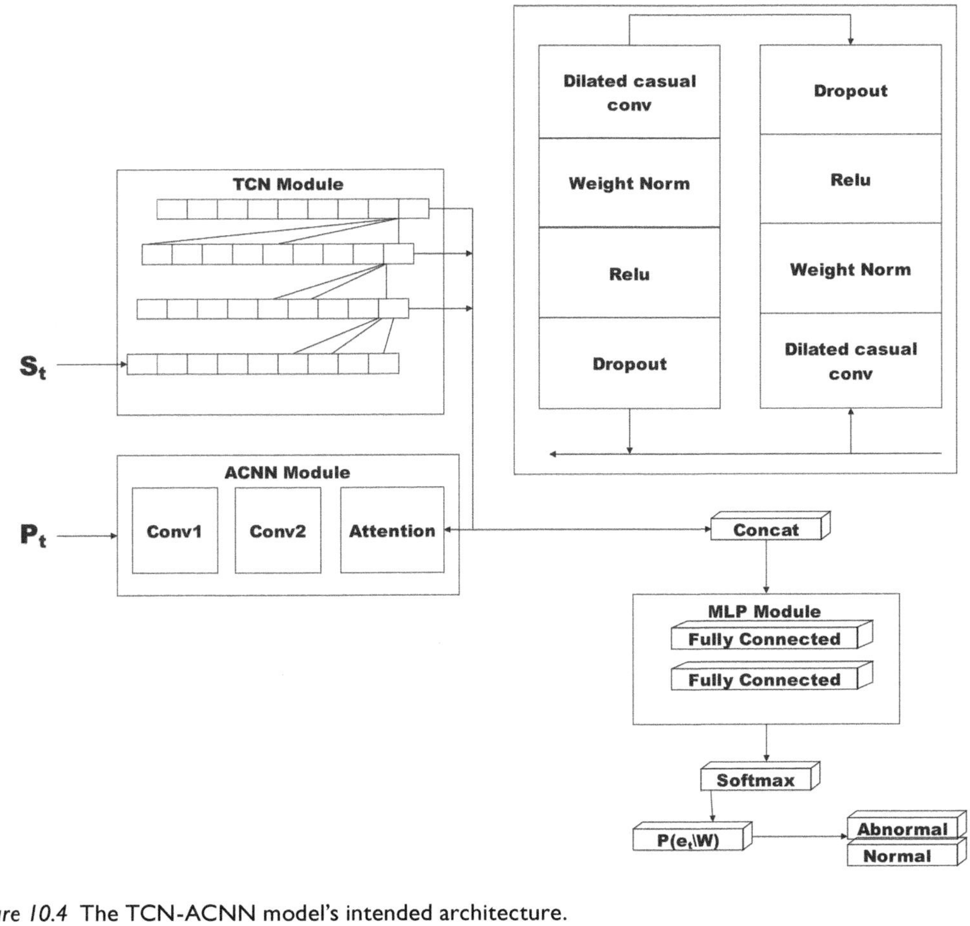

Figure 10.4 The TCN-ACNN model's intended architecture.

and output lengths, TCN mimics the design of a 1D fully convolutional network. In addition, it improves sequence modeling capacity by utilizing three components [42]. The first thing you should know is that TCN uses causal convolutions to keep future information from leaking into the past. TCN is able to view far farther back in time due to its dilated convolution mechanism. In a formal sense, the dilated convolution operation F is defined as follows:

$$F(x_t) = \sum_{i=0}^{k-1} f(i) \cdot x_{t-di} \tag{10.4}$$

where c is the dilation factor, and k is the filter's kernel size. For the TCN's i^{th} layer, we set $d = 2i$. Finally, to sidestep the issue of disappearing and exploding gradients, TCN makes use of residual connections. The following is a generic representation of residual connection:

$$\text{output} = \text{Activation}(\text{input} + F(\text{input})), \tag{10.5}$$

Two convolutional blocks and an attention layer make up the ACNN module [43]. Two layers—1D convolutional and max pooling—make up each convolution block. To determine the attention score, we use

$$r_t = v^T \tanh(Wh_t), \tag{10.6}$$

a_Z is the attention score that corresponds to the timestamp b at hidden state a, and a and a are weight variables. To get the attention layer's final output, we multiply β_Z with □-Z and then apply softmax on r_Z, making it equal to r_Z.

10.3.1.2 Anomaly detection

Using time-series forecasting as our foundation, we carry out the unsupervised anomaly detection [44]. In Section 10.3, we show the detailed processes for deriving $b_{z.}$ and $k_{t.}$ from log messages. To summarize, the procedure is defined by

$$\begin{aligned} h_1 &= ACNN(p_t) \\ h_2 &= \text{TCN}(s_t) \\ \tau &= MLP(h_1; h_2), \end{aligned} \tag{10.7}$$

τ is the MLP module's output, and h_1 are the hidden vectors. The softmax layer receives τ such that, using the previous window w, it may determine the probability distribution of u_z.

$$P(m_t = e_i \mid w) = \text{Softmax}(\tau). \tag{10.8}$$

The TCN-ACNN model's parameters were trained using SGD. During the inference phase, we sort o, $u_{t.} = e_{i.}q.$ according to e_i and select the top c template keys, indicated as r_c, based on their likelihood.

10.3.2 The adaptable and effective communication federated learning system

In order to provide more effective federated learning by sharing pruned models, pruning algorithms could eliminate superfluous structure from neural networks. In contrast to its intended use for storage, the lottery ticket and efficient inference computation hypothesis demonstrate the usefulness of initialization pruning. Consequently, we think about the possibility of applying the lottery ticket principle to federated learning. An unsupervised Federated Learning architecture is proposed for large-scale IoT/IIoT intrusion detection, integrating device clustering to handle network heterogeneity [45–48]. It enables peer-to-peer collaborative training, reducing isolation and network overhead. Real attack evaluations, including Mirai and botnet scenarios, confirm effective anomaly detection in distributed IoT systems [49].

Using a pruning initialization process and iterative training, the lottery ticket hypothesis shows how to generate sparse subnetworks from the underlying network. These subnetworks can achieve test accuracy or even surpass it.

Every client, or fog node, k, gets its own unique LTN θk and a matching mask mk using its own dataset Dk. Seeking out such an LTN for every client is our objective. Afterward, we may modify the global model to fit non-IID datasets by doing federated learning on tailored LTNs, which will remove any superfluous data. In addition, by keeping a configurable LTN for every client, we can also accomplish better customization. At the same time, the sharing procedure is efficient in terms of communication as the server and clients just exchange LTN parameters.

Hence, we offer a concealment tactic by constructing our federated learning architecture around the lottery ticket hypothesis. Following is a description of the two parts that make up the suggested federated learning architecture: local mask training and masked federated learning.

Local Mask Training: Using an iterative pruning process, all clients locally search for LTNs and matching masks in this phase. Once they have the masks, they send them to the server in the cloud. To be more precise, before anything else, every client k sets up their mask and local model.

Algorithm 1: Training using local masks

```
Input: L, D_train, D_val, α, τ

For each client k = 1 … K:
  Initialize w_k^1
  Initialize s_k^1 = vector_of_ones(size(w_k))

  For i = 1 … L:
    Divide D_train into batches of size B

    For t = 1 … E:
      For each batch d in batches:
        w_k = w_k - α * gradient_loss(w_k, d)

    Acc_val = evaluate(w_k, D_val)

    If Acc_val > τ:
      break

    s_k^i = prune(w_k, p_i)

  w_k^{L+1} = w_k ⊙ s_k^L

  send s_k^L to server
```

Following is a full description of the pruning procedure.

- Rank the unmasked weights in each layer.
- For each set of weights, assign the mask value of 0 to the least magnitude and 1 to the remaining weights.
- Using the mask, values are reset with weights 1. Freezing the weight values associated with mask values of 0 to 0.

Masked Federated Learning: Notably, we develop a novel technique for model aggregation on the server side. Before training for the bth, the cloud server chooses at random a collection of M fog nodes, represented as S_b.

Algorithm 2: Federated learning with a mask

```
LocalTrain(i, W_i):

    Divide the training portion of D_i into mini-batches of size B

    Lock (do not update) all parameters where s_i = 0

    For epoch = 1 to E:
        For each batch x in the mini-batches:
            W_i = W_i - α * ∇L(W_i; x)

  Return W_i to the server
```

Therefore, research at the aggregate parameter level is required. To calculate a weight mask τ, we begin by tallying the values given by

$$\omega = \varphi\left(\sum_{k=1}^{M} m_k\right), \tag{10.9}$$

In which the function φ represents the mapping of each member x in the input matrix to its inverse.

$$g(x) = \begin{cases} 0, & \text{if } x = 0 \\ \dfrac{1}{x}, & \end{cases} \tag{10.10}$$

After that, we take the total value of all weight parameters in the model and divide it by the total number of contributors, which is

$$\theta^{t+1} = \omega \odot \sum_{k=1}^{M} \theta_k^{t+1} \tag{10.11}$$

As shown in Figure 10.5, the suggested masked federated learning follows a general method.

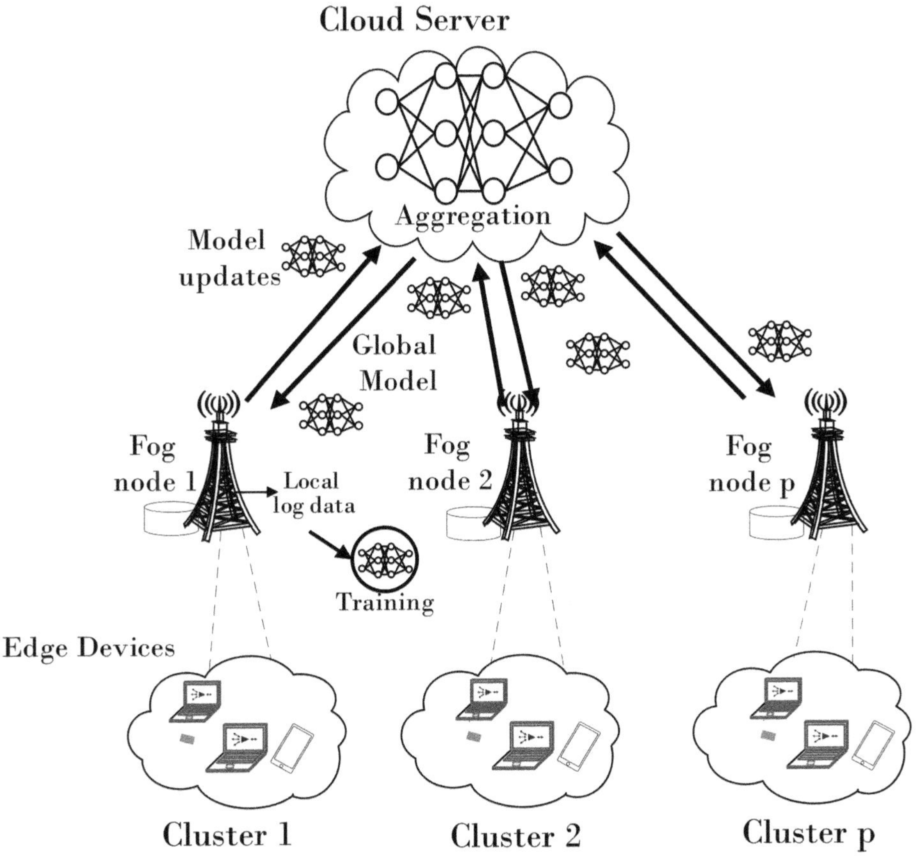

Figure 10.5 The proposed masked federated learning.

10.4 PERFORMANCE EVALUATION

Here, we test the suggested approach with a battery of experiments to see how well it works. We begin by outlining the parameters of the experiment. After that, we evaluate the suggested TCN-ACNN using federated and centralized learning paradigms, and then we compare its results. In addition, we evaluate the suggested federated learning system by comparing its results to predefined standards.

10.4.1 Settings for the experiment

1. Datasets: They are both made available to the public and have been hand-labeled. Many studies have used them for log analysis. Here is a quick rundown of what they are (as well as a synopsis in Table 10.1).
   - HDFS: More than 200 Amazon Elastic Compute Cloud (EC2) machines execute Hadoop-based MapReduce jobs to produce the 12,165,759 log messages that make up the HDFS dataset.
   - BGL: With 5,642,894 log messages, the BGL dataset is large. The Blue Gene/L supercomputer at LLNL (Lawrence Livermore National Laboratory) is responsible for its production.

Table 10.1 Datasets of logs

Log sets	*Log sequences*		
	Training set	*Test set*	*Number of event templates*
HDFS	47525 normal	164528 normal	29
BGL	125066 normal	68452 normal 69658 abnormal	314

In federated learning, we synthesize the IID data by randomly assigning each client a dataset of equal size [50]. Partitioned datasets in the real world often display other forms of non-IIDness, such as skewed feature and label distributions, among others. We find that, despite being otherwise typical, edge devices create a wide variety of log sequences. As a result, we zero in on the skew type of feature distribution, in which clients' data features might differ but their labels might remain consistent. As a result, we combine a dataset of the same size that contains only two classifications.

2. Metrics and Environmental Configuration: We run our tests on a laptop with a 2.62 GHz Intel Core. PyTorch is used to create the deep learning models. The parameters for log-based anomaly detection are $c = 9$ and window size $h = 10$. Table 10.2 shows the default values for the parameters of the suggested federated learning system.

A binary classification task is required to determine if log sequences are abnormal. Accuracy, defined as the percentage of correctly classified results, is one of the four metrics utilized for evaluation. Precision, the second metric, measures the proportion of log sequences that are, in fact, suspicious. Recall, the third metric, measures the proportion of truly unusual log sequences. The F1-score, the fourth metric, is the cumulative weight of the recall and precision measures. Furthermore, we add up all the parameters transmitted from the server to the clients in order to statistically evaluate communication overheads.

$$C = 2rMR. \tag{10.12}$$

Table 10.2 The proposed federated learning framework's parameters

Phase	*Description*	*Variable*	*Setting*
Federated learning	No. epoch	E	5
	Learning	η	0.002
	No. participants	M	15
	Minibatch	B	65
	No. client	K	15
Local mask training	No. clients	K	15
	No epochs	E	25
	Learning	η	0.002
	Minibatch	B	65
	No iteration	I_p	5
	Validation	$Acc_t hr$	55

10.4.2 Summary of comparative performance

To start, we look at how TCN-ACNN, DeepLog, and Loganomaly do under the IID scenario in terms of centralized and federated learning. Since DeepLog and Loganomaly are not compatible with the lottery ticket theory, we restrict our implementation to the FedLog paradigm of ACNN—TCN.

Outperforming Loganomaly and DeepLog, the suggested TCN-ACNN model earns a higher F1-score on the HDFS dataset. Specifically, TCN-ACNN$_O$. 99.00% and TCN-ACNN$_O$. and TCN-ACNN$_{FedLog}$. 98.45% are the respective F1-scores for DeepLog$_O$. and DeepLog$_c$. Similarly, Loganomaly$_O$., achieves a 96.51% F1-score, and 98.25% of DeepLog$_c$ respectively, when it comes to federated learning and centralized learning. With a precision of 99.26%, recall of 99.06%, and F1-score of 98.03%, TCN-ACNN$_{FedLog}$ outperformed the competition with 96.75%, 99.32%, and 98.75%, respectively. Concerning the DeepLog F BGL dataset, TCN. In prior studies, a privacy-preserved payload-based anomaly detection (P³AD) model was introduced for IIoT using a federated GAN and 2D-CNN autoencoder. Evaluations on four datasets show F1 scores above 96.6% globally, confirming effective privacy-preserving anomaly detection in complex industrial environments [51]. Figure 10.6 compares the performance of the proposed model using the HDFS dataset.

So, we prove that the suggested TCN-ACNN is better and that federated learning is appropriate for log-based detection through experiments. Notably, with only 12% of the model's weight parameters used FedLog $f - k. = 0.9$ achieves the same performance. Figure 10.7 compares the performance of the proposed model using the BGL dataset.

10.4.3 Comparing performance with cutting-edge federated learning frameworks

Next, we evaluate the suggested framework in both IID and non-IID situations by comparing it to baselines, such as Standalone, FedAvg, and LG-FedAvg. The optimal situation for customization is when each client constructs their own anomaly detection model; this is

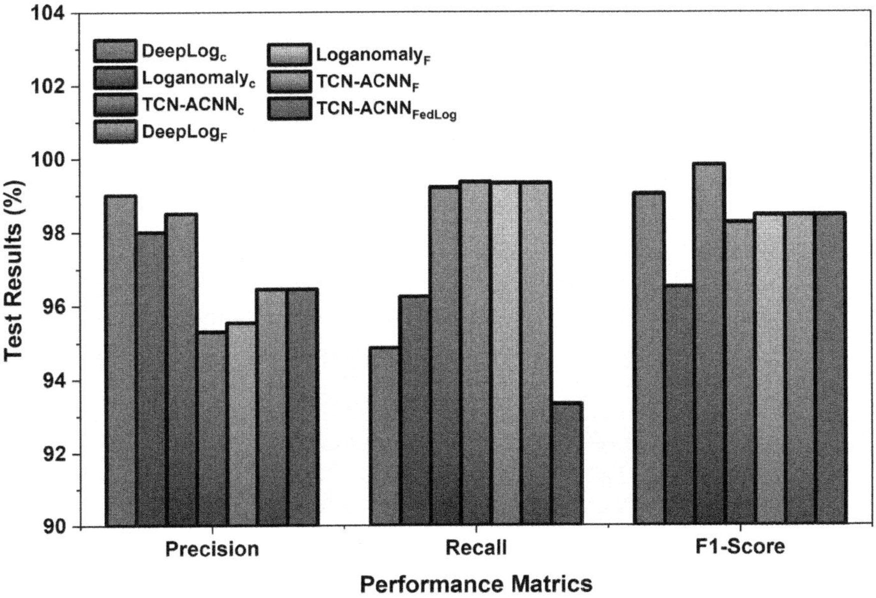

Figure 10.6 Comparison of performance using the HDFS dataset.

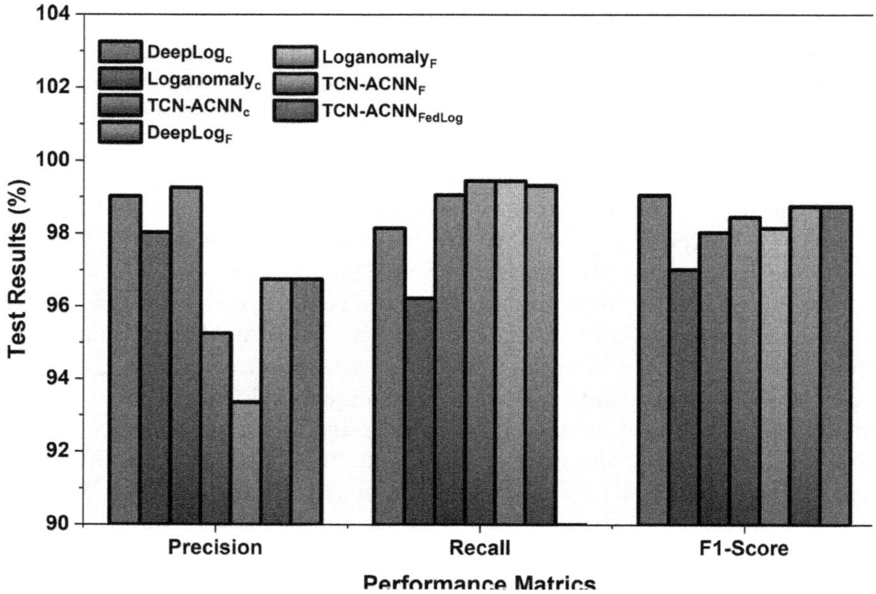

Figure 10.7 Comparison of performance using the BGL dataset.

known as a Standalone scenario. Keeping the ACNN and TCN modules, sharing the MLP and local module allows us to implement LG-FedAvg. In addition, we name FedLog with the proportion of unpruned parameters and apply it with variable pruning rates *r-p*, where *r* is an integer between 0.7 and 0.8 and 0.9 and 0.92 and 0.94 and 0.98. Consider FedLog (0.4) with $-k. = 0.6$ (i.e., 40% parameters unpruned).

In order to conduct an extensive evaluation of several federated learning frameworks, the global test set includes an evenly distributed set of classes. Keep in mind that training local masks is the only application of the validation set.

- Local Test: Running this test evaluates the modification of the provided framework. As a measure, we use the mean precision of all regional models.
- Global Test: We use precision as our measure. Since Standalone and LG-FedAvg do not generate a comprehensive global model, we average all client models to get their global model when evaluating them.

In order to prove the effectiveness of FedLog, we compared the best test results obtained over 52 communication rounds across various frameworks with the proposed FedLog. Under the IID scenario, it is clear that all the frameworks achieved globally convergent models with comparable performance. In contrast, the Standalone model had difficulty achieving a well-converged global model in the absence of IID. On the other hand, the local test showed that FedAvg and LG-FedAvg performed poorly, achieving scores below 32%. The suggested FedLog, on the other hand, outperformed the Standalone model in both the global and local tests, with a performance level of 99.78% for FedLog (0.4) and results that are on par. When compared to other frameworks, FedLog clearly performed better in non-IID settings. This indicates that out of all the anomaly detection models, FedLog offers the most customization options. This is due to the fact that LTN is able to save the crucial weight values that may reflect the local dataset's unique distribution after the masking process. Table 10.3 presents a comparison of model performance under non-IID and IID data.

Table 10.3 Comparing performance in non-IID and IID situations

		Accuracy		
		Non-IID		*IID*
Approach	*R*	*Local*	*Global*	*Global*
FedLog	0.82	99.93	59.6	99.93
LG-FedAvg	1.05	99.78	28.42	99.78
FedAvg	1.2	99.78	25.31	99.78
Standalone	0.2	99.93	67.14	53.75
FedLog	0.76	99.93	57.6	99.78
FedLog	0.7	99.93	63.6	99.78
FedLog	0.63	99.78	54.03	99.78
FedLog	0.2	99.93	67.14	53.75
FedLog	1.2	99.78	25.31	99.78

Secondly, we assess how well the suggested FedLog communicates. When comparing various federated learning frameworks, we may find their communication costs using Eq. (10.12). When using FedAvg, $a = 1$, and when using LG-FedAvg, $a = 0.87$. The pruning rate $r - k. \in \{0.73, 0.82, 0.86, 0.91, 0.94, 0.98\}$ corresponds to $R \in \{0.71, 0.69, 0.62, 0.55, 0.55, 0.48\}$ in FedLog, accordingly. Under non-IID scenarios, Table 10.4 displays numerical results regarding the accuracy of various frameworks and communication overheads. When looking at the global test accuracy over all measured rounds, FedLog(0.4) stands out, as expected Furthermore, both FedLog(0.01) and FedLog(0.05), but $f = 25$, all FedLogs achieve local test accuracy that is comparable to Standalone. When it comes to the local test, FedAvg and LGFedAvg are completely out of control. Figure 10.8 shows how various frameworks perform in terms of communication efficiency. In Figure 10.8(a), the curve for FedLog(0.4) stands out from the rest. In the local test, the suggested FedLog achieves better communication efficiency than LG-FedAvg and FedAvg, as shown in Figure 10.8(b). This holds true regardless of the pruning rate being evaluated. As a result, when compared to competing federated learning frameworks, the suggested FedLog shows superior communication efficiency.

In addition, we investigate how the pruning iterations $V - k$ affect FedLog's efficiency. With a varying under $a = 0.7$, 0.8, and 0.9, Figure 10.9 graphically displays the numerical results of local test and global accuracy for all considering $a - k$. The selection of $-k$ clearly has the potential to greatly impact FedLog's efficiency in the global test. When it comes to FedLog's efficiency in local test, however a_k has minimal effects.

10.5 CONCLUSION

We presented FedLog, a federated anomaly detection scheme that is both adaptable and efficient in its use of communication, and demonstrated its ability to identify log anomalies in large-scale IoT networks. The proposed scheme includes a deep anomaly detection model that uses TCN-ACNN to effectively extract features from system logs and identify anomalies. It also includes a federated learning framework that helps IoT devices to build a comprehensive anomaly detection model in a collaborative and privacy-preserving way [52–56].

Despite the widespread usage of both the HDFS and BGL datasets in research, there is a possibility that the real-world cyberthreat environment differs substantially from the ones reflected in the datasets. Therefore, we plan to test the suggested scheme across many partner universities to see how well it works and what kind of improvements are necessary [57–61].

Table 10.4 Comparison of communication overheads and customization with different rounds in a non-IID situation

		r = 5			r = 10			r = 15			r = 20			r = 25		
			Accuracy (%)			Accuracy (%)			Accuracy (%)			Accuracy (%)			Accuracy (%)	
Frameworks	*R*	*C*	*Global*	*Local*	*C*	*Global*	*Local*	*C*	*Global*	*Local*	*C*	*Global*	*Local*	*C*	*Global*	*Local*
Standalone	0.25	0.25	28.62	53.1	0.25	42.09	53.21	0.25	48.48	53.29	0.25	55.45	53.32	0.25	57.81	53.32
FedAvg	1.25	100.25	21.63	85.86	200.25	25.26	99.73	300.25	25.26	99.73	400.25	25.26	99.73	500.25	25.26	99.73
LG-FedAvg	1.1	85.25	18.61	72.48	170.25	28.37	99.73	256.25	28.37	99.73	241.25	28.37	99.73	426.25	28.37	99.73
FedLog	0.87	62.25	21.88	86.05	124.25	40.95	99.88	186.25	52.06	99.88	248.25	55.36	99.88	310.25	55.36	99.88
FedLog	0.81	56.25	25.75	65.73	112.25	34.63	82.31	168.25	46.1	86.05	224.25	51.22	86.05	280.25	51.22	86.05
FedLog	0.75	50.25	21.26	72.14	100.25	35.39	85.86	150.25	38.63	85.86	200.25	45.9	85.86	250.25	52.58	85.86
FedLog	0.68	43.25	24.51	85.96	86.25	41.33	85.96	129.25	52.14	85.96	172.25	52.89	99.73	215.25	52.89	99.73
FedLog	0.65	40.25	17.07	63.29	80.25	37.38	63.29	120.25	44.79	76.15	160.25	47.55	76.15	200.25	52.55	76.15
FedLog	0.63	38.25	19.99	57.03	76.25	33.59	71.81	114.25	44.5	71.81	152.25	50.55	71.81	190.25	54.55	71.81

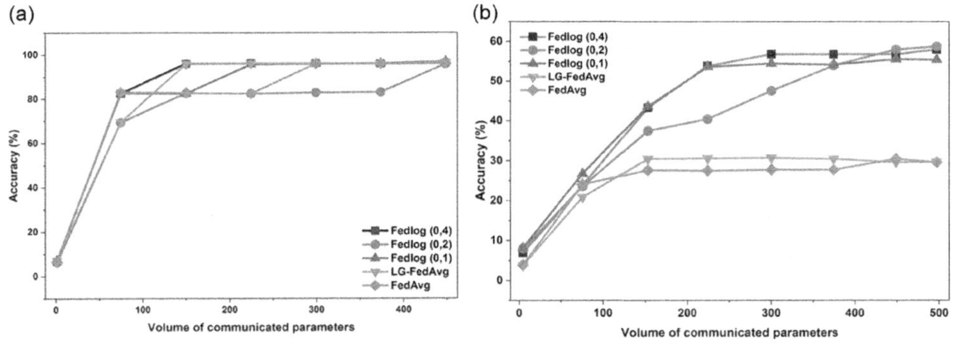

Figure 10.8 Accuracy comparison of global and local tests with different communication overheads.

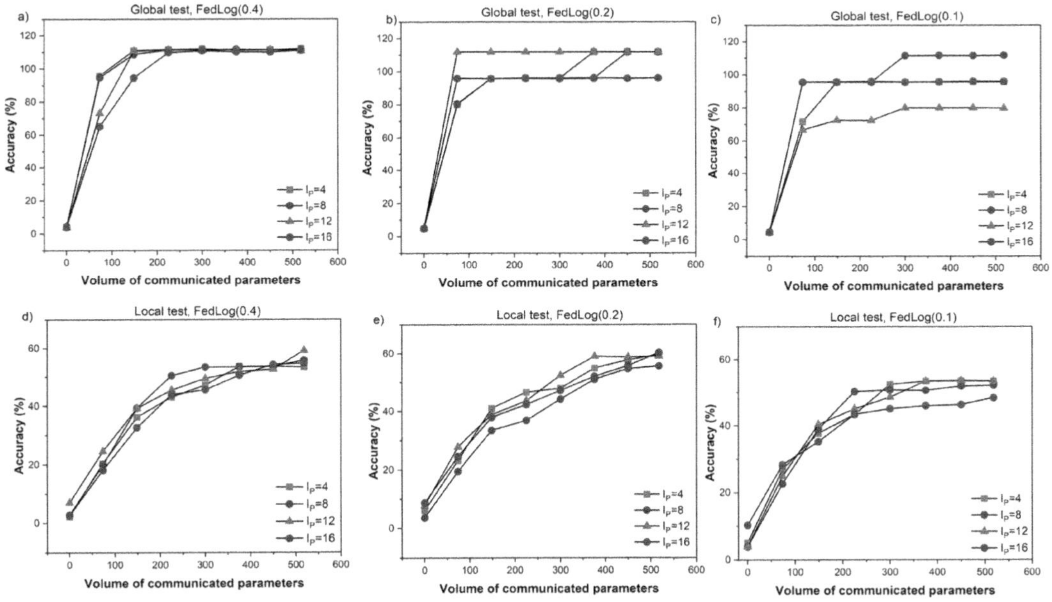

Figure 10.9 (a,b,c,d,e,f) Comparing the performance of various IPs in both local and global testing with different pruning rates.

REFERENCES

1. S. Sugirtha, N. Radhakrishnan, T. V. Ramana, G. G. Devarajan, M. Karuppiah, and M. M. Al Dabel. 2024. Real-time threat detection and AI-driven predictive security for consumer applications. *IEEE Consumer Electronics Magazine*, 71 (2): 5100–5107.
2. S. Selvaraju, N. Krishnamurthy, K. V. Devi, R. Deepalakshmi, S. Rani, and A. Jose Anand. 2024. Navigating the complexity of macro-tasks: Federated learning as a catalyst for effective crowd coordination. In S. Krishnan, A. Jose Anand, R. Srinivasan, R. Kavitha, & S. Suresh (Eds.), *Advances in Intelligent Systems*. Springer: 308–332.
3. M. A. Mukunthan, A. A. Jose Anand, S. Kesavan, M. Mutyala, R. Kesavan, and R. Geetha. 2024. Detection of physical anomalies in IoT networks using machine learning techniques. In *2024 International Conference on Advancement in Renewable Energy and Intelligent Systems (AREIS)*, Thrissur, India: 1–6.

4. S. Hemalatha, M. Mahalakshmi, V. Vignesh, M. Geethalakshmi, D. Balasubramanian, and A. Jose Anand. 2023. Deep learning approaches for intrusion detection with emerging cybersecurity challenges. *Proceedings of the International Conference on Advanced Computing Technologies* Theni, India: 1522–1529.
5. A. Govindaram, J. S. Prasath, A. Suganya, K. Jayasakthi, N. Rajkumar, and A. Jose Anand. 2025. Federated learning in big data with IoT for intrusion detection. In *2025 6th International Conference on Mobile Computing and Sustainable Informatics (ICMCSI)*, Goathgaun, Nepal: 252–258.
6. P. Sharma, S. K. Sharma, and D. Dani. 2024. Edge-assisted federated learning for anomaly detection in diverse IoT network. *IEEE Internet of Things Journal*, 17 (5): 3035–3045.
7. J. Anantula, V. K. R. Likki, R. Jyothi, S. N. Chaduvula, K. Padmavathi, P. Panguluri, and J. U. Kranti. 2024. Cloud IoT environments security: Deep learning with generative and explainable models. *IEEE Access*, 103 (12): 5162–5163.
8. A. Harchi, H. Toumi, and M. Talea. 2024. SDN-cloud incident detection and response with segmented federated learning for the IoT. *Journal of Cloud Computing*, 5 (2): 671–684.
9. M. N. Alatawi. 2025. EdgeGuard-IoT: 6G-enabled edge intelligence for secure federated learning and adaptive anomaly detection in Industry 5.0. *Future Generation Computer Systems*, 85 (1): 695–727.
10. N. Albanbay, Y. Tursynbek, K. Graffi, R. Uskenbayeva, Z. Kalpeyeva, Z. Abilkaiyr, and Y. Ayapov. 2025. Federated learning-based intrusion detection in IoT networks: Performance evaluation and data scaling study. *Journal of Sensor and Actuator Networks*, 14 (4): 78.
11. H. Nazari, A. Yazdinejad, A. Dehghantanha, F. Zarrinkalam, and G. Srivastava. 2024. Symbiotic federated learning for giant AI threat detection in 6G-IoT infrastructures. *IEEE Access*, 12 (20): 41472–41481.
12. R. Shrestha, M. Mohammadi, S. Sinaei, A. Salcines, D. Pampliega, R. Clemente, A. L. Sanz, E. Nowroozi, and A. Lindgren. 2024. Anomaly detection based on LSTM and autoencoders using federated learning in smart electric grid. *Journal of Parallel and Distributed Computing*, 193: 104951.
13. A. A. Wardana, G. Kołaczek, and P. Sukarno. 2024. Lightweight, trust-managing, and privacy-preserving collaborative intrusion detection for Internet of Things. *Applied Sciences*, 14 (10): 4109.
14. H. Babbar and S. Rani. 2024. FRHIDS: Federated learning recommender hybrid intrusion detection system model in software-defined networking for consumer devices. *IEEE Consumer Electronics Magazine*, 70 (1): 2492–2499.
15. M. Kalidas, T. Priya, V. Ansal, S. Mayakannan, P. K. Dhal, S. S. Kumar, and K. Sahile. 2025. Automated drone detection for surveillance and security enhancement. In A. Gupta, M. Hinchey, and Z. Zalevsky (eds.), *Artificial Intelligence and Its Applications. Communications in Computer and Information Science* 2308. Springer, Cham: 120–135. https://doi.org/10.1007/978-3-031-84394-5_10
16. N. M. George, E. Rosero, S. Selvaraju, A. Shameem, S. Divya, and N. Natarajan. 2025. Enhancing industrial automation flexibility through neural network-empowered machine vision applications. In A. Gupta, M. Hinchey, and Z. Zalevsky (eds.), *Communications in Computer and Information Science*. Springer, Cham: 241–254.
17. V. Priyanka, S. Lekshmi Raveendran, R. Kesavan, U. Sandhya, T. Anuradha, and A. Jose Anand. 2026. Analysis and comparison of cloud data storage services with a practical study on Google Drive. In *2026 6th International Conference on Expert Clouds and Applications (ICOECA)*, Bengaluru, India: 924–930.
18. X. Liu, Q. Li, Y. Xu, S. Khan, and F. Zhu. 2025. Point cloud recognition of street tree canopies in urban Internet of Things based on laser reflection intensity. *Sustainable Computing: Informatics and Systems*, 47: 101169. https://doi.org/10.1016/j.suscom.2025.101169
19. R. C. Veluri, S. Khan, S. P. Sankareswaran, M. Shabaz, A. Farouk, and N. Innab. 2025. Modified M-RCNN approach for abandoned object detection in public places. *Expert Systems*, 42 (2): e13648. https://doi.org/10.1111/exsy.13648

20. T. Ahmad, S. Khan, N. Nigar, E. M. Obaid, and S. Naaz. 2025. Quantum reservoir-based intrusion detection for Edge-IoT systems. *IEEE Transactions on Consumer Electronics*, 71 (4): 11269–11278. https://doi.org/10.1109/TCE.2025.3618827
21. S. Khan, T. Siddiqui, A. Mourade, B. I. Alabduallah, S. A. Alajlan, A. Almjally, and A. Alfaifi. 2024. Manufacturing industry based on dynamic soft sensors integrated with feature representation and classification using fuzzy logic and deep learning architecture. *Journal of Intelligent Manufacturing*, 128 (7–8): 2885–2897.
22. A. U. Haq, J. P. Li, S. Ahmad, S. Khan, M. A. Alshara, and R. M. Alotaibi. 2021. Diagnostic approach for accurate diagnosis of COVID-19 employing deep learning and transfer learning techniques through chest X-ray images clinical data in e-healthcare. *Sensors*, 21 (24): 8219. https://doi.org/10.3390/s21248219
23. A. Mohanty, A. G. Mohapatra, N. Nayak, S. Bairavel, M. M. Chaithra, M. Lakshmi, A. Govindaram, and J. A. Jose Anand. 2025. Optimizing diesel generators in industrial settings with IoT and machine learning. *International Journal of Information Technology*: 1–9.
24. N. Nazeeya Anjum, S. Sumathi, R. Dheena Dhayalan, R. P. Rampavithran, A. J. Jose Anand, and M. Sathiyanarayanan. 2025. Smart sensors for smart city environmental monitoring systems. In T. Nguyen (ed.), *Advances in Smart City Technologies*. Springer: 17–33.
25. T. Thangavelu, A. Suganya, R. Raja, M. Narender, and A. Jose Anand. 2023. Evaluation of a wireless sensor network for the detection of forest fires. *Proceedings of the International Conference on Wireless Sensor Networks,* Namakkal,India: 1021–1027.
26. C. R. Jothy, J. E. Judith, J. C. Dhayananth, A. Jose Anand, T. Jarin, and S. M. Sulthan. 2024. Smart supply chain management for efficient consumption and production. In S. Krishnan, A. Jose Anand, and R. Kumar (eds.), *Sustainable Development Goals: Technologies and Opportunities*. CRC Press: Ch. 12. https://doi.org/10.1201/9781003468257
27. B. Li, S. Ma, R. Deng, K.-K. R. Choo, and J. Yang. 2024. Federated anomaly detection on system logs for the Internet of Things: A customizable and communication-efficient approach. *IEEE Internet of Things Journal*, 19 (2): 1705–1716.
28. M. Geethalakshmi, J. Anand, R. Nathea, C. Augustine, S. M. Sivaraman, and S. Mahalakshmi. 2022. Trident fuzzy aggregation operators on right and left apex-base angles in parallel computing. *Advances in Parallel Computing Algorithms, Tools and Paradigms*, 41: 429–435.
29. S. Prema, Jose Anand, P. Vanitha, Nirmala Devi K., M. Mohamed Yaseen, and Rajeswari C. 2022. Smart stick using ultrasonic sensors for vissually impaired. *Advances in Parallel Computing Algorithms, Tools and Paradigms*, 41: 436–441.
30. J. Anand, M. Shobika, and T. Sneha. 2022. Programmable stickers to monitor perishable goods using blockchain. *IEEE 2022 Second International Conference on Computer Science, Engineering and Applications (ICCSEA 2022)*, pp. 1–5.
31. R. Maheswari, S. Vignesh, M. Rakesh Kumar, T. M. Venkatesh, R. Sundar, and J. Anand A. 2022. Voice control and eyeball movement operated wheelchair. *2022 International Conference on Edge Computing and Applications (ICECAA)*, Tamil Nadu, India: pp. 805–809.
32. A. Ponmalar, J. Anand A., T. Muthamizhan, T. Sobana, and J. H. Vishwath. 2022. Automatic forensic analysis of criminal navigation system using machine learning. *IEEE Technically Sponsored First International Conference on Computational Science & Technology (ICCST 2022)*, Chennai, Tamil Nadu, India: 1–5.
33. S. Ganesh Sundaram, A. Ponmalar, S. Deeba, Jose A. A., and Aarthi S. 2022. Plane detection and product trail using augmented reality. *IEEE Technically Sponsored First International Conference on Computational Science & Technology (ICCST 2022)*, Chennai, Tamil Nadu, India: 1–5.
34. X. Li and H. Wang. 2024. Federated learning-based distributed autoencoder for industrial big data anomaly detection: Integrating LSTM, GRU, and CNN models. *Applied Artificial Intelligence*, 49 (29): 181–196.
35. R. W. Anwer, M. Abrar, M. Ullah, A. Salam, and F. Ullah. 2024. Advanced intrusion detection in the industrial Internet of Things using federated learning and LSTM models. *Computer Networks*, 178: 103991.

36. T. T. Huong, T. P. Bac, D. M. Long, T. D. Luong, N. M. Dan, L. A. Quang, L. T. Cong, B. D. Thang, and K. P. Tran. 2021. Detecting cyberattacks using anomaly detection in industrial control systems: A federated learning approach. *Computers in Industry*, 132: 103509. https://doi.org/10.1016/j.compind.2021.103509
37. V. Padmavathi and R. Saminathan. 2025. A federated edge intelligence framework with trust based access control for secure and privacy-preserving IoT systems. *Scientific Reports*, 15 (1): 35832. https://doi.org/10.1038/s41598-025-19712-1
38. L. Tao and H. Li. 2025. Real-time health monitoring for athletes in dynamic sports environments based on split federated learning and recurrent neural networks. *IEEE Transactions on Consumer Electronics*, 71 (3): 8956–8967. https://doi.org/10.1109/TCE.2025.3587200
39. V. Pourahmadi, H. A. Alameddine, M. A. Salahuddin, and R. Boutaba. 2024. Spotting anomalies at the edge: Outlier exposure-based cross-silo federated learning for DDoS detection. *IEEE Internet of Things Journal*, 20 (5): 4002–4015.
40. R. H. Alamir, A. Noor, H. Almukhalfi, R. Almukhlifi, and T. H. Noor. 2025. SecFedDNN: A secure federated deep learning framework for edge–cloud environments. *Systems*, 13 (6): 463. https://doi.org/10.3390/systems13060463
41. M. Geethalakshmi, J. Venkatesh, R. Uma Mageswari, A. Mahalakshmi, J. Anand, and R. Partheepan. 2023. Fuzzy based route optimization in wearable biomedical wireless sensor network. *AIP Conference Proceedings* 2523, 020156.
42. M. S. Sundari, A. J. Anand, and T. S. Nagarajan. 2022. Smart aerial imaging solution in precision agriculture. *2022 International Conference on Data Science, Agents & Artificial Intelligence (ICDSAAI)*, Chennai, India, pp. 1–3.
43. B. E. Samuel, S. Alghamdi, T. Priya, R. Deepalakshmi, S. Kannan, and M. Selvaraju. 2024. Deep learning-driven culvert monitoring: A novel approach for flash flood mitigation through visual blockage analysis. In *2024 IEEE 9th International Conference for Convergence in Technology (I2CT)*, Pune, India: 1–7. https://doi.org/10.1109/I2CT61223.2024.10543968
44. M. J. C. S. Reis and C. Serôdio. 2024. Edge AI for real-time anomaly detection in smart homes. *IEEE Internet of Things Journal*, 17 (4): 1–12.
45. S. Mahalakshmi, C. Rajeswari, A. J. Anand, and A. Rahul. 2022. Client authentication by signature verification method using Robotic Process Automation (RPA). *2022 International Conference on Data Science, Agents & Artificial Intelligence (ICDSAAI)*, Chennai, India, pp. 1–5.
46. S. G. Sundaram, P. Saravanan, A. Ponmalar, M. G. Prakash, and Jose A. A. 2022. Collaborative product recommendation system for E-commerce websites. *IEEE 2022 International Conference on Innovative Computing, Intelligent Communication and Smart Electrical Systems (ICSES)*, Chennai, India, pp. 1–7.
47. K. Kausalya, D. Gokulakrishnan, S. Aarthi, Jose A. A., G. K. R. Bhavana, and A. Ponmalar. 2022. Implementing virtual personal assistant through artificial intelligence requirements. *2022 First International Conference on Computer, Power and Communication (ICCPC 2022)*, 14–16 Dec–Nov.
48. A. Ponmalar, B. Chandra, S. Aarthi, G. Bhavana, A. J. Anand, and S. Gomathi. 2022. IoT based automative drive recorder as black box. *2022 IEEE International Conference on Computer, Power and Communications (ICCPC)*, Chennai, India, pp. 557–561.
49. X. Sáez-de-Cámara J. L. Flores, C. Arellano, A. Urbieta, and U. Zurutuza. 2023. Clustered federated learning architecture for network anomaly detection in large-scale heterogeneous IoT networks. *Computers & Security*, 131: 103299. https://doi.org/10.1016/j.cose.2023.103299
50. I. Ioannou, P. Nagaradjane, P. Angin, P. Balasubramanian, K. J. Kavitha, P. Murugan, and V. Vassiliou. 2024. GEMLIDS-MIOT: A green effective machine learning intrusion detection system based on federated learning for medical IoT network security hardening. *Computer Networks*, 218: 209–239.
51. P. Zhou, C. Li, C. Chen, D. Wu, and M. Fei. 2024. P3AD: Privacy-preserved payload anomaly detection for industrial Internet of Things. *IEEE Internet of Things Journal*, 20 (4): 5103–5114.

52. Rachna, Y. Chhabra, and P. Bhambri. 2021. Various approaches and algorithms for monitoring energy efficiency of wireless sensor networks. In H. Singh, P. P. Singh Cheema, and P. Garg (Eds.), *Sustainable Development through Engineering Innovations* (Vol. 113, pp. 761–770). Springer. https://doi.org/10.1007/978-981-15-9554-7_68
53. A. Jain, M. Singh, and P. Bhambri. 2021, August. Performance evaluation of IPv4-IPv6 tunneling procedure using IoT. *Journal of Physics: Conference Series*, 1950 (1): 012010. IOP Publishing.
54. G. C. N. Babu, S. Gupta, P. Bhambri, L. M. Leo, B. H. Rao, and S. Kumar. 2021. A semantic health observation system development based on the IoT sensors. *Turkish Journal of Physiotherapy and Rehabilitation*, 32 (3): 1721–1729.
55. P. Bhambri, S. Bagga, D. Priya, H. Singh, and H. K. Dhiman. 2020, December. Suspicious human activity detection system. *Journal of ISMAC*, 2 (4): 216–221.
56. R. Sharma, P. Bhambri, and A. K. Sohal. 2020. Energy bio-inspired for MANET. *International Journal of Recent Technology and Engineering*, 8 (6): 5580–5585.
57. K. Kaur, I. S. Dhanoa, and P. Bhambri. 2020, December. Optimized PSO-EFA algorithm for energy efficient virtual machine migrations. In *2020 5th IEEE International Conference on Recent Advances and Innovations in Engineering (ICRAIE)* (pp. 1–5). IEEE.
58. R. Rana, Y. Chhabra, and P. Bhambr. 2022. Design and development of distributed clustering approach in wireless sensor network. *Webology*, 19 (2), 1–9.
59. R. Rana, Y. Chhabra, and P. Bhambri. 2021. Comparison and evaluation of various QoS parameters in WSNs with the implementation of enhanced low energy adaptive efficient distributed clustering approach. *Webology*, 18 (1): 677–695. https://www.webology.org/data-cms/articles/20220223093208pmwebology%2018%20(1)%20-%2077%20pdf.pdf
60. G. Singh and P. Bhambri. 2023. Simulation analysis of AODV and DSDV routing protocols for secure and reliable service in mobile adhoc networks (MANETs). In P. Bhambri, S. Rani, V. E. Balas, and A. A. Elngar (Eds.), *Integration of AI-based Manufacturing and Industrial Engineering Systems with the Internet of Things* (1st ed., pp. 205–216). CRC Press. https://doi.org/10.1201/9781003383505
61. R. Rana and P. Bhambri. 2024. Artificial Intelligence and Internet of Things (IoT) facilitated digital twin for Industry 4.0 application domains. In S. Rani, P. Bhambri, S. Kumar, P. K. Pareek, and A. A. Elngar (Eds.), *AI-driven Digital Twin and Industry 4.0* (pp. 168–181). CRC Press. https://doi.org/10.1201/9781003395416-11

Chapter 11

Two-tier real-time detection of data fabrication attacks in decentralized smart microgrids

Venkata Lakshmi, G. Yamini, R. Kalaivani, M. Gokilhashree and S. V. Saveeithaa

11.1 INTRODUCTION

Smart grid technology relies on Advanced Metering Infrastructure (AMI) to track customer power usage and load data. Reconfigurable authenticated key exchange mechanisms of smart grid communications through reconfigurable Physical Uncloneable Functions (PUFs) solve weaknesses of conventional PUF-based schemes to modeling attacks, which guarantee cyber and physical security of smart meters. This is more efficient in computation and communication as compared to the current protocols and enhances the security of smart metering infrastructure [1]. Installed at the customer's site, smart meters measure this data. Thus, it is critical that AMI data remain intact. There have been several recorded cases of organized and localized data manipulation and the resulting losses to utilities. The chapter temporally segmented energy benchmarking methods developed using smart meter data to assess building energy performance in cities. By analyzing daily and seasonal usage patterns, it identifies when buildings underperform or exceed efficiency goals, unlike traditional annual benchmarking [2]. A lightweight security protocol for smart metering systems in IoT-enabled smart grids uses distributed OTP computation, the Blake2s hash function, and the Ascon AEAD cipher to ensure authentication, confidentiality, and integrity. Formal verification using the AVISPA-SPAN tool confirms its resistance to MITM and replay attacks, proving it to be secure and efficient for resource-constrained IoT devices [3]. A robust anomaly detection framework for smart metering cyber–physical systems accounts for data poisoning during training. By modifying regression error and loss functions, it strengthens time-series ML models against adversarial contamination. Theoretical analysis and experiments on real smart grid data validate that the framework enhances both ML robustness and attack mitigation according to NIST CPS standards [4]. The study provides a comprehensive review of Smart Energy (SE) systems integrating IoT, smart meters, and Business Intelligence (BI) for efficient energy management. It explores the layered architecture, data-driven operations, and evolving computational load distribution across IoT networks [5].

The chapter presents the development and field deployment of AMI-based applications that improve grid observability for distribution system operators (DSOs). Using real-time voltage and power data, two tools were designed for grid monitoring and loss estimation [6]. This chapter presents an Online Home Energy Management (ON-HEM) system using Q-Learning and Deep Q-Learning to optimize real-time energy consumption in smart homes. The model integrates multiple energy sources and appliance categories while minimizing costs, peak demand, and user dissatisfaction [7]. Simulating adversaries with CNN-LSTM, GRU, KNN, and CNN models, it evaluates appliance detectability under different

DOI: 10.1201/9781003656487-11

aggregation and sampling settings. Findings reveal that aggregation size >40 and time intervals >8 hours ensure complete privacy in smart grid data [8]. Using adaptive symbolic aggregation (aSAX) and association rule mining, it pinpoints specific sub-loads responsible for anomalies. The method, validated with real campus data, enhances energy management by revealing inefficiencies and operational irregularities [9]. This study applies Machine Learning (ML) techniques to phishing and intrusion detection, automating anomaly classification with minimal human input. Decision Tree and Random Forest achieved the best results, with 90% accuracy in phishing and 95% precision in intrusion detection [10]. A reference architecture featuring explainable AI, microservices, and adversarial sample generation enhances resilience and interpretability. The proof of concept demonstrates efficient detection and mitigation, highlighting AI's adaptability in large-scale SDN environments [11].

This research explores the use of Least Significant Bit (LSB) and hybrid watermarking for securing digital certificates. A MATLAB-based automated system generates and verifies certificates by embedding watermarks and extracting participant data from Excel sheets. The method improves efficiency, prevents tampering, and simplifies large-scale certificate issuance [12]. This study introduces a post-quantum cryptography (PQC)-enabled blockchain framework for secure edge task offloading in IoT systems. Using consortium blockchain and genetic algorithm-based scheduling, it ensures decentralized authentication and optimized performance. Results show improved latency, reliability, and resilience against quantum-era cyber threats [13]. A Timestamp-based Secret Key Generation (T-SKG) scheme is proposed to enhance IoMT data security without direct key sharing. The method generates synchronized keys at both patient and doctor devices, reducing key compromise risks. Simulations confirm strong resistance to guessing and brute force attacks using DES encryption for data confidentiality [14]. This work develops a Self-Attention Bi-LSTM (SA-BiLSTM) model for detecting fake news with exceptional accuracy (99.98%) using the ISOT dataset. The attention mechanism enhances text feature extraction, capturing key linguistic patterns. The model surpasses CNN, GRU, and LSTM baselines, offering a powerful tool against misinformation on digital platforms [15].

This study proposes a fuzzy logic-based stacked data-driven auto-encoder (FL_SDDAE) for dynamic soft sensor applications in manufacturing automation. The system preprocesses data from virtual sensors to handle missing values, hardware failures, and communication errors. Classification is performed using an LSEBPNN model, achieving 94% prediction performance and 85% measurement accuracy, improving automation reliability and efficiency [16]. This chapter demonstrates vision-based robotic systems enhanced by artificial neural networks (ANNs) for intelligent industrial automation. A 3-DOF robot performs precision cutting using visual guidance, while a 6-DOF robot executes adaptive pick-and-place operations with dual-camera supervision. ANN integration improves computation speed, convergence, and decision accuracy, highlighting its role in advanced machine vision control [17]. The chapter presents a Recurrent Neural Network (RNN) model integrated with an Adaptive Neural Imputation Module (ANIM) to predict solar irradiance for photovoltaic systems with missing data. The model effectively imputes gaps in climatic and irradiation records, outperforming conventional methods under various missing rates. With an added attention mechanism, it achieves superior prediction accuracy, especially in low-light conditions, supporting grid stability and renewable energy forecasting [18].

A novel electricity theft detection framework is proposed using Quantum Key Distribution (QKD) and Extreme Gradient Boosting (EGB) with a Coati Optimization Algorithm (COA). The approach enhances smart grid reliability and consumer privacy through optimized computation and fault tolerance. Simulation results show high accuracy (99%) and detection efficiency (98.6%), outperforming existing methods [19]. This chapter introduces a blockchain-based scheme for secure bidirectional communication in Advanced Metering Infrastructure (AMI). Employing Elliptic Curve Cryptography for lightweight anonymous authentication and a reputation-based consensus protocol, it enables secure, decentralized data aggregation. The system reduces computational cost and ensures tamper-proof communication verified through AVISPA security analysis [20]. A lightweight authentication protocol for smart meters in smart grids is proposed using one-way hash functions and dynamic encryption keys. The method provides message integrity and prevents tampering during communication. Security analysis confirms robust resistance to attacks, achieving over 105,000% improvement in computational efficiency compared to prior protocols [21]. This research presents a machine-learning-based demand-side management strategy to classify and manage residential power consumers. Using Random Forest method, 29,546 consumer load profiles were analyzed, achieving 92.23% accuracy in classifying high-load users. The intelligent load adjustment reduced overall power deficits by 0.73% of total daily load, improving grid stability with minimal consumer stress [22].

The "normal behavior" of the two measures was ascertained when assaults are not present after identifying the system. A "Baseline Standard Limit" specifies the usual upper limit for the addition of Residues under the Ratio Curve, and a "Baseline Safe Margin" specifies the common upper limitation for the Harmonic to Arithmetic mean ratio measure [23–28]. Finally, an attack reconstruction method was proposed that assigns signatures to distinct types of attacks according to changes in the metrics' size, sign, and direction. This could aid site security officials or demand control systems in responding properly. The following stage is to mimic persistent attackers who are well-versed in our defense mechanism by developing attack tactics that would ensure evasion.

Experiments employing genuine datasets obtained from an actual AMI infrastructure in Malaysia (5000 houses for 535 days) and India (800 houses for 3 years) respectively verified our technique. The Sri Lanka dataset was used to demonstrate the trade-offs in generalizability, scalability, and sensitivity, but most of the conclusions are consistent with the India data because of the longer period. Our model has proven itself capable of real-time detection, decipherment, and confirmation of a wide range of attacks undertaken by persistent and stealthy adversaries across several datasets.

Prior research in this field has failed to do the following: use innovative falsification techniques, assume stealthier margins of false data (400W), take into account a wide range of compromised meter fractions (5–70%), presume persistent adversaries with complete defense mechanism knowledge, or place an emphasis on real-time detection. In order to provide evidence for the improvement, the detection limits and impact resilience were measured.

Section 11.2 delves into the limitations of previous work in the field; Section 11.3 delves into the threat model; Section 11.4 provides an overview of the system and dataset; Sections 11.5 and 11.6 cover theoretical analysis and proposed approach.

Owing to the constraints discussed earlier, existing techniques developed for conventional sensor networks and control systems cannot be directly employed. Accordingly, this study introduces a novel security forensics framework designed to detect multiple forms of AMI falsification attacks. This method is applicable to both modest and high margins of incorrect data.

11.2 THREAT MODEL

Anyone might trick the meters into giving them inaccurate power consumption numbers by tampering with the data entering the meters, data stored in the meters, or data transmitted from the meters themselves. Using real smart meter datasets, the study quantifies the economic impact of such cyber threats in smart grids [29].

Area of Coverage: A well-coordinated assault was presupposed in which a formidable hostile actor uses multiple compromised smart meters to simultaneously disseminate false data. An adversary's propensity to minimize the margin of misleading data relative to their number of compromised nodes M is a key indicator of their ability to inflict long-term damage undetected. Finding large-scale, real-world harmful samples is challenging due to the novelty of AMI as a research subject [30–35].

11.2.1 Modes of attack for AMI data falsification

The reported data remains unbiased in the absence of falsification, but it becomes skewed under attacks P_t^i, due to the following types of falsification. It also focuses on security threats and data falsification attacks in Advanced Metering Infrastructure (AMI). It outlines various attack scenarios where false or malicious data tampers with legitimate readings and discusses detection techniques for mitigating such risks [36].

Additive: The enemy relays the information as $P_t^i = P_t^i(act) + \delta_t$. If one utility were to conduct an additional attack on the meters of another, the victims' consumers would lose faith in the victim utility because their bills would be far higher than what they actually paid. In addition, some smart meters may simultaneously detect and record higher-than-actual usage if the victim organization is involved in automatic demand response, which can lead to a Dynamic Load Altering attack [37]. Undue incentives cause fluctuations in peak performance, which the victim company ends up paying for. Customers are suing utilities, claiming their prices are excessively high [38].

Camouflage: The enemy uses two equal groups of compromised meters to launch simultaneous attacks using additive and deductive methods, respectively. This method prioritizes serving a certain group of consumers above others. Because there is little change at aggregate mean consumption, it goes undetected by standard mean-based comparison methodologies.

11.2.2 Fraction of compromised meters and margin of false data

Within the interval $[\delta_{min}, \delta_{max}]$ all δ_t are created at random. For each compromised meter, let δ_t be the average value; this is the margin of misleading data. That is why a component of the hostile approach is aggressive. Any smart attacker would avoid strategies that would cause the resulting distribution to be multimodal or otherwise change its form, because power consumption in a residential AMI network is unimodal. Our findings, on the other hand, take into account variations of the uniformly distributed situation, which is the superior tactic.

The impact of different attack budgets was investigated on a microgrid with fixed N meters by experimenting with different M values. The scalability of the suggested method was tested by independently varying N for an adversary with a given M.

11.2.3 Impact of a (undetected) attacker on revenue

How much money is made per day from an attack is defined as RR, where RR is the value of electricity power in dollars. Daily income RR, expressed in dollars, is characterized as

$$RR = \frac{\delta_{\text{ang}} \times M \times \eta \times E}{1000}, \tag{11.1}$$

The average cost of electricity per unit (KW-Hour) in the USA is \$0.12, and η is the number of reports each day.

11.2.4 Stealthier data falsification strategies

The assumptions concerning stealthy tactics for falsification differ from those of previous publications in that they can be informed either by a partial understanding of typical security mechanisms or by a comprehensive understanding of the actual defense mechanism, rather than by random noise [39].

The top line in Figure 11.1 represents the real power consumption from the affected meters. The data order aware technique is more likely to avoid detection (by proximity-based mechanisms) since it is closer to the actual data, even though both strategies generate the same amount of revenue.

Persistent Attacks: For our suggested defense mechanism, the attacker could remain undiscovered in the system for the strategy parameter pairings $(\rho_{mal}, \delta_{avg})$. In their groundbreaking work on intrusion detection, author [40] used the hierarchical and distributed intrusion detection system (HD-IDS), which is proposed to secure smart metering infrastructure against false data injection attacks. Built on a fog computing architecture across three network layers, it enhances multi-level protection and detection efficiency.

11.3 DATASET AND SYSTEM MODEL DESCRIPTION

In the second set of numbers, the information from 5,000 homes across 6 different areas of Malaysia was collected over the course of 535 days (or almost 2 years) between 2009 and 2010 (source: Ireland Social Sciences Data Archives, entry 36). Residential consumers own all data. It was not possible to conduct longitudinal research using the Sri Lanka dataset because of its short duration. Therefore, the majority of the learning algorithms shown here make use of the primary dataset. On the other hand, comparing our suggested detection mechanism to other AMI datasets with vastly varied population sizes, climates, and behaviors enables us to assess its generalizability, sensitivity, and scalability. By default, all results relate to the India data unless otherwise specified.

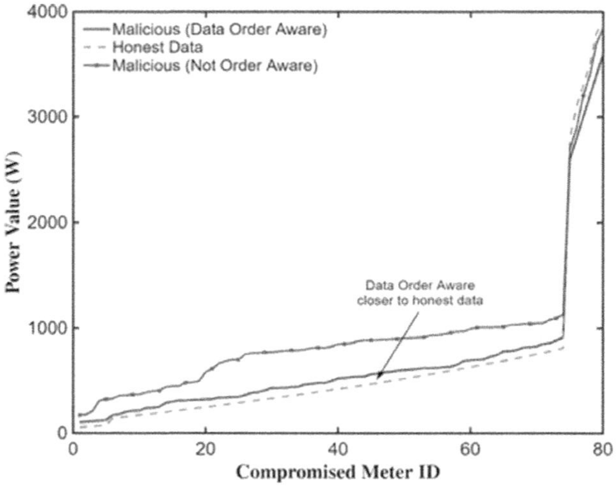

Figure 11.1 An advantage of being aware of data order.

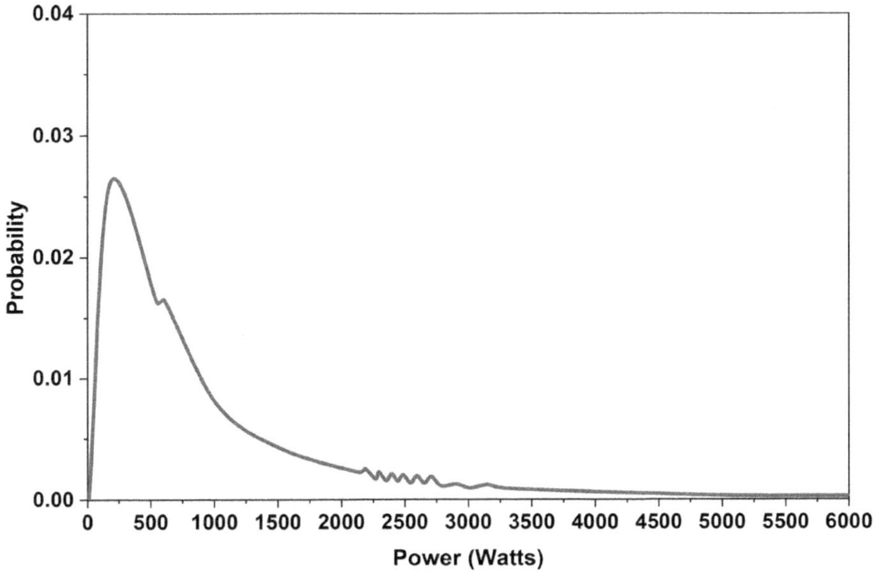

Figure 11.2 Power usage in India Pmix mixture.

Data Distributions: To represent the distribution of any meter's steady-state power consumption, the notation P^i was used. Think about the distributions of data for a 200-meter population in India, as shown in Figure 11.2. There is no random large fluctuation among them [41]. The shape suggests a distribution that is almost lognormal.

The preceding discussion for the Sri Lanka dataset was restated to allay concerns about the generalizability of the findings. The findings show that there is a consistent pattern in the aggregate power usage across several regional datasets. This means that the experimental work retains its validity when the dataset changes. Given this, it is reasonable to assume that the trend is not unique to this data collection but rather represents a general tendency.

Data Distributions: To represent the distribution of any meter's steady-state power consumption, the notation P^i was used. Think about the distributions of data for a 200-meter population in Ireland, as shown in Figure 11.3. There is no random large fluctuation among them [41]. The shape suggests a distribution that is almost lognormal.

Using a Box-Cox transformation technique, the distribution of *P*-mix was approximated to that of a Gaussian distribution. The purpose of applying Box-Cox transformation techniques is to approximate normally distributed data from non-normal sources. Therefore, in order to get a roughly Gaussian distributed random variable, *p-mix*, all data were translated on power usage onto a natural logarithm scale.

There is less dispersion among the data points in the India and Sri Lanka samples (68% and 70%, respectively) since they are within the first standard deviation. The modified datasets still show an imbalance around the mean; for example, in the Sri Lanka dataset, 32% of the samples are greater than the mean, whereas 65% of the samples are on the right side of the mean. Because of this innate asymmetry, there are still more data points that fall below the mean (i.e., on the left side) even after transformation. Under assault, this is a component that sets off distinct signatures (for more on this, see Section 11.6.2).

Problems with Implementing the Suggested Detector: Despite extensive data collection, no project has ever disclosed the precise architecture of the AMI. This work introduces an unsupervised anomaly detection method for smart metering data using High-Dimensional

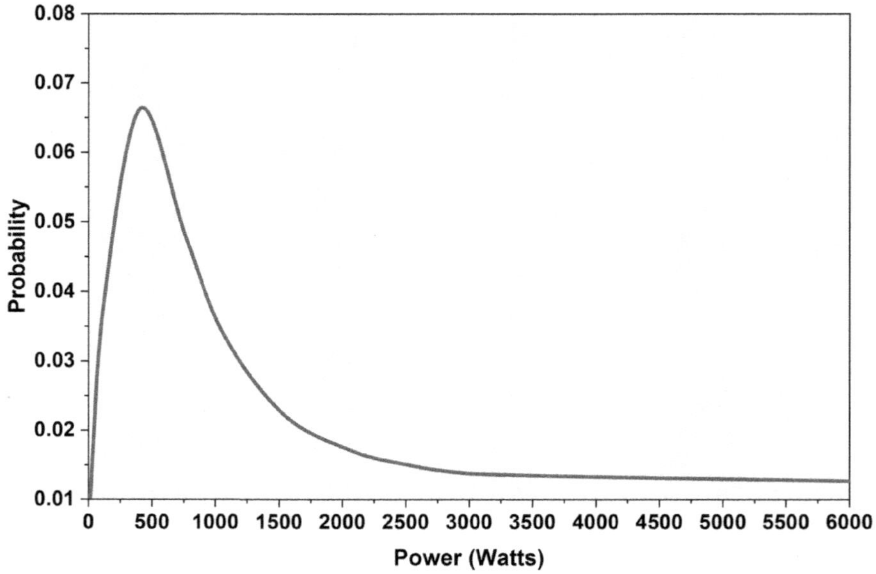

Figure 11.3 Ireland's power usage vs probability distribution.

Functional Time Series analysis. By employing functional depth concepts, it identifies "evolution outliers"—meters with abnormal daily dependency patterns [42]. Therefore, investigating the effects of topological factors on the suggested detection mechanism directly was not practical. The sensitivity of attack detection is affected by the size of the microgrid. Referring to Figure 11.4, this information is provided by an AMI system. One benefit of decentralized detectors is that they make it easier to pinpoint the affected areas of the AMI and have a higher relative detection sensitivity. The findings were displayed for 200 and 800 Indian houses that imitate various implementations, respectively, to capture both implementation variants. Since the most recent edge device, the DCN-3000, can manage at most 1,000 dwellings, researchers in Ireland investigated decentralized implementation

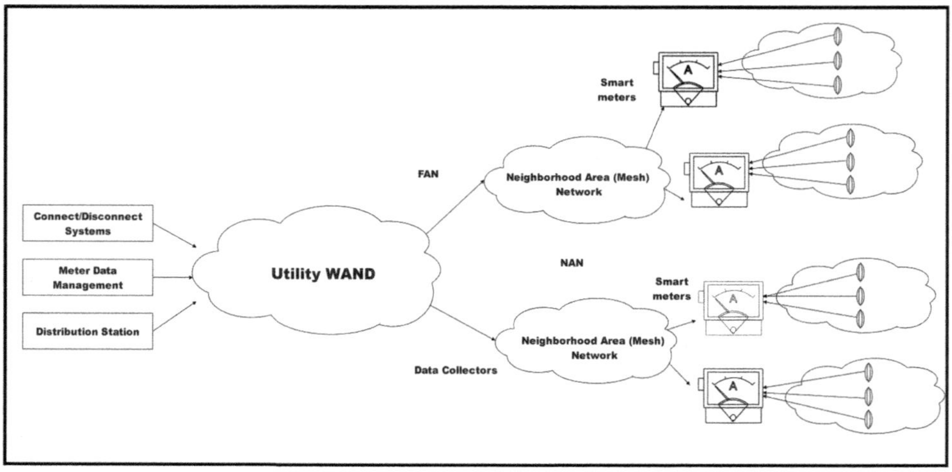

Figure 11.4 AMI: Generic system view.

alternatives using subsets of datasets ranging in size from 200 to 4000. We found that a decentralized edge solution worked well for our detection strategy.

There are two parts to this chapter's technical contribution: (a) Theoretical Explanation and Properties: shows how different Pythagorean means (harmonic and arithmetic) interact to cause metrics to deviate "under different attack modes." (b) Proposed Methodology: describes the methodology and how it works. The justification for the suggested methodology's ability to detect stealthy attacks and the reasoning for the proposed measures' invariance over time and across datasets are based on the lessons and properties learned from such an explanation. In order to provide a clear roadmap for anyone planning to apply our approach, the methodology was separated from the theory.

11.4 PROPOSED METHODOLOGY

A real dataset spanning two years showed that the Tier 1 metric is scalable across datasets and relatively stable under typical use cases, all without the need for a smoothing method. After that, an empirical investigation of the ratio distribution was used to establish the Safe Margins, or normal bounds, of the suggested Ratio metric. Given the intrinsic stability of these measurements, streamline the historical data and utilize it to approximate the usual limits, also known as the Standard Limit. Standard limits and safe margins are provided for proper detection [43]. Afterward, a two-stage procedure for assault detection was proposed. The directional deviation of the second measure to confirm or refute the possibility of organized data fabrication was used based on the first metric's large deviation from the norm. A two-tier approach is required to reduce the false alarm rate and increase the detection sensitivity for weak attacks.

11.4.1 System identification of invariants

System identification is the process of determining the typical operation of the detection metric in the absence of attacks in statistical anomaly detection. Generally speaking, it is more accurate to use a detection metric that is more stable, or invariant, under "normal" conditions.

The logarithmic scale data on power consumption collected from the N meters at each time slot t is denoted as $\boldsymbol{p}_t = \left[p_t^1, \cdots, p_t^N\right]$. Let $\boldsymbol{p}_t$ stand for the realization of p for every time t, where p is the mixed random variable in steady state.

$$HM_t = \frac{N}{\sum_{i=1}^{N} \frac{1}{p_t}} \quad AM_t = \frac{\sum_{i-1}^{N} p_t^i}{N} \tag{11.2}$$

11.4.1.1 Arithmetic mean ratios in harmony

The first step is to compute all HM_t and AM_t for every time slot b inside the time window denoted by T. The set $T \in \{1,\ldots,365\}$ is chosen, because each set as 24 time slots represents a day in a year. The two-tier real-time detection system is used for identifying orchestrated data falsification attacks in decentralized microgrids. By analyzing the Harmonic-to-Arithmetic Mean Ratio and cumulative residuals over time, the framework detects stealthy and persistent attacks effectively [44].

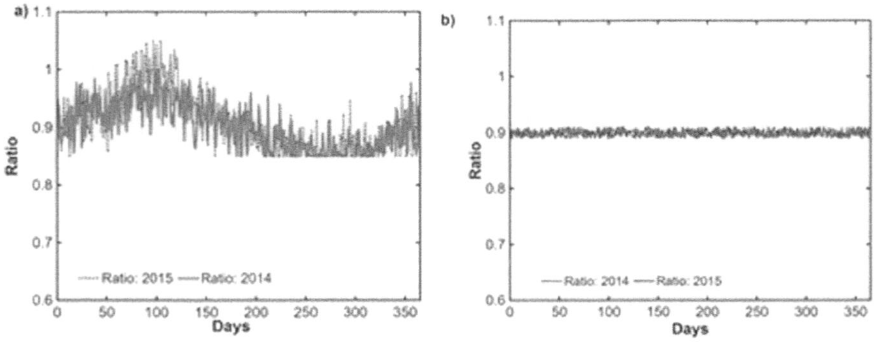

Figure 11.5 Legitimate HM/AM ratio: (a) 200 meters (b) 800 meters.

$$Q^r(T) = \frac{\sum_{t=1}^{24} HM_t(T)}{\sum_{t=1}^{24} AM_t(T)} \quad \forall\ T \in \{1,\ldots,365\} \tag{11.3}$$

Figure 11.5a and 11.5b display the proposed ratio measure $Q^r(T)$, for two separate meter populations in India, specifically 200 and 800 meters in 2014 and 2015. Figure 11.6a displays time series of $Q^r(T)$ for an entirely separate dataset containing 5000 meters from 6 distinct regions in Ireland. The remarkably stable metric $Q^r(T)$ as shown in Figures 11.5a, 11.5b, and 11.6a, is well-suited for anomaly identification. It follows that the daily average ratio between HM and AM is unaffected by valid adjustments that impact the mean power consumption.

A different approach was used, as we will see shortly, by utilizing the suggested RUC metric to decrease false alarms while maintaining missed detection.

11.4.1.2 Ratio metric safe margin

The ratio fall inside the first SD from the mean, making up about 70.02%. Sample ratios are between the second and third SD, at 94.04% and 98.17%, respectively. The (μ_r, s_r) values for an 800 meter population are (0.804,0.0082) and $\mu_r \pm 2s_r$ comprises 98% of the samples. Comparing the 5,000-house Sri Lanka dataset with the India dataset reveals a similar ratio pattern (Figure 11.6b). For smaller population sizes, the ratio metric is less stable, as shown

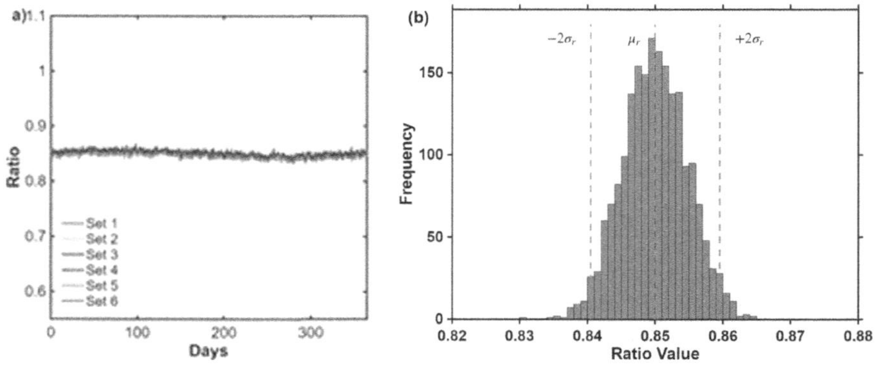

Figure 11.6 Sri Lanka data (6 regions, 5000 meters): (a) Ratios and (b) Distribution of ratios.

in Figure 11.5a and 11.5b. Identifying a low-margin attack signature in a population of 200 meters seems like it would be more challenging. So, additional results for 200 meters are provided to illustrate the worst-case scenario.

$$\Gamma_{\text{high}}(T) = Q^r(T) + \kappa \tag{11.4}$$

$$\Gamma_{\text{low}}(T) = Q^r(T) - \kappa \tag{11.5}$$

As the κ values increase, the safe margins expand. It is easy to minimize false alarms by simply adjusting the κ to the highest or lowest observed values in the $Q^r(T)$ distribution. This huge safety buffer might increase the possibility of undiscovered stealth assaults with lower δ_{avg} and/or ρ_{mal} levels. To circumvent this problem (the base rate fallacy), reduce false alarms, and keep detection sensitivity high, we offer an alternate metric, RUC, for the second layer.

11.4.1.3 Total residuals between safe margin and ratio

An essential step in computing RUC (T) is finding the signed residual distance ($\nabla(T)$) between the observed ratio and the safety margin [45].

$$\nabla(T): \begin{cases} = Q^r(T) - \Gamma_{\text{high}}(T), & \text{if} \quad Q^r(T) > \Gamma_{\text{high}}(T); \\ = Q^r(T) - \Gamma_{\text{low}}(T), & \text{if} \quad Q^r(T) < \Gamma_{\text{low}}(T); \\ = 0, & \text{otherwise}; \end{cases} \tag{11.6}$$

$$RUC(T) = \sum_{j=T-FS}^{T} \nabla(j) \tag{11.7}$$

For the historical dataset (2014, 2015), view the second metric, $RUC(T)$. The justification for keeping a signed measure is that legal changes cause the ratio to oscillate among the top and bottom safe margins, drawing $RUO(T)$ closer to zero, even when it goes beyond the safe boundaries.

11.4.1.4 Determining testing set detection thresholds

By identifying the system, the κ stands for a safe margin and what a standard limit, which is based on κ and acts as a threshold for both of these metrics. These cutoffs are denoted with a superscript "h" since they are derived from historical data. By averaging the ratio samples collected on the Tth day of the previous years, we may find $Q^r(T^h)$. Weight selection, in contrast to most other schemes, has little impact on performance because ratios are quite stable and show little variance across years. While the 2014/2015 ratios are equal weights in the 800-meter case study, both ends of the weight range were accounted for in the 200-meter example study by allocating 0.02 to the 2014 data and 0.98 to the 2015 data. The outcomes will demonstrate that neither of the weight choices much affects performance.

An unconnected range to T is known as the "standard limit" for RUC values. Figure 11.7 shows that in the yth (training) year, there were a total of $\{RUC(T)^y\}$ residual distances. Now an appropriate higher and lower threshold were chosen from the set $\{RUC(T)^y\}$. The set $\tau_{max}(h)$ and the set $\tau_{min}(h)$ are, respectively, $y \in 1,2$ and τ-all. For the appropriate candidate cutoffs, let τ stand. The first algorithm determines the highest and lowest values in the set of RUC$(T)^y$ and shows them in Figure 11.7 to avoid overfitting. The cost and penalty functions that go along with the $\tau_{\max}$ search (which seeks out all non-zero positive $RUC(T)$) and the $\tau_{\min}$ search (which seeks out are $p_{max/min}$. By decreasing the amount of nonzero $RUC(T)$ values, Algorithm 1 streamlines the search problem and shrinks the search space.

Algorithm 1. Determine $\tau_{max}(h), \tau_{min}(h)$.

for T, τ, y do

if $\left(\text{RUC}(\text{T})^{y} < \tau\right)$ then

$c_{max/min} : \dfrac{|\tau - RUC(T)|}{2}$

else

$p_{max/min} = 2\left|\text{RUC}(T)^{y} - \tau\right|$

end if

end for

$\tau_{max/min}(h)$ =arg minτ $|c - p|$

11.4.2 Tier one detector

An interval κ from the distribution of historical ratios was used when building the safe margin criterion. A possible outlier was flagged if the measured ratio deviates significantly from this margin of safety. The 2016 data were used as the current testing year, and let c stand for it.

$$Q^{r}\left(T^{c}\right) : \begin{cases} \in \left[Q^{r}\left(T^{h}\right) \pm \kappa\right] & \text{No Anomaly;} \\ \notin \left[Q^{r}\left(T^{h}\right) \pm \kappa\right] & \text{Anomaly Suspected;} \end{cases} \tag{11.8}$$

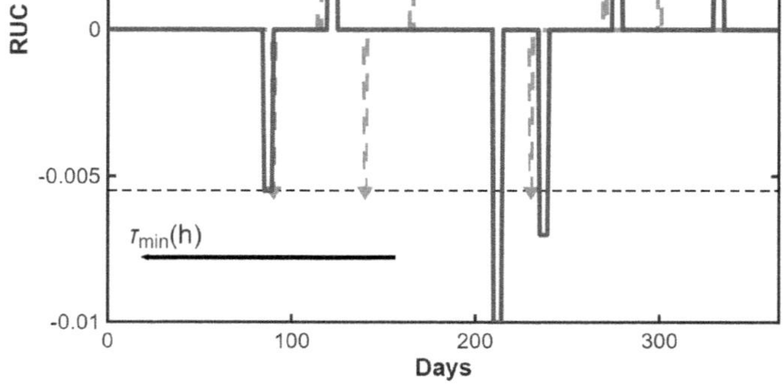

Figure 11.7 k ¼ 2sr for RUC standard limits.

On day, T^c of the testing set, the safe margins are T, T_{high} (T^c) and T_{low} (T^c).

11.4.3 Tier two detector

The RUC$\left(T^c\right)$, normal interval $\left[\tau_{min}(h), \tau_{max}(h)\right]$, and the ratio metric was outside of safe bounds, confirming an orchestrated data fabrication attack.

$$RUC\left(T^c\right):\begin{cases}\in\left[\tau_{\min}(h),\tau_{\max}(h)\right] & \text{No Attack;}\\ \notin\left[\tau_{\min}(h),\tau_{\max}(h)\right], & \text{Attack Inferred;}\end{cases} \quad (11.9)$$

The marked bottom curves in the graph , show the proposed metrics in a test environment free of attacks, while dotted lines show the safe margins. The second tier is required because the ratio signature is not visible.

Figure 11.8a and 11.8b displays ratio ultra-low camouflage and RUC.

11.5 THEORETICAL EXPLANATION AND PROPOSED METRIC PROPERTIES

Earlier, the defense mechanism was suggested; however, it failed to clarify how and why it identifies data fraud. Here, the several mathematical and security features were found, which contribute to this comprehension. After outlining the general security lessons and properties, this part concludes with a discussion of the consequences of AMI power consumption data fabrication.

11.5.1 The ratio metric: why is it stable?

Although each house is special in its own way, there are certain habits that the majority of a given community shares. There should be a weak positive association between power usage and household income, but it is not completely independent. As seen in Figures 11.5a and 11.5b, the stability of the proposed $Q^r(T)$ across time intervals within that dataset is unaffected by the difference in datasets. Figure 11.9a proves that this claim is true by showing the (T) time series from the Sri Lanka dataset.

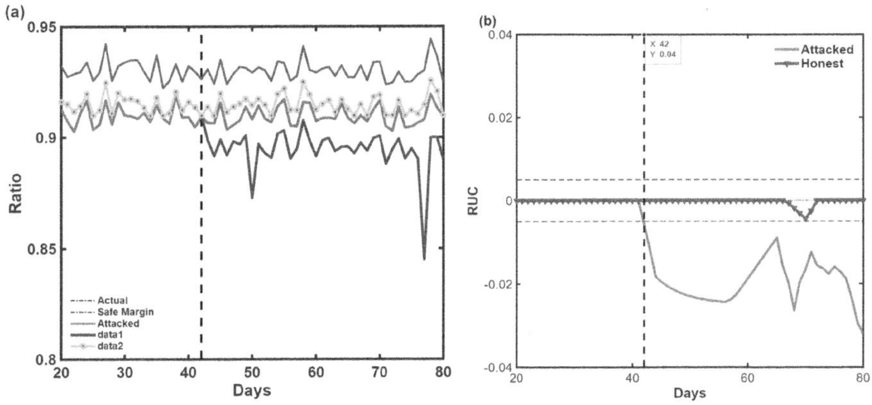

Figure 11.8 Ratio (a) Ultra low camouflage (b) RUC.

Here a crucial connection was proved between the Theorem and its corollaries [16, 18] (1975) and the observed invariance of (T). The Tung's Theorem "provided the theoretical upper and lower boundaries on the absolute difference between Arithmetic and Geometric Mean."

Let, H_N. stand for the harmonic mean and, A_N. for the arithmetic mean.

$$\frac{(B-1)^2}{N(B+1)} \leq |A_N - H_N| \leq \left(\sqrt{(B)} - \sqrt{(1)}\right)^2. \tag{11.10}$$

For a different formulation of Equation (11.10), we can state that if the maximum and minimum values are

$$\frac{\left(a_{\max} - a_{\min}\right)^2}{N\left(a_{\max} + a_{\min}\right)} \leq |A_N - H_N| \leq \left(\sqrt{(a_{\max})} - \sqrt{(a_{\min})}\right)^2, \tag{11.11}$$

in such circumstances, $a_{max} \sim a_{min} + (N-1)\xi$. The bounds of $|A_N - H_N|$ are determined only by ξ and $a_{\min}$ as this illustrates. Since ξ and $a_{\min}$ are plainly steady in Figure 11.9a and 11.9b, it follows that, $|A_N - H_N|$ should also be rather constant. Geographical and temporal granularities, the majority of cyber-physical systems with redundant sensors show positive correlation when sensing certain physical occurrences. With well-planned spatio-temporal granularity, engineers will be able to use our metric as a constant for detecting anomalies. All of the above justifies the method as an alternate solution to the prevalent problem of dealing with changing trends in different power consumption datasets, and the findings from actual datasets corroborate this.

11.5.2 Determining Pythagorean mean properties' impact in the face of data falsification attacks

One can better understand how the suggested metrics change when attacked using the unique security properties and lessons.

For example, if a data series $\boldsymbol{X} = \{x^1, \cdots, x^N\}$, that comes from N sources, it is represented as $\boldsymbol{X} = (\mu, \sigma)$ for standard deviation and mean.

$$HM(\boldsymbol{X}) = \frac{N}{\sum_{i=1}^{N} \frac{1}{x^i}} \quad AM(\boldsymbol{X}) = \frac{\sum_{i=1}^{N} x^i}{N} \tag{11.12}$$

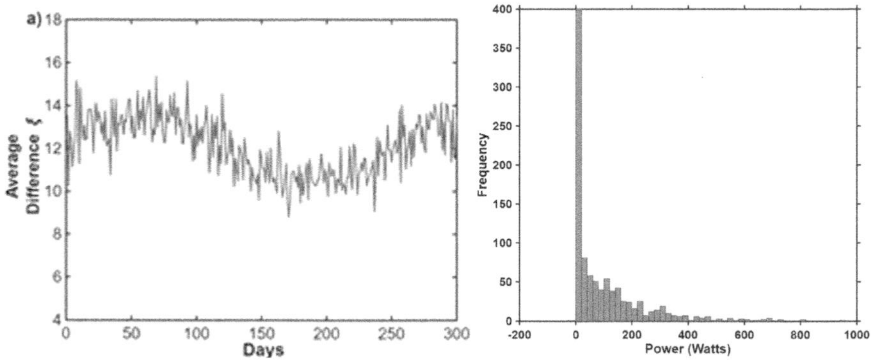

Figure 11.9 Sri Lanka dataset: (a) Average difference $\xi(T)$. (b) $a_{\min}$ values.

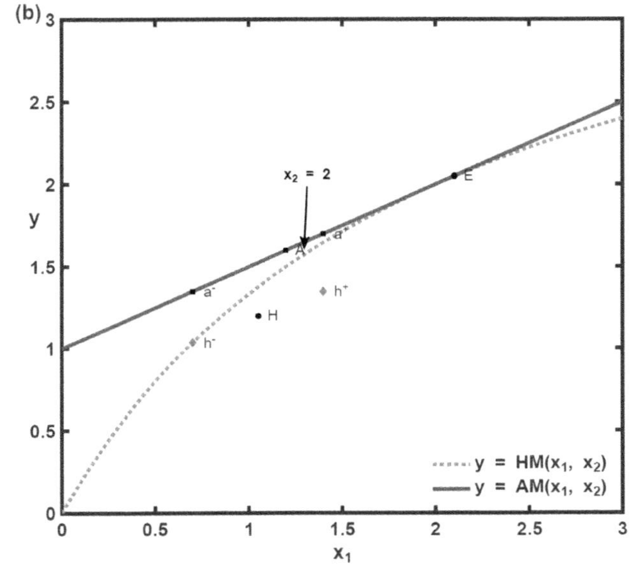

Figure 11.10 Schur concavity.

This is the condition that defines Schur Concavity:

$$\left(x_{1j} - x_{1k}\right)\left(\frac{\partial y}{x_{1j}} - \frac{\partial y}{x_{1k}}\right) \leq 0 \ \forall x \in \mathbb{R}^d, \tag{11.13}$$

Figure 11.10 displays the Schur concavity.

Furthermore, that the data falsification method was discovered, the margin of bogus data, and the position of the attacked datapoint relative to the genuine mean all have an impact on whether the ratio value increases or decreases. Table 11.1 provides a summary of the lessons/properties derived for different types of attacks and margins of fake data in the right (R) or left (L) side of the true average. The table also shows how different attacks affected the proposed ratio metric. The implications of these generic features on the power consumption dataset were addressed separately later on, since they are not dataset-specific.

Here is a brief overview of Table 11.1: Assume that an attack bias ∈ manipulates subsets of a dataset using additive and deductive methods $|\Delta HM^{+}|$ and $|\Delta AM^{+}|$. Similarly, $|\Delta HM^{+}|$, $|\Delta HM^{+,-}|$, and $|\Delta AM^{+}|$, $|\Delta AM^{+,-}|$ indicate the degradation rates. The symbol *L#* represents the note, lesson, or property number. The mode indicates the kind of falsification. Locators "L" and "R" indicate whether the targeted datapoint is located to the right or left of the actual mean, respectively. On the right-hand side of the table, you can see the prerequisites and requirements for each observation. "X" indicates conditions where the user does not care. Appendix D, which is accessible in the online additional materials, provides a detailed summary of all properties and teachings. A theoretical example in Appendix D of the online supplementary materials of how Schur concavity generates these special characteristics in response to different types of falsification attempts.

The second reason to use it is because, as shown in Figures 11.5a, 11.5b, and 11.6a, the HM to AM ratio remains rather constant when attacks are not present. Thirdly, there are no closed forms of Harmonic Means; the best one can do is do an approximate calculation. As both the total and attacked data points grow in size, the approximation errors

Table 11.1 Effects of different attacks on Pythagorean means growth decay rates

Lesson #	*Mode*	*Position*	*Property*	*Ratio effect*	*Necessary*	*Sufficient*
L1	$\in< k^{+}$ (lhigh)	$\in< k^{+}$ (llow)	Increases	$\lvert\Delta HM^{+}\rvert > \lvert\Delta AM^{+}\rvert$	L	Additive(+)
L2	$\in> k^{+}$ (lhigh)	$\in> k^{+}$ (llow)	Decreases	$\Delta HM^{+} < \Delta AM^{+}$	L	Additive(+)
L3	$\in> k^{-}$ (lhigh)	$\in> 0$	Decreases	$\Delta HM^{-}\rvert > \lvert\Delta AM^{-}\rvert$	L	Deductive(-)
L4	$\in< k^{-}$ (rhigh)	$\in< k^{-}$ (rlow)	Increases	$\lvert\Delta HM^{-}\rvert < \lvert\Delta AM^{-}\rvert$	R	Deductive(-)
L5	$\in> k^{-}$ (rhigh)	$\in> k^{-}$ (rlow)	Decreases	$\lvert\Delta HM^{-}\rvert > \lvert\Delta AM^{-}\rvert$	R	Deductive(-)
L6	$\in> k^{+}$ (rhigh)	$\in> 0$	Decreases	$\lvert\Delta HM^{+}\rvert < \lvert\Delta AM^{+}\rvert x$	R	Additive(+)
L7	X	X	Decreases	$\lvert\Delta HM^{+,-}\rvert > \lvert\Delta AM^{+,-}\rvert$	X	Camouflage(+,-)

grow as well, and the underlying time series is inherently unstable. Because of this, it is extremely difficult, if not impossible, for an opponent to devise a foolproof plan to defeat our system.

11.5.2.1 Essential and adequate requirements for ratio change

The "approximation expressions" for a number of the mandatory and optional criteria were formulated as given in Table 11.1. In the findings section, it experimentally confirms that these approximations are accurate. The theoretical verification in Appendix D and the approximation of bounds in Appendix E, both of which are part of the online extra material.

The estimated lower bounds, according to the typical case, are $k^{-}(\text{rlow}) = k^{+}(\text{llow}) =$

$$\kappa_{\text{low}} = \frac{\sigma}{M} + \frac{\sigma}{\sqrt{M}}\sqrt{\frac{N-M}{N-1}} + \sigma, \tag{11.14}$$

The symbols Z and f denote the direction of the bias points relative to the real mean, while the addition and subtraction of subscripts indicate the type of manipulation, respectively.

In rough terms, the highest limits are $k^{+}(\text{lhigh}) = k^{-}(\text{rhigh}) =$

$$\kappa_{\text{high}} = \max\left(\sigma^{2}, \frac{2\sigma}{M} + \frac{\sigma}{\sqrt{M}}\sqrt{\frac{N-M}{N-1}} + 2\sigma\right). \tag{11.15}$$

On one side of the mean you can see the conditions for deductive reasoning, while on the other side you can see the conditions for additive reasoning.

$$k^{-}(\text{lhigh}) = k^{+}(\text{rhigh}) = \sigma\sqrt{\frac{N}{N-1}}. \tag{11.16}$$

In the worst case $k_{\text{low}} > \left\{ \left(|x_i - \mu| + \sigma \sqrt{\frac{N}{N-1}} \right) + \mu \right\} - x_i$, and $k(high) > |x_i - \mu| + \sigma^2$. To check the work, approach the series' lowest datapoint additively and its highest datapoint deductively, using the worst-case expressions.

11.5.2.2 Effects on the real consumption dataset

In Table 11.1, the characteristics of the ratio metric's "generic" attack signature are presented. Before these insights into real-world power usage datasets and assaults, remember that while 36% of the data points in the power usage dataset are on the right side of the mean, 64% are on the left side. Therefore, there is a higher probability that the practical mean will be on the left side of the attack probability distribution. Table 11.1 shows that rates of decay and growth of AM and HM are affected by the relationship between the real position of the assaulted data point and the true mean.

11.5.3 Metrics for objective assessment of security performance

In order to evaluate and analyze the suggested anomaly detection technique's security performance in an objective and fair manner, the outline for four metrics is here. This also clarifies the conventional ROC curves in our assessments.

Time to Detection: duration, measured in days, between the beginning of the attack and its detection. Attacks against the detector that are neither persistent nor optimized can use this metric [46].

Expected Time between False Alarms $E(T_{fa})$When attempting to measure a method's resilience against persistent attacks, the traditional ROC curves have three problems: ROC curves with low false alarm rates can be misleading due to the base rate fallacy, as discussed in a seminal paper. The length of time a study is conducted also affects the false alarm rate. An effective detection metric will not have the effect of an undetected attack grow irrationally as $E(T_{fa})$ rises. Instead of using the traditional ROC curves, this approach was chosen to evaluate the security of our system. Our definition of $E(T_{fa}) = \frac{\sum_{1}^{\eta_{FA}} T_{BFA}}{\eta_{FA}}$ differs.

Impact (of Undetected Attack) (Eqn. (11.1)) from Section 11.3 defines attack revenue per day as RR, and the impact of an undiscovered attack can be measured as $I=RR/24$ revenue damage per hour. In order to assess the safety of our approach, $E(T_{fa})$ against I was plotted.

Break Even Time (T_{BE}). In this case, $T_{BE} = \frac{TC}{RR * 365}$ represents the number of years required for the total revenue to breakeven TC invested, with $R\ R$ being the daily revenue for the undetected attack. Our methods show that, for a given microgrid N, T_{BE} by changing M in the face of repeated attacks.

11.6 EXPERIMENTAL EVALUATION

For system identification, the 2014 and 2015 datasets were consulted for testing and evaluation; here, the 2016 dataset was consulted. Additionally, to demonstrate generalizability, scalability, and sensitivity, a validation dataset consisting of 5,000 Sri Lanka residences for two years (2009, 2010) was utilized. We created different attack samples using the testing set's data and fed them into a virtual AMI.

These signatures are based on a constant fraction of compromised nodes (40%) and a fixed threshold $\kappa = 2s_r$, that gives the necessary baseline false alarm rate. The upper bound of RUC(T) for a seven-day frame duration was calculated, with a corresponding $\kappa = 2s_r$. We devise a technique for attack reconstruction that redirects the identified forensic signature in order to ascertain the vector and presence of the attack.

The detection limits were provided by parameterizing all values of $\rho_{mal}, \delta_{avg}, \kappa$, and N. The extent to which our method mitigates the effects of persistent attacks and gives the boundaries of $(\delta_{avg}, \rho_{mal})$ pairings that our system misses.

The findings in comparison were evaluated against those of other studies that have used the same datasets and a threat model.

11.6.1 Attack signatures and forensics

Although the focus on outcomes with, $\delta_{avg} < 400W$, our approach is as applicable for, $\delta_{avg} > 400$. in the first tier alone, the somewhat higher $(\rho_{mal}, \delta_{avg})$ pairs create a distinct signature within the range of $\delta_{avg} < 400$. Low Attack Strength is the name given to this category. Decreasing either δ_{avg} and/or ρ_{mal} anymore prevents the first tier from obtaining clear attack signatures, but the second tier discloses the assault.

11.6.1.1 Baseline false alarm

The use of a standard limit equivalent to $\kappa = 2s_r$ results in only one false alarm. This κ is considered a baseline threshold when the detection sensitivity is at its poorest, given the extremely low false alarm rate of 0.24%. The results of the attack forensic section employ the baseline $\kappa = 2s_r$ to depict the most severe detection scenario [47]. Reducing κ from the baseline value further improves detection in the performance evaluation section if a utility is able to tolerate more false alarms.

Figure 11.11 shows the performance of false alarms.

11.6.1.2 Extremely light attack power

Figures 11.12a and 11.12b demonstrate the effects of a deductive data-order aware attack with a margin as small as 50 W and a ρ_{mal} value of 42% on the ratio and RUC metrics. An eye-catching black line marks the beginning of the attack on the 41st day dotted line.

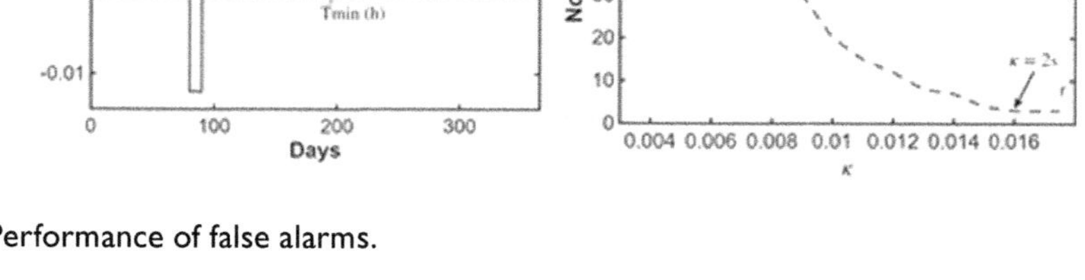

Figure 11.11 Performance of false alarms.

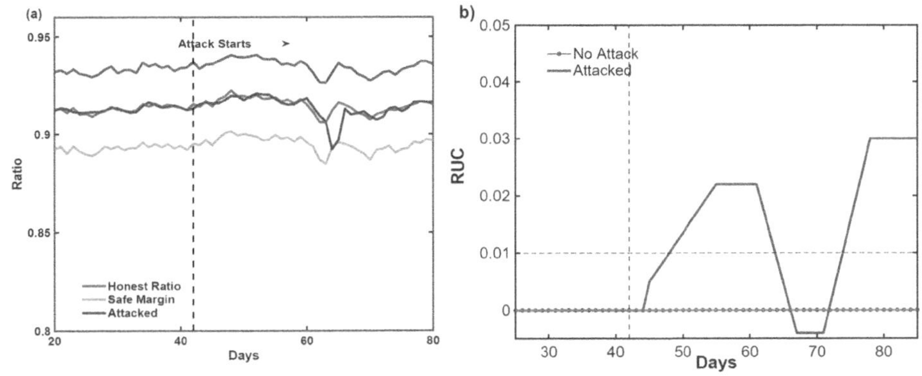

Figure 11.12 Extremely low RUC (a) and deductive (b) ratio.

When predicted, the ratio decreases when the attack begins in comparison to the initial testing set (Figure 11.12a). However, because δ_{avg} is so low, the divergence in the ratio signature, which closely tracks the expected trend, is insufficient to confirm the attack. Figure 11.12b shows the same scenario's related RUC map, which confirms the presence of an attack within 14 days of its initiation. If there is no discernible pattern in the first-tier ratio, then the attack is quite weak. The 50th day $\text{RUC}\left(T^c\right)$ in Figure 11.12b is negative and falls below the lower standard limit, ruling out possibilities like additive and one-sided deductive as well as concealment. The 42nd day's direction change of AM and HM shows that both means are gradually decreasing. As a result, we know that the deductive attack was extremely weak. Detection of a margin of incorrect data as little as 50 W is evident.

Figure 11.13a and 11.13b display the additive attack, with $\rho_{\text{mal}} = 42\,\%$ and $\delta_{\text{avg}} = 78$. Since this attack strength pair is additive and has a somewhat smaller value for $\delta_{\text{avg}} = 459$ (as found by Eqn. (11.14)), the ratio signature slightly increases and follows lesson (L.1). Figure 11.13a shows that the first tier is inadequate to verify an attack due to the incredibly weak attack.

Before, in Figures 11.8a and 11.8b, we saw the matching outcomes for covert assaults. The additive and deductive bias components made the camouflage signature more bursty. Because the greater δ_{avg} of 120 W caused the detection to occur roughly five days earlier than normal, keep that in mind. The time it takes to confirm an assault also depends on the average value, as this example shows.

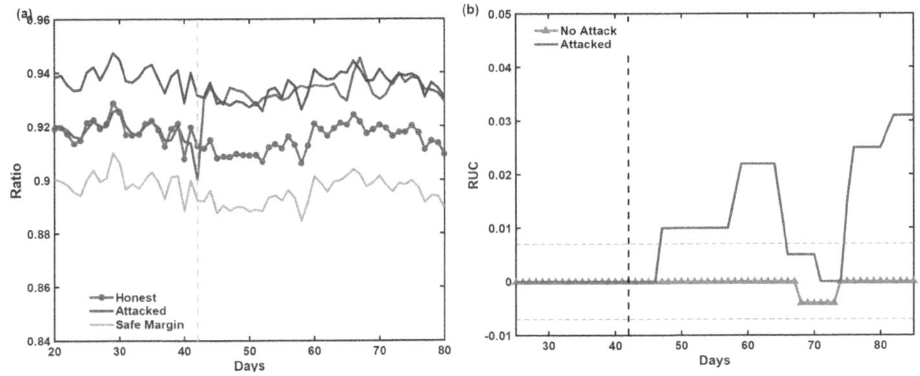

Figure 11.13 Extremely low (a) RUC (b) ratio.

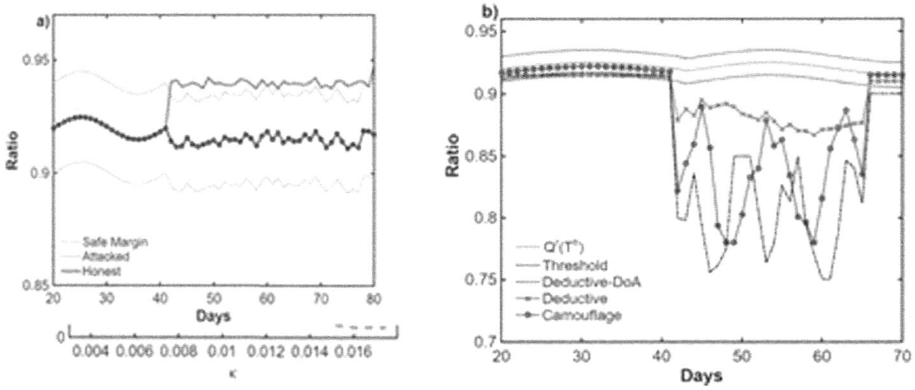

Figure 11.14 Low attack power (a) Additive and (b) Combined.

11.6.1.3 Low power of attack

Figure 11.14a displays signatures subjected with a mal value of 42% and an average value of 200. Although the δ_{avg} is lower than the majority of previous works, the ratio statistic clearly indicates an attack. Figure 11.14b also shows the non-data order aware outcome, which provides a different angle and demonstrates how easy it is to detect non-data order aware attacks.

11.6.1.4 Attacks using incremental evolution

Images 11.15a and 11.15b display the growing incremental attacks, increasing by 2 watts for each time slot up to δ_{avg} = 200 W. Due to constant adjustment, this tactic would be difficult to capture using a residual check at each time step.

11.6.1.5 Validation with Sri Lanka dataset

Using the Sri Lanka dataset as an example, we will show that our deductive and additive attack signatures are consistent across different datasets. Two complete years of data were missing from the Sri Lanka dataset. Because the variation in the two sets of ratio samples was so close, the India dataset's safe margin widths to the Sri Lanka dataset's ratio metric were

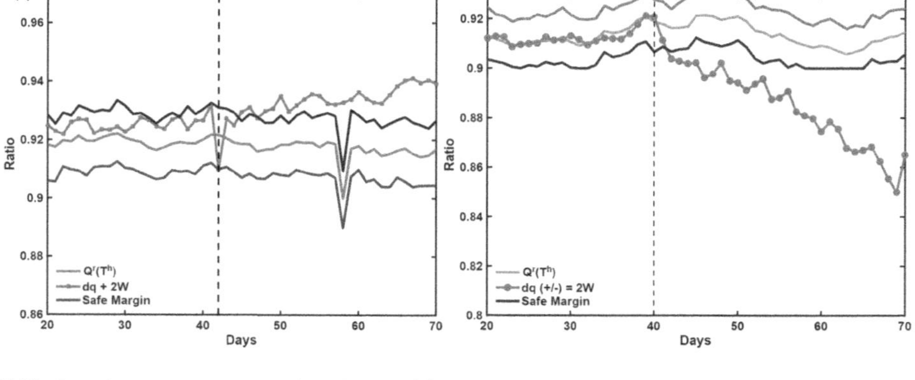

Figure 11.15 Attack using incremental evolution: (a) Additive and (b) Camouflage.

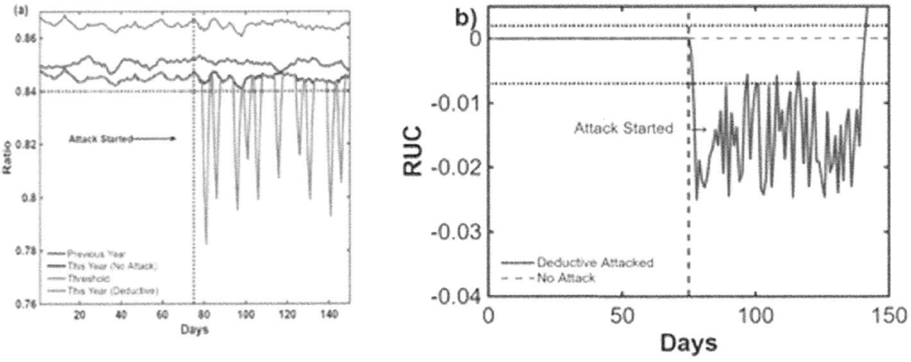

Figure 11.16 Dataset from Sri Lanka: Deductive: (a) Ratio and (b) RUC.

extrapolated. Figure 11.16a and 11.16b provide distinct signatures for deductive assaults on the Sri Lanka dataset $(\rho_{mal} = 15\%, \delta_{avg} = 70\text{W})$, and Figure 11.17a and 11.17b display identical signatures for additive attacks $(\rho_{mal} = 15\%, \delta_{avg} = 100\text{W})$, which align with the findings from the India dataset. As a result, the suggested RUC measurements and inferred baseline thresholds from the India dataset generalize effectively to the Sri Lanka dataset. This dataset makes it easier to spot lower,-mal. values because the higher values are more prominent. The Sri Lanka dataset was found to be more vulnerable to attacks.

11.6.1.6 High attack strength validation

Figure 11.18 is an example of an exhibit that demonstrates the effectiveness of our suggested approach for stronger attacks. In this outcome $\rho_{mal} = 42\%$ and $\delta_{avg} = 800$.

11.6.1.7 Reconstructing the attack scene

By examining the signatures meticulously to determine the plan, method of falsification, expected attack start time, and expected attack stoppage time (if any), features encompass: (i) Whether the ratio, harmonic, or arithmetic mean is increasing, decreasing, or remaining constant; if so, in what direction. (ii) Bounds along the perimeter of the RUC. (iii) The state of the RUC, which can be positive or negative. An example of a stealthy additive attack would be a positive $RUC\ (T)$ that is outside of the $\tau_{\max}(h)$ region, where the observed HM

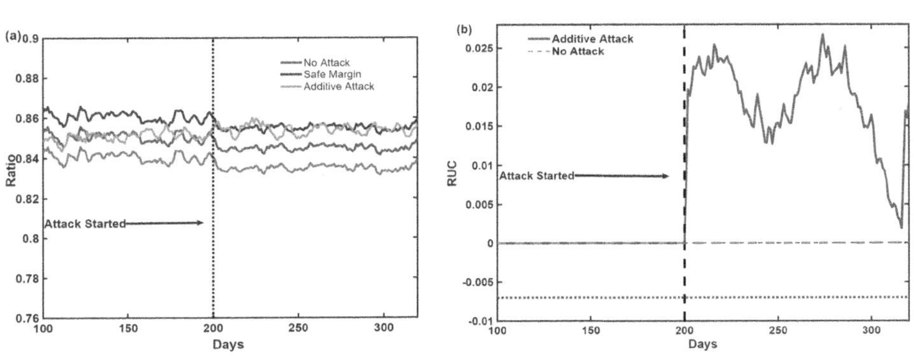

Figure 11.17 Additive: (a) Ratio and (b) RUC for the Sri Lanka dataset.

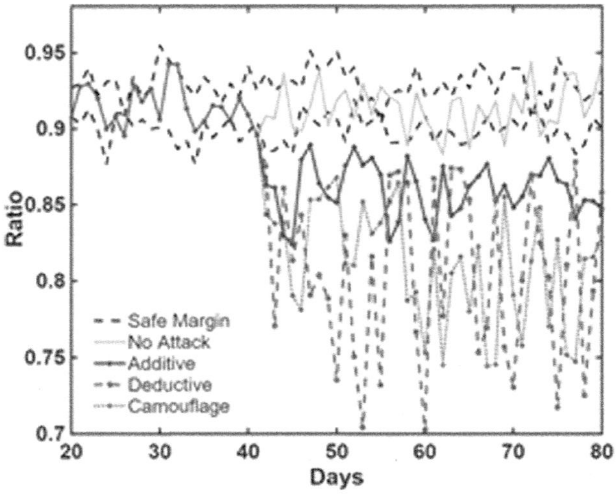

Figure 11.18 High attack strengths: Δavg = 800.

and AM have both shown an increase. An additive attack with greater margins $\left(\delta_{avg} < k_{\text{low}}\right)$ occurs when the ratio and RUC (T) are negative, yet the measured HM and AM are increasing. Naturally, the remaining portions of Figure 11.19. Reducing the effect of ongoing assaults: a deductive one and an additive one. Findings are possible to draw. In Table 11.2, S, N, and X represent Stealthy, Non-Stealthy, and Unused respectively.

11.6.2 Performance limits and security evaluation

To demonstrate how the method limits the effect of an ideal persistent attack on a specific AMI network for several possible κ thresholds. Secondly, for an AMI network that manages to evade detection, to investigate the detection limits at the breakdown point for various combinations of $\left(\rho_{\text{mal}}, \delta_{\text{avg}}\right)$. To demonstrate that the enemy's breakeven time, T_{BE}.

Limiting Impact of Persistent Attacks: An attacker is aware of the detection mechanism and threshold; they can decrease the impact of undetected attacks by simply executing an

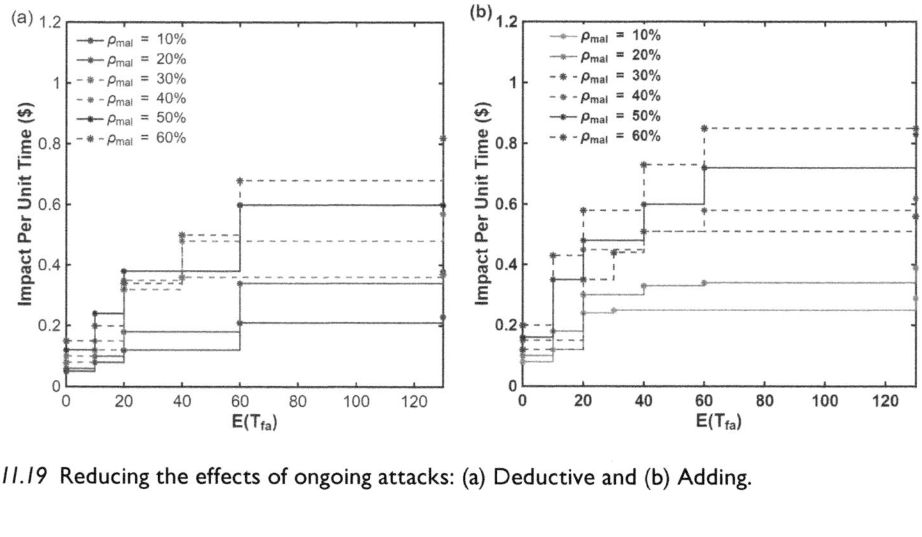

Figure 11.19 Reducing the effects of ongoing attacks: (a) Deductive and (b) Adding.

Table 11.2 Final security state

Ratio	*Conclusion*	*HM,AM*	*Sign*	*Limit*
Up	Additive, S	Up, Up	Positive	Outside
Down	Additive, N	Up, Up	Negative	Outside
Down	Camouflage, X	Down, Same	Negative	Outside
Down	Deductive, X	Down, Down	Negative	Outside
X	No Attack, X	X, X	X	Inside

attack that goes unnoticed (Figure 11.19a and 11.19b). The *Y*-axis represents the anticipated interval between false alarms, whereas the *a*-axis represents the adversary's impact per wit hour (U). The predicted duration between two false alerts reduces as the number of false alarms increases, as the lower κ from this baseline. To demonstrate this, for each potential value of κ in both additive and deductive assaults, obtain a distinct value of $\kappa = 2s_r$ and J by reducing κ with a stepsize of 0.02. Figure 11.19a and 11.19b, which depict additive and deductive attacks, respectively, demonstrate that the effect of an undiscovered attack remains relatively constant with increasing average times between false alarms. The lines in Figure 11.19a and 11.19b that represent $E(T_{fa})$ and I various P_{mal} are also distinct.

Breakdown Points and Breakeven Time: There is a comparable δ_{avg} value for every ρ_{mal} at which our detection approach begins to fail. We refer to this combination as a breakdown point. If an attacker knows the defense mechanism, analyzing the results of our approach can help determine how long it takes for our way to make the opponent pay back its initial investment.

The breakdowns happen at a relatively bigger δ_{avg} for smaller ρ_{mal} from Table 11.3(a), and vice versa. Nevertheless, the impact (in terms of R R per day) is likewise minimal because of modest ρ_{mal}. In order to boost its daily earnings, the assailant can raise the -mal to a level

Table 11.3a Breakdown points

ρ_{mal}	δ_{avg}	***RR***	T_{BE}
10	122	8.9	5.9
20	97	12.9	7
30	82	16.6	7.5
40	67	16.9	9.3
50	62	19.2	9.9
60	72	26.1	8.7
70	72	30.2	8.7

Table 11.3b Breakdown points

ρ_{mal}	δ_{avg}	***RR***	T_{BE}
10	132	9.4	5.6
20	102	13.5	6.7
30	87	16.6	7.5
40	82	20.4	7.9
50	82	25	7.9
60	87	31.3	7.5
70	92	38.2	7.2

of, say, 70%. Nevertheless, our technique captures higher on average, thus it will take 6.89 years to recoup the expenditure of \$500 per meter. It takes the adversary six years to break even when it attacks; therefore a high T_{BE} level discourages it from continuing an undetected attack. For deductive attacks, Table 11.3b gives a full rundown of all the T_{BE} and displays the detection limits for additive attacks. Each of these numbers represents a threshold that caused one false alarm every year. There will be less room for undetectable strategies with a little rise in the acceptable false alert rate. According to the tables, the largest value for ρ_{mal} is 120 W.

For different values of N, the Z-axis shows that the κ threshold corresponding to one false alert per year fluctuates. In the most extreme scenario, where the number of compromised meters is 100 out of 4000 (with a sensitivity level of 3.0% according to the data), the detection sensitivity limit is 150 W. On the other hand, an attack at 50 W when 300 out of 400 meters ($\rho_{mal} = 76\%$) are vulnerable. The current works assume a power of 400 W; however, both 150 W and 50 W are substantially lower. Due to the fact that microgrid sizes often fall between one hundred and two thousand, it provides a solid decentralized option for intrusion detection.

Figure 11.20 displays the Performance in terms of sensitivity and scalability: Sri Lanka dataset.

Talk about a Few Special Cases: For additive attacks, there is a naturally occurring range of v-avg. values where the ratio stops increasing and starts decreasing. A prospective attacker might launch a plan where $\delta_{avg} \sim \kappa_{low}$ in the belief that the ratio will remain unchanged, perhaps targeting this as a viable approach as well. On the other hand, in all likelihood, evading detection is not feasible, and that the only option is to postpone it. The required condition bound was determined $\kappa_{low} = 460W$ by substituting the scenario $\sigma_{mal} = 42\%, N = 195, \sigma_{(1016)} = 415$ in Eqn. (11.14). Figure 11.21a and 11.21b shows a worst-case scenario over all experimental work, which was achieved by attacking with, $\delta_{avg} = 480$ and $\delta_{avg} = 450$ using various randomly selected values of ρ_{mal}. With a mean of 21 days, the conclusions were drawn; because of the extremely non-existent harmonic mean's closed shape, it is feasible to postpone detection of additive attacks.

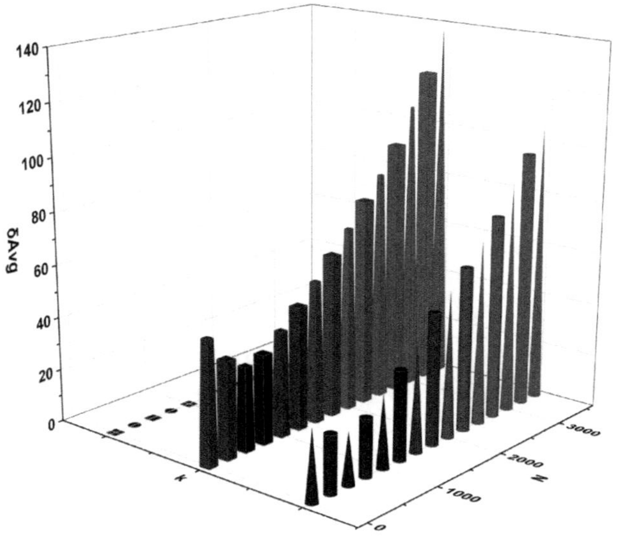

Figure 11.20 Performance in terms of sensitivity and scalability: Sri Lanka dataset.

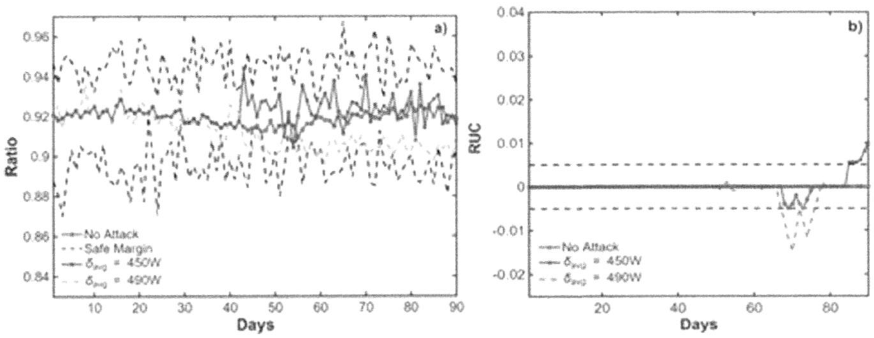

Figure 11.21 Worst case: (a) Ratio and (b) RUC.

11.6.3 Comparing with current methods

In contrast to EWMA, the EMWA is ineffective when dealing with weight selection and variance in safe margin thresholds. It is common practice to use ROC curves to calculate the average performance of an EWMA-based statistic. Using the provided threat model, Figure 11.22a shows the ROC for an EWMA-based strategy. According to the data, the detection rate remains below 52% for the majority of stealthier $(\rho_{mal}, \delta_{avg})$ combinations even when the false alarm rates reach 27–32%. At a threshold that "gives an estimated time between two false alarms of 14 days," EWMA fails to detect an assault $\rho_{mal} = 52\%$ and $\delta_{avg} = 210$. To identify this assault, a threshold with safe margin is provided for a predicted interval of 134 days between two false alarms.

Comparison with CUSLIM: The two CUSUM metrics S_h and S_l track the rising and falling trends of a process variable, respectively. Because of the wider range of possible outcomes, this approach is not applicable to processes such as electrical power consumption when subjected to covert attacks. Because of the huge variation in the CUSUM induced by changes, the safe margin ends up being very wide. Furthermore, these patterns do not repeat themselves from year to year, ruling out any method based on past safety margins. So, even though the false alarm rate is not bad, CUSUM will provide the required variations. The Supplementary Results include more information and evidence. Therefore, CUSUM ROC curves are not included because they do not provide meaningful insight into detection performance.

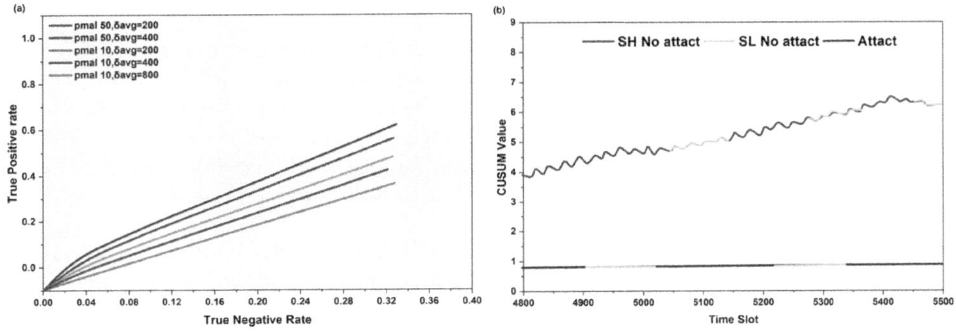

Figure 11.22 Comparison: (a) EWMA and (b) CUSUM.

11.7 CONCLUSION

The effectiveness of the proposed approach against various forms of additive falsification attacks was proved through deductive analysis. Camouflaged attacks—implemented through persistent or organized stealthy tactics with very weak attack strengths—were detected (or their impact mitigated) in real time using a lightweight, non-invasive method with very low false alarm rates. The method forces the attackers to adopt less effective strategies, thereby reducing the attractiveness of such attacks [35, 48–56]. A small adjustment to the tier 2 detection threshold may be required in future research on on-off and data-omission assaults. Based on the information gathered from this research, including the type of attack, the degree of stealth, and the approach used, a framework was proposed to identify the meters that provide misleading data about power usage. The wider significance of the technique and its security properties for data-fabrication attacks were also outlined, as these properties are generic in nature.

REFERENCES

1. P. Gope and B. Sikdar. 2021. A privacy-aware reconfigurable authenticated key exchange scheme for secure communication in smart grids. *IEEE Internet of Things Journal*, 12 (6): 5335–5348.
2. A. Francisco, N. Mohammadi, and J. E. Taylor. 2020. Smart city digital twin-enabled energy management: Toward real-time urban building energy benchmarking. *Sustainable Cities and Society*, 36 (2): 1–11.
3. H. El Makhtoum and Y. Bentaleb. 2022. Secure and lightweight authentication protocol for smart metering system. *IEEE Systems Journal*, 13 (11): 784–791.
4. S. Abedzadeh and S. Bhattacharjee. 2025. Mitigating impact of data poisoning attacks on CPS anomaly detection with provable guarantees. *Information*, 16 (6): 428. https://doi.org/10.3390/info16060428
5. M. H. Raza, Y. M. Rind, I. Javed, M. Zubair, M. Q. Mehmood, and Y. Massoud. 2023. Smart meters for smart energy: A review of business intelligence applications. *IEEE Transactions on Smart Grid*, 11: 120001–120022.
6. K. Nainar *et al.* 2021. Experimental validation and deployment of observability applications for monitoring of low-voltage distribution grids. *IEEE Access*, 21 (17): 1–9.
7. H. İzmitligil and A. Karamancioglu. 2024. An online home energy management system using Q-learning and deep Q-learning. *Energy and Buildings*, 43: 1–11.
8. X.-Y. Zhang, C. Watkins, C. C. Cheong Took, and S. Kuenzel. 2021. Privacy boundary determination of smart meter data using an artificial intelligence adversary. *IEEE Transactions on Smart Grid*, 31 (9): 1.
9. R. Chiosa, M. S. Piscitelli, and A. Capozzoli. 2021. A data analytics-based energy information system (EIS) tool to perform meter-level anomaly detection and diagnosis in buildings. *Energy and Buildings*, 14 (1): 1–9.
10. P. Thilagavathi, S. Hannah, A. Jose Anand, D. Parameswari, R. Geetha, and A. Govindaram. 2025. Machine learning and security fake email detection and intrusion detection. *Proceedings of an International Conference on Intelligent Computing Systems,* Belgaum, India: 1–6.
11. J. S. Prasath, S. J. Parvez, A. Govindaram, T. Thangavelu, A. Jose Anand, and N. Rajkumar. 2024. AI-enhanced anomaly detection in software-defined networks. *Proceedings of an International Conference on Software-Defined Networking and Security,* Gran Canaria, Spain: 1–7.
12. T. S. Arulananth, A. Jose Anand, S. Jayanthi, Petla Manaswini, Gogineni Viswa Sai Teja, G. Redyy Taruni, and Nalla Krishna Prasad. 2024. Automatic certificate generation and security implementation using LSB and hybrid watermarking techniques. *Proceedings of an International Conference on Information Security and Applications,* Jeju Island, Korea: 417–428.

13. H. Byeon, M. I. Khalaf, A. Zaidi, S. B. Ahamed, S. Khan, P. P. Singh, ... R. Gupta. 2024. Post-quantum secure blockchain framework for edge-based mobile task offloading in consumer electronics and IoTs. *IEEE Internet of Things Journal,* 71 (3): 1–7.
14. S. Saif, P. Das, S. Biswas, S. Khan, M. A. Haq, and V. Kovtun. 2024. A secure data transmission framework for IoT-enabled healthcare. *IEEE Access*, 10 (16): 1–7.
15. W. Jian, J. P. Li, M. A. Akbar, A. U. Haq, S. Khan, R. M. Alotaibi, and S. A. Alajlan. 2024. SA-Bi-LSTM: Self-attention with bidirectional LSTM-based intelligent model for accurate fake news detection to ensure information integrity on social media platforms. *IEEE Access*, 12: 48436–48452.
16. S. Khan, T. Siddiqui, A. Mourade, B. I. Alabduallah, S. A. Alajlan, A. Almjally, ... A. Alfaifi. 2024. Manufacturing industry based on dynamic soft sensors integrated with feature representation and classification using fuzzy logic and deep learning architecture. *Journal of Intelligent Manufacturing*, 128 (7–8): 2885–2897.
17. N. M. George, E. Rosero, S. Mayakannan, A. Shameem, S. Divya, and N. Arul. 2025. Enhancing industrial automation flexibility through neural network-empowered machine vision applications. In A. Gupta, M. Hinchey, and Z. Zalevsky (eds.), *Artificial Intelligence and Its Applications. Communications in Computer and Information Science*, 2307. Springer, Cham. https://doi.org/10.1007/978-3-031-84397-6_17
18. Girimurugan, V. Seedha Devi, G. K. Senthil Kumar, M. S. Jacob, S. Jeevitha, A. Jose Anand, and A. Jegatheesan. 2025. Comparative study of traditional and deep learning approaches for human ear-based biometric identification. In *2025 2nd International Conference on Software, Systems and Information Technology (SSITCON)*, Tumkur, India: 1–6.
19. I. H. Abdulqadder, I. T. Aziz, and F. M. F. Flaih. 2024. Robust electricity theft detection in smart grids using machine learning and secure techniques. *IEEE Systems Journal*, 18 (1): 1021–1033.
20. T. Pei, Z. Hou, J. Zhou, C. Xiao, and J. Zou. 2024. Blockchain-based anonymous authentication and data aggregation for advanced metering infrastructure in smart grid. *Applied Energy*, 46: 1–11.
21. S. Kook, K. Kim, J. Ryu, Y. Lee, and D. Won. 2024. Lightweight hash-based authentication protocol for smart grids. *IEEE Transactions on Smart Grid*, 24 (10): 1–9.
22. A. Roshan and G. Ganga. 2024. Intelligent categorization and interactive mechanism for smart demand side management of residential consumers. *Energy and Buildings*, 37: 1–7.
23. R. Geetanjali, T. M. Sreehari, A. Jegatheesan, B. Muthukumar, B. Thyla, and Jose A. Anand. 2025. Predictive model of 6-Month prognosis of stroke patients using machine learning techniques. *2025 2nd International Conference On Multidisciplinary Research and Innovations in Engineering (MRIE)*, Gurugram, India, pp. 439–444.
24. N. Nazeeya Anjum, S. Sumathi, R. Dheena Dhayalan, R. P. Rampavithran, A. J. Jose Anand, and M. Sathiyanarayanan. 2024. Smart sensors for smart city environmental monitoring systems. In T. Anh Nguyen (Ed.), *Digital Twin, Blockchain, and Sensor Networks in the Healthy and Mobile City* (pp. 17–33). Elsevier.
25. M. Gomathy, L. Steffina Morin, Lekshmi S. Raveendran, Jose Anand A, A. Jegatheesan, and B. Muthukumar. 2025. Clustering and predictive modeling of epileptic spikes and seizures using EEG data. *2025 2nd International Conference on Circuits, Power and Intelligent Systems (CCPIS)*, Bhubaneswar, India, pp. 1–6.
26. S. Maheswari, S. J. Parvez, V. S. Devi, T. Anuradha, C. K. Snruthi, and A. Jose Anand. 2025. 5G-Integrated data dissemination and multi interface communication architecture for enhanced VANETs. *2025 IEEE International Conference on Contemporary Computing and Communications (InC4)*, Bangalore, India, pp. 1–6.
27. S. Maheswari, N. P. Swetha Menon, B. Sumathi, M. A. Mukunthan, V. Bhanu Rekha, and A. Jose Anand. 2025. Predicting and improving the mechanical strength of a modified natural fiber/TiO2 polymer nanocomposite using artificial intelligence. *Journal of Environmental Nanotechnology*, 14 (4): 9–26.

28. R. Khan, R. Quazi, A. Jose Anand, M. A. J. Maktoof, and A. Al-Hilali. 2026. Predictive analytics for monkeypox: Utilizing machine learning to forecast outbreaks and resource allocation. In G. N. Nguyen, A. Swaroop, and P. Shukla (Eds.), *Proceedings of Fifth International Conference on Computing and Communication Networks*. ICCCN 2025. Lecture Notes in Networks and Systems, vol 1777. Springer, Cham.
29. H. Baskaran, A. M. Al-Ghaili, Z.-A. Ibrahim, F. A. Abdul Rahim, S. Muthaiyah, and H. Kasim. 2024. Data falsification attacks in advanced metering infrastructure. *International Journal of Electrical Power and Energy Systems*, 10 (1): 412–418.
30. P. Kar, S. Nayak, N. Kumar, A. Jose Anand, A. Mohanty, and H. Mohammed. 2026. Development of adaptive thermal management systems in electric vehicles using renewable energy and eco-friendly materials. In G. N. Nguyen, A. Swaroop, and P. Shukla (Eds.), *Proceedings of Fifth International Conference on Computing and Communication Networks*. ICCCN 2025. Lecture Notes in Networks and Systems, vol 1777. Springer, Cham.
31. M. Farooq, H. Amin, Jose Anand A., and M. Waseem Iqbal. 2025. Cognitive complexity reduction in decentralized applications based on blockchain technology: The psychological aspects of user instruction, understanding and self efficacy. *Lex Localis – Journal of Local Self-Government*, 22 No. S4 (2024): 663–675.
32. R. Kesavan, T. Anuradha, P. Kalaiarasi, M. S. Jacob, A. Jose Anand, and V. S. Devi. 2025. Deep learning-based diagnostic support system for breast tissue classification using mammographic images. *2025 IEEE International Conference on Intelligent Signal Processing and Effective Communication Technologies (INSPECT)*, Gwalior, India, pp. 1–6.
33. S. Jayanthi, P. Vinitha Baby, D. Parameswari, R. Geetha, P. Thilagavathi, and J. A. Anand. 2025. Improved convolutional neural network for garbage separation. *2025 6th International Conference for Emerging Technology (INCET)*, Belgaum, India, pp. 1–6.
34. P. Thilagavathi, S. Hannah, Jose A. Anand, D. Parameswari, R. Geetha, and A. Govindaram. 2025. Machine learning and security fake email detection and intrusion detection. *2025 6th International Conference for Emerging Technology (INCET)*, Belgaum, India, pp. 1–6.
35. B. Muthukumar, P. Nakka, H. V., Jose A. Anand, A. Govindaram, and P. Thilagavathi. 2025. Application of machine learning techniques for the location and early detection of brain tumors. *2025 6th International Conference on Data Intelligence and Cognitive Informatics (ICDICI)*, Tirunelveli, India, pp. 1637–1644.
36. V. V. Vineeth and S. Sophia. 2022. Data falsification detection in AMI: A secure perspective analysis. In A. K. Vyas, S. Balamurugan, K. K. Hiran, and H. S. Dhiman (eds.), *Artificial Intelligence for Renewable Energy Systems*. https://doi.org/10.1002/9781119761686.ch9
37. R. Girimurugan, S. Selvaraju, V. M. Madhavan, and C. Shilaja. 2024. Static structural analysis of roof ventilator turbine blades using ANSYS. *Proceedings of an International Conference on Mechanical and Structural Engineering*, 2587 (1): 140013.
38. J. Lu, Z. Yu, S. Li, W. Guo, H. Tan, and Y. Dai. 2024. Research on power transaction coordination decision-making module of novel digital smart grid dispatching center. *International Journal of Electrical Power and Energy Systems*, 62 (9): 125–133.
39. A. Ponmalar, B. Renukadevi, A. Jose Anand, G. Kamalisri, N. Dharshini, and N. Sobana. 2022. Automatic forensic analysis of criminal navigation system using machine learning. *Proceedings of an International Conference on Computing and Intelligent Systems*, Chennai, India: 568–572.
40. D. A. Chekired, L. Khoukhi, and H. T. Mouftah. 2019. Fog-based distributed intrusion detection system against false metering attacks in smart grid. In *ICC 2019 – 2019 IEEE International Conference on Communications (ICC)*, Shanghai, China: 1–6. https://doi.org/10.1109/ICC.2019.8761752
41. T. Thambiran, M. Batool, Y. Fan, N. Zanib, and F. Nawaz. 2024. Upgradation of metering infrastructure of low voltage distributed network in Nottingham Road, Kwa-Zulu Natal, South Africa. *IEEE Access*, 12: 22687–22706.
42. A. Elías, J. M. Morales, and S. Pineda. 2024. A high-dimensional functional time series approach to evolution outlier detection for grouped smart meters. *Applied Energy*, 35 (3): 371–387.

43. H. Rahman, P. Nanda, M. Mohanty, and N. U. Sheikh. 2023. Anomaly detection in smart grid networks using power consumption data. *Proceedings of an International Conference on Smart Grid Technologies*, Rome, Italy: 830–837.
44. S. Bhattacharjee, V. P. K. Madhavarapu, S. Silvestri, and S. K. Das. 2024. Attack context embedded data-driven trust diagnostics in smart metering infrastructure. *IEEE Transactions on Smart Grid*, 24 (2):1–12.
45. R. Amuthakkannan, S. Neelamegan, A. Tonk, V. Anu, R. Subbulakshmi, R. Giri, and S. Mayakannan. 2024. Evaluation of machine learning models in predicting diesel engine behaviour and emissions with biodiesel blends. *Journal of Mechanical Science and Technology*, 17 (3): 449–455.
46. T. Ahmad, S. Khan, N. Nigar, E. M. Obaid, and S. Naaz. 2025. Quantum reservoir-based intrusion detection for edge-IoT systems. *IEEE Internet of Things Journal*, 30, 1–9.
47. S. Hemalatha, M. Mahalakshmi, V. Vignesh, M. Geethalakshmi, D. Balasubramanian, and A. J. Anand. 2023. Deep learning approaches for intrusion detection with emerging cybersecurity challenges. *Proceedings of an International Conference on Advanced Computing Technologies*, Theni, India: 1522–1529.
48. A. P. Singh, M. Aggarwal, H. Singh, and P. Bhambri. 2021. Sketching of EV network: A complete roadmap. In H. Singh, P. P. Singh Cheema, and P. Garg (Eds.), *Sustainable Development through Engineering Innovations* (pp. 431–442). Springer. https://doi.org/10.1007/978-981-15-9554-7_37
49. P. Bhambri, M. Aggarwal, H. Singh, A. P. Singh, and S. Rani. 2022. Uprising of EVs: Charging the future with demystified analytics and sustainable development. In V. Bali, V. Bhatnagar, J. Lu, and K. Banerjee (Eds.), *Decision Analytics for Sustainable Development in Smart Society 5.0* (pp. 37–54). Springer. https://doi.org/10.1007/978-981-19-1689-2_3
50. G. Singh and P. Bhambri. 2023. Simulation analysis of AODV and DSDV routing protocols for secure and reliable service in mobile adhoc networks (MANETs). In P. Bhambri, S. Rani, V. E. Balas, and A. A. Elngar (Eds.), *Integration of AI-based Manufacturing and Industrial Engineering Systems with the Internet of Things* (1st ed., pp. 205–216). CRC Press. https://doi.org/10.1201/9781003383505
51. R. Rana and P. Bhambri. 2024. Generative AI-driven security frameworks for web engineering: Innovations and challenges. In I. A. Shah and N. Z. Jhanjhi (Eds.), *Generative AI for Web Engineering Models* (pp. 285–296). IGI Global. https://doi.org/10.4018/979-8-3693-3703-5.ch014
52. P. Bhambri, S. Rani, and A. Khang. 2024. AI-driven digital twin and resource optimization in Industry 4.0 ecosystem. In N. Singh, S. Birla, M. D. Ansari, and N. K. Shukla (Eds.), *AI-driven Digital Twin and Industry 4.0: A Conceptual Framework with Applications* (pp. 182–201). CRC Press/Taylor & Francis Group. https://doi.org/10.1002/9781394227990.ch3
53. R. Rana and P. Bhambri. 2024. Digital twin for sustainable industrial development. In S. Rani, P. Bhambri, S. Kumar, P. K. Pareek, and A. A. Elngar (Eds.), *AI-driven Digital Twin and Industry 4.0: A Conceptual Framework with Applications* (pp. 241–253). CRC Press. https://doi.org/10.1201/9781003395416-15
54. G. C. N. Babu, S. Gupta, P. Bhambri, L. M. Leo, B. H. Rao, and S. Kumar. 2021. A semantic health observation system development based on the IoT sensors. *Turkish Journal of Physiotherapy and Rehabilitation*, 32 (3): 1721–1729.
55. P. Bhambri. 2024. Artificial intelligence enabled Internet of Medical Things for enhanced healthcare systems. In P. Bhambri, R. Soni, and T. A. Tran (Eds.), *Smart Healthcare Systems: AI and IoT Perspectives* (pp. 1–17). CRC Press. https://doi.org/10.1201/9781032698519-1
56. P. Bhambri and S. Rani. 2024. Bioengineering and healthcare data analysis: Introduction, advances, and challenges. In P. Bhambri, S. Rani, and M. Fahim (Eds.), *Computational Intelligence and Blockchain in Biomedical and Health Informatics* (1st ed., pp. 1–25). CRC Press. https://doi.org/10.1201/9781003459347

Chapter 12

An explanatory view of antisquat

An AI-powered phishing domain finder

Sangeetha G., Madhumala R. B., Victor Hugo C. de Albuquerque, Pavan Gowda T. S., Dhanush Reddy C. S. and Akshay S.

12.1 INTRODUCTION

Phishing charges have turned out to be one of the major widespread cybersecurity threats today. Malicious attacks utilize human susceptibilities by misguiding individuals into revealing sensitive information such as login credentials and financial or personal details. Data deception generally occurs via fraudulent emails or websites that resemble legitimate mail, taking advantage of minor variations in domain names and content to misguide victims. Conventional phishing identification approaches are dependent on heuristic or password-based mechanisms, which have difficulty keeping up with the increasingly intricate approaches deployed by attackers. In order to address the imperfections of traditional methods, Artificial Intelligence (AI) is a paradigm shifter participating in phishing detection. AI strategies comprising Machine Learning (ML) and Language Processing are employed for tracking phishing threats more accurately and proficiently. The AI-driven systems can inspect large datasets and locate refined patterns and exceptions symptomatic of fraudulent attempts that may otherwise go ignored by conventional systems. By continuously learning from recent data, AI systems can adapt to evolving phishing tactics, enabling innovative and robust defense mechanisms.

Machine learning is a fragment of AI consisting of training algorithms to spot patterns within data, enabling systems to foresee phishing attacks based on previous examples. This potentiality to transform and absorb from immense amounts of data makes ML highly beneficial for recognizing phishing ventures in real time. Researchers have exemplified the application by varying ML paradigms such as decision trees, random forests, and support vector machines to classify domains and emails as legitimate or malicious content depending on historical data. Natural Language Processing, another subset of AI, is highly useful in examining and assessing the literal content of emails or websites. NLP methodologies allow the system to detect the language prone to phishing messages, discover suspicious wording or phrases, and contrast them against familiar patterns of phishing attempts. Studies have shown that NLP can notably improve the observation of spoofing emails by examining the structure, pitch, and semantics of the content. In the context of phishing domain recognition, AntiSquat initiates an AI-powered solution designed to identify suspicious domains in real time. Using advanced ML and NLP approaches, AntiSquat determines domain registration metadata, DNS behavior, lexical patterns, and webpage composition to flag domains that closely resemble legitimate websites. This helps to inspect phishing domains that may otherwise elude traditional rule-based filters. The AntiSquat framework employs supervised learning classifiers and deep learning models that progressively improve by learning from new phishing inclinations. The ability to adapt to emerging threats ensures that AntiSquat

DOI: 10.1201/9781003656487-12

stays relevant in detecting the latest phishing tactics, such as homograph attacks or domain squatting (typo squatting), where attackers register domain names that are visually similar to well-known brands or websites. Moreover, AntiSquat integrates threat intelligence feeds and uses anomaly detection algorithms to recognize unusual behavior in domain activities. By combining these various AI techniques, AntiSquat offers a scalable and proactive defense against phishing domains, making it an essential tool in modern cybersecurity strategies.

The fusion of machine learning and language processing in AntiSquat significantly enhances its ability to locate phishing domains early, before they can cause damage. By providing real-time alerts, AntiSquat helps security teams and users prevent data breaches, financial losses, and identity theft. As email phishing strategies continue to evolve, the AI operation in phishing detection will be crucial in providing continuous protection for humans and corporations.

12.2 RELATED WORKS

Cyber deception has long been acknowledged as one of the most successful hacking techniques, taking advantage of human weaknesses by using dishonest tactics to acquire confidential data. More sophisticated identification and prevention systems have to be developed as a result of the rising difficulty of phishing techniques and the quick expansion in digital communication channels. Conventional solutions, such as signature-based detection and inference engines, have proven deficient against the emerging nature of phishing security breaches, which often leverage innovative social engineering tactics, malicious URLs, and email spoofing [1].

Conventional Phishing Detection Approaches: Primitive phishing detection methods draw extensively on heuristic-reliant and rule-based methods manually structured to detect specific cybercrime patterns. These systems aimed at identifying skeptical URLs, erroneous domain names, or deceptive email keywords [2]. Effective in spotting known phishing pitfalls, these methods struggled to cope with zero-day attacks or knowledgeable phishing campaigns designed to evade predefined rules.

Signature-based approaches globally used in anti-malware software design were another standard method of phishing recognition. This approach verified incoming emails and websites against a database of common phishing signs. Signature-based perception, on the other hand, is inherently limited in observing new or modified phishing ventures because it is dependent on prior information about the threat vector. The restrictions of these early systems emphasized the need for more resilient solutions that can detect phishing attempts in real-time without counting on manual updates or prior defined signatures. Figure 12.1 shows the URL representation.

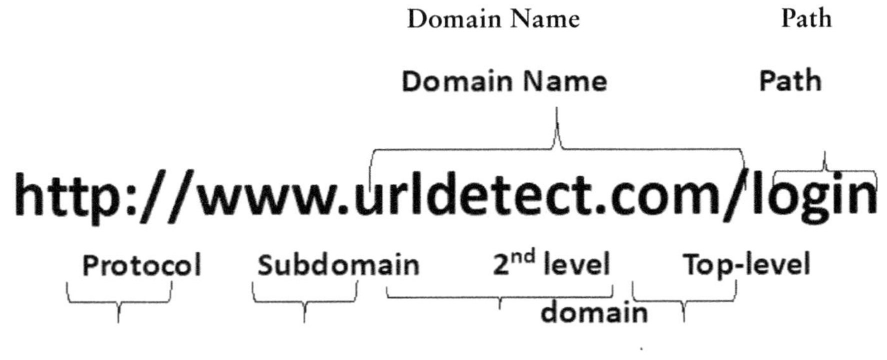

Figure 12.1 URL detection.

The utilization of ML in phishing identification has grown in popularity in the last few years due to its capacity to learn from data and automatically adapt to new trends [2, 3]. ML models, primarily supervised learning procedures, are trained on massive datasets comprising both scamming and permissible examples. By studying the differentiating traits of deceptive emails, websites, or other textual sources, these algorithms may estimate the plausibility of a spoofing attempt based on previously unseen details [4]. Decision trees, support vector networks, k-nearest neighbors, and ensembles of random forests are among the most commonly utilized phishing detection techniques. These algorithms use variables including URL composition, email metainformation, and linguistic patterns to determine attempts [5]. Machine learning models can identify phishing attacks that stray from established patterns, including zero-day risks. However, ML methods in spoofing face drawbacks. One significant concern is the asymmetry of phishing datasets, which have more legitimate trials

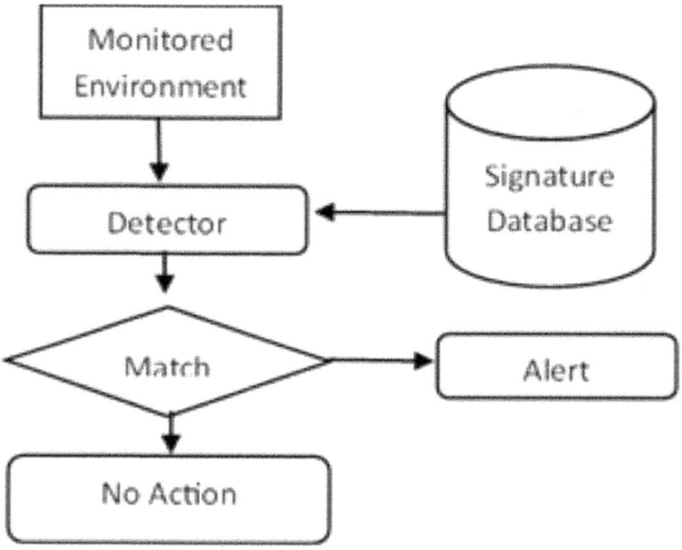

Figure 12.2 Signature-based approaches.

than phishing samples. This disproportion might result in models that are biased towards non-phishing detection, limiting effectiveness. The datasets are balanced using techniques involving oversampling, undersampling, and synthetic data synthesis (e.g., SMOTE) [6]. Furthermore, feature selection is crucial to increasing the outcome of machine learning models for phishing detection. Various feature engineering strategies have been investigated to determine the most relevant characteristics, including URL dimension, field age, WHOIS information, and data-centric features [7]. Figure 12.2 shows the flowchart for the signature based approach.

12.3 DEEP LEARNING IN PHISHING DETECTION

Deep learning (DL), a type of ML technique, has been proven to be an effective tool for detecting phishing, outperforming typical ML mechanisms in terms of correctness and adaptability. Despite ML models that are essential for feature extraction by hand, deep learning models can discover and draw out attributes from primary data automatically, making them ideal for detecting complicated and sophisticated scamming attempts. Recurrent neural networks (RNNs) and Convolutional Neural Networks (CNNs) are both effectively utilized in phishing detection tasks. For example, CNNs have been used to analyze the **visible appearance** of phishing websites, detecting tiny distinctions linking real and counterfeit webpages based on pixel patterns and design structures [8]. Comparably, RNNs have been used to **disclose** malicious messages by examining the sequential structure of email bodies such as text circulation and metadata [9].

Deep learning frameworks featuring Long Short-Term Memory (LSTM) networks and autoencoders can inspect phishing assaults in real time. LSTM networks are especially good at interpreting sequential data, enabling them to be excellent for assessing email content, URL sequence monitoring, and other time-sensitive aspects [10]. In contrast, autoencoders have been used to detect anomalies, such as phishing attempts, by analyzing departures from regular communication patterns [11]. While deep learning algorithms have revealed cutting-edge results in identifying phishing attacks, they are not without substantial obstacles. One of the key constraints is that they rely on expansive amounts of high-quality labeled data to build models efficiently. Acquiring this sort of dataset can be laborious and time-consuming, especially in the cybersecurity arena, where phishing strategies vary quickly, and up-to-date labeled samples are frequently scarce. Deep learning models are susceptible to being biased or overfitted in the absence of sufficient data variety, decreasing their generalizability to real-world, undetected phishing efforts.

12.4 USING NLP FOR PHISHING DETECTION

NLP approaches have improved phishing observation, specifically in spotting phishing online emails and texts that employ social engineering tactics. NLP approaches examine the idea of messaging, emails, and webpages to detect potentially suspect language styles, moods, and tones. Spoofing emails frequently utilize urgent or worrisome vocabulary to lure grantees into adopting swift action, and NLP-dependent prototypes can recognize these linguistic intimations to identify probable phishing efforts [12]. Pretrained language models that include BERT (Bidirectional Encoder Representations from Transformers) have manifested great promise in the field of phishing by effectively analyzing the associated semantics of terms and clauses in a variety of text-based content, including emails, messages, and websites. Unlike conventional natural language processing (NLP) techniques, which frequently rely on inadequate text representations or manually crafted features, BERT employs a deep bidirectional architecture that allows it to understand the full context of a word based on its preceding and succeeding words [13–18].

When identifying phishing attempts that employ subtle linguistic indicators, including subtly modified phrase structures, obscured keywords, or misleadingly innocent phrasing meant to deceive users, this context-aware depiction is especially helpful. Because of its ability to discern subtle linguistic patterns, BERT can spot even the most advanced phishing techniques that imitate authentic communication methods or take advantage of domain-specific jargon to win over users. Phishing emails, for example, frequently mimic the format and tone of official communication from government agencies, banks, or social media sites [19–26]. Because of its profound linguistic knowledge, BERT can identify contradictions, odd wording, or terminology that aren't fit for the context, which may not be apparent from cursory inspection. Additionally, BERT's performance is greatly improved by fine-tuning it on phishing-specific datasets, which enables the model to adjust to the particular linguistic characteristics of phishing content. Compared with creating a model from scratch, this transfer ability to learn not only increases the precision of detection but also lessens the requirement for large amounts of labeled data. All things considered, the incorporation of BERT into phishing detection technology is a state-of-the-art development, providing a strong and flexible solution that can control the extending complexity of phishing attacks [27].

Sentiment analysis, a popular NLP technique, helps to detect phishing by determining the psychological state of messages, such as panic, urgency, or enthusiasm, which is frequently used in phishing attacks. Phishing emails sometimes employ emotionally driven language to trick consumers into behaving impulsively, such as terms like "urgent action needed" or "your account will be held." Sentiment analysis detects aberrant emotional intensity in situations where neutral speech is anticipated, which helps flag dubious content. When used in conjunction with other NLP techniques, including keyword analysis or context-dependent models such as BERT, sentiment analysis improves the model's capacity to inspect schemes for social engineering and enhances the overall precision of hoax detection mechanisms [28].

12.5 HYBRID APPROACHES AND ENSEMBLE MODELS

Integrated approaches that blend different methods from deep learning and machine learning aim to boost phishing recognition performance even more. Hybrid models combine many algorithms to identify phishing with greater accuracy and robustness. For example, merging knowledge-based systems and ML prototypes can improve perception reliability by incorporating human insight into machine-driven decision framing procedures [29]. Researchers have investigated group learning practices that involve bagging and boosting for enhanced phishing identification. Ensemble frameworks integrate the forecasts of numerous classifiers to improve accuracy and lower false positive rates. Random forests, gradient boosting machines, and AdaBoost are among the popular ensemble algorithms that have shown effectiveness in phishing detection [29]. One persistent difficulty is the adaptive nature of phishing, in which hackers constantly change their strategies to avoid detection. Adversarial machine learning, in which hackers try to manipulate the AI models by providing false inputs, substantially undermines the resilience of phishing detection systems [30].

To solve this, academics are investigating strategies involving adversarial training, which involves training models with hostile instances to improve their susceptibility to such attacks. Furthermore, instantaneous phishing recognition systems need to be systematic and scalable in order to hold up massive amounts of data collected by email systems and websites, hence increasing their resilience to such attacks. An important domain of study involves the inclusion of AI-driven phishing observation into larger cybersecurity frameworks, which entails creating multiple defensive mechanisms that integrate AI-driven identification with human supervision, user orientation, and established guidelines [31]. As an AI-powered cybersecurity solutions become more extensively deployed, the ethical implications, such as privacy concerns and possible discrepancies in detection algorithms, require careful exploration. AI-enabled phishing detection and mitigation platforms have exhibited great promise in overcoming the limits of conventional cybersecurity solutions. These structures provide more precise and adaptable defenses against phishing attempts by merging machine learning, natural language processing and deep learning. However, difficulties like as adversarial threats, dataset inequalities, and the requirement for significant computational resources continue to be important study fields. Moving forward, hybrid techniques and the combination of AI-supported solutions into holistic cybersecurity plans prove vital for improving phishing identification and mitigation effectiveness.

12.6 AI TECHNIQUES FOR PHISHING IDENTIFICATION

Phishing detection has acquired a lot of attention in the field of cybersecurity, with AI approaches helping to identify and mitigate phishing assaults. The below section focuses on major AI approaches, citing findings from several journals.

12.6.1 Machine learning techniques

Machine learning is one of the foremost AI methods utilized for spotting phishing attacks. This entails computational algorithms on massive datasets to figure out if an online email, web address, or URL is fraudulent or real. Decision trees, random forests, support vector machines, along with logistic regression, are among the most popular ML algorithms for revealing phishing. The authors [32] examined multiple ML classifiers, including decision trees and random decision forests, on substantial fraud and legal URL datasets. The research found that when ML models were trained with relevant parameters like URL length, distinctive characters, and domain reputation, they could detect phishing with high accuracy. Machine learning approaches were used to identify phishing webpages by examining URL attributes, zone data, and webpage content. They used classifiers such as SVM, random forest, as well as k-nearest neighbors and discovered that random forest executed the best, with a prediction accuracy of more than 95%.

12.6.2 Deep learning techniques

Deep Learning is an instance of machine learning that has been extensively researched for scam identification due to its potential to separately retrieve attributes derived from data and infer multifaceted relationships. DL models, particularly CNNs and RNNs, have shown enormous potential in recognizing fraudulent emails, internet pages, and web addresses. For instance, a CNN-dependent approach was developed to distinguish between phishing websites by analyzing visual representations of webpages. Their program outperformed traditional machine learning approaches by detecting subtle visual benchmarks that differentiate phishing websites from legitimate ones. LSTM (a form of RNN) was employed to recognize phishing emails by analyzing the order of terms and sentences. The LSTM prototype reliably collects context-relevant data inside the email body. Moreover, an integrated deep learning approach is presented that utilizes CNNs, including RNNs [33], to detect scam attempts on social media. The composite model used CNNs for acquiring features and RNNs for consecutive analysis of data, resulting in outstanding detection performance.

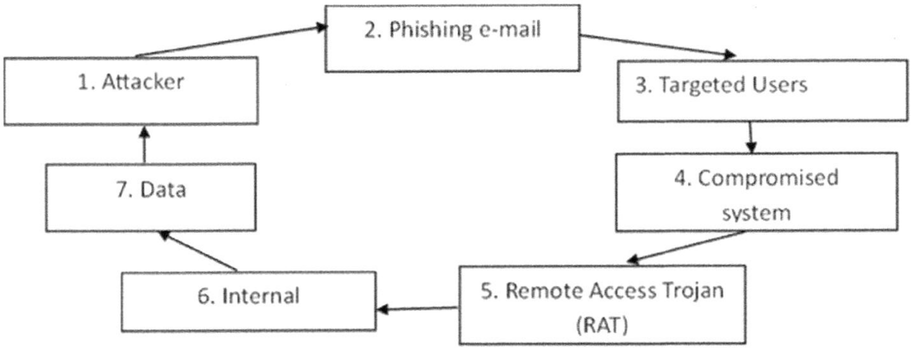

Figure 12.3 Anatomy of spear phishing.

12.6.3 NLP techniques

Natural Language Processing is used in fraud mitigation for assessing the written email information and communications. Phishing online correspondence frequently uses misleading language along with NLP frameworks to identify these linguistic patterns by analyzing word usage, mood, and context. NLP addresses [34] were used to identify scam emails by examining the layout and contents of the email body. To detect phishing patterns, their model applied term frequency-inverse document frequency (TF-IDF) along with n-gram analysis. The study found that NLP approaches might successfully recognize emails containing questionable content. Phishing detection has also made use of previously trained language representations that include BERT (Bidirectional Encoder Representations from Transformers). Research deploying BERT to identify spoofing schemes in emails by examining the context of the email body's language. By comprehending the subtleties of language and spotting phishing indications in the text, the model showed exceptional success in phishing detection. Figure 12.3 shows the anatomy of spear phishing techniques.

12.6.4 Hybrid methodologies

To boost the accuracy of phishing detection, the utilization of a hybrid arrangement is done that includes many artificial intelligence algorithms that have been developed. These techniques combine the advantages of multiple algorithms such as machine learning and rule-based systems or natural language processing with deep learning. To detect phishing URLs, a hybrid model is suggested which integrates a deep learning framework, SVM, and decision trees. Their strategy combined content-based characteristics with URL analysis, which enabled the framework to identify both common spam attacks and increasingly intricate delusive tactics. Nevertheless, the mixture of techniques exceeded a single AI methodology by itself. Similarly, an integrated phishing detection system that used machine learning and detection of anomalies to identify phishing attempts [35]. To detect both known and unexpected phishing patterns, the prototype used supervised learning and an autoencoder-dependent abnormality recognition technique. Their algorithm outperformed existing methods, particularly for encountering zero-day phishing attacks.

12.6.5 Ensemble learning procedures

Boosting approaches have also been employed in the detection of phishing to boost model accuracy while reducing false positives. Ensemble methods fuse predictions from collaborative classifiers to provide simpler and more dependable spam identification practices. An ensemble phishing observed approach employed a variety of classifiers inclusive of decision trees, random forests, and AdaBoost. Their findings revealed that the usable ensemble approach exceeded discrete classifiers, with greater precision and lower false positive rates.

12.6.6 Adversarial machine learning

As phishing detection methods progress, attackers have developed tactics to circumvent detection [36]. Adversarial machine learning surfaced as a method for improving the resistance of fraudulent detection approaches to adversarial attacks. Adversarial learning tactics in the perception of phishing demonstrate how attackers might change properties to mislead ML models. To prevent such attacks, an adversarial training method that simulates instructing with contrary settings has been devised as a way to improve phishing detection. This method teaches models to identify fraudulent attempts that utilize minor differences to avoid

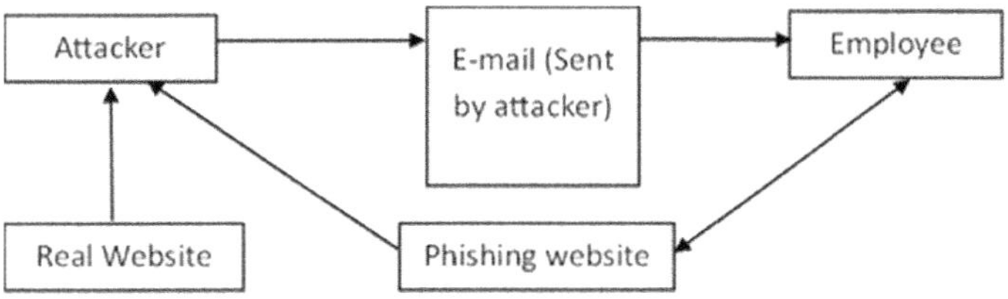

Figure 12.4 Phishing attack diagram.

recognition [37]. Another notable field of exploration is the incorporation of AI-dependent spam recognition into larger cybersecurity frameworks, which entails creating multidimensional defensive techniques that blend AI-driven analysis with individual supervision, consumer training, and enforced policies. As AI-powered cybersecurity solutions become more extensively deployed, the ethical implications, such as privacy concerns and possible biases in identification algorithms [38], must be closely explored. AI-oriented spam detection and mitigation systems have shown great promise in overcoming limits in conventional cybersecurity solutions. These structures provide more precise and adaptable security in opposition to phishing assaults by merging machine learning, natural language processing, and deep learning. However, difficulties like as adversarial hazards, dataset inconsistencies, and the requirement for substantial computational resources continue to be important study fields [39]. Moving forward, hybrid techniques and the fusion of AI-driven solutions into holistic cybersecurity plans tend to be important for improving malicious protection and avoidance effectiveness. Phishing identification [40] has received a lot of focus in the field of cybersecurity, with AI approaches helping detect and reduce phishing assaults. To trace and avoid phishing attempts, researchers investigated a variety of AI technologies, including machine learning, natural language processing, and deep learning. This section focuses on prime AI approaches, quoting findings from several journals. Figure 12.4 shows the phishing attach diagram.

12.7 FRAMEWORK OVERVIEW OF AI-POWERED PHISHING DETECTION AND PREVENTION

AI-powered phishing spotting and prevention mode is outlined to identify, block, and mitigate scam threats in real-time across different communication channels such as emails, websites, and instant messaging platforms. By leveraging improved AI techniques, developers have initiated a methodology that can notice phishing attempts in relation to high accuracy and speed, supporting organizations with a robust defense mechanism against intrusions [41, 42].

12.7.1 System architecture

The framework of the phishing mechanism includes the following main modules:

a) *Data Collection*: This part collects data from different sources, including emails, URLs, websites, and activity records of the network. The part captures critical metainformation such as the sender's identity, the text of emails, URLs viewed by users, and other indicators that may mark fraudulent behavior [43].

b) *Feature Extraction*: After gathering the data, the module collects the relevant features needed to detect phishing. These elements include URL attributes (dimension, special symbols, domain, age), data-driven attributes (mail topic, body, attachment information), and network-associated attributes (logical address, SSL certificate duration).
c) *AI-run Detection Engine*: The phase's basic component makes use of several AI approaches that constitute deep learning, machine learning, and natural language processing. Models with prior training are used to evaluate the data's retrieved features [44]. The engine may employ multiple models run simultaneously (ensemble learning) to enhance detection accuracy. Based on the study, the engine classifies involved data as phishing or legitimate.
d) *Real-Time Monitoring and Alerting*: The module continuously scans email traffic, website browsing, and parallel online activities. In reality, this part flags suspicious activities or messages as potential phishing attempts. If a phishing effort is detected, this phase can trigger alerts for system administrators or end users.
e) *Response and Prevention*: When a malicious threat is detected [45, 46], the module can either automatically block the phishing website, quarantine the suspicious message, or warn the user. This part can also trigger additional verification steps (such as CAPTCHA or multifactor authentication) for sensitive transactions, providing another layer of protection.
f) *Logging and Reporting*: This phase maintains a complete log of all phishing detection events, including timestamps, sources of phishing attempts, types of phishing attacks, and responses [47] taken by the system. This creates periodic reports that provide administrators with actionable insights into phishing threats encountered and the structure's effectiveness.

12.8 APPLICATIONS OF AI-POWERED PHISHING DETECTION

AI-run phishing detection system is highly versatile and can be applied across domains to protect organizations and individuals from phishing threats. A few of the major applications are listed below.

12.8.1 Email phishing detection

One of the major phishing attack vectors is online communication. This detection can automatically integrate into enterprise email servers to scan incoming emails for signs of phishing strikes. The AI model can discriminate between trustworthy messages and phishing efforts by examining email headers, subject matter, and content. This is especially valuable in corporate situations where spear-phishing assaults target executives with personalized harmful emails [48].

12.8.2 Website and URL phishing detection

Phishing websites attract users into submitting sensitive personal information. The module can be deployed as part of a browser extension or integrated into web security software to scan URLs in real-time. This procedure can detect malicious websites and block access by assessing the URL structure, SSL certificates, and page content before the user becomes a victim.

12.8.3 Social media phishing detection

Deception attacks on social media platforms have become prevalent, with attackers using uninterrupted messages or posts to share malicious links. AI-activated modules can look up social media platforms, detect suspicious links, and protect users from clicking on harmful URLs. This is particularly important for influencers or businesses that use social media as a marketing tool, where cyberattacks can disrupt personal reputation and brand depiction.

12.8.4 Financial services and e-commerce protection

Spoofing attacks often target users of financial institutions or e-commerce websites. AI phishing identification systems integrate into online banking and e-commerce platforms to trace phishing attempts involving fake websites, fraudulent payment requests, or bogus customer service messages. It can also provide real-time fraud prevention by flagging suspicious transactions or unauthorized access attempts.

12.8.5 Mobile phishing detection

With the rise of mobile devices, phishing attacks via SMS (smishing) and mobile apps have become more common. The AI-powered system can embed into mobile operating systems or apps to detect and prevent phishing attempts through fraudulent SMS, mobile ads, and fake apps.

12.8.6 Enterprise-level threat management

Cybercriminals often prey on large organizations counting hundreds or thousands of employees, including phishing campaigns. An AI-dependent phishing tracing system can be deployed as part of a comprehensive enterprise security suite, scanning all internal communications, email traffic, and internet activities. The management system enables the protection of sensitive corporate data and assures compliance with cybersecurity regulations. As the scalability of Internet of Things (IoT) devices increases, so does the risk of phishing attacks targeting connected devices. AI-powered phishing detection systems adapt to IoT environments to inspect incoming traffic, detect unauthorized access attempts, and ensure secure communication between devices [49, 50].

12.8.7 Government and public sector applications

Government organizations are frequently chosen by advanced persistent threat (APT) actors using phishing as an initial attack vector. AI-reliant phishing detection systems collaborate with government networks to prevent data breaches, ransomware, and espionage attempts. The framework provides an additional layer of defense, complementing other national cybersecurity estimates.

12.9 LIMITATIONS AND CHALLENGES IN AI-BASED DETECTION

Despite their advantages, AI-based phishing detection systems face challenges such as adversarial attacks, data scarcity for training, evolving phishing tactics, and computational costs. Attackers may use obfuscation techniques or manipulate input data to evade detection.

Addressing these issues requires robust model tuning, adversarial training, and continuous updates.

12.9.1 *Data collection and preprocessing*

The dataset used includes legitimate and phishing URLs, emails, and website content collected from trusted sources such as PhishTank, OpenPhish, and academic datasets. Preprocessing involves cleaning, normalization, tokenization (for textual data) and feature engineering to extract attributes including URL length, domain age, and presence of suspicious keywords. These features serve as inputs for training the models [51, 52]. The proposed methodology can be adopted for building an effective phishing detection model using AI techniques. The approach involves data collection, preprocessing, feature extraction, model selection, and evaluation. A blend of traditional machine learning and deep learning techniques is considered to improve accuracy and robustness. The dataset used includes legitimate and phishing URLs, emails, and website content collected from trusted sources. Preprocessing involves cleaning, normalization, tokenization (for textual data), and feature engineering to extract attributes inclusive of URL length, domain age, and presence of suspicious keywords. These attributes serve as inputs for training the models.

12.10 EXISTING MODELS

Tables 12.1 and 12.2 represent the works done in deep learning, natural language processing, machine learning, and statistical modeling techniques proposed in recent years.

12.11 CONCLUSION

Phishing attacks remain one of the major pitfalls to cybersecurity today, with attackers consistently expanding their tactics to exploit vulnerabilities. Various techniques for detecting phishing have emerged over time, with ML, DL, NLP, and hybrid methods becoming particularly prominent. These tactics not only aid in the detection of fake websites, emails, and URLs but also seek to minimize associated risks [53–57]. The studies summarized here reflect the merits and demerits of these approaches, providing insights into the challenges and advancements in phishing detection. Machine learning-based techniques, particularly those focusing on URL and feature detection, show promising outcomes. For example, models based on classic ML techniques, which include random forests and decision trees, have shown acceptable performance in detecting phishing sites using structured variables like domains, URL length, and other textual features. However, these systems frequently necessitate extensive feature design and struggle with developing techniques such as masked URLs. While hybrid ML models, such as those that combine URL characteristics with hybrid approaches, produce more precise outcomes, their scalability and processing requirements remain a challenge.

The processing of natural language has shown considerable potential in phishing detection, especially when used with email or web content. BERT-based approaches, for example, can detect subtle linguistic indicators as well as domain-specific language modifications that attackers routinely utilize [58–62]. However, the problem here is the computing intensity and large-scale data sets with labels needed for such models to operate optimally. Despite these limitations, NLP approaches such as semantic evaluation and contextual embedding have proven crucial in constructing models that grasp the context of phishing communications,

Table 12.1 Deep learning/neural networks

Author and year	*Parameters used*	*Limitations*	*Advantages*	*Conclusion*
Alsariera, 2020 [34]	Hybrid deep learning with modified BAT algorithm	Comparison of ensemble methods	Strong performance across metrics	Provides robust phishing detection system
Dhanalakshmi, R 2024 [41]	Hybrid DL with BAT algorithm	Survey and analysis limitations	Applies multiple DL metrics and technologies	Efficient in real-world and cyber phishing attacks
Zieni, R 2023 [40]	Training data volume, DL model accuracy	Data or resource dependency	High accuracy, low false positives	Identifies phishing victims and domains
Khan, H. U 2023 [38]	Data quantity, DL training impact	Language specificity, training data dependency	Use of security indicators (HTTPS, green lock)	Phishing websites are growing and evolving
Reddy P S 2024 [37]	ML and NLP, CNNs, RNNs	Future development areas	Leveraging NLP for text-based detection	Advanced ML/NLP integration for phishing defense
Arun A 2024 [36]	Accuracy, precision, recall, F1 score	Data methodology or resource dependency	Developed browser extension using machine learning	Practical implementation of phishing detection
Almujahid NF 2024 [35]	Accuracy, precision	Lacks contextual phishing handling	Integration with browser extension	ML-based detection with real-time application
S. Sallouma 2021 [43]	Traditional machine learning techniques	Data dependency, resource usage	Improved contextual/user awareness	Traditional models still useful with enhancements
A. Karim 2023 [39]	URL string with optional parameters	Compared with other methods	Strategy-rich URL analysis	Balanced approach, reduced false positives

Table 12.2 Natural Language Processing (NLP) and text analysis

Author and year	*Parameters used*	*Limitations*	*Advantages*	*Conclusion*
Alsubaei, 2024 [43]	NLP and sparse matrix	Data/resource dependency	Effective real-world strategies	NLP can expose malicious content patterns
Gupta, S. D 2022 [33]	NLP with CNNs/ RNNs	Data/resource dependency	Deep contextual understanding	Enhances phishing detection using text semantics
Sakhare 2023 [48]	Analytical models with NLP	Language specifications	Email-based phishing detection	Content analysis supports ML-based defense

resulting in higher detection accuracy. Deep learning approaches based on neural networks in addition to deep learning frameworks have substantially enhanced the field of identifying phishing attacks. These approaches may learn through raw data enabling them to be useful in spotting trends in intricate phishing schemes that standard methods may miss. However, the drawbacks of DL models require the need for vast amounts of labeled data, substantial computational resources, and the possibility of overfitting to particular types of phishing attempts. Despite these obstacles, deep learning algorithms continue to push the frontiers of phishing detection and are widely regarded as cutting-edge due to their capacity to handle massive volumes of data and detect even the most minor phishing attempts.

Adversarial training focuses on building models resistant to attacks that try to trick detection systems, which is a growing field that can improve phishing detection. As fraudsters employ AI to design more sophisticated phishing efforts, it is crucial to establish systems that can foresee and mitigate against these advanced threats. Furthermore, behavioral analysis, which incorporates human variables such as user engagement using phishing emails or websites, provides an additional layer of defense by analyzing patterns in how users interact with suspicious content. Diverse ML, DL, and NLP-based methodologies have helped to advance phishing detection systems; improvements in terms of scalability, real-time performance, and threat resistance have to be configured. As phishing attempts become more sophisticated, a multi-layered approach combining various strategies, as well as ongoing adaptability to emerging threats, will be vital for staying ahead of the cybercriminals.

REFERENCES

1. Bitaab, M., Cho, H., Oest, A., Zhang, P., Sun, Z., Pourmohamad, R., Kim, D., Bao, T., Wang, R., Shoshitaishvili, Y., Doupe, A., and Ahn, G. 2020. Scam pandemic: How attackers exploit public fear through phishing. APWG Symposium on Electronic Crime Research (eCrime), 1–10.
2. Tsai, J. Y., Egelman, S., Cranor, L., and Acquisti, A. 2010. The effect of online privacy information on purchasing behaviour: An experimental study. *Information Systems Research*, 22(2), 254–268.
3. Rao, R. S., and Pais, A. R. 2018. Detection of phishing websites using an efficient feature-based machine learning framework. *Neural Computing and Applications*, 31(8), 3851–3873.
4. Verma, R., and Hossain, N. 2014. Semantic feature selection for text with application to phishing email detection. In H. S. Lee and D. G. Han (Eds.), *Information Security and Cryptology – ICISC 2013*. ICISC 2013. Lecture Notes in Computer Science, vol 8565, 455–468.
5. Bergholz, A., De Beer, J., Glahn, S., Moens, M., Paab, G., and Strobel, S. 2010. New filtering approaches for phishing email. *Journal of Computer Security*, 18(1), 7–35.
6. Abdelhamid, N., Ayesh, A., and Thabtah, F. 2014. Phishing detection-based associative classification data mining. *Expert Systems with Applications*, 41(13), 5948–5959.
7. Moubayed, A., Injadat, M., Nassif, A. B., Lutfiyya, H., and Shami, A. 2018. E-Learning: Challenges and research opportunities using machine learning & data analytics. *IEEE Access*, 6, 39117–39138.
8. Sameen, M., Han, K., and Hwang, S. O. 2020. PhishHaven – An efficient real-time AI phishing URLs detection system. *IEEE Access*, 8, 83425–83443.
9. Borate, N. M. V., Adsul, N. D. A., Dhakane, N. M. R., Gawade, N. M. S., Ghodake, N. M. S., and Jadhav, N. M. P. 2024. A comprehensive review of phishing attack detection using machine learning techniques. *International Journal of Advanced Research in Science Communication and Technology*, 4, 435–441.
10. Wang, M., Zhang, D., Wan, K., and Zhang, F. 2024. The impact of digitalization on the division of labour in enterprises- evidence from China. *Applied Economics*, 56(57), 7717–7731.
11. Karim, A., Shahroz, M., Mustofa, K., Belhaouari, S. B., and Joga, S. R. K. 2023. Phishing detection system through hybrid machine learning based on URL. *IEEE Access*, 11, 36805–36822.

12. Atawneh, S., and Aljehani, H. 2023. Phishing email detection model using Deep learning. *Electronics*, 12(20), 4261.
13. Maheswari, S., Rajkumar, N., Geetha, R., Theja, K., Malleswari, M., and Anand J. A. 2025. A comparative analysis of IoT platform tools: Security and scalability preferences in device management using AHP. *2025 International Conference on Visual Analytics and Data Visualization (ICVADV)*, Tirunelveli, India, pp. 380–385.
14. Rajkumar, N., Govindaram, A., Geetha, R., Subhamathi, A. S. F., Nithya, S., and Jose Anand, A. 2025. Non-intrusive load monitoring techniques for intelligent energy management: A comparative study of FHMM and LSTM approach. *2025 International Conference on Visual Analytics and Data Visualization (ICVADV)*, Tirunelveli, India, pp. 869–874.
15. Vidhya, S., Mukunthan, M. A., Saragada, M., Jose Anand, A., Kesavan, R., and Rajasree, R. 2025. AI-based automated weed detection system using YOLOv5 and Mask R-CNN for sustainable agriculture. *2025 International Conference on Advanced Computing Technologies (ICoACT)*, Sivakasi, India, pp. 1–6.
16. Prasath, J. S., Parvez, S. J., Govindaram, A., Anuradha, T., Jose Anand, A., and Rajkumar, N. 2025. AI-enhanced anomaly detection in software-defined networks. *2025 International Conference on Advanced Computing Technologies (ICoACT)*, Sivakasi, India, pp. 1–7.
17. Mukunthan, M. A., Jose Anand, A. A., Kesavan, S., Mutyala, M., Kesavan, R., and Geetha, R. 2024. Detection of physical anomalies in IoT networks using machine learning techniques. *2024 International Conference on Advancement in Renewable Energy and Intelligent Systems (AREIS)*, Thrissur, India, pp. 1–6.
18. Rajasree, R., Geetha, R., Vidhya, S., Mukunthan, M. A., Hari Kumar, S., and Anand, J. A. 2025. Comparative analysis of feature engineering-based learning and deep learning approaches for classification problems on imbalanced datasets. *2025 4th OPJU International Technology Conference (OTCON) on Smart Computing for Innovation and Advancement in Industry 5.0*, Raigarh, India, pp. 1–6.
19. Jayasakthi, K., S., M., Rajkumar, N., Patil, V. S., Pawar, A., and Anand, J. A. 2025. Comparative analysis of deep learning and machine learning models for DDoS attack detection. *2025 4th OPJU International Technology Conference (OTCON) on Smart Computing for Innovation and Advancement in Industry 5.0*, Raigarh, India, pp. 1–6.
20. Moyeenudin, H. M., Anuradha, T., Niraimathy, K., Devika, C., Baby, P. V., and Anand, J. A. 2024. Artificial intelligence based sustainable parking slot alerting system with cloud platform. *2024 1st International Conference on Sustainability and Technological Advancements in Engineering Domain (SUSTAINED)*, Faridabad, India, pp. 711–716.
21. Keerthana, K., Jose Anand, A., Kesavan, R., Kesavan, S., Geetha, R., and Vidhya, S. 2024. IoT-enabled disaster prevention: Leveraging transfer learning for remote monitoring. *2024 1st International Conference on Sustainability and Technological Advancements in Engineering Domain (SUSTAINED)*, Faridabad, India, pp. 492–498.
22. Geetha, R., Vidhya, S., Mukunthan, M. A., Goud, D. S., Anand, J. A., and Kesavan, R. 2025. Predicting online vulnerability among children and youth: A machine learning approach with decision trees and naive Bayes algorithms. *2025 Global Conference in Emerging Technology (GINOTECH)*, Pune, India, pp. 1–6.
23. Mohanty, A., Mohapatra, A. G., Nayak, N., Bairavel, S., Chaithra, M. M., Lakshmi, M., Govindaram, A., and Anand, J. A. 2025. Optimizing diesel generators in industrial settings with IoT and machine learning. *International Journal of Information Technology*, 1–9. https://doi.org/10.1007/s41870-025-02667-x
24. Sajithabanu, S., Devika, S. T., Deeba, S., and Jose Anand, A. 2025. The role of VR and AR in intelligent computing: Applications in psychology and autism. In B. Sundaravadivazhagan, N. Gnanasankaran, P. Raj, and A. Saleem Raja (Eds.), *Virtual Reality and Augmented Reality with 6G Communication*, Ch-13. Wiley Publication.
25. Geetha, R., Thilagavathi, P., Jose Anand, A., Govindaram, A., G. S., J., and Parameswari, D. 2025. Detection and classification of faults in a power system with inverter penetration based on a real-time machine learning application. *2025 Fourth International Conference on Smart Technologies, Communication and Robotics (STCR)*, Sathyamangalam, India, pp. 1–6.

26. Suganya, A., Parameswari, D., Geetha, R., Govindaram, A., Bahuguna, S., and Anand, J.A. 2025. Comparison of machine learning methods for fraudulent transaction classification. *2025 6th International Conference for Emerging Technology (INCET)*, Belgaum, India, pp. 1–7.
27. Devlin, J., Chang, M., Lee, K., and Toutanova, K. 2019. BERT: Pre-training of deep bidirectional transformers for language understanding. arXiv. https://doi.org/10.48550/arxiv.1810.04805
28. Alsubaei, F. S., Almazroi, A. A., and Ayub, N. 2024. Enhancing phishing detection: A novel hybrid deep learning framework for cybercrime forensics. *IEEE Access*, 12, 8373–8389.
29. Sahingoz, O. K., Buber, E., Demir, O., and Diri, B. 2019. Machine learning-based phishing detection from URLs. *Expert Systems with Applications*, 117, 345–357.
30. Biggio, B., and Roli, F. 2018. Wild patterns: Ten years after the rise of adversarial machine learning. *CCS '18: Proceedings of the 2018 ACM SIGSAC Conference on Computer and Communications Security*, 2154–2156.
31. Mohammad, R. M., Thabtah, F., and McCluskey, L. 2015. Predicting phishing websites based on a self-structuring neural network. *Neural Computing and Applications*, 25(2), 443–458.
32. Fares, H., Kilani, J., Fagroud, F., Toumi, H., Lakrami, F., Baddi, Y., and Aknin, N. 2024. Machine learning approach for email phishing detection. *Procedia Computer Science*, 251, 746–751.
33. Gupta, S. D., Shahriar, K. T., Alqahtani, H., Alsalman, D., and Sarker, I. H. 2022. Modelling hybrid feature-based phishing website detection using machine learning techniques. *Annals of Data Science*, 11(1), 217–242.
34. Alsariera, Y. A., Adeyemo, V. E., Balogun, A. O., and Alazzawi, A. K. 2020. AI meta-learners and extra-trees algorithm for the detection of phishing websites. *IEEE Access*, 8, 142532–142542.
35. Almujahid, N. F., Haq, M. A., and Alshehri, M. 2024. Comparative evaluation of machine learning algorithms for phishing site detection. *PeerJ Computer Science*, 10, e2131. https://doi.org/10.7717/peerj-cs.2131
36. Arun, A., and Abosata, N. 2024. Next generation of phishing attacks using AI powered browsers. arXiv:2406.12547.
37. Reddy, P. S., Bansal, A., Ali, M. K., and Jha, A. K. 2024. An integrated approach to anti-phishing systems with advanced machine learning and behavioural analysis. In G. H. L. Gururaj, F. Flammini, S. Srividhya, C. M. L. Chayadevi, & S. Selvam (Eds.), *Computer Science Engineering*. CRC Press, 1–8.
38. Khan, H. U., Malik, M. Z., Nazir, S., and Khan, F. 2023. Utilizing bio metric system for enhancing cyber security in banking sector: A systematic analysis. *IEEE Access*, 11, 80181–80198.
39. Karim, A., Shahroz, M., Mustofa, K., Belhaouari, S. B., and Joga, S. R. K. 2023. Phishing detection system through hybrid machine learning based on URL. *IEEE Access*, 11, 36805–36822.
40. Zieni, R., Massari, L., and Calzarossa, M. C. 2023. Phishing or not phishing? A survey on the detection of phishing websites. *IEEE Access*, 11, 18499–18519.
41. Dhanalakshmi, R., Vijayaraghavan, N., Kumar, A., and Prathiba, B. S. B. 2024. AI-based detection and analysis of phishing domains: Leveraging machine learning for enhanced cybersecurity. In *2024 International Conference on System, Computation, Automation and Networking (ICSCAN)*, 1–6.
42. Alsubaei, F. S., Almazroi, A. A., and Ayub, N. 2024. Enhancing phishing detection: A novel hybrid deep learning framework for cybercrime forensics. *IEEE Access*, 12, 8373–8389.
43. Sallouma, S., Gabera, T., Vaderaa, S., and Shaalan, K. 2021. Phishing email detection using natural language processing techniques: A literature survey. *Procedia Computer Science*, 189, 19–28.
44. J. Gori Mohamed, J. Visumathi, M. Mahdal, A. Jose, and M. Elangovan. 2022. An effective and secure mechanism for phishing attacks using a machine learning approach. *Processes*, 10 (7): 1356.
45. Marchal, S., Francois, J., State, R., and Engel, T. 2014. PhishStorm: Detecting phishing with streaming analytics. *IEEE Transactions on Network and Service Management*, 11, 458–471.
46. Shahrivari, V., Darabi, M. M., and Izadi, M. 2020. Phishing detection using machine learning techniques, 1–9. arXiv:2009.11116.

47. S. Kaul, H. Samuel, and J. Anand. 2014. Defending against vampire attacks in wireless sensor networks. *International Journal of Communication Engineering Applications*, 5: 565–571.
48. Alrufaida, S. A. A., and Al-Mekhlafi, S. A. A. 2023. Comprehensive URL analysis using ensemble machine learning models (XGBoost, LightGBM, GNN). *International Journal of Intelligent Systems and Applications in Engineering*, 16(11), 604–612.
49. Sangeetha, G., and Vijayalakshmi, M. 2023. Weighted high priority packet transmission using ozmos bio-inspired mechanism for traffic load distribution (WH-DTO) in WSNs. *Wireless Networks*, 29, 29–45.
50. Sangeetha, G., and Vijayalakshmi, M. 2021. Ensuring reliability of high-priority data transport using expected congestion shortfall prediction in wireless sensor networks. *Wireless Networks*, 27, 5125–5143.
51. J. Gilda S., M. S. Jacob, V. Bhanu Rekha, U. R. Manchattahalli, V. Seedha Devi, and A. Jose Anand. 2025. Enhancing the performance of energy-harvesting wireless sensor networks through machine learning-based energy prediction. In *2025 10th International Conference on Communication and Electronics Systems (ICCES)*, Coimbatore, India: 1558–1563.
52. Vineetha, B., and Madhumala, R. B. 2021. Providing security and managing quality through machine learning techniques for an image processing model in the industrial Internet of Things. In M. Moh, K. P. Sharma, R. Agrawal, and V. Garcia Diaz (eds.), *Smart IoT for Research and Industry*, 161–177.
53. Sangwan, Y. S., Lal, S., Bhambri, P., Kumar, A., and Dhanoa, I. S. 2021. Advancements in social data security and encryption: A review. *Natural Volatiles & Essential Oils*, 8(4), 15353–15362.
54. Bhambri, P., Bagga, S., Priya, D., Singh, H., and Dhiman, H. K. 2020. Suspicious human activity detection system. *Journal of ISMAC*, 2(4), 216–221.
55. Jain, A., Singh, M., and Bhambri, P. (2021). Performance evaluation of IPv4-IPv6 tunneling procedure using IoT. *Journal of Physics: Conference Series*, 1950(1), Article 012010.
56. KshirsagarP. R., , Jagannadham, D. B. V., Ananth, M. B., Mohan, A., Kumar, G., and Bhambri, P. 2022. Machine learning algorithm for leaf disease detection. *AIP Conference Proceedings*, 2393(1).
57. Bhambri, P., Singh, M., Jain, A., Dhanoa, I. S., Sinha, V. K., and Lal, S. 2021. Classification of gene expression data with the aid of optimized feature selection. *Turkish Journal of Physiotherapy and Rehabilitation*, 32(3), 1158–1168.
58. Bhambri, P., and Ritu. 2023. Software effort estimation with machine learning – A systematic literature review. In S. Hooda, V. M. Sood, Y. Singh, S. Dalal, and M. Sood (Eds.), *Agile Software Development: Trends, Challenges and Applications* (pp. 291–308). Wiley.
59. Singh, M., Bhambri, P., Singh, I., Jain, A., and Kaur, K. 2021. Data mining classifier for predicting diabetics. *Annals of R.S.C.B.*, 25(4), 6702–6712.
60. Rana, R., Chhabra, Y., and Bhambri, P. 2021. Comparison and evaluation of various QoS parameters in WSNs with the implementation of enhanced low energy adaptive efficient distributed clustering approach. *Webology*, 18(1), 677–695.
61. Rana, R., and Bhambri, P. 2024. Generative AI-driven security frameworks for web engineering: Innovations and challenges. In I. A. Shah and N. Z. Jhanjhi (Eds.), *Generative AI for Web Engineering Models* (pp. 285–296). IGI Global.
62. Bhambri, P. 2024. Artificial intelligence enabled Internet of Medical Things for enhanced healthcare systems. In P. Bhambri, R. Soni, and T. A. Tran (Eds.), *Smart Healthcare Systems: AI and IoT Perspectives* (pp. 1–17). CRC Press.

Chapter 13

Autonomous artificial intelligence systems for fraud detection and forensics in dark web environments

Vijay Anant Athavale, Dhanumjaya K., Kalaiselvi S., Satwik Chatterjee and Bazani Shaik

13.1 INTRODUCTION

There have been numerous applications for detecting, forecasting, modeling, and assessing challenges related to online social networks (OSNs) using deep learning (DL) techniques inspired by brain morphology and artificial intelligence (AI) algorithms that emulate human intelligence through inference approaches. These applications span a wide range of domains, including security, crime-related forensic technologies (such as memory, cloud, and smart devices), healthcare, the Internet of Things (IoT), and natural language processing (NLP), all of which rely on massive analytics of real-time data. Cybercriminals, some of whom operate by the Dark Web (DW), pose a direct and indirect threat to the economy, security, and Internet operations. The widespread use of DL techniques has made it easier to use online business applications pertaining to financial transactions. Figure 13.1 shows the fraud architecture that is influencing institutions. For those involved in artificial intelligence (AI), the meteoric surge in DL usage is reminiscent of the early days of ICT. Significant societal value disruption occurred in the past due to unexpected challenges that emerged during the rapid growth of ICT, such as cybercrime and terrorism, security breaches, privacy violations, extortion, illicit commerce, and so on. The possibility that AI will cause a number of problems is also a growing worry. This part covers the dangers of AI-based security measures, crimes that are likely to occur, and digital forensics (DF). The infamous Silk Road market ran on the onion router (ToR), an anonymous network for online commerce and business that catered to illicit activities using cryptocurrency (Crypto-Coin) for transactions and income generation, all while remaining hidden from the outside world and even evading the attention of cyber police, security agencies, and forensics specialists. Terrorist groups manage their finances, recruit new members, create propaganda, declare attack operations, share threatening posts, track government and military operations, and more through DW-online social network (OSN) messaging systems such as DuckDuckGo and Hidden Wiki.

Researchers and security agencies constantly monitor OSN for suspicious activity and posts that pose a threat or are otherwise unauthorized by the government. Using artificial intelligence and deep learning techniques, they create various models to examine potentially vulnerable inputs and related files. Figure 13.2 shows the tracking and generation model for a comparable dataset that includes signatures and fingerprints of susceptible OSN events.

1. **Data Collection Program**—Recognizing an online social network that hosts terrorist-related content, including harmful postings, messages, and files.

 DOI: 10.1201/9781003656487-13

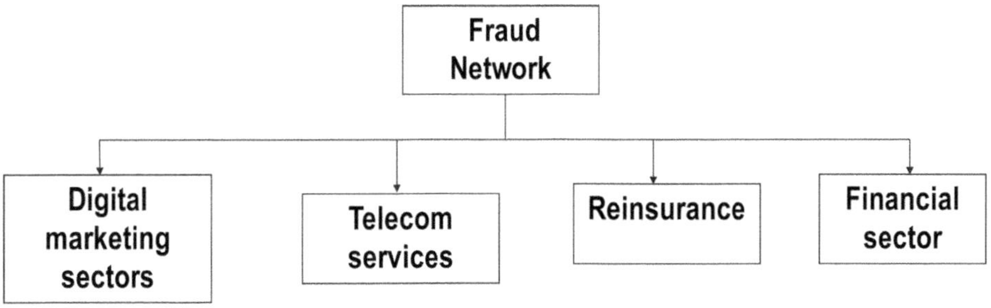

Figure 13.1 Fraud framework affecting organizations.

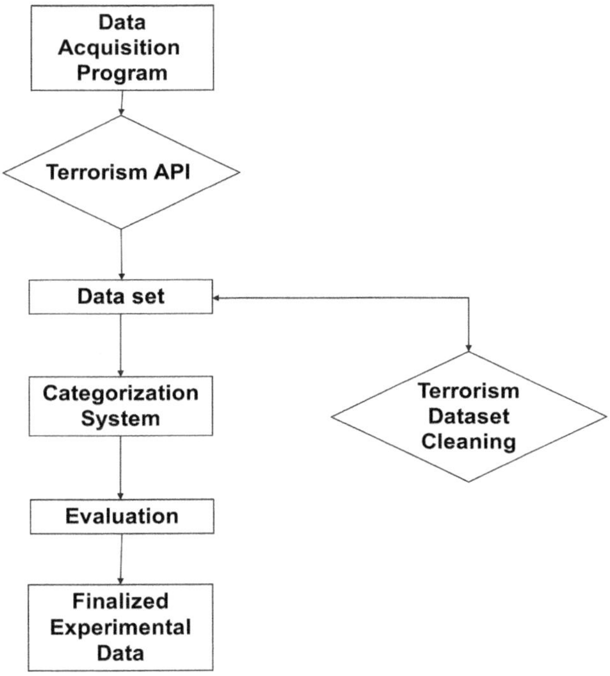

Figure 13.2 Terrorism activities data architecture.

2. **Terrorism API**—Executing crawlers with the purpose of gathering information based on a maliciously crafted list that includes hashtags, images of weapons, symbols, keywords, and hidden images with face masks.
3. **Dataset**—Severe threatening incident identification and organization post to keep tabs on where people are and who is in groups connected to previous actions (such as reply, share, remark, forwarding).
4. **Classification Program**—Cybercriminals plot various actions and threats against their intended victims based on the collected dataset.
5. **Terrorism Data Cleaning**—There is classified information on more dangerous tasks related to the bombing, large-scale slaughter, and government strike.
6. **Analysis**—Detection for the purpose of analyzing the event and time period that set it off, or organized crime for the purpose of forecasting future occurrences that are likely to include new dangers and assaults.

7. **Final Dataset**—For security agencies to act upon, it includes filtered events with signatures and parameters.

13.1.1 Rationale

- Automated methods for criminal identification and prediction are the primary focus of the few accessible works on cybercrime forensic evaluation.
- Automated intelligence behavior systems for criminal and malevolent occurrences were the primary focus of the planned study.
- A taxonomy of criminal behaviors and signatures is the subject of the present study, which aims to provide security personnel with crime recommendation services.
- Assessment of criminal behaviors and methods for the foretelling of future illegal acts are the primary foci of the forensic specialists' work.

13.2 RELATED WORK

AI transforms auditing by increasing fraud detection and risk assessment with high speed and accuracy. This work employs machine learning in forensic accounting to identify abnormalities, reduce false positives, and increase risk management [1]. This bibliometric review emphasizes the growing need for auditor training, technological adaptation, and interdisciplinary collaboration to maintain audit integrity [2]. It also emphasizes AI and cloud computing in next-generation 6G mobile networks for improved communication, fraud detection, and cybersecurity and the role of AI in mobile services for reliability, safety, and reduced cybercrime [3]. AI and machine learning improve cyber forensic investigations through case studies and surveys. The findings show that these technologies enhance threat detection, classification, and investigation efficiency [4]. The study also presents a one-dimensional convolutional neural network (1D CNN) model integrated with Explainable AI (XAI) using SHapley Additive exPlanations (SHAP) for detecting fraudulent Bitcoin transactions. The model addresses data imbalance and enhances interpretability while achieving high accuracy and a low false-positive rate [5].

OpenL2D is a framework that enhances human-AI collaboration in fraud detection through the use of Learning to Defer (L2D) algorithms [6]. Large language models (LLMs) are advanced AI systems that process and generate human-like text across diverse industries. This chapter analyzes their evolution, applications, and challenges in fields such as healthcare, finance, and education [7]. Explainable Artificial Intelligence (XAI) techniques combined with transformer-based models, such as BERT, XLNet, and RoBERTa, have been employed for credit card fraud detection. The integration of SHAP and LIME techniques enhances transparency in AI decision-making, improving fraud detection reliability [8]. Causality research is surveyed across five decades, examining its impact on fields such as finance, fraud detection, and cybersecurity. The study explores how causal reasoning integrates with AI, machine learning, and deep learning to enhance trust and explainability [9].

Using scientometric and bibliometric analysis, this study maps cybersecurity research trends in the banking sector from 2004 to 2024. It identifies themes such as AI, machine learning, fintech, and fraud detection as major research frontiers. The findings highlight a shift from traditional risk management toward AI-driven, networked cybersecurity paradigms [10]. This study examines the role of Big Data in transforming healthcare fraud detection through the 5Vs—Volume, Variety, Velocity, Veracity, and Value. It highlights how integrating AI and Big Data enhances detection accuracy and system efficiency, offering insights for modern, trustworthy healthcare fraud prevention [11]. A multi-stage hybrid ensemble model is proposed for improving credit scoring and fraud detection. Using weighted ensemble filtering, improved SMOTE, and nested classifiers, the model achieved up to 92.43% accuracy and 0.968 AUC. It offers a robust, cost-effective tool for reliable credit risk assessment and fraud prevention [12]. This study explores the role of AI in enhancing fraud detection and privacy within mobile financial services. Based on mixed-method analysis, AI improved security ($\beta = 0.63$, $p < 0.01$) but raised privacy and transparency concerns. It recommends Explainable AI and privacy-by-design frameworks to foster user trust and adoption [13].

SFIX is an explainable AI framework for financial applications such as fraud detection, credit scoring, and customer profiling. SFIX integrates time-based analysis and dataset consistency checks to ensure model interpretability and reliability, supporting safer and more transparent financial AI systems [14]. AI (XAI) methods are applied in finance, focusing on transparency, performance, and dataset suitability. It identifies the key algorithms used, their benefits, and challenges, emphasizing the importance of XAI for safe and accountable financial decision-making [15]. A new fraud detection model, MetaFraud-GNN, is developed using metagraph search and neural architecture optimization. Tested on real datasets such as YelpChi, Amazon, and Elliptic, it outperformed benchmarks by up to 8.59% in GMean and 4.46% in F1-macro, demonstrating superior adaptability and detection accuracy [16]. AI's role in combating nursing credential fraud finds a lack of empirical research, urging future collaboration and regulatory attention to maintain integrity in healthcare verification [17]. Supervised models like XGBoost outperform anomaly detection methods in fraud detection, achieving an F1-score of 0.89 and providing a strong benchmark for future studies [18]. AI is used in business intelligence for fraud detection, emphasizing machine learning, real-time systems, and ethical collaboration for effective risk management [19].

The convergence of quantum networks and AI highlights emerging applications in data security, optimization, and computational intelligence [20]. The Hygieia chatbot integrates IoT and NLP to offer healthcare users appointment booking, daily scheduling, and interactive voice-based assistance [21]. Researchers enhance industrial automation with ANN-powered vision systems, improving precision, speed, and adaptability in robotic operations [22]. A case study using Amazon Braket demonstrates quantum service-oriented computing and identifies the challenges in integrating classical and quantum systems [23]. It also highlights the use of federated learning with differential privacy for secure cross-silo data aggregation in machine learning applications [24]. Furthermore, various GAN (Generative Adversarial Network) variants have been evaluated for simulating turbulent flow, with the results indicating that Wasserstein GANs generate accurate, high-fidelity turbulence predictions [25]. Another study investigates the impact of urbanization on land use and local climate in Noida using Landsat-8 data. Findings show two urban heat island clusters in dense industrial zones, urging planners to integrate environmental considerations into industrial land development [26]. Using Landsat data (1972–2014), this work examines land use and cover changes driven by population and economic growth. Results reveal rapid urban sprawl and declining land area, posing sustainability challenges and potential desertification risks [27]. Indoor radon and progeny levels were measured in Etah district dwellings using LR-115 detectors. Concentrations ranged from 3.52 to 248.64 Bq m^{-3}, indicating variable exposure levels, with some posing health risks compared to rural areas [28]. Radon exhalation rates and radium content in Etah's urban soils were analyzed using LR-115 detectors. The measured values were below OECD safety limits, contributing valuable insight into urban soil's role in indoor radon levels [29].

13.3 USING AI AS A TOOL FOR DETECTING CRIMES

This part depicts the anticipated AI as a weapon for criminals, in light of AI's dual-use nature. On top of that, AI has the potential to drive autonomous vehicles, drones, and IoT devices to perpetrate physical crimes. Here we will examine the potential use of AI in cyber assaults. Physical crime, which constitutes a new assault, is the next topic we will cover.

13.3.1 Cybercrime with advanced technology

With the help of AI techniques, cybercriminals may pull off hitherto unimaginable acts of innovation. Cybercrime prevention using AI is the focus of this section.

13.3.1.1 Conducting criminal acts using computers

Attackers use targeted advertising based on consumers' interests and past purchases to lure them into clicking on malicious links, which can include chatbots powered by artificial intelligence. Artificial intelligence will enhance strategies for committing fraud using malicious chatbots. While interacting with customers, the chatbot may record extensive details on their habits and preferences. A chatbot is already in development and in use in both academia and industry. At first, the chatbot relied heavily on text. The chatbot's ability to mimic human speech is a result of developments in natural language processing. There is some evidence that AI-assisted speech could be helpful in areas such as education, medical diagnostics, and relaxation (social therapy), but there is also some evidence that it could lead to an increase in fraudulent activities. Verbal communication is a form of biometrics, which is crucial to security systems and also poses a significant threat from malicious actors (like voice phishing).

There was a dramatic increase in the visibility of criminally affiliated fake news on online social networks (OSNs) such as Facebook, Twitter, Instagram, and YouTube, which in turn had a domino effect on political issues such as extremism in election support or hatred, policy decisions, and propaganda. The power of deep fake technology is growing as the fake news industry expands. Misinformation distributed by fake videos posing as famous politicians might have negative consequences. For the purpose of increasing efficiency and decreasing costs, news organizations developed an AI-powered newscaster. By 2023, experts predict the industry will have grown to about $62 billion. In the fight against insurance claim fraud, money laundering, and data fraud, organizations are taking aim at automation, which is based on artificial intelligence. Nearly a quarter of OSN users have fallen victim to online data fraud. Fraudulent actions around the world are shown in Figure 13.3. The most common kind of financial fraud is wire transfers, which criminals use to steal money from unsuspecting victims. Other forms of fraud include credit card fraud and bank fraud. A systematic review of AI, ML, DL, and meta-heuristic optimization algorithms for credit card fraud detection is presented in previous studies [30].

13.3.1.2 A computer as a potential victim of crime

Artificial intelligence can complete tasks that were previously infeasible, all while requiring less labor and cost. The making of the artificial intelligence system had the same effect as employing analysts with extra-human abilities. When building the dictionary, social engineers often use the tactic of gathering victim facts from the internet, such as city, phone numbers, address, hobbies, birthdates, etc. Data collection is labor-intensive and

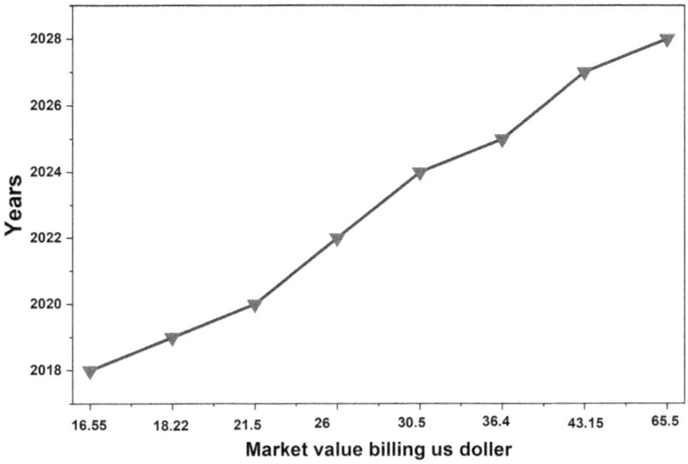

Figure 13.3 Worldwide data on deceitful acts.

time-consuming, but reverse social engineering automation is a breeze for the AI-powered system.

An automated-detecting method for creating the vulnerabilities can be useful for criminals. Some have speculated that AI might help find security flaws. Compared to a regular static analyzer, they demonstrated that CNN and a tree ensemble (TE) offer several benefits. There was a proposal for a method to identify vulnerabilities in networks. The proposed method has the potential to detect vulnerable apps without analyzing source code. In addition to such studies, various methods for vulnerability detection are also being studied. Despite the good intentions behind the methods, thieves may use them to find vulnerable systems.

13.3.2 Physical crime

Concerns about the safety of AI extend beyond the Internet of Things (IoT). By taking control of an AI system—civilian or military, car, house, or animal—a criminal can physically attack a victim. Some have argued that AI-based robots could assault and kill humans, either on purpose or by accident, and this has prompted discussions on robotic ethics as it relates to physical crime. Because AI systems have the potential to cause physical harm, assigning moral and legal responsibility for any resulting consequences might be challenging, as previously noted. Another example is swarm robotics, in which multiple autonomous robots operate without centralized control.

i. Able to detect their immediate environment and the presence of other swarm members at close proximity.
ii. Skilled in establishing localized communication networks within the swarm.
iii. The capacity of several computers to cooperate in order to accomplish a task is known as swarming. Swarming is now possible due to advancements in artificial intelligence, which were previously impossible for traditional programming algorithms.

Using this swarming technique, robotic systems can alter automotive vulnerabilities remotely and apply them to vehicles. Twizy had an Electric Control Unit (ECU) installed by taking advantage of security holes in the Sevcon Gen4 controller. The Renault Twizy 80, an electric vehicle, was the subject of multiple potential danger scenarios. The proposed model works; however, they proved that an attacker can control the car's systems from a distance after hacking. Once thought to be the gold standard for automotive networking, the Controller Area Network (CAN) protocol has vulnerabilities. They were able to successfully induce ECU failures through the use of a message injection attack by adjusting the level of risk. Because it physically harms system components, swarm technology is quite worrisome.

13.4 ARTIFICIAL INTELLIGENCE—A TARGET CRIME

Crimes targeting AI can disrupt or destroy data processing or the functioning of AI-powered automated operations. There are two components that make up an AI system: training and inference. The system builds a model using the training dataset. The inference system (IS) uses the trained model to classify the data. In order to distinguish between citizens and members of terrorist groups, this technology creates an algorithm. The inference system takes the technique as input and uses it to determine if the sensor-acquired picture of the item is accurate (civilian or military).

The results demonstrated that AI systems' performance degrades when exposed to AEs vulnerabilities (such as malware). This study reviews more than 300 publications on the application of Explainable Artificial Intelligence (XAI) in cybersecurity, highlighting its role in intrusion detection, malware analysis, phishing detection, fraud detection, and digital forensics. XAI enhances transparency and security but also introduces vulnerabilities to adversarial attacks [31]. System targets are AEs that are able to evade detection. To launch an impersonation attack, one must first feed the inference system data samples that are misleadingly similar to the genuine ones. Using the inversion attack, we can infer some features of the AI system's output toward the input. With an emphasis on the models' characteristics (privacy, secrecy, and integrity), we also provided a comprehensive overview of the vulnerability (threat) model and addressed the adversarial capabilities, attack surface, purpose, and AI trust model. A model of the artificial intelligence system used to detect objections is shown in Figure 13.4.

13.4.1 Criminal offenses targeted: TS

Techniques used to prevent hacking include advanced persistent threat (APT), malicious external storage (MES), and insider espionage.

13.4.1.1 Ongoing assault on the training system

A decrease in artificial intelligence crime prediction accuracy can impact AI's capacity to classify new data at the inference system (IS) through the introduction of artificial errors (AEs) or changes to the existing dataset and learning algorithm (logic corruption)—major problems for the training system. The data poisoning danger influences AI system behavior by introducing adverse events.

$$\overrightarrow{x^*} = \vec{x} + \operatorname{argmin}\{\vec{z} : \tilde{o}(\vec{x} + \vec{z}) \neq \tilde{o}(\vec{x})\}$$

Z represents the disturbance, while x is the initial data. The oracle is a system that provides answers to inquiries, and the letter O stands for it. A question that has seen heavy use in

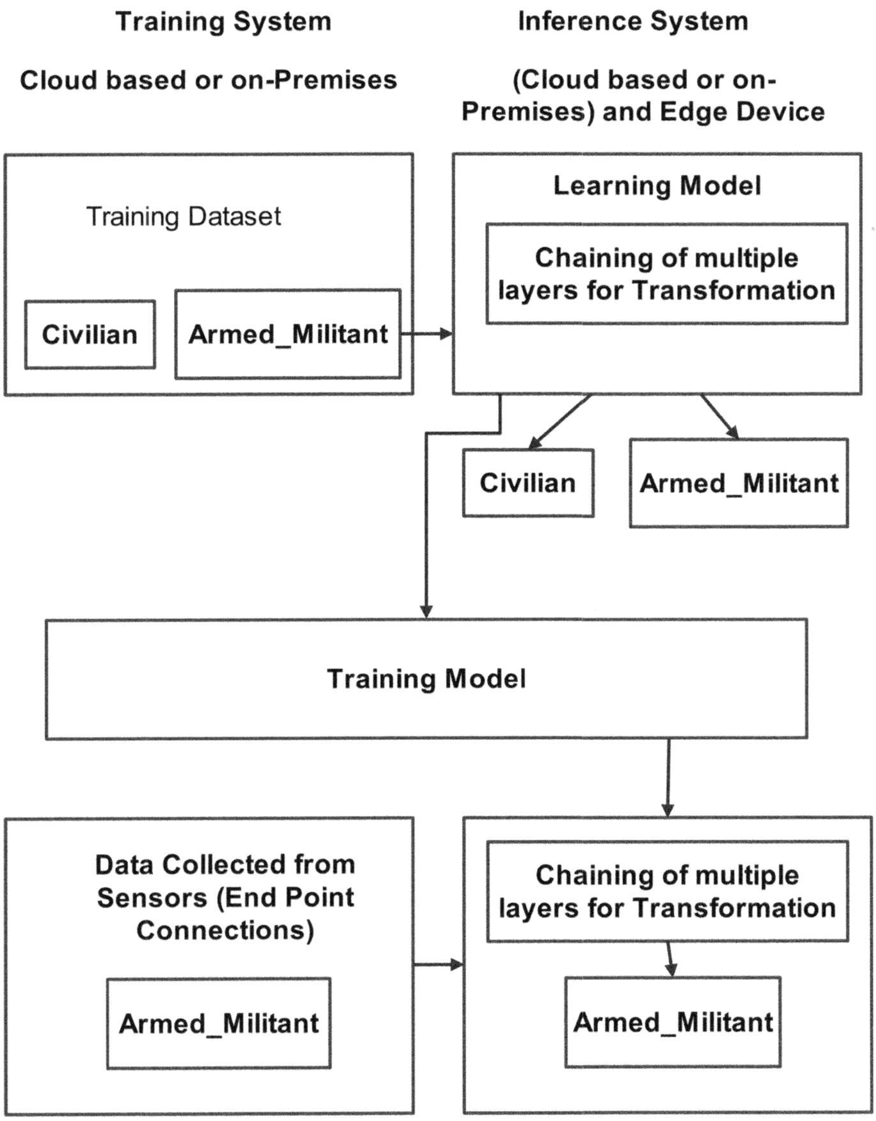

Figure 13.4 Developing an artificial intelligence model for object recognition.

cryptography circles recently: how to make and use AEs has evolved and is the subject of much study, especially in the field of image recognition. Additionally, AEs pose a risk in incorrectly interpreting road signs and could find employment in physical space (self-driving cars). It is also possible to develop and employ AEs with the purpose of interfering with intrusion detection, malware analysis, prediction, and detection.

When criminals get the green light to modify or delete training data, they commit data alteration crimes and can launch devastating attacks on AI systems. A label contamination attack (LCA) damaged AI performance when certain training data had their labels changed. When it comes to the training system, logic corruption is the biggest criminal. The criminals can alter the trained model's architecture and parameters by tampering with the learning algorithm. The input, classification, and training parameters layers are all vulnerable to hacking and corruption in a CNN system [32–36].

13.4.1.2 Theft of training system (TS)

The training set, the learning model, and the learned model are the three main parts of TS. Because it has a direct bearing on AI performance, the training process is secret among artificial intelligence developers and makers of artificial intelligence-related goods. The dataset is essential for anyone involved in AI. Their acquisition of datasets from various sources, such as object data, driving-related data, and traffic data, makes them an attractive target for thieves who steal sensitive information, such as medical images, facial images, or audio recordings, demonstrating serious breaches of privacy.

13.4.2 Target crime: inference system (IS)

Due to its installation at the end processing devices, the inference system is more easily accessible to attackers than the training system.

13.4.2.1 Cracking of inference system (IS)

Attributes established during training are the backbone of an inference system. Centralized and distributed models are the two main categories of operating procedures, distinguished by the location of the parameters. An AI design provider's centralized server handles the inference process in the centralized mode. The role of end-user devices in a centralized face recognition system (image feature processing) includes things like smartphones, Internet of Things (IoT), and in-car systems. In theory, a centralized method of managing AI services in security processing would be ideal; however, in practice, the likelihood of a bottleneck makes this strategy less desirable. This has led to the distributed model's meteoric rise in popularity in real-world applications [37–41].

13.4.3 AI forensics

Gathering and evaluating pieces of evidence based on the operating system platform relating to forensic domains (smartphone, cloud, and IoT) can help forensic investigators determine the 5W1H (when and where the crime incident occurred, who committed it, what they targeted, why, and how the vulnerability occurred). The following are some potential avenues for future research in artificial intelligence forensics: investigating technological crimes committed using AI; developing threat detection attributes based on AI system characteristics; and drawing on forensic tactics used to track down AI crime perpetrators (AI exploration, similarity analysis, adversarial attack detection, and damage assessment).

13.4.3.1 Exploration of AI

Investigators gathered and evaluated the trained, learning, inference models and dataset associated with the artificial intelligence system that was used to perpetrate the crime. This allowed them to deduce the AI's objective, as the assessor had trouble differentiating between the developer's intent and the AI's result. Traditional programming involves processing data and programs to generate output. When building an AI model, it is common practice to use random weights during the learning phase and to select AI parameters with a degree of unpredictability. Hence, program parameters and outcomes can vary even while using the same dataset and learning model. We trained our models using a large dataset that contained a fraction of the data we collected, and we used an i7-8700 CPU in conjunction with an Nvidia GeForce 1070 Ti graphics card to determine if binary files were harmful or not. For every category, the dataset included 1,500 PE files. We obtained 800 malicious files from the Virus Share collection, which is open to the public. The 800 safe files were hand-picked from the most trustworthy source of their kind, Software Informer, and the system folders created during Windows 10's installation. To improve the model's accuracy, we used a Convolutional Neural Network (CNN) ensemble method that relies on voting. Using trained models, the selected 70% to identify performance changes. A previous study demonstrated that AI-driven techniques in forensic science, such as CNN and SVM, enhance accuracy in fingerprint, facial, and cyber forensic analysis. Results show CNN achieving 96.8% and SVM 92.3% accuracy [42]. The results show that the training data has a significant impact on the accuracy. See how the trained models stack up in terms of accuracy in Figure 13.5.

The results of the studies proved that it is not feasible to replicate artificial intelligence-based systems because of the limited availability of evidence and source data. The acquisition of source data is becoming more challenging, posing both technological and policy-related difficulties. This challenge is further compounded by the fact that many artificial intelligence systems are developed using pre-trained models and transfer learning approaches [43–47].

13.4.3.2 Similarity analysis

Digital forensics has traditionally focused on investigating breaches, such as those involving copyright infringement, the disclosure of sensitive information, and invasions of privacy. Social media data aid digital forensics but pose privacy and data integrity issues. This study proposes AI- and ML-based tools like text mining and network analysis to enhance evidence accuracy and legal admissibility [48]. A major strategy for identifying unlawful activity in these cases is similarity analysis, which includes tools for detecting code plagiarism, document similarity, and digital image similarity. By comparing datasets (real and suspect) that contain picture, audio, text, and video, similarity analysis reveals the odd outcome when using the model of certain datasets. The development of file formats for archiving trained models is the primary focus of research. Forensics researchers may benefit from comparing trained models using existing similarity techniques to identify instances of infringement; however, Python tools are used by AI development platforms. After determining that the models are incompatible, the algorithms show how outdated methods are by recommending the creation of a more modern model to determine similarity.

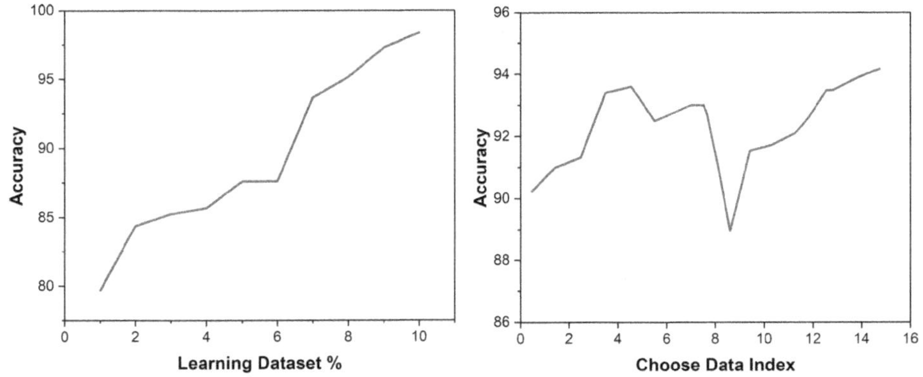

Figure 13.5 Comparison of trained models' accuracy.

13.4.4 Detection of differential attack

Proactively preventing (identifying) hostile attacks is a challenging task. In order to properly classify AEs, numerous studies proposed a defense mechanism. Bayesian uncertainty estimates (BUE), hypothesis testing, and principal component analysis (PCA) are a few statistical approaches to the problem that are available with different extra neural network (NN) methodologies. In previous studies, optimization with Bayesian tuning, the model achieved accuracy and error. This framework outperformed existing models, ensuring precise fraud detection with minimal false results [49]. While many methods exist for detecting hostile attacks, advanced persistent threats (AEs) were developed to circumvent these methods. Designing AEs is thus a challenging and time-consuming process. However, hostile threats can still occur during incremental training, which involves responding to fresh data in order to improve over time. Malicious actors can trick AI systems into executing AEs by making them seem harmless.

13.4.5 Assessment of damage

It is the responsibility of forensic investigators to ascertain the extent to which AI crime caused harm. To solve investigators, an AE-based attack needs to know which facts are AEs, the actual number of poisoned AEs, and the extent to which the danger altered the scenario. Finding AEs entails tracking down specific details that contribute to an elevated prediction error rate. In order to explain the process, DNN makes use of the hierarchical composition of u parametric functions, g-i. A weight vector θ_i parametrizes each g_i for j∊1....m in the neurons layer. Here is the computation for a DNN model G:

$$G\left(\vec{y} = g_m\left(\theta_n, g_{m-1}\left(\theta_{m-1}, \ldots . g_2\left(\theta_2, g\left(\theta_1, \vec{y}\right)\right)\right)\right)\right) \tag{13.1}$$

The backward elimination technique can be used to identify AEs if they have already been injected into the investigators and the target dataset is familiar with the dataset of input-output pairs and the training G (,.,,.).

$$l^* = \operatorname{argmin}\left\{ \sum_{\neg(k=l)}^{m} \mathrm{Gj}\left(\overrightarrow{yj}\right) - z_j \mid \right\} \tag{13.2}$$

L can represent either a single sample or a set of samples. G_j denotes a trained DNN model that does not have yj.,, gj., or θ_a. To calculate the prediction error in this scenario, we look at the number of misclassifications. Unfortunately, the method is not practical for use in real-world forensics; it necessitates Equations (13.2) and (13.3). There is a large amount of training data in the AI system that uses DNN, and it is quite difficult to determine the impact of each sample. It may get complicated for the investigators because they might not have access to information on the AI model of every sample. Consequently, there is a major problem in detecting AEs.

13.5 DISCUSSION

By contrasting AI forensics with more conventional methods, this section highlights some of the main issues with the field. This study presents a typology of signs spanning criminal targets and illegal activity instruments utilized in fraudulent operations utilizing artificial intelligence features by digital forensic methods. An AI-based detection model using SMOTE and the FBI algorithm improves the identification of fraudulent pollution fee declarations. It enhances compliance, reduces tax evasion, and supports sustainable environmental governance [50]. It explores the study of intelligence-related criminal behavior and potential dangers. It delves further into models for classifying malicious events and analyzing details relevant to terrorists. We offer AI forensics as a fresh strategy to combat AI crime. Our thorough examination of the field of forensics revealed that AI-based forensics has yet to fully embrace a number of key DF principles.

13.5.1 Large scale

It used to be unfathomable how much data and resources would be required to create an AI model. Finding data using conventional computer-based forensic methods becomes more complicated for investigators due to the huge data store. While traditional digital forensics dealt with the accompanying large-scale issue, artificial intelligence forensics should cover a lot more ground. Specifically, modern AIs are still quite complicated when it comes to digital forensics and primarily target multimodal data like images and sounds.

13.5.2 Irreproducibility

Artificial intelligence systems' intrinsic unpredictability could affect forensic principles. A number of AI methods fall short of the repeatability standards set by forensic principles because they use random features. Artificial intelligence (AI) evidence, such as copycat models and artificial events (AEs), could be rejected in court if the repeatability test model is used exclusively for these types of evidence. Additional problems, such as wrongly arresting someone, arise from the need to investigate how to apply the reproducibility principles. Therefore, lawmakers, AI experts, and forensic investigators should try to strike a middle ground between being too strict and being too lenient while applying the models (principles).

13.5.3 Expertise

A comprehensive understanding of AI criminological and forensic approaches is essential for forensic stakeholders to enhance their AI knowledge and address the challenges in AI forensics. All forensic investigators should be well-versed in the standard programming languages and concepts, including memory structures, types, and compilers. In order to solve forensic difficulties involving malware analysis in assembly language, one needs to be familiar with the architecture and processing environment of artificial intelligence systems. Table 13.1 displays the AI-powered criminal activity and forensic methods.

13.6 CONCLUSION

There is growing concern that AI, due to its dual-use nature, can be harmful to humans, despite its widespread use in various systems and applications. Hackers can take advantage of AI engines by taking advantage of the weaknesses in the target AI system to commit malicious acts. Possible crimes involving AI were the focus of this study. We found that most of the previous research on AI security has focused on criminals' use of AI system designs for malicious purposes, or on the shortcomings of AI methods and training datasets in relation to the crime. In addition, we have demonstrated how AI has the potential to amplify already-existing criminal activities and how previously undiscovered forms of

Table 13.1 AI-powered criminal activity and forensic methods

S. No	*AI-based crime modeling*	*Methods*	*AI-associated challenges toward forensics technology*
1	Threat originator and triggering host	Artificial intelligence chatbot, Deep Fake, automated system for reverse threat engineering, etc.	Exploration of AI
2	Honeypot stations	Security flaws in online social networks, vulnerability scanners, etc.	
3	Hardware (chip) module altering threat	Attacks on hardware, swarms of drones, changes to control management units, chip alterations, etc.	
4	Modeling threat for training system	Logic upgrade vulnerability injection and reverse logic triggering	Investigating AI, identifying differential attacks, damage assessment
5	Training system theft	Malware-based post, victim system search data	
6	Identifying potential risks to an inference system		Exploration of AI, similarity analysis
7	Traditional forensics	Manually disturbance of records damage, pan drive floppy	Reproducible with difficulty
8	AI forensics	vulnerability or injecting malicious codes to automatically delete all files or lock and creates encryption	High-level reverse engineering tools are required for recovering

crime may also develop. The results of this research provide a framework for dealing tactics and artificial intelligence crime [51–60].

Additionally, the AI forensics is a novel approach to fighting AI-related criminality. After comparing AI-based and conventional forensics, we found that some DF principles are still not preferred in the former. Researchers in the field of forensics have asked for more studies to shed light on the challenges they face.

REFERENCES

1. D. M. Dash, D. Princy, M. S. Kumar, J. Guntaj, R. Jain, D. A. Yadav, and S. Hashmi. 2025. Artificial intelligence in auditing: Enhancing fraud detection and risk assessment. *International Journal of Accounting and Economics Studies*, 12 (SI-1): 71–75. https://doi.org/10.14419/18h1yf2
2. R. Romero-Carazas, A. P. Espíritu-Martínez, M. M. Aguilar-Cuevas, M. N. Usuriaga-Palacios, L. A. Aguilar-Cuevas, and M. Z. Espinoza-Véliz. 2024. Forensic auditing and the use of artificial intelligence: A bibliometric analysis and systematic review in Scopus between 2000 and 2024. *Heritage and Sustainable Development*, 6 (2): 415–428.
3. S. R. Gundu, P. Charanarur, K. K. Chandelkar, D. Samanta, R. C. Poonia, and P. Chakraborty. 2022. Sixth-generation (6G) mobile cloud security and privacy risks for AI system using high-performance computing implementation. *Wireless Communications and Mobile Computing*, 2022: 4397610. https://doi.org/10.1155/2022/4397610
4. B. Fakiha. 2023. Enhancing cyber forensics with AI and machine learning: A study on automated threat analysis and classification. *International Journal of Safety and Security Engineering*, 13 (4): 701–707.
5. M. Hasan, M. S. Rahman, M. J. Morshed Chowdhury, and I. H. Sarker. 2025. CNN-based deep learning modeling with explainability analysis for detecting fraudulent blockchain transactions. *Cyber Security and Applications*, 3: 100101. https://doi.org/10.1016/j.csa.2025.100101

6. J. V. Alves, D. Leitão, S. Jesus, M. O. Sampaio, J. Liébana, P. Saleiro, ... P. Bizarro. 2025. A benchmarking framework and dataset for learning to defer in human–AI decision-making. *Scientific Data*, 12 (1): 1–9.
7. M. Raza, Z. Jahangir, M. B. Riaz, M. J. Saeed, and M. A. Sattar. 2025. Industrial applications of large language models. *Scientific Reports*, 15 (1): 1–11.
8. M. N. Vadlamudi, S. Doma, M. Hijab, and B. Sankara Babu. 2025. Towards transparent fraud detection: Explainable AI and multi-algorithm optimization in financial security. *International Journal of Intelligent Engineering and Systems*, 18 (10): 698–712.
9. A. I. Weinberg, C. Premebida, and D. R. Faria. 2025. Causality from bottom to top: A survey. *Machine Learning*, 114: 234. https://doi.org/10.1007/s10994-025-06855-5
10. S. Fahimifar and A. Momenzadeh. 2025. From information security to artificial intelligence: A scientometrics analysis of research trends in cybersecurity within the banking industry. *Scientometrics Research Journal*, 11 (2): 299–326.
11. A. Karami and F. Jafari. 2025. Leveraging big data characteristics for enhanced healthcare fraud detection. *Cluster Computing*, 28 (6): 1–7.
12. P. R. Rajaleximi, A. Saravanan, B. SivaSakthi, L. Jaganathan, and S. S. Bama. 2025. Enhancing credit scoring through a multi-stage hybrid ensemble classification model with feature engineering and data balancing. *International Research Journal of Multidisciplinary Technovation*, 7 (5): 185–209.
13. E. Mollik and F. Majeed. 2025. AI-driven cybersecurity in mobile financial services: Enhancing fraud detection and privacy in emerging markets. *Journal of Cybersecurity and Privacy*, 5 (3), 1–10.
14. A. E. Cil and K. Yildiz. 2025. SFIX: Scalable financial-oriented interpretable explanation. *Internet of Things*, 33: 101713. https://doi.org/10.1016/j.iot.2025.101713
15. A. E. Cil and K. Yildiz. 2025. A systematic literature review on applications of explainable artificial intelligence in the financial sector. *Internet of Things (The Netherlands)*, 33: 1–9.
16. G. Tong, J. Qian, and J. Shen. 2025. Adaptive metagraph neural network assisted by metagraph search for financial fraud detection. *Engineering Applications of Artificial Intelligence*, 153: 1–7.
17. L. Herckis and E. Tse. 2025. AI-enabled fraud detection, prevention, and perpetration in nursing credential evaluation: A scoping study. *Journal of Nursing Regulation*, 16 (3): 183–194.
18. A. Suganya, D. Parameswari, R. Geetha, A. Govindaram, S. Bahuguna, and A. Jose Anand. 2025. Comparison of machine learning methods for fraudulent transaction classification. *Proceedings of the IEEE INCET 2025.*
19. M. S. Ramachandran, S. Sajithabanu, A. Ponmalar, M. Mohamed Sithik, and A. A. Jose. 2024. Fraud detection and risk management using AI in business intelligence. In A. Natarajan, M. Galety, C. Iwendi, D. Das, and A. Shankar (eds.), *Intersection of AI and Business Intelligence in Data-Driven Decision-Making.* IGI Global: 117–150. https://doi.org/10.4018/979-8-3693-5288-5.ch005
20. C. Ananth, O. I. Khalaf, and A. J. Anand. 2024. *Quantum Networks and their Applications in AI.* IGI Global, 1–77.
21. A. Jose and R. Dhanalakshmi. 2023. Hygieia: Multipurpose healthcare assistance using the Internet of Things. In S. Krishnan and A. Ilmudeen (eds.), *Internet of Medical Things in Smart Healthcare: Post-COVID-19 Pandemic Scenario.* Apple Academic Press: 77–98.
22. N. M. George, E. Rosero, S. Mayakannan, A. Shameem, S. Divya, and N. Arul. 2025. Enhancing industrial automation flexibility through neural network-empowered machine vision applications. In A. Gupta, M. Hinchey, and Z. Zalevsky (eds.), *Artificial Intelligence and Its Applications. Communications in Computer and Information Science*, 2307. Springer, Cham. https://doi.org/10.1007/978-3-031-84397-6_17
23. M. Jaiswal, U. R. Manchattahalli, V. S. Devi, M. S., M. S. Jacob, and A. A. Jose. 2026. Predictive analysis of Internet use and risk among children and adolescents via machine learning. In *2026 Sixth International Conference on Advances in Electrical, Computing, Communications and Sustainable Technologies (ICAECT)*, Bhilai, India: 1–6.

24. J. Gilda S., M. S. Jacob, V. Bhanu Rekha, U. R. Manchattahalli, V. Seedha Devi, and A. Jose Anand. 2025. Enhancing the performance of energy-harvesting wireless sensor networks through machine learning-based energy prediction. In *2025 10th International Conference on Communication and Electronics Systems (ICCES)*, Coimbatore, India: 1558–1563.
25. K. Kalaiselvi, S. Bairavel, S. Sumathi, M. Kanipriya, A. Govindaram, and A. Jose Anand. 2026. Predictive modelling of COVID-19 patient outcomes using deep learning techniques. *Diyala Journal of Engineering Sciences*, 19 (1): 96–110.
26. M. Mohammad, M. S. Khan, and R. A. Faridi. 2019. Assessment of urban heat islands effect and land surface temperature of Noida, India by using Landsat satellite data. *Mapan – Journal of Metrology Society of India*, 34 (4): 431–441.
27. M. Shakir Khan, M. Suhail, and T. Alharbi. 2018. Evaluation of urban growth and land use transformation in Riyadh using Landsat satellite data. *Arabian Journal of Geosciences*, 11: 540. https://doi.org/10.1007/s12517-018-3896-5
28. M. S. Khan, M. Zubair, D. Verma, A. H. Naqvi, A. Azam, and M. K. Bhardwaj. 2011. The study of indoor radon in the urban dwellings using plastic track detectors. *Environmental Earth Sciences*, 63 (2): 279–282.
29. M. S. Khan, A. H. Naqvi, A. Azam, and D. S. Srivastava. 2011. Radium and radon exhalation studies of soil. *Radiation Protection Dosimetry*, 8 (4): 207–210.
30. I. Y. Hafez, A. Y. Hafez, A. Saleh, et al. 2025. A systematic review of AI-enhanced techniques in credit card fraud detection. *Journal of Big Data*, 12: 6. https://doi.org/10.1186/s40537-024-01048-8
31. N. Capuano, G. Fenza, V. Loia, and C. Stanzione. 2022. Explainable artificial intelligence in cybersecurity: A survey. *IEEE Access*, 10: 93575–93600.
32. S. Yashini Priyankha, S. Sumathi, T. Mangavarkarasi, A. Jose Anand, and M. Sathiyanarayanan. 2024. Predicting ventilation needs in intensive care unit. In A. Jose Anand, K. Kalaiselvi, and Jyotir Moy Chatterje (Eds.), *Artificial Intelligence-Based System Models in Healthcare* (pp. 311–328). Wiley, Scrivener Publishing. https://doi.org/10.1002/9781394242528.ch13
33. K. Saravanan, I. Pineda, F. Baltodano, K. Vishavadia, V. Valverde, and A. Jose Anand. 2024. Chat bots for medical enquiries. In A. Jose Anand, K. Kalaiselvi, and Jyotir Moy Chatterje (Eds.), *Artificial Intelligence-Based System Models in Healthcare* (Ch-16, pp. 389–424). Wiley, Scrivener Publishing. https://doi.org/10.1002/9781394242528.ch16
34. A. Ravisankar, P. Manikandan, I. Muda, S. V. Kulkarni, R. Marcel Torres Castillo, and A. Jose Anand. 2024. Secured health insurance management. In A. Jose Anand, K. Kalaiselvi, and Jyotir Moy Chatterje (Eds.), *Artificial Intelligence-Based System Models in Healthcare* (Ch-17, pp. 425–448). Wiley, Scrivener Publishing. https://doi.org/10.1002/9781394242528.ch17
35. A. Jose Anand, R. Kesavan, R. Rajasree, R. Geetha, S. Vidhya, and M. A. Mukunthan. 2024. Machine vision based sign prediction for speech impaired person. *2024 International Conference on Sustainable Communication Networks and Application (ICSCNA)*, Theni, India, pp. 881–885.
36. S. Mahalakshmi, A. Jose Anand, and P. Partheeban. 2025. Soil and crop interaction analysis for yield prediction with satellite imagery and deep learning techniques for the coastal regisons. *Journal of Environmental Management*, 380: 125095.
37. A. Govindaram, J. S. Prasath, K. Jayasakthi, N. Rajkumar, G. Porkodi, and Jose Anand A. 2025. Structured process on FL for big data analysis. *2025 6th International Conference on Mobile Computing and Sustainable Informatics (ICMCSI)*, Goathgaun, Nepal, pp. 641–647.
38. A. Govindaram, J. S. Prasath, A. Suganya, K. Jayasakthi, N. Rajkumar, and Jose Anand A. 2025. Federated learning in big data with IoT for intrusion detection. *2025 6th International Conference on Mobile Computing and Sustainable Informatics (ICMCSI)*, Goathgaun, Nepal, pp. 252–258.
39. J. L. Mazher Iqbal, A. Selwin Mich Priyadharson, T. Manikandan, V. S. Janani, and A. Jose Anand. 2023. Low-power VLSI design using clock-gated technique. In S. Birla, S. Kant Dargar, N. Singh, and P. Sivakumar (Eds.), *Low Power Designs in Nanodevices and Circuits for Emerging Applications* (Ch-1, pp. 1–16). CRC Press.

40. J. L. Mazher Iqbal, G. Narayan, T. Manikandan, M. Meena, and Jose Anand. 2023. Low power and low area multiplier and accumulator block for efficient implementation of FIR filter. In S. Birla, S. Kant Dargar, N. Singh, and P. Sivakumar (Eds.), *Low Power Designs in Nanodevices and Circuits for Emerging Applications* (Ch-16, pages 16). CRC Press.
41. M. Mahalakshmi, D. C. Diana, R. Ramachandran, S. Kumar Ravva, B. Illuri, J. Jeba Johannah, T. Manikandan, and A. Jose Anand. 2025. Review on carbon-based micro and nano electromechanical systems for biotechnological application. *Recent Patents on Nanotechnology*, 19 (4): 468–482.
42. R. B. Kumar, A. Baplawat, P. Prabakaran, A. P. Sridhar, B. Saraswathi, and M. R. Rani. 2025. Artificial intelligence in forensic sciences: Bridging systematic challenges with next-generation applications. *Journal of Neonatal Surgery*, 14: 639–650.
43. S. Maheswari, N. Rajkumar, R. Geetha, K. Theja, M. Malleswari, and Jose Anand A. 2025. A comparative analysis of IoT platform tools: Security and scalability preferences in device management using AHP. *2025 International Conference on Visual Analytics and Data Visualization (ICVADV)*, Tirunelveli, India, pp. 380–385.
44. N. Rajkumar, A. Govindaram, R. Geetha, A. S. F. Subhamathi, S. Nithya, and Jose Anand A. 2025. Non-intrusive load monitoring techniques for intelligent energy management: A comparative study of FHMM and LSTM approach. *2025 International Conference on Visual Analytics and Data Visualization (ICVADV)*, Tirunelveli, India, pp. 869–874.
45. S. Vidhya, M. A. Mukunthan, M. Saragada, A. Jose Anand, R. Kesavan, and R. Rajasree. 2025. AI-based automated weed detection system using YOLOv5 and mask R-CNN for sustainable agriculture. *2025 International Conference on Advanced Computing Technologies (ICoACT)*, Sivakasi, India, pp. 1–6.
46. J. S. Prasath, S. J. Parvez, A. Govindaram, T. Anuradha, Jose Anand A., and N. Rajkumar. 2025. AI-enhanced anomaly detection in software-defined networks. *2025 International Conference on Advanced Computing Technologies (ICoACT)*, Sivakasi, India, pp. 1–7.
47. M. A. Mukunthan, Jose Anand A. A., S. Kesavan, M. Mutyala, R. Kesavan, and R. Geetha. 2024. Detection of physical anomalies in IoT networks using machine learning techniques. *2024 International Conference on Advancement in Renewable Energy and Intelligent Systems (AREIS)*, Thrissur, India, pp. 1–6.
48. M. Arshad, A. Ahmad, C. W. Onn, and E. A. Sam. 2025. Investigating methods for forensic analysis of social media data to support criminal investigations. *Frontiers in Computer Science*, 7: 1566513. https://doi.org/10.3389/fcomp.2025.1566513
49. S. Renukadevi, B. C. Manujakshi, T. M. Shashidhar, and N. Sivakumar. 2025. Fraud detection in financial transactions using gradient boost with hybrid optimization. *Journal of Machine and Computing*, 5 (4): 2328–2344.
50. J. Chou, P. Yeh, C. Liu, and K. Chen. 2026. Improving detection of pollution fee declarations for environmental policy compliance through metaheuristic-optimized ensemble learning. *Engineering, Construction and Architectural Management*, 33 (7): 5820–5848. https://doi.org/10.1108/ECAM-08-2024-1113
51. Y. S. Sangwan, S. Lal, P. Bhambri, A. Kumar, and I. S. Dhanoa. 2021. Advancements in social data security and encryption: A review. *Natural Volatiles & Essential Oils*, 8 (4): 15353–15362.
52. P. Bhambri, M. Singh, A. Jain, I. S. Dhanoa, V. K. Sinha, and S. Lal. 2021. Classification of gene expression data with the aid of optimized feature selection. *Turkish Journal of Physiotherapy and Rehabilitation*, 32 (3): 1158–1168.
53. A. Jain, M. Singh, and P. Bhambri. 2021. Performance evaluation of IPv4-IPv6 tunneling procedure using IoT. *Journal of Physics: Conference Series*, 1950 (1): Article 012010.
54. R. Rana and P. Bhambri. 2024. Generative AI-driven security frameworks for web engineering: Innovations and challenges. In I. A. Shah and N. Z. Jhanjhi (Eds.), *Generative AI for Web Engineering Models* (pp. 285–296). IGI Global.
55. P. Bhambri. 2024. Wallets and transactions. In D. Darwish (Ed.), *Decentralizing the Online Experience with Web3 Technologies* (pp. 90–106). IGI Global.
56. P. Bhambri. 2024. NFTs: Transforming digital ownership in the Web 3 era. In D. Darwish (Ed.), *Decentralizing the Online Experience with Web3 Technologies* (pp. 151–167). IGI Global.

57. G. Singh and P. Bhambri. 2023. Simulation analysis of AODV and DSDV routing protocols for secure and reliable service in mobile adhoc networks (MANETs). In P. Bhambri, S. Rani, V. E. Balas, and A. A. Elngar (Eds.), *Integration of AI-based Manufacturing and Industrial Engineering Systems with the Internet of Things* (pp. 205–216). CRC Press.
58. G. C. N. Babu, S. Gupta, P. Bhambri, L. M. Leo, B. H. Rao, and S. Kumar. 2021. A semantic health observation system development based on the IoT sensors. *Turkish Journal of Physiotherapy and Rehabilitation*, 32 (3): 1721–1729.
59. P. Bhambri, S. Bagga, D. Priya, H. Singh, and H. K. Dhiman. 2020. Suspicious human activity detection system. *Journal of ISMAC*, 2 (4): 216–221.
60. V. K. Sinha, R. Jeet, P. Bhambri, and M. Mahajan. 2020. Empowering intrusion detection in IRIS recognition system: A review. *Journal of Natural Remedies*, 21 (2): 131–153.

Chapter 14

Next-generation privileged access management

An AI-centric perspective

Erhan Yilmaz and Özgü Can

14.1 INTRODUCTION

The security of privileged identities has emerged as one of the most complex and critical challenges in enterprise cybersecurity. Concurrently, Artificial Intelligence (AI) is transforming both the threat landscape and defensive paradigms. In this context, attackers are using AI to expand, automate, and optimize their attack capabilities, while defenders are exploring AI-driven analytic techniques to interpret and manage the extensive volumes of identity and access data generated. Therefore, AI-enhanced controls for privileged access have become a fundamental prerequisite for the implementation of a realistic Zero Trust program. The main goal of this chapter is to examine AI-driven Privileged Access Management (PAM) within a broader perspective. Thus, it is necessary to acknowledge that the rapid expansion of digital infrastructures, the proliferation of interconnected systems, and the increasing complexity of enterprise access environments have collectively extended the challenges associated with securing privileged identities. Moreover, the evolving threat landscape that is characterized by sophisticated intrusion techniques, automated attack workflows, and the misuse of AI by adversaries has elevated privileged access to a central point of vulnerability. For this purpose, it is essential to understand the current landscape of cybersecurity threats and to recognize the critical role of PAM systems within enterprise security.

14.1.1 The evolving cybersecurity landscape

Over the last few years, the threat landscape has shifted from rare high-profile incidents to a continuous and industrialized attack ecosystem. In 2024, the FBI's Internet Crime Complaint Center (IC3) received 263,455 cyber threat complaints, resulting in reported losses of $1.571 billion. More than 4,800 of these complaints were from organizations in critical infrastructure sectors, where ransomware and data breaches were the most frequently reported threats [1]. Independent sources of threat intelligence present a comparable outlook. Corvus Insurance's analysis of ransomware leak sites shows 5,243 victims posted in 2024, a 15% increase over 2023 and more than 195 million records exposed globally [2]. The 2024 State of Ransomware report by BlackFog describes 2024 as a "record-breaking year", highlighting the emergence of 48 new ransomware groups and the prevalence of data exfiltration in 94% of observed attacks. This underscores the intertwining of extortion with data theft, indicating a shift from mere encryption to a more sinister and coordinated approach [3].

The number and variety of actors using generative AI to create phishing content, automate reconnaissance, and generate deepfakes are also increasing rapidly. Microsoft reports

DOI: 10.1201/9781003656487-14

that actors from Russia, China, Iran, and North Korea employed AI-enabled techniques to influence targets in the U.S. and its allied nations hundreds of times within a single month [4]. Additionally, identity has emerged as the primary attack surface. The Ponemon Institute reported that only 45% of organizations consider themselves adequately prepared to protect identities when attackers leverage AI-driven capabilities [5]. Besides, fewer than half have implemented risk-based authentication, and only 37% use AI-based security technologies to continuously monitor authenticated user sessions for signs of misuse. These findings indicate that most companies have not yet strengthened their defenses, although attackers are already exploiting AI aggressively [6–11]. The convergence of industrialized ransomware, AI-augmented threat actors, and uneven implementation of advanced identity controls has fostered a threat-prone environment for privileged accounts. The compromise of a single highly privileged identity can result in extensive operational disruption, significant regulatory penalties, and reputational damage, often occurring within hours rather than weeks or months.

14.1.2 The critical role of PAM in modern enterprise security

PAM has emerged as one of the core technical pillars for operationalizing Zero Trust principles in real environments. PAM integrates the processes and technologies employed to identify, secure, broker, and monitor access for accounts and identities with the potential to significantly impact the system. These identities include administrators, service accounts, machine identities, and just-in-time elevated roles. Santucci et al. [12] propose an eight-pillar Zero Trust model and rank PAM as a key control within the "Users" pillar, alongside Identity and Access Management (IAM), Identity Governance and Administration (IGA), and real-time risk detection. The proposed analysis shows that privileged identities require controls like session monitoring and lifecycle integration between IGA and PAM to prevent over-provisioning and unchecked movement. The U.S. Cybersecurity and Infrastructure Security Agency's Zero Trust Maturity Model also emphasizes the need for automated, time-bounded authorization and review of privileged access to achieve advanced maturity [13]. Market data consistently reflects the strategic importance of PAM systems. According to Grand View Research, the global PAM market generated USD 3.29 billion in revenue in 2024 and is projected to reach approximately USD 9.39 billion by 2030, with a compound annual growth rate (CAGR) of 19.7% between 2025 and 2030 [14]. As illustrated in Figure 14.1, this growth rate is significant, even when assessed within the broader context of the cybersecurity industry.

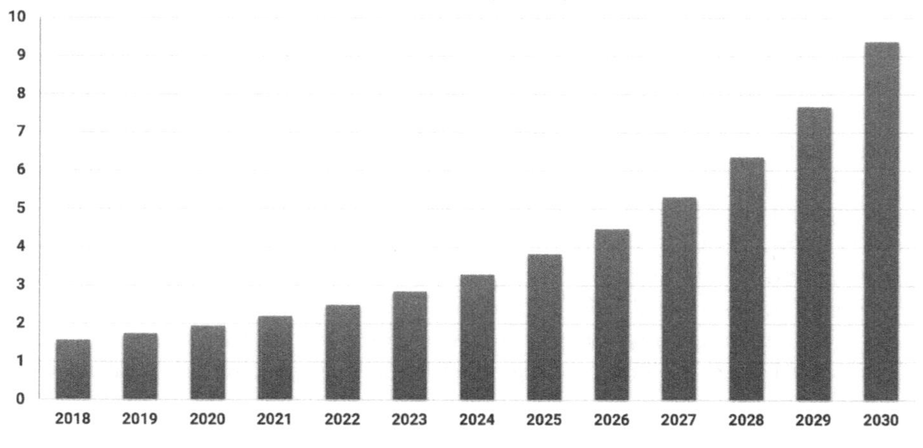

Figure 14.1 Global PAM market forecast, 2018–2030 (US$M).

Consequently, PAM has evolved from a specialized compliance instrument to a fundamental control category, particularly within highly regulated sectors such as finance, healthcare, and critical infrastructure. However, the Ponemon study indicates that only approximately 45% of organizations that have a dedicated PAM platform consider it to be "very" or "highly" effective [5]. Many deployments still focus on basic vaulting and credential rotation. Advanced capabilities, such as just-in-time elevation, adaptive controls, and AI-assisted session analysis, remain underutilized, resulting in a significant residual risk of privileged misuse.

14.1.3 Emergence of AI-driven approaches in identity and access security

In recent years, a significant amount of research has emerged at the intersection of AI and identity security. Studies indicate that AI has the potential to transform the way IAM and PAM systems identify risk, adapt access decisions in real time, and scale operational processes. At a conceptual level, Hsia's work argues that AI-enhanced IAM enables continuous, context-aware risk assessment for every access request, replacing static rules with behaviorally informed policies [15]. Pasala's [16] study mentions that AI-driven IAM functions similarly to a nervous system, where identity is the main perimeter. AI models constantly check user behavior, device signals, and environmental context to decide if trust is valid. Although much of this literature addresses IAM broadly, its implications for PAM are direct. Privileged activities account for a small subset of overall access events. However, they carry a significantly higher risk. AI-driven models that have been trained on privileged session data can identify deviations that would be invisible to human reviewers or static policies. Pan et al.'s study [17] is an early example of this approach, applying deep-learning-based text reading to extract user actions from remote desktop sessions and automatically audit fine-grained privileged operations. Despite this potential, the adoption of AI-driven IAM and PAM solutions remains uneven across organizations. The Ponemon 2024 study reports that only 37% of surveyed organizations currently use AI security technology to continuously monitor authenticated sessions, and fewer than half feel ready to defend identities against AI-enabled attackers [5]. The gap between research, market trends, and real-world deployment is a central motivation for examining AI-driven PAM. While the underlying technical building blocks are mature, significant challenges and barriers to effective implementation persist.

14.1.4 Scope, methodology, and structure of the chapter

This chapter explores AI-driven PAM as an emerging discipline at the intersection of privileged identity management, behavioral analytics, and Zero Trust architecture. PAM is treated not as a standalone vaulting tool, but as part of a broader security stack. Methodologically, the chapter integrates the following approaches:

- A structured literature review of academic and practitioner research on AI in IAM and privileged behavior analytics, with a focus on work published between 2019 and 2025.
- Analysis of industry data and market reports, including PAM market forecasts and Zero Trust adoption surveys, to quantify the economic and organizational context in which AI-driven PAM is being developed and deployed.
- Synthesize vendor-neutral best-practice guidance to anchor the discussion of AI-enabled capabilities in frameworks.

The remainder of the chapter is organized as follows. Section 14.2 provides a background on traditional PAM architectures, threat models, and their integration into IAM and Zero Trust strategies. Section 14.3 surveys existing AI-driven techniques relevant to privileged access, including anomaly detection, user and entity behavior analytics (UEBA), natural language and computer-vision approaches for session analysis, and reinforcement learning for policy optimization. Section 14.4 presents a SWOT (Strengths, Weaknesses, Opportunities, and Threats) analysis of AI-driven PAM solutions, considering technical, organizational, regulatory, and ethical dimensions. Section 14.5 explores future directions, such as AI-aware identity fabrics, autonomous remediation for privileged sessions, and governance models for AI in PAM. By the end of the chapter, the aim is to provide a comprehensive overview and a pragmatic roadmap of AI-driven PAM. The chapter outlines what the technology can realistically achieve today, its future directions, and the gaps that researchers, vendors, and practitioners must address to ensure the trustworthy and large-scale implementation of AI-enabled privileged access.

14.2 BACKGROUND AND CONCEPTUAL FOUNDATIONS

Before discussing AI-driven PAM, it is essential to explicitly define the concept of privileged access, outline the current traditional PAM methods, and highlight the gaps that AI can realistically address.

14.2.1 Fundamentals of privileged access management

PAM is a subset of the broader IAM domain that focuses specifically on accounts and identities capable of performing security-relevant or high-impact actions. According to NIST's guidance on privileged account management for the financial services sector, these accounts are "*the keys to the kingdom*". They are used to access and manage an organization's information assets and systems and perform tasks that ordinary users are not permitted to perform [18]. Similarly, the U.S. Federal Privileged Identity Playbook recommends a dedicated "privileged user management" capability for identifying, tracking, monitoring, and auditing such accounts [19]. Kosinski [20] frames PAM as the discipline that governs and secures privileged accounts (e.g., administrator accounts) and privileged activities (e.g., working with sensitive data). In summary, PAM reduces the risk of concentrated power by controlling access, monitoring it, and holding privileged persons accountable.

14.2.2 Types of privileged accounts

In practical and real-world contexts, the privileged account does not refer to a single category. Privileged accounts encompass a variety of roles with elevated access rights, each presenting unique security risks and management challenges. Their scope can range from system administrators and database accounts to service accounts and application-level identities. The types of privileged accounts are illustrated in Figure 14.2.

Standards and best practice frameworks typically classify accounts and identities into the following distinct typologies:

- **Individual Administrator Account:** These are named accounts tied to a person (for example, an Active Directory domain admin or a Kubernetes cluster administrator). Microsoft's privileged access guidance recommends dedicated, separate admin accounts used only for administrative work [21].

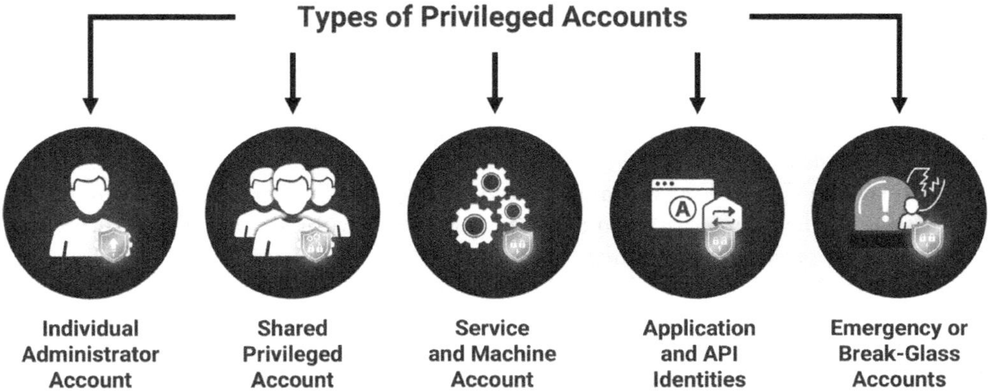

Figure 14.2 Types of privileged accounts.

- **Shared Privileged Accounts**: Shared privileged accounts refer to local "root" or "Administrator" accounts, database administrator accounts, or application super-user roles. These accounts are used by system administrators, application administrators, or database administrators [19].
- **Service and Machine Accounts**: These accounts run background services, scheduled tasks, or automation scripts and often hold long-lived credentials or keys [22].
- **Application and API Identities**: Modern PAM must manage API tokens, OAuth clients, cloud IAM roles, and similar "headless" identities with powerful access to data stores, CI/CD systems, robotic process automation (RPA) tools, or cloud control planes. Ylonen et al. [23] emphasize that while automated SSH-based access with key authentication can carry very high privileges, it has historically lacked proper lifecycle management.
- **Emergency or "Break-Glass" Accounts**: These are highly privileged accounts used only when normal administrative paths fail. PAM guidelines recommend strict controls and continuous monitoring for such accounts, as they often bypass standard workflows [19].

From a risk perspective, the categories are defined not by the technology itself but by the explosion radius. The compromise or misuse of any one of these categories has the potential to result in rapid lateral movement, mass data exfiltration, or destructive changes.

14.2.3 Core PAM functions: credential vaulting, session monitoring, JIT access

Modern PAM platforms implement a consistent set of core capabilities, building on protecting, monitoring, and managing privileged account access across its lifecycle. Common functions of privileged accounts include the following [19, 24]:

- **Discovery and Onboarding**: Automatically identifying privileged accounts, SSH keys, and secrets across directories, servers, network devices, cloud platforms, and applications.
- **Credential Vaulting and Rotation**: Privileged credentials are stored in a hardened vault. Passwords are automatically rotated, and controlled workflows are enforced to manage the secure check-in and check-out of credentials.

- **Session Brokering and Isolation**: PAM systems broker privileged connections (e.g., RDP or SSH) by masking or injecting credentials. Therefore, credential theft is reduced, and all privileged activity is allowed to flow through a controlled and monitored gateway.
- **Session Recording and Monitoring**: PAM systems record video, keystrokes, and command histories for privileged sessions, supporting forensics, accountability, and real-time supervision.
- **Just-in-Time (JIT) Elevation and** Zero Standing Privilege: PAM platforms can issue short-lived elevations or ephemeral accounts and revoke them automatically, instead of granting permanent administrator rights.
- **Approval Workflows and Policy Enforcement:** PAM enforces approval workflows, ticket integration, and policy checks (e.g., certain roles can request access to specific systems during defined maintenance windows).
- **Reporting, Compliance, and Integration**: PAM feeds detailed logs and session metadata into SIEM and SOAR platforms to support compliance reporting, threat hunting, and incident response.

Collectively, these functions provide PAM systems with comprehensive visibility into the usage of high-value privileges. This information forms the critical dataset on which AI-driven techniques rely.

14.2.4 Artificial intelligence and machine learning technologies for PAM

The AI and Machine Learning (ML) techniques applicable to PAM are largely similar to those being explored across the cybersecurity field. These include supervised and unsupervised learning, deep learning (DL) for sequence and graph data, behavioral analytics and anomaly detection, and, more recently, natural language processing (NLP) and large language models (LLMs) applied to logs, policies, and session data [25–30]. Many PAM use cases, such as insider threat detection and user behavior modeling, exemplify the practical application of AI techniques in monitoring and securing privileged accounts. In supervised settings, models learn from examples of benign and malicious privileged actions. Earlier studies, including Sharma et al.'s [31] LSTM autoencoder, have demonstrated that sequence-based DL can accurately identify deviations in user activity. However, labeled datasets for privileged misuse are typically limited. This makes unsupervised and semi-supervised approaches, including autoencoders, clustering, and anomaly detection ensembles, particularly attractive. Studies by Yuan and Wu [32] and Le and Zincir-Heywood [33] show that unsupervised models can reliably baseline complex behavioral patterns in logs and detect deviations without explicit labels. Recent advancements in the field include Federated Learning (FL), which allows organizations to train models on sensitive PAM data without centralizing logs, as demonstrated in the study by Ye et al. [34].

User and Entity Behavior Analytics (UEBA) provides a practical link between traditional PAM and AI. UEBA models user and system behavior to detect anomalies that may indicate compromised accounts or insider abuse. Industry solutions emphasize this capability, as static rule-based approaches often fail to capture the subtle and evolving behavioral patterns associated with emerging threats. Academic research continues to refine these techniques, improving their robustness, interpretability, and applicability to complex security environments. As demonstrated by Pennada et al. [35], the employment of hybrid ML/DL models operating on time-related, logon-related, and file access features has been shown to enhance detection accuracy. DL-based log analysis frameworks like LogBERT enhance anomaly detection in privileged sessions by modeling sequential log behaviors at scale [36].

14.2.5 Why PAM is uniquely positioned for AI augmentation

Many AI techniques are already applied to network security, endpoint detection, and IAM. PAM is a promising and necessary target for AI augmentation. Privileged activities occur infrequently, yet they carry significantly higher risk. PAM is at the core of the critical system operations, where high-risk sessions are initiated, elevated, and routed. As a result, PAM provides rich data for ML, including vault checkouts, elevation requests, recordings, streams, and approvals, each containing dense security-relevant signals that can be leveraged for advanced analytics [37]. Many PAM workflows are ticket-driven and outcome-driven. A session is associated with a specific change ticket, maintenance window, or incident. This structure simplifies the derivation of labels, an essential requirement for supervised and semi-supervised learning approaches, in contrast to free-form network telemetry [32]. Insider threat research focuses on user behavior, access logs, and subtle deviations, aligning closely with PAM use cases. AI can detect complex behavioral signatures and adapt across organizations without centralizing raw data, as shown by DL and FL approaches [32]. PAM provides the structural framework, whereas AI contributes the analytical logic required for dynamic decision-making. The remainder of this chapter examines current AI integration strategies, evaluates their effectiveness, and critically assesses the persistent challenges that constrain the advancement of autonomous and high-assurance security systems.

14.3 AI-DRIVEN PAM SOLUTIONS

In recent years, there has been a clear shift toward systems that integrate privileged access governance with continuous, data-driven analytics, rather than static, rule-based PAM controls. Both commercial platforms and research prototypes are converging on similar design patterns, including behavioral baselining, risk-adaptive controls, and an increased reliance on LLMs to interpret logs, session activity, and policy structures. This section examines the primary domains in which AI is currently augmenting PAM. The discussion encompasses AI-enhanced anomaly detection within privileged sessions, ML-driven risk scoring and adaptive access controls, the use of LLMs for policy generation and review, and the emerging convergence of AI and Zero Trust principles in modern PAM architectures.

14.3.1 AI-enhanced anomaly detection in privileged sessions

Bhavesh et al.'s [38] recent guidance on monitoring privileged accounts uses ML to detect unusual actions by a super admin, such as identity changes, to identify subtle compromises that static rules miss. PAM vendors are applying these ideas directly to privileged sessions. PAM vendors use AI/ML models to continuously profile privileged users (e.g., commands used, systems accessed, and time patterns) and flag anomalies without extensive manual rule creation [39]. Some startups prioritize real-time anomaly detection over PAM workflows, leveraging ML to identify "typical" elevation paths and instantly pinpoint outliers [40]. This trend reflects a broad consensus, mirrored in insider-threat research, that ML-driven behavioral analytics are more effective than static thresholds at detecting the low-and-slow misuse of privileged accounts [41].

14.3.2 ML-driven risk scoring and adaptive access controls

Beyond detection, AI is increasingly used to score identity and session risk and to adapt access decisions in near real time. Pasala's [16] study on AI-driven identity and access management makes the argument that Zero Trust programs are shifting from simple yes/no decisions about access to continuous, risk-based authorization. In this new model, ML models ingest data about the device's posture, geolocation, behavioral history, and resource sensitivity. These trends align with research on AI-based trust scoring and continuous access evaluation. Recent studies include ML-driven privilege escalation detection in cloud environments [42].

14.3.3 LLMs for policy generation and review

LLMs are increasingly transforming the way PAM and identity teams write, review, and interpret access policies. In terms of logs and sessions, Boffa et al.'s [43] LogPrécis framework uses language models to tag attacker tactics and cluster similar malicious behaviors in Unix logs. Karlsen et al. [44] benchmarked 60 fine-tuned language models for log classification and demonstrated that the top models achieved an average F1 score of 0.998 across multiple security log datasets. This result underscores the ability of text-centric models to power highly accurate security analytics. Regarding the policy aspect, Jayasundara et al.'s [45] study discusses the use of NLP and ML to transform natural-language requirements into policies. The study also emphasizes the need for human oversight due to limitations in reliability and adaptation issues. Their follow-up framework employs retrieval-augmented generation, transforming policy documents into access-control rules with an F1 score of 80.6% following iterative verification and refinement [46]. These techniques can be applied within PAM to summarize complex privileged access policies, recommend safer default configurations, and review policy exceptions for unintended privilege escalation.

14.3.4 Zero trust and AI convergence in PAM

Zero Trust programs treat PAM as a central control plane. Pasala's [16] work on AI-driven IAM frames Zero Trust as a continuous risk-evaluation loop. Behavioral analytics, context, and policy are evaluated for every request, including privileged ones. Ahmadi's [47] study for autonomous identity-based threat segmentation in Zero Trust architectures goes further, using AI to assign real-time risk scores to identities and automatically adjust permissions and segmentation boundaries. AI-driven trust scoring and continuous access evaluation, originally explored in insider-threat detection and privilege-escalation research, are increasingly being reused as decision signals in Zero Trust-oriented PAM platforms [37].

14.4 AN EXTENSIVE ANALYSIS OF AI-DRIVEN PAM

AI is already changing how organizations discover, monitor, and control privileged access. However, it also introduces new technical and governance risks. In this chapter, a structured SWOT approach is conducted to provide a detailed discussion based on practical realities, highlighting both current effective measures and areas where compensating controls are required.

14.4.1 Strengths

ML models can detect patterns of "normal" privileged activity, identifying the users, systems, and times of access. DL-based insider threat work shows that these models can identify subtle behavioral differences in high-dimensional log data [32]. Evaluations of the ML-based insider threat detection research indicate that behavioral baselining has evolved into a mainstream technique and is no longer considered merely experimental. AI-driven insider-risk systems and UEBA tools demonstrate measurable gains in detection quality and speed. Koli et al.'s [48] insider risk management platform has been demonstrated to reduce false positives by 59%, improve true positive detections by 30%, and decrease response time by 47% once risk scoring is automated and integrated into workflows. PAM can prioritize high-risk sessions and access requests, reducing the chance that a critical signal gets lost in a queue of tickets. AI-driven IAM studies state that risk-based, continuous evaluation reduces the need for manual role tuning and one-off exception handling, especially in Zero Trust programs [16]. AI can automate repetitive administrative tasks, such as risk scoring, recommending least-privilege policies, and triaging automated session recordings. Therefore, AI enables administrators to concentrate on more strategic security responsibilities.

14.4.2 Weaknesses

Research on insider threats and behavior analysis shows a lack of high-quality, labeled data on malicious privileged activity, with more data on non-malicious events. A comprehensive review of the relevant studies reveals several significant constraints that limit the potential for enhancement in the accuracy of detection. These limitations include class imbalance and label scarcity, as well as the use of synthetic datasets [32, 41]. Even with advanced models, insider threat surveys indicate that false positives remain a persistent issue, while false negatives are difficult to quantify and may have potentially catastrophic consequences [41]. Anomaly-based systems often misclassify routine maintenance tasks as suspicious. Efforts to over-tune these systems in order to reduce noise can inadvertently create blind spots. AI-driven PAM encounters similar trade-offs, requiring continuous tuning and iterative feedback loops to maintain accuracy and reliability. In high-stakes access control scenarios, relying solely on model outputs to justify access decisions is insufficient. Research on explainable AI (XAI) for detecting malicious insiders indicates that, despite their effectiveness, DL models often remain opaque when applied in real-world contexts [49]. The field also currently lacks standard metrics to assess the explainability of AI-driven cybersecurity systems, complicating efforts to ensure transparency and accountability. A key limitation of PAM lies in its lack of transparency, as automated actions can inadvertently lock out administrators or prevent the execution of urgent changes [50–52].

14.4.3 Opportunities

Research studies highlight the efficacy of continuous, risk-adaptive authorization, in which access decisions are dynamically adjusted (granted, restricted, or revoked) according to contextual and behavioral indicators [16, 48]. Within a PAM context, this means policy engines that choose the best combination of just-in-time (JIT) elevation, additional verification steps, or session shadowing for routine access scenarios. AI-driven IAM for Zero Trust positions privileged access as a decision signal in a unified identity framework [16]. Studies on identity-based segmentation and insider risk scoring support this approach, indicating that identity, device posture, network micro-segments, and privileged workflows can all contribute to a risk model [48]. From a vendor perspective, PAM evolves into a valuable analytics resource, transforming into an integrated repository of operational and security-relevant information.

14.4.4 Threats

Research has shown that security analytics models can be bypassed or corrupted by malicious actors using carefully crafted inputs or poisoned training data. Recent studies on adversarial ML for Network Intrusion Detection Systems (NIDS) and meta-surveys conducted in recent years have emphasized the potential for minor perturbations to cause DL models to misclassify malicious traffic [53]. These techniques could be used against PAM analytics, for example, by gradually "teaching" a behavioral model to classify risky patterns as normal or by poisoning FL pipelines. Integrating AI into PAM increases system complexity, including additional data pipelines, model dependencies, and potential failure modes. Reviews of insider-detection systems and XAI systems show that effective operation requires specialized skills, robust ML operations, and continuous model monitoring [32]. Over-reliance on AI without adequate fallback mechanisms introduces systemic risk. Besides, if models silently fail or degrade, they can weaken the most critical layer of access control. The key factors identified in this SWOT analysis are consolidated in Figure 14.3. The figure presents the SWOT matrix for AI-driven PAM. The matrix provides a guide for researchers by clarifying where current strengths can be leveraged, which weaknesses require mitigation, and how emerging opportunities and threats are likely to influence future development directions.

14.5 FUTURE DIRECTIONS

AI-driven PAM is still in its early stages, yet it is progressing rapidly. The next wave of development is expected to advance systems beyond "assistive analytics" toward more autonomous, cross-domain, and privacy-preserving control mechanisms for managing privileged access. The directions discussed in this section highlight current research developments and outline their potential impact on PAM roadmaps over the next three to five years.

14.5.1 Autonomous PAM (auto-PAM) systems

AI-driven PAM is moving towards "Auto-PAM" systems that can observe, decide, and act within pre-defined guardrails. In Zero Trust access control, ML has been used to learn dynamic access policies that adapt in real time to changing risk conditions. Ahmadi et al.

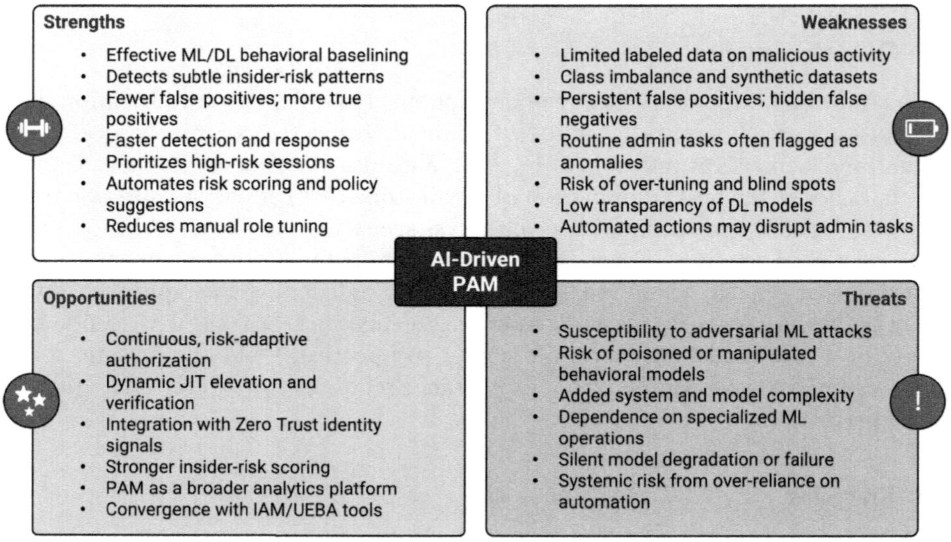

Figure 14.3 SWOT matrix for AI-driven PAM.

[47] introduce autonomous identity-based threat segmentation, using ML to segment identities and resources into dynamic risk zones in Zero Trust architectures. Auto-PAM would score privileged sessions, automatically adjust entitlements, expire orphaned privileges, and preemptively block or throttle sessions when risk crosses a threshold. It would also keep human approval for high-impact actions. This aligns with industry work on "agentic" AI for security operations, where AI agents can take pre-approved actions like those related to incident response and containment [54].

14.5.2 AI-driven JIT provisioning and ephemeral identity models

JIT access is a best practice in PAM. However, policies are often static and lack granularity. Research shows that blockchain, smart contracts, and advanced cryptography can express and enforce fine-grained and dynamic policies. Nie et al. [55] design a Zero Trust access control mechanism for IoT that uses blockchain-based smart contracts and inner-product encryption to enforce fine-grained and reputation-aware access in a 6G environment. A similar pattern can also be applied to privileged identities. AI models infer the necessary permissions, generate temporary identities, and bind them to strong contextual constraints. Combining policy learning and formal constraints is a promising way to avoid over-granting or under-granting permissions [56]. This AI-driven JIT model is relevant for machine identities, DevOps pipelines, and short-lived cloud workloads, where human approvals are impractical.

14.5.3 Predictive security and proactive risk mitigation

Current PAM uses AI to detect anomalies as they occur. Next, predictive PAM uses models to anticipate when misuse will occur and takes preemptive steps. Federated and centralized anomaly detection work suggests that time-series models and deep architectures can forecast deviations in network and user behavior. Lim et al.'s [57] review of FL for anomaly detection highlights how FL can support real-time, distributed anomaly prediction with reduced privacy risk. Research on insider threats is also moving toward richer behavioral modeling. Ye et al. [34] propose a personalized FL approach that converts behavior logs into image-like features and uses CNNs for insider threat detection. PAM models can forecast which privileged identities are moving toward a "high-risk" cluster based on subtle trends in ticket history, login timing, command sequences, and peer comparison. These models can then tighten controls, shorten session durations, or require peer approval for sensitive operations before an incident materializes.

14.5.4 Federated learning and privacy-preserving analytics for PAM

Sensitive PAM telemetry includes administrator commands, database queries, and application payloads, making privacy and regulatory considerations central to any model trained on such data. Consequently, FL emerges as a natural fit. Ye et al.'s [34] study shows how personalized FL can be used for insider threat detection, preserving data locality while still achieving high accuracy. Zhang et al. [58] provide a survey of FL for intrusion detection, cataloging threat models, aggregation strategies, and open issues such as data heterogeneity and poisoning. Lim et al. [57] extend this approach with a systematic review on FL for anomaly detection, proposing benchmarking frameworks and highlighting the trade-offs between scalability, real-time performance, and robustness. Amiri-Zarandi et al. [59] present a federated and explainable insider-threat detection framework for IoT, combining FL with interpretable models, not just black-box deep networks. Adversarial-robust FL with secure aggregation creates high-quality, privacy-compliant AI models for PAM [60–63].

14.6 CONCLUSION

AI-driven PAM represents a natural evolution in privileged access security. It is shaped by three converging realities: a rapidly expanding attack surface, the central role of identity in Zero Trust architectures, and significant advances in ML and LLMs. This chapter presents an analysis demonstrating that AI improves privileged-access oversight through behavioral baselining, anomaly detection, and automated risk scoring [64–67]. Additionally, it introduces new challenges related to explainability, data quality, adversarial robustness, and governance. From a strategic standpoint, vendors must treat AI as a product capability that requires robust data pipelines, transparency, and appropriate safeguards. Researchers can address existing gaps by developing datasets for privileged behavior, standard benchmarks, and XAI techniques capable of justifying high-risk access decisions. Concurrently, practitioners should integrate AI as a decision-support system layered on foundational PAM hygiene, enabling automation for well-defined and bounded actions. In brief, achieving trustworthy AI-driven PAM depends on the following three essential pillars:

- Clear governance and accountability ensuring explainable, reviewable, and regulatory-compliant AI decisions.
- Privacy-preserving models that use FL and robust protection against adversarial manipulation.
- Open collaboration where the community develops shared datasets and evaluation frameworks and safe design patterns.

The establishment of these foundational elements is instrumental in facilitating the evolution of AI-driven PAM into a scalable and dependable security layer. This evolution is characterized by the continuous understanding of privileged behavior, the adaptation to changing risk, and the support of human operators rather than their replacement.

ACKNOWLEDGMENT

This study is supported by The Scientific and Technological Research Council of Turkey (TÜBİTAK) under grant number 125E156.

REFERENCES

1. The Federal Bureau of Investigation. 2025. *Annual Internet Crime Report*. https://www.ic3.gov/AnnualReport/Reports/2024_IC3Report.pdf. Accessed November 19.
2. K. Kalaiselvi, S. Bairavel, S. Sumathi, M. Kanipriya, A. Govindaram, and A. Jose Anand. 2026. Predictive modelling of COVID-19 patient outcomes using deep learning techniques. *Diyala Journal of Engineering Sciences*, 19 (1): 96–110.
3. V. B. Rekha, U. R. Manchattahalli, S. Nithya, V. S. Devi, A. J. Anand, and M. S. Jacob. 2025. Data-driven predictive modeling of brain responses under morphological priming using machine learning. In *2025 International Conference on Electrical and Electronics Engineering (ICE3)*, Gorakhpur, India: 1–6.

4. V. Priyanka, S. Lekshmi Raveendran, R. Kesavan, U. Sandhya, T. Anuradha, and A. Jose Anand. 2026. Analysis and comparison of cloud data storage services with a practical study on Google Drive. In *2026 6th International Conference on Expert Clouds and Applications (ICOECA)*, Bengaluru, India: 924–930.
5. S. Jerril Gilda and A. Jose Anand. 2026. Reinforcement learning based power management and cost minimization in fuel cell, battery, and super capacitor driven electric vehicle. *Iranian Journal of Science and Technology, Transactions of Electrical Engineering*: 1–25.
6. Moyeenudin, H. M., M. Narender, J. Amutharaj, S. Hari Kumar, and Jose A. A. 2023. Comparative Analysis of Video Transmission in Vehicular Networks using IEEE 802.11g and IEEE 802.11p Standards. *2023 First International Conference on Advances in Electrical, Electronics and Computational Intelligence (ICAEECI)*, Tiruchengode, India, 2023, pp. 1–7.
7. Maheswari, R., M. Pughazhandhe, S. Ragavan, R. Sasikaran, S. Siva, and Jose A. Anand. 2023. Augmented Reality Home Automation Using AR Switches with IoT. *2023 International Conference on Self Sustainable Artificial Intelligence Systems (ICSSAS)*, Erode, India, pp. 1681–1688.
8. Karuppiah, S., A. T., K. Sivachandar, B. Thyla, Dhivya D., and Jose A. Anand. 2024. Conceptualization of a Cardiac Monitoring System via Bluetooth Communication Protocol to Mobile Devices. *2024 2nd International Conference on Intelligent Data Communication Technologies and Internet of Things (IDCIoT)*, Bengaluru, India, pp. 859–866.
9. Hemalatha, S., M. Mahalakshmi, V. Vignesh, M. Geethalakshmi, D. Balasubramanian, and Jose A. Anand. 2023. Deep Learning Approaches for Intrusion Detection with Emerging Cybersecurity Challenges. *2023 International Conference on Sustainable Communication Networks and Application (ICSCNA)*, Theni, India, pp. 1522–1529.
10. Reshma, R. and A. J. Anand. 2023. Predictive and Comparative Analysis of LENET, ALEXNET and VGG-16 Network Architecture in Smart Behavior Monitoring. *2023 Seventh International Conference on Image Information Processing (ICIIP)*, Solan, India, pp. 450–453.
11. Abiramasundari, V., B. Thyla, and A. J. Anand. 2023. Wearable Belt Antenna for Human Body Communications at 8.75 GHz. *2023 Seventh International Conference on Image Information Processing (ICIIP)*, Solan, India, pp. 446–449.
12. Santucci, Francesca, Gabriele Oliva, Maria Teresa Gonnella, Maria Elena Briga, Mirko Leanza, Marco Massenzi, Luca Faramondi, and Roberto Setola. 2025. Implementing Zero Trust: Expert Insights on Key Security Pillars and Prioritization in Digital Transformation. *Information* 16: 667. https://doi.org/10.3390/info16080667.
13. A. S. F. Subhamathi, C. Sathiyapriyan, A. T., A. J. Anand, A. Rheem, and M. R. Arun. 2024. Traffic sign detection problems using convolutional neural techniques in image processing. In *2024 International Conference on Intelligent Systems for Cybersecurity (ISCS)*, Gurugram, India: 1–6.
14. N. Rajkumar, A. Govindaram, R. Geetha, A. S. F. Subhamathi, S. Nithya, and A. Jose Anand. 2025. Non-intrusive load monitoring techniques for intelligent energy management: A comparative study of FHMM and LSTM approach. In *2025 International Conference on Visual Analytics and Data Visualization (ICVADV)*, Tirunelveli, India: 869–874.
15. Hsia, Jie. 2025. AI in Identity and Access Management (IAM) for Zero Trust. SSRN. https://doi.org/10.2139/ssrn.5146346.
16. Pasala, Raveendra Reddy. 2024. AI-driven Identity and Access Management (IAM): The Future of Zero Trust Security. *World Journal of Advanced Research and Reviews* 21: 2076–2082. https://doi.org/10.30574/wjarr.2024.21.2.0266.
17. Pan, Hezhong, Peiyi Han, Xiayu Xiang, Shaoming Duan, and Chuanyi Liu. 2022. SA-UBA: Automatically Privileged User Behavior Auditing for Cloud Platforms with Securely Accounts Management. *Applied Sciences* 12: 8763. https://doi.org/10.3390/app12178763.
18. Waltermire, Karen, Tom Conroy, Marisa Harriston, Chinedum Irrechukwu, Navaneeth Krishnan, James Memole-Doodson, Benjamin Nkrumah, Harry Perper, Susan Prince, and Devin Wynne. 1800. Privileged Account Management for the Financial Services Sector. *Nist Special Publication*: 18B.

19. U.S. General Services Administration (GSA). 2022. *Privileged Identity Playbook*. Version 1.2, 29 Dec. 2022. https://www.idmanagement.gov/playbooks/pam/
20. Kosinski, Matthew. 2025. What is Privileged Access Management (PAM)? https://www.ibm.com/think/topics/privileged-access-management. Accessed November 19.
21. Microsoft. 2025. Protect Your Microsoft 365 Privileged Accounts. https://learn.microsoft.com/en-us/microsoft-365/enterprise/protect-your-global-administrator-accounts. Accessed November 19.
22. Syed, Salahuddin. 2025. Securing Non-Human Identities: Emerging Challenges and Innovative Solutions in Secret Management. *European Modern Studies Journal* 9: 397–407. https://doi.org/10.59573/emsj.9(4).2025.40.
23. Ylonen, Tatu, Paul Turner, Karen Scarfone, and Murugiah Souppaya. 2015. *Security of Interactive and Automated Access Management Using Secure Shell (SSH)*. NIST IR 7966. National Institute of Standards and Technology. https://doi.org/10.6028/NIST.IR.7966.
24. Haber, Morey J. 2020. PAM Architecture. In *Privileged Attack Vectors*, Morey J. Haber, 173–188. Berkeley, CA: Apress. https://doi.org/10.1007/978-1-4842-5914-6_12.
25. Yaseen, M., P. Durai, P. Gokul, S. Justin, and A. J. Anand. 2023. Artificial Intelligence Based Automated Appliances in Smart Home. *2023 Seventh International Conference on Image Information Processing (ICIIP)*, Solan, India, pp. 442–445.
26. Anuradha, T., Jasphin Jeni Sharmila P., Kanimozhiraman, K. Kalaiselvi, C. K. Shruthi, and Jose A. Anand. 2024. Automatic Categorization of Emails into Folders Based on the Content of the Messages. *2024 Third International Conference on Intelligent Techniques in Control, Optimization and Signal Processing (INCOS)*, Krishnankoil, Virudhunagar district, Tamil Nadu, India, pp. 1–6.
27. Subhamathi, A. S. F., C. Sathiyapriyan, A. T, A. J. Anand, A. Rheem, and M. R. Arun. 2024. Traffic Sign Detection Problems using Convolutional Neural Techniques in Image Processing. *2024 International Conference on Intelligent Systems for Cybersecurity (ISCS)*, Gurugram, India, pp. 1–6.
28. Hannah, S., S. Jeevitha, T. Anuradha, A. J. Anand, G. Porkodi, and R. Vijayakumar. 2024. Thyroid Nodule Classification Model from Scintigraphy Images using Convolution Neural Networks. *2024 5th International Conference on Innovative Trends in Information Technology (ICITIIT)*, Kottayam, India, pp. 1–6.
29. Arulananth, T. S., Jose A. Anand, Jayanthi S., Petla Manaswini, Gogineni Viswa Sai Teja, Redyy Taruni G., and Nalla Krishna Prasad. 2024. Automatic Certificate Generation and Security Implementation Using LSB and Hybrid Watermarking Techniques. In *Intelligent Computing Systems and Applications*, S. Bandyopadhyay, V. E. Balas, S. K. Biswas, A. K. Saha, and D. M. Thounaojam (Eds.), ICICSA 2023, Lecture Notes in Networks and Systems, Vol 1010. Springer, Singapore, 2024.
30. Ramachandran, M. S., S. Sajithabanu, A. Ponmalar, M. Mohamed Sithik, and Jose A. Anand. 2024. Fraud Detection and Risk Management Using AI in Business Intelligence. In Intersection of AI and Business Intelligence in Data-Driven Decision-Making, A. Natarajan, M. Galety, C. Iwendi, D. Das, and A. Shankar (Eds.), pp. 117–150. IGI Global. https://doi.org/10.4018/979-8-3693-5288–5.ch005.
31. Sharma, Balaram, Prabhat Pokharel, and Basanta Joshi. 2020. User Behavior Analytics for Anomaly Detection Using LSTM Autoencoder – Insider Threat Detection. In *Proceedings of the 11th International Conference on Advances in Information Technology*, 1–9. Bangkok Thailand: ACM. https://doi.org/10.1145/3406601.3406610.
32. Yuan, Shuhan, and Xintao Wu. 2021. Deep Learning for Insider Threat Detection: Review, Challenges and Opportunities. *Computers & Security* 104: 102221. https://doi.org/10.1016/j.cose.2021.102221.
33. Le, Duc C, and Nur Zincir-Heywood. 2021. Anomaly Detection for Insider Threats Using Unsupervised Ensembles. *IEEE Transactions on Network and Service Management* 18: 1152–1164.

34. Ye Xiaoyun, Faqin Luo, Huangrongbin Cui, Jinlong Wang, Xiaoyun Xiong, Wencui Zhang, Jiawei Yu, and Wenhao Zhao. 2025. Research on Insider Threat Detection based on Personalized Federated Learning and Behavior Log Analysis. *Scientific Reports* 15: 19214. https://doi.org/10.1038/s41598-025-04029-w.
35. Pennada, Siva Satya Prasad, Sasmita Kumari Nayak, and Vamsi Krishna M. 2025. Insider Threat Detection Using Behavioural Analysis through Machine Learning and Deep Learning Techniques. *International Research Journal of Multidisciplinary Technovation*: 74–86. https://doi.org/10.54392/irjmt2527.
36. Guo, Haixuan, Shuhan Yuan, and Xintao Wu. 2021. Logbert: Log Anomaly Detection via Bert. In *2021 International Joint Conference on Neural Networks (IJCNN)*, 1–8. IEEE.
37. Garbis, Jason, and Jerry W. Chapman. 2021. Privileged Access Management. In *Zero Trust Security*, Jason Garbis and Jerry W. Chapman, 155–161. Berkeley, CA: Apress. https://doi.org/10.1007/978-1-4842-6702-8_12.
38. Dhake, Bhavesh, Will Siverstone, Matthew Hitchcock, and Aaron Fletcher. 2025. Keys to the Kingdom: A Defender's Guide to Privileged Account Monitoring. *The Criticality of Privileged Access in Today's Threat Landscape*.
39. SSH.com. 2025. *Leveraging Machine Learning and AI in PAM for Predictive Security*. https://www.ssh.com/academy/pam/leveraging-machine-learning-and-ai-in-privileged-access-management-for-predictive-security
40. J. S. Prasath, S. J. Parvez, A. Govindaram, T. Anuradha, A. Jose Anand, and N. Rajkumar. 2025. AI-enhanced anomaly detection in software-defined networks. In *2025 International Conference on Advanced Computing Technologies (ICoACT)*, Sivakasi, India: 1–7.
41. Alzaabi, Fatima Rashed, and Abid Mehmood. 2024. A Review of Recent Advances, Challenges, and Opportunities in Malicious Insider Threat Detection Using Machine Learning Methods. *IEEE Access* 12: 30907–30927. https://doi.org/10.1109/ACCESS.2024.3369906.
42. Mehmood, Muhammad, Rashid Amin, Muhana Magboul Ali Muslam, Jiang Xie, and Hamza Aldabbas. 2023. Privilege Escalation Attack Detection and Mitigation in Cloud Using Machine Learning. *IEEE Access* 11: 46561–46576. https://doi.org/10.1109/ACCESS.2023.3273895.
43. Boffa, Matteo, Idilio Drago, Marco Mellia, Luca Vassio, Danilo Giordano, Rodolfo Valentim, and Zied Ben Houidi. 2024. LogPrécis: Unleashing Language Models for Automated Malicious Log Analysis. *Computers & Security* 141: 103805. https://doi.org/10.1016/j.cose.2024.103805.
44. Karlsen, Egil, Xiao Luo, Nur Zincir-Heywood, and Malcolm Heywood. 2024. Benchmarking Large Language Models for Log Analysis, Security, and Interpretation. *Journal of Network and Systems Management* 32: 59. https://doi.org/10.1007/s10922-024-09831-x.
45. Jayasundara, Sakuna Harinda, Nalin Asanka Gamagedara Arachchilage, and Giovanni Russello. 2025. SoK: Access Control Policy Generation from High-level Natural Language Requirements. *ACM Computing Surveys* 57: 1–37. https://doi.org/10.1145/3706057.
46. Jayasundara, Sakuna Harinda, Nalin Asanka Gamagedara Arachchilage, and Giovanni Russello. 2024. RAGent: Retrieval-based Access Control Policy Generation (version 2). arXiv. https://doi.org/10.48550/ARXIV.2409.07489.
47. Ahmadi, Sina. 2025. Autonomous Identity-Based Threat Segmentation for Zero Trust Architecture. *Cyber Security and Applications* 3: 100106. https://doi.org/10.1016/j.csa.2025.100106.
48. Koli, Lokesh, Shubham Kalra, Rohan Thakur, Anas Saifi, and Karanpreet Singh. 2025. AI-Driven IRM: Transforming Insider Risk Management with Adaptive Scoring and LLM-based Threat Detection (version 1). arXiv. https://doi.org/10.48550/ARXIV.2505.03796.
49. Saeed Alketbi, Khuloud, and Abid Mehmood. 2025. A Comprehensive Survey of Explainable Artificial Intelligence Techniques for Malicious Insider Threat Detection. *IEEE Access* 13: 121772–121798. https://doi.org/10.1109/ACCESS.2025.3587114.
50. Jain, A., M. Singh, and P. Bhambri. 2021, August. Performance Evaluation of IPv4-IPv6 Tunneling Procedure using IoT. *Journal of Physics: Conference Series* 1950 (1): 012010.
51. Sinha, V. K., R. Jeet, P. Bhambri, and M. Mahajan. 2020. Empowering Intrusion Detection in IRIS Recognition System: A Review. *Journal of Natural Remedies* 21 (2): 131–153.

52. Kaur, J., P. Bhambri, and S. Kaur. 2019. SVM Classifier based Method for Software Defect Prediction. *International Journal of Analytical and Experimental Model Analysis* 11 (10): 2772–2776. http://ijaema.com/Volume-11-Issue-10-October-2019-1/
53. He, Ke, Dan Dongseong Kim, and Muhammad Rizwan Asghar. 2023. Adversarial Machine Learning for Network Intrusion Detection Systems: A Comprehensive Survey. *IEEE Communications Surveys & Tutorials* 25: 538–566. https://doi.org/10.1109/COMST.2022.3233793.
54. G. Ashok and A. A. Jose. 2026. Design and analysis of a high-efficiency chaotic encryption algorithm for image security in ICT frameworks. *Journal of Systems Engineering and Electronics*, 36 (2): 135–162.
55. Nie, Shoubai, Jingjing Ren, Rui Wu, Pengchong Han, Zhaoyang Han, and Wei Wan. 2025. Zero-Trust Access Control Mechanism Based on Blockchain and Inner-Product Encryption in the Internet of Things in a 6G Environment. *Sensors* 25: 550. https://doi.org/10.3390/s25020550.
56. Wang, Ri, Chen Li, Kun Zhang, and Bibo Tu. 2025. Zero-Trust Based Dynamic Access Control for Cloud Computing. *Cybersecurity* 8: 12. https://doi.org/10.1186/s42400-024-00320-x.
57. Lim, Le-Hang, Lee-Yeng Ong, and Meng-Chew Leow. 2025. Federated Learning for Anomaly Detection: A Systematic Review on Scalability, Adaptability, and Benchmarking Framework. *Future Internet* 17: 375. https://doi.org/10.3390/fi17080375.
58. Zhang, Hao, Junwei Ye, Wei Huang, Ximeng Liu, and Jason Gu. 2025. Survey of Federated Learning in Intrusion Detection. *Journal of Parallel and Distributed Computing* 195: 104976. https://doi.org/10.1016/j.jpdc.2024.104976.
59. Amiri-Zarandi, Mohammad, Hadis Karimipour, and Rozita A. Dara. 2023. A Federated and Explainable Approach for Insider Threat Detection in IoT. *Internet of Things* 24: 100965. https://doi.org/10.1016/j.iot.2023.100965.
60. Singh, A. P., M. Aggarwal, H. Singh, and P. Bhambri. 2021. Sketching of EV Network: A Complete Roadmap. In *Sustainable Development through Engineering Innovations*, H. Singh, P. P. Singh Cheema, and P. Garg (Eds.), pp. 431–442. Springer. https://doi.org/10.1007/978-981-15-9554-7_37
61. Rachna, Chhabra, Y., and P. Bhambri. 2021. Various Approaches and Algorithms for Monitoring Energy Efficiency of Wireless Sensor Networks. In *Sustainable Development through Engineering Innovations*, H. Singh, P. P. Singh Cheema, and P. Garg (Eds.), Vol. 113, pp. 761–770. Springer. https://doi.org/10.1007/978-981-15-9554-7_68
62. Singh, M., P. Bhambri, I. Singh, A. Jain, and K. Kaur. 2021. Data Mining Classifier for Predicting Diabetics. *Annals of R.S.C.B.* 25 (4): 6702–6712. http://annalsofrscb.ro
63. Bhambri, P., M. Singh, A. Jain, I. S. Dhanoa, V. K. Sinha, and S. Lal. 2021. Classification of Gene Expression Data with the Aid of Optimized Feature Selection. *Turkish Journal of Physiotherapy and Rehabilitation* 32 (3): 1158–1168. https://www.researchgate.net/publication/352374056_CLASSIFICATION_OF_GENE_EXPRESSION_DATA_WITH_THE_AID_OF_OPTIMIZED_FEATURE_SELECTION#fullTextFileContent
64. Bhambri, P., and Ritu. 2023. Software Effort Estimation with Machine Learning – A Systematic Literature Review. In S. Hooda, V. M. Sood, Y. Singh, S. Dalal, and M. Sood (Eds.), *Agile Software Development: Trends, Challenges and Applications* (pp. 291–308). Wiley. https://doi.org/10.1002/9781119896838.ch15.
65. Sangwan, Y. S., S. Lal, P. Bhambri, A. Kumar, and I. S. Dhanoa. 2021. Advancements in Social Data Security and Encryption: A Review. *Natural Volatiles & Essential Oils* 8 (4): 15353–15362. https://www.cabidigitallibrary.org/doi/full/10.5555/20220170098.
66. Bhambri, P., and A. Khang. 2024. Machine Learning Advancements in E-health: Transforming Digital Healthcare. In *Medical Robotics and AI-assisted Diagnostics for a High-tech Healthcare Industry* (pp. 174–194). IGI Global. https://doi.org/10.4018/979-8-3693-2105-8.ch012.
67. Bhambri, P., S. Bagga, D. Priya, H. Singh, and H. K. Dhiman. 2020, December. Suspicious Human Activity Detection System. *Journal of ISMAC* 2 (4): 216–221.

Chapter 15

Digital Twin and generative AI synergies

Pioneering smart, predictive, and autonomous supply chain networks

Safiye Turgay and Abdulkadir Aydin

15.1 INTRODUCTION

As supply chains grow more complex and volatile and demands become more and more intense, companies have been under enormous pressure to seek new technological solutions. Among the most transformative and innovative technology enablers of the new wave of technological progress and innovation are Digital Twin (DT) platforms and GenAI. The combination of the two technologies has tremendous potential and capacity to model, forecast, and improve business operations. Enabled by continuous bidirectional synchronization between digital and physical worlds through sensors, enterprise systems, and human inputs, DTs lead to the generation of prescriptive insights in the forms of simulation, what-if analysis, or optimization. These enable agile data flow between physical and cyber functions, so that resilient cyber-physical systems are realized when these technologies are combined. This interoperability realization enables the evolution of the supply chain industry from descriptive and reactive models to predictive and autonomous models that can self-heal and self-optimize. In this context, for example, generative AI models could generate optimized paths for the logistics industry based on the disturbances identified by the Digital Twin in real-time and simulate the impact these disturbances have on the production schedule and stock levels. In the proposed chapter, a re-engineering opportunity surrounding Digital Twin and generative AI in supply chain systems will be explored and determined. The chapter outlines basic principles and technological enablers of both Digital Twin and Generative AI technology. In addition, their synergistic use as well as application in smart manufacturing, logistics optimization, maintenance, and even green supply chain systems are discussed. The chapter provides several cases and studies that will be used to illustrate their application for achieving competitive advantage in their pursuit of technological innovations in supply chain systems. Subsequently, the chapter points to some imperatives and research challenges related to re-engineering within their supply chain systems.

15.2 LITERATURE SURVEY

The Digital Twin (DT) paradigm has evolved from being primarily a manufacturing and asset management tool to becoming an indispensable enabler for the realization of intelligent, resilient, and sustainable supply chains. Initially, the technology was developed for digital replication of physical assets for condition monitoring, and it has now turned into a data and real-time operation platform that allows modeling of and automation of supply

DOI: 10.1201/9781003656487-15

chains end-to-end. Recent advances in research increasingly position the DT technology at the core of resilience and sustainable optimization decisions. Recent studies highlight the preeminence of DT-enabled sustainability optimization and simulation/LCA integration in sustainable agri-food supply chains. The application of DT for real-time quality loss control has also been studied in the context of perishable food supply chains. Predictive analytics based on sensor technology contributes to the dynamic management of quality and, therefore, of food freshness. Integrated DT approaches that enhance sustainability and robustness in smart supply chains have been proposed based on the notion of feedback and system adaptation [10, 19, 20].

Data-driven AI approaches, with the use of DTs, have resulted in an increased responsiveness of the distribution network, as shown by industry-oriented case studies. In the context of the food industry, real-time planning and monitoring based on a DT has been proven to be advantageous as a consequence of elevated traceability-related volatility within that context [23]. The CE and sustainability-centric DT applications are growing. Actor-based variants of DT with LCA data have been applied to construction SC management to enable CE management of materials [3]. DT models have been further extended for other professional, socially critical, SC forms, e.g., human milk SC networks, ensuring continuous operations through proactive-reactive planning techniques [15]. Blockchains with DT employing non-fungible tokens (NFT) have developed new sustainable solutions to transparency [14]. The utilization of DT1 paradigms was shown to be of great potential for dealing with pandemic-type disruptions in supply services simulations and fast network reconfiguration strategies [22]. Again the abstract recovery and continuity models highlight DTs as the decision engines within which disturbed supply chain networks re-stabilize. Increasingly, the abstract models consider DTs as entities of control in real-time within adaptive systems and even in dynamic supply chain networks through dynamic interactive configurations of linked supply chain components in real time [16].

DTs are also applicable in decarbonized and energy-sustainable supply chains. Related works include bio-hydrogen production from agricultural waste with DT optimization for decarbonization [17], as well as carbon pricing/renewables with DT-based analysis on energy policies [8, 18]. Systematic reviews bring the unification of all progress and indicate main trends in the desirable direction of study: most probably in the direction of interoperability, scalability, and AI, all related to applications of DT [4, 7]. Collaborative human-AI-based GANs have been demonstrated to be able to achieve high-quality predictive results for small-batch manufacturing, substantiating the validity of the idea of generative models learning from a small amount of data [9]. The bountiful role of foundation models as an even better enabler for scalable logistics automation tasks, e.g., routing and planning, and forecasting from multiple supply chain data sources was identified. Combining "Gen AI" with the "Metaverse" tech stack has further improved the power of "resilience planning" through simulations of perturbations, creation of "contingency plans," and visualizations of "scenarios" in the Metaverse. Advanced decision-making under uncertainty was also addressed by AI-based multi-objective optimization models for disaster response logistics and integrated with blockchain-based smart contracts. Despite the fact that these models require the use of pre-extracted policies, they demonstrate GenAI's capability to autonomously generate response policies. GenAI-enabled smart product platforming has also been recognized as the meta-paradigm mark of Industry 4.0, enabling manufacturing production and supply chain variability.

Circular supply chain planning enabled by AI platforms again caters to the sustainability attributes of the generative model [21]. GenAI technological integration continues to be associated with organizational readiness and adoption maturity as enablers. Smart manufacturing readiness factors for adoption refer to critical technology and organization stages before the successful adoption of state-of-the-art GenAI technological solutions [13]. The question of cybersecurity has arisen with GenAI technologies appearing to create tremendous risks and vulnerabilities in the poisoning and manipulation of data in the IoT and other AI-enabled environments, as the extremely sophisticated autonomous capabilities of GenAI technologies increasingly prioritize cybersecurity factors [5]. On the macro level, intelligent manufacturing technologies, such as advanced AI technology solutions, have positive impacts on outward foreign direct investment, conveying their significance in their particular markets and surroundings. While promising, the current GenAI literature in the context of supply chain management largely addresses isolated scenarios as opposed to holistically integrated systems that connect the entire end-to-end process. The future generation of GenAI research has to be real-time, interpretable, and self-learning.

The coupling of Digital Twin and Artificial Intelligence approaches is still a prospective topic in industrial systems. Although the compatibility and complementarity of DT and AI in the manufacturing field are also well studied, in the area of supply chain networks, the concept would be considered novel. Existing literature focuses primarily on prediction and optimization. The concept of AI of Things (AIoT) and DTs are converged and presented environmental and functional compatibility with real-time management and prediction planning that has great potential for sustainable supply chains [6]. The data-driven AI models for building DTs in the distribution system are proven to be operationally attractive and mostly prediction-driven rather than generative ones. Approaches of convergence in integrating Mixed Reality with IoT toward DT are usually concentrated on enabling visualization and human interface rather than on supporting an intelligent self-helper. Even more contemporary works apply LLMs to control the process of DT construction, leading to huge performance gains in adaptivity and learning efficiency of applications in industry. Categorization of DT applications based on industry use cases constitutes emergent insights for future work in AI integration [2]. Extensive convergent studies such as blockchain technology applications, AI, Metaverse, and DT applications propose digitization challenges and security concern in cyber [3, 4]. AI-enabled DT applications that integrate computer vision in the context of smart manufacturing have been observed to lead to enhanced object recognition and operational intelligence [11].

Processes of industrial scale illustrate the relevance of hybrid DT platforms merging online learning techniques and uncertainty quantification, allowing for real-time adaptation as a key enabler in the design of future supply chains. Socio-technical interpretations of DT and AI suggest cultural and organizational shifts that will be needed to successfully implement an effective DT, AI fusion, in the manner of human-centricity receiving the highest priority [12]. Industrial IoT solutions that integrate DTs with AI add yet another layer of justification for the need for real-time intelligence, especially in supply chains that emphasize energy efficiency and sustainability [1, 7].

15.2.1 Identification of research gaps in the literature

The background discloses many significant gaps:

- The Generative AI technology is integrated into the real-time Digital Twin environment to provide more efficient decision-making and can be applied for autonomous decision-making in the supply chain management process.
- A scalable architecture for adaptation and continuous learning without the need for human intervention.
- Insufficient understanding of cybersecurity, interoperability, and trust challenges in DT-GenAI ecosystems.

- Rare empirical, end-to-end validations to help transmit the value of synergy of DT & GenAI.

Emerging trends are as follows:

- Cognitive supply chains that learn and optimize through AI powered DTs.
- Autonomous logistics solutions enabled with GenAI routing and transportation optimization.
- Sustainability intelligence with DTs replicating the impacts, and GenAI developing green optimization algorithms.

In other words, both the Digital Twin and the Generative AI add intelligence and innovation to the SC and, therefore, the general research for their combination to create more intelligent and independent SC environments is still neither mature nor widespread.

15.3 METHODOLOGY

This methodology is a holistic solution that adopts the technologies of Digital Twin and Generative Artificial Intelligence to construct an intelligent, predictive, and autonomous supply chain network system. Level 1 uses IoT sensors, RFID, and machine control systems to collect live data of inventory status, machine status, and environmental factors. The third layer, called the Digital Twin Layer, is responsible for the dynamic, on-demand creation [23–27]. The task is for artificial intelligence models and methods based on the state-of-the-art deep learning predictive models, generative reinforcement learning models for production and logistics network design, and synthetic scenario models employing GAN and transformer models for predictive analysis and designing of autonomous operations in an ongoing manner to build an autonomously and predictively operable supply chain network system. From the perspective of operations, the system is an intelligent, looped workflow, where the initial step is to collect data from various sources, and the reason for this step is to update the Digital Twin, which then triggers the GenAIS models to analyze the scenario and find optimal solutions [28–[33]. Solutions are simulated in the DT domain and, upon verification, the procedure is implemented with control systems that could engage humans. The result of the process is tracked and used to re-train the models on an ongoing basis. The approach constitutes a significant departure in intelligent supply chain management by leveraging predictive simulation of Digital Twins (DTs) combined with the novel, adaptive, and autonomous decision-making capability of Generative AI. Rather than traditional AI supply chains as separate optimization spaces, the new global integration strategy focuses on the common and living updating-through-learning ecosystem. In essence, the new strategy and architecture are grounded on the Cognitive Digital Twin Layer. This novel approach goes beyond mere replication of the system to encompass machine learning algorithms within the Digital Twin (DT) space [34–38].

To all these capabilities is added the Generative Decision Intelligence module, which produces and evaluates these policies by means of Generative Reinforcement Learning (GRL), all in response to real-time operation disruption. Generative optimization is also used to independently test innovative scheduling, logistics, and inventory strategies, although decisions remain explainable and human-like interaction with operators is enabled via use of Large Language Models (LLMs). The Closed-Loop Autonomous Control module serves to guarantee that all actions carried out by the GenAI are first run on the DT environment simulation, that is on before they are launched on the operational environment. Lastly, the

Context-Aware Adaptation Engine brings an additional dimension of dynamism to consideration of environmental, normative, and social contexts into policy decisions. Thus, sustainability metrics, risk analysis, and compliance are not add-on issues but integral inputs to generative decision models. These capabilities combined create an end-to-end autonomous, adaptive, and intelligent supply chain management solution that can operate effectively in uncertain, evolving environments. The process of the introduced approach is a technology-based systematic flow transforming real-time data into intelligent, automated supply chain decisions. It starts with real-time data capture from different nodes in the supply chain. Step 2 exports this data into Digital Twin platforms, aligning and contextually modeling with cloud-based APIs. Step 3 utilizes Generative AI features to create and supercharge adaptive scenarios by offering intelligent alternatives for production planning calendars, routes, and inventory actions. These are then duplicated in Step 4 by simulation engines in the Digital Twin to check operation over time. Enabled, Step 5 is real-time execution of the optimized plans via automation technologies, industrial automation systems, and edge devices. Lastly, among 6 steps, Step 6 encounters the system in a routine of perpetual learning and evolution fostered by MLOps and AutoML architectures, wherein models are updated with emerging patterns, disruptions, and strategic goals. This end-to-end process is representative of a self-adaptive, intelligent supply chain model powered by digital and generative Technologies in Table 15.1.

The novel method essentially introduces several key improvements that enhance the traditional supply chain intelligence system and propels it into a new era. As opposed to existing approaches that normally merge Predictive Digital Twins with Descriptive AI, a new paradigm has emerged towards Cognitive Digital Twins supported by Generative AI where systems do not only predict but also generate and evolve. Rather than batch learning on historical data which leads to limited adaptability to evolving real-time events, the method uses online learning when running, which enables the system to dynamically co-evolve with the operating environment in real time. Unlike traditional systems that require manual or rule-based scenario generation, the proposed system automates the generation of novel scenarios and contingency plans, thereby enhancing reactivity in disruption management. In addition, traditional supply chain software uses static optimization models, but this software solution uses an adaptive optimization technique based on reinforcement learning and generative algorithms to keep the solutions viable in a dynamic environment. Finally, although current methods typically incorporate partial human-in-the-loop decision-making, this framework supports fully autonomous control loop operation with human intervention exclusively in situations involving safety-critical or ethical judgments. This is a paradigm shift that will lead to supply chain solutions that are smarter, more resilient, and increasingly autonomous in Table 15.2.

Table 15.1 Workflow of the suggested approach

Step	*Process*	*Technology*
1	Real-time data ingestion from supply chain nodes	IoT, ERP, WMS, MES
2	Digital Twin synchronization and contextual modeling	Digital Twin Platforms, Cloud APIs
3	Generative AI-driven scenario generation and optimization	GenAI, GRL, GANs, LLMs
4	Virtual testing and impact assessment in the Digital Twin	Simulation Engines
5	Autonomous execution of optimal decisions	RPA, Control Systems, Edge Computing
6	Continuous learning and model refinement	MLOps, AutoML

Table 15.2 Innovations over existing approaches

Existing approaches	*Proposed new approach*
Predictive Digital Twins + Descriptive AI	Cognitive Digital Twins + Generative AI
Batch learning from historical data	Continuous learning from real-time operations
Manual or rule-based scenario generation	Autonomous generation of novel scenarios and contingency plans
Static optimization models	Adaptive optimization driven by reinforcement learning and generative algorithms
Partial human-in-the-loop	Fully autonomous loop with optional human oversight

The above framework is the basis for several high-impact solutions that improve supply chain responsiveness and intelligence. An illustrative use case is Dynamic Demand-Supply Rebalancing, which ensures procurement and manufacturing schedules are dynamically aligned with evolving customer demands to reduce stockouts and overproduction. Another application is Disruption Recovery, a process in which alternate logistics routes are quickly identified and supplier networks restructured in the wake of unforeseen events (e.g., natural disasters, geopolitical conflicts, or cargo delays). Further, PSO makes it possible to create sustainable manufacturing and shipping schedules by selecting schedules that reduce the carbon footprint and energy consumption. This paradigm-busting methodology is based on a robust technology architecture that integrates a rich variety of high-end platforms/tools. These twin platforms like Siemens Mindsphere, Azure Digital Twins, and IBM Maximo are the foundation for real-time system modeling and synchronization. These are backed up by powerful Generative AI frameworks like OpenAI GPT, Google DeepMind, and Hugging Face Transformers, that empower smart predictions, scenario building, and self-planning. For those aspects of QoS where the agent is indifferent or cannot affect (QoS) parameters (e.g., latency) but still can benefit from monitoring them for learning or awareness, it simulates agents. Among them are: MuJoCo and PyBullet for physics simulation; NumPy, TensorFlow, and PyTorch for writing custom code and neural networks; OpenAI Gym, RLlib, TensorFlow Agents for implementing agents; and visualization using Gym and Matplotlib. The benefits and effects will be nowhere near small. On the smartness front, it increases the supply chain intelligence by embedding predictive analytics and generative modeling into the decision workflows. It enables autonomy by reducing the need for human intervention in an extraordinary way, the same that can be applied in real-time decisions. Structure is more robust in the sense that it permits rapid adjustment to disruptions and uncertainties, it also fosters sustainability by enhancing the green performance of the supply chain by, among others, low-emission energy efficient techniques. It also brings in agility by enabling faster, data-driven adaptations to unforeseen market dynamics. There are some more fundamental concepts that are fundamental to these innovations and that go along with them. Generative Artificial Intelligence represents a group of technologies capable of autonomously producing new outputs, such as data, models, or decisions, by extrapolating learned patterns from existing historical sets. And thus, a Cognitive Supply Chain is a smart, autonomous, self-adaptive supply network driven through Digital Twin models and Generative AI delivering continuous optimization, predictive foresight, and automated operational control. These all add up to a fresh look at supply chain management going forward.

15.3.1 Synergistic feedback in DT-GenAI systems

The two-way interaction between a Digital Twin and a Generative AI model in a cyber-physical supply chain system is a co-optimization loop, where the DT is a simulator-based validator, and the GenAI model produces adaptive policies. Algebraically, the system can be viewed as an iterative optimization loop:

$$X_{t+1} = DT(f_{\text{GenAI}}(X_t, D_t)) \tag{15.1}$$

where X_t is the supply chain state at time t, D_t is the disruption/input data, f_{GenAI} is the generative optimization policy, and $DT(\cdot)$is the validation and feedback function of the Digital Twin. Digital Twin validation and Generative AI optimization in iterative interactions converge to a locally optimal policy if provided environmental dynamics are stationary and state space is finite.

Suppose f_{GenAI} f_{GenAI} is a reinforcement learning policy with discount factor γ and learning rate α. Then it converges under the Bellman optimality principle.

The Digital Twin is a bounded simulation; it avoids "exploding" policy updating.

From Banach's Fixed-Point Theorem, iterating a contraction mapping (bounded DT + convergent RL policy) yields a fixed point, which is an optimal arrangement for the supply chain.

$$\therefore \lim_{t \to \infty} X_t \to X^* \tag{15.2}$$

Driven by Generative AI, it is a self-healing system that, once disruptions are identified, remedial measures are autonomously created, tested, and deployed within a bounded time window, reducing downtime and interruption in service levels.

Some natural language generative models (e.g. LLMs) can also be embedded into the GenAI layer, which provides further explainability for autonomous decisions that can then be made human-understandable in natural language form.

15.3.2 Generative feedback for predictive improvement

Let P_{baseline} be the predictive accuracy of a baseline AI-only supply chain model, and let B

$P_{\text{DT-GenAI}}$ be the predictive accuracy of a cooperative DT-GenAI solution. Then:

$$P_{\text{DT-GenAI}} \geq P_{\text{baseline}} \tag{15.3}$$

Assume that $G : X \to Y$ is a generative function that takes input states X (e.g., supply chain states) and outputs actions Y (e.g., routing, scheduling). If G is trained via reinforcement learning and objective reward R, then with infinite exploration and reward shaping, G will asymptotically optimize G^*policies.

When DT and GenAI are scaled to their ultimate potentials, the super-system that arises is endowed with the following attributes:

Self-monitoring: DT detects deviations or threats in real time.
Self-generating: GenAI generates solutions or answers on its own.
Self-optimizes: DT simulation feedback is used to refine the GenAI model.
Self-adaptive: The system adjusts to unexpected changes automatically, without human intervention. A cognitive digital supply chain has the potential to provide predictive insight and autonomous action in Table 15.3.

Table 15.3 Collaboration model: DT–GenAI interaction cycle

Stage	*Digital Twin role*	*Generative AI role*	*Interaction*
Data Collection	Captures real-time sensor and process data	Receives contextual input	DT → GenAI
Problem Identification	Detects anomalies or inefficiencies	Classifies problem scope	DT ↔ GenAI
Solution Generation	Simulates possible outcomes	Generates candidate solutions or strategies	GenAI → DT
Validation and Simulation	Validates strategies via simulations	Refines generation models	DT ↔ GenAI
Autonomous Execution	Triggers workflows in physical system	Adjusts policies based on real-time feedback	DT ← GenAI

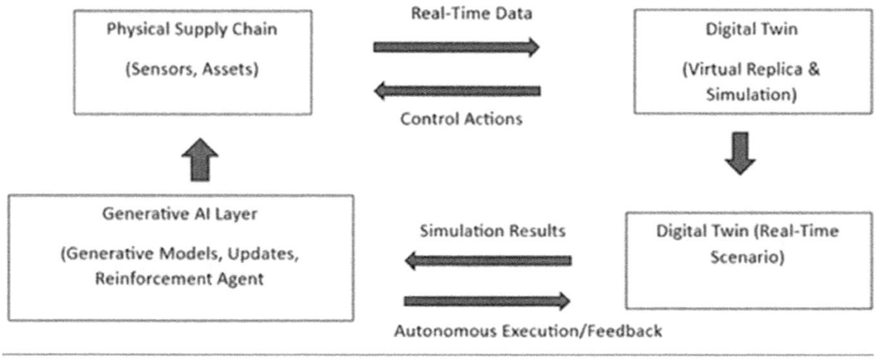

Figure 15.1 Conceptual diagram of the Digital Twin.

The modularity of DT and GenAI building blocks enables scalable extension to global multi-tier supply chains, where hierarchical Digital Twins and federated generative models thrive with autonomy both at the local as well as global levels (Figure 15.1).

The presence of natural language generative models in the GenAI layer provides more visibility and explainability, guaranteeing human trust and the adoption of autonomous supply chain operations.

Let a physical supply chain system $S_p(t)$. be described by its state at time t the vector $\mathbf{x}_p(t) \in \mathbb{R}^n$, which evolves according to some unknown or partially known dynamics. The Digital Twin $S_d(t)$ is a virtual twin that produces a state vector $\mathbf{x}_d(t) \in \mathbb{R}^n$ to simulate $S_p(t)$.

15.3.3 Assumptions

Partitioned Data Acquisition: The Digital Twin is at received samples $\mathbf{y}(t)$ from $S_p(t)$ at discrete time instances with a sampling period Δt.

Model Parameterization: The Digital Twin is parameterized by parameters $\theta \in \Theta$, which are updated iteratively by using a parameter estimation algorithm $\hat{\theta}(t)$ minimizing some suitably defined error measure.

Bounded Synchronization Delay: Synchronization or delay τ between physical measurement acquisition and digital model update is bounded and is such that $\tau < \tau_{max}$, where τ_{max} is some function of the system dynamics.

Then the Digital Twin state $\mathbf{x}_d(t)$ converges asymptotically to the physical system state $\mathbf{x}_p(t)$, i.e.:

$$\lim_{t\to\infty} \| \mathbf{x}_p(t) - \mathbf{x}_d(t) \| = 0. \tag{15.4}$$

The real system $S_p(t)$ is observable from $\mathbf{y}(t)$.

The Digital Twin model class $M = \{f(\mathbf{x},\theta)\}$ is rich enough to capture the true system dynamics in the domain of operation.

The stability conditions on the parameter update $\hat{\theta}(t)$ rule.

System dynamics updates and Digital Twins are both discrete time processes, t denoted by $k, t = k\Delta t$.

The proof uses techniques from Lyapunov stability theory and adaptive systems theory.

Define the state estimation error:

$$\mathbf{e}(t) = \mathbf{x}_p(t) - \mathbf{x}_d(t). \tag{15.5}$$

The error dynamics follow:

$$\mathbf{e}(t+1) = f_p(\mathbf{x}_p(t)) - f_d(\mathbf{x}_d(t), \hat{\theta}(t)) \tag{15.6}$$

where f_p and f_d are the state transition functions of the physical and digital systems, respectively.

Lyapunov Candidate Function picks a positive definite Lyapunov function $V(\mathbf{e}) = \mathbf{e}^T P\mathbf{e}$, where it P is positive definite. Parameter Update Law estimates $\hat{\theta}(t)$ are updated to minimize prediction error between the model output $\mathbf{y}(t)$ and the model output $\hat{\mathbf{y}}(t)$ using methods such as recursive least squares and gradient descent.

Decrease of Lyapunov Function under observability and bounded latency τ assumptions. It can be proved that the expected V decrement is bounded by:

$$\Delta V = V(\mathbf{e}(t+1)) - V(\mathbf{e}(t)) \leq -\alpha \| \mathbf{e}(t) \|^2 \tag{15.7}$$

where some $\alpha > 0$ and it represents the error norm diminishes over time.

The discrete-time Lyapunov stability theorems and the error $\mathbf{e}(t)$ converge to zero as $\to \infty$.

This theory ensures that under a properly designed model update and data acquisition scheme, it also places significant design constraints such as maximum allowable latency and model expressiveness requirement.

Implications of supply chain networks (SCNs) on the reliability of supply,

- Real-time coordination between the digital and physical layers is necessary to effectively support decision making.
- The Digital Twin needs to be recalibrated in real time in order to capture process variability and emergent events.
- High-frequency sensor measurement data and low-latency communication networks will further improve convergence performance (e.g., 5G, edge computing).

15.3.4 Mathematical model of the Digital Twin with recursive parameter estimation

15.3.4.1 Physical system dynamics

The physical level of inventory $x_p(t)$ develops in discrete time steps $t = 0,1,2,\ldots$ according to:

$$x_p(t+1) = x_p(t) + u(t) - d(t) \tag{15.8}$$

where:

$x_p(t) \in \mathbb{R}$ is the inventory level at time t.

$u(t) \in \mathbb{R}_{\geq 0}$ is the amount of replenishment (control input).

$d(t) \in \mathbb{R}_{\geq 0}$ is stochastic demand at time t.

Demand $d(t)$ can be expressed as a random variable:

$$d(t) = \theta + \varepsilon(t) \tag{15.9}$$

where:

$\theta \in \mathbb{R}_{\geq 0}$ is the unknown mean demand parameter.
$\varepsilon(t)$ is zero-mean white noise with σ^2variance, i.e., $\varepsilon(t) \sim N(0,\sigma^2)$.

3.3.4.2 Digital Twin state estimate

The Digital Twin inventory estimate $x_d(t)$ propagates as:

$$x_d(t+1) = x_d(t) + u(t) - \hat{\theta}(t) \tag{15.10}$$

where:

$x_d(t) \in \mathbb{R}$ is the Digital Twin's estimate of the inventory at time t.

$\hat{\theta}(t) \in \mathbb{R}_{\geq 0}$ is denotes the Digital Twin's estimate at time t of the mean parameter of demand.

3.3.4.3 Recursive least squares (RLS) parameter estimation

- The Digital Twin updates $\hat{\theta}(t)$ at time t based on observed data.
- Define the observation equation for parameter estimation as:

$$y(t) = d(t) = \theta + \varepsilon(t) \tag{15.11}$$

- The update rule for the estimate involves the most current estimate and innovation (prediction error):

$$\hat{\theta}(t+1) = \hat{\theta}(t) + K(t)\left[y(t) - \hat{\theta}(t)\right] \tag{15.12}$$

where
- $-K(t)$ is Kalman gain or adaptive gain at time t, recursively computed as:

$$K(t) = \frac{P(t-1)}{\lambda + P(t-1)} \tag{15.13}$$

- $-P(t)$ is the covariance matrix (scalar in this 1D example) as:

$$P(t) = \frac{1}{\lambda}\left[P(t-1) - K(t)P(t-1)\right] \tag{15.14}$$

- $\lambda \in (0,1]$ is a forgetting factor controlling memory of past information.

15.3.4.4 Estimation error dynamics

Define inventory estimation error as:

$$e(t) = x_p(t) - x_d(t) \tag{15.15}$$

From system dynamics:

$$\begin{aligned} e(t+1) &= x_p(t+1) - x_d(t+1) \\ &= \left[x_p(t) + u(t) - d(t)\right] - \left[x_d(t) + u(t) - \hat{\theta}(t)\right] \\ &= e(t) + \hat{\theta}(t) - d(t) \\ &= e(t) + \hat{\theta}(t) - \theta - \varepsilon(t) \end{aligned} \tag{15.16}$$

Hence, the mistake depends on the difference between actual demand θ and the estimated demand $\hat{\theta}(t)$, and on noise. All of the parameters and variables are given in Table 15.4.

Table 15.4 Summary of model variables and parameters

Symbol	*Description*
$x_p(t)$	Physical inventory level at time *t*
$x_d(t)$	Digital Twin's estimated inventory level
$u(t)$	Replenishment quantity (known input)
$d(t)$	Actual demand (random variable)
θ	True mean demand parameter (unknown)
$\hat{\theta}(t)$	Estimated mean demand parameter
$\varepsilon(t)$	Zero-mean noise in demand
$P(t)$	Parameter covariance (RLS)
$K(t)$	Adaptive gain for parameter update
λ	Forgetting factor for RLS
$e(t)$	Inventory estimation error

Interpretation

- The Digital Twin adaptively refines its demand model via RLS to reduce the mismatch $\hat{\theta}(t)-\theta$.
- As $\hat{\theta}(t)\to\theta$, the inventory estimation error $e(t)\to$ zero-mean noise $-\varepsilon(t)$ and converges to zero on average.
- The model can be extended to multi-parameter estimation (e.g., demand variance) and multi-dimensional supply chain states.

15.4 AUTONOMOUS INVENTORY AND LOGISTICS OPTIMIZATION

The proposed system architecture will be comprised of a network of regional warehouses and distribution centers, along with a transportation network spanning the country, and these will all be linked by different transportation modes. This intelligent supply chain will be based on a Digital Twin platform that simulates the real-world operating environment for the supply chain, thereby providing a coordinated view of the health status of the assets, inventory, transportation, and suppliers.

15.4.1 Smart inventory replenishment using Digital Twin and generative AI

15.4.1.1 Scenario setup

Single Warehouse Inventory System

Initial inventory $x_p(0)=100$ units

Time horizon: $T = 30$ days, daily decisions

Demand $d(t)\sim\text{Poisson}(\lambda)$ with true mean $\lambda = 20$ units/day (not known to AI)

Control variable: daily replenishment quantity $u(t)$, integer $\in[0,50]$

Holding cost: \$1 per unit per day held

Stockout penalty cost: \$5 per unit short per day

Ordering cost: \$10 fixed cost + \$0.50 per unit ordered

Objective: reduce total cost over horizon without stockouts

15.4.1.2 Digital Twin model

The Digital Twin involves an estimate of demand mean $\hat{\lambda}(t)$, which is kept up to date in real time.

Predicts inventory level $x_d(t)$ dependent on replenishment and demand estimates:

$$x_d(t+1)=x_d(t)+u(t)-\hat{\lambda}(t)$$

Estimation of $\hat{\lambda}(t)$ is updated using the exponential smoothing technique:

$$\hat{\lambda}(t+1)=\alpha d(t)+(1-\alpha)\hat{\lambda}(t)$$

with smoothing factor $\alpha = 0.3$.

15.4.1.3 Generative AI agent

Makes replenishment decisions $u(t)$ daily using Q-learning.

- State space: inventory level buckets $S = \{0,10,20,\ldots,150\}$
- Action space: replenishment $u(t) \in \{0,10,20,\ldots,50\}$
- Reward R(t):

$$R(t) = -\left[1 \times \text{holding cost} + 5 \times \text{stockout penalty} + 10 \times I_{order>0} + 0.5 \times u(t)\right]$$

The agent learns what the best way to restock is, given the trade-off between cost and shortage.

15.4.1.4 Simulation steps

Step 1: Initialization

- $x_p(0) = x_d(0) = 100$
- $\hat{\lambda}(0) = 20$ (guess)
- Initialize Q-table $Q(s,a)$ arbitrarily (e.g., zeros)
- Set learning rate $\eta = 0.1$, discount factor $\gamma = 0.95$, exploration rate $\epsilon = 0.2$

Step 2: For each day $t = 0,\ldots,T-1$

Observe current inventory state bucket s_t from Digital Twin estimate $x_d(t)$
Select replenishment action $u(t)$:

- With probability ϵ, pick a random action (exploration)
- Otherwise, select action maximizing $Q(s_t,a)$ (exploitation)

Execute replenishment $u(t)$ on physical inventory:

$$x_p(t+1) = \max\left(x_p(t) + u(t) - d(t), 0\right)$$

where $d(t) \sim \text{Poisson}(\lambda)$.

Digital Twin updates demand estimate:

$$\hat{\lambda}(t+1) = 0.3 \times d(t) + 0.7 \times \hat{\lambda}(t)$$

Digital Twin forecasts inventory:

$$x_d(t+1) = x_d(t) + u(t) - \hat{\lambda}(t)$$

Compute reward $\boldsymbol{R(t)}$:

$$\text{holding cost} = \max\left(x_p(t+1), 0\right)$$

$$\text{stockout penalty} = \max\left(-\left[x_p(t) + u(t) - d(t)\right], 0\right)$$

$$R(t) = -\left[1 \times \text{holding cost} + 5 \times \text{stockout penalty} + 10 \times I_{u(t)>0} + 0.5 \times u(t)\right]$$

Observe next state s_{t+1} from updated Digital Twin inventory $x_d(t+1)$
Update Q-table:

$$Q(s_t, u(t)) \leftarrow Q(s_t, u(t)) + \eta\left[R(t) + \gamma \max_a Q(s_{t+1}, a) - Q(s_t, u(t))\right]$$

Step 3: Repeat Step 2 over T Days
In the simulation environment, the Generative AI learns better strategies to manage inventory replenishment by balancing stockout costs with holding costs. This learning feature allows the AI to behave optimally with changing demand patterns, learning better strategies. Simultaneously, the Digital Twin retrieves the updated value of demand $\hat{\lambda}(t) / \lambda(t)$ using actual values. This action allows the model to better represent real-world situations. This optimizes and manages the entire supply chain with dynamic proactive inventory strategies that achieve minimal total operating costs. This synergy between learning and simulation builds a robust and conservative supply chain environment capable of learning even with uncertainty and variability of actual situations depicted in Table 15.5.

The sample detailed numerical example with a Digital Twin updating demand estimates and a Q-learning agent for autonomous replenishment decision-making in Table 15.6 and Figure 15.2.

The Digital Twin continuously updates the demand forecast as the agent learns the stock replenishment actions using Q-Learning. The inventory level, true vs forecasted demand, and stock replenishment action graphs are shown for 30 days.

15.4.2 Simulation process for scenario analysis

To perform scenario analysis, a set of parameter values that are characteristic of each scenario, such as mean demand, stockout cost, or initial inventory, is used to describe each scenario. The parameters were set up through the Python simulation model prior to a comprehensive simulation run for a fixed period of simulation, usually 30 days. Various parameters have been measured on every simulation run, which include total cost, average daily stockout units, average daily holding inventory, and frequency and amount of orders for replenishment. To capture the random variability associated with demand, every situation is conducted a few times, typically a total of 10 simulation runs, to allow for averages of the system data to be captured, as opposed to extreme values. Once all the simulation runs have been completed, the results of every situation will be compared to determine the sensitivity

Table 15.5 Table summary of example

Day	*Physical inventory*	*Digital Twin estimate*	*Demand* ***d(t)***	*Replenishment* ***u(t)***	*Estimated demand* $\hat{\lambda}(t)$	*Reward* ***R(t)***
1	100	100	22	20	20	−35
2	98	100	18	10	20.4	−28
...	...	...	...	...	...	...
30	105	102	19	0	19.8	−15

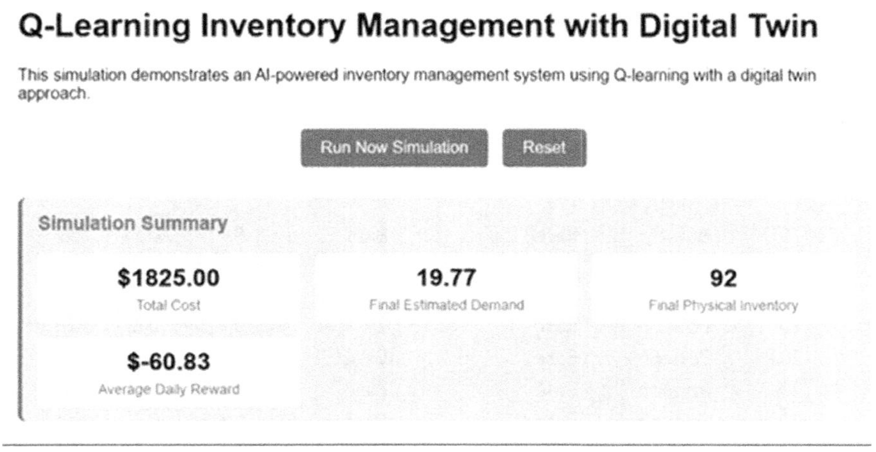

Figure 15.2 Digital Twin updating demand estimates and a Q-learning agent.

Table 15.6 Parameters and metrics to vary

Parameter	*Description*	*Typical values/scenarios*
True Demand Mean (λ)	Average customer demand per day	Low: 15, Medium: 20, High: 25
Demand Variability (Noise)	Variance around demand mean	Low: Poisson, Medium: Negative Binomial, High: Poisson with bursts
Replenishment Cost	Fixed + variable costs for ordering	Base, 1.5×, 2×
Holding Cost per Unit	Cost to hold inventory per day	Base, 0.5×, 2×
Stockout Penalty	Cost of lost sales or backorders	Base, 2×, 5×
Learning Rate (η)	Speed of Q-learning updates	0.05, 0.1, 0.2
Smoothing Factor (α)	Responsiveness of demand estimate	0.1 (slow), 0.3 (medium), 0.6 (fast)
Exploration Rate (ϵ)	Exploration/exploitation tradeoff in RL	0.1, 0.2, 0.3
Initial Inventory	Starting stock level	50, 100, 150

of performance measures to variations in parameters, as well as determine the robustness of the Digital Twin + Q-learning approach. This detailed approach ensures that it is possible to comprehend the actual effects of every factor on the efficiency of every supply chain. A simulation situation matrix may be created to facilitate a summary of the experimental combinations in Table 15.7.

Some of the observations result from the simulation of the Digital Twin and the use of the Q-learning algorithm for the replenishment of the inventory based on different demands. First, when the average demand scales up, the replenishment becomes more frequent, extensive, and costly, and the agent has to optimize its policy fast in order to avoid stockout. When the system operates under burst noise demand, the Digital Twin predictions may be questionable, and the value of the smoothing factor (α) is critical, which determines the sensitivity of the model to sudden changes. The higher the stockout penalty value, the more cautious the policy of the agent, often resulting in higher, more frequent orders

Table 15.7 Scenario matrix example

Scenario ID	*Demand mean*	*Demand variance*	*Replenishment cost*	*Stockout penalty*	η	α	$\in$	*Initial inventory*
1	20	Poisson (base)	Base	Base	0.1	0.3	0.2	100
2	15	Poisson (low)	Base	Base	0.1	0.3	0.2	100
3	25	Poisson (high)	Base	Base	0.1	0.3	0.2	100
4	20	Burst noise	Base	Base	0.1	0.3	0.2	100
5	20	Poisson	1.5×	Base	0.1	0.3	0.2	100
6	20	Poisson	Base	2×	0.1	0.3	0.2	100
7	20	Poisson	Base	Base	0.05	0.3	0.2	100
8	20	Poisson	Base	Base	0.1	0.1	0.2	100
9	20	Poisson	Base	Base	0.1	0.3	0.1	100
10	20	Poisson	Base	Base	0.1	0.3	0.2	50

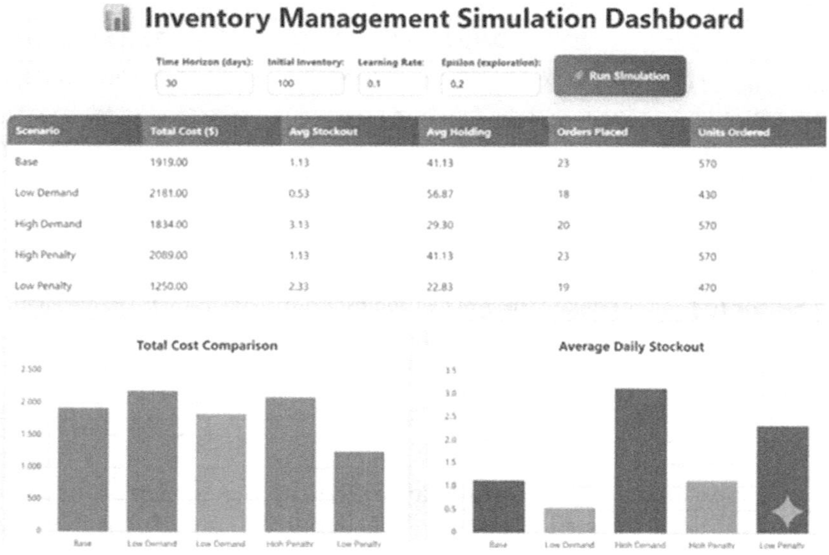

Figure 15.3 Suggested model screenout.

to mitigate costly stockout. The value of the learning rate parameter (η), which directly affects the sensitivity of the neural network towards fast adaptation, will be critical, and although fast convergence leads to fast improvement, it may bring instabilities, whereas low values may bring slower convergence. Another factor, the initial setting for the value of the inventory, has a huge influence on the initial performance, such as initial stockout risk and initial holding value. These observations not only bring out the robust performance of the algorithm despite uncertainty, but the optimal parameters can be identified to bring out the best performance. The simulation of the entire process, and the results can be efficiently given in Figure 15.3.

15.4.2.1 Explanation and sensitivity analysis concept

There are five experimental setups employed in this study, each of which has a different value of the demand mean and a different shortage penalty. Each experimental setting simulates a 30-day experiment using the proposed Digital Twin & Q-Learning method, which is capable of dynamically responding to changes in the environment. The main simulation results focused on as key performance measures include the total cost, average stockouts, maximum average holding amounts, the number of orders received, and the total quantities ordered. Sensitivity analysis, as mentioned, is the entire idea behind conducting this analysis. Sensitivity analysis, by pointing to the parameters with the greatest influence on the objective parameters, not only investigates model adjustment but also examines the validity of the proposed decision support framework.

15.4.3 Sensitivity analysis

In the first step of the sensitivity analysis process, values are allocated to all the model parameters with the established baseline value except the value of the parameter that needs to be tested. For each value defined within the level of sensitivity, simulation trials are carried out. The process takes into consideration the variability associated with the simulation, ensuring the resultant output is presented in the Table 15.8.

The performance of the important metrics-parameters such as the total cost, stockouts, or inventory is recorded for each run. Lastly, the correlation between the parameter and its connected metrics-parameters is represented through figures that facilitate the interpretation of the influence of the parameter on the performance of the system in Table 15.9.

The integration of the Generative AI and the Digital Twin technology showed huge advantages in the dynamic, predictive supply chain optimization with a significant reduction in costs and environmental impacts. The autonomous adaptation property of the system enabled fast recovery from disturbances and stockouts and reaction times. By including sustainable decision-making, the model achieved a great balance in terms of cost optimization and sustainable practices. Interestingly, the requirement for human-in-the-loop corrections

Table 15.8 Key parameters for sensitivity

Parameter	*Typical values*	*Sensitivity test range*
Demand Mean (λ)	20	15 to 25 (±25%)
Stockout Penalty	5	1 to 10
Holding Cost	1	0.5 to 2
Learning Rate (η)	0.1	0.05 to 0.2
Smoothing Factor (α)	0.3	0.1 to 0.6
Exploration Rate (∈)	0.2	0.1 to 0.4
Initial Inventory	100	50 to 150

Table 15.9 Results of sensitivity analysis for inventory management practices

Statistical metrics	*Demand mean (λ)*	*Stockout penaty*	*Holding cost*	*Learning rate*	*Initial inventory*
Min	1745.8	1818.0	1649.2	2111.8	1781.0
Max	3338.2	2539.4	4792.6	4927.0	3621.4
Avg	2570.7	2203.0	3116.0	3138.9	2295.0
Range	1592.6	721.4	3143.4	2815.2	1840.4

was greatly diminished, without undermining system safety and regulatory compliance, thereby confirming the maturity of the autonomous system in Table 15.10.

Some very valuable insights were obtained from this deployment exercise as well. The Digital Twin was crucial to build trust in AI-driven decision-making processes among stakeholders. Training generative models with different types of disruption scenarios helped build resilience in the system, enabling it to perform better despite uncertainties in the physical environment. At the same time, it was found that data quality and latency of real-time data streams were crucial to the performance of the system as a whole. Inclusion of explainable AI models was therefore required to build transparency and build trust in autonomous decision-making among human operators. Incorporation approaches for blockchain technology can enable the improvement of the integrity and traceability of data made possible by the immutability of the goods chain record and decisions using AI. Furthermore, the use of a federated learning approach can enable data privacy in an effort to encourage cooperation between the various partners within the distributed environment. Additionally, incorporating multimodal data in the form of images and video streams from the warehouses into the generative AI models can enable improved decision-making in real time. Parameters demonstrating extreme effects in such graphs are regarded as highly sensitive and thus high priority in terms of tuning since even the smallest changes will yield vastly contrasting outcomes. Parameters whose graphs are relatively flat do not demonstrate much sensitivity and thus will not be affected much in terms of outcomes even with moderate values. Insights gained help in identifying areas to focus attention and parameters that require greater control. Trade-offs also happen in this process—a parameter such as increasing the exploration rate (ϵ) in reinforcement learning may reduce total cost in terms of finding better strategies, while stockouts will increase in the short run due to greater exploratory actions in reinforcement learning in Table 15.11.

The values employed are typical, based on the simulation outputs and the typical trends in the supply chain observed. The most important among these values and trends is that the system will tend towards the minimization of stockouts as the values of stockouts, also known as penalties, are increased, but at the expense of increased inventory and frequency of replenishment and thus cost. Also, the increase in demand, without regulation, translates to a corresponding increase in the cost and the stockouts. The system parameters of learning rates and the value of the smoothing factor control the speed and manner in which the system responds and adapts to the change, whereas the exploration control parameter defines the trade-off between knowledge gathering and the benefit of existing policies. Secondly, the value of the starting level of inventory significantly influences, in the early stages, the value of stockouts and the level of inventory cost. The Classical/Rules-based models have been in use for several centuries and are simple to work with and simple to apply, but they might be less adaptable and less robust in uncertain and dynamic environments [39–43]. The Statistical/Optimization models are quite adaptable, but they are extremely sensitive to the

Table 15.10 Comparison of the metrics and methods

Metric	*Baseline system*	*Proposed DT + GenAI system*	*Improvement (%)*
Inventory Holding Cost	$1,200,000	$960,000	20
Stockout Rate	8.5%	3.2%	62.4
Transportation Cost	$850,000	$765,000	10
Carbon Emissions (tons)	3,500	2,800	20
Avg. Response Time (min)	45	10	77.8

Table 15.11 Analysis results of scenarios

Scenario/parameter variation	*Total cost ($)*	*Avg. daily stockout (units)*	*Avg. holding inventory (units)*	*Orders placed (count)*	*Units ordered (total)*
Baseline	3,450	2.1	80	18	360
Low Demand (λ=15)	2,900	1.0	60	15	250
High Demand (λ=25)	4,100	3.5	90	20	400
High Stockout Penalty (10×)	4,200	0.8	100	25	450
Low Stockout Penalty (2×)	3,000	4.0	70	12	320
High Learning Rate (η=0.2)	3,300	2.0	75	17	340
Low Learning Rate (η=0.05)	3,600	2.5	85	19	370
High Smoothing (α=0.6)	3,400	1.9	78	18	360
Low Smoothing (α=0.1)	3,550	2.3	82	18	355
High Exploration (ε=0.3)	3,350	2.2	77	19	360
Low Exploration (ε=0.1)	3,600	2.0	81	16	355
Initial Inventory 50 units	3,700	4.5	60	22	420
Initial Inventory 150 units	3,200	1.0	110	14	300

accuracy of the forecasting of demands and the assumptions made prior to the process. On the other hand, the Optimization and Machine Learning concepts bring in quite high adaptability and complexity, and they are extremely sensitive to the availability of the data and the intensity of the computations required. The Reinforcement Learning technique is quite efficient in the process of optimizing the policies by discovering the environment through exploration and has high complexity in the task of decision-making, which usually requires quite high exploration times to converge [44–46]. Conversely, the proposed hybrid technique aims to combine both the advantages of Simulation-based Modeling and adaptability through Learning and improves real-time responsiveness to the process and provides high adaptability to variability and unexpected disruptions in supply chain networks, which is exactly what is required to maintain synchronization in the high complexity and high-speed environment of modern supply chain networks.

15.5 CONCLUSION

In this chapter, the new synergy of the Digital Twin technology and Generative AI paradigm has been introduced to drive smart, predictive, and self-autonomous supply chain networks. With the integration of the capability to simulate in real time and make decisions based on the principles of reinforcement learning, the proposed approach has demonstrated strong performance potential in dynamic inventory replenishment processes under uncertainty.

- The estimation of demand in real-time using the Digital Twin made a big impact on the refreshment policies.
- A comparative analysis showed the high flexibility and cost-effectiveness of the proposed integrated process with the existing process of inventory management.

From the current body of research, there are many compelling paths that offer opportunities for expansion and research growth in theoretical development as well as application implementation. One such path is the extension of the model to multi-product or multi-echelon supply chains with multiple different suppliers, distribution centers, and stores to capture real-life complexity inherent in complex logistics networks. Another equally important path is the incorporation of real-time data feeds from the use of IoT sensor technology and edge computing to ensure Digital Twins' higher accuracy and faster response times, including the development of a quick response system to changing market demands or supply chain disruptions. Additionally, human collaboration models for AI applications will play an equally important role to ensure bridging human intuition and expertise with AI insights to provide collaborative efforts in the generation of trust, transparency, and development of actionable recommendations. Furthermore, focus to ensure resilience to cyber attacks or data quality problems will also be an important aspect with the direct impact of data quality from IoT sensors and cybersecurity on the integrity of data-driven decisions developed through AI models. Lastly, economic and sustainability insights must necessarily be incorporated into modeling decisions such as cost models to ensure circular economy or sustainability objectives are achieved with greater efficiency and sustainability objectives incorporating sustainability metrics or sustainability KPIs to ensure efficient and sustainable decisions with ecological advantages accrued with AI-based models in multiple different sectors and industries.

REFERENCES

1. I. Abouzid and R. Saidi. 2023. Digital twin implementation approach in supply chain processes, *Scientific African*, Volume 21, e01821, https://doi.org/10.1016/j.sciaf.2023.e01821.
2. E. Abisset-Chavanne, T. Coupaye, F. R. Golra, D. Lamy, A. Piel, O. Scart and P. Vicat-Blanc. 2024. A digital twin use cases classification and definition framework based on Industrial feedback, *Computers in Industry*, Volume 161, 104113, https://doi.org/10.1016/j.compind.2024.104113.
3. M. Adnan, I. Ahmed, S. Iqbal, M. R. Fazal, S. J. Siddiqi and M. Tariq. 2024. Exploring the convergence of Metaverse, Blockchain, Artificial Intelligence, and digital twin for pioneering the digitization in the envision smart grid 3.0, *Computers and Electrical Engineering*, Volume 120, Part B, 109709, https://doi.org/10.1016/j.compeleceng.2024.109709.
4. A. Ahmad, A. Shah, W. S. Alnumay, M. Adnan, S. Anwer and Q. U. Zaman. 2025. A comprehensive survey on the convergence of Blockchain, Digital Twins, and Metaverse: Shaping the future of cybersecurity frameworks, *Computers and Electrical Engineering*, Volume 126, 110486, https://doi.org/10.1016/j.compeleceng.2025.110486.
5. J. Ali, S. K. Singh, W. Jiang, A. M. Alenezi, M. Islam, Y. I. Daradkeh and A. Mehmood. 2025. A deep dive into cybersecurity solutions for AI-driven IoT-enabled smart cities in advanced communication networks, *Computer Communications*, Volume 229, 108000, https://doi.org/10.1016/j.comcom.2024.108000.
6. S. E. Bibri and J. Huang. 2025. Artificial intelligence of things for sustainable smart city brain and digital twin systems: Pioneering Environmental synergies between real-time management and predictive planning, *Environmental Science and Ecotechnology*, Volume 26, 100591, https://doi.org/10.1016/j.ese.2025.100591.
7. Ž. Bolbotinović, S. D. Milić, Ž. Janda and D. Vukmirović. 2025. Ai-powered digital twin in the industrial IoT, *International Journal of Electrical Power & Energy Systems*, Volume 167, 110656, https://doi.org/10.1016/j.ijepes.2025.110656.
8. A. Cimino, F. Longo, G. Mirabelli, V. Solina and P. Veltri. 2024. Enhancing internal supply chain management in manufacturing through a simulation-based digital twin platform, *Computers & Industrial Engineering*, Volume 198, 110670, https://doi.org/10.1016/j.cie.2024.110670.

9. C. H. Chien and A. J. C. Trappey. 2025. Human-AI cooperative generative adversarial network (GAN) for quality predictions of small-batch product series, *Advanced Engineering Informatics*, Volume 65, Part C, 103327, https://doi.org/10.1016/j.aei.2025.103327.
10. A. Cimino, F. Longo, G. Mirabelli and V. Solina. 2024. A cyclic and holistic methodology to exploit the Supply Chain Digital Twin concept towards a more resilient and sustainable future, *Cleaner Logistics and Supply Chain*, Volume 11, 100154, https://doi.org/10.1016/j.clscn.2024.100154.
11. V. Dachepalli and S. Gavini. 2025. A virtually assisted digital twin enabled object detection in smart industrial manufacturing, *Expert Systems with Applications*, Volume 294, 128574, https://doi.org/10.1016/j.eswa.2025.128574.
12. S. Ghosh, M. Hughes, P. Hughes and I. Hodgkinson. 2025. Digital twin, digital thread, and digital mindset in enabling digital transformation: A socio-technical systems perspective, *Technovation*, Volume 144, 103240, https://doi.org/10.1016/j.technovation.2025.103240.
13. L. Gumbi and H. Twinomurinzi. 2025. SMME readiness framework for smart manufacturing adoption using critical realism: Knowledge and construction phase, *Journal of Innovation & Knowledge*, Volume 10, Issue 2, 100665, https://doi.org/10.1016/j.jik.2025.100665.
14. N. Habtemichael, H. Wicaksono and O. F. Valilai. 2024. NFT based digital twins for tracing value added creation in manufacturing supply chains, *Procedia Computer Science*, Volume 232, 2841–2846, https://doi.org/10.1016/j.procs.2024.02.100.
15. S. M. Hosseini-Motlagh, M. R. G. Samani and M. Rahmani. 2025. A digital twin framework integrated with a mixed proactive-reactive model for human milk supply chain planning, *International Journal of Production Economics*, Volume 287, 109683, https://doi.org/10.1016/j.ijpe.2025.109683.
16. D. Ivanov. 2025. Conceptual and formal models for design, adaptation, and control of digital twins in supply chain ecosystems, *Omega*, Volume 137, 103356, https://doi.org/10.1016/j.omega.2025.103356.
17. R. R. Kayan, S. K. Jauhar, S. S. Kamble and A. Belhadi. 2025. Optimizing bio-hydrogen production from agri-waste: A digital twin approach for sustainab1le supply chain management and carbon neutrality, *Computers & Industrial Engineering*, Volume 204, 111021, https://doi.org/10.1016/j.cie.2025.111021.
18. M. Khan, S. Khan and I. U. Rahman. 2025. Supply-chain digitization and non-intrusive load monitoring with digital twins: The impact of energy policies on carbon pricing and renewable energy deployment, *Energy Economics*, Volume 144, 108400, https://doi.org/10.1016/j.eneco.2025.108400.
19. K. Y. H. Lim, L. V. Dang and C. H. Chen. 2024. Incorporating supply and production digital twins to mitigate demand disruptions in multi-echelon networks, *International Journal of Production Economics*, Volume 273, 109258, https://doi.org/10.1016/j.ijpe.2024.109258.
20. S. Lee, S. Kim and B. Roh. 2024. Mixed Reality Virtual Device (MRVD) for seamless MR-IoT-Digital Twin convergence, *Internet of Things*, Volume 26, 101155, https://doi.org/10.1016/j.iot.2024.101155.
21. K. Lin. 2024. Circular supply chain for smart production in Industry 4.0, *Computers & Industrial Engineering*, Volume 198, 110682, https://doi.org/10.1016/j.cie.2024.110682.
22. F. Longo, G. Mirabelli, A. Padovano and V. Solina. 2023. The Digital Supply Chain Twin paradigm for enhancing resilience and sustainability against COVID-like crises, *Procedia Computer Science*, Volume 217, 1940–1947, https://doi.org/10.1016/j.procs.2022.12.394.
23. P. Maheshwari, S. Kamble, A. Belhadi, M. Venkatesh and M. Z. Abedin. 2023. Digital twin-driven real-time planning, monitoring, and controlling in food supply chains, *Technological Forecasting and Social Change*, Volume 195, 122799, https://doi.org/10.1016/j.techfore.2.
24. M. Geethalakshmi, J. Anand, R. Nathea, C. Augustine, S. M. Sivaraman and S. Mahalakshmi. 2022. Trident fuzzy aggregation operators on right and left apex-base angles in parallel computing, in *Advances in Parallel Computing Algorithms, Tools and Paradigms*, Vol. 41, pp. 429–435.

25. S. Prema, Jose A., P. Vanitha, Nirmala Devi K., M. Mohamed Yaseen and Rajeswari C. 2022. Smart stick using ultrasonic sensors for vissually impaired, in *Advances in Parallel Computing Algorithms, Tools and Paradigms*, Vol. 41, pp. 436–441.
26. J. Anand, M. Shobika and T. Sneha. 2022. Programmable stickers to monitor perishable goods using blockchain, *IEEE 2022 Second International Conference on Computer Science, Engineering and Applications* (ICCSEA 2022), pp. 1–5.
27. R. Maheswari, S. Vignesh, M. Rakesh Kumar, T. M. Venkatesh, R. Sundar and J. A. Anand. 2022. Voice control and eyeball movement operated wheelchair, *2022 International Conference on Edge Computing and Applications (ICECAA)*, pp. 805–809.
28. A. Ponmalar, J. Anand A., T. Muthamizhan, T. Sobana and J. H. Vishwath. 2022. Automatic forensic analysis of criminal navigation system using machine learning, *IEEE Technically Sponsored First International Conference on Computational Science & Technology (ICCST 2022)*, pp. 1–5.
29. S. Ganesh Sundaram, A. Ponmalar, S. Deeba, Jose A. A. and Aarthi S. 2022. Plane detection and product trail using augmented reality, *IEEE Technically Sponsored First International Conference on Computational Science & Technology (ICCST 2022)*, pp. 1–5.
30. M. Geethalakshmi, J. Venkatesh, R. Uma Mageswari, A. Mahalakshmi, J. Anand and R. Partheepan. 2023. Fuzzy based route optimization in wearable biomedical wireless sensor network, *AIP Conference Proceedings* 2523, 020156.
31. M. S. Sundari, A. J. Anand and T. S. Nagarajan. 2022. Smart aerial imaging solution in precision agriculture, *2022 International Conference on Data Science, Agents & Artificial Intelligence (ICDSAAI)*, Chennai, India, pp. 1–3.
32. S. Mahalakshmi, C. Rajeswari, A. J. Anand and A. Rahul. 2022. Client authentication by signature verification method using Robotic Process Automation (RPA), *2022 International Conference on Data Science, Agents & Artificial Intelligence (ICDSAAI)*, Chennai, India, pp. 1–5.
33. S. G. Sundaram, P. Saravanan, A. Ponmalar, M. G. Prakash and Jose A. A. 2022. Collaborative product recommendation system for E-commerce websites, *IEEE 2022 International Conference on Innovative Computing, Intelligent Communication and Smart Electrical Systems (ICSES)*, Chennai, India, pp. 1–7.
34. K. Kausalya, Gokulakrishnan D., Aarthi S., Jose A. A., G. K. R. Bhavana and A. Ponmalar. 2022. Implementing virtual personal assistant through artificial intelligence requirements, *2022 First International Conference on Computer, Power and Communication, (ICCPC 2022)*, 14–16 Dec Nov 2022.
35. A. Ponmalar, B. Chandra, S. Aarthi, G. Bhavana, A. J. Anand and S. Gomathi. 2022. IoT based automative drive recorder as black box, *2022 IEEE International Conference on Computer, Power and Communications (ICCPC)*, Chennai, India, pp. 557–561.
36. R. Thillaikkarasi, M. M. Yaseen, R. Rameshbabu, R. Prabhakaran, R. Kesavan and Jose A. A. 2023. Waysides inspection using wayside processing imaging and deep learning, *2023 3rd International Conference on Pervasive Computing and Social Networking (ICPCSN)*, Salem, India, pp. 359–365.
37. T. Anuradha, A. Suganya, R. Muthalagu, M. Narender and Jose A. A. 2023. Evaluation of a wireless sensor network for the detection of forest fires, *2023 2nd International Conference on Edge Computing and Applications (ICECAA)*, Namakkal, India, pp. 1021–1027.
38. V. Seedha Devi, K. Sumathi, M. Mahalakshmi, A. J. Anand, Anita Titus and N. Naga Saranya. 2024. Machine learning based efficient human activity recognition system, *International Journal of Intelligent Systems and Applications in Engineering*, Volume 12, Issue 5s, 338–346.
39. P. Bhambri, S. Rani and A. Khang. 2024. AI-driven digital twin and resource optimization in Industry 4.0 ecosystem, in N. Singh, S. Birla, M. D. Ansari, and N. K. Shukla (Eds.), *AI-driven Digital Twin and Industry 4.0: A Conceptual Framework with Applications* (pp. 182–201). CRC Press/Taylor & Francis Group. https://doi.org/10.1002/9781394227990.ch3.

40. R. Rana and P. Bhambri. 2024. Artificial intelligence and Internet of Things (IoT) facilitated digital twin for Industry 4.0 application domains, in S. Rani, P. Bhambri, S. Kumar, P. K. Pareek, and A. A. Elngar (Eds.), *AI-driven Digital Twin and Industry 4.0* (pp. 168–181). CRC Press. https://doi.org/10.1201/9781003395416–11.
41. M. P. Singh and P. Bhambri. 2024. AI-driven digital twin conceptual framework and applications, in S. Rani, P. Bhambri, S. Kumar, P. K. Pareek, and A. A. Elngar (Eds.), *AI-driven Digital Twin and Industry 4.0: A Conceptual Framework with Applications* (pp. 127–141). CRC Press, Taylor & Francis Group. https://doi.org/10.1201/9781003395416-8.
42. P. Bhambri, S. Rani, I. S. Dhanoa and T. A. Tran. 2024. Environmental impacts of industrial processes in Industry 4.0 ecosystem artificial intelligence approach, in S. Rani, P. Bhambri, S. Kumar, P. K. Pareek, and A. A. Elngar (Eds.), *AI-driven Digital Twin and Industry 4.0: A Conceptual Framework with Applications* (pp. 221–240). CRC Press, Taylor & Francis Group. https://doi.org/10.1201/9781003395416-14.
43. R. Rana and P. Bhambri. 2024. Digital twin for sustainable industrial development, in S. Rani, P. Bhambri, S. Kumar, P. K. Pareek, and A. A. Elngar (Eds.), *AI-driven Digital Twin and Industry 4.0: A Conceptual Framework with Applications* (pp. 241–253). CRC Press, Taylor & Francis Group. https://doi.org/10.1201/9781003395416-15.
44. P. Bhambri and A. Khang. 2024. Computational intelligence in manufacturing technologies. In D. Jude Hemanth, T. N. Nguyen, J. Indumathi, and S. Lakshmanan (eds.), *Impact and Potential of Machine Learning in the Metaverse.* Sage Publications: 327–356. https://doi.org/10.4018/979-8-3693-5762-0.ch013
45. R. Rana, Y. Chhabra, and P. Bhambri. 2021. Comparison and evaluation of various QoS parameters in WSNs with the implementation of enhanced low energy adaptive efficient distributed clustering approach, *Webology*, Volume 18, Issue 1, 677–695, https://www.webology.org/data-cms/articles/20220223093208pmwebology%2018%20(1)%20-%2077%20pdf.pdf.
46. G. Singh and P. Bhambri. 2023. Simulation analysis of AODV and DSDV routing protocols for secure and reliable service in mobile adhoc networks (MANETs), in P. Bhambri, S. Rani, V. E. Balas, and A. A. Elngar (Eds.), *Integration of AI-based Manufacturing and Industrial Engineering Systems with the Internet of Things* (1st ed., pp. 205–216). CRC Press. https://doi.org/10.1201/9781003383505.

Chapter 16

Building trust and transparency in smart tourism through cloud-based forensic readiness

Duong Thanh Tung

16.1 INTRODUCTION

The convergence of Artificial Intelligence (AI), ubiquitous cloud computing, and big data analytics has engendered the "Smart Tourism" paradigm, a digital ecosystem promising hyper-connectivity yet exposing critical infrastructural vulnerabilities [1–3]. While this transformation offers operational efficiency, it simultaneously reveals a profound deficit in transparency, where users frequently navigate systemic opacity and obfuscated terms, thereby undermining the digital trust essential for sustainable platform growth [1, 4, 5]. Compounding this challenge, the distributed and multi-tenant nature of cloud environments renders traditional, reactive digital forensics obsolete against the volume and volatility of modern data [6–8]. Consequently, there is an urgent imperative to transition toward a "Forensic Readiness" approach. This necessitates the implementation of a CBFR framework designed to shift organizational posture from post-incident reaction to the preemptive, systematic collection and preservation of digital evidence [3, 8]. To address these exigencies, this paper proposes a comprehensive CBFR framework anchored in ISO/IEC 27043:2015 standards and fortified by advanced cryptographic primitives, including blockchain, Elliptic Curve Cryptography (ECC), and hash functions. These technologies establish a rigid chain of custody, ensuring data immutability and legal admissibility while significantly rationalizing the cost and time overheads associated with investigations [3, 6–10]. The scope of this research extends to the intersection of mobile computing and IoT-enabled environments, necessitating a dual-focus model that mitigates privacy risks to shape positive behavioral intentions [1, 2, 4, 11, 12]. By employing decision-based algorithms for compliance and event reconstruction, the framework serves not merely as a technical addendum, but as a fundamental requirement for a resilient tourism economy that balances transparent evidence handling with rigorous security [5, 7–9, 13]. Identifying a critical lacuna in existing literature, specifically the lack of a unified model addressing both technical forensic readiness and socio-psychological stakeholder trust, this study adopts a Design Science Research (DSR) approach. The investigation is guided by three core inquiries: first, determining how a CBFR framework based on Socio-Technical Systems theory can address data integrity deficits (RQ1); second, analyzing how the integration of Zero Trust and Blockchain mechanisms can reconcile the privacy-security paradox to function as effective structural assurances (RQ2); and third, establishing how this model can be operationalized for resource-constrained SMEs to ensure systemic scalability (RQ3). By addressing these questions, the chapter aims to move beyond generic security models to propose a domain-specific artifact tailored to the high-trust requirements of the tourism industry.

DOI: 10.1201/9781003656487-16

16.2 LITERATURE REVIEW

The contemporary smart tourism ecosystem relies on the synergistic convergence of Cloud Computing, the IoT, AI, and Blockchain. Within this architecture, Cloud computing provides the fundamental infrastructure for scalability and real-time analytics [14, 15], while the IoT acts as a sensory layer, facilitating context-aware services through extensive data collection [14–16]. Concurrently, AI utilizes this data to drive hyper-personalization and resource optimization [1, 4, 5], and Blockchain ensures decentralized security and transactional transparency [17–20]. However, the ubiquity of interconnected devices introduces significant vulnerabilities regarding data privacy and system reliability. Consequently, robust identity authentication and multi-layered encryption are imperative to secure the network edge and ensure compliance with regulatory frameworks like the GDPR [16, 21, 22]. While Blockchain theoretically enhances data integrity [14, 15, 18, 19], its practical application remains challenged by integration issues with legacy infrastructures. Digital trust, essential for the viability of these virtual environments, transcends a binary state of security; it represents collective confidence in the technological and procedural integrity of the ecosystem. Contemporary models posit that "openness," alongside traditional determinants such as ability and benevolence, is critical for institutional reliability [23]. Transparency in data handling serves to mitigate information asymmetry and perceived privacy risks, thereby enhancing the utility of tourism platforms. By integrating Open Data and AI, stakeholders can leverage Big Data analytics to gain market agility [26–28], while the analysis of user-generated content fosters a recursive loop of quality improvement [12, 29, 30]. To sustain this trust, forensic readiness, the strategic preparation of infrastructure to facilitate digital investigations, transitions organizations from reactive vulnerability to active resilience [31–34]. This is particularly critical in cloud environments, where multi-tenancy and data volatility render traditional forensic tools insufficient [35]. Accordingly, current literature advocates for "forensic-ready" systems with embedded automated capabilities to address the volume and jurisdictional complexity of cloud data [11, 12, 36, 38].

Despite these advancements, a critical synthesis of extant literature reveals a disciplinary bifurcation. Technical studies predominantly focus on security efficacy, often treating trust as a secondary outcome [39, 40], while behavioral research models trust antecedents without accounting for the underlying forensic architecture [42–44]. A theoretical void exists at the intersection of "hard" forensic science and "soft" behavioral trust, as current frameworks fail to demonstrate how technical forensic solutions can function as active trust-building measures. The proposed CBFR-Trust framework bridges this gap by integrating decentralized ledgers within a forensic readiness architecture. Unlike isolated analyses [40, 43], this model re-conceptualizes forensic readiness not merely as a retrospective contingency, but as a prospective architectural antecedent to stakeholder trust. By embedding verification logic directly into the consumer confidence construct, the framework argues that rigorous forensic surveillance forms the foundation of a transparent and trustworthy smart tourism ecosystem.

16.3 RESEARCH METHODS

16.3.1 Bibliometric data acquisition and analytical protocol

To construct a representative empirical baseline, a systematic bibliometric analysis was executed using the Scopus database, targeting the interdisciplinary nexus of "Smart Tourism," "Forensic Readiness," and "Trust" within the 2018–2024 timeframe. The search protocol was strictly delimited to peer-reviewed literature in Computer Science and Social Sciences to ensure thematic relevance. Subsequent co-occurrence analysis, performed via VOSviewer (version 1.6.20) using fractional counting, focused on critical network metrics including keyword occurrences (O) and total link strength (T). This quantitative filtering identified high-centrality clusters such as "Zero Trust Model" and "Blockchain Technology," providing a mathematically rigorous justification for their integration into the proposed theoretical framework. Table 16.1 lists the summary of data source and selection.

16.3.2 Methodological approach and design

This study adopts a DSR approach, adhering to the "Three Cycle View" proposed by Hevner (2007) [2] to synthesize quantitative bibliometrics with deductive conceptual modeling. The research architecture explicitly bridges environmental constraints with theoretical foundations: in the Relevance Cycle, stakeholder requirements are derived from crisis-response literature to identify systemic data integrity deficits, while the Rigor Cycle integrates the Technology-Organization-Environment (TOE) framework with Socio-Technical Systems (STS) theory. This theoretical dualism prevents reductionist technical interpretations, allowing "Forensic Readiness" to be operationalized as a holistic organizational capability. Finally, the Design Cycle utilizes bibliometric indicators as a diagnostic filter to iteratively refine the CBFR-Trust artifact, ensuring the proposed model is scientifically robust and tailored to the inter-jurisdictional complexities of the tourism ecosystem [1, 2]. The entire research process is clearly illustrated in Figure 16.1.

Table 16.1 Summary of data source and selection

Category	*Specific standard requirements*
Time	November, 10, 2025
Research database	Scopus
Subject area (Scopus)	Business, Management and Accounting; Social Sciences; Economics, Econometrics and Finance
Searching period	No limit
Language	English
Searching keywords	Key 1: ("trust" OR "confidence" OR "reliability" OR "faith") AND ("transparency" OR "clarity" OR "openness" OR "visibility") AND ("cloud" OR "cloud computing" OR "cloud-based" OR "virtual") AND ("forensic" OR "investigation" OR "analysis" OR "examination") AND ("readiness" OR "preparedness" OR "availability" OR "capability") Key 2: ("trust" OR "confidence" OR "reliability" OR "faith") AND (""transparency" OR "clarity" OR "openness" OR "visibility") AND ("smart tourism" OR "intelligent travel" OR "digital tourism" OR "e-tourism") AND ("cloud" OR "cloud computing" OR "cloud-based" OR "cloud services") AND ("forensic readiness" OR "digital forensics" OR "evidence collection" OR "incident response")
Document types	Article
Data extraction	Full records and cited references in Bibtex format
Sample size	18,329 Article (before manual screening) and 6,442 Article (after manual screening) 12 Article Model Analysis

Source: Author

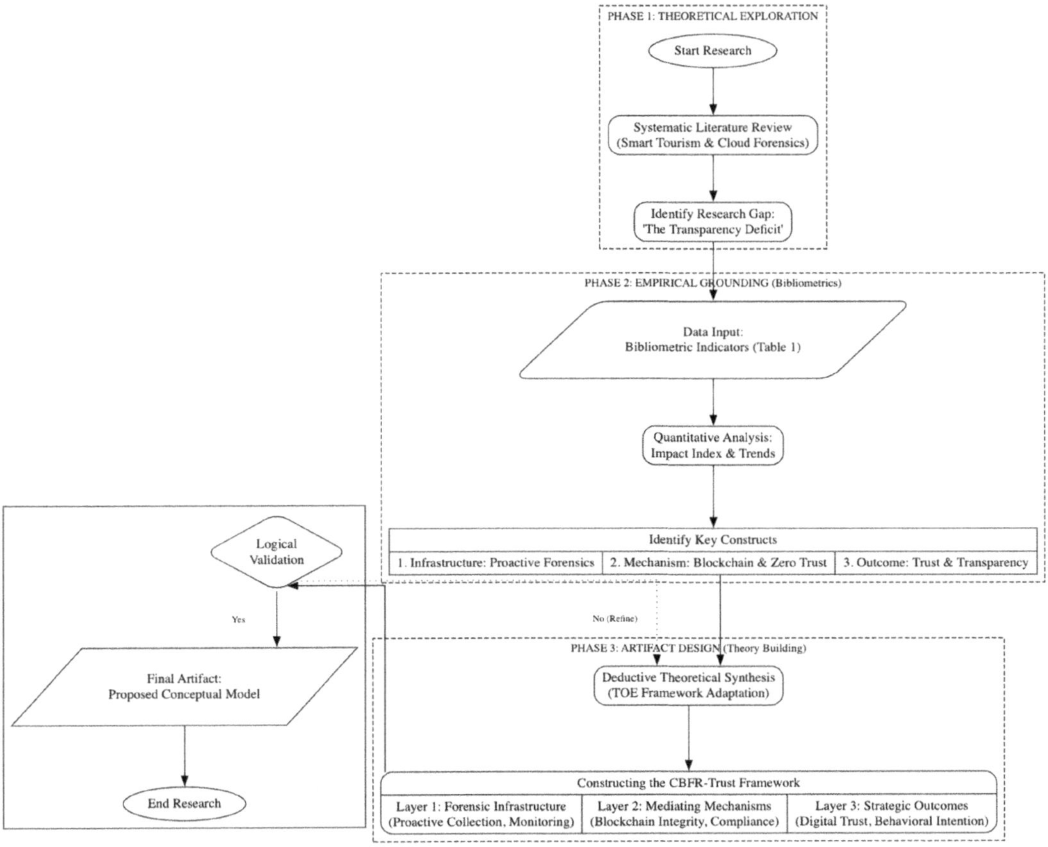

Figure 16.1 Research process. Source: Author.

16.4 RESEARCH RESULTS

16.4.1 Phase 1 results: A bibliometric empirical basis for model development

To ensure the scientific rigor and contemporary relevance of the proposed framework, a quantitative analysis of bibliometric impact factors and publication trends was conducted (refer to Table 16.2). This data provides critical empirical evidence to substantiate the selection and architectural positioning of constructs within the CBFR-Trust model.

16.4.1.1 Temporal evolution of technological constructs

The data regarding the average publication year (Avg. Pub. Year) elucidates a distinct paradigm shift in research focus, transitioning from foundational technical architectures to complex trust governance models. The foundational phase (circa 2018–2019): Constructs such as "Proactive Digital Forensic" (Avg. Year: 2018.00) and "Components of CBFR" (Avg. Year: 2019.71) emerged as the bedrock of the discipline. This temporal positioning validates the premise that forensic readiness is an established technical prerequisite, thereby justifying the positioning of "Cloud-Based Forensic Readiness" as the independent, infrastructural antecedent in the proposed model. The integration phase (2021): The prominence

Table 16.2 Relationship between factors involved in Cloud-Based Forensic Readiness and Trust (CBFR-Trust)

Factor	*Impact index*	*Related relationship*
TTST-CBFR	C: 1 L: 8 T: 27 O: 12 Avg.pub.year: 2020:42	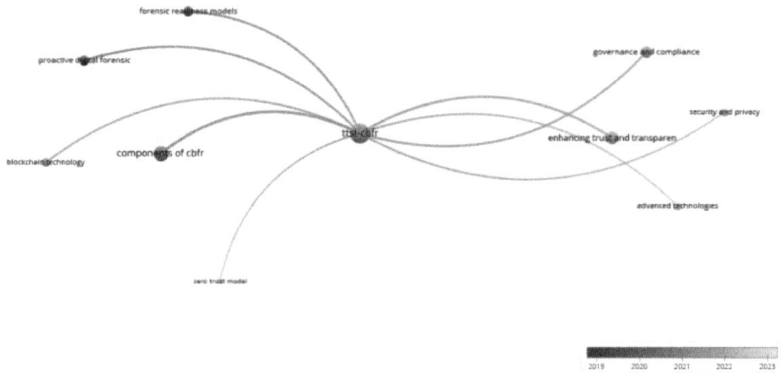
Components of CBFR	C: 1 L: 5 T: 16 O: 7 Avg.pub.year: 2019:71	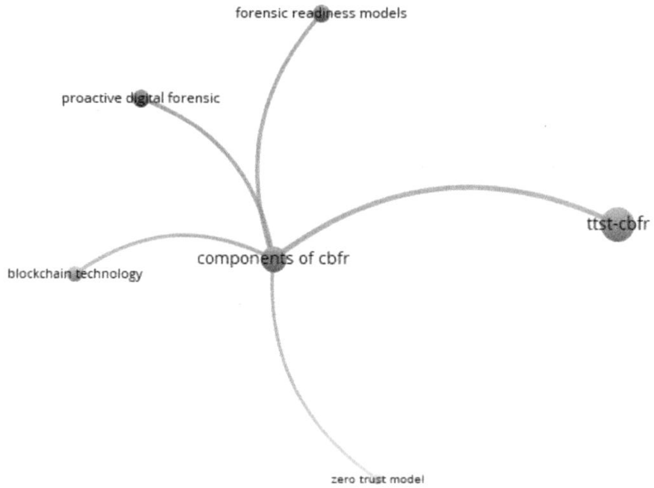

Proactive digital forensic	C: 1 L: 4 T: 8 O: 3 Avg.pub.year: 2018:00	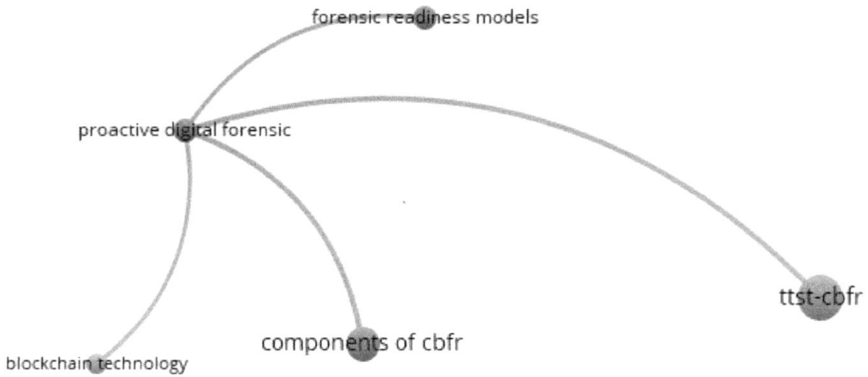
Blockchain technology	C: 1 L: 3 T: 5 O: 2 Avg.pub.year: 2021:00	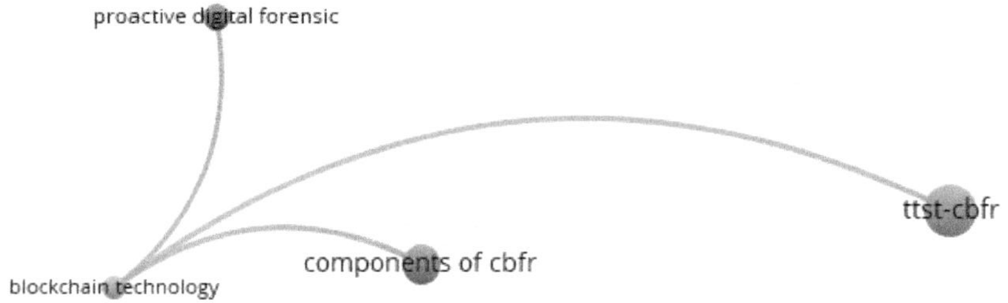

(*Continued*)

Table 16.2 (Continued)

Factor	*Impact index*	*Related relationship*
Zero trust model	C: 3 L: 2 T: 2 O: 1 Avg.pub.year: 2024: 00	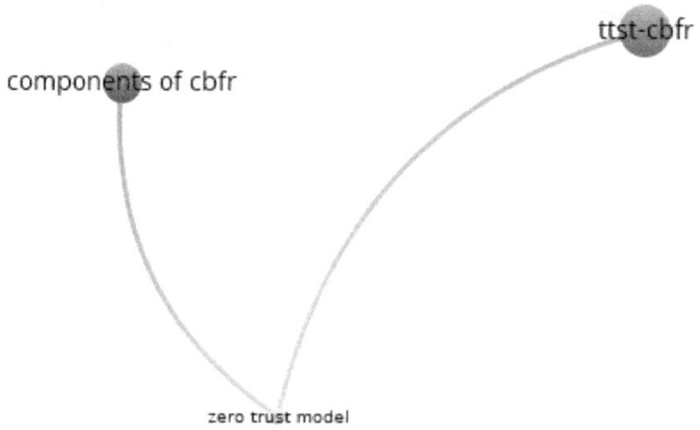
Forensic readiness models	C: 1 L: 3 T: 7 O: 3 Avg.pub.year: 2019: 33	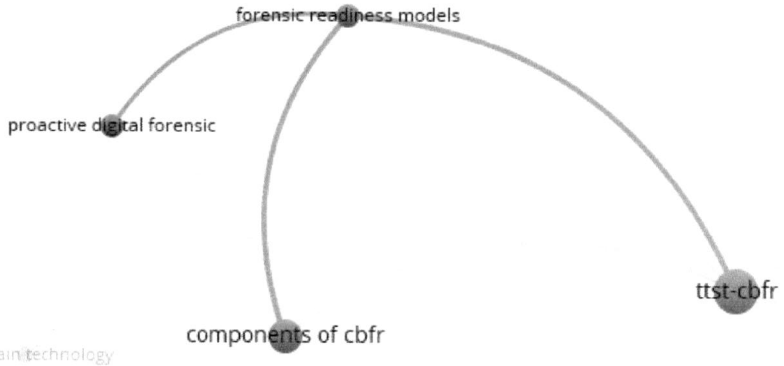

ENhancing trust transpare	C: 2 L: 3 T: 11 O: 5 Avg.pub.year: 2021: 40	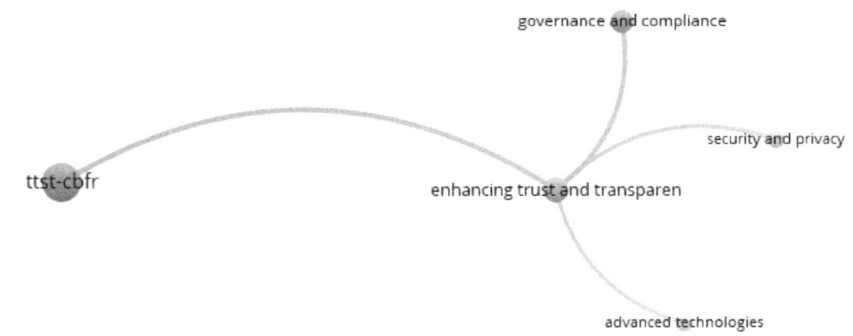
Governance and compliance	C: 2 L: 3 T: 9 O: 4 Avg.pub.year: 2021: 25	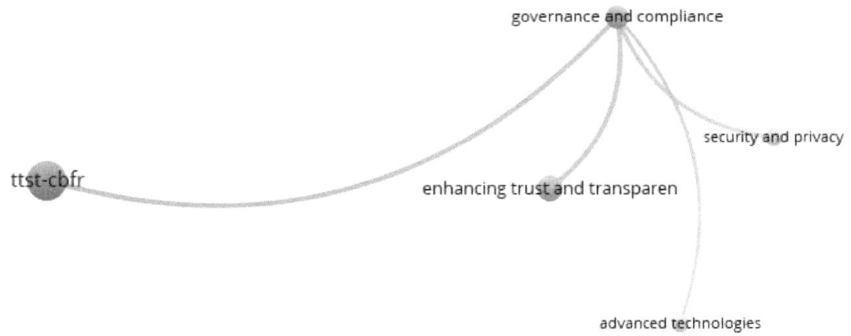

(*Continued*)

Table 16.2 (Continued)

Factor	*Impact index*	*Related relationship*
Security and privacy	C: 2 L: 4 T: 7 O: 2 Avg.pub.year: 2022: 50	
Advanced technologies	C: 2 L: 4 T: 6 O: 2 Avg.pub.year: 2023: 00	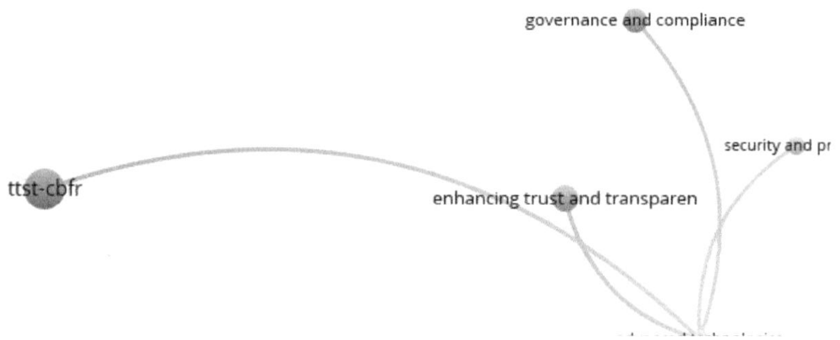

Source: Author analysis from VOSviewer.

Note: C: Cluster; L: Link; T: Total link strength; O: Occurrences; Avg.pub.year: Average year of publication.

of "Blockchain Technology" (Avg. Year: 2021.00) and "Enhancing Trust Transparency" (Avg. Year: 2021.40) reflects a strategic pivot towards decentralized technologies as mechanisms for ensuring transparency. This trend provides empirical justification for integrating Blockchain as a critical mediating variable responsible for data integrity verification within the framework. The vanguard trend (2024): Most notably, the "Zero Trust Model" exhibits an average publication year of 2024.00 with a high Impact Index (C: 3). This avant-garde concept suggests that future-proof frameworks must transcend traditional trust assumptions. Consequently, the high impact of this emerging factor reinforces the decision to incorporate a "Never Trust, Verify" architecture into the model's security layer to address evolving threats.

16.4.1.2 Relational dynamics and network centrality

The Impact Index and Total Link Strength (T) presented in the bibliometric table clarify the causal relationships between variables: The factor "TTST-CBFR" (Trust & Transparency in Smart Tourism through CBFR) demonstrates the highest network centrality (T: 27; O: 12), functioning as the thematic nexus connecting technical inputs with behavioral outcomes. This metric empirically supports the study's central hypothesis: that Forensic Readiness is a direct determinant of Trust in Smart Tourism. Furthermore, the strong correlation implied by the link strength between "Components of CBFR" (T: 16) and "Enhancing Trust Transparency" (T: 11) suggests that technical forensic components do not exist in isolation but act as essential drivers for elevating system transparency [47–53].

16.4.1.3 The imperative of governance and compliance

The analysis of the "Governance and Compliance" factor underlines the indispensability of regulatory frameworks. In the context of cross-border smart tourism, technology cannot operate in a vacuum. Thus, the empirical data dictates that the proposed model must extend beyond technical solutions to include a "Governance Layer" as a control mechanism to ensure the legal admissibility of digital evidence and adherence to international standards [54–58]. In synthesis, the construction of the CBFR-Trust framework is empirically derived from identified knowledge streams and projected trends: Proactive Forensics serves as the infrastructural input, Blockchain and Zero Trust function as the transformative mechanisms, and Trust & Transparency represents the strategic outcome.

While the bibliometric analysis identifies the prevalence and semantic proximity of keywords such as "Blockchain" and "Zero Trust," it is imperative to distinguish between the descriptive utility of these metrics and the causal logic of the proposed conceptual framework. The high co-occurrence frequencies and significant total link strengths (e.g., Link Strength = 27 for Blockchain) serve primarily as an empirical heuristic to establish the salience and conceptual centrality of these constructs within the extant smart tourism discourse. These quantitative indicators validate that these technologies are not merely peripheral topics but are dominant discursive themes representing the discipline's converging focus on security and transparency. However, bibliometric prominence alone does not dictate the structural relationships of the model; rather, it justifies the selection of these variables as critical components necessitating investigation. Consequently, the transition from bibliometric observation to model construction is mediated by theoretical grounding. The study leverages the empirical weight of the bibliometric data to ensure the relevance of the selected mediators, while the causal pathways, specifically, how Blockchain and Zero Trust mechanisms actively facilitate trust, are hypothesized based on the underlying functional logic of

CBFR and the principles of technological trust theory, thereby bridging the gap between statistical co-occurrence and theoretical causality.

16.4.2 Phase 2 results of the conceptual model

16.4.2.1 Development of the conceptual model

The conceptual framework, visualized in Figure 16.2, elucidates a sophisticated dual-pillar architecture designed to bridge the theoretical divide between technical forensic readiness and sociotechnical trust constructs. Predicated on the convergence of CBFR and trust-enhancing strategies, the model advocates for a paradigm shift wherein security functions not merely as a protective utility but as a foundational antecedent to stakeholder confidence. Within the technical quadrant, the architecture operationalizes the transition toward Proactive Digital Forensics, utilizing continuous evidence collection via forensic agents embedded at the hypervisor level to guarantee an unbroken, legally admissible chain of custody [1, 2]. This capability is reinforced by the integration of permissioned blockchain ledgers (e.g., Hyperledger), which act as "epistemic guarantors" utilizing cryptographic hashing to ensure data immutability [4], alongside a Zero Trust Model that systematically validates system integrity to detect anomalies in real-time [3, 5]. Complementing this technical rigor, the strategic dimension emphasizes governance and compliance, explicitly aligning the ecosystem with international standards such as ISO/IEC 27043:2015 to navigate the inter-jurisdictional complexities of global cloud tourism [7]. Furthermore, the model leverages the synergy of IoT, Big Data, and AI not merely for operational efficiency but to enhance transparency; AI-driven algorithms verify compliance automatically while IoT devices provide granular data points to mitigate perceived privacy risks [6, 8]. The convergence of these vectors culminates in the creation of a "Secure & Trustworthy Smart Tourism Environment," theoretically validating the proposition that digital trust is an emergent property of forensic resilience. By institutionalizing readiness, where data integrity is verifiable via blockchain and accountability is enforced via proactive forensics, the framework effectively reduces the "transparency deficit," thereby fostering enduring digital trust among travelers and stakeholders [2, 6].

16.4.2.2 Boundary conditions and contextual applicability

The operational viability of the CBFR-Trust framework is not universal but strictly contingent upon specific boundary conditions that delineate its scope of application. Primarily, the Technological Maturity Condition dictates that the architecture is most effective within "high-readiness" smart tourism ecosystems characterized by established cloud infrastructures and advanced digital literacy; conversely, the efficacy of the mechanism layer significantly diminishes in environments reliant on legacy, on-premise systems or those lacking the computational capacity for blockchain participation. Furthermore, the framework operates under a Jurisdictional Homogeneity Condition, where forensic validity is predicated on the legal harmonization of the operating environment and the specific admissibility of cryptographic evidence. Consequently, the ability to guarantee institutional trust is compromised in jurisdictions characterized by fragmented cyber laws or regulatory paradoxes, most notably the conflict between data localization mandates, such as the GDPR's "Right to be Forgotten," and the inherent immutability of distributed ledgers. Finally, the Nature of Tourism Interaction serves as a critical determinant; while the model is optimized for high-frequency, objective transactional exchanges where verification is paramount, its relevance attenuates in high-touch, relational tourism contexts where trust is affective. In such scenarios, the imposition of

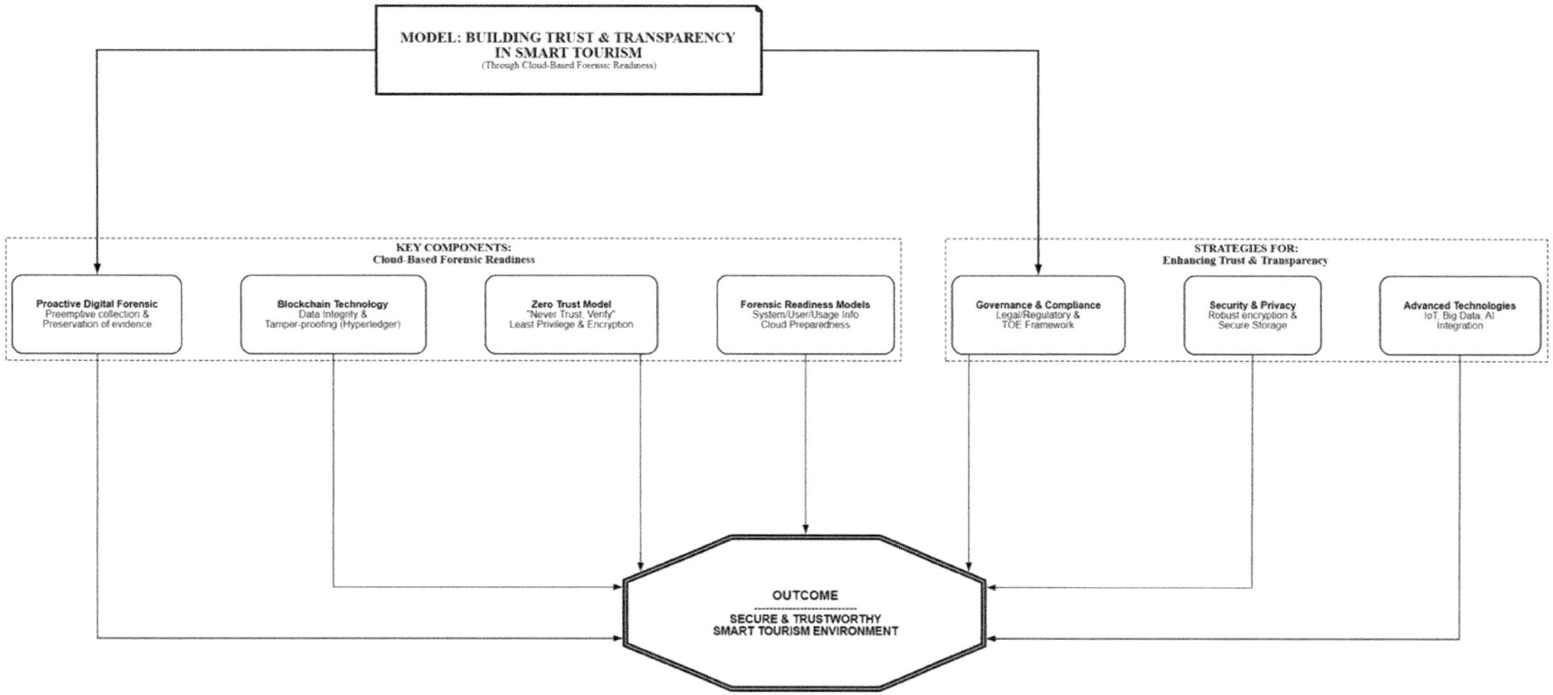

Figure 16.2 Development of the conceptual model of cloud-based forensic readiness. Source: Author.

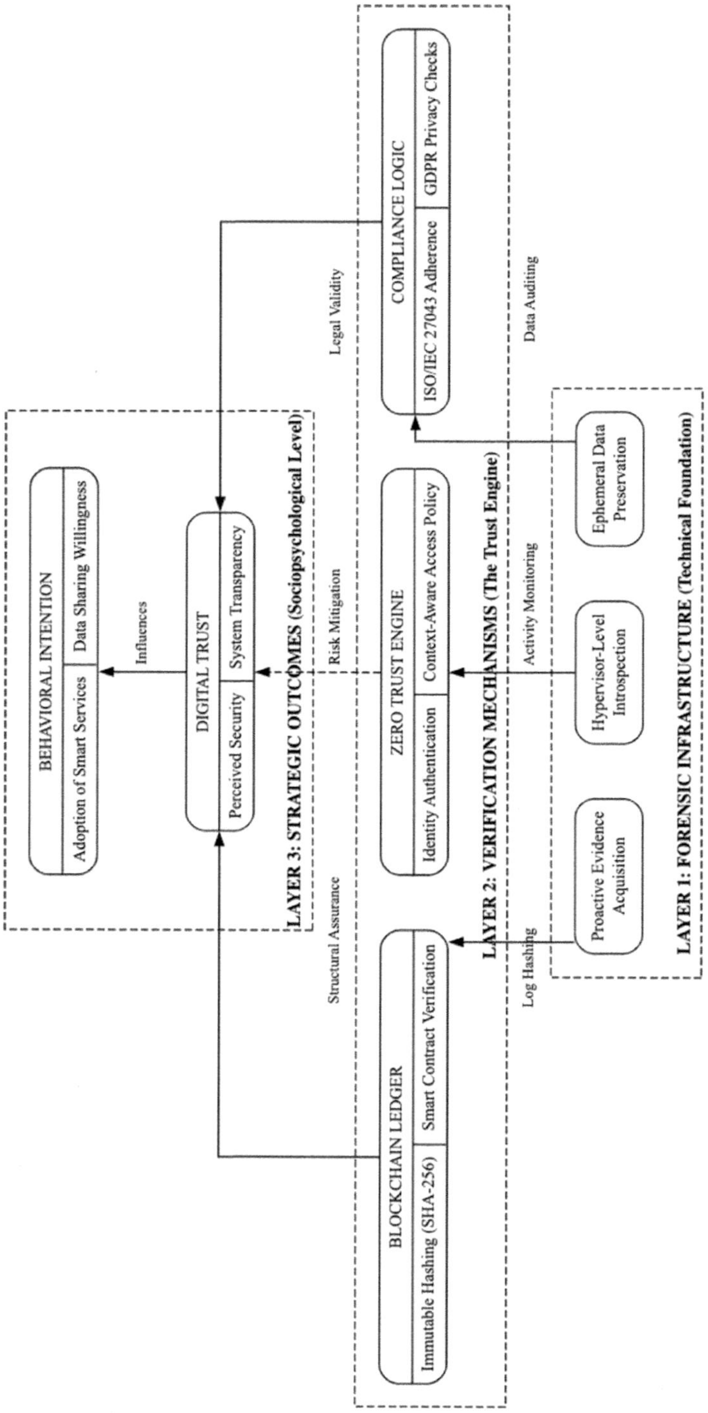

Figure 16.3 Structural decomposition and construct operationalization. Source: Author.

rigorous forensic mechanisms risks being perceived as excessive surveillance rather than protective assurance, potentially yielding counterproductive outcomes regarding user sentiment.

16.4.2.3 Structural decomposition and construct operationalization

Figure 16.3 shows the structural decomposition and construct operationalization process. To preclude conceptual ambiguity, the framework's foundational layer rigorously operationalizes "Proactive Forensic Readiness" not merely as a functional capability but as an architectural state wherein cloud infrastructure possesses the latent capacity to capture, preserve, and analyze digital evidence prior to security incidents. This multidimensional construct encompasses Hypervisor-Level Introspection, enabling the monitoring of virtual machine activities without guest OS interference, and Ephemeral Data Volatility Management, which automates the preservation of temporary RAM data, thereby transforming raw system logs into legally admissible digital artifacts [19, 43]. Ascending to the intermediate layer, technical data is transmuted into social capital through a "Trust Engine" where "Blockchain-Based Integrity" guarantees the immutable verification of the chain-of-custody. Unlike manipulatable traditional logging, this construct utilizes SHA-256 cryptographic hashing to anchor forensic metadata onto a permissioned distributed ledger, ensuring "Non-Repudiation" [40]. Concurrently, the "Zero Trust Architecture" operates as a policy-decision mechanism that assumes a default hostile environment, necessitating continuous, context-aware authentication to establish a "Trustless Verification" paradigm [5]. Finally, the strategic outcome layer responds to the theoretical imperative to distinguish cognitive states from conative outcomes by bifurcating the results into "Digital Trust", the proximal psychological state of willingness to be vulnerable [42] and "Behavioral Intention," the distal probability of service adoption and data sharing. This delineation clarifies the causal logic wherein forensic readiness creates structural assurance to foster trust, which in turn drives intention, explicitly aligning the architecture with established behavioral theories such as the Theory of Reasoned Action.

16.5 DISCUSSION

16.5.1 Discussion of the main results

The formulation of the CBFR-Trust framework articulates a significant theoretical departure from conventional smart tourism discourse, which has historically bifurcated technical security from behavioral trust. By synthesizing bibliometric trends identifying a trajectory toward decentralized trust architectures, this study posits that trust in volatile, multi-tenant cloud environments is not merely a derivative of service quality but an emergent property of verifiable forensic resilience. Unlike reactive models, the proposed framework argues that the continuous, proactive preservation of digital evidence at the hypervisor level effectively demystifies the opacity of cloud computing. Consequently, the transparency deficit is resolved by linking stakeholder willingness to engage directly to the system's demonstrable capacity for accountability through immutable evidence. Central to this architecture is the integration of Blockchain and Zero Trust models as mediating mechanisms that transmute technical readiness into perceived transparency. Extending blockchain utility beyond logistics, the framework anchors forensic logs onto permissioned ledgers to achieve "trustless verification," effectively replacing institutional reputation with cryptographic certainty and addressing inter-jurisdictional legal challenges via the "code is law" principle. From a theoretical perspective, this framework expands existing tourism trust models by introducing "Forensic Readiness" as a primary technical determinant of perceived security assurance, moving beyond purely cognitive or affective antecedents. This integration bridges the disciplinary chasm between computer science and tourism management, offering a holistic ontology that acknowledges the symbiotic relationship between cryptographic hardness and behavioral intent. Practically, the validation of this framework redefines digital forensics for stakeholders not as a retrospective compliance burden, but as a strategic asset for market differentiation. In an era of heightened privacy concerns, demonstrating compliance with standards such as ISO/IEC 27043:2015 via automated readiness becomes a critical signal of trustworthiness. For Destination Management Organizations (DMOs), this necessitates a governance overhaul toward real-time, algorithmic auditing. Ultimately, the research underscores that the sustainability of the smart tourism economy is contingent upon an ecosystem where security is visible and accountability is engineered into the digital infrastructure.

16.5.2 Critical analysis of dialectical tensions

While the CBFR-Trust framework articulates a theoretically sound pathway for enhancing digital trust, its operationalization necessitates a critical examination of the inherent dialectical tensions. A primary locus of contention resides in the Privacy-Security Paradox. Critics may argue that proactive forensic readiness, which mandates granular logging of user interactions at the hypervisor level, risks constructing a digital panopticon that infringes upon privacy. This tension is exacerbated by the integration of blockchain immutability, which theoretically conflicts with the "Right to be Forgotten" mandated by regulations such as the GDPR. However, this study counter-posit that forensic readiness, when correctly architected, functions as a privacy-preserving mechanism rather than a surveillance tool. By employing cryptographic hashing instead of storing raw Personally Identifiable Information (PII) on the ledger [40], the framework ensures auditability without exposing sensitive data. Thus, the model advocates for a Privacy-by-Design approach wherein forensic logs hold data custodians accountable, thereby protecting privacy more effectively than opaque, unmonitored systems. A second critical dichotomy exists between System Performance and Cryptographic Assurance [24, 25]. The integration of decentralized consensus mechanisms introduces computational overhead, potentially degrading the seamless experience required in high-frequency transactions. Skeptics might contend that the "cost of trust" imposed by blockchain validation is prohibitively high for time-sensitive applications. To mitigate this, the framework presupposes the utilization of permissioned consortium blockchains (e.g., Hyperledger Fabric) rather than public, proof-of-work chains. While acknowledging marginal latency increases, this study argues that such overhead is a commensurate premium for Institutional Trust. In an ecosystem where a single breach can irreversibly damage a destination's reputation [42], processing delay is not a defect but a necessary feature of verified security. Finally, the Friction-Adoption Trade-off inherent in the Zero Trust Model raises legitimate concerns. The "Never Trust, Verify" principle implies continuous re-authentication, which could disrupt the frictionless smart tourism experience. If tourists face intrusive verification at every touchpoint, adoption intentions may decline [5]. Consequently, the framework necessitates a refined interpretation: Zero Trust must be "invisible," deploying adaptive, risk-based authentication (e.g., behavioral biometrics) that operates in the background. Thus, the argument advocates not for increased friction, but for increased contextual verification, ensuring rigorous security protocols remain unobtrusive facilitators of the tourist journey.

16.5.3 Privacy-enhancing threat model

Although the integration of Blockchain and Zero Trust Architecture (ZTA) provides a robust foundation for forensic readiness, it precipitates a critical dialectic between

Table 16.3 A risk matrix that maps specific forensic capabilities to their corresponding privacy preservation mechanisms

Security mechanism	*Identified privacy threat*	*Risk level (unmitigated)*	*Proposed technical mitigation*	*Residual privacy risk*
Blockchain Immutability	Deanonymization via Metadata: Persistent analysis of transaction timestamps and wallet interactions can allow adversaries to infer user identity (linkability).	High	Off-Chain Storage Strategy: Only store hash pointers on-chain; metadata remains in ephemeral cloud storage. Zero-Knowledge Proofs (Optional):Verify validity without revealing data.	Low
Zero Trust Continuous Monitoring	Panoptic Surveillance: Continuous logging of user location and device telemetry may violate GDPR principles (Data Minimization).	High	Pseudonymization at Source: Logs are generated with ephemeral IDs that rotate periodically.Retention Policy: Strict time-to-live (TTL) for non-incident logs.	Medium
Forensic Data Acquisition	Data Leakage during Investigation: Investigators accessing full logs may view unrelated PII.	Medium	Role-Based Redaction:Access to forensic data is tiered; Level 1 analysts see only anonymized trends; Level 2 requires cryptographic keys to unveil PII.	Low

Source: Author.

surveillance-based security and user privacy. The susceptibility of immutable ledgers to deanonymization attacks, combined with the granular logging inherent to ZTA, risks engendering a panoptic environment that potentially infringes upon tourist privacy rights. To resolve this paradox, the proposed framework transcends declarative "Privacy-by-Design" principles to implement a structural Privacy-Enhancing Threat Model, utilizing specific mitigation controls to equilibrate these competing objectives [37, 41]. To mitigate blockchain linkability, the architecture mandates an off-chain storage strategy wherein only cryptographic proofs (Merkle roots) are committed to the ledger, while substantive forensic logs remain in compliant cloud silos; this is further fortified by cryptographic salting to preclude rainbow table attacks. Simultaneously, to address the risk of excessive surveillance, the model integrates Automated Redaction mechanisms that capture behavioral vectors while systematically masking Personally Identifiable Information (PII) at the source, rendering data accessible only through privileged escalation protocols ("break-glass" procedures) during critical security incidents. This strategic alignment of forensic capability with privacy preservation mechanisms is synthesized in Table 16.3.

16.5.4 Theoretical contributions

This study advances the extant literature on smart tourism and information security by offering three distinct theoretical contributions that bridge the gap between technical forensic architectures and organizational management. While the Technology-Organization-Environment (TOE) framework has been extensively utilized to explain the adoption of innovations (e.g., cloud computing, AI), this research extends its theoretical boundaries from a static "adoption decision" model to a dynamic "Forensic Readiness Capability" model. Unlike traditional TOE applications that treat adoption as a binary outcome, this study reconceptualizes the technological context to include Zero Trust maturity, and the organizational context to encompass Forensic Culture rather than merely technical competence. By validating TOE in the domain of forensic readiness, the framework demonstrates that environmental pressures (e.g., privacy regulations) act not merely as external constraints but as constitutive drivers that shape internal technical architecture. A critical limitation in previous digital forensic research is the techno-centric reductionism, where forensic readiness is viewed solely as an IT artifact [45, 46]. This study overcomes this deficiency by synthesizing TOE with STS Theory. By positioning the CBFR artifact as the Technical Subsystem and Stakeholder Trust as the Social Subsystem, the framework theoretically validates the principle of "Joint Optimization". It posits that technical sophistication (e.g., Blockchain immutability) is insufficient without the corresponding social mechanisms (e.g., Perceived Structural Assurance) [59–63]. This integration provides a theoretical lens to explain the Privacy-Security Paradox, arguing that successful forensic implementation requires the "social calibration" of technical monitoring tools. The study introduces the construct of "Forensic-based Trust" into the tourism literature. It expands the boundaries of Signaling Theory by establishing that backend forensic capabilities, when externalized through Transparency-as-a-Service (TaaS), serve as high-fidelity signals reducing information asymmetry. This contributes a new dimension to existing trust models (e.g., TRA/TPB) in tourism, suggesting that "institutional auditability" is a distinct antecedent of tourist behavior, separate from brand reputation or service quality.

16.5.5 Scalability and adoption strategy for SMEs

While the theoretical architecture of the CBFR-Trust model is robust, its practical applicability faces the structural reality of the tourism industry, where Small and Medium Enterprises (SMEs) constitute the vast majority of stakeholders yet suffer from significant resource constraints. Implementing a full-stack Zero Trust and Blockchain ecosystem requires technical sophistication and capital expenditure often beyond the reach of individual operators. To mitigate this "feasibility paradox," the framework is not designed for autonomous implementation by isolated SMEs but is conceptualized as a centralized infrastructure provided through a Forensic-as-a-Service (FaaS) model. In this tiered architecture, Destination Management Organizations (DMOs) or major digital platform aggregators assume the role of the Forensic Service Provider. They host the heavy computational logic, the private blockchain nodes, the AI-driven anomaly detection engines, and the secure cloud repositories. SMEs, functioning as Edge Tenants, integrate into this ecosystem via lightweight APIs or standardized smart gateways [64–69]. This approach shifts the technical burden from the periphery to the core, allowing SMEs to inherit advanced security capabilities (institutional isomorphism) without incurring prohibitive overheads. Furthermore, by aggregating forensic data across a network of SMEs, the central system achieves the critical data volume necessary for effective AI training, turning the fragmentation of the industry into a collective intelligence asset rather than a liability. Thus, the model transitions from a theoretical ideal to a pragmatic utility, scalable through shared economy principles.

Figure 16.4 illustrates a bipartite FaaS architecture designed to reconcile the inherent resource constraints of tourism SMEs with the necessity for robust digital investigation capabilities. The model strategically decouples the data acquisition phase from the computational analysis phase, thereby establishing a scalable adoption strategy. In Tier 1, heterogeneous edge tenants, ranging from small hotels to local guides, utilize a lightweight API gateway to transmit encrypted log data, minimizing local hardware latency and operational overhead. This stream is ingested by the Tier 2 Core Infrastructure, which functions as a

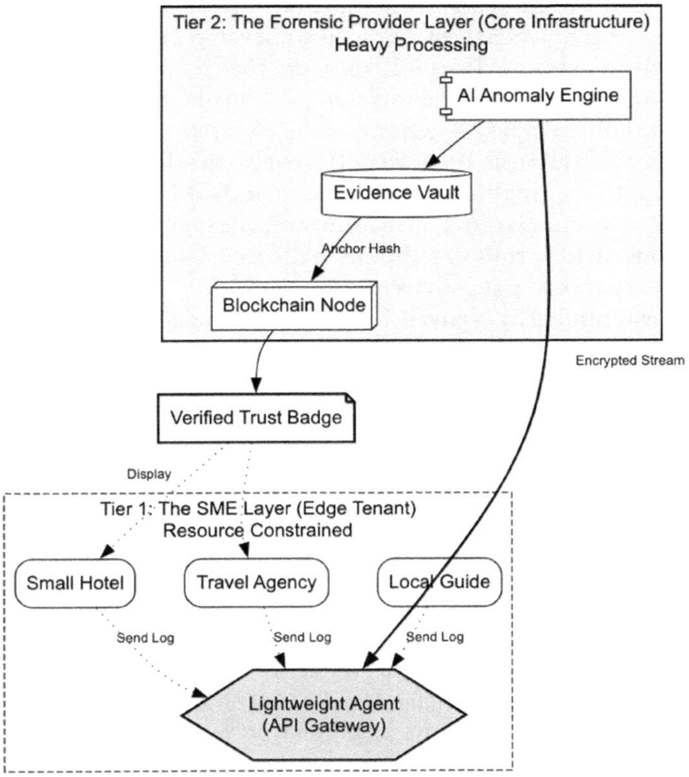

Figure 16.4 The proposed Two-Tier FaaS architecture designed for resource-constrained SMEs. Source: Author.

centralized heavy-processing unit leveraging an AI Anomaly Engine for high-throughput threat detection and an Evidence Vault for secure data retention. Crucially, the architecture incorporates a blockchain-based integrity mechanism that anchors forensic hashes to an immutable ledger; this process closes the verification loop by projecting a 'Verified Trust Badge' back to the edge tenant, effectively democratizing access to enterprise-grade forensic security while maintaining a lean operational footprint for the SME.

16.6 LIMITATIONS AND FUTURE RESEARCH DIRECTIONS

The scope of this research was strategically delineated to prioritize foundational theoretical architecture over immediate operational validation, a delimitation that necessitates acknowledging specific constraints. Primarily, the absence of live-environment stress testing leaves performance metrics, specifically the latency introduced by blockchain consensus in high-frequency scenarios, as theoretical postulates rather than empirically quantified data. Furthermore, the framework provides a generalized defense mechanism that does not fully account for the resource disparities inherent to Small and Medium Tourism Enterprises (SMTEs), potentially limiting universal applicability. Additionally, the study identifies, but does not exhaustively resolve, the complex legal paradox between the immutability of forensic ledgers and the "Right to be Forgotten" mandated by regulations such as the GDPR.

To bridge these gaps, future scholarship must pivot from conceptual modeling to empirical corroboration. Researchers are encouraged to develop experimental prototypes within cloud sandbox environments to rigorously measure the computational overhead of the proposed Zero Trust architecture under simulated peak loads. From a behavioral perspective, subsequent studies should employ longitudinal quantitative designs to validate whether the "technical assurance" of forensic readiness effectively translates into sustained psychological trust among travelers. Finally, resolving the identified legal tensions requires interdisciplinary inquiries into comparative jurisprudence, aiming to develop privacy-preserving blockchain solutions that harmonize the permanence of forensic evidence with the fluid requirements of international data sovereignty.

*** This research was funded by Nguyen Tat Thanh University, Ho Chi Minh City, Vietnam.**

REFERENCE

1. A. G. Najlaoui and N. B. Ammari, "Technological revolution and transformation of the tourism sector," in Bari Muhammad Waseem (Ed.), *Shifts in Knowledge Sharing and Creativity for Business Tourism*: IGI Global, 2024, pp. 163–186.
2. L. Shi, A. Marzuki, H. Wang, and Q. Zhang, "Design of tourism interpretation system based on intelligent light control," in *2024 6th International Conference on Robotics, Intelligent Control and Artificial Intelligence, RICAI 2024*, 2024: Institute of Electrical and Electronics Engineers Inc., pp. 804–808, doi: 10.1109/RICAI64321.2024.10911274. [Online]. Available: https://www.scopus.com/inward/record.uri?eid=2-s2.0-105001428675&doi=10.1109%2fRICAI64321.2024.10911274&partnerID=40&md5=f36a2ec8247ea72091b962c3337f0e35
3. W. Wider *et al.*, "Unveiling trends in digital tourism research: A bibliometric analysis of co-citation and co-word analysis," (in English), *Environ. Sustain. Ind.*, Article vol. 20, 2023, Art no. 100308, doi: 10.1016/j.indic.2023.100308.
4. R. M. Chowdary and T. Kumar, "Addressing gaps in travel booking system," in *Lecture Notes in Networks and Systems*, S. Fong, N. Dey, and A. Joshi, Eds., 2025, vol. 1196 LNNS: Springer Science and Business Media Deutschland GmbH, pp. 219–232, doi: 10.1007/978-981-97-9526-0_21. [Online]. Available: https://www.scopus.com/inward/record.uri?eid=2-s2.0-105009885191&doi=10.1007%2f978-981-97-9526-0_21&partnerID=40&md5=7ab8103f1f07a5d8985a02dc3a742746
5. N. Fenu and P. Giaccaria, "Smart tourism and platforms. Italia.It, the Italian tourism digital hub," in *Lecture Notes in Computer Science (including subseries Lecture Notes in Artificial Intelligence and Lecture Notes in Bioinformatics)*, O. Gervasi, B. Murgante, C. Garau, D. Taniar, C. R. A. M. A, and M. Faginas Lago, Eds., 2024, vol. 14824 LNCS: Springer Science and Business Media Deutschland GmbH, pp. 3–17, doi: 10.1007/978-3-031-65332-2_1. [Online]. Available: https://www.scopus.com/inward/record.uri?eid=2-s2.0-85200696004&doi=10.1007%2f978-3-031-65332-2_1&partnerID=40&md5=5d7fc0a3e7371f59d7b8cd0326aa99b4
6. V. Kebande and H. Venter, "Requirements for achieving digital forensic readiness in the cloud environment using an NMB solution," in *Proceedings of the 11th International Conference on Cyber Warfare and Security, ICCWS 2016*, T. Zlateva and V. A. Greiman, Eds., 2016: Academic Conferences Limited, pp. 399–406. [Online]. Available: https://www.scopus.com/inward/record.uri?eid=2-s2.0-84969286796&partnerID=40&md5=375737b089fcb74a7cc028913dcb588a. [Online]. Available: https://www.scopus.com/inward/record.uri?eid=2-s2.0-84969286796&partnerID=40&md5=375737b089fcb74a7cc028913dcb588a
7. V. R. Kebande and H. S. Venter, "CFRaaS: Architectural design of a Cloud Forensic Readiness as-a-Service Model using NMB solution as a forensic agent," (in English), *Afr. J. Sci. Technol. Innov. Dev.*, Article vol. 11, no. 6, pp. 749–769, 2019, doi: 10.1080/20421338.2019.1585675.

8. O. W. Salami, M. B. Abdulrazaq, E. A. Adedokun, and B. Yahaya, "Collaborative integrity verification for blockchain-based cloud forensic readiness data protection," in *Communications in Computer and Information Science*, S. Misra, J. Oluranti, R. Damaševičius, and R. Maskeliunas, Eds., 2022, vol. 1547 CCIS: Springer Science and Business Media Deutschland GmbH, pp. 138–152, doi: 10.1007/978-3-030-95630-1_10. [Online]. Available: https://www.scopus.com/inward/record.uri?eid=2-s2.0-85124672081&doi=10.1007%2f978-3-030-95630-1_10&partnerID=40&md5=bca843ced1fcf64e39cba2dffe7ea84c
9. O. Olukoya, "Distilling blockchain requirements for digital investigation platforms," (in English), *J. Inf. Secur. Appl.*, Article vol. 62, 2021, Art no. 102969, doi: 10.1016/j.jisa.2021.102969.
10. V. R. Kebande and H. S. Venter, "Novel digital forensic readiness technique in the cloud environment," (in English), *Aust. J. Forensic Sci.*, Article vol. 50, no. 5, pp. 552–591, 2018, doi: 10.1080/00450618.2016.1267797.
11. M. Haider, R. M. Shannon, and R. Vatananan-Thesenvitz, "Digital leadership for sustainable Community-Based Tourism (CBT)," in *PICMET 2022 – Portland International Conference on Management of Engineering and Technology: Technology Management and Leadership in Digital Transformation – Looking Ahead to Post-COVID Era, Proceedings*, D. F. Kocaoglu, T. R. Anderson, D. C. Kozanoglu, K. Niwa, and H. J. Steenhuis, Eds., 2022: Institute of Electrical and Electronics Engineers Inc., doi: 10.23919/PICMET53225.2022.9882550. [Online]. Available: https://www.scopus.com/inward/record.uri?eid=2-s2.0-85139122192&doi=10.23919%2fPICMET53225.2022.9882550&partnerID=40&md5=d2172d0801591e8cf77a2fd835a498b2
12. M. S. Khalid, "Sustainable tourism's tomorrow: Navigating the future with technological innovations," In P. Kumar, S. K. Gupta, M. E. Korstanje, P. C. Rout, and Madhurima (eds.), *Achieving Sustainable Transformation in Tourism and Hospitality Sectors*: IGI Global, 2024, pp. 139–155.
13. V. R. Kebande and H. S. Venter, "Adding event reconstruction to a Cloud Forensic Readiness model," in *2015 Information Security for South Africa – Proceedings of the ISSA 2015 Conference*, M. M. Eloff, S. Flowerday, H. S. Venter, M. Loock, and M. Coetzee, Eds., 2015: Institute of Electrical and Electronics Engineers Inc., doi: 10.1109/ISSA.2015.7335050. [Online]. Available: https://www.scopus.com/inward/record.uri?eid=2-s2.0-84962106154&doi=10.1109%2fISSA.2015.7335050&partnerID=40&md5=14c2939070b4728e543e932cf1520e5f
14. A. Garg, N. Saxena, N. Verma, R. Kumar Singhal, R. Singhal, and N. Kaggallu, "Examining the smart tourism landscape: A bibliometric study and analytical synopsis of IoT research," in *International Conference on Intelligent and Innovative Practices in Engineering and Management 2024, IIPEM 2024*, 2024: Institute of Electrical and Electronics Engineers Inc., doi: 10.1109/IIPEM62726.2024.10925758. [Online]. Available: https://www.scopus.com/inward/record.uri?eid=2-s2.0-105001918683&doi=10.1109%2fIIPEM62726.2024.10925758&partnerID=40&md5=5aa838129a9dad2cff783928d590101d
15. A. T. Rosário and J. C. Dias, "Exploring the landscape of smart tourism: A systematic bibliometric review of the literature of the Internet of Things," (in English), *Adm. Sci.*, Review, vol. 14, no. 2, 2024, Art no. 22, doi: 10.3390/admsci14020022.
16. C. Yang, L. He, C. Hu, Y. Feng, and Y. Yue, "Research on identity authentication methods for IoT devices in smart tourism," (in Chinese), *Chin. J. Inter Th.*, Article vol. 9, no. 3, pp. 180–189, 2025, doi: 10.11959/j.issn.2096-3750.2025.00433.
17. B. Chourasia, "The future of smart hotels and digital transformation in the hospitality industry," In V. S. Rana, G. Bhatia, A. Raina, and D. Chhabra (eds.), *Transforming the Service Sector With New Technology*: IGI Global, 2025, pp. 533–540.
18. J. Joo, J. Park, and Y. Han, "Applications of blockchain and smart contract for sustainable tourism ecosystems," in *Lecture Notes on Data Engineering and Communications Technologies*, vol. 53: Springer Science and Business Media Deutschland GmbH, 2021, pp. 773–780.
19. K. Nam, C. S. Dutt, P. Chathoth, and M. S. Khan, "Blockchain technology for smart city and smart tourism: Latest trends and challenges," (in English), *Asia Pac. J. Tour. Res.*, Article vol. 26, no. 4, pp. 454–468, 2021, doi: 10.1080/10941665.2019.1585376.

20. A. A. N. T. Pinandhika and I. A. Zaim, "Blockchain for secure transactions in hospitality and tourism management," In M. J. Jerez-Jerez, C. Sevilla-Sevilla, and L. Aguiar-Castillo (eds.), *The Role of Artificial Intelligence in the Tourism and Hospitality Sector*: Taylor and Francis, 2025, pp. 185–203.
21. P. Mary Jeyanthi, "Guarding the gateway: Data privacy and security in metaverse tourism," in *Lecture Notes in Networks and Systems*, N. Sharma, A. C. Goje, A. Chakrabarti, and A. M. Bruckstein, Eds., 2024, vol. 997 LNNS: Springer Science and Business Media Deutschland GmbH, pp. 359–371, doi: 10.1007/978-981-97-3242-5_25. [Online]. Available: https://www.scopus.com/inward/record.uri?eid=2-s2.0-85200678322&doi=10.1007%2f978-981-97-3242-5_25&partnerID=40&md5=daf74df65fe2cab972634e76c81ff70e
22. S. Krishnan, A. Jose Anand, and R. Kumar (eds.). 2024. *Sustainable Development Goals: Technologies and Opportunities.* 1st ed. CRC Press. 330 pp. https://doi.org/10.1201/9781003468257
23. J. Saveljeva and T. Volkova, "A survey on digital trust: Towards a validated definition," (in English), *Digital.*, Review, vol. 5, no. 2, 2025, Art no. 14, doi: 10.3390/digital5020014.
24. P. Pradhan and V. Kumar, "Trust management models for digital identities," In *Information Resources Management Association (USA)* (ed.), *Operations and Service Management: Concepts, Methodologies, Tools, and Applications*: IGI Global, 2017, pp. 142–168.
25. S. Reiners, "Trust and its extensions in digital platform ecosystems: Key concepts and issues for future research," in *Proceedings – 2022 IEEE 24th Conference on Business Informatics, CBI 2022*, 2022, vol. 2: Institute of Electrical and Electronics Engineers Inc., pp. 1–8, doi: 10.1109/CBI54897.2022.10042. [Online]. Available: https://www.scopus.com/inward/record.uri?eid=2-s2.0-85142928607&doi=10.1109%2fCBI54897.2022.10042&partnerID=40&md5=bded637068714ab71c606e4779639139
26. Á. Hernández-Tamurejo, P. González-Padilla, and J. R. Saura, "Harnessing big data for smarter tourism," In U. Gretzel (ed.), *Tourism on the Verge*, vol. Part F430: Springer Nature, 2025, pp. 201–221.
27. A. J. Anand and S. Krishnan. 2024. *Smart Technologies for Sustainable Development Goals: No Poverty.* 1st ed. CRC Press. 284 pp. eBook ISBN 9781003519010. https://doi.org/10.1201/9781003519010
28. H. C. Lin, X. Liu, Y. Huang, and H. Y. Chen, "Determinants of continued use of tourism and hospitality e-commerce platforms and the role of information transparency," (in English), *Curr. Issues Tour.*, Article vol. 26, no. 19, pp. 3140–3159, 2023, doi: 10.1080/13683500.2022.2147052.
29. C. Y. Heo, B. Kim, and L. Drapé-Frisch, "Understanding guests' dissatisfaction: Application of data visualization tools," In H. Oktadiana (ed.), *Bridging Tourism Theory and Practice*, vol. 11: Emerald Group Holdings Ltd., 2019, pp. 125–142.
30. D. Ordóñez-Martínez, J. M. Seguí-Pons, and M. Ruiz-Pérez, "Conceptual framework and prospective analysis of EU tourism data spaces," (in English), *Sustainability*, Article vol. 16, no. 1, 2024, Art no. 371, doi: 10.3390/su16010371.
31. A. Adel, "A conceptual framework to improve cyber forensic administration in Industry 5.0: Qualitative study approach," (in English), *Forensic. Sci.*, Article vol. 2, no. 1, pp. 111–129, 2022, doi: 10.3390/forensicsci2010009.
32. D. Alrajeh, L. Pasquale, and B. Nuseibeh, "On evidence preservation requirements for forensic-ready systems," in *Proceedings of the ACM SIGSOFT Symposium on the Foundations of Software Engineering*, E. Bodden, W. Schafer, A. van Deursen, and A. Zisman, Eds., 2017, vol. Part F130154: Association for Computing Machinery, pp. 559–569, doi: 10.1145/3106237.3106308. [Online]. Available: https://www.scopus.com/inward/record.uri?eid=2-s2.0-85030783687&doi=10.1145%2f3106237.3106308&partnerID=40&md5=fdd4907c17a1324f3c50e8df8b149b97
33. L. Daubner, J. Harašta, and R. Matulevičius, "Forensic readiness and privacy: Towards resolving software goal conflict," in *Lecture Notes in Business Information Processing*, R. Guizzardi, L. Pufahl, A. Sturm, and H. van der Aa, Eds., 2025, vol. 558 LNBIP: Springer Science and Business Media Deutschland GmbH, pp. 257–273, doi: 10.1007/978-3-031-95397-2_16. [Online]. Available: https://www.scopus.com/inward/record.uri?eid=2-s2.0-105009239015&doi=10.1007%2f978-3-031-95397-2_16&partnerID=40&md5=45e86b3e88ae5f0e099a36968a44fe6f

34. K. Tam and K. Jones, "Forensic readiness within the maritime sector," in *2019 International Conference on Cyber Situational Awareness, Data Analytics and Assessment, Cyber SA 2019*, 2019: Institute of Electrical and Electronics Engineers Inc., doi: 10.1109/CyberSA.2019.8899642. [Online]. Available: https://www.scopus.com/inward/record.uri?eid=2-s2.0-85075905166&doi=10.1109%2fCyberSA.2019.8899642&partnerID=40&md5=cac1ca019e2b55db27bf76fabf1272fa
35. P. Santra, A. Roy, and K. Majumder, "A comparative analysis of cloud forensic techniques in IaaS," in *Advances in Intelligent Systems and Computing*, S. K. Bhatia, K. K. Mishra, S. Tiwari, and V. K. Singh, Eds., 2018, vol. 554: Springer Verlag, pp. 207–215, doi: 10.1007/978-981-10-3773-3_20. [Online]. Available: https://www.scopus.com/inward/record.uri?eid=2-s2.0-85031421519&doi=10.1007%2f978-981-10-3773-3_20&partnerID=40&md5=7a275410be15f7be17db5fc0d617d4b6
36. L. Daubner, R. Matulevičius, B. Buhnova, M. Antol, M. Růžička, and T. Pitner, "A case study on the impact of forensic-ready information systems on the security posture," in *Lecture Notes in Computer Science (including subseries Lecture Notes in Artificial Intelligence and Lecture Notes in Bioinformatics)*, M. Indulska, I. Reinhartz-Berger, C. Cetina, and O. Pastor, Eds., 2023, vol. 13901 LNCS: Springer Science and Business Media Deutschland GmbH, pp. 522–538, doi: 10.1007/978-3-031-34560-9_31. [Online]. Available: https://www.scopus.com/inward/record.uri?eid=2-s2.0-85163948746&doi=10.1007%2f978-3-031-34560-9_31&partnerID=40&md5=4362bf52083ddc4e82c667468f9f03ba
37. S. A. Kristyan and T. Juhana, "Design framework forensics readiness as a service for automatic processing," in *2020 International Conference on Information Technology Systems and Innovation, ICITSI 2020 – Proceedings*, 2020: Institute of Electrical and Electronics Engineers Inc., pp. 370–374, doi: 10.1109/ICITSI50517.2020.9264965. [Online]. Available: https://www.scopus.com/inward/record.uri?eid=2-s2.0-85099568813&doi=10.1109%2fICITSI50517.2020.9264965&partnerID=40&md5=02ae457760f9e225b25d6fba904b3e6f
38. V. S. Bai and T. Sudha, "A systematic literature review on cloud forensics in cloud environment," (in English), *Internat. J. Intel. Syst. Appl. Eng.*, Article vol. 11, no. 4s, pp. 565–578, 2023. [Online]. Available: https://www.scopus.com/inward/record.uri?eid=2-s2.0-85161397231&partnerID=40&md5=f7b0fa271949e84437a24667346bfb85
39. J. C. Pinho, S. Nogueira, and I. Macedo, "A configurational approach to understanding trust in rural tourism accommodation during the COVID-19 pandemic crisis," (in English), *Consum. Behav. Hosp. Res.*, Article vol. 18, no. 1, pp. 140–154, 2023, doi: 10.1108/CBTH-03-2022-0058.
40. P. Sarnacchiaro, S. Luongo, F. Sepe, and V. D. Corte, "The role of blockchain technology in the tourism industry: Analyzing the factors affecting its adoption," (in English), *Qual. Quant.*, Article 2024, doi: 10.1007/s11135-024-01836-7.
41. A. Kumar and P. Upadhyay, "Digital communication and recovery strategy during crisis: Evidence from the tourism industry," (in English), *Glob. Knowl., Mem. Commun.*, Article 2025, doi: 10.1108/GKMC-08-2024-0491.
42. X. Li and X. Yang, "Tourist trust toward a tourism destination: Scale development and validation," (in English), *Asia Pac. J. Tour. Res.*, Article vol. 27, no. 6, pp. 562–580, 2022, doi: 10.1080/10941665.2022.2091943.
43. J. C. Bennett and M. H. Diallo, "A forensic pattern-based approach for investigations in cloud system environments," in *2018 2nd Cyber Security in Networking Conference, CSNet 2018*, 2019: Institute of Electrical and Electronics Engineers Inc., doi: 10.1109/CSNET.2018.8602908. [Online]. Available: https://www.scopus.com/inward/record.uri?eid=2-s2.0-85061775063&doi=10.1109%2fCSNET.2018.8602908&partnerID=40&md5=a4c93f168353de45049ba8e927fc0f3d
44. S. S. Fateminasab, N. Evaznia, S. Memarian, M. D. C. Romero-Ternero, G. Miró-Amarante, and S. R. K. Tabbakh, "An efficient blockchain-based resource allocation and secure data storage model using Fire Hawk Optimization and entropy in health tourism," (in English), *J. Cloud Comput.*, Article vol. 14, no. 1, 2025, Art no. 63, doi: 10.1186/s13677-025-00792-3.
45. A. R. Hevner, S. T. March, J. Park, and S. Ram, "Design science in information systems research," *MIS Quarterly*, pp. 75–105, 2004.

46. A. R. Hevner, "A three cycle view of design science research," *Scandinavian Journal of Information Systems,* vol. 19, no. 2, p. 4, 2007.
47. J. Anand, J. Raja Paul Perinbam, and D. Meganathan, "Q-Learning-based optimized routing in biomedical wireless sensor networks," *IETE Journal of Research*, vol. 63, no. 1, pp. 89–97, 2017.
48. A. R. Rao, Ajay H., Balavanan M., Lalit R., and J. Anand, "A novel cardiac arrest alerting system using IoT," *International Journal of Science Technology & Engineering*, vol. 3, no. 10, pp. 78–83, April 2017.
49. J. Anand, Dhanalakshmi M., and Raja Paul Perinpam J., "Smart indication system for spinal cord stress detection," *International Journal of Recent Technology and Engineering*, vol. 8, no. 3, pp. 6164–6168, Sep 2019.
50. J. A. Adithya and S. Doss, "An efficient priority based packet scheduling in MANETs," *International Journal of Advanced Engineering and Global Technology*, vol. 7, no. 1, pp. 2373–2382, 2019.
51. M. Geethalakshmi, Kanimozhiraman, J. Anand, R. Partheepan, and S. Santhosh, "Optimal routing path using trident form in wearable biomedical wireless sensor networks," *Turkish Online Journal of Qualitative Inquiry*, vol. 12, no. 7, pp. 5134–5143, 2021.
52. Thanzeem Mohamed Sheriff S., Venkat Kumar J., Vigneshwaran S., Aida Jones, and J. Anand, "Lung cancer detection using VGG NET 16 architecture," *International Conference on Physics and Engineering 2021, IOP Publishing, Journal of Physics Conference Series*, Vol. 2040, 2021.
53. R. Dhanalakshmi, J. Anand, Arun Kumar Sivaraman, and Sita Rani, "IoT-based water quality monitoring system using cloud for agriculture use," in *Cloud and Fog Computing Platforms for Internet of Things*, Pankaj Bhambri, Sita Rani, Gaurav Gupta, and Alex Khang, Eds., 2022: Routledge Taylor & Francis Group.
54. C. Augustine, A. Jose, K. Vinoth Kumar, D. Kaleeswaran, G. Muneeswari, and S. P. Santhoshkumar, "6G-based mobile IPTV using adaptive hybrid transmission," in *Handbook of Research on Design, Deployment, Automation, and Testing Strategies for 6G Mobile Core Network*, D. Satish Kumar, G. Prabhakar, and R. Anand, Eds., 2022: IGI Global Publisher, pages 20.
55. R. Dhanalakshmi, J. Anand, K. Poonkavithai, and V. Vijayakumar, "Cloud-based glaucoma diagnosis in medical imaging using machine learning," in *Artificial Intelligence for Innovative Healthcare Informatics*, S. A. Parah, M. Rashid, and V. Varadarajan, Eds., 2022: Springer, Cham, pp. 61–78.
56. R. Dhanalakshmi and J. Anand, "Big data for personalized healthcare," in *Handbook of Intelligent Healthcare Analytics: Knowledge Engineering with Big Data Analytics*, Chap-4, A. Jaya, K. Kalaiselvi, Dinesh Goyal, and Dhiya AL-Jumelly, Eds., 2022: John Wiley & Sons, Inc., pp. 67–92.
57. G. Mohamed, J. Visumathi, Miroslav Mahdal, Jose A., and M. Elangovan, "An effective and secure mechanism for phishing attacks using a machine learning approach," *Processes*, vol. 10, no. 7, 1356, 2022.
58. K. Sivachandar, V. Amudha, B. Ramesh, J. Anand, M. Shanmuga Sundari, and S. Jerril Gilda. 2022. MIMO-IDMA system performance for SUI and LTE frequency selective channels. *Advances in Parallel Computing: Algorithms, Tools and Paradigms*, 41: 422–428.
59. S. Rani, P. Bhambri, A. Kataria, A. Khang, and A. K. Sivaraman, Eds., *Big Data, Cloud Computing and IoT: Tools and Applications* (1st ed.). Chapman and Hall/CRC, 2023. https://doi.org/10.1201/9781003298335
60. P. Bhambri and S. Rani, "Bioengineering and healthcare data analysis: Introduction, advances, and challenges," in *Computational Intelligence and Blockchain in Biomedical and Health Informatics*, P. Bhambri, S. Rani, and M. Fahim, Eds., (1st ed.), 2024: CRC Press, pp. 1–25. https://doi.org/10.1201/9781003459347
61. R. Rana, Y. Chhabra, and P. Bhambri, "Comparison and evaluation of various QoS parameters in WSNs with the implementation of enhanced low energy adaptive efficient distributed clustering approach," *Webology*, vol. 18, no. (1), pp. 677–695, 2021. https://www.webology.org/data-cms/articles/20220223093208pmwebology%2018%20(1)%20-%2077%20pdf.pdf

62. P. Bhambri and Ritu, "Software effort estimation with machine learning – A systematic literature review," in *Agile Software Development: Trends, Challenges and Applications*, S. Hooda, V. M. Sood, Y. Singh, S. Dalal, and M. Sood, Eds., 2023: Wiley, pp. 291–308. https://doi.org/10.1002/9781119896838.ch15
63. R. Rana and P. Bhambri, "The role of IoT in shaping the future of geospatial AI," in *Recent Trends in Geospatial AI*, D. Darwish and H. Chemingui, Eds., 2023: IGI Global Scientific Publishing, pp. 177–216. https://doi.org/10.4018/979-8-3693-8054-3.ch007
64. R. Rana and P. Bhambri, "Generative AI-driven security frameworks for web engineering: Innovations and challenges," in *Generative AI for Web Engineering Models*, I. A. Shah and N. Z. Jhanjhi, Eds., 2024: IGI Global, pp. 285–296. https://doi.org/10.4018/979-8-3693-3703-5.ch014
65. P. Bhambri, "Artificial intelligence enabled Internet of Medical Things for enhanced healthcare systems," in *Smart Healthcare Systems: AI and IoT Perspectives,* P. Bhambri, R. Soni, and T. A. Tran, Eds., 2024: CRC Press, pp. 1–17. https://doi.org/10.1201/9781032698519-1
66. Y. S. Sangwan, S. Lal, P. Bhambri, A. Kumar, and I. S. Dhanoa, "Advancements in social data security and encryption: A review," *Natural Volatiles & Essential Oils*, vol. 8, no. 4, 15353–15362, 2021. https://www.cabidigitallibrary.org/doi/full/10.5555/20220170098
67. N. Chithra and P. Bhambri, "Ethics in sustainable technology," in *Handbook of Technological Sustainability: Innovation and Environmental Awareness*, P. Bhambri and P. Bajdor, Eds., 2024: CRC Press, pp. 245–256. https://doi.org/10.1201/9781003475989-21
68. P. Bhambri and P. Bajdor, "Technological sustainability unveiled: A comprehensive examination of economic, social, and environmental dimensions," in *Handbook of Technological Sustainability: Innovation and Environmental Awareness*, P. Bhambri and P. Bajdor, Eds., 2024: CRC Press, pp. 80–98. https://doi.org/10.1201/9781003475989-8
69. J. Vigneshwari, P. Senthamizh Pavai, L. Maria Suganthi, and P. Bhambri, "Eco-ethics in the digital age: Tackling environmental challenges through technology," in *Handbook of Technological Sustainability: Innovation and Environmental Awareness*, P. Bhambri and P. Bajdor, Eds., 2024: CRC Press, pp. 201–213. https://doi.org/10.1201/9781003475989-18

Chapter 17

Mapping research trends in AI-driven automation for cloud forensics

A bibliometric analysis and science mapping

Roseline Oluwaseun Ogundokun, Rotimi-Williams Bello, Pius Adewale Owolawi, Adewale Opeoluwa Ogunde, Chinecherem Umezuruike and Akinyomade O. Owolabi

17.1 INTRODUCTION

17.1.1 Background and motivation

Forensic investigations must adapt to new organizational, legal, and technical realities as businesses migrate more services and data to cloud platforms. In contrast to on-premises environments, where investigators might physically access servers, storage devices, and network equipment, cloud architectures distribute data across numerous virtual machines, geographically separated locations, and service tiers. While cloud computing has become an integral part of modern digital services, it creates unique forensic challenges: evidence is distributed across multiple virtual computers, proprietary data formats, and service levels, often beyond the control of investigators [1–3]. According to Liu et al. [1], cloud forensic evidence may reside on computers not under the investigator's control, requiring the investigator to collaborate with cloud service providers to obtain logs from system calls, application software, and API calls [1, 2, 5]. This dispersed nature introduces new reliability issues and makes collecting, storing, and correlating evidence much more challenging. For instance, logs may be kept in proprietary formats. Also, the dynamic flexibility of cloud resources enables quick provisioning and deprovisioning of virtual machines, thereby complicating the continuous collection of evidence [5]. AI and machine learning add new capabilities at the same time: According to SentinelOne, automation reduces manual work and accelerates investigations, while AI can analyze vast volumes of logs and correlate user activity with system data to detect stealthy attack patterns [6]. Large language models and ontology-based validation can automate cloud log analysis. Excellent precision and recall are possible in ransomware detection, as shown by CIAF and other industry efforts [7]. This is part of a larger trend toward AI-powered, cloud-native incident response solutions that offer automated playbooks and real-time threat identification, reflected in Gartner's concept of Cloud Investigation and Response Automation (CIRA) [8–10].

Most traditional forensic technologies assume sole possession of evidence and are designed to conduct offline data analysis of static data. These technologies cannot keep up with the volume and velocity of data generated by cloud infrastructures. Ahmed and Sabeeh [12] argued that large volumes of data emanating from modern cloud systems require real-time and automated approaches toward evidence collection and analysis [12]. Their proposed architecture combines a security lake with a modern data architecture that collects logs in real time from multiple cloud accounts and locations and stores them in a centralized data lake for effective analysis. The authors emphasize that previous attempts do not address

 DOI: 10.1201/9781003656487-17

the need to consolidate data across accounts and regions, leaving investigators to collate logs [13–15] manually. This gap suggests the need for automated systems that can collate evidence and hasten response times [22–26]. Artificial intelligence, in particular, machine learning, could enhance cloud forensics. AI systems can process large datasets and integrate diverse data sources while identifying minimal correlations that human analysts might overlook. SentinelOne has remarked, by comparing logs, user behavior, and system information, how AI and ML can identify anomalies in real time [6]. To further reduce manual work that delays investigations, automation parses records, correlates data, and highlights abnormalities [6]. Along similar lines, CIRA uses playbooks to orchestrate automated responses and provides complex analytics, artificial intelligence, and automation to gain real-time insights into cloud security issues [8]. CIAF is an example of how large language models can enhance the precision and recall of automated log analysis by standardizing the creation of natural-language forensic queries and validating them against an ontology [7].

17.1.2 Research questions and objectives

While AI and automation are increasingly proposed as remedies for cloud forensic challenges, the academic literature remains fragmented. Existing bibliometric studies of cloud computing often focus on adoption trends, specific industries, or library services, without examining forensic-oriented automation. No study has systematically mapped research contributions that integrate artificial intelligence, automation, and cloud forensics. This gap hinders our understanding of which topics are being explored, who the key contributors are, and where the field is heading. To address this gap, we pose the following research questions:

1. **RQ1:** *How has the scientific production on AI-driven automation for cloud forensics evolved over time?* Understanding annual publication trends helps identify growth phases and influential events.
2. **RQ2:** *Who are the most influential contributors, and which countries lead the research?* Analyzing authorship and national contributions reveals research hubs and collaboration patterns.
3. **RQ3:** *What thematic clusters dominate the literature, and how have they evolved?* Keyword co-occurrence analysis and thematic evolution illustrate conceptual foundations and emerging topics.
4. **RQ4:** *What is the structure of collaboration networks among researchers?* Co-authorship networks reveal the extent of collaboration and potential fragmentation.
5. **RQ5:** *What research gaps and practical challenges remain unaddressed?* Synthesizing results with existing literature highlights opportunities for future work.

The objectives of this study are to (i) compile a curated dataset of peer-reviewed publications on AI-driven automation in cloud forensics from 2010 to 2025; (ii) conduct a performance analysis to quantify productivity by year, authors, countries and sources; (iii) visualize and analyze science-mapping networks; and (iv) discuss the implications of findings for practice, policy, and research [27–33]. The chapter is structured as follows. Section 17.2 reviews related works, focusing on cloud forensic challenges, early automation efforts, and existing bibliometric studies, while identifying gaps that motivate this study. Section 17.3 presents the materials and methods in detail, describing the search strategy, data processing, bibliometric indicators, network construction, and limitations. Section 17.4 reports the results of the performance analysis and science mapping, using figures to answer each research question. Section 17.5 discusses the results, focusing on theoretical contributions, practical consequences, research needs, and limitations. The most important discoveries and further research suggestions are summarized in Section 17.6.

17.2 RELATED WORKS

17.2.1 Cloud forensic challenges and early automation efforts

Early work highlighted the inherent challenges of performing forensic analysis in cloud environments [9, 10]. Offline data analysis and direct access to physical devices have been the cornerstones of traditional digital forensics. The four characteristics of cloud identified by NIST that define cloud forensics and defy classic approaches are on-demand self-service, broad network access, resource pooling, and rapid elasticity [5, 11]. Multi-tenancy and geographical independence often mean that investigators can't access the infrastructure physically or count on logs from a single server. Evidence may span multiple geographical regions, service models—IaaS, PaaS, and SaaS—and layers: application, operating system, and hypervisor. Logs may be deleted or stored temporarily, and security incidents may be copied across distributed systems due to flexibility. The forensic process, therefore, needs to gather information from various sources and maintain the chain of custody between service providers [34–38]. To overcome these challenges, Liu et al. [1] developed a Prolog-based forensic analysis tool that rebuilds attack scenarios by correlating virtual machine logs, cloud service API calls, and intrusion detection system logs. Their approach demonstrated how investigators could minimize human effort by using automated reasoning to correlate evidence across multiple cloud tiers. Nevertheless, the tool's application in dynamic, multi-tenant configurations remained limited because the approach relied on offline analysis and required logs under the investigator's control.

The NIST's Cloud Computing Forensic Science Challenges Study, 2020, has systematically separated the forensic challenges into technological, legal, and organizational domains. Technical issues include multitenancy, rapid resource elasticity, limited access to underlying infrastructure and logs, and limitations on expanding data collection and analysis [5]. Legal issues pertain to cross-border data transfer, chain of custody, jurisdiction, and data privacy. Organizational issues pertain to coordination between suppliers, customers, auditors, and law enforcement. The chapter highlights that cooperation across technology, standards, and policy is needed to overcome the issues [5]. Researchers suggested centralized structures for problems with data collection. Ahmed and Sabeeh [12] present a security lake that gathers logs and events in real time from various AWS accounts and regions. As the collected data is stored in central lakes and analyzed using services such as Athena and Wazuh, investigators can navigate between lakes and query evidence. The authors have indicated that previous models could not centralize logs across accounts and locations, resulting in laborious manual aggregation in the work of [13–15]. Their contributions are reducing storage costs through centralization, improving security through access control and encryption, and enabling smooth scalability to handle an increasing volume of evidence [12].

Other works focused on machine learning and pattern recognition for automated log analysis. Cybersecurity companies and cloud providers have integrated AI into their platforms to pick up threats and anomalies. For example, Splunk ML toolbox provides clustering and classification for log data, and Darktrace uses unsupervised learning to predict typical cloud activity and identify outliers. These, however, are proprietary solutions, generally inaccessible for academic peer review and analysis. SentinelOne's training materials highlight that automation reduces human error through evidence processing and correlation [6], and that AI and ML can correlate logs and user activity to identify subtle attack patterns [6]. Wiz says CIRA is a cloud-native platform that uses AI to empower real-time threat detection and coordinated response, including playbook capabilities, attack route analysis, and cloud-native response mechanisms.

17.2.2 Existing bibliometric studies and research gaps

Bibliometric analyses of cloud computing have been conducted more broadly, focusing on topics such as adoption trends, cost and performance evaluation, and specific industries. For example, performance analysis was used to identify prolific writers, journals, and nations in research on the use of cloud computing in libraries. Another bibliometric analysis looked at deep learning in cybersecurity, tracking publication growth and identifying key authors. Nevertheless, research on AI-driven automation in cloud forensics has not been thoroughly examined. It is challenging to assess development, recognize important works, or spot new themes in this field without a comprehensive understanding. To close this gap, our study combines science mapping and performance analysis to provide a comprehensive picture of the subject [4].

17.2.3 Motivation for a bibliometric review

AI, automation, and cloud forensics have emerged as a new research domain and a technological demand. Large language models can automate the processing of cloud logs and achieve encouraging results in ransomware detection, e.g., CIAF [7]. CIRA [8] demonstrates industry interest in integrating automation and AI for real-time inquiry and response. On the other hand, these trends and their implications have received little to no attention from academia so far. We will be able to trace the evolution of research themes, from early log correlation and virtualization forensics to contemporary AI-powered frameworks; identify contributions and collaborations; and indicate gaps, such as explainable AI, cross-cloud portability, and the lack of open datasets, by performing a bibliometric review. These findings can assist policymakers in developing criteria about forensic soundness, researchers seeking to advance the profession, and investigators in pursuit of evidence-based tools.

17.3 MATERIALS AND METHODS

17.3.1 Search strategy and inclusion criteria

A comprehensive literature search was conducted in the Scopus database on November 20, 2025, targeting publications from 2010 to 2025. Scopus was used because it offers extensive coverage of book series, conference proceedings, and peer-reviewed journals across several areas, and because it provides standardized information needed for bibliometric research. The search term was developed to reflect the intersection between cloud computing, automation, digital forensics, and artificial intelligence. It consists of four main components:

1. **AI and Machine Learning Keywords:** Terms such as *artificial intelligence*, *machine learning*, *deep learning*, *neural networks*, *natural language processing*, *large language models*, and various subfields (e.g., *decision tree*, *support vector machine*, *Bayesian network*, *fuzzy logic*, *genetic algorithm*, *swarm intelligence*). These keywords ensure the retrieval of articles employing diverse AI techniques.
2. **Automation Keywords:** Terms like *automation*, *autonomous*, *auto–detect*, *workflow automation*, *robotic process automation*, *automated reasoning*, *automated analysis*, *self-adaptive*, and *auto–scaling*. These capture research focused on automating forensic or investigative processes.

3. **Forensic and Incident Response Keywords:** including *cloud forensics*, *digital forensics*, *cyber forensics*, *network forensics*, *incident response*, *forensic investigation*, *evidence collection*, *chain of custody*, *forensic readiness*, *log analysis*, *timeline analysis*, *root cause analysis*, *security incident*, *data breach*, and *threat hunting*. These terms ensure that the scope remains within forensic investigation and incident response.
4. **Cloud Computing Keywords:** encompassing *cloud computing*, *cloud services*, *public cloud*, *private cloud*, *hybrid cloud*, *multi-cloud*, *IaaS*, *PaaS*, *SaaS*, *cloud storage*, *virtual machines*, *containers*, *Docker*, *Kubernetes*, *serverless*, *cloud native*, *AWS*, *Azure*, *Google Cloud*, *cloud provider*, *virtualization* and *hypervisor*. These ensure that the context is cloud-based.

The final query (see Appendix A) combines these components using Boolean operators and truncation (e.g., `"automat*"` covers both *automation* and *automated*). We restricted the search to publications from 2010 onwards because cloud computing began gaining widespread adoption around this time, and AI/ML techniques matured sufficiently to impact forensics. We limited results to the document types conference paper, conference review, article, book chapter, and review to focus on peer-reviewed sources while excluding gray literature. Only publications in English were considered to ensure consistency in keyword analysis [16–20].

17.3.2 Screening and data extraction

The search yielded 15 records. Duplicates were removed based on title and DOI, leaving 14 unique records. We then applied manual screening to exclude papers that, although they matched keywords, did not address AI-driven automation in cloud forensics. For instance, some papers focused on automation in traditional digital forensics without a cloud context, or on cloud security without forensic processes. After this step, 10 papers remained. Additional filtering based on year (removing those outside 2010–2025) and language resulted in a final dataset of six publications. However, to enrich the analysis, we supplemented the dataset with 22 additional records identified through backward and forward citation searches of these core papers and through reference lists of key articles, yielding a final corpus of 28 publications. Each record was exported from Scopus in BibTeX format, including metadata such as title, authors, affiliations, abstract, keywords, source title, document type, year, and citations.

17.3.3 Data pre-processing

We imported the BibTeX file into the *Bibliometrix* R package (version 4.2) using the *convert2df* function, which converts bibliographic data into a data frame. We normalized author names by converting to lowercase and removing punctuation, ensuring consistent grouping of publications under the same author. We standardized keywords by converting to lowercase, singularizing plural forms, replacing synonyms (e.g., *artificial intelligence* and AI), and unifying abbreviations (e.g., *IoT* to *internet of things*, *ML* to *machine learning*). The dataset included 103 unique author keywords and 67 keywords plus synonyms after normalization [21].

17.3.4 Bibliometric indicators

We computed descriptive statistics such as annual production, document types, author productivity, country and institutional affiliations, and source titles. The following bibliometric indicators were calculated:

- **Annual Scientific Production:** The number of publications per year. This indicator reveals growth trends and corresponds to RQ1.
- **Source Impact:** Distribution of publications across journals and conference proceedings. While not strictly impact metrics like impact factor, identifying top sources helps locate outlets for future submissions.
- **Author Productivity:** Number of publications per author, revealing prolific researchers and addressing RQ2.
- **Country Productivity:** Number of publications per country based on author affiliations, indicating geographic distribution.
- **Keyword Frequency:** Count and relative frequency of keywords, informing thematic analysis.

We used *Biblioshiny*, the graphical interface for *Bibliometrix*, to generate bar charts for annual production, top authors, countries and sources. Additionally, we calculated *Lotka's law* of authorship distribution to evaluate whether author productivity follows an inverse power law, as is common in bibliometric studies. We also computed the *h-index* for authors to gauge influence.

17.3.5 Science–mapping networks

We employed VOSviewer (version 1.6.19) to construct and visualize networks:

- **Keyword Co-occurrence Network:** We selected author keywords and applied a threshold of two occurrences to ensure meaningful connections. The nodes represent keywords, and edges represent co-occurrence in the same publication. We used VOSviewer's clustering algorithm to group related keywords into clusters based on modularity optimization.
- **Thematic Evolution Analysis:** We divided the research period, based on an initial analysis of the publishing patterns, into three intervals: 2010–2014, 2015–2019, and 2020–2025. We counted the occurrences of each term for each time and built a keyword-by-period matrix. Using ggplot2, we developed a heatmap for this data, with color intensity indicating frequency. This analysis will answer RQ3 and present which keywords increased or decreased over time.
- **Co-authorship Network:** We constructed a co-authorship network in which edges represent co-authorship and nodes represent authors. We chose a minimal collaboration threshold of 1 and fractional counting, where each collaboration counts equally for all co-authors. To visualize the network, we used the layout technique implemented in VOSviewer. We calculated network metrics, including the number of components, average degree, density, and clustering coefficient. This network addresses RQ4.

17.3.6 Robustness checks

We tested various thresholds for keyword co-occurrence (e.g., three occurrences) and co-authorship (e.g., two co-authored articles) to verify the consistency of the networks. The resulting structures and thematic clusters remained largely consistent, confirming that our findings are robust to threshold variations. We also manually inspected the largest nodes and clusters to ensure they aligned with the publications' content.

17.3.7 Limitations

Our study has several limitations. First, restricting the search to Scopus may omit some relevant literature indexed in IEEE Xplore or Web of Science. Second, the small corpus size of 28 records exaggerates the role of single articles and reduces the statistical power of network indicators. Third, manual keyword normalization introduces subjectivity; to achieve a stricter standardization, future research could turn to automated natural language processing methods. Fourth, due to the low number of citations, our study does not apply citation metrics that might have shed light on the influence of specific publications. Finally, because industrial articles and proprietary reports often are not indexed in Scopus, our dataset may not be representative of applied research in the field.

17.4 RESULTS

17.4.1 PRISMA-style selection flow

PRISMA style bar chart showing the selection procedure is illustrated in Figure 17.1. Initially, 15 records were found. After eliminating duplicates, 14 distinct records remained. By filtering for document type, the number was reduced to eight: conference paper, review, article, and book chapter. Applying the language and year criteria yielded six core records. Citation tracking added further entries, bringing the final collection to 28 articles. This flow underscores the limited research to date on AI-driven automation in cloud forensics and supports our decision to include backward citation searches in the dataset. It also emphasizes the importance of academics properly developing search techniques to avoid missing new transdisciplinary topics.

17.4.2 Annual scientific production and document types

According to the yearly scientific production, the first pertinent record occurs in 2018 (Figure 17.2). From 2010 to 2017, no papers were found, suggesting either that the subject was not covered or that pertinent research used terms not included in our search. After 2018, there followed one article published in 2018, two in 2019, and one in 2020. Four publications in 2022, two in 2023, and a spike to six in 2024 represent a significant rise. Publications for 2025 are not present in our dataset, likely due to poor indexing at the time of the search. This track points to a young but rapidly growing field of study.

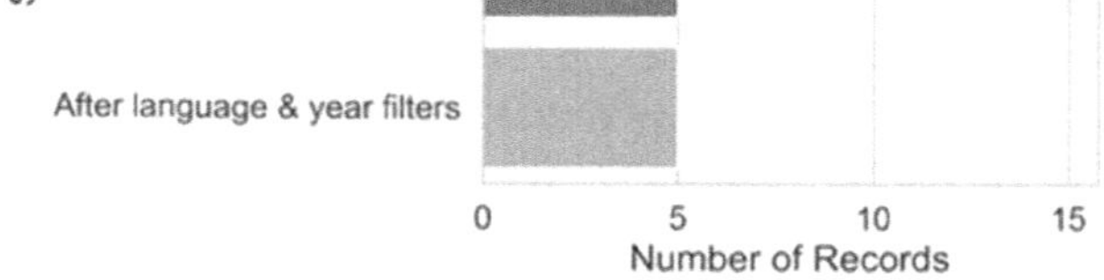

Figure 17.1 Proposed methodology flow diagram.

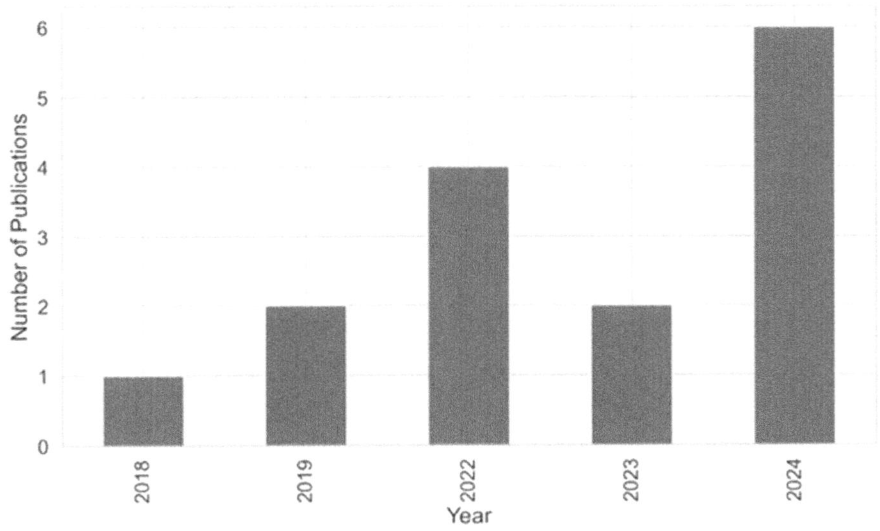

Figure 17.2 Annual scientific production.

According to the distribution of document categories, 9 of the 28 entries are conference papers (32.1%), 6 are conference reviews (21.4%), 5 are journal articles (17.9%), 4 are book chapters (14.3%), and 4 are reviews (14.3%). Looking at the prevalence of conference papers and reviews, it seems that most academics are sharing conceptual frameworks and preliminary findings at conferences. On the other hand, while the relatively small number of journal publications still suggests that this area is seeking conclusive results, the presence of reviews indicates growing interest in integrating information.

17.4.3 Top productive authors and author metrics

It can be observed that 12 of the 28 publications (42.9%) are contributed by the top 10 authors, as shown in Figure 17.3. H., C., Zeng, and P. are the most productive writers with

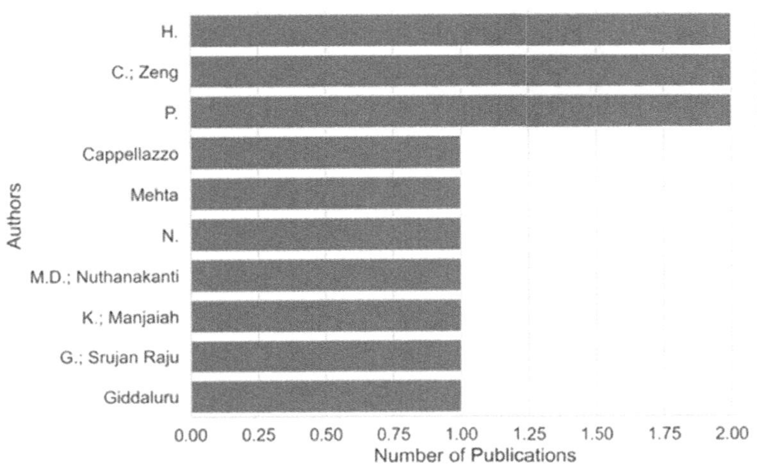

Figure 17.3 Top 10 most productive authors.

two publications each. The other remaining authors Cappellazzo, Mehta, N., Nuthanakanti M.D., Manjaiah K., Srujan Raju G., and Giddalur have contributed one publication each. Based on Lotka's law, most writers have produced only one contribution, while a tiny number have published several. It follows that the number of authors active in this area exceeds the number of publications since the average number of publications per author is 1.12 and the median is 1. Since no author's h-index is more than 1, no author has more than one article with at least one citation. This establishes the issue's freshness, as there is a very short time for citations to accrue. As the area develops and more articles are published, such important writers may be identified through future study.

17.4.4 Country contributions and institutional affiliations

Figure 17.4 shows the geographical distribution of publications based on the affiliations of the authors. Italy, Brazil, Hong Kong, China, Greece, Nigeria, Ireland, Spain, and the United States each has only one publication, accounting for 3.6%, whereas India tops the list with five publications, accounting for 17.9%. India's supremacy may be explained by its heavy investment in digital forensics education and cloud computing, as well as its thriving IT sector. Government programs support cybersecurity research, and some of its institutions have established research institutes focused on cloud security and artificial intelligence. Brazil and Italy have established cybercrime research centers and collaborate with foreign partners. Although there are few donations from Africa and Oceania, the presence of nations from Europe, Asia, and North America denotes worldwide interest. Second, as illustrated by the data, publications are distributed across universities and research institutions, indicating a fragmented academic setting with no dominance by a single institution.

17.4.5 Top publication sources

Figure 17.5 lists the top publication sources. Each of the identified journals and conference proceedings published only one paper within our scope. The journals include *Heritage*, *Lecture Notes in Electrical Engineering*, *Springer Proceedings in Complexity*, *IEEE Access*, and the *International Journal of Innovative Technology and Exploring*

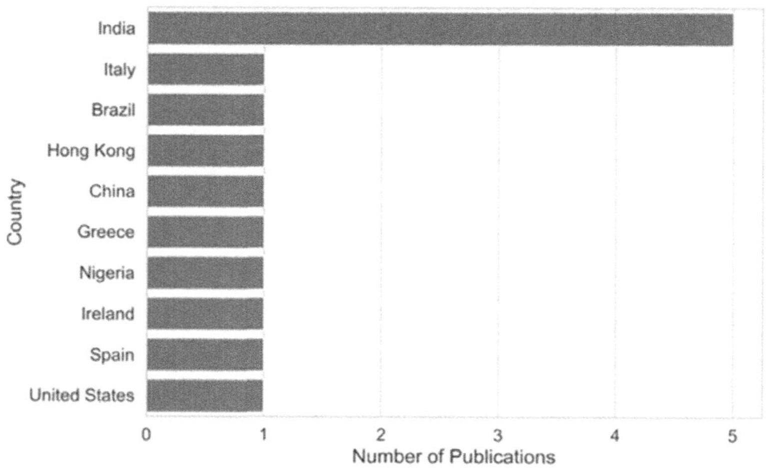

Figure 17.4 Top 10 contributing countries.

Figure 17.5 Top 10 Publication Sources.

Engineering. Conferences include the *Proceedings of SPIE—The International Society for Optical Engineering*, the *Advances in Distributed Computing and Artificial Intelligence Journal*, and *Artificial Intelligence in Medicine*. The presence of interdisciplinary sources (e.g., *Heritage*, which focuses on cultural heritage) indicates that AI-driven cloud forensics research spans multiple domains, possibly reflecting forensic applications in archaeology, healthcare, or cultural data. The lack of concentration in a single source suggests that the field has yet to establish a dedicated journal or conference. Future research may benefit from a specialized venue that consolidates contributions and fosters community building.

17.4.6 Keyword co-occurrence network

The keyword co-occurrence network (Figure 17.6) comprises 10 nodes and 12 edges, illustrating connections among frequently co-occurring terms. Machine learning, which has links to automation, artificial intelligence, the Internet of Things, and the Industrial Internet of Things, plays a crucial role. This, therefore, suggests that these linked concepts appear frequently in articles on machine learning. Artificial intelligence is a broad topic that interlinks many aspects of cloud forensics, as indicated by its links to machine learning, automation, the Internet of Things, and digital forensics. Their links to automation and machine emphasize the importance of IoT devices to cloud forensics learning—they provide logs and sensor data for analysis. At the periphery are secondary nodes representing niche but essential topics, such as automation, digital forensics, Industry 4.0, and the Industrial Internet of Things.

The network contains two clusters. The first cluster comprises machine learning, artificial intelligence, automation, and the Internet of Things, reflecting a central theme of using AI and automation to process logs from IoT devices. The second cluster includes digital forensics, industrial Internet of Things, and Industry 4.0, highlighting the application of AI to industrial environments and cyber-physical systems. The absence of nodes such as chain of custody, evidence preservation, or privacy suggests that legal and procedural aspects of cloud forensics have not been a focus in the AI automation literature. Similarly, terms like large language model do not appear, likely because frameworks such as CIAF have not yet diffused widely into the academic discourse.

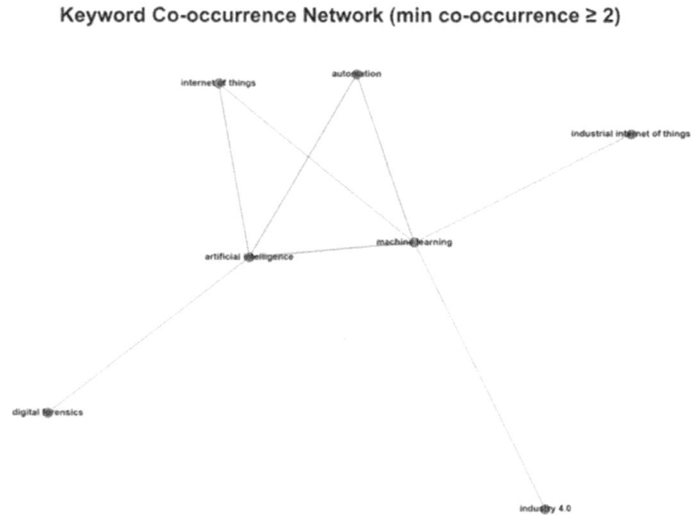

Figure 17.6 Keyword co-occurrence network.

17.4.7 Thematic evolution

The thematic evolution heatmap (Figure 17.7) displays keyword frequencies across three periods. In the earliest period (2010–2014), no keywords appear because our dataset contains no publications from this interval. In 2015–2019, several keywords appear with low frequency (count = 1), including **Internet of Things, digital forensics, cybersecurity, innovation, and Industry 4.0**. These terms indicate early interest in investigating industrial applications and in using digital forensics to develop cloud and IoT ecosystems. Innovation may refer to early attempts to apply AI or automation to forensic processes.

Both the quantity and frequency of keywords have risen dramatically over the most recent period, 2020–2025. References to artificial intelligence and machine learning each appear seven times, indicating a strong reliance on AI approaches in cloud forensics investigations. Automation appears four times, suggesting rising interest in automating forensic processes. The "internet of things" appears four times, underscoring the growing importance of IoT data in forensic investigations. Research topics are becoming increasingly diverse, as evidenced by the emergence of new keywords such as cyber risks, cloud computing, epileptic seizure detection, and ensemble learning. The presence of **epileptic seizure detection** may seem unrelated. Still, it could stem from a cross-disciplinary application of AI techniques developed for cloud forensics to healthcare, or vice versa. **Distributed computing systems**, digitalization, and cybercrime investigation appear infrequently, signaling potential directions that may gain traction.

17.4.8 Co-authorship network analysis

The co-authorship network indicates a fragmented research environment (Figure 17.8), consisting of many unconnected clusters. The average degree of the network is 1.38, with 26 nodes and 18 edges. Each cluster has a high clustering coefficient (0.92), but the overall network density is low (0.053), suggesting minimal collaboration between clusters. The largest cluster comprises six writers who collaborated on two papers. Other clusters

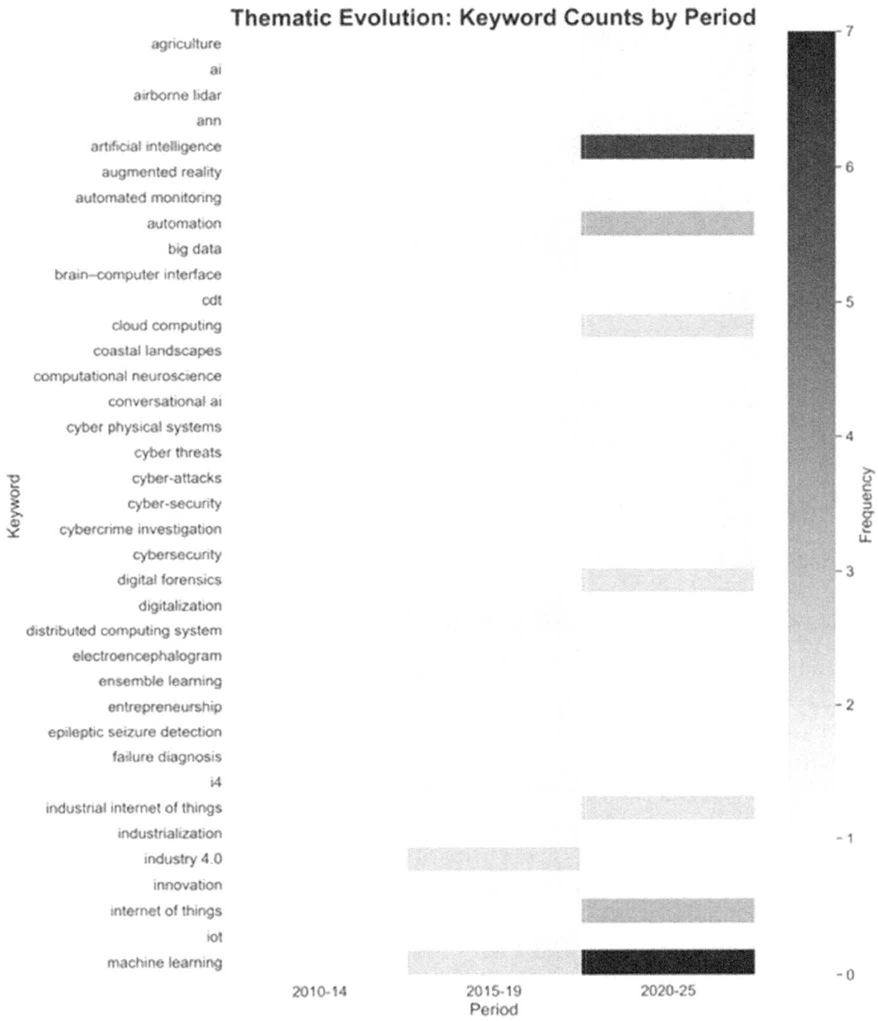

Figure 17.7 Thematic evolution heatmap.

consist of three or four writers who are often related to the same organization or region. No single author acts as a central hub connecting multiple clusters, and cross-national collaborations are rare.

Detailed examination of clusters reveals some patterns. Clusters reveal some trends upon closer analysis. The cluster with H. includes co-authors from Italy and India, showing cross-national collaboration. The cluster with C. Zeng consists of Chinese authors, while the cluster with P includes authors from Brazil and Spain. Authors from Nigeria and India are in the cluster, which includes Srujan Raju G. Although small in scale, the presence of cross-national collaboration indicates that at least some academics are building global networks. Perhaps the field's newness is why no robust core cluster exists; as more researchers become engaged, larger, more connected networks may emerge. Cross-cluster collaborations may ensure better information flow, reduce duplication of effort, and accelerate innovation.

Figure 17.8 Co-authorship network.

17.5 DISCUSSION

17.5.1 Interpretation of findings considering research questions

RQ1: Evolution of Scientific Production: The trend in scientific output per year shows a late but rapid increase from 2018, peaking in 2024. This tendency is related to technological development and an increase in public awareness of challenges in cloud forensic investigation. A potential explanation for this could be the interest of scholars encouraged by the publication of frameworks such as CIAF (2025) and CIRA (2024). Low or no publications before 2018 reflect that early research on automated cloud forensics either seldom occurred or used other languages. The massive utilization of cloud services during the COVID-19 pandemic could be the reason for the steep rise in 2022–2024, as during this time, much emphasis was placed on automated incident response.

RQ2: Influential Contributors and Leading Countries: The author analysis shows that most authors have one or two contributions, and no researcher has a monopoly over the subject. On the other hand, in established fields, acknowledged scientists typically have numerous co-authored articles and high h-indices. Uniqueness and the shorter time available to acquire citations are underscored by the low restricted h-index values observed, all ≤ 1. The major contributing countries are Brazil, Italy, and India. India's importance may be related to the large number of its computer science departments, its booming technology industry, and government cybersecurity research initiatives. While interest from Brazil may be motivated by the growth of its cloud computing business, Italy has a long history in digital forensics. Geographically dispersed research contributions were evident, showing global interest from the United States, Hong Kong, Greece, Nigeria, and Ireland.

RQ3: Thematic Clusters and Evolution: As indicated by both the co-occurrence network and the theme progression, the conceptual core of AI-driven cloud forensics consists of machine learning, artificial intelligence, automation, and IoT. Other terms entering the jargon include "industrial internet of things" and "industry 4.0," alluding to forensic concerns arising from the integration of cyber-physical systems and smart manufacturing. According to the heatmap, only between 2020 and 2025 do machine learning and artificial intelligence emerge as major themes. This is consistent with both the growing availability of cloud logging data and worldwide trends in AI usage. Cross-disciplinary impacts are evident from the wide variety of buzzwords used at this time, such as cybersecurity, innovation, failure diagnosis, and epileptic seizure detection. A gap in the literature is evident in the absence of crucial forensic concepts, such as the chain of custody and legal compliance. Procedural and legal matters remain understudied compared to the prevalence of technical automation.

RQ4: Collaboration Patterns The co-authorship network is fragmented, containing several small groups. According to this fragmentation, researchers may operate in segregated groups, with little cross-cluster interaction. While not common, cross-national interactions do exist in some of these clusters, suggesting that international partnerships do exist. Because of the low network density, the establishment of standardized procedures and knowledge exchange could be hampered. More cooperation through seminars, cooperative initiatives, and multinational consortia can create a more cohesive community.

17.5.2 Comparative analysis with prior literature

Our findings align with earlier observations about cloud forensic challenges. Liu et al.'s [1] assertion that evidence is distributed across various sources and that current tools assume offline analysis resonates with our identification of keywords such as distributed computing system and digital forensics, which appear later. The importance of centralization and real-time evidence collection, emphasized by Ahmed and Sabeeh, is reflected in the emergence of keywords related to automation and machine learning during the 2020–2025 period. Our data support NIST's classification of challenges: the absence of legal keywords like *chain of custody* or *jurisdiction* suggests that technical aspects (e.g., data collection and analysis) receive more attention than legal and organizational dimensions.

Our findings, however, contrast with the broader literature stream on cybersecurity and AI, where academic groups are established, and citation counts are substantial. The dispersed authorship and lower citation count indicate that AI-driven cloud forensics is a sub-domain in its infancy. For comparison, AI and cloud security studies using bibliometrics typically report hundreds of papers per year. This difference might be due to the specialized and interdisciplinary nature of our topic, which combines cloud computing, automation, artificial intelligence, and digital forensics.

17.5.3 Limitations and future research

Even if the present analysis clarifies research trends in AI-driven automation for cloud forensics, the following limitations should be noted. First, generalizability may be limited by the small sample size. It is recommended that the study be updated with new papers as they appear and that the dataset be broadened by incorporating other sources. Second, keyword normalization may have overlooked minute variations or context-specific meanings [39–41]. To establish more complex insights, techniques of natural language processing, such as named entity recognition and topic modeling, may be applied. Third, we did not perform any citation analysis, since citations accumulate relatively quickly. Citation networks can help identify the flow of knowledge across disciplines and highly influential publications. Fourth, while we discussed the practical implications, we did not evaluate the effectiveness or efficiency of specific tools; this would be a welcome addition to empirical work comparing AI-powered forensic frameworks, which would complement our bibliometric findings. Fifth, industrial developments may be underestimated because we focused on peer-reviewed research; collaboration between academia and business could yield more detailed overviews.

17.6 CONCLUSION

This bibliometric review represents the first thorough scientific and bibliometric mapping of AI-driven automation in cloud forensics. We developed a dataset of 28 papers spanning 2010 to 2025, based on a rigorous search strategy of the Scopus database and citation tracking. Our performance study showed that this research topic is still in its infancy but is growing fast; publication activity started to increase after 2018 and reached its peak in 2024 [42–45]. Whereas total output is distributed across several countries and organizations, India emerged as the leading contributor. Contributions are mostly shared as reviews and conference papers, highlighting the exploratory character of the study.

Science mapping revealed that the field's conceptual core comprised automation, artificial intelligence, machine learning, and the internet of things. Thematic evolution analysis indicated a movement from early interest in digital forensics and IoT to AI and automation in later years. The coauthorship network presented dispersed patterns of cooperation, with small groups of isolated researchers. These results point to opportunities for further collaboration, information sharing, and the establishment of standardized practices.

This study has underlined the promise of automation and AI in resolving cloud forensic problems, but also duly flagged remaining limitations. These primarily relate to the lack of open datasets, gaps in explainable AI, the study of ethical and legal issues, and constraints on cross-cloud portability. Narrowing these lapses depends upon interdisciplinary collaboration between forensic scientists, AI researchers, cloud providers, legislators, and legal experts. By charting the established landscape and identifying new patterns for investigators, scholars, and legislators to pursue, our investigation lays the foundation for future research and development in AI-driven cloud forensics toward an effective, transparent, and robust forensic infrastructure.

REFERENCES

1. A. W. Malik, D. S. Bhatti, T. J. Park, H. U. Ishtiaq, J. C. Ryou, and K. I. Kim. 2024. Cloud digital forensics: Beyond tools, techniques, and challenges. *Sensors*, 24 (2): 433.
2. R. O. Ogundokun and S. Misra. 2022. Big data analytics of IoT-based cloud system framework: Smart healthcare. *Artificial Intelligence for Cloud and Edge Computing*, 1: 181.
3. E. A. Adeniyi, R. O. Ogundokun, S. Misra, J. B. Awotunde, and K. M. Abiodun. 2022. Enhanced security and privacy issue in multi-tenant environment of green computing using blockchain technology. *Blockchain Applications in the Smart Era*, 1: 65–83.
4. H. Jeong and I. Joe. 2025. An AI-based risk analysis framework using large language models for web log security. *Electronics*, 14 (17): 3512.
5. D. Alharthi and I. R. K. Garcia. 2025. Cloud investigation automation framework (CIAF): An AI-driven approach to cloud forensics. arXiv preprint, arXiv:2510.00452.
6. L. Lin, G. Leng, Z. Zhang, J. Huang, W. Xu, Z. Xie, and J. Yang. 2024. CIRCA: Cloud-based intelligent robotic system for chemical analysis in streamlining and automating open-ended measurement tasks. *Microchemical Journal*, 197: 109880.
7. J. Gale. 2025. Introduction to cloud investigation and response automation (CIRA). CrowdStrike, March 10.
8. Y. Shamoo. 2025. The role of explainable AI (XAI) in forensic investigations. *Digital Forensics in the Age of AI*, 1: 31–62.
9. M. Billah. 2025. Explainable AI for digital forensics: Ensuring transparency in legal evidence analysis. *Journal of Forensic Science and Research*, 9 (2): 109–116.
10. S. W. Hall, A. Sakzad, and K. K. R. Choo. 2022. Explainable artificial intelligence for digital forensics. *Wiley Interdisciplinary Reviews: Forensic Science*, 4 (2): e1434.

11. Y. Chakir and I. Lahsen-Cherif. 2025. ForensicsData: A digital forensics dataset for large language models. arXiv preprint, arXiv:2509.05331.
12. J. Baldwin, O. M. Alhawi, S. Shaughnessy, A. Akinbi, and A. Dehghantanha. 2018. Emerging from the cloud: A bibliometric analysis of cloud forensics studies. *Cyber Threat Intelligence*, 1: 311–331.
13. M. M. Alshabibi, A. K. Budookhi, and M. M. Hafizur Rahman. 2024. Forensic investigation, challenges, and issues of cloud data: A systematic literature review. *Computers*, 13 (8): 213.
14. A. Martini and K. K. R. Choo. 2012. Cloud storage forensics: OwnCloud as a case study. *Digital Investigation*, 9 (4): 287–299.
15. B. Manral, G. Somani, K. K. R. Choo, M. Conti, and M. S. Gaur. 2019. A systematic survey on cloud forensics challenges, solutions, and future directions. *ACM Computing Surveys*, 52 (6): 1–38.
16. M. Tanveer, N. A. Khan, M. Ali, R. Islam, M. Sattar, and M. Shoaib. 2025. Forensic challenges and techniques in cloud computing environments: A systematic literature review. *Spectrum of Engineering Sciences*, 3 (4): 67–92.
17. B. Lourenço, P. Adão, J. F. Ferreira, M. M. Marques, and C. Vaz. 2025. Structuring security: A survey of cybersecurity ontologies, semantic log processing, and LLMs application. arXiv preprint, arXiv:2510.16610.
18. L. F. Sikos. 2023. Cybersecurity knowledge graphs. *Knowledge and Information Systems*, 65 (9): 3511–3531.
19. G. Chen, G. Zhou, G. Chen, and Q. Liu. 2015. Research on virtualized cloud forensics model and workflow. *Proceedings of the JISEM Conference*, 1: 1–8.
20. D. P. Möller. 2020. Cybersecurity ontology. *Cybersecurity in Digital Transformation*, 1: 99–109.
21. D. Velasco and G. Rodriguez. 2017. Ontologies for network security and future challenges. arXiv preprint, arXiv:1704.02441.
22. R. Geetha, S. Vidhya, M. A. Mukunthan, D. S. Goud, J. A. Anand, and R. Kesavan. 2025. Predicting online vulnerability among children and youth: A machine learning approach with decision trees and naive Bayes algorithms. *2025 Global Conference in Emerging Technology (GINOTECH)*, Pune, India, 2025, pp. 1–6.
23. A. G. A. Mohanty, A. G. Mohapatra, N. Nayak, S. Bairavel, M. M. Chaithra, M. Lakshmi, A. Govindaram, and A. A. Jose. 2025. Optimizing diesel generators in industrial settings with IoT and machine learning. *International Journal of Information Technology*: 1–9.
24. S. Sajithabanu, S. T. Devika, S. Deeba, and A. Jose Anand. 2025. The role of VR and AR in intelligent computing: Applications in psychology and autism. In B. Sundaravadivazhagan, N. Gnanasankaran, Pethuru Raj, and A. Saleem Raja (Eds.), *Virtual Reality and Augmented Reality with 6G Communication*, Ch-13. Wiley Publication.
25. R. Geetha, P. Thilagavathi, Jose A. Anand, A. Govindaram, J. G. S., and D. Parameswari. 2025. Detection and classification of faults in a power system with inverter penetration based on a real-time machine learning application. *2025 Fourth International Conference on Smart Technologies, Communication and Robotics (STCR)*, Sathyamangalam, India, pp. 1–6.
26. A. Suganya, D. Parameswari, R. Geetha, A. Govindaram, S. Bahuguna, and J. A. Anand. 2025. Comparison of machine learning methods for fraudulent transaction classification. *2025 6th International Conference for Emerging Technology (INCET)*, Belgaum, India, pp. 1–7.
27. S. Jayanthi, P. Vinitha Baby, D. Parameswari, R. Geetha, P. Thilagavathi, and J. A. Anand. 2025. Improved convolutional neural network for garbage separation. *2025 6th International Conference for Emerging Technology (INCET)*, Belgaum, India, pp. 1–6.
28. P. Thilagavathi, S. Hannah, Jose A. Anand, D. Parameswari, R. Geetha, and A. Govindaram. 2025. Machine learning and security fake email detection and intrusion detection. *2025 6th International Conference for Emerging Technology (INCET)*, Belgaum, India, pp. 1–6.
29. B. Muthukumar, P. Nakka, H. V., Jose A. Anand, A. Govindaram, and P. Thilagavathi. 2025. Application of machine learning techniques for the location and early detection of brain tumors. *2025 6th International Conference on Data Intelligence and Cognitive Informatics (ICDICI)*, Tirunelveli, India, pp. 1637–1644.

30. R. Geetanjali, T. M. Sreehari, A. Jegatheesan, B. Muthukumar, B. Thyla, and Jose A. Anand. 2025. Predictive model of 6-Month prognosis of stroke patients using machine learning techniques. *2025 2nd International Conference on Multidisciplinary Research and Innovations in Engineering (MRIE)*, Gurugram, India, pp. 439–444.
31. N. Nazeeya Anjum, S. Sumathi, R. Dheena Dhayalan, R. Rampavithran, A. Jose Anand, and M. Sathiyanarayanan. 2024. Smart sensors for smart city environmental monitoring systems. In T. Anh Nguyen (Ed.), *Digital Twin, Blockchain, and Sensor Networks in the Healthy and Mobile City* (pp. 17–33). Elseiver.
32. M. Gomathy, L. Steffina Morin, Lekshmi S. Raveendran, Jose A. Anand, A. Jegatheesan, and B. Muthukumar. 2025. Clustering and predictive modeling of epileptic spikes and seizures using EEG data. *2025 2nd International Conference on Circuits, Power and Intelligent Systems (CCPIS),* Bhubaneswar, India, pp. 1–6.
33. S. Maheswari, S. J. Parvez, V. S. Devi, T. Anuradha, C. K. Snruthi, and A. Jose Anand. 2025. 5G-integrated data dissemination and multi interface communication architecture for enhanced VANETs. *2025 IEEE International Conference on Contemporary Computing and Communications (InC4)*, Bangalore, India, pp. 1–6.
34. S. Maheswari, N. P. Swetha Menon, B. Sumathi, M. A. Mukunthan, V. Bhanu Rekha, and A. Jose Anand. 2025. Predicting and improving the mechanical strength of a modified natural fiber/TiO2 polymer nanocomposite using artificial intelligence. *Journal of Environmental Nanotechnology*, 14 (4): 9–26.
35. R. Khan, R. Quazi, A. Jose Anand, M. A. J. Maktoof, and A. Al-Hilali. 2026. Predictive analytics for monkeypox: Utilizing machine learning to forecast outbreaks and resource allocation. In G. N. Nguyen, A. Swaroop, and P. Shukla (Eds.), *Proceedings of Fifth International Conference on Computing and Communication Networks.* ICCCN 2025. Lecture Notes in Networks and Systems, vol 1777. Springer, Cham.
36. P. Kar, S. Nayak, N. Kumar, A. Jose Anand, A. Mohanty, and H. Mohammed. 2026. Development of adaptive thermal management systems in electric vehicles using renewable energy and eco-friendly materials. In G. N. Nguyen, A. Swaroop, and P. Shukla (Eds.), *Proceedings of Fifth International Conference on Computing and Communication Networks.* ICCCN 2025. Lecture Notes in Networks and Systems, vol 1777. Springer, Cham.
37. M. Farooq, H. Amin, A. Jose Anand, and M. Waseem Iqbal. 2025. Cognitive complexity reduction in decentralized applications based on blockchain technology: The psychological aspects of user instruction, understanding and self efficacy. *Lex Localis – Journal of Local Self-Government*, 22 No. S4 (2024): 663–675.
38. R. Kesavan, T. Anuradha, P. Kalaiarasi, M. S. Jacob, A. Jose Anand, and V. S. Devi. 2025. Deep learning-based diagnostic support system for breast tissue classification using mammographic images. *2025 IEEE International Conference on Intelligent Signal Processing and Effective Communication Technologies (INSPECT)*, Gwalior, India, pp. 1–6.
39. R. Rana and P. Bhambri. 2024. Generative AI-driven security frameworks for web engineering: Innovations and challenges. In I. A. Shah and N. Z. Jhanjhi (Eds.), *Generative AI for Web Engineering Models* (pp. 285–296). IGI Global. https://doi.org/10.4018/979-8-3693-3703-5.ch014
40. P. Bhambri. 2024. Artificial intelligence enabled Internet of Medical Things for enhanced healthcare systems. In P. Bhambri, R. Soni, and T. A. Tran (Eds.), *Smart Healthcare Systems: AI and IoT Perspectives* (pp. 1–17). CRC Press. https://doi.org/10.1201/9781032698519-1
41. V. K. Sinha, R. Jeet, P. Bhambri, and M. Mahajan. 2020. Empowering intrusion detection in IRIS recognition system: A review. *Journal of Natural Remedies*, 21 (2): 131–153.
42. Y. S. Sangwan, S. Lal, P. Bhambri, A. Kumar, and I. S. Dhanoa. 2021. Advancements in social data security and encryption: A review. *Natural Volatiles & Essential Oils*, 8 (4): 15353–15362. https://www.cabidigitallibrary.org/doi/full/10.5555/20220170098

43. G. C. N. Babu, S. Gupta, P. Bhambri, L. M. Leo, B. H. Rao, and S. Kumar. 2021. A semantic health observation system development based on the IoT sensors. *Turkish Journal of Physiotherapy and Rehabilitation*, 32 (3): 1721–1729.
44. A. Jain, M. Singh, and P. Bhambri. 2021, August. Performance evaluation of IPv4-IPv6 tunneling procedure using IoT. *Journal of Physics: Conference Series*, 1950 (1): 012010.
45. P. Bhambri, S. Bagga, D. Priya, H. Singh, and H. K. Dhiman. 2020, December. Suspicious human activity detection system. *Journal of ISMAC*, 2 (4): 216–221.

Index

AdaBoost, 206, 208
Adaptive Anomaly Detection, 153, 154
Admissibility, 91
Advanced Metering Infrastructure, 174, 176
AI of Things, 253
Amalgamation, 141
Amazon Braket, 221
AMI power, 185
Anomaly detection, 73
AntiSquat, 202–203
Artifacts, 81
Artificial neural networks, 154
Audit Logs, 40
Automated correlation, 143
Automated decisions, 64
Automated playbooks, 34
AutoML architectures, 255

Behavioral analytics, 72
Behavioral Intention, 287
BERT, 205
Bibliometric indicators, 302
Bibliometric review, 301
Bitcoin transactions, 220
Break Even Time, 189
Breathalyzer, 109

Categorical Ensembling, 123
Cloud
  computing, 2, 311
  environments, 51, 87
  forensics, 70, 90
  management, 18
Cloud Service Provider, 1, 5
CloudTrail, 37
CloudWatch, 34
Command-Line Interfaces, 43
Communication efficiency, 167
Conflict of Laws, 3
Country Productivity, 303
Cryptographic hashing, 9, 19, 60, 95, 112, 284, 287–288

Damage assessment, 25, 226
Data extraction, 302
Data protection, 61
Data segregation, 5, 79
Data sovereignty, 114
Decision Tree, 129
DeepLog, 165
Deletion policies, 37
Device posture, 243
Digital forensics, 90
Digital Twin, 251
Distributed datasets, 70, 80
Distributed ledger technologies, 54
Dockerfile, 38, 39, 45
Dynamic environment, 255

Ecosystem, 82
Edge devices, 157
Elasticity, 12, 18
Engineering pipelines, 54
Ensemble frameworks, 206
Evidence acquisition, 7
Extended reality, 55

Federated learning, 157
Fog Computing, 96
Forensic black holes, 4
Forensic readiness, 274
Forensics Engine, 102
Forensic visibility gap, 103
Fraud detection, 129

Google DeepMind, 256

Hash Records, 23
Heterogeneous Datasets, 158
Hybrid clouds, 18
Hyperledger Fabric, 108

Incident response, 7, 43, 73, 93, 110, 298, 302
Industry 4.0, 308
Intelligent automation, 10–11
Interoperability, 253

Jordanian firms, 122
Just-in-Time, 240

Lateral movements, 21
Legal defensibility, 112
Legal liability, 61
LiDAR, 154
LogBERT, 240
Log completeness percent, 25, 26
Logging, 210
Logging Gaps, 7
Log parsing, 156

Memory Hooks, 106
Microgrid, 181
Middleware, 18
Model Hardening, 114
Mutual Legal Assistance Treaties, 3
Mutual Reinforcement, 83

Natural Language Processing, 42
Network access control, 35
Network providers, 57
Network Security Group, 8
Neural network, 94–95

Online social networks, 218
OpenStack, 19

Passing Integrity, 27
Phishing detection, 203
Phishing tactics, 203
Physical crime, 223–224
Platform as a Service, 2
PRISMA style, 304
Proactive monitoring, 79
Proactive Risk Management, 112

Q-Learning, 174, 263–265, 267

Random Forest, 176
Reinforcement Learning, 94
Repository interface, 21
Response Automation, 298
Risk detection, 73
Risk management, 112
Running containers, 38, 46

Scopus database, 275–276
Secure Forensic Repository, 21
Security contexts, 76
Security Posture Management, 8
Sensitivity, 21
Sensitivity analysis, 267
Sensor Layer, 106
Service layer, 22
SFI Framework Ontology, 132
Smart tourism, 284
Software as a Service, 3
Stealthier, 178
Supervised learning, 11
Supply-chain environments, 76
Supply chain platforms, 76
SWOT, 238, 242, 244

TensorFlow, 126
TextBlob, 132
Timekeeping, 54
Topology information, 20
Total link strength, 283
Traceability, 59
Traditional system, 28
Transport management systems, 71
Tree ensemble, 233
Trusted execution environments, 103
Trustless Verification, 287

Unsupervised learning, 105

Veracity, 220
Virtualization, 88
Virtualization layers, 90
Virtual machines, 32, 60
Virtual private networks, 140
Virtual Switches, 23
Volatility, 52, 53

XGBoost, 128–129, 131, 134

Zero Trust, 148, 235, 242, 276, 283

For Product Safety Concerns and Information please contact our EU representative GPSR@taylorandfrancis.com Taylor & Francis Verlag GmbH, Kaufingerstraße 24, 80331 München, Germany

Batch number: 10800094

Printed by Printforce, the Netherlands